THE BARBOUR COLLECTION OF CONNECTICUT TOWN VITAL RECORDS

THE BARBOUR COLLECTION OF CONNECTICUT TOWN VITAL RECORDS

GRISWOLD 1815–1848

GROTON 1704–1853

Compiled by

Jerri Lynn Burket

General Editor

Lorraine Cook White

Genealogical Publishing Co., Inc.
Baltimore, Maryland

Library of Congress Catalogue Card Number 94-76197
International Standard Book Number 0-8063-1592-X
Made in the United States of America

INTRODUCTION

As early as 1640 the Connecticut Court of Election ordered all magistrates to keep a record of the marriages they performed. In 1644 the registration of births and marriages became the official responsibility of town clerks and registrars, with deaths added to their duties in 1650. From 1660 until the close of the Revolutionary War these vital records of birth, marriage, and death were generally well kept, but then for a period of about two generations until the mid-nineteenth century, the faithful recording of vital records declined in some towns.

General Lucius Barnes Barbour was the Connecticut Examiner of Public Records from 1911 to 1934 and in that capacity directed a project in which the vital records kept by the towns up to about 1850 were copied and abstracted. Barbour previously had directed the publication of the Bolton and Vernon vital records for the Connecticut Historical Society. For this new project he hired several individuals who were experienced in copying old records and familiar with the old script.

Barbour presented the completed transcriptions of town vital records to the Connecticut State Library where the information was typed onto printed forms. The form sheets were then cut, producing twelve small slips from each sheet. The slips for most towns were then alphabetized and the information was then typed a second time on large sheets of rag paper, which were subsequently bound into separate volumes for each town. The slips for all towns were then interfiled, forming a statewide alphabetized slip index for most surviving town vital records.

The dates of coverage vary from town to town, and of course the records of some towns are more complete than others. There are many cases in which an entry may appear two or three times, apparently because that entry was entered by one or more persons. Altogether the entire Barbour Collection--one of the great genealogical manuscript collections and one of the last to be published--covers 137 towns and comprises 14,333 typed pages.

TABLE OF CONTENTS

ABBREVIATIONS

ae. - - - - - - age
b. - - - - - - - born, both
bd. - - - - - - buried
B.G. - - - - - Burying Ground
d. - - - - - - - died, day, or daughter
Deac. - - - - Deacon
decd. - - - - - deceased
Eld. - - - - - Elder
f. - - - - - - - father
h. - - - - - - - hour
J. P. - - - - - Justice of Peace
m. - - - - - - married or month
Min. - - - - - Minister
res. - - - - - - resident
s. - - - - - - - son
st. - - - - - - - stillborn
V. D. M. - - minister (volun dues)
w. - - - - - - wife
wid. - - - - - widow
wk. - - - - - - week
y. - - - - - - - year

THE BARBOUR COLLECTION OF CONNECTICUT TOWN VITAL RECORDS

GRISWOLD VITAL RECORDS
1815 - 1848

Page

ABEL, Avilata, of Franklin, m. Phillip **OLIN**, of Griswold, Jan. 24, 1822, by Rev. Caleb Read 77
Elisha J., m. Fanny **BOARDMAN**, Sept. 2, 1804 10
Elizabeth, d. Elisha & Fanny, b. Oct. 8, 1813 10
Fanny Boardman, d. Elisha & Fanny, b. Sept. 2, 1809; d. Aug. 23, 1811 10
Hannah More, d. Elisha & Fanny, b. Oct. 13, 1815 10
Henry, s. Elisha & Fanny, b. Aug. 2, 1811 10
Lucretia, d. Elisha & Fanny, b. May 1, 1808 10
Mary, d. Elisha & Fanny, b. Nov. 30, 1805 10

ADAMS, Ebenezer T., of Mystic, m. Catharine B. **GRAVES**, of Griswold, Apr. 17, 1839, by Rev. William R. Jewett 183
Mary Graves, twin with Sarah Gardiner, d. Ebenezer T. & Catharine B., b. July 13, 1844 183
Priscilla, m. Henry **BENNETT**, Apr. 11, 1822 150
Reuben, of Worcester, Mass., m. Emily **BROWN**, of [Griswold?], Nov. 8, 1847, by Tho[ma]s S. Shipman 26
Sarah Gardiner, twin with Mary Graves, d. Ebenezer T. & Catherine B., b. July 13, 1844 183

ALDRICH, W[illia]m W., of Webster, Mass., m. Eliza G. **BOWEN**, of [Jewett City], Aug. 9, 1847, by Tho[ma]s S. Shipman 220

ALEXANDER, Alvin, m. Mary **PAINE**, b. residing in Griswold, Oct. 19, 1823, by Amos Read, Elder 126
Ambrose, m. Melora **CUTLER**, b. of Griswold, Apr. 5, 1824, by Rev. Amos Read 148
James D., of Voluntown, m. Betsey **DURFEY**, of Griswold, Feb. 27, 1832, by Rev. S. D. Jewett 18
Samuel, of Voluntown, m. Nancy **AVERY**, of Griswold, Aug. 21, 1821, by Rev. Horatio Waldo 75
Sarah Ann, m. Benjamin **GORTON**, b. residing in Griswold, Oct. 19, 1823, by Amos Read, Elder 125

ALLEN, Lucinda P., m. P. P. **CADY**, b. of Pomfret, Dec. 1, 1833, in Jewett City, by Bela Hicks, of Pomfret 304
Lucy Maria, d. George W. & Maria M., b. Dec. 3, 1845 28

ANDREWS, Maria, m. George D. **LAWTON**, June 16, 1816 60

APLEY, Lydia, of Plainfield, m. Thomas **HERRINGTON**, of Lisbon, Jan. 2, 1823, by Elisha Partridge, J.P. 118

ARMSBEE, Albert H., of Boston, Mass., m. Mary A. P. **SHERMAN**, of Griswold, Mar. 23, 1841, at Jewett City, by Rev. B. Cook 167

ARMSTRONG, Clarrissa, m. Jedediah **BAKER**, Sept. 27, 1807 84
Elizabeth, of Canterbury, m. Perry **CLARK**, of Griswold, Dec. 21, 1823, by Rev. Horatio Waldo 131

AUSTIN, James, m. Dorcas A. **TANNER**, b. of Griswold, Mar. 9, 1845, by Rev. B. Cook, of Jewett City 305

	Page
AVERELL, Charles, s. James & Lucy, b. Apr. 23, 1825	34
George, s. James & Lucy, b. Oct. 18, 1816	34
James, s. James & Lucy, b. May 29, 1815	34
Lucy, wid. Capt. James, d. June 18, 1817	33
Lucy R., of Griswold, m. Charles **HINCKL[E]Y**, of Plainfield, May 1, 1839, by Rev. William R. Jewett	183
Lucy Read, d. James & Lucy, b. Nov. 3, 1818	34
Olive, d. James & Lucy, b. May 19, 1822	34
Olive, m. Josias **BYLES**, b. of Griswold, Oct. 2, 1839, by Rev. William R. Jewett	304
AVERY, Anna, d. [John & Lucy], . Apr. 2, 1787	103
Betsey, d. [John & Lucy], b. Apr. 18, 1791	103
Cynthia, d. [John & Lucy], b. Feb. 22, 1793	103
Cynthia, m. Charles **COOK**, Dec. 14, 1815	34-A
Elbridge, m. Mary O. **BIGELOW**, b. of Griswold, Nov. 24, 1845, by Tho[ma]s S. Shipman	199
Elisha, s. [John & Lucy], b. Jan. 4, 1783	103
Esther w., d. Fred[eric]k A. & Rachel, b. Mar. 20, 1816	75
Eunice, of Preston, m. W[illia]m **HUNTINGTON**, of Griswold, Nov. 17, 1847, by Rev. C. Terry	299
Frederick A., m. Rachel **MOREY**, Feb. 2, 1817	75
Giles C., s. Frederick A. & Rachel, b. Dec. 6, 1820	75
Hannah, d. [John & Lucy], b. Feb. 19, 1789	103
Hannah, of Griswold, m. John **PARK[E]**, of White Hall, N.Y., July 28, 1825, by Rev. Horatio Waldo	70
Henry, s. [John & Clarina], b. Dec. 20, 1818	103
John, of Preston, b. Dec. 14, 1755; m. Lucy **AYER**, of Groton, Feb. 25, 1779	103
John, s. [John & Lucy], b. Nov. 23, 1780	103
John, s. John & Lucym m. Clarina **HALSEY**, May 28, 1812	103
John, Sr., d. Mar. 18, 1815	112
John Watson, s. John & Clarina, b. Feb. 14, 1813	103
Joseph Ayer, s. [John & Clarina], b. Nov. 12, 1820; d. May 10, 1822	103
Lucy, d. [John & Lucy], b. Mar. 17 1785	103
Mariah, d. [John & Lucy], b. June 22, 1795; d. Feb. 2, 1796	103
Mary, of Plainfield, m. James **HOXSIE**, of Griswold, May 8, 1845, by Tho[ma]s S. Shipman	247
Nancy, of Griswold, m. Samuel **ALEXANDER**, of Voluntown, Aug. 21, 1821, by Rev. Horatio Waldo	75
Nancy D., m. William **CLIFT**, June 5, 1813	17
Sally A., d. Fredderick A. & Rachel, b. July 20, 1819	75
Stephen W., s. Frederick A. & Rachel, b. Mar. 26, 1818	75
Susan, d. [John & Clarina], b. Sept. 30, 1814	103
Susan, of Griswold, m. William P. **HARRIS**, of Groton, Nov. 12, 1833, by Rev. S. D. Jewett	300
Thankful P., d. Frederick A. & Rachel, b. May 26, 1822	75
Timothy, m. Patty **FRINK**, b. of Preston, Aug. 20, 1826, by Nathan Stanton, J.P.	178
William, s. W[illia]m P. & Olive H., b. July 7, 1845	215
William P., Rev., m. Olive **HUNTINGTON**, Oct 2., 1844, by Rev. Roswell Whitman	215
William Pitt, s. [John & Clarina], b. Oct. 2, 1816	103
AYER, Lucy, of Groton, b. July 21, 1759; m. John **AVERY**, of Preston, Feb. 25, 1779	103
BAKER, Henry Damon, s. Jedediah & Clarissa, b. Mar. 20, 1814	84
Jedediah, m. Clarrissa **ARMSTRONG**, Sept. 27, 1807	84

	Page
BAKER, (cont.)	
Jedediah Calkins, s. Jedediah & Clarissa, b. Aug. 28, 1808	84
Marvin, of Norwich, m. Rebecca S. **BROWNELL**, of Pomfret, Oct. 11, 1841, by Rev. William Wright, of Jewett City	152
Mary, m. James M. **BREWSTER**, Sept. 3, 1832, by Rev. S. D. Jewett	285
Patty, of Brooklyn, m. Daniel **DEWEY**, of Lebanon, Feb. 2, 1824, by Rev. Horatio Waldo	138
William, s. Jedediah & Clarissa, b. Aug. 16, 1810	84
BALDWIN, Bridget, b. Aug. 31, 1779; m. Robert M. **PALMER**, Feb. 3, 1801	39
Eunice, b. Mar. 16, 1775; m. Stephen **TUCKER**, Jan. 17, 1793	19
Harriet A., of Canterbury, m. Walter R. **PALMER**, of Griswold, Nov. 27, 1837, by Rev. Geo[rge] Perkins	232
Mary E., d. W[illia]m H. & Sally, b. July 24, 1845	279
Nancy, of Griswold, m. Charles **STONE**, of Brooklyn, Ct, [ ], by Rev. William Wright	35
Sarah E., d. W[illia]m H. & Sally, b. Apr. 6, 1844	279
BARBER, Alice, [d. Gardiner & Ellenor(?)], b. May 4, 1818, at Groton	292
Celestiana L.A.W., of Westerly, R.I., m. Elisha S. **BILL**, of Griswold, July 23, 1837, by Deac. Comfort D. Fillmore	97
Charles C., [s. Gardiner & Ellenor(?)], b. Oct. 9, 1812, at Hopkinton, R.I.	292
Delia A., m. Chester A. **MORGAN**, b. of Griswold, Sept. 13 1842, by Rev. William R. Jewett	164
Diantha F., [d. Gardiner & Ellenor(?)], b. Apr. 26, 1822, at Voluntown, Ct.	292
Diathia, d. Reuben & Sally, b. Oct. 24, 1819	36
Edward, m. Martha M. **ECCLESTON**, b. of Griswold, Oct. 6, 1844, by Rev. B. Cook, of Jewett City	265
Edward, m. Martha M. **ECELESTON**, b. of Griswold, Oct. 6, 1844, by Rev. B. Cook, of Jewett City	274
Eliza, [d. Gardiner & Ellenor(?)], b. Dec. 26, 1810, at Exeter, R.I.	292
Eliza Ann, d. Reuben & Sally, b. Aug. 13, 1821	36
Gardiner, b. Dec. 10, 1787, at Exeter, R.I.; m. Ellenor Lewis (?)	292
Hannah, [d. Gardiner & Ellenor(?)], b. Mar. 20, 1820, at N. Stonington	292
Henry C., m. Hannah E. **CLARK**, b. of Griswold, Oct. 26, 1846, by Rev. B. Cook, of Jewett City	108
Mary, w. Reuben, d. June 3, 1818	36
Mary, of Voluntown, m. Sam[ue]l **BROWN**, of Griswold, June 23, 1833, by Alexander Stewart, J.P.	297
Mary Ann, [d. Gardiner & Ellenor(?)], b. Oct. 8, 1833, at Griswold	292
Nelson, m. Prudence Ann **UTLEY**, b. of Griswold, June 7, 1834, by Rev. Nathan E. Shailer	213
Rebecca, of Richmantown, R.I., m. Geo[rge] H. **NIE**, of Hopkinton, R.I., Mar. 31, 1844, at Jewett City, by Rev. B. Cook, of Jewett City	271
Reuben, m. Sally **HUTCHINSON**, Dec. 13, 1818	36
Ruth, [d. Gardiner & Ellenor(?)], b. Oct. 10, 1808, at Exeter, R.I.	292
Ruth, m. Reuben **PARTRIDGE**, b. of Griswold, Feb. 1, 1827, by Elisha Partridge, J.P.	195
Sally, [d. Gardiner & Ellenor(?)], b. Apr. 16, 1814, at N. Stonington	292
Susannah, [d. Gardiner & Ellenor(?)], b. May 16, 1816, at Hopkinton, R.I.	292
Thankful Ang[a]l[ine], [d. Gardiner & Ellenor(?)], b. Aug. 6, 1827, at Griswold	292
William M., [s. Gardiner & Ellenor(?)], b. May 7, 1824, at Griswold	292
BARKELY, Mene, of Plainfield, m. John **HENRY**, of Griswold, Oct. 22, 1840, by Rev. William Wright, of Jewett City	244

Page

BARKER, William, m. Clarissa **CUTLER**, b. of Griswold, Dec. 3, 1826, by Rev. Seth Bliss 187

BARNES, Elijah, of Preston, m. Hannah **PALMER**, of Griswold, Nov. 25, 1839, by Rev. William Wright, of Jewett City 307

Sarah, of Preston, m. Douglass **TRACY**, of Lisbon, Sept. 24, 1834, by Rev. George Perkins 312

BARRETT, Gardner, of McKean Co., Penn., m. Elizabeth **COGSWELL**, of Griswold, June 15, 1842, by Rev. William R. Jewett 204

BARROWS, Eliza, m. Ezra **STILLMAN**, b. of Jewett City, July 16, 1843, by Rev. B. Cook, of Jewett City 25

BATES, James G., of Thompson Ct., m. Lucy F. **HYDE**, of Jewett City, Apr. 18, 1847, by Rev. B. Cook, of J[ewett] City 270

Sabin T., s. Sabin & Fanny, b. Jan. 6, 1831 62

BECKWITH, Denison, m. Mariah **BURDICK**, Jan. 17, 1828, by Thomas Stewart, J.P. 213

Sally Ann, of Canterbury, m. George **BURROWS**, of Norwich, Nov. 15, 1835, in Griswold, by Rev. George Perkins 300

Sarah M., m. William **HALL**, b. of Lisbon, June 28, 1840, by Rev. William Wright 295

BELCHER, Lucy, w. Nathan, d. Oct. 1, 1848 60

Nathan, d. Aug. 12, 1840 60

BENJAMIN, BENJAMINS, Ezra Gardiner, s. Rames & Prudence, b. Jan. 26, 1825 41

Hannah, d. Rames & Prudence, b. Sept. 22, 1813 41

Hannah, m. Thomas **RIX**, b. of Griswold, Mar. 9, 1845, by Comfort D. Fillmore, Elder 225

Henry Josiah, s. Hiram & Marilla, b. June 3, 1844 279

Hiram, m. Marilla **BRUMLEY**, June 14, 1842, by Rev. Levi Wallace 279

Laura, of Griswold, m. Benjamin F. **BENTLEY**, of N. Stonington, Dec. 30, 1839, by Rev. Nathan F. Shailer, of Preston 72

Lucy Ann, d. Rames & Prudence, b. Nov. 18, 1817 41

Prudence B., m. Jeptha G. **BILL**, of Griswold, Feb. 15, 1848, by Rev. Ebenezer Blake 257

Prudence P., d. Rames & Prudence, b. June 8, 1821 41

BENNETT, Dwight Waldo, s. Jacob & Esther, b. Aug. 24, 1825 95

Emily, twin with Emma, d. Elisha, b. June 6, 1815 116

Emily C., m. Albert E. **BROWN**, b. of Jewett City, Apr. 2, 1843, by Rev. B. Cook, of Jewett City 24

Emma, twin with Emily, d. Elisha, b. June 6, 1815 116

George Allen, s. [Jacob & Ether], b. July 25, 1823 95

Hannah, d. Elisha, b. Mar. 5, 1822 116

Henry, m. Priscilla **ADAMS**, Apr. 11, 1822 150

Henry, s. Henry & Priscilla, b. Apr. 19, 1824 150

Jacob, m. Esther **LAWRENCE**, May 9, 1822, by Rev. Horatio Waldo 95

Jacob, d. May 22, 1830 95

Julia, d. Elisha, b. Sept. 10, 1819 116

Lora Esther, d. Jacob & Esther, b. Aug. 14, 1827 95

Mary Loiza, d. Jacob & Esther, b. Sept. 18, 1830 95

Nancy Maria, d. Elisha, b. May 22, 1817 116

William R., m. Mary Ann **GREEN**, b. of Jewett City, Oct. 4, 1847, by Rev. B. Cook, of J[ewett] City 313

BENTLEY, Benjamin F., of N. Stonington, m. Laura **BENJAMIN**, of Griswold, Dec. 30, 1839, by Rev. Nathan F. Shailer, of Preston 72

BICKNELL, Lydia, of London, m. James M. **BUDDINGTON**, of Groton, June 10, 1838, by Seth Bliss, of Jewett City 91

Page

BIGELOW, Mary O., m. Elbridge **AVERY**, b. of Griswold, Nov. 24 1845, by Tho[ma]s S. Shipman 199
BILL, Ann Elizabeth, d. Elisha S., b. Nov. 7, 1825 97
Elisha S., of Griswold, m. Celestiana L. A. W. **BARBER**, of Westerly, R.I., July 23, 1837, by Deac. Comfort D. Fillmore 97
James L, m. Lucy A. **MAINE**, b. of Griswold, Mar. 12, 1843, by Rev. N. O. Shailer, of Preston 203
James Leonard, s. Elisha S., b. Aug. 16, 1821 97
Jeptha G., m. Prudence B. **BENJAMINS**, b. of Griswold, Feb. 15, 1848, by Rev. Ebenezer Blake 257
Jephthet Geer, s. Elisha S., b. Sept. 7, 1823 97
Maria D., of Griswold, m. Horatio **BORDEN**, of Norwich, Sept. 6, 1842, by Rev. B. Cook, of Jewett City 144
Sally M., of Griswold, m. Silas **FITCH**, of Westerly, R.I., Feb. 4, 1838, by Deac. Comfort D. Fillmore 151
BILLINGS, Alfred Gardner, s. Peleg, 2d, b. Mar. 20, 1823 122
Charles, m. Sally **LEWIS**, Aug. 24, 1823 140
Coddington, m. Catharine **SPENCER**, Sept. 13, 1832, by Rev. S. D. Jewett 286
George Frederick, s. Peleg & Abby, b. Jan. 13, 1825 122
Joseph W., s. Peleg, b. Mar. 7, 1836 122
Lucy, of Griswold, m. Asher **COATS**, of N. Stonington, Apr. 18, 1826, by David Coats, J.P. 68
Lucy A., of Griswold, m. Charles H. **SAUNDERS**, of Griswold, Nov. 1, 1846, by Rev. Jesse B. Denison. Witnesses: Jacob O. Lathrop, Charlotte A. Lathrop 160
Lucy Adams, d. [Charles & Sally], b. Jan. 24, 1824 140
Mary B., d. Peleg, b. July 13, 1840 122
Polly E., d. Peleg, b. May 7, 1832 122
Robert, m. Calista **KINNEY**, b. of Griswold, Nov. 29, 1827, by Alexander Stewart, Jr., J.P. 211
Theophilus, m. Violata **OLIN**, b. of Griswold, Dec. 22, 1839, by Rev. William R. Jewett 308
BITGOOD, Dolly, m. James GORTON, b. of Griswold, Sept. 5, 1824, by Rev. Horatio Waldo 147
BLACKMAN, Mary, m. Daniel **WALTON**, June 27, 1815, in Canterbury, by Daniel Frost, J.P. 8
BLISS, Francis, of Canterbury, m. Lydia **HOPKINS**, of Griswold, Nov. 6, 1831, by Welcome A. Browning, J.P. 271
BOARDMAN, Alfred, s. John & Abby, b. July 15, 1825 259
Almira, d. John & Abby, b. June 4, 1836 259
Byron, s. John & Abby, b. Apr. 14, 1831 259
Clement, s. John & Abby, b. Oct. 28, 1829 259
David, m. Mary **BROWN**, May 20, 1815 38
Emily, d. John & Abby, b. Oct. 23, 1820 259
Emily, m. Archibald **KINNE**, Mar. 27, 1845, by Rev. Russell Whitmore 99
Eunice, m. Jonas **HEWETT**, b. of Preston, Sept. 10, 1815, by Alexander Stewart, J.P. 56
Fanny, m. Elisha J. **ABEL**, Sept. 2, 1804 10
George, s. Hezekiah & Frances M., b. Apr. 6, 1846 260
Harris, s. John & Abby, b. Feb. 14, 1824 259
Harvey, s. John & Abby, b. Oct. 14, 1833 259
Hezekiah, m. Frances Mariah **PRENTICE**, b. of Griswold, [ ] 20, [18], by Rev. S. D. Jewett 260

Page

BOARDMAN, (cont.)
James, s. John & Abby, b. May 20, 1822 259
Jemima, w. David, d. July 30, 1814 38
Joseph, s. Hezekiah & Frances M., b. Aug. 30, 1833 260
Olive, m. Alpheas **KINGSLEY**, Mar. 1, 1843, by Rev. H. Torbush 195
BOLLES, Delight P., of Griswold, m. Ebenezer **WILLIAMS**, of Thompson, May 17, 1821, by Rev. Caleb Read 70
Joanna W., of Griswold, m. Ebenezer **WILLIAMS**, of Hampton, Dec. 27, 1826, by Rev. Seth Bliss 188
BORDEN, Horatio, of Norwich, m. Maria D. **BILL**, of Griswold, Sept. 6, 1842, by Rev. B. Cook, of Jewett City 144
BOSS, Phebe M., m. Edward **RICHMOND**, Sept. 8, 1827, by Thomas Stewart, J.P. 212
BOTTOM, Charles Henry, s. [William & Betsey], b. Apr. 23, 1827 42
Elizabeth N., d. [William & Betsey], b. Apr. 10, 1820 42
George, s. [William & Betsey], b. Oct. 16, 1821 42
Sobriety Fitzerland, d. [William & Betsey], b. Feb. 9, 1825 42
William, m. Betsey **BRUMLEY**, Mar. 23, 1818 42
BOWEN, Eliza G., of [Jewett City], m. W[illia]m W. **ALDRICH**, of Webster, Mass., Aug. 9, 1847, by Tho[ma]s S. Shipman 220
BRAMAN, Mariah, m. Thomas H. **EAGLESTON**, b. of Griswold, Oct. 13, 1839, by Welcome A. Browning, J.P. 82
Sarah Ann, of Griswold, m. Denison D. **TILLINGHAST**, of W. Greenwich, R.I., July 3, 1837, by Rev. Levi Nelson 189
BRANCH, Elisha, m. Abby **HERRICK**, b. of Griswold, Nov. 6, 1823, by Rev. Isaac Jennison 128
Ethel, s. Thomas & Mary, d. Mar. 13, 1828, ae. 67 y. 226
Lucy, d. Thomas & Mary, d. Apr. 10, 1826, ae 56 y. 226
Mary, wid. of Thomas, d. Dec. 17, 1825, ae 90y. 226
BRATON, Frances Patience, d. Pardon P. & Freelove, b. June 3, 1833 168
James J., s. Pardon P. & Freelove, b. Jan. 5, 1839 168
John J., s. Pardon P. & Freelove, b. Mar. 18, 1842 168
BREWSTER, Albert Gordon, s. Ephraim M. & Esther, b. Sept. 10, 1835 309
Ann Lathrop, d. Ephraim M. & Esther, b. Dec. 19, 1831 309
Betsey H., of Griswold, m. Robert N. **BABCOCK**, of N. Stonington, Dec. 11, 1845, by Rev. Roswell Whitman 151
Caroline Morgan, twin with Catharine Wilson, d. Simon, 2d, & Martha, b. Dec. 13, 1840 148
Catharine Wilson, twin with Caroline Morgan, d. Simon, 2d, & Martha, b. Dec. 13, 1840 148
Dwight Tyler, s. Frederick & Abby, b. Jan. 8, 1833 186
Edward, s. Frederick & Abby, b. Dec. 18, 1828 186
Elias, m. Sally **CORNING**, b. of Griswold, Mar. 30, 1824, by Rev. Horatio Waldo 143
Elias, d. Mar. 12, 1834 143
Elias Morgan, s. Ephraim M. & Esther, b. May 29, 1834 309
Emily Huntington, d. Frederick & Abby, b. Aug. 1, 1843 186
Frederick, m. Abby **TYLER**, b. of Griswold, Nov. 15, 1826, by Rev. Horatio Waldo 186
Frederick, Jr., [s. Frederick & Abby], b. Dec. 4, 1830 186
George, s. Frederick & Abby, b. Aug. 17, 1827 186
George, s. Frederick & Abby, b. Oct. 3, 1830 186
George, m. Olive **CRASS**, May 4, 1834, by Rev. S. D. Jewett 174
Hetty Ann, of Griswold, m. David F. **GORDON**, of Lisbon, Aug. 9, 1841, by Rev. W[illia]m R. Jewett 147
James M., m. Mary **BAKER**, Sept. 3, 1832, by Rev. S. D. Jewett 285

Page

BREWSTER, (cont.)
Jane, d. Frederick & Abby, b. Dec. 18, 1839 186
John Corning, s. Simon, 2d, & Martha, b. Mar. 5 1839 148
John T., s. Frederick & Abby, b. Apr. 15, 1835; d. June 25, 1836 186
Louisa Gennett, d. Ephraim M. & Esther, b. Dec. 16, 1839 309
Margary, w. Elias, d. Jan. 11, 1823 143
Martha, of Griswold, m. Capt. Moses **HILL[I]ARD**, of Preston, Feb. 4, 1824, by Rev. Horatio Waldo 139
Mary Tyler, d. Frederick & Abby, b. May 28, 1837 186
Simon, 2d, m. Martha **CORNING**, b. of Griswold, Oct. 8, 1837, by Rev. George Perkins 148
Simon Ashley, s. Simon & Martha, b. Jan. 18, 1842 148
Susan, of Griswold, m. James **WILSON**, of Lisbon, Mar. 4, 1827, by Welcome A. Browning, J.P. 192
Sybel, of Griswold, m. Appleton **MEECH**, of Preston, June 6, 1821, by Rev. Horatio Waldo 69

BRIGGS, Harvey D., m. Fanny K. **DOUGLASS**, Oct. 1, 1843, by Rev. C. S. Weaver, of Voluntown 214
Lewis W., of Coventry, R.I., m. Almira T. **TIFFANY**, of Griswold, Aug. 13, 1844, by Rev. B. Cook, of Jewett City. 274
Robert, of Cranston, R.I., m. Deborah **LEWIS**, of Griswold, July 22, 1821, by Rev. Caleb Read 71

BROMLEY, [see under **BRUMLEY**]

BROOKS, Agness E., d. George & Marian, b. Feb. 12, 1834 79
Charlotte W., d. George & Almira, b. Dec. 31, 1838 79
George W., of Norwich, m. Cynthia **LAW**, of Griswold, Aug. 31, 1836, at Jewett City (Griswold), by Rev. Tubal Wakefield 73
Isabella C., d. George & Marian, b. May 12, 1832 79
Marian S., d. George & Almira, b. Sept. 18, 1842 79
W[ilia]m J., s. George & Almira, b. Mar. 1, 1836 79

BROWN, Abby, of Griswold, m. Joshua **CASWELL**, of Preston, Dec. 29, 1829, by Levi Meech, Elder 245
Abigail, of Griswold, m. Nathaniel **MAIN**, of N. Stonington, June 8, 1829, by Alexander Stewart, Jr., J.P. 233
Albert E., m. Emily C. **BENNETT**, b. of Jewett City, Apr. 2, 1843, by Rev. B. Cook, of Jewett City 24
Alfred F., m. Abigail A. **MASON**, b. of Griswold, Oct. 30, 1842, by Rev. Benajah Cook, of Jewett City 286
Amanda, of Preston, m. Jesse **PHILLIPS**, of Plainfield, Nov. 7, 1825, by Rev. Seth Bliss, of Jewett City 157
Billings, of Preston, m. Mary A. **TYLER**, of Griswold, Feb. 24, 1825, by Rev. David Austin, of Bozrah 153
Calista R., m. Samuel A. **DAVIS**, b. of Preston, Jan. 22, 1846, by Rev. Roswell Whitman 260
Charles H., m. Abigail E. **PRATT**, b. of Jewett City, May 11, 1846, by Rev. B. Cook, of Jewett City
Daniel, of Preston, m. Mary **STANTON**, of Griswold, Oct. 7, 1840, by Rev. William R. Jewett 310
Dorothy, m. Samuel **KINNEY**, Apr. 24, 1826, by Nathan Stanton, J.P. 78
Eliza H., [d. Stephen?], b. Dec. 10, 1839 29
Elizabeth, m. John **COGSWELL**, b. of Preston, Oct. 14, 1790 50
Elizabeth Margaret, d. John H. & Emeline, b. Apr. 18, 1831 261

Page

BROWN, (cont.)
Emily, of [Griswold?], m. Reuben **ADAMS**, of Worcester, Mass., Nov. 8, 1847, by Tho[ma]s S. Shipman 26
Esther, d. Joseph & Mary Ann, b. Mar. 4, 1840 0
George P., s. Palmer A. & Sarah, b. Jan. 24, 1846 284
George Washington, s. Joseph & Mary Ann, b. Jan. 1, 1845 0
Isaac M., of Preston, m. Nancy **BROWN**, of Griswold, Nov. 25, 1830, by Rev. Joseph Treson 255
James Munroe, s. Wheeler & Louis, b. May 20, 1817 32
Lot R., of Preston, m. Mary D. **BURDICK**, of Griswold, Feb. 25, 1846, by Comfort D. Fillmore, Elder 48
Lucinda, m. Spencer **KINNEY**, b. of Griswold, Sept. 11, 1825, by Alexander Stewart, Jr., J.P. 156
Lucy U., [d. Stephen?], b. July 27, 1845 29
Maria M., of Jewett City, m. Newman **PERKINS**, of Griswold, Aug. 30, 1846, by Rev. B. Cook, of Jewett City 272
Martha D., [d. Stephen?], b. Apr. 12, 1844 29
Mary, m. David **BOARDMAN**, May 20, 1815 38
Mary Ann, d. John H. & Emeline, b. Sept. 6, 1829 261
Mary Buddington, d. Joseph & Mary Ann, b. Jan. 24, 1843 0
Mary F., of Griswold, m. Christopher B. **HOLMES**, of Stonington, Jan. 5, 1826, by Rev. Horatio Waldo 167
Mary F., [d. Stephen?], b. Dec. 6, 1847 29
Mary J., d. Palmer A. & Sarah, b. Sept. 16, 1847 284
Nancy, of Griswold, m. Isaac M. **BROWN**, of Preston, Nov. 25, 1830, by Rev. Joseph Treson 255
Nathan Lafayette, s. John H. & Emeline, b. Feb. 22, 1834 261
Oscar, s. Joseph & Mary Ann, b. Nov. 23, 1848 0
Patty, m. Nathaniel **PHILLIPS**, Jr., Mar. 19, 1809 111
Patty M., m. Daniel **STALKER**, Oct. 31, 1834, by Rev. Alfred Gates 164½
Prudence, of Griswold, m. Lemuel CAPRON, Mar. 26, 1822, by Alexander Stewart, Jr., J.P. 83
Sally, m. Calvin **KINNEY**, b. of Griswold, Apr. 17, 1836, by Alexander Stewart, Jr., J.P. 245
Sally Ann, d. John H. & Emeline, b. May 19, 1835 261
Sally Augusta, d. Walter and Sally Ann, b. Sept. 16, 1827 174
Sam[ue]l, of Griswold, m. Mary **BARBER**, of Voluntown, June 23, 1833, by Alexander Stewart, J.P. 297
Shepard F., [s. Stephen?], b. Jan. 14, 1853 29
Susan A., [d. Stephen?], b. June 1, 1842 29
Susan Maria, d. John H. & Emeline, b. Mar. 29, 1837 261
Sybel, d. Stephen & Lucy, b. Jan. 11, 1817 29
Sybel M., [d. Stephen?], b. Jan. 25, 1838 29
Walter Hyram, s. Walter & Sally Ann, b. Aug. 17, 1825 174
William, of North Kingstown, R.I., m. Amelia **YERRINGTON**, of Griswold, Jan. 1, 1822, by Welcome A. Browning, J.P. 82

BROWNELL, Rebecca S., of Pomfret, m. Marvin **BAKER**, of Norwich, Oct. 11, 1841, by Rev. William Wright, of Jewett City 152

BROWNING, Almira D., m. Henry L. **JOHNSON**, b. of [Griswold], May 14, 1834, by Rev. Geo[rge] Perkins 76
Beriah H., of Brooklyn, m. Sarah E. **CAMPBELL**, of Griswold, Nov. 21, 1842, by Rev. William R. Jewett 201

Page

BROWNING, (cont.)
Susan, of Griswold, m. William S. **BROWNING**, of S. Kingstown, R.I., Nov. 21, 1838, by Rev. William Wright, of Jewett City 158
William S., of S. Kingstown, R.I., m. Susan **BROWNING**, of Griswold, Nov. 21, 1838, by Rev. William Wright, of Jewett City 158
BRUMLEY, BROMLEY, Abigail, d. [Israel & Lucy], b. Jan. 8, 1803; d. Jan. 31, 1803 209
Alas D., s. [Israel & Lucy], b. Apr. 17, 1798 209
Amanda F., of Griswold, m. Josephus **DRESSER**, of Coventry, Dec. 1, 1833, by Rev. Alfred Gates 303
Amanda Fitzerlina, d. [Israel & Lucy], b. June 26, 1807 209
Amos G., of Preston, m. Eliza Ann **HERRICK**, Dec. 3, 1837, by Rev. Nathan E. Shailer, of Preston 74
Andrew, [s. Orrin P. & Mary A.], b. Mar. 29, 1848 121
Angellana, d. [Israel & Lucy], b. Dec. 29, 1812; d. Nov. 11, 1814 209
Appleton, s. [Israel & Lucy], b. Mar. 8, 1801; d. Apr. 27, 1823 209
Betsey, m. William **BOTTOM**, Mar. 23, 1818 42
Dwight, [s. Orrin P. & Mary A.], b. Sept. 29, 1840 121
Elizabeth, d. [Israel & Lucy], b. June 18, 1799 209
Esther, d. [Israel & Lucy], b. June 20, 1805 209
Esther, m. Ralph **FLINT**, Sept. 1, 1824, by Nathan Stanton, J.P. 146
Eunice, [d. Orrin P. & Mary A.], b. Jan. 19, 1852 121
George W., [s. Orrin P. & Mary A.], b. Mar. 10, 1842 121
Harriet Ann, m. W[illia]m **READ**, Apr. 9, 1848, by Nathan Stanton, J.P. 79
Israel, m. Lucy **TRACY**, Feb. 2, 1795 209
Joel Jefferson Madison Munroe, s. [Israel & Lucy], b. Sept. 7, 1817; d. Sept. 23, 1820 209
Jonathan, m. Polly C. **RAY**, b. of Griswold, Sept. 10, 1826, by Rev. Levi Walker 177
Lucy Tracy, d. [Israel & Lucy], b. May 19, 1809 209
Luther Safford, s. [Israel & Lucy], b. May 24, 1815; d. Sept. 22, 1815 209
Marilla, m. Hiram **BENJAMINS**, June 14, 1842, by Rev. Levi Wallace 279
Mary, [d. Orrin P. & Mary A.], b. Feb. 13, 1847 121
Orrin P., m. Mary A. **BURDICK**, Aug. 11, 1839, by Nathan Stanton, J.P. 121
Phillip D., s. [Israel & Lucy], b. July 10, 1796; d. Mar. 25, 1797 209
Sindra Marela, d. [Israel & Lucy], b. Apr. 23, 1811 209
Sophia, d. [Israel & Lucy], b. Mar. 29, 1804 209
Sophia, of Griswold, m. W[illia]m B. **MULKEY**, of Norwich, Jan. 1, 1832, by Rev. S. D. Jewett 279
Zerviah Morgan, d. [Israel & Lucy], b. Feb. 5, 1820 209
BUCK, Erastus, of Griswold, m. Eliza **MUNROE**, of Lebanon, Feb. 10, 1833, by Rev. S. D. Jewett 291
Jedediah, m. Mary E. **NEDSON**, b. of Griswold, Jan. 28, 1835, by David Avery 315
BUDDINGTON, James M., of Groton, m. Lydia **BICKNELL**, of [New] London, June 10, 1838, by Seth Bliss, of Jewett City 91
BUDLONG, William D., m. Louisa **SALSBURY**, b. of Griswold, Feb. 23, 1834, by Welcome A. Browning, J.P. 306
BUMP, Henry G., m. Ann **MAKES**, b. of Griswold, Oct. 21, 1832, by Welcome A. Browning, J.P. 287
BURBANK, Abiah, m. Denison B. **TUCKER**, Nov. 8, 1826, by Rev. Reuben S. Hazen of Agawam & Feeding Hills, W. Springfield 203
BURCH, Harriet, of Griswold, m. Albert L. **TRACY**, of Lisbon, Mar. 10, 1825, by Rev. Horatio Waldo 69
BURDICK, Charles, m. Nancy **RIX**, b. of Griswold, Feb. 14, 1838, by Rev. William R. Jewett 314

Page

BURDICK, (cont.)
Eleanor, of [Jewett City], m. Nathan B. **PECKHAM**, of Lisbon, Nov. 6, 1842, by Rev. B. Cook, of Jewett City 282
Elias, of Griswold, m. Mary M. **HOWE**, of Canterbury, Mar. 24, 1840, by Rev. William Wright, of Jewett City 153
James B., m. Eunice **RIX**, b. of Griswold, Mar. 8, 1848, by Rev. Jesse B. Denison 175
John, s. Mason, b. Oct. 8, 1818 57
John N., m. Maria P. **RIX**, b. of Griswold, Mar. 22, 1844, by Rev. Roswell Whitman 62
Louisa, m. Edward W. **SHEPHARD**, b. of Plainfield, Dec. 20, 1831, by Rev. S. D. Jewett 275
Lucy, d. Mason, b. Feb. 27, 1827 57
Lucy A., m. Samuel F. **WILBUR**, Mar. 29, 1841, by Deac. Comfort D. Fillmore 81
Mariah, m. Denison **BECKWITH**, Jan. 17, 1828, by Thomas Stewart, J.P. 213
Mary A., m. Orrin P. **BRUMLEY**, Aug. 11, 1839, by Nathan Stanton, J.P. 121
Mary D., of Griswold, m. Lot R. **BROWN**, of Preston, Feb. 25, 1846, by Comfort D. Fillmore, Elder 48
Rowland, of Lisbon, m. Eliza **JONES**, of Preston, Oct. 25, 1826, by Welcome A. Browning, J.P. 181
Sabra M., m. Harris S. **HOLMES**, b. of Griswold, Mar. 29, 1848, by Jesse B. Denison 280

BURLISON, Matilda, m. Joseph W. **HOLMES**, b. of Griswold, Oct. 12, 1828, by Rev. Seth Bliss, of Jewett City 223

BURROWS, George, of Norwich, m. Sally Ann **BECKWITH**, of Canterbury, Nov. 15, 1835, in Griswold, by Rev. George Perkins 300

BURTON, Albert, m. Lucinda **REYNOLDS**, b. of Griswold, Sept. 1, 1844, by Rev. Roswell Whitman 200
Amos, m. Betsey **RAY**, of [Griswold], Feb. 11, 1822, by Rev. Levi Walker 89-90
Betsey, of Griswold, m. Russell **RIX**, of Preston, Feb. 1, 1821, by Rev. Horatio Waldo 61
Julia A., m. Henry **MEECH**, b. of Griswold, Dec. 20 1832, by Rev. S. D. Jewett 288
Louisa, m. Erastus **KINNEY**, b. of Griswold, Oct. 19, 1837, by Rev. William R. Jewett 231
Lucy, of Griswold, m. Erastus **KINNEY**, of Plainfield, Apr. 1, 1829, by Rev. Horatio Waldo 231
Marintha, of Griswold, m. Zephaniah P. **HATCH**, of Thompson, N.Y., Apr. 1, 1841, by Rev. William R. Jewett 170
Mary, of Griswold, m. John E. **KINNEY**, of Thompson, N.Y., Feb. 19, 1829, by Rev. Horatio Waldo 228
Sally, m. Samuel **WORDEN**, Feb. 28, 1822, by Levi Walker, Elder 98

BUTTON, Edward, s. Joel & Eunice, b. July 16, 1829 201
Jane, d. Joel & Eunice, b. Mar. 23, 1827 201
Joel, m. Eunice **HINCKLEY**, Apr. 26, 1826 201
Joseph, Capt., of Griswold, m. Rachel **READ**, of Lisbon, Sept. 12, 1827, in Lisbon, by Rev. Levi Nelson 202
Olive, w. Joseph, d. Apr. 2, 1826 202
Olive, m. Charles **DABNEY**, b. of Griswold, Feb. 2, 1830, by Rev. Horatio Waldo 244
Sabra P., of Preston, m. Martin **OBRIEN**, of Norwich, May 5, 1845, by Tho[ma]s L. Shipman 5
Sibbel, of Griswold, m. Josiah **JONES**, of Hebron, Mar. 12, 1823, by Rev. Horatio Waldo 101

BYLES, Josias, m. Olive **AVERELL**, b. of Griswold, Oct. 2, 1839, by Rev. William R. Jewett 304

Page

CADY, Anne, of Griswold, m. Samuel **HEATH**, of Corinth, Vt., Dec. [ ], 1831, by Rev. Daniel Dorchester 276

P. P., m. Lucinda P. **ALLEN**, b. of Pomfret, Dec. 1, 1833, in Jewett City, by Bela Hicks, of Pomfret 304

CAMPBELL, Alpha R., of Voluntown, m. Clarissa **COOK**, of Griswold, Sept. 24, 1822, by Elisha Partridge, J.P. 107

Ezra K., of Voluntown, m. Mariah **COOK**, of Griswold, Dec. 7, 1820, by Rev. Horatio Waldo 58½

Harvey, of Voluntown, m. Eliza **COOK**, of [Griswold], July 8, 1828, by Rev. Orin Fowler 219

Jeanette, m. John **CAMPBELL**, b. of Voluntown, July 5, 1852, at Jewett City, by Rev. Daniel D. Lyon, of Jewett City 291

John, m. Jeanette **CAMPBELL**, b. of Voluntown, July 5, 1852, at Jewett City, by Rev. Daniel D. Lyon, of Jewett City 291

Sarah E., of Griswold, m. Beriah H. **BROWNING**, of Brooklyn, Nov. 21, 1842, by Rev. William R. Jewett 201

CAPRON, Lemuel, m. Prudence **BROWN**, of Griswold, Mar. 26, 1822, by Alexander Stewart, Jr., J.P. 83

CARPENTER, W[illia]m P., m. Huldah A. **HYDE**, of Franklin, Dec. 18, 1843, by Joshua Tracy, J.P. 224

CARR, Tabatha, of Griswold, m. Stafford **SCRANTON**, of Brooklyn, Aug. 13, 1837, by Rev. Benj[ami]n M. Walker 105

CASWELL, Joshua, of Preston, m. Abby **BROWN**, of Griswold, Dec. 29, 1829, by Levi Meech, Elder 245

CHACE, [see under **CHASE**]

CHALFANT, Samuel, m. Ziporah **MOTT**, Jan. 3, [18], by Levi Kneeland 242

CHAPIN, Otis, m. Est[h]er M. **FLINT**, b. of Hampton, Dec. 1, 1839, by Rev. Jacob Allen 167

CHAPLAIN, John M., of Lebanon, m. Eliza **DAVENPORT**, Nov. 16, 1835, by Rev. A. D. Jewett 42

CHAPMAN, Abner Butler, s. Dyer & Zipporah, b. Jan. 1, 1816 12

Archah, of Griswold, m. Allen **THURBER**, of Pittstown, N.Y., June 9, 1835, by Rev. S. D. Jewett 32

Betsey, m. Waterman **HARRIS**, b. of Griswold, Nov. 30, [1834], by Rev. George Perkins 312

Betsey P., m. Ephraim H. **UTLEY**, Feb. 9, 1815, by Rev. Horatio Waldo 5

Dyer, m. Zipporah **KINNEY**, Apr. 16, 1815 12

Eliza, of Griswold, m. Henry L. **JEWETT**, of Norwich, Nov. 8, 1838, by Rev. William R. Jewett 262

George A., m. Mary Ann **CHAPMAN**, Mar. 17, 1843, by Rev. H. Torbush 195

Henry, s. Joseph B. & Sarah, b. Nov. 7, 1826 257

Jane, d. Joseph B., & Sarah, b. Feb. 6, 1819 257

John Henry, of Paris, Oneida Co., N.Y., m. Abby Amanda **GATES**, of Jewett City, Mar. 26, 1846, at Jewett City, by Rev. B. Cook, of Jewett City 272

Mary Ann, d. Joseph B. & Sarah, b. Mar. 16, 1822 257

Mary Ann, m. George A. **CHAPMAN**, Mar. 17, 1843, by Rev. H. Torbush 195

Mary Olive, b. Nov. 21, 1860; d. Nov. 14, 1861. Reported by her father [George A.?] 195

Sarah, d. Joseph B. & Sarah, b. Jan. 14, 1828 257

Stewart, of N. Stonington, m. Betsey **COOK**, of Griswold, Nov. 10, 1829, by Comfort D. Fillmore, J.P. 239

Terzah, of Griswold, m. William **DABNEY**, of Brooklyn, Mar. 9, 1824, by Rev. Horatio Waldo 141

Page

COGSWELL, (cont.)
James M., b. Sept. 1, 1801 185
James M., m. Charlotte **COIT**, b. of Griswold, Nov. 6, 1826, by Rev. Horatio Waldo 185
Jane, d. James M. & Charlotte, b. Aug. 13, 1827 185
Joann, of Griswold, m. Edwin **TUCKER**, of Plainfield, Apr. 13, 1831, by Rev. S. D. Jewett 263
John, of Preston, m. Hannah **GALLUP**, of Voluntown, May 13, 1784 50
John, m. Elizabeth **BROWN**, b. of Preston, Oct. 14, 1790 50
John, s. [Nathaniel & Huldah], b. Dec. 28, 1847[sic] (1747) 120
Joseph, s. [Nathaniel & Bridget], b. June 8, 1760 120
Judeth, d. [Nathaniel & Huldah], b. Jan. 30, 1745/6 120
Louis, d. [Nathaniel & Huldah], b. Apr. 17, 1744 120
Martha, d. [Nathaniel & Hulday], b. Feb. 9, 1749 120
Nathan, twin with Elizabeth, s. [Nathaniel & Huldah], b. Oct. 11, 1754 120
Nathan, s. [Nathaniel & Huldah], b. Jan. 28, 1759 120
Nathaniel, m. Huldah **KINNEY**, b. of Preston, Dec. 8, 1737 120
Nathaniel, s. [Nathaniel & Huldah], b. May 16, 1742 120
Nathaniel, of Preston, m. Bridget **WEDGE**, of Canterbury, May 25, 1757 120
Nathaniel, Capt., of Preston, m. Eunice **WILLIAMS**, May 30, 1782 121
Nathaniel, Capt., d. Nov. 4, 1810 121
Patty, d. John & Elizabeth, b. Oct. 1, 1792 50
William, s. [Nathaniel & Bridget], b. Nov. 7, 1761 120
Zerviah, d. [Nathaniel & Huldah], b. July 14, 1752 120
COIT, Betsey, w. Nathaniel, d. Mar. 13, 1831 59½
Charles, of Norwich, m. Lucretia **TYLER**, of Griswold, May 14 1821, by Rev. Horatio Waldo 68
Charles, of Chelsea, m. Lydia **TYLER**, of Griswold, Jan. 21, 1824, by Rev. John Hyde 134
Charlotte, b. Sept. 20, 1805 185
Charlotte, m. James M. **COGSWELL**, b. of Griswold, Nov. 6, 1826, by Rev. Horatio Waldo 185
Hannah M., m. Charles **JOHNSON**, b. of Griswold, Mar. 9, 1830, by Seth Bliss, of Jewett City 247
Martha, m. Capt. Joseph **LESTER**, b. of Griswold, Sept. 8, 1816, by Rev. Horatio Waldo 104
Mary, of Preston, m. Amos **CLIFT**, of Windham, Feb. 12, 1761 92
Nathaniel, m. Betsey **PRENTICE**, Feb. 1, 1832, by Rev. S. D. Jewett 59½
Nathaniel, d. Mar. 11, 1848 59½
Ruth A., m. Rev. Andrew **DUNNING**, b. of Plainfield, [ ], by Tho[ma]s S. Shipman 58
COLBURN, Lois Ann, of Griswold, m. William **SMITH**, June 2, 1839, by Rev. William R. Jewett 223
Olive, m. Hiram **LEWIS**, b. of Griswold, Oct. 30, 1842, by Rev. Benajah Cook, of Jewett City 285
Sylvanus, m. Mehetable **EVERET[T]**, b. of Griswold, Jan. 28, 1828, by Elisha Partridge, J.P. 216
COLE, Julia A., m. Charles H. **FANNING**, b. of Griswold, Mar. 9, 1834, by Rev. George Perkins 311
Mewry B., m. Zilpha A. **HOWE**, b. of Griswold, Nov. 13, 1842, by Rev. B. Cook, of Jewett City 140
Silas, of Foster, R. I., m. Abby Ann **STONE**, of Griswold, Jan. 1, 1826, by Amos Read, Elder 160

Page

COLE, (cont.)
Stephen H., m. Sarah G. **COLVER**, b. of Griswold, Jan. 8, 1844, at Jewett City, by Rev. Benajah Cook 288
Sumner B., m. Clementine **HOWE**, b. of Griswold, Aug. 17, 1828, by Rev. Seth Bliss, of Jewett City 220
[**COLLIER**], **COLIER**, **COLYEAR**, Cabot, of Griswold, m. Mary **LATHAM**, of Groton, Sept. 4, 1826, by Welcome A. Browning, J.P. 175
Henry T., m. Mary Ann **HOPKINS**, b. residing in Griswold, Oct. 9, 1831, by Amos Read, Elder 273
Mary Loiza, d. Cabot & Mary, b. Sept. 5, 1828 175
COLVER, [see also **CULVER**], Sarah G., m. Stephen H. COLE, b. of Griswold, Jan. 8, 1844, at Jewett City, by Rev. Benajah Cook 288
COMSTOCK, Esth[h]er, m. James **JOHNSON**, b. of Norwich, Nov. 27, 1834, by Rev. Herman Perry 18
CONGDON, Dorcas, of Exeter, R.I., m. Daniel **KINNEY**, of Thompson, Dec. 19, 1830, by Alexander Stewart, J.P. 256
James, of Preston, m. Sarah **WAMSLEY**, of Griswold, Jan. 23, 1825, by Rev. Horatio Waldo 165
Stephen, of Preston, m. Henrietta **WAMSLEY**, of Griswold, Mar. 2, 1823, by Rev. Horatio Waldo 99
COOK, Abby E., d. Samuel & Abby, b. Mar. 28, 1825 267
Adin, of Preston, m. Sarah S. **CUSHMAN**, of Tunbridge, Vt., Apr. 25, 1822, by Rev. John Hyde 93
Alexander Hambleton, s. John & Thankful, b. Jan. 10, 1808 15
Avis E., of Griswold, m. Dwight **BAILEY**, of Franklin, Jan. 23, 1831, by Comfort D. Fillmore, J.P. 259
Benedic Franklin, s. John & Thankful, b. May 25, 1812 15
Betsey, of Griswold, m. Stewart **CHAPMAN**, of N. Stonington, Nov. 10, 1829, by Comfort D. Fillmore, J.P. 239
Betsey C., d. Esquire C. & Sally, b. Dec. 9, 1845 266
Charles, m. Cynthia **AVERY**, Dec. 14, 1815 34-A
Charles Edwin, s. Charles & Cynthia, b. Nov. 27, 1817; d. the same day 34-A
Clarissa, of Griswold, m. Alpha R. **CAMPBELL**, of Voluntown, Sept. 24, 1822, by Elisha Partridge, J.P. 107
Clark Robbins, s. Esquire C. & Sally, b. Dec. 6, 1835 266
Desire Abigail, d. John & Thankful, b. Mar. 7, 1810 15
Edward, s. Samuel & Abby, b. Oct. 14, 1830 267
Eliza, of [Griswold], m. Harvey **CAMPBELL**, of Voluntown, July 8, 1828, by Rev. Orin Fowler 219
Ellen B., d. S[amuel] & A[bby], b. Jan. 22, 1836 267
Esquire C., m. Sally **KINNEY**, b. of Griswold, Mar. 30, 1831, by Comfort D. Fillmore, J.P. 266
Eunice Permela, d. John & Thankfull, b. Aug. 15, 1814 15
Frances Maria, d. Esquire C. & Sally, b. July 10, 1841 266
Harriet Roxa, d. Esquire C. & Sally, b. Dec. 26, 1837 266
Henry Stewart, s. Nathan & Eliza, b. Apr. 3, 1816 16
John, m. Thankful **ECCLESTONE**, Apr. 7, 1803, in Stonington 15
John, s. John & Thankful, b. Dec. 30, 1805 15
Nathan, m. Eliza **STEWART**, Dec. 31, 1812 16
Orlando, s. Samuel & Abby, b. Aug. 24, 1827 267
Riland E., s. S[amuel] & A[bby], b. Oct. 17, 1834 267
Roxanna, m. Clark **SAUNDERS**, b. of Griswold, Mar. 30, 1834, by Alexander Stewart, J.P. 31

Page

COOK, (cont.)
Sally Jane, d. Esquire C. & Sally, b. Aug. 1, 1833 266
Samuel, m. Abby **CRARY**, Nov. 14, 1822 267
Samuel Avery, s. Nathan & Eliza, b. Jan. 23, 1814 16
Samuel C., s. Samuel & Abby, b. Feb. 12, 1824 267
Sarah, s.[sic][d.], Samuel & Abby, b. Oct. 10, 1832 267
Sidney, s. S[amuel] & A[bby], b. Sept. 17, 1838 267
Solomon(?), of Griswold, m. Daniel **KEGWIN**, of Voluntown, May 1, 1822, by Rev. Horatio Waldo 94
Susan A., d. Charles & Cynthia, b. July 27, 1822 34-A
Thankful, d. John & Thankful, b. Apr. 17, 1804 15
William P., s. Charles & Cynthia, b. May 24, 1819 34-A
-----, infant s. S[amuel] & A[bby], b. Oct. 31, 1838(sic) 267
COOPER, Elizabeth, d. John* & Abby Ann, . Feb. 20, 1845 [*Rev.] 247
COPP, Eliza S., of Griswold, m. Shubael **MEECH**, Sept. 26, 1842, by Rev. William A. Jewett 0
COPUT, Lewis W., of Uxbridge, Mass., m. Maria F. **GLASH**, of Griswold, Dec. 25, 1825, by Levi Meech, Elder 77
COREY, Charles C., m. Amy Ann **TILLINGHAST**, Aug. 18, 1831, by Rev. S. D. Jewett 268
Dwight T., m. Mary Ann **RATHBURN**, Jan. 3, 1847, by C. Terry 268
Eleanor, m. Samuel **WATSON**, Jr., Apr. 26, 1824, by Thomas Stewart, J.P. 100
George B., m. Olive A. **LAW**, b. of Griswold, May 4, 1834, by Welcome A. Browning, J.P. 308
Martin, m. Elizabeth **RICHARDSON**, July 21, 1822, by Thomas Stewart, J.P. 110
Roland R., m. Alice **LETSON**, b. of Voluntown, Sept. 15, 1831, by Rev. S. D. Jewett 269
Sally, m. Frederic **YARRINGTON**, b. of Griswold, Mar. 17, 1825, by Stephen Meech, J.P. 152
William G., m. Hannah **PERKINS**, b. of Griswold, May 19, 1822, by Caleb Read, Elder 99
CORNING, Martha, m. Simon **BREWSTER**, 2d, b. of Griswold, Oct. 8, 1837, by Rev. George Perkins 148
Sally, m. Elias **BREWSTER**, b. of Griswold, Mar. 30, 1824, by Rev. Horatio Waldo 143
COTTRELL, Jesse D., of W. Greenwich, m. Hannah **NICHOLS**, of Coventry, R. I., Oct. 24, 1847, by Rev. C. Terry 143
COUCH, Paul, Rev. of W. Newbury, Mass., m. Harriet **TYLER**, of Griswold, May 28, 1827, by Rev. Horatio Waldo 199
CRANDALL, CRANDAL, Lydia, m. Phillip **ELLICE**, b. residing in Griswold, Aug. 17, 1831, by Amos Read, Elder 272
Maria, of J[ewett] City, m. John **FROST**, June 19, 1847, by Rev. B. Cook, of Jewett City 269
Mary, of Griswold, m. Samuel **PECKHAM**, of Lisbon, Mar. 2, 1834, by Rev. George Perkins 311
Phinehas, Rev., of Talmouth, Mass., m. Deborah B. **TINKHAM**, of Griswold, Apr. 9, 1824, by Isaaac Jennison, Elder 115
CRARY, Abby, m. Samuel **COOK**, Nov. 14, 1822 267
CRASS, [see also **CROSS**], Olive, m. George **BREWSTER**, May 4, 1834, by Rev. S. D. Jewett 174
CROSS, [see also **CRASS**], Charles H., b. [ ], 1860 31
Ella J., b. [ ], 1855 31
Francis F., b. [ ], 1854 31
Sarah O., b. [ ], 1877 31

Page

CRUM, Sybel, m. James **SWEET**, b. of Griswold, Aug. 5, 1827, by Rev. Horatio Waldo 200
CULVER, [see also **COLVER**], Eliza, of Jewett City, m. John W. **WILLARD**, Sept. 21, 1847, by Tho[ma]s S. Shipman 132
CUMMINS, W[illia]m, m. Eliza M. **TANNER**, b. of Killingly, Dec. 30, 1843, by Rev. Roswell Whitman 223
CUSHMAN, Sarah S., of Tunbridge, Vt., m. Adin **COOK**, of Preston, Apr. 25, 1822, by Rev. John Hyde 93
CUTLER, Benjamin, of Killingly, m. Nancy Jane **PALMER**, of Plainfield, July 2, 1848, at Walter **PALMER**'s house, in Griswold, by Rev. Henry Robinson, of Plainfield 116
Charles, m. Roxanna **PORTER**, b. of Griswold, Jan. 28, 1827, by Rev. Seth Bliss 190
Clarissa, m. William **BARKER**, b. of Griswold, Dec. 3, 1826, by Rev. Seth Bliss 187
Melora, m. Ambrose **ALEXANDER**, b. of Griswold, Apr. 5, 1824, by Rev. Amos Read 148
Samuel H., m. Lucretia **WADE**, b. of Griswold, Dec. 25, 1825, by Rev. Silad Bliss, of Jewett City 161
DABNEY, Ann, d. William & Terzah, b. Feb. 14, 1825 141
Charles, m. Olive **BUTTON**, b. of Griswold, Feb. 2, 1830, by Rev. Horadio Waldo 244
Charles William, s. William & Terzah, b. Jan. 8, 1827 141
Mary Chapman, d. William & Terzah, b. Nov. 2, 1829 141
William, of Brooklyn, m. Terzah **CHAPMAN**, of Griswold, Mar. 9, 1824, by Rev. Horatio Waldo 141
DANIELS, Eliza, m. William **FRAZIER**, b. of Griswold, Jan. 1, 1829, by Rev. Seth Bliss, of Jewett City 226
James, m. Hannah **HULETT**, b. of Griswold, Nov. 28, 1839, by Rev. William Wright, of Jewett City 307
DARLING, Lemuel, m. Lucy **LATHAM**, b. of Griswold, Jan. 1, 1829, by Welcome A. Browning, J.P. 227
DAVENPORT, Eliza, m. John M. **CHAPLAIN**, of Lebanon, Nov. 16, 1835, by Rev. A. D. Jewett 42
Gurdon J., m. Sarah E. **LAWRANCE**, b. of Norwich, Sept. 21, 1845, by Rev. W[illia]m Potter 84
DAVIS, Alfred, m. Sally **WHIPPLE**, May 9, 1824, by Nathan Stanton, J.P. 57
Amos Palmer, s. Martin & Eunice Ann, b. Mar. 23, 1843 154
Andrew M., of Norwich, m. Susan E. **DOUGLASS**, of Jewett City, Nov. 7, 1847, by Rev. B. Cook, of J[ewett] City 264
Emmy Ann, d. Martin & Eunice Ann, b. May 8, 1841 54
Harmony C., of Griswold, m. Elias **GIDDINGS**, of Preston, Feb. 4, 1821, by Caleb Read, Elder 62
Milo S., of Montville, Ct., m. Matilda **SPRAGUE**, of Mass., Oct. 2, 1847, at Jewett City, by Rev. B. Cook, of J[ewett] City 269
Samuel, m. Olive Eddy, b. of Griswold, Mar. 3, 1840, by Rev. Tubal Wakefield 283
Samuel A., m. Calista R. **BROWN**, b. of Preston, Jan. 22, 1846, by Rev. Roswell Whitman 260
DAWLEY, Nathan, m. Lucretia **JACKSON**, b. of Warwick, R.I., Aug. 1, 1848, by Rev. Ebenezer Blake, in Griswold, Ct. 121
DENISON, Hannah P., m. Moses T. **GEER**, Feb. 1, 1816 23
DENNIS, Elvia, [d. James], b. May 26, 1832 133
Lucy B., [d. James], b. Jan. 24, 1827 133
Munroe, s. James, b. Jan. 31, 1821 133
Zipporah A., [d. James], b. Oct. 13, 1835 133
DEWEY, Daniel, of Lebanon, m. Patty **BAKER**, of Brooklyn, Feb. 2, 1824, by Rev. Horatio Waldo 138

Page

DICKINSON, DICKENSON, Charles B., Dr., of Hardford, m. Harriet **GEER**, of Griswold, Jan. 1, 1827, by Rev. Horatio Waldo 189

Mary B. of Washington, Vt., m. John **GRAVES**, of Griswold, May 29, 1845, by Rev. Roswell Whitman 184

DILLABY, Asa, of Norwich, m. Orcelia **THOMPSON**, [ ] 10, [ ], by Cha[rle]s E. Leonard, J.P. 217

DORRANCE, Gordon, Rev., of Sunderland, M[as]s., m. Wid. Olive **TYLER**, of [Griswold], Nov. 21, 1835, by Rev. S. D. Jewett 33

DOUGLASS, Daniel M., m. Polly **STANTON**, Aug. 19, 1822, by Thomas Stewart, J.P. 110

Emma Burrows, d. Stephen A. & Emma, b. June 25, 1833 282

Fanny K., m. Harvey D. **BRIGGS**, Oct. 1, 1843, by Rev. G. S. Weaver, of Voluntown 214

Stephen A., of Voluntown, m. Emma C. **STEWART**, of Griswold, Mar. 18, 1832, by Alexander Stewart, J.P. 282

Susan E., of Jewett City, m. Andrew M. **DAVIS**, of Norwich, Nov. 7, 1847, by Rev. B. Cook, of J[ewett] City 264

William W., m. Esther **WILCOX**, b. of Griswold, Oct. 26, 1828, by Levi Kneeland 225

DOWDELL, Daniel, m. Eliza Ann **SMITH**, b. of Norwich, Sept. 13, 1827, by Rev. Seth Bliss, of Jewett City 205

DOWNING, Hellen Mariah W., d. Eleazer B., b. July 30, 1818 64

Louisa Tyler, d. Eleazer B. & w., b. July 30, 1818 64

Lucy H., m. Henry B. **RAY**, Feb. 11, 1819 48

DRAPER, James, m. Ann **CHEESEBOROUGH**, b. of Griswold, Apr. 15, 1832, by Welcome A. Browning, J.P. 283

Rowland, of Norwich, m. Emeline **EGGLESTON**, of Griswold, Nov. 24, 1833, by Welcome A. Browning, J.P. 302

DRESSER, Josephus, of Coventry, m. Amanda F. **BRUMLEY**, of Griswold, Dec. 1, 1833, by Rev. Alfred Gates 303

DROWN, Mary, of Lisbon, m. Russell **HATCH**, of East Greenwich, R.I., June 2, 1822, by Rev. Horatio Waldo 100

DUCE, William, m. Eliza **JEFFREY**, b. residing in New London, July 30, 1837, by Amos Read, Elder 234

DUNN, Arnold, m. Elizabeth **RANDALL**, b. of Griswold, Sept. 8, 1829, by Rev. Seth Bliss 237

DUNNING, Andrew, Rev., m. Ruth A. COIT, b. of Plainfield, [ ], by Tho[ma]s S. Shipman 58

DURFEY, Alice, of Griswold, m. Joseph **LATHAM**, of Hebron, Apr. 24, 1823, by Rev. Horatio Waldo 94

Betsey, of Griswold, m. James D. **ALEXANDER**, of Voluntown, Feb. 27, 1832, by Rev. S. D. Jewett 18

Lucy K., of Griswold, m. Harlan **HYDE**, of Norwich, Apr. 28, 1841, by Rev. William R. Jewett 172

EAGLES, Charles, m. Mary M. **HERSKEL**, b. of Norwich, Sept. 13, 1827, by Rev. Seth Bliss, of Jewett City 204

EAGLESTON, [see also **ECCLESTON** and **EGGLESTON**], Thomas H., m. Mariah **BRAMAN**, b. of Griswold, Oct. 13, 1839, by Welcome A. Browning, J.P. 82

EAMES, Lucy Kinney, m. Walter **PALMER**, Jr., Nov. 24, 1812 2

EATON, Lucy, m. Thomas H. **WILSON**, Sept. 14, 1814 46

ECCLESTON, ECCLESTONE, [see also **EGGLESTON** and **EAGLESTON**], George L., m. Lucy R. **GATES**, b. of Jewett City, July 16, 1843, by Rev. B. Cook, of Jewett City 23

James N., of N. Stonington, m. Betsey **TIFT**, of Griswold, July 4, 1844, at Jewett City, by Rev. B. Cook, of Jewett City 224

Page

ECCLESTON, ECCLESTONE, (cont.)
Martha M., m. Edward **BARBER**, b. of Griswold, Oct. 6, 1844, by Rev. B. Cook, of Jewett City 265
Martha M., m. Edward **BARBER**, b. of Griswold, Oct. 6, 1844, by Rev. B. Cook, of Jewett City 274
Nelson, of Bozra[h]ville, m. Rosanna **MATHEWSON**, of Griswold, Nov. 16, [1834], by Rev. George Perkins 312
Rebecca, m. Sanford **MAIN**, May 30, 1816 18
Thankful, m. John **COOK**, Apr. 7, 1803, in Stonington 15
EDDY, Olive, m. Samuel **DAVIS**, b. of Griswold, Mar. 3, 1840, by Rev. Tubal Wakefield 283
EDMOND, EDMUNDS, Abby C., d. A[ndrew] & Mary E., b. Jan. 24, 1851 294
John T., s. A[ndrew] & Mary E., b. Mar. 15, 1848 294
Mary E., m. Benajah **GAY**, b. of Griswold, June 14, 1843, by Rev. William R. Jewett 218
Mary Frances, d. Andrew & Mary E., b. Dec. 19, 1845 294
EDWARDS, Christopher, of Voluntown, m. Deliverance **REYNOLDS**, of Griswold, Aug. 5, 1820, by Alexander Stewart, Jr., J.P. 55
Perry, Jr., of Canterbury, m. Sally **GREEN**, of Griswold, Aug. 16, 1826, by Elisha Partridge, J.P. 105
Perry, Jr., of Canterbury, m. Sally **GREEN**, of Griswold, Aug. 16, 1826, by Elisha Partridge, J.P. 179
EGGLESTON, [see also **ECCLESTON** and **EAGLESTON**], Emeline, of Griswold, m. Rowland **DRAPER**, of Norwich, Nov. 24, 1833, by Welcome A. Browning, J.P. 302
ELLIS, ELLICE, Else, of Griswold, m. Samuel W. **WHEELER**, June 24, 1821, by Rev. Caleb Read 72
Phillip, m. Lydia **CRANDALL**, b. residing in Griswold, Aug. 17, 1831, by Amos Read, Elder 272
Sabrina, of Griswold, m. Griswold **LATHAM**, of Preston, Mar. 21, 1834, by Rev. George Perkins 311
ENSWORTH, Andrew W., Jr., s. Andrew W. & Charity H., b. Nov. 20, 1844 142
EVERET[T], Mehetable, m. Sylvanus **COLBURN**, b. of Griswold, Jan. 28, 1828, by Elisha Partridge, J.P. 216
FANNING, Charles H., m. Julia A. **COLE**, b. of Griswold, Mar. 9, 1834, by Rev. George Perkins 311
John H., of Norwich, m. Elizabeth **PRIDE**, of Griswold, Mar. 1, 1831, by Rev. Seth Bliss 264
John M., s. [John W. & Mary], b. Nov. 22, 1825 149
John W., m. Mary **WILSON**, b. of Griswold, Oct. 7, 1824, by Rev. Horatio Waldo 149
FAULKNER, Frank, b. Nov. 2, 1860. Testified to by Betsey A. **FAULKNER** and Calvin **YOUNG** 188
Franklin, of Norwich, m. Betsey Ann **SPICER**, of Jewett City, Aug. 16, 1846, by Tho[ma]s S. Shipman 188
FENNER, Asa, m. Betsey **LAW**, . of Jersey City, Jan. 17, 1830, by Rev. Levi Kneeland 243
Asa, m. Sophia M. **LAW**, b. of Griswold, Nov. 20, 1836, by Rev. Shubael Wakefield 243
Betsey, w. Asa, d. Mar. 22, 1833 243
Charles, s. Joshua & Lucy Ann, b. May 3, 1830 294
Charles E., twin with Frederick, s. Asa & Sophia M., b. Feb. 19, 1853 243
Frank A., s. Asa & Sophia M., b. June 25, 1848 243
Frederick, twin with Charles E., s. Asa & Sophia M., b. Feb. 19, 1853 243
Henry W., s. Asa & Sophia M., b. Sept. 22, 1857 243
John A., s. Asa & Sophia M., b. June 15, 1846 243
Julia B., d. Asa & Sophia M., b. Oct. 1, 1839 243

Page

FENNER, (cont.)
William, s. Joshua & Lucy Ann, b. Feb. 11, 1832 294
FISHER, Isaac P., of Gourvenor, N.Y., m. Lydia N. **JOHNSON**, of Griswold, Sept. 5, 1842, by Tho[ma]s L. Shipman 3
FITCH, Martha J., m. James D. **RAY**, b. of Griswold, Sept. 18, 1842, by Rev. William R. Jewett 149
Silas, of Westerly, R.I., m. Sally M. **BILL**, of Griswold, Feb. 4, 1838, by Deac. Comfort D. Fillmore 151
FLETCHER, Caroline C., of Plainfield, m. Samuel **WHITFORD**, of Griswold, Oct. 17, 1847, by Tho[ma]s S. Shipman 285
FLINT, Est[h]er M. m. Otis **CHAPIN**, b. of Hampton, Dec. 1, 1839, by Rev. Jacob Allen 167
Levi Kneeland, s. Ralph & Esther, b. July 26, 1830; d. May 27, 1831; ae 10 m. 1 d. 146
Marietta, d. Ralph & Esther, b. Oct. 4, 1825 146
Ralph, m. Esther **BRUMLEY**, Sept. 1, 1824, by Nathan Stanton, J.P. 146
Ralph, s. Ralph & Esther, b. Feb. 23, 1827 146
FRAZIER, Alathea S., m. Edwin **MORGAN**, b. of Griswold, Jan. 1, 1838, by Rev. William R. Jewett 278
Alethear Sharp, d. John & Alethear, b. May 11, 1820 26
Frances Adaline, d. John & Alethear, b. Sept. 16, 1822 26
John, m. Alethear **STEVENS**, Nov. 10, 1816 26
Mary Elizabeth, d. John & Alethear, b. July 4, 1828 26
William, m. Eliza **DANIELS**, b. of Griswold, Jan. 1, 1829, by Rev. Seth Bliss, of Jewett City 226
FRENCH, Henry, of Hartford, m. Mary A. **LESTER**, of Griswold, Oct. 11, 1842, by Rev. William R. Jewett 215
FRINK, Marshall, of Norwich, m. Mary **GEER**, of Griswold, Sept. 16, 1827, by Elisha Partridge, J.P. 207
Patty, m. Timothy **AVERY**, b. of Preston, Aug. 20, 1826, by Nathan Stanton, J.P. 178
FROST, David, of Griswold, m. Mary **WALLACE**, Jan. 31, 1841, by Charles E. Leonard, J.P. 74
John, m. Maria **CRANDALL**, of J[ewett] City, June 19, 1847, by Rev. B. Cook, of J[ewett] City 269
FRY, Betsey, m. Samuel **PARTRIDGE**, b. of Griswold, Mar. 28, 1831, by Rev. Seth Bliss, of Jewett City 265
Caroline, of Plainfield, m. Allen **TENNANT**, of Voluntown, Aug. 30, 1835, by Erastus Benton 72
Orilla, m. Nicholas **MATHEWSON**, b. of Griswold, Jan. 31, 1832, by Rev. Joseph Ayer, Jr. 280
FULLER, Alonzo, m. Anne S. **YOUNG**, b. of Griswold, [Feb.?] 14, [1822?], by Tho[ma]s S. Shipman 88
GALLUP, Alban W., m. Rachel M. **LAWTON**, b. of [Griswold?], Mar. 12, 1833, by Levi Kneeland 293
Densy, m. Thomas A. **TIFFANY**, Nov. 30, 1843, at Hopeville, Griswold, by Rev. B. Cook, of Jewett City 29
Hannah, of Voluntown, m. John **COGSWELL**, of Preston, May 13, 1784 50
Henry W., of Sterling, m. Rebecca M. **PHILLIPS**, of Griswold, Sept. 26, 1843, by Rev. Jacob Allen 52
Rebecca, of Plainfield, Ct., m. Henry D. **HULL**, of Caneva, N.Y., Oct. 10, 1830, by Rev. Seth Bliss, of Jewett City 251
Sarah S., d. Alexis F. & Elizabeth L., b. Apr. 12, 1845 210
GARDINER, Eason, of Norwich, Ct., m. Hannah **TIFT**, of Griswold, Mar. 16, 1823, by Amos Read, Elder 24

	Page
GARDNER, Jasper G., of Mansfield, m. Olive **WOODSWORTH**, of Griswold, July 14, 1839, at Jewett City, by Rev. William R. Jewett	125
GASKILL, Henry Clay, s. Benjamin & Phebe, b. Nov. 9, 1829	230
Mary Elizabeth, d. Benjamin & Phebe, b. Jan. 27, 1828	230
GATES, Abby Amanda, of Jewett City, m. John Henry **CHAPMAN**, of Paris, Oneida Co., N.Y., Mar. 26, 1846, at Jewett City, by Rev. B. Cook, of Jewett City	272
Almira, d. Levi & Polly, b. Nov. 17, 1812	43
Betsey, d. Levi & Polly, b. May 16, 1816	43
Elijah, of W. Greenwich, R.I., m. Maata **PHILLIPS**, of Griswold, Oct. 11, 1825, by Rev. Horatio Waldo	169
Grovener Billings, s. Simon, b. June 18, 1809	47
John, s. Levi & Polly, b. June 4, 1824	43
John Bitgood, s. Simon, b. Apr. 5, 1810	47
Lucy R., m. George L. **ECCLESTON**, b. of Jewett City, July 16, 1843, by Rev. B. Cook, of Jewett City	23
Lydia, m. Alexander **WILLIAMS**, b. of Plainfield, Oct. 28, 1830, by Rev. S. D. Jewett	253
Mariah, d. Levi & Polly, b. July 15, 1814	43
Mary, d. Levi & Polly, b. Mar. 15, 1820	43
Nelson, s. Levi & Polly, b. July 1, 1819	43
Samuel Darcut, s. Simon, b. Aug. 6, 1816; d. Nov. 20, 1817	47
Samuel Darcut, s. Simon, b. Oct. 9, 1818 (twin with unnamed son)	47
Simon Horatio, s. Simon, b. Nov. 11, 1814	47
-----, twin with Samuel Darcut, s. Simon, b. Oct. 9, 1818; d. Oct. 17, 1817	47
GAY, Benajah, m. Mary E. **EDMUNDS**, b. of Griswold, June 14, 1843, by Rev. William R. Jewett	218
GEER, Abel, d. Aug. 10, 1816	24
Charles Averell, s. Fitch & Anna, b. Nov. 14 1831	124
David Austin, s. Elijah D. & Dorothy, b. Aug. 7, 1824	85
Delia Jane, d. Elijah D. & Dorothy, b. Mar. 13, 1827	85
Elbridge, s. Fitch & Anna, b. Sept. 29, 1826	124
Elijah Denison, s. Elijah D., b. Nov. 15, 1817; d. Feb. 6, 1818	85
Eliza Tyler, [d. John D.], b. July 31, 1838	276
Ethan Denison, s. Moses T. & Hannah P., b. Apr. 12, 1823	86
Fitch, m. Anna **TOWNSEND**, b. of Griswold, Nov. 18, 1819, by Rev. Horatio Waldo	124
Frances, d. Fitch & Anna, b. Apr. 21, 1824	124
Frances. d. Fitch & Anna, b. July 26, 1825	124
Hannah Loiza, d. Moses T. & Hannah P., b. July 26, 1826	86
Harriet, of Griswold, m. Dr. Charles B. **DICKINSON**, of Hardford, Jan. 1, 1827, by Rev. Horatio Waldo	189
Harriet A., of [Griswold], m. Ethan A. **PEIRCE**, of Truxton, N.Y., May 8, 1842, by Tho[ma]s S. Shipman	80
Harriet Abbey, d. Moses T. & Hannah P., b. Oct. 28, 1817	86
Harriet Paulina, [d. John D.], b. Jan. 23, 1843	276
John Wheeler, s. Moses T. & Hannah P., b. Dec. 16, 1828	86
Joseph Stoddard, s. Nathan, Jr., & Prescilla L., b. Apr. 9, 1831	284
Mary, of Griswold, m. Marshall **FRINK**, of Norwich, Sept. 16, 1827, by Elisha Partridge, J.P.	207
Mary, d. Nathan, [Jr.], & Prescilla L., b. Apr. 17, 1836	284
Mary Elizabeth, d. Fitch & Anna, b. Nov. 10, 1833	124
Mary Ellen, d. Elijah D., b. Nov. 29, 1819	85
Moses Edward, s. Moses T. & Hannah P., b. Dec. 14, 1819	86
Moses T., m. Hannah P. **DENISON**, Feb. 1, 1816	23

Page

GEER, (cont.)
Nathan, s. Nathan, Jr., & Prescilla L., b. Apr. 8, 1825 284
Nathan, d. Aug. 6, 1836 276
Olive, w. Nathan, d. Dec. 23, 1834 276
Robert Stoddard, s. Nathan, Jr., & Prescilla L., b. Mar. 19, 1828 284
Sally, m. Constant **TABOR**, b. of Griswold, Oct. 8, 1826, by Rev. Horatio Waldo 184
Samuel, of Griswold, m. Elizabeth **WILBUR**, of Norwich, Mar. 22, 1821, by Rev. John Sterry, of Norwich 114
Samuel Leonord, [s. John D.], b. Aug. 5, 1840 276
Sarah Caroline, d. Moses T. & Hannah P., b. Oct. 22, 1832 86
Sarah Maria, m. Edwin B. **MEECH**, b. of Griswold, May 17, 1836, by George Perkins 53
Semantha, m. John **GREENMAN**, b. of Jewett City, Aug. 30, 1835, by J. W. Newton 301
William, s. Fitch & Anna, b. Sept. 9, 1821 124
William Stanton, s. Elijah D. & Dorothy, b. May 21, 1822 85
GIBSON, Sutton, m. Sally **HOPKINS**, b. of Griswold, July 22, 1821, by Thomas Stewart, J.P. 73
GIDDINGS, Elias, of Preston, m. Harmony C. **DAVIS**, of Griswold, Feb. 4, 1821, by Caleb Read, Elder 62
GLASH, Maria F., of Griswold, m. Lewis W. **COPUT**, of Uxbridge, Mass., Dec. 25, 1825, by Levi Meech, Elder 77
GLASKO, Eliza, d. Isaac, b. June 11, 1811 96
Isaac Moodey, s. Isaac, b. Nov. 16, 1813 96
Mary Ann, d. Isaac, b. May 30, 1805 96
Mary Ann, of Griswold, m. James **WALLIS**, of New York, Dec. 31, 1826, by Levi Meech, Elder 221
Mirando, d. Isaac, b. Aug. 20, 1820 96
GLEASON, Arthur, of Pomfret, m. Sarah **NORTH[R]UP**, of Griswold, Nov. 4, 1824, by Rev. Horatio Waldo 64
GOLD, Eve C., of [Griswold], m. Pashall N. **TUOSKSBURY**, of Hartland, Vt., Jan. 30, 1837, by Geo[rge] Perkins 196
GORDON, [see also **GORTON**], Almira, of Lisbon, Ct., m. Thaddeus **PRENTICE**, of Munden, Mass., July 26, 1818 79
David F., of Lisbon, m. Hetty Ann **BREWSTER**, of Griswold, Aug. 9, 1841, by Rev. W[illia]m R. Jewett 147
Ruth Jane, d. Gideon W. & Sophronia, b. Feb. 23, 1834 71
GORTON, [see also **GORDON**], Benjamin, m. Sarah Ann **ALEXANDER**, b. residing in Griswold, Oct. 19, 1823, by Amos Read, Elder 125
James, m. Dolly **BITGOOD**, b. of Griswold, Sept. 5, 1824, by Rev. Horatio Waldo 147
GRANT, Charles H., of Preston, m. Elizabeth A. **PRENTICE**, of Griswold, June 8, 1841, by Rev. William R. Jewett 171
GRAVES, Abby P., d. June 2, 1816 184
Catharine B., of Griswold, m. Ebenezer T. **ADAMS**, of Mystic, Apr. 17, 1839, by Rev. William R. Jewett 183
Catharine Bradford, d. John & Mary, b. Oct. 28, 1816 81
John, m. Mary **PENNIMAN**, Apr. 7, 1814 81
John, s. John & Mary, b. May 29, 1819 81
John, of Griswold, m. Mary B. **DICKENSON**, of Washington, Vt., May 29, 1845, by Rev. Roswell Whitman 184
John, d. Mar. 31, 1855 184
Joseph, d. Aug. 21, 1827 184
Joseph Leonord, s. John & Mary, b. Apr. 8, 1823 81
Mary, d. John & Mary, b. Aug. 10, 1828 81

Page

GRAVES, (cont.)
Mary, d. May 30, 1842 184
GREEN, Bennett, of Canterbury, m. Malissa Ann **WHITMAN**, of Griswold, Nov. 24, 1838, by Elisha Partridge, J.P. 157
Charles, m. Delany **GREEN**, b. of Canterbury, Sept. 2, 1827, by Elisha Partridge, J.P. 206
Delany, m. Charles **GREEN**, b. of Canterbury, Sept. 2, 1827, by Elisha Partridge, J.P. 206
Diana, d. Samuel & Phebe, b. Oct. 15, 1806 9
Emila, d. Samuel & Phebe, b. Apr. 14, 1816 9
Frederick, alias Frederick Olin, s. Betsey **GREEN**, b. Feb. 25, 1801 76
John Leland, s. Samuel & Phebe, b. Aug. 2, 1809 9
Mary, of Plainfield, m. Elisha **TYLER**, of Griswold, Mar. 9, 1830, by Rev. Seth Bliss 246
Mary, w. John, d. Sept. 5, 1849, ae. 63 y. 38
Mary Ann, m. William R. **BENNETT**, b. of Jewett City, Oct. 4, 1847, by Rev. B. Cook, of J[ewett] City 313
Mary Jane, d. Samuel & Phebe, b. Oct. 25, 1824 9
Peggy, of Plainfield, m. Wheeler **MORGAN**, of Voluntown, Nov. 27, 1826, by Alexander Stewart, J.r, J.P. 183
Sally, of Griswold, m. Perry **EDWARDS**, Jr., of Canterbury, Aug. 16, 1826, by Elisha Partridge, J.P. 105
Sally, of Griswold, m. Perry **EDWARDS**, Jr., of Canterbury, Aug. 16, 1826, by Elisha Partridge, J.P. 179
Samuel, s. Samuel & Phebe, b. Oct. 2, 1818 9
Sarah Ann, d. Samuel & Phebe, b. Mar. 24, 1821 9
William Randolph, s. Samuel & Phebe, b. Mar. 5, 1814 9
GREENMAN, Dwight, s. James & Sarah L., b. Oct. 16, 1837 241
George, s. James & Sarah L., b. Jan. 27, 1843 241
James, m. Sarah L. **MORSE**, Mar. 21, 1836, by Rev. S. D. Jewett 241
John, m. Semantha **GEER**, b. of Jewett City, Aug. 30, 1835, by J. W. Newton 301
Sarah Morse, d. James & Sarah L., b. May 23, 1840 241
-----, s. James & Sarah [L.], b. Dec. [ ], 1846 241
GRISWOLD, Caleb, of Franklin, m. Mahala **PARTRIDGE**, of Griswold, Apr. 26, 1821, by Rev. Horatio Waldo 67
GUILE, Charles, m. Lucy **RAY**, b. of Griswold, Feb. 22, 1824, by Levi Meech, Elder 136
Charles Loring, s. Charles & Lucy, b. Mar. 30, 1832 136
Daniel S., s. Henry & Eleanor, b. Oct. 12, 1831 114
Gilbert, m. Lucy **TURNER**, b. of Griswold, Dec. 23, 1824, by Levi Meech, Elder 151
Susan Ann, d. Charles & Lucy, b. July 23, 1828 136
William S., s. Henry & Eleanor, b. July 14, 1829 114
HAKES, Ann, m. Henry G. **BUMP**, b. of Griswold Oct. 21, 1832, by Welcome A. Browning, J.P. 287
Mary Ann, d. Elisha & Mary, b. June 29, 1830 165
HALL, Ichabod, d. Sept. 19, 1847, ae. 65 y. 38
James M., m. Lydia **SMITH**, Feb. 23, 1823, by Thomas Stewart, J.P. 98
William, m. Sarah M. **BECKWITH**, b. of Lisbon, June 28, 1840, by Rev. William Wright 295
William P., m. Susan **PELHAM**, b. of Griswold, Jan. 11, 1846, by Rev. Roswell Whitman 296
HALLOWAY, Abby, m. John E. **KINNEY**, Jan. 1, 1832, by Thomas Stewart, J.P. 278
HALSEY, Clarina, b. Feb. 23, 1783 103
Clarina, m. John **AVERY**, s. John & Lucy, May 28, 1812 103

Page

HAMILTON, Mary, m. Ezekiel **SIMONS**, b. of Griswold, Aug. 7, 1831, by Elisha Partridge, J.P. 71
HAMMOND, Maduria, m. Festus C. **LITCHFIELD**, b. of Southbridge, Mass., Oct. 27, [1834], by Rev. George Perkins 312
HARRIS, Waterman, m. Betsey **CHAPMAN**, b. of Griswold, Nov. 30, [1834], by Rev. George Perkins 312
William P., of Groton, m. Susan **AVERY**, of Griswold, Nov. 12, 1833, by Rev. S. D. Jewett 300
HARVEY, Betsey, of Griswold, m. William **TILLEY**, European, Oct. 7, 1821, by Amos Read, Elder 78
Charles E., s. George & Mary, b. Feb. 13, 1834 252
Elizabeth M., d. George & Mary, b. May 22, 1825 252
Emily L., d. George & Mary, b. Apr. 8, 1838 251
George, b. Nov. 5, 1800 252
George, s. George & Mary, b. Aug. 13, 1821 252
Jane F., d. George & Mary, b. Mar. 22, 1830 252
Mary, b. Feb. 19, 1801 252
Mary A., d. George & Mary, b. June 10, 1818 252
Olive, d. George & Mary, b. May 11, 1836 251
Sarah, d. George & Mary, b. Mar. 2, 1828 252
William H., s. George & Mary, b. June 12, 1832 252
HATCH, Betty, d. Dec. 22, 1818 35
Elisha, d. May 14, 1839 35
Hannah, d. Jan. 6, 1823 80
Russell, of East Greenwich, R.I., m. Mary **DROWN**, of Lisbon, June 2, 1823, by Rev. Horatio Waldo 100
Zephaniah P., of Thompson, N.Y., m. Marintha **BURTON**, of Griswold, Apr. 1, 1841, by Rev. William R. Jewett 170
Zerviah, d. May 10, 1817 35
HAWKINS, Alexander S., s. John & Sally, b. Dec. 25, 1838 111
John C., s. John & Sally, b. Sept. 7, 1834 111
Julia S., d. [John & Sally], b. Mar. 10, 1842 111
Lucy B., d. [John & Sally], b. Aug. 15, 1833 111
Sarah M., [d. John & Sally], b. Oct. 13, 1844 111
William H., s. John & Sally, b. Dec. 6, 1816 [1836?] 111
HAZIN, Frances A., of Griswold, Ct., m. John E. **MAYNARD**, of Shrewsbury, Vt., Nov. 6, 1843, by Rev. Henry Torbush 217
HEALEY, William A., of Packersville, m. Susan C. **MOORE**, of Jewett City, July 26, 1841, by Rev. B. Cook, of Jewett City 146
HEATH, Samuel, of Corinth, Vt., m. Anne **CADY**, of Griswold, Dec. [ ], 1831, by Rev. Daniel Dorchester 276
HEFLIN, Mary, m. George A. **YARRINGTON**, b. of Preston, Nov. 16, 1826, by Welcome A. Brownig, J.P. 182
HENRY, John, of Griswold, m. Mene **BARKELY**, of Plainfield, Oct. 22, 1840, by Rev. William Wright, of Jewett City 244
HERRICK, HERRECK, Abby, m. Elisha **BRANCH**, b. of Griswold, Nov. 6, 1823, by Rev. Isaac Jennison 128
Calista, d. Robert & Eliza, b. June 17, 1827 66
Eliza Ann, d. Robert & Eliza, b. Aug. 30, 1821 66
Eliza Ann, m. Amos G. **BROMLEY**, of Preston, Dec. 3, 1837, by Rev. Nathan E. Shailer, of Preston 74
Ephraim, d. Oct. 3, 1825 30
Eunice Benjamins, d. Robert & Eliza, b. Sept. 15, 1825 66

Page

HERRICK, HERRECK, (cont.)
Hannah Ann, d. Robert & Eliza, b. June 20, 1829 66
Lucy, d. Robert & Eliza, b. Aug. 24, 1823 66
Persus, m. Augustus **PARISH**, [ ], by Rev. H. Forbush 51
Robert, m. Eliza **LOCK**, b. of Griswold, Nov. 23, 1820, by Levi Walker 66
Robert Avery, s. Robert & Eliza, b. Sept. 8, 1831 66
Sarah, w. Ephraim, d. Nov. 20, 1816 112
HERRINGTON, [see also **YARRINGTON**], Thomas, of Lisbon, m. Lydia **APLEY**, of Plainfield, Jan. 2, 1823, by Elisha Partridge, J.P. 118
HERSKEL, Mary M., m. Charles **EAGLES**, b. of Norwich, Sept. 13, 1827, by Rev. Seth Bliss, of Jewett City 204
HEWETT, Horatio Boardman, s. Jonas & Eunice, b. Sept. 13, 1816 56
Jonas, m. Eunice **BOARDMAN**, b. of Preston, Sept. 10, 1815, by Alexander Stewart, J.P. 56
Jonas, d. Jan. 31, 1823 56
Mary Brown, d. Jonas & Eunice, b. Apr. 5, 1823 56
Thomas Holmes, s. Jonas & Eunice, b. Sept. 25, 1819 56
HILL[I]ARD, Moses, Capt., of Preston, m. Martha **BREWSTER**, of Griswold, Feb. 4, 1824, by Rev. Horatio Waldo 139
HILLMAN, Charles, m. Sally **REXFORD**, b. of Griswold, Feb. 6, 1842, by Rev. William Wright 73
HINCKLEY, HINCKLY, Charles, of Plainfield, m. Lucy R. **AVERELL**, of Griswold, May 1, 1839, by Rev. William R. Jewett 183
Eunice, m. Joel **BUTTON**, Apr. 26, 1826 201
Lucy Landon, d. Orin & Catharine B., b. June 16, 1846 265
HISCOX, Clarinda N., m. Henry N. **RAY**, b. of Jewett City, Aug. 1, 1842, by Rev. B. Cook, of Jewett City 216
HITCHCOCK, William T., d. Nov. 27, 1841 130
HOLDRIDGE, Phinehas, of Groton, m. Fanny **STARR**, of Griswold, June 26, 1828, by Rev. Seth Bliss, of Jewett City 218
HOLMES, A. Bartlett, [s. Harris S.? & Sabra M.?], b. Nov. 15, 1849 280
Christopher B., of Stonington, m. Mary F. **BROWN**, of Griswold, Jan. 5, 1826, by Rev. Horatio Waldo 167
Harris S., m. Sabra M. **BURDICK**, b. of Griswold, Mar. 29, 1848, by Jesse B. Denison 280
Joseph W., m. Matilda **BURLISON**, b. of Griswold, Oct. 12, 1828, by Rev. Seth Bliss, of Jewett City 223
HOPKINS, Lydia, of Griswold, m. Francis **BLISS**, of Canterbury, Nov. 6, 1831, by Welcome A. Browning, J.P. 271
Mary Ann, m. Henry T. **COLYEAR**, b. residing in Griswold, Oct. 9, 1831, by Amos Read, Elder 273
Sally, m. Sutton **GIBSON**, b. of Griswold, July 22, 1821, by Thomas Stewart, J.P. 73
HOWARD, Edward Milton, s. George F. & Mary F., b. Mar. 19, 1852 239
Phila, m. Dexter B. **SHAW**, b. of Cumberland, R.I., Aug. 21, 1847, by Rev. Jesse B. Denison. Witnesses: E. Bill, Abby W. Denison. 141
HOWE, HOW, Catharine, of Canterbury, m. Ezra W. **KEIGWIN**, of Griswold, Dec. 30, 1832, by Rev. S. D. Jewett 289
Clementine, m. Sumner B. **COLE**, b. of Griswold, Aug. 17, 1828, by Rev. Seth Bliss, of Jewett City 220
Daniel, of Canterbury, m. Mary Ann **PHILLIPS**, of Griswold, Mar. 29, 1847, by Cha[rle]s Noble 249
Mary M., of Canterbury, m. Elias **BURDICK**, of Griswold, Mar. 24, 1840, by Rev. William Wright, of Jewett City 153

	Page
HOWE, HOW, (cont.)	
Silas, m. Rebecca **RUTH[ER]FORD**, Jan. 29, 1826, by Rev. Seth Bliss	162
Zilpha A., m. Mewry B. **COLE**, b. of Griswold, Nov. 13, 1842, by Rev. B. Cook, of Jewett City	140
HOXSIE, James, of Griswold, m. Mary **AVERY**, of Plainfield, May 8, 1845, by Tho[ma]s S. Shipman	247
Phebe M., of Richmond, R.I., m. Job **KENYON**, of Exeter, R.I., Apr. 7, 1854, by Rev. Charles Dixon	286
HULETT, Hannah, m. James **DANIELS**, b. of Griswold, Nov. 28, 1839, by Rev. William Wright, of Jewett City	307
Matilda, m. Edward **NYLES**, b. of Griswold, Dec. 8, 1839, by Rev. William Wright, of Jewett City	307
HULL, Henry D., of Geneva, N.Y., m. Rebecca **GALLUP**, of Plainfield, Ct., Oct. 10, 1830, by Rev. Seth Bliss, of Jewett City	251
HUNTINGTON, Abigail, d. Daniel & Elizabeth, b. Nov. 27, 1806	14
Andrew, s. Daniel & Elizabeth, b. July 29, 1808	14
Andrew, d. Jan. 31, 1830	30
Betsey, m. John **PRENTICE**, Jan. 19, 1810	65
Dan, of Lebanon, m. Emily **WILSON**, of Griswold, Mar. 5, 1838, by Welcome A. Browning, J.P.	106
Daniel, b. Oct. 20, 1775; m. Elizabeth **LORD**, Apr. 24, 1800	14
Daniel, s. William & Elizabeth, b. July 31, 1844	299
Elizabeth, w. Daniel, d. July 21, 1844	49
Elizabeth, w. W[illia]m, d. [ ]	299
George, s. Daniel & Elizabeth, b. Mar. 30, 1805	14
George, s. Daniel & Elizabeth, wrecked at sea on board the steamboat Pulaski, June 14, 1838, and lost	49
Hannah, d. William & Elizabeth, b. Mar. 21, 1840	299
Henry, s. Daniel & Elizabeth, b. Feb. 25, 1801	14
Henry, s. Daniel & Elizabeth, b. Dec. 3, 1807	14
Lucy, d. Daniel & Elizabeth, b. Apr. 15, 1803	14
Lucy, w. Andrew, d. Feb. 10, 1815	30
Lucy, d. Daniel & Elizabeth, d. Nov. 15, 1838	49
Olivee, d. Daniel & Elizabeth, b. Jan. 19, 1817	14
Olive, m. Rev. William P. **AVERY**, Oct. 2, 1844, by Rev. Roswell Whitman	215
Sarah, d. William & Elizabeth, b. Oct. 4, 1836	299
Simon, s. Daniel & Elizabeth, b. July 24 1810	14
Sybel, d. Daniel & Elizabeth, b. Sept. 22, 1818	49
Sybil, d. Daniel & Elizabeth, d. June 30, 1849	49
William, s. Daniel & Elizabeth, b. July 9, 1812	14
William, m. Elizabeth **TYLER**, b. of Griswold, Nov. 6, 1833, by Rev. S. D. Jewett	299
W[illia]m, of Griswold, m. Eunice **AVERY**, of Preston, Nov. 17, 1847, by Rev. C. Terry	299
HUTCHENS, Asa, of Thompson, m. Susan **TUCKER**, of Griswold, Oct. 28, 1822, by Rev. Horatio Waldo	115
HUTCHINSON, Amos, d. Feb. 15, 1817	28
Daniel, d. Apr. 2, 1814	80
Daniel, s. Daniel & Sally, b. Nov. 24, 1824	80
Elizabeth, d. Ralph & Eliza, b. Apr. 15, 1821	22
Merebah, of Griswold, m. Roger **WILLIAMS**, of Groton, June 21, 1820, by Phillip Gray, J.P.	54
Prosper Kimball, s. Ralph & Eliza, b. Aug. 29, 1817	22
Ralph, m. Eliza **KIMBALL**, Oct. 6, 1816	22

Page

HUTCHINSON, (cont.)
Sally, m. Reuben **BARBER**, Dec. 13, 1818 36
HYDE, Charles, s. John & Sally, b. Nov. 25, 1823 109
Harlan, of Norwich, m. Lucy K. **DURFEY**, of Griswold, Apr. 28, 1841, by Rev. William R. Jewett 172
Harriet, m. Henry C. **TYLER**, b. of Griswold, Mar. 13, 1823, by Rev. Horatio Waldo 123
Huldah A., of Franklin, m. W[illia]m P. **CARPENTER**, Dec. 18, 1843, by Joshua Tracy, J.P. 224
Jerusha Jane, d. John & Sally, b. Dec. 27, 1826 109
John, of Preston, m. Sally **YER[R]INGTON**, of Griswold, Oct. 6, 1822, by Welcome A. Browning, J.P. 109
Lucy F., of Jewett City, m. James G. BATES, of Thompson, Ct., Apr. 18, 1847, by Rev. B. Cook, of J[ewett] City 270
JACKSON, Abigail, d. Thomas, b. June 9, 1817 52
Albert, s. Thomas, b. Dec. 1, 1815 52
Esther, d. Thomas, b. Feb. 20, 1811 52
Horace, s. Thomas, b. Oct. 24, 1818 52
Lucretia, m. Nathan **DAWLEY**, b. of Warwick, R.I., Aug. 1, 1848, in Griswold, Ct., by Rev. Ebenezer Blake 121
Mary, d. Thomas, b. July 20, 1814 52
Mary, m. Ezra **WHIPPLE**, Jr., b. of Griswold, Apr. 10, 1836, by Alexander Stewart, Jr., J.P. 242
Thomas, s. Thomas, b. Nov. 19, 1808 52
JEFFREY, Eliza, m. William **DUCE**, b. residing in New London, July 30, 1837, by Amos Read, Elder 234
JEWETT, Henry, s. Spafford D. & Abigail G., b. June 20, 1833 277
Henry L., of Norwich, m. Eliza **CHAPMAN**, of Griswold, Nov. 8, 1838, by Rev. William R. Jewett 262
Jane, d. Spafford D. & Abigail G., b. Oct. 13, 1831; d. Apr. 10, 1832 277
Spafford D., Rev., of Griswold, m. Abigail G. **SHIPMAN**, of Berlin, Dec. 22, 1830 277
William R., m. Hannah Ann C. **LESTER**, b. of Griswold, Sept. 24, 1838, by Rev. Samuel Rockwell 293
JOHNSON, Almira B., d. H[enry] L. & A[lmira] D., b. Sept. 30, 1839; d. Feb. 4, 1841 76
Charles, m. Hannah M. **COIT**, b. of Griswold, Mar. 9, 1830, by Seth Bliss, of Jewett City 247
Daniel, s. Stephen & Lydai, b. May 22, 1813 7
Dwight, of New York, m. Mary **TUCKER**, of Griswold, Sept. 2, 1844, by Rev. Roswell Whitman 262
Frank, s. John & Lydia, b. Feb. 8, 1819; d. Apr. 8, 1819 51
Henry, s. Nathan & Ruth F., b. Jan. 9, 1828 249
Henry L., m. Almira D. **BROWNING**, b. of [Griswold], May 14, 1834, by Rev. Geo[rge] Perkins 76
Henry Larned, s. H[enry] L. & A[lmira] D., b. July 11, 1837 76
Isabella, d. H[enry] L. & A[lmira] D., b. Jan. 3, 1844, at E. Haddam 76
James, m. Est[h]er **COMSTOCK**, b. of Norwich, Nov. 27, 1834, by Rev. Herman Perry 18
Julia, m. Geo[rge] W. **CLARK**, b. of Griswold, [Nov. 27, 1837], by Rev. Geo[rge] Perkins 232
Laura, m. Joseph **LEONORD**, Jr., May 24, 1826, by Seth Bliss, Pastor 173
Lucy, d. Nathan & Mary, d. Jan. 17, 1824 249
Lydia L., d. Stephen & Lydia, b. Nov. 7, 1823 7
Lydia N., of Griswold, m. Isaac P. **FISHER**, of Gourvenor, N.Y., Sept. 5, 1842, by Tho[ma]s L. Shipman 3

Page

JOHNSON, (cont.)
Martha Hull, d. Henry L. & Almira D., b. Apr. 20, 1835 76
Mary, w. Nathan, d. Dec. 28, 1823 249
Mary, d. Nathan & Mary, d. Mar. 15, 1825 249
Mary Hubbard, d. Nathan & Ruth F., b. Sept. 10, 1826 249
Mary K., m. Dwight R. **TYLER**, Feb. 23, 1846 132
Olive, m. Dr. Lucius **TYLER**, b. of Griswold, Mar. 23, 1824, by Rev. Horatio Waldo 142
Sally, of Griswold, m. Joseph B. **PALMER**, of Norwich, Aug. 7, 1825, by Rev. Horatio Waldo 138
Sanford, s. Stephen & Lydia, b. Nov. 26, 1817 7
Sarah Hilliard, d. Nathan & Ruth F., b. Apr. 20, 1831 249
Stephen, s. Henry L. & A[lmira] D., b. May 10, 1846 76
Thomas Meech, s. Nathan & Ruth F., [b.] Oct. 21, 1829 249
William, s. Stephen & Lydia, b. Aug. 13, 1815; d. Mar. 26, 1816 7

JONES, Eliza, of Preston, m. Rowland **BURDICK**, of Lisbon, Oct. 25, 1826, by Welcome A. Browning, J.P. 181
Emma Barber, d. Josiah & Sybel, b. June 16, 1829 101
Joel, s. Josiah & Sybel, b. Jan. 18, 1824 101
Josiah, of Hebron, m. Sibbel **BUTTON**, of Griswold, Mar. 12, 1823, by Rev. Horatio Waldo 101
Olive Prentice, d. Josiah & Sybel, b. July 25, 1827 101

JUSTIN, Almira, of Griswold, m. Elisha **YAR[R]INGTON**, of Preston, Mar. 6, 1827, by Amos Read, Elder 198
Fanny, of Griswold, m. Charles S. **WHITING**, of Lisbon, Nov. 24, 1825, by Amos Read, Elder 159
James, m. Betsey **MONEY**, b. of Griswold, Nov. 25, [ ], by Welcome A. Browning, J.P. 254
James L., s. William & Mercy, b. July 8, 1810 236

KEIGWIN, KEGWIN, Clarissa, w. John, d. Sept. 6, 1823 170
Daniel, of Voluntown, m. Solomon(?) **COOK**, of Griswold, May 1, 1822, by Rev. Horatio Waldo 94
Dwight R., s. Ezra W. & Catharine D., b. July 16, 1837 289
Eunice, m. Warren **CLARK**, Dec. 6, 1822, by Thomas Stewart, J.P. 83
Ezra W., of Griswold, m. Catharine **HOWE**, of Canterbury, Dec. 30, 1832, by Rev. S. D. Jewett 289
George Westly, s. Ezra W. & Catharine D., b. Feb. 13, 1843 289
John, b. May 24, 1778; m. Clarissa **SMITH**, Jan. 7, 1802 170
John, m. Thisbe **PHILLIPS**, Jan. 1, 1823 [sic] 170
John, d. Apr. 15, 1827 170
John Gordon, s. John & Thisbe, b. Jan. 29, 1825 170
John H., s. Ezra W. & Catharine D., b. Nov. 23, 1833 289
Sarah, of Griswold, m. George **SHAY**, of Plainfield, Jan. 25, 1824, by Rev. Horatio Waldo 137

KELLEY, John, m. Sarah N. **POST**, b. of Griswold, Apr. 18, 1847, by Rev. J. W. Case 172

KENYON, Job, of Exeter, R.I., m. Phebe M. **HOXSIE**, of Richmond, R.I., Apr. 7, 1854, by Rev. Charles Dixon 286

KILBURN, Pamelia, of Griswold, m. Freeman **PHILLIPS**, Sept. 11, 1826, by Elisha Partridge, J.P. 180

KIMBALL, David Dwight, s. Charles & Sarah, b. May 31, 1834 138
Eliza, m. Ralph **HUTCHINSON**, Oct. 6, 1816 22
Prosper, s. Charles & Sarah Ann, b. Nov. 27, 1836 138

KIMPTON, Millings G., of Smithfield, R.I., m. Eliza E. **PALMER**, of Griswold, Apr. 3, 1825, by Amos Read, E!der 154

Page

KINGSLEY, Alpheas, m. Olive **BOARDMAN**, Mar. 1, 1843, by Rev. H. Torbush 195
KINNEY, KINNE, KINEY, Archibald, m. Emily **BOARDMAN**, Mar. 27, 1845, by Rev. Roswell Whitmore 99
Buel, of Homer, N.Y., m. Charlotte A. **LEONARD**, of [Griswold], Sept. 21, 1831, by Rev. S. D. Jewett 166
Calista, m. Robert **BILLINGS**, b. of Griswold, Nov. 29, 1827, by Alexander Stewart, J.P. 211
Calvin, m. Sally **BROWN**, b. of Griswold, Apr. 17, 1836, by Alexander Stewart, J.P. 245
Caroline B., m. John **RIPLEY**, Mar. 14, 1831, by Thomas Stewart, J.P. 262
Charles Leonard, s. Prentice & Mary L., b. Mar. 15, 1828 166
Daniel, of Thompson, m. Dorcas **CONGDON**, of Exeter, R.I., Dec. 19, 1830, by Alexander Stewart, J.P. 256
Elisha, s. Woodbury & Zerviah, b. July 11, 1816 176
Erastus, of Plainfield, m. Lucy **BURTON**, of Griswold, Apr. 1, 1829, by Rev. Horatio Waldo 231
Erastus, m. Louisa **BURTON**, b. of Griswold, Oct. 19, 1837, by Rev. William R. Jewett 231
Huldah, m. Nathaniel **COGSWELL**, b. of Preston, Dec. 8, 1737 120
John E., of Thompson, N.Y., m. Mary **BURTON**, of Griswold, Feb. 19, 1829, by Rev. Horatio Waldo 228
John E., m. Abby **HALLOWAY**, Jan. 1, 1832, by Thomas Stewart, J.P. 278
Joseph, s. Woodbury & Zerviah, b. Aug. 22, 1814 176
Joseph B., s. Prentice & Mary L., b. Mar. 4, 1830 166
Mary, d. Woodbury & Zerviah, b. July 22, 1819 176
Mary, d. Woodbury & Zerviah, d. Aug. 23, 1823 176
Mary Ann, d. Prentice & Mary L., b. Aug. 21, 1826 166
Olive F., m. Theophilus F. **STANTON**, Apr. 29, 1838, by Nathan Stanton, J.P. 59
Prentice, m. Mary L. **LEONARD**, b. of Griswold, Sept. 1, 1825, by Rev. Horatio Waldo 166
Sally, m. Esquire C. **COOK**, b. of Griswold, Mar. 30, 1831, by Comfort D. Fillmore, J.P. 266
Samuel, m. Dorothy **BROWN**, Apr. 24, 1826, by Nathan Stanton, J.P. 78
Spencer, m. Lucinda **BROWN**, b. of Griswold, Sept. 11, 1825, by Alexander Stewart, J.P. 156
William, s. Woodbury & Zerviah, b. Oct. 2, 1812 176
Woodbury, of Preston, m. Zerviah **KIN[N]EY**, of Plainfield, Feb. 14, 1808 176
Zerviah, of Plainfield, m. Woodbury **KINNEY**, of Preston, Feb. 14, 1808 176
Zerviah, w. Woodbury, d. May 4, 1820 176
Zipporah, m. Dyer **CHAPMAN**, Apr. 16, 1815 12
KNOWLES, Mary, m. James T. **OLNEY**, Oct. 3, 1819 35
LAMB, Andrew, m. Lettice **LAMB**, b. of Griswold, Dec. 9, 1827, by Rev. S. Bliss 210
Lettice, m. Andrew **LAMB**, b. of Griswold, Dec. 9, 1827, by Rev. S. Bliss 210
LARKIN, Irena, of Griswold, m. William **WILCOX**, of W. Greenrich, R.I., July 15, 1821, by Rev. Horatio Waldo 74
LATHAM, Andrew M., s. Thomas & Alice, b. Apr. 16, 1833 298
George, s. Thomas & Alice, b. Oct. 6, 1827, in Norwich 298
Griswold, of Preston, m. Sabrina **ELLIS**, of Griswold, Mar. 21, 1834, by Rev. George Perkins 311
Henry T., s. Thomas & Alice, b. Jan. 20, 1830, in Griswold 298
Joseph, of Hebron, m. Alice **DURFEY**, of Griswold, Apr. 24, 1823, by Rev. Horatio Waldo 94

Page

LATHAM, (cont.)
Lucy, m. Lemuel **DARLING**, b. of Griswold, Jan. 1, 1829, by Welcome A. Browning, J.P. 227
Lydia Ann, d. Thomas & Alice, b. Dec. 15, 1831 298
Margaret, m. Phillip **OLIN**, Sept. 7, 1810 77
Mary, of Groto, m. Cabot COLIER, of Griswold, Sept. 4, 1826, by Welcome A. Browning, J.P. 175
LATHROP, Elisha, of Griswold, m. Susan B. **LEWIS**, of Westerly, R.I., Mar. 6, 1828, by Rev. Horatio Waldo 217
Eunice, m. Jonathan **REYNOLDS**, b. of Norwich, Apr. 15, 1829, by Alexander Stewart, Jr., J.P. 232
Jason, m. Susan E. **PECKHAM**, b. of Griswold, Sept. 14, 1840, by Rev. William R. Jewett 308
Lucinda, m. James **PECKHAM**, b. of Norwich, Dec. 11, 1841, by Rev. W[illia]m R. Jewett 113
Mahala, d. Dixwell & Mahala, b. Aug. 31, 1816 33
LAW, Betsey, m. Asa **FENNER**, b. of Jersey City, Jan. 17, 1830, by Rev. Levi Kneeland 243
Cynthia, of Griswold, m. George W. **BROOKS**, of Norwich, Aug. 31, 1836, at Jewett City (Griswold), by Rev. Tubal Wakefield 73
Olive A., m. George B. **COREY**, b. of Griswold, May 4, 1834, by Welcome A. Browning, J.P. 308
Sophia M., m. Asa **FENNER**, b. of Griswold, Nov. 20, 1836, by Rev. Shubael Wakefield 243
LAWRENCE, LAWRANCE, Esther, m. Jacob **BENNETT**, May 9, 1822, by Rev. Horatio Waldo 95
Sarah E., m. Gurdon J. **DAVENPORT**, b. of Norwich, Sept. 21, 1845, by Rev. W[illia]m Potter 84
LAWTON, Caroline, d. George & Mariah, b. Feb. 8, 1821 60
George D., m. Maria **ANDREWS**, June 16, 1816 60
Mariah, d. George D. & Mariah, b. May 14, 1819; d. Oct. 11, 1819 60
Rachel M., m. Alban W. **GALLUP**, b. of [Griswold?], Mar. 12, 1833, by Levi Kneeland 293
Thomas Cary, s. George D. & Mariah, b. Sept. 4, 1817 60
LEE, John, m. Asia **TIFFANY**, b. of Griswold, June 29, 1834, by David Avery 313
LEONARD, LEONORD, Betsey, m. Hezekiah **PRENTICE**, Jan. 23, 1817 45
Betsey Brown, d. James, b. Dec. 21, 1825 197
Charles B., m. Maria A. **LESTER**, May 21, 1834, by Rev. S. D. Jewett 310
Charlotte A., of [Griswold], m. Buel **KINNEY**, of Homer, N.Y., Sept. 21, 1831, by Rev. S. D. Jewett 166
George Edwin, s. Joseph, Jr. & Laura, b. June 17, 1831 173
Harriet, d. Joseph & Mary, d. Feb. 7, 1817 25
Havord, s. Joseph, Jr. & Laura, b. June 4, 1842 173
James, s. James & Betsey, b. Aug. 26, 1828 197
Joseph, Jr., m. Laura **JOHNSON**, May 24, 1826, by Rev. Seth Bliss 173
Joseph, d. July 12, 1843 25
Joseph Edward, s. Joseph, Jr. & Laura, b. Sept. 6, 1839 173
Laura Ann, d. Joseph, Jr. & Laura, b. Nov. 13, 1841 173
Lucy Maria, d. Charles E. & Maria A., b. Feb. 2, 1838 310
Maria Johnson, d. Joseph, Jr. & Laura, b. Jan. 31, 1834 173
Mary L., m. Prentice **KINNEY**, b. of Griswold, Sept. 1, 1825, by Rev. Horatio Waldo 166
Mary Thrusa(?), d. Cha[rle]s E. & Maria A., b. Dec. 25, 1840 310
Samuel, s. Joseph, Jr. & Laura, b. Apr. 28, 1827 173
Sarah, d. Joseph, Jr. & Laura, b. Aug. 18, 1829 173

	Page
LEONARD, LEONORD, (cont.)	
William J., s. Joseph, Jr. & Laura, b. Mar. 1, 1836	173
William J., s. Joseph, Jr. & Laura, d. Sept. 9, 1839	173
LESTER, Alexander Hamilton, s. Daniel M. & Abigail, b. May 30, 1813	63
Charles F., d. Oct. 30, 1821	30
Daniel M., m. Abigail **LORD**, Jan. 4, 1809	63
Elijah, d. Aug. 22, 1823	80
Elizabeth Lord, s. Daniel M. & Abigail, b. Jan. 28, 1822	63
George, m. Maria A. **PARKMAN**, b. of Griswold, Sept. 7, 1829, by Rev. Horatio Waldo	234
George William, s. John & Mary D., b. Sept. 13, 1831	87
Hannah Ann C., m. William R. **JEWETT**, b. of Griswold, Sept. 24, 1838, by Rev. Samuel Rockwell	293
Henry, s. Moses W. & Sarah B., b. Dec. 13, 1830	104
John, Capt., m. Lucy* D. **TUCKER**, b. of Griswold, Jan. 15, 1822, by Rev. Horatio Waldo. (*Name is Mary in the record of the births of the children)	87
Joseph, Capt., m. Martha **COIT**, b. of Griswold, Sept. 8, 1816, by Rev. Horatio Waldo	104
Lemuel Hart, s. John & Mary D., b. Sept. 18, 1825	87
Lucy, m. George Loring, Mar. 23, 1809	135
Maria A., m. Charles B. **LEONARD**, May 21, 1834, by Rev. S. D. Jewett	310
Mary, d. Elisha & Betsey, d. July 22, 1822	117
Mary, d. John & Mary D., b. May 9, 1823	87
Mary A., of Griswold, m. Henry **FRENCH**, of Hartford, Oct. 11, 1842, by Rev. William R. Jewett	215
Mary Ann, d. James D. & Lucy, d. Sept 24, 1840, at New York	25
Moses, Capt., m. Sarah B. **TUCKER**, b. of Griswold, Sept. 23, 1829, by Rev. Horatio Waldo	235
Nathaniel Lord, s. Daniel M. & Abigail, b. Oct. 10, 1820	63
Rebecca, m. John P. **PRENTICE**, b. of Griswold, Mar. 29, 1835, by Rev. S. D. Jewett	316
Sarah Ann, d. Daniel M. & Abigail, b. Mar. 15, 1826	63
Sarah E., of Griswold, m. Joseph **WOODBRIDGE**, of Stockbridge, Mass., Oct. 16, 1828, by Seth Bliss	54
Sarah W., m. Henry **TUCKER**, b. of Griswold, Sept. 4, 1837, by Rev. William R. Jewett	233
Sarah Wight, d. [Capt. Joseph & Martha], b. Dec. 5, 1817	104
LETSON, Alice, m. Roland R. **COREY**, b. of Voluntown, Sept. 15, 1831, by Rev. S. D. Jewett	269
LEWIS, Albert, m. Patty **RIX**, b. of Voluntown, Nov. 17, 1833, by Alexander Stewart, J.P.	301
Caroline, of Packersville, Ct., m. Jared F. **PHILLIPS**, of Hampton, Oct. 20, 1847, at Jewett City, by Rev. B. Cook	197
Deborah, of Griswold, m. Robert **BRIGGS**, of Cranston, R.I., July 22, 1821, by Rev. Caleb Read	71
Elias, m. Sally **PRENTICE**, b. of Griswold, Nov. 2, 1823, by Rev. Horatio Waldo	129
Ellenor, b. June 2, 1791, at Exeter, R.I.; [m.(?) Gardiner **BARBER**(?)]	292
Hiram, m. Olive **COLBURN**, b. of Griswold, Oct. 30, 1842, by Rev. Benajah Cook, of Jewett City	285
Lucy Ann, of Voluntown, m. Leonord **CHASE**, of Brookfield, Worcester Cty., Mass., May 6, 1824, by Elisha Partridge, J.P.	28
Sally, m. Charles **BILLINGS**, Aug. 24, 1823	140
Susan B., of Westerly, R.I., m. Elisha **LATHROP**, of Griswold, Mar. 6, 1828, by Rev. Horatio Waldo	217

Page

LILLIBRIDGE, John, Jr., of Exeter, R.I., m. Phebe **SWAN**, of [Griswold], June 4, 1820, by Rev. Levi Walker 53
LIPPITT, Christopher H., m. Celia T. **MEECH**, Mar. 4, 1833, by Rev. George Perkins 296
Maria C. W., of Griswold, m. Samuel **SMITH**, of Westerly, R.I., Oct. 15, [1834], by Rev. George Perkins 312
LITCHFIELD, Festus C., m. Maduria **HAMMOND**, b. of Southbridge, Mass., Oct. 27, [1834], by Rev. George Perkins 312
LOCK, Eliza, m. Robert **HERRICK**, b. of Griswold, Nov. 23, 1820, by Levi Walker 66
LORD, Abigail, m. Daniel M. **LESTER**, Jan. 4, 1809 63
Elizabeth, b. May 17, 1779; m. Daniel **HUNTINGTON**, Apr. 24, 1800 14
Hezekiah, s. William & Prudence, b. Nov. 18, 1827 215
Levi Hart, s. William & Prudence, b. Apr. 11 1834 215
William, of Griswold, m. Prudence MORGAN, of Groton, Dec. 26, 1826 215
LORING, Frances Ann, d. George & Lucy, b. Feb. 24, 1812 135
George, m. Lucy **LESTER**, Mar. 23, 1809 135
Henry Isaac, s. George & Lucy, b. July 19, 1814 135
Lucy, d. George & Lucy, b. Apr. 6, 1810 135
Lucy, d. George & Lucy, b. July 27, 1819 135
Sarah, d. George & Lucy, b. Oct. 2, 1821 135
William, s. George & Lucy, b. Feb. 3, 1817 135
MACOMBER, MACCUMBER, Clarinda M., m. Charles **PHILLIPS**, b. of Jewett City, Oct. 27, 1843, by Rev. B. Cook, of Jewett City 22
William C., m. Betsey **PHILLIPS**, b. of Griswold, July 5, 1847, by Rev. C. Terry 287
MAIN, Lewis, s. Rufus, b. May 17, 1784, in Preston 6
Lucy A., m. James L. **BILL**, b. of Griswold, Mar. 12, 1843, by Rev. N. O. Shailer, of Preston 203
Nathaniel, of N. Stonington, m. Abigail **BROWN**, of Griswold, June 8, 1829, by Alexander Stewart, Jr., J.P. 233
Prudence, d. Rufus, b. Nov. 14, 1793, in Preston 6
Ruth, d. Rufus, b. Sept. 7, 1786, in Preston 6
Sally, d. Rufus, b. Aug. 23, 1791, in Preston 6
Sanford, s. Rufus, b. Oct. 1, 1796, in Preston 6
Sanford, m. Rebecca **ECCLESTON**, May 30, 1816 18
MANNING, Betsey, m. William WITHEY, Apr. 1, 1806 155
MARVIN, Henry A. M., s. W[illia]m A., b. July 30, 1841 202
MASON, Abigail A., m. Alfred F. **BROWN**, b. of Griswold, Oct. 30, 1842, by Rev. Benajah Cook, of Jewett City 286
MA[T]THEWSON, Nicholas, m. Orilla **FRY**, b. of Griswold, Jan. 31, 1832, by Rev. Joseph Ayer, Jr. 280
Rosanna, of Griswold, m. Nelson **ECCLESTON**, of Bozra[h]ville, Nov. 16, [1834], by Rev. George Perkins 312
MAYNARD, John E., of Shrewsbury, Vt., m. Frances A. **HAZIN**, of Griswold, Ct., Nov. 6, 1843, by Rev. Henry Torbush 217
McCOY, Charles, m. Rhoda **TILLOTSON**, b. of Griswold, Mar. 24, 1834, by Welcome A. Browning, J.P. 307
MEDBURY, David, of Griswold, m. Louis **PHILLIPS**, of Plainfield, Feb. 6, 1827, by Welcome A. Browning, J.P. 191
MEECH, Adeline, of Griswold, m. Aaron **STEPHENS**, of Norwich, Nov. 23, 1841, by Rev. William R. Jewett 113
Andrew Huntington, s. Edwin B. & Sarah M., b. Mar. 15, 1839 53
Ann Eliza, d. Shubael & Eliza S., b. Dec. 27, 1846 0
Appleton, of Preston, m. Sybel **BREWSTER**, of Griswold, June 6, 1821, by Rev. Horatio Waldo 69

Page

MEECH, (cont.)
Celia T., m. Christopher H. **LIPPITT**, Mar. 4, 1833, by Rev. George Perkins 296
Charles Shubael, s. Shubael & Eliza S., b. Oct. 22, 1843 0
Edwin, s. Edwin B. & Sarah M., b. Aug. 2, 1845 53
Edwin B., m. Sarah Maria **GEER**, b. of Griswold, May 17, 1836, by George Perkins 53
Ellen, d. Edwin B. & Sarah M., b. June 17, 1837 53
Henry, m. Julia A. **BURTON**, b. of Griswold, Dec. 20, 1832, by Rev. S. D. Jewett 288
Mary D., d. Edwin B. & Sarah M., b. Mar. 7, 1843 53
Sally, wid. Shadrach*, d. Nov. 28, 1839. (*First written "Shubael") 135
Sarah M., d. Edwin B. & Sarah M., b. Dec. 24, 1840 53
Shadrach, d. Nov. 4, 1839 135
Shubael, m. Eliza S. **COPP**, of Griswold, Sept. 26, 1842, by Rev. William A. Jewett 0
MILLARD, Adaline A., m. Bertrand **ROUNDS**, Jr., b. of [Griswold?], Mar. 25, 1827, by Rev. Seth Bliss 194
MINER, Betsey O., m. James M. **STARR**, b. of Griswold, Aug. 19, 1832, by Rev. George Perkins 295
MONEY, Betsey, m. James **JUSTIN**, b. of Griswold, Nov. 25, [ ], by Welcome A. Browning, J.P. 254
MOODRY, Andrew Lamb, s. Thaddeus & Martha, b. Jan. 18, 1824 44
Daniel Dick, s. Thaddeus, b. Aug. 22, 1811 44
Martha, d. Thaddeus & Martha, b. Aug. 4, 1819 44
Philotha, d. Thaddeus & Martha, b. Mar. 9, 1821 44
Ruth, d. Tidal & Eunice, b. Nov. 6, 1791 222
Thaddeus, m. Martha **WAMSLEY**, Dec. 10, 1818, by Rev. Horatio Waldo 44
Thaddeus Downer, s. Thaddeus & Martha, b. Apr. 22, 1822 44
MOORE, Susan C., of Jewett City, m. William A. **HEALEY**, of Packerville, July 26, 1841, by Rev. B. Cook, of Jewett City 146
MOREY, Rachel, m. Frederick A. **AVERY**, Feb. 2, 1817 75
MORGAN, Albert, s. Allen A. & Charlotte, b. May 9, 1831 281
Chester A., m. Delia A. **BARBER**, b. of Griswold, Sept. 13, 1842, by Rev. William R. Jewett 164
Daniel, Major, d. Nov. 10, 1820 27
Edwin, m. Alathea S. **FRAZIER**, b. of Griswold, Jan. 1, 1838, by Rev. William R. Jewett 278
Henry, s. Allen A. & Charlotte, b. Apr. 9, 1829 281
Henry, s. Edwin & Alathea S., b. Mar. 8, 1841 278
Hezekiah L., m. Frances **TYLER**, Dec. 25, 1833, by Rev. S. D. Jewett 187
Mary A., m. Nathan **STANDISH**, b. of Norwich, June 21, 1841, by Rev. William R. Jewett, in Griswold 98
Prudence, of Groton, m. William **LORD**, of Griswold, Dec. 26, 1826 215
Sally, m. William **TUCKER**, Jr., May 5, 1814, by Rev. Horatio Waldo 4
Sarah, d. Hezekiah L. & Frances, b. Jan. 29, 1835 187
Susanna, d. Edwin & Alathea S., b. Jan. 31, 1839 278
Wheeler, of Voluntown, m. Peggy **GREEN**, of Plainfield, Nov. 27, 1826, by Alexander Stewart, Jr., J.P. 183
MORSE, Alma S., of Jewett City, m. Charles C. **STETSON**, of Lisbon, Aug. 19, 1844, by Rev. B. Cook, of Jewett City 275
Hannah, d. W[illia]m M. & Hannah, b. June 22, 1811 37
Lydia, d. W[illia]m M. & Hannah, b. Sept. 27, 1815 37
Lydia, of Canterbury, m. Calvin **ROUSE**, of Laurens, N.Y., Sept. 23, 1830, by Seth Bliss, of Jewett City 251
Moses, s. W[illia]m M. & Hannah, b. Oct. 21, 1821 37
Patty, d. W[illia]m M. & Hannah, b. Mar. 23, 1817 37

Page

MORSE, (cont.)

Sarah L., m. James **GREENMAN**, Mar. 21, 1836, by Rev. S. D. Jewett 241

Sarah Leffingwell, d. W[illia]m M. & Hannah, b. Jan. 5, 1814 37

Thirzah, m. Henry C. **TYLER**, Mar. 25, 1828, by Seth Bliss of Jewett City 123

Thomas G., of Dover, N.H., m. Lydia L. **TIFFANY**, of Griswold, May 16, 1847, at J[ewett] City, by Rev. B. Cook, of J[ewett] City 264

William, s. William M. & Hannah, b. Mar. 20, 1819 37

William M., m. Hannah **WOODWARD**, Nov. 30, 1809 37

MOTT, John T., m. Joan F. **STEWART**, Oct. 2, 1828, by Thomas Stewart, J.P. 224

Nancy Ann, of Groton, m. Ephraim **PIKE**, Jr., of Sterling, Nov. 20, 1831, by Rev. Seth Bliss, of Jewett City 274

Ziporah, m. Samuel **CHALFANT**, Jan. 3, [18], by Levi Kneeland 242

MULKEY, W[illia]m B., of Norwich, m. Sophia **BRUMLEY**, of Griswold, Jan. 1, 1832, by Rev. S. D. Jewett 279

MULKIN, Mary, m. Erastus **NEWKY**, Feb. 18, 1828, by Thomas Stewart, J.P. 214

MUMFORD, Louisa, m. Richard B. **RUGGLES**, b. of Norwich, Sept. 3, 1848, by Tho[ma]s S. Shipman 85

MUNROE, Eliza, of Lebanon, m. Erastus **BUCK**, of Griswold, Feb. 10, 1833, by Rev. S. D. Jewett 291

NEDSON, Mary B., m. Jedediah **BUCK**, b. of Griswold, Jan. 28, 1835, by David Avery 315

NEWKY, NUKEY, Erastus, m. Mary **MULKIN**, Feb. 18, 1828, by Thomas Stewart, J.P. 214

Sally, m. William OLIN, Apr. 17, 1827, by Thomas Stewart, J.P. 109

NEWTON, Charlotte, of Voluntown, Ct., m. Stephen **REYNOLDS**, of Griswold, Ct., Nov. 22, 1846, by Rev. Ebenezer Blake, of Voluntown 219

NICHOLS, Hannah, of Coventry, R.I., m. Jesse D. **COTTRELL**, of W. Greenwich, Oct. 24, 1847, by Rev. C. Terry 143

NIE, Geo[rge] H., of Hopkinton, R.I., m. Rebecca **BARBER**, of Richmantown, R.I., Mar. 31, 1844, at Jewett City, by Rev. B. Cook, of Jewett City 271

NILES, [see under **NYLES**]

NOFF, Axa, of Griswold, m. Henry **OLIN**, of Canterbury, Oct. 5, 1837, by George Perkins 154

NOONAN, James, m. Eliza **PRATT**, b. of Griswold, Aug. 28, 1839, by Rev. W[illia]m Wright, of Jewett City 128

NORTHAM, Eliza P., m. Thomas C. **WILBUR**, b. of Griswold, Jan. 26, 1823, by Rev. Horatio Waldo 12

NORTH[R]UP, Eliza Ann, m. Charles C. **SPENCER**, b. of Griswold, Oct. 6, 1846, by Rev. Roswell Whitman 156

Sarah, of Griswold, m. Arthur **GLEASON**, of Pomfret, Nov. 4, 1824, by Rev. Horatio Waldo 64

Sarah, of Griswold, m. Arthur **GLEASON**, of Pomfret, Nov. 4, 1824, by Rev. Horatio Waldo 163

Simon Y., m. Abby L. **PHILLIPS**, b. of Griswold, June 28, 1846, by Rev. Anson Gleason 179

NUKEY, [see under **NEWKY**]

NYLES, Edward, m. Matilda **HULETT**, b. of Griswold, Dec. 8, 1839, by Rev. William Wright, of Jewett City 307

OBRIEN, Martin, of Norwich, m. Sabra P. **BUTTON**, of Preston, May 5, 1845, by Tho[ma]s L. Shipman 5

OLIN, Edward, m. Anne **SPICER**, b. of Griswold, Nov. 17, 1842, by Rev. B. Cook, of Jewett City 95

Elisha, of Canterbury, m. Jemima **RATHBONE**, of Lisbon, Mar. 1, 1841, by Rev. B. Cook, of Jewett City 168

Eunice, m. Ezra M. **SPAULDING**, Oct. 20, 1822, by Amos Read, Elder 113

Page

OLIN, (cont.)
Frederic, alias Frederic **GREEN**, s. Betsey **GREEN**, b. Feb. 25, 1801 76
Frederic, m. Hannah **WISE**, b. of Griswold, Oct. 16, 1825, by Welcome A. Browning, J.P. 93
Frederic, of Griswold, m. Charity D. **RATHBURN**, of Hopkinton, R.I., Sept. 14, 1828, by Seth Bliss, of Jewett City 93
Hannah, w. Frederick, d. Mar. 1, 1828 93
Henry, of Canterbury, m. Axa **NOFF**, of Griswold, Oct. 5, 1837, by George Perkins 154
Joann, m. Harkless **PHILLIPS**, b. residing in Griswold, Oct. 12, 1823, by Amos Read, Elder 127
Margaret, w. Phillip, d. June 11, 1821 77
Phillip, m. Margaret **LATHAM**, Sept. 7, 1810 77
Phillip, of Griswold, m. Avilata **ABEL**, of Franklin, Jan. 24, 1822, by Rev. Caleb Read 77
Violata, m. Theophilus **BILLINGS**, b. of Griswold, Dec. 22, 1839, by Rev. William R. Jewett 308
William, m. Saly **NUKEY**, Apr. 17, 1827, by Thomas Stewart, J.P. 109

OLNEY, Dwight, s. James T. & Mary, b. Jan. 15, 1822 35
George, s. James T. & Mary, b. Dec. 27, 1819 35
James T., m. Mary **KNOWLES**, Oct. 3, 1819 35

PAINE, Mary, m. Alvin **ALEXANDER**, b. residing in Griswold, Oct. 19, 1823, by Amos Read, Elder 126

PALMER, Abby B., d. Robert M. & Bridget, b. July 15, 1812 39
Betsey B., d. Robert M. & Bridget, b. Apr. 29, 1810 39
Charles York, s. William P. & Fanny, b. Aug. 5, 1826 91
Eliza E., of Griswold, m. Millings G. **KIMPTON**, of Smithfield, R.I., Apr. 3, 1825, by Amos Read, Elder 154
George Benjamin, s. George D. & Harriet B., b. May 24, 1843 222
Hannah, d. Walter, Jr. & Lucy K., b. Sept. 3, 1815, in Preston 2
Hannah, of Griswold, m. Elijah **BARNES**, of Preston, Nov. 25, 1839, by Rev. William Wright, of Jewett City 307
Harvey C., of Exeter, R.I., m. Phebe T. **SAUNDERS**, of Voluntown, Nov. 1, 1841, by Rev. Moses Standish 36
James A., m. Alice Z. **WILBUR**, b. of Griswold, Feb. 13, 1848, by Rev. Cyrus Miner 277
John Crary, s. William P. & Fanny, b. May 29, 1825 91
Joseph B., s. Robert M. & Bridget, b. Oct. 18, 1801 39
Joseph B., of Norwich, m. Sally **JOHNSON**, of Griswold, Aug. 7, 1825, by Rev. Horatio Waldo 138
Joseph T., s. Walter, Jr. & Lucy K., b. July 21, 1819 2
Leroy Fuller, s. Walter K., & Harriet A., b. Dec. 20, 1844 232
Lydia, d. Walter, Jr. & Lucy K., b. Aug. 31, 1813, in Preston; d. Aug. 24, 1814 2
Lydia R., d. Robert M. & Bridget, b. June 13, 1806 39
Nancy B., d. Robert M. & Bridget, b. Oct. 3, 1803 39
Nancy Jane, of Plainfield, m. Benjamin **CUTLER**, of Killingly, July 2, 1848, at Walter **PALMER**'s house in Griswold, by Rev. Henry Robinso, of Plainfield 116
Robert M., b. Jan. 10, 1777; m. Bridget **BALDWIN**, Feb. 3, 1801 39
Walter, Jr., m. Lucy Kinney **EAMES**, Nov. 24, 1812 2
Walter, Jr., d. Sept. 6, 1819 2
Walter Atwood, s. Walter K. & Harriet A., b. Mar. 14, 1840 232
Walter K., d. Nov. 8, 1845, ae. 28 y. 232
Walter Kinney, s. Walter, Jr. & Lucy [K.], b. May 5, 1817 2

Page

PALMER, (cont.)
Walter R., of Griswold, m. Harriet A. **BALDWIN**, of Canterbury, Nov. 27, 1837, by Rev. Geo[rge] Perkins 232
William Randall, s. William P. & Fanny, b. Jan. 15, 1822 91
PARK[E], George B., s. Norman & Emma, b. Dec. 30, 1841 11
John, of White Hall, N.Y., m. Hannah **AVERY**, of Griswold, July 28, 1825, by Rev. Horatio Waldo 70
Susanna F., d. Norman & Emma, b. Aug. 10, 1840 11
PARKER, Daniel, 2d, of Groton, m. Mariah Ann **SMITH**, of Griswold, July 25, 1822, by Elias Brewster, J.P. 102
John H., m. Betsey M. **WALKER**, b. of Griswold, Nov. 1, 1829, by Seth Bliss, of Jewett City 240
PARKMAN, Maria A., m. George **LESTER**, b. of Griswold, Sept. 7, 1829, by Rev. Horatio Waldo 234
PARRISH, PARISH, Anna, of Griswold, m. Eliphalet **PERKINS**, of Frankful [Franklin?], July 20, 1823, by Comfort D. Fillmore, J.P. 76
Augustus, M. Persus **HERRICK**, [ ], by Rev. H. Forbush 51
PARTELOW, Elizabeth C., d. Philetus P. & Rebecca M., b. Jan. 5, 1833 273
Joann Fish, d. Philetus P. & Rebecca M., b. Feb. 6, 1841 273
Lucy Ann, d. Philetus P. & Rebecca M., b. Jan. 13, 1831 273
Palmer P., of Voluntown, m. Sabra **STANTON**, of Griswold, Jan. 1, 1824, by Rev. Horatio Waldo 133
Philetus Kneeland, s. Philetus P. & Rebecca M., b. May 4, 1835 273
Rebecca Jane, d. Philetus P. & Rebecca M., b. Jan. 9, 1838 273
PARTRIDGE, Cyrus, m. Sally **WHIPPLE**, Mar. 29, 1820 58
Cyrus, of Lisbon, m. Mary **PRENTICE**, of Griswold, Mar. 18, 1838, by Rev. W[illia]m R. Jewett 58
Eliphal, w. Asa, d. Oct. 16, 1817, ae 78y. 36
Mahala, of Griswold, m. Caleb **GRISWOLD**, of Franklin, Apr. 26, 1821, by Rev. Horatio Waldo 67
Reuben, d. Oct. 23, 1820 59½
Reuben, m. Ruth **BARBER**, b. of Griswold, Feb. 1, 1827, by Elisha Partridge, J.P. 195
Samuel, m. Betsey **FRY**, b. of Griswold, Mar. 28, 1831, by Rev. Seth Bliss, of Jewett City 265
PASH, Phebe, of Griswold, m. Erastus **SAFFORD**, of Preston, Mar. 18, 1834, by Rev. George Perkins 311
PECKHAM, James, m. Lucinda **LATHROP**, b. of Norwich, Dec. 11, 1841, by Rev. W[illia]m R. Jewett 113
Nathan B., of Lisbon, m. Eleanor **BURDICK**, of [Jewett City], Nov. 6, 1842, by Rev. B. Cook, of Jewett City 282
Samuel, of Lisbon, m. Mary **CRANDAL**, of Griswold, Mar. 2, 1834, by Rev. George Perkins 311
Susan E., m. Jason **LATHROP**, b. of Griswold, Sept. 14, 1840, by Rev. William R. Jewett 308
PELHAM, Susan, m. William P. **HALL**, b. of Griswold, Jan. 11, 1846, by Rev. Roswell Whitman 296
PELLET, Elijah M., of Norwich, m. Abby E. **PHILLIPS**, of Griswold, Sept. 6, 1840, by Rev. Jacob Allen 169
PENNIMAN, Mary, m. John GRAVES, Apr. 7, 1814 81
PERKINS, Eliphalet, of Frankful [Franklin?], m. Anna **PARRISH**, of Griswold, July 20, 1823, by Comfort D. Fillmore, J.P. 76
Hannah, m. William G. **COREY**, b. of Griswold, May 19, 1822, by Caleb Read, Elder 99

Page

PERKINS, (cont.)
Mary, m. Willard **UNDERWOOD**, b. of Griswold, Apr. 1, 1824, by Rev. Horatio Waldo 144
Newman, of Griswold, m. Maria M. **BROWN**, of Jewett City, Aug. 30, 1846, by Rev. B. Cook, of Jewett City 272
PHILLIPS, Abby E., of Griswold, m. Elijah M. **PELLET**, of Norwich, Sept. 6, 1840, by Rev. Jacob Allen 169
Abby L., m. Simon Y. **NORTH[R]UP**, b. of Griswold, June 28, 1846, by Rev. Anson Gleason 179
Benjamin B., now of Smithfield, R.I., m. Betsey M. **PHILLIPS**, of Griswold, Apr. 20, 1824, by Samuel C. Morgan, J.P. 145
Betsey M., of Griswold, m. Benjamin B. **PHILLIPS**, now of Smithfield, R.I., Apr. 20, 1824, by Samuel C. Morgan, J.P. 145
Betsey M., m. William C. **MACCUMBER**, b. of Griswold, July 5, 1847, by Rev. C. Terry 287
Betsey Matilda, d. Harkless & Joann, b. July 4, 1829 127
Charles, s. Harkless & Joann, b. Jan. 20, 1825 127
Charles, m. Clarinda M. **MACOMBER**, b. of Jewett City, Oct. 27, 1843, by Rev. B. Cook, of Jewett City 22
Charles F., s. Frederic F. & Mehitable, b. Mar. 12, 1826 55
Freeman, m. Pamelia **KILBURN**, of Griswold, Sept. 11, 1826, by Elisha Partridge, J.P. 180
Harkless, m. Joann **OLIN**, b. residing in Griswold, Oct. 12, 1823, by Amos Read, Elder 127
Henry Jourdon, s. [Nathaniel, Jr. & Patty], b. Feb. 2, 1816 111
James Munroe, s. [Nathaniel, Jr. & Patty], b. Feb. 24, 1818 111
Jared F., of Hampton, m. Caroline **LEWIS**, of Packersville, Ct., Oct. 20, 1847, at Jewett City, by Rev. B. Cook 197
Louis, of Plainfield, m. David **MEDBURY**, of Griswold, Feb. 6, 1827, by Welcome A. Browning, J.P. 191
Lucinda Maria, d. [Nathaniel, Jr. & Patty], b. Apr. 11, 1820 111
Maata, of Griswold, m. Elijah **GATES**, of W. Greenwich, R.I., Oct. 11, 1825, by Rev. Horatio Waldo 169
Mary, m. Elisha R. **POTTER**, Jr., b. of Canterbury, Dec. 19, 1847, at Jewett City, by Rev. B. Cook 197
Mary Ann, of Griswold, m. Daniel **HOWE**, of Canterbury, Mar. 29, 1847, by Cha[rle]s Noble 249
Nathaniel, Jr., m. Patty **BROWN**, Mar. 19, 1809 111
Nathaniel Wilbur, s. [Nathaniel, Jr. & Patty], b. Jan. 25, 1812 111
Patty Brown, d. [Nathaniel, Jr. & Patty, b. Jan. 11, 1810 111
Rebecca, m. Bushnell **TURNER**, b. of Griswold, Nov. 24, 1825, by Rev. Seth Bliss, of Jewett City 158
Rebecca M., of Griswold, m. Henry W. **GALLUP**, of Sterling, Sept. 26, 1843, by Rev. Jacob Allen 52
Samuel Nelson, s. [Nathaniel, Jr. & Patty], b. May 8, 1814 111
Sarah Ann, d. Atwood & Sally, b. May 9, 1828 229
Thisbe, b. Sept. 22, 1802; m. John **KEIGWIN**, Jan. 1, 1823[sic] 170
[PIERCE],PEIRCE, Eseck, m. Desire **SIMONS**, b. of Griswold, Mar. 30, 1830, by Seth Bliss, of Jewett City 250
Ethan A., of Truxton, N.Y., m. Harriet A. **GEER**, of [Griswold], May 8, 1842 by Tho[ma]s S. Shipman 80
PIKE, Ephraim, Jr., of Sterling, m. Nancy Ann **MOTT**, of Groton, Nov. 20, 1831, by Rev. Seth Bliss, of Jewett City 274

	Page
PORTER, Roxanna, m. Charles **CUTLER**, b. of Griswold, Jan. 28, 1827, by Rev. Seth Bliss	190
POST, Sarah N., m. John **KELLEY**, b. of Griswold, Apr. 18, 1847, by Rev. J. W. Case	172
POTTER, Elisha R., Jr., m. Mary **PHILLIPS**, b. of Canterbury, Dec. 19, 1847, at Jewett City, by Rev. B. Cook	197
Eliza, m. Reynolds **WILCOX**, b. of Griswold, Feb. 16, 1834, by Welcome A. Browning, J.P.	305
Frances Wayland, s. Nathan P. & Lucy A., b. Sept. 7, 1852	240
PRATT, Abigail E., m. Charles H. **BROWN**, b. of Jewett City, May 11, 1846, by Rev. B. Cook, of Jewett City	271
Eliza, m. James **NOONAN**, b. of Griswold, Aug. 28, 1839, by Rev. W[illia]m Wright, of Jewett City	128
PRENTICE, Abby Ann, d. Nathan & Alice, b. May 26, 1827	248
Abby C., of Griswold, m. Prentice **WILLIAMS**, of Groton, Dec. 29, 1824, by Rev. Horatio Waldo	164½
Almira, d. [Thaddeus & Almira], b. Jan. 12, 1825	79
Amos, s. [John & Betsey], b. Aug. 5, 1792	65
Amos, of Griswold, m. Lucy **WYLIE**, of Voluntown, Jan. 11, 1816, by John Wylie, J.P.	3
Amos Wylie, s. Amos & Lucy, b. Dec. 20, 1816	3
Andrew, s. John & Betsey, b. May 29, 1816	65
Betsey, m. Nathaniel **COIT**, Feb. 1, 1832, by Rev. S. D. Jewett	59½
Betsey Clift, d. [John & Betsey], b. Apr. 15, 1805	65
Caroline Abbey, d. [John & Betsey], b. Mar. 12, 1812	65
Charlotte, d. [John & Betsey], b. Oct. 20, 1802	65
Elizabeth, d. Hezekiah & Betsey, b. Dec. 4, 1820	45
Elizabeth A., of Griswold, m. Charles H. **GRANT**, of Preston, June 8, 1841, by Rev. William R. Jewett	171
Frances Maria, d. [John & Betsey], b. Mar. 5, 1809	65
Frances Mariah, m. Hezekiah **BOARDMAN**, b. of Griswold, [ ] 20, [18], by Rev. S. D. Jewett	260
Fred[eri]c, s. [John & Betsey], b. May 14, 1796	65
Hezekiah, m. Betsey **LEONARD**, Jan. 23, 1817	45
Hezekiah Leonord, s. Hezekiah & Betsey, b. Feb. 13, 1819	45
James, s. Thaddeus & Almira, b. Jan. 18, 1821	79
Jane Grey, d. Hezekiah & Betsey, b. Aug. 4, 1825	45
John, m. Betsey **CLIFT**, Dec. 25, 1791	65
John, s. [John & Betsey], b. Nov. 28, 1800	65
John, m. Betsey **HUNTINGTON**, Jan. 19, 1810	65
John P., m. Rebecca **LESTER**, b. of Griswold, Mar. 29, 1835, by Rev. S. D. Jewett	316
Laura Ann, d. Rufus & Wealthy, b. June 19, 1826	196
Lucy, d. John & Betsey, b. Nov. 10, 1818	65
Manassah, d. Mar. 10, 1825	27
Mary, of Griswold, m. Cyrus **PARTRIDGE**, of Lisbon, Mar. 18, 1838, by Rev. W[illia]m R. Jewett	58
Mary Ann, m. Charles R. **SPENCER**, b. of Griswold, Feb. 6, 1822, by Rev. Horatio Waldo	88
Mary Jane, d. Nathan & Alice, b. June 27, 1829	248
Mehetable, wid., d. Mar. 25, 1825	27
Nathan, of Groton, m. Alice A. **SPENCER**, of Griswold, June 13, 1822, by Rev. Horatio Waldo	101
Nathan, s. Nathan & Alice, b. Aug. 26, 1831	248
Nathan Mallory, s. Nathan & Alice, b. Apr. 18, 1823	101

Page

PRENTICE, (cont.)
Nathan Mallory, s. Nathan & Alice, d. Oct. 7, 1826 248
Nehemiah Reynolds, s. Nathan & Alice, b. Feb. 27, 1842 101
Rufus, m. Wealthy **STARKWEATHER**, Aug. 14, 1823 196
Sally, d. [John & Betsey], b. May 21, 1792 65
Sally, m. Elias **LEWIS**, b. of Griswold, Nov. 2, 1823, by Rev. Horatio Waldo 129
Samuel T., m. Sarah A. **WOODWARD**, b. of Griswold, Mar. 7, 1843, by Rev. William R. Jewett 136
Samuel Tyler, s. Amos & Lucy, b. Jan. 9, 1820 3
Thaddeus, of Munden, Mass., m. Almira **GORDON**, of Lisbon, Ct., July 26, 1818 79
Thaddeus, s. [Thaddeus & Almira], b. Mar. 17, 1823 79
W[illia]m Clift, s. [John & Betsey], b. Mar. 6, 1807 65

PRESTON, Ebenezer Clark, s. Daniel & Abigail, b. Sept. 23, 1825 168
Elisha Aaron, s. Daniel & Abigail, b. June 22, 1816 168

PRIDE, Elizabeth, of Griswold, m. John H. **FANNING**, of Norwich, Mar. 1, 1831, by Rev. Seth Bliss 264

RANDALL, Elizabeth, m. Aarnold **DUNN**, b. of Griswold, Sept. 8, 1829, by Rev. Seth Bliss 237

RATHBURN, RATHBONE, Charity D., of Hopkinton, R.I., m. Frederic **OLIN**, of Griswold, Sept. 14, 1828, by Rev. Seth Bliss, of Jewett City 93
Jemima, of Lisbon, m. Elisha **OLIN**, of Canterbury, Mar. 1, 1841, by Rev. B. Cook, of Jewett City 168
Mary Ann, m. Dwight T. **COREY**, Jan. 3, 1847, by C. Terry 268
William M., m. Harriet **TERRY**, b. of Griswold, Nov. 26, 1846, by Rev. Charles Noble 281

RAWSON, Calvin G., s. Calvin, b. May 18, 1816 130
Sybel B., d. Calvin, b. Sept. 24, 1814 130

RAY, Betsey, of [Griswold], m. Amos **BURTON**, Feb. 11, 1822, by Rev. Levi Walker 89-90
Henry B., m. Lucy H. **DOWNING**, Feb. 11, 1819 48
Henry N., m. Clarinda N. **HISCOX**, b. of Jewett City, Aug. 1, 1842, by Rev. B. Cook, of Jewett City 216
Henry Nelson, s. Henry B. & Lucy, b. Dec. 14, 1819 48
James D., m. Martha J. **FITCH**, b. of Griswold, Sept. 18, 1842, by Rev. William R. Jewett 149
James Leonard, s. Henry B. & Lucy, b. Mar. 4, 1823 48
Lucy, m. Charles **GUILE**, b. of Griswold, Feb. 22, 1824, by Levi Meech, Elder 136
Polly C., m. Jonathan **BRUMLEY**, b. of Griswold, Sept. 10, 1826, by Rev. Levi Walker 177
Robert J., m. Mary Ann **WRIGHT**, b. of Jewett City, Oct. 2, 1843, by Tho[ma]s S. Shipman 202
Samuel Billings, s. Henry B. & Lucy, b. Jan. 27, 1821 48

RAYMAN, Mary, d. June 26 1827 30

READ, Rachel, of Lisbon, m. Capt. Joseph **BUTTON**, of Griswold, Sept. 12, 1827, in Lisbon, by Rev. Levi Nelson 202
W[illia]m, m. Harriet Ann **BRUMLEY**, Apr. 9, 1848, by Nathan Stanton, J.P. 79

REXFORD, Sally, m. Charles **HILLMAN**, b. of Griswold, Feb. 6, 1842, by Rev. William Wright 73

REYNOLDS, Deliverance, of Griswold, m. Christopher **EDWARDS**, of Voluntown, Aug. 5, 1820, by Alexander Stewart, Jr., J.P. 55
Jonathan, m. Eunice **LATHROP**, b. of Norwich, Apr. 15, 1829, by Alexander Stewart, Jr., J.P. 232
Lucinda, m. Albert **BURTON**, b. of Griswold, Sept. 1, 1844, by Rev. Roswell Whitman 200

Page

REYNOLDS, (cont.)
Melissa Ann, m. John **WHITMAN**, b. of Canterbury, Sept. 1, 1832, by Elisha Partridge, J.P. 104
Stephen, of Griswold, Ct., m. Charlotte **NEWTON**, of Voluntown, Ct., Nov. 22, 1846, by Rev. Ebenezer Blake, of Voluntown 219
RICHARDSON, Elizabeth, m. Martin **COREY**, July 21, 1822, by Thomas Stewart, J.P. 110
RICHMOND, Edward, m. Phebe M. **BOSS**, Sept. 8, 1827, by Thomas Stewart, J.P. 212
Mary C., m. Dudley F. **SAUNDERS**, Feb. 6, 1848, by Rev. John W. Case 211
RIPLEY, John, m. Caroline B. **KINNEY**, Mar. 14, 1831, by Thomas Stewart, J.P. 262
RIX, Betsey, w. Russell, d. Mar. 4, 1843 61
Charles, s. Russell & Betsey, b. Nov. 9, 1821, in Preston; d. Oct. 7, 1822 61
Charles Leonard, s. Russell & Esther, b. Dec. 20, 1844 61
Ella Ann, d. Russell & Esther, b. Dec. 13, 1848 212
Eunice, m. James B. **BURDICK**, b. of Griswold, Mar. 8, 1848, by Rev. Jesse B. Denison 175
George Davison, s. Russel[l] & Esther, b. Oct. 18, 1846 212
Giles Eaton, s. Russell & Betsey, b. May 9, 1824 61
Hannah, of Griswold, m. Henry **SAFFORD**, of Preston, Oct. 27, 1830, by Rev. S. D. Jewett 252
Henry Frances, s. Russell & Betsey, b. June 29, 1828 61
John Frances, s. Ephraim B. & Lucy H., b. Apr. 12, 1839 108
Maria P., m. John N. **BURDICK**, b. of Griswold, Mar. 22, 1844, by Rev. Roswell Whitman 62
Martha Jane, d. Russell & Betsey, b. June 10, 1832 61
Mary Esther, d. Ephraim & Susan, b. Feb. 28, 1822 258
Nancy, m. Charles **BURDICK**, b. of Griswold, Feb. 14, 1838, by Rev. William R. Jewett 314
Patty, m. Albert **LEWIS**, b. of Voluntown, Nov. 17, 1833, by Alexander Stewart, J.P. 301
Russell, of Preston, m. Betsey **BURTON**, of Griswold, Feb. 1, 1821, by Rev. Horatio Waldo 61
Russell, m. Esther **STILLMAN**, b. of Griswold, Mar. 15, 1844, by Rev. Roswell Whitman 61
Susan B., d. Ephraim & Susan, b. Apr. 21, 1820 258
Thomas, m. Hannah **BENJAMINS**, b. of Griswold, Mar. 9, 1845, by Comfort D. Fillmore, Elder 225
ROBINSON, Robert, m. Polly **WILCOX**, b. of Griswold, Sept. 7, 1820, by Alexander Stewart, Jr., J.P. 56
ROSE, Edwin, s. Elijah & Lydia, b. Feb. 20, 1829 241
John, M. Nancy **WHEELER**, Sept. 8, 1839, by Nathan Stanton, J.P. 126
ROSS, Louis, m. Russell **YARRINGTON**, Mar. 30, 1817 40
ROUNDS, Bertrand, Jr., m. Adaline A. **MILLARD**, b. of [Griswold?], Mar. 25, 1827, by Rev. Seth Bliss 194
ROUSE, Calvin, of Laurens, N.Y., m. Lydia **MORSE**, of Canterbury, Sept. 23, 1830, by Seth Bliss, of Jewett City 251
Nelson, of Preston, m. Matilda B. **TIFT**, of Griswold, Sept. 24, 1837, by Rev. William R. Jewett 134
RUGG, Salome, of Uxbridge, Mass., m. Thomas **WILCOX**, of Griswold, Mar. 22, 1836, by Benedict Johnson, Elder 250
RUGGLES, Richard B., m. Louisa **MUMFORD**, b. of Norwich, Sept. 3, 1848, by Tho[ma]s S. Shipman 85
RUTH[ER]FORD, Rebecca, m. Silas **HOW[E]**, Jan. 29, 1826, by Rev. Seth Bliss 162
SAFFORD, Erastus, of Preston, m. Phebe **PASH**, of Griswold, Mar. 18, 1834, by Rev. George Perkins 311

Page

SAFFORD, (cont.)
Henry, of Preston, m. Hannah **RIX**, of Griswold, Oct. 27, 1830, by Rev. S. D. Jewett 252
SALSBURY, Louisa, m. William D. **BUDLONG**, b. of Griswold, Feb. 23, 1834, by Welcome A. Browning, J.P. 306
SAUNDERS, Clark, m. Roxanna **COOK**, b. of Griswold, Mar. 30, 1834, by Alexander Stewart, J.P. 31
Dudley F., m. Mary C. **RICHMOND**, Feb. 6, 1848, by Rev. John W. Case 211
Phebe T., of Voluntown, m. Harvey C. **PALMER**, of Exeter, R.I., Nov. 1, 1841, by Rev. Moses Standish 36
SCRANTON, Stafford, of Brooklyn, m. Tabatha **CARR**, of Griswold, Aug. 13, 1837, by Rev. Benj[ami]n M. Walker 105
SEAGRAVES, Sylvanus T., of Uxbridge, Mass., m. Caroline **SLACK**, of Stonington, Oct. 30, 1825, by Levi Meech, Elder 107
SHAW, Dexter B., m. Phila **HOWARD**, b. of Cumberland, R.I., Aug. 21, 1847, by Rev. Jesse B. Denison. Witnesses: E. Bill, Abby W. Denison. 141
SHAY, George, of Plainfield, m. Sarah **KEIGWIN**, of Griswold, Jan. 25, 1824, by Rev. Horatio Waldo 137
James, of Plainfield, m. Lucy L. **WHIPPLE**, of Griswold, Aug. 22, 1847, by Rev. John W. Case 129
SHEPHARD, Edward W., m. Louisa **BURDICK**, b. of Plainfield, Dec. 20, 1831, by Rev. S. D. Jewett 275
SHERMAN, Mary A. P., of Griswold, m. Albert H. **ARMSBEE**, of Boston, Mass., Mar. 23, 1841, at Jewett City, by Rev. B. Cook 167
SHIPMAN, Abigail G., of Berlin, m. Rev. Spafford D. **JEWETT**, of Griswold, Dec. 22, 1830 277
SIMONS, Desire, m. Eseck **PEIRCE**, b. of Griswold, Mar. 30, 1830, by Seth Bliss, of Jewett City 250
Ezekiel, m. Mary **HAMILTON**, b. of Griswold, Aug. 7, 1831, by Elisha Partridge, J.P. 71
SLACK, Caroline, of Stonington, m. Sylvanus T. **SEAGRAVES**, of Uxbridge, Mass., Oct. 30, 1825, by Levi Meech, Elder 107
SMITH, Adah, of Jewett City, m. Ira **WHEELER**, of Colchester, July 13, 1841, by Rev. B. Cook, of Jewett City 169
Clarissa, b. Oct. 8, 1785; m. John **KEIGWIN**, Jan. 7, 1802 170
Eliza Ann, m. Daniel **DOWDELL**, b. of Norwich, Sept. 13, 1827, by Rev. Seth Bliss, of Jewett City 205
Hiram, m. Mary **WILKINS**, b. of Griswold, Aug. 3, 1834, by David Avery 314
Lydia, m. James M. **HALL**, Feb. 23, 1823, by Thomas Stewart, J.P. 98
Mariah Ann, of Griswold, m. Daniel **PARKER**, 2d, of Groton, July 25, 1822, by Elias Brewster, J.P. 102
Samuel, of Westerly, R.I., m. Maria C. W. **LIPPITT**, of Griswold, Oct. 15, [1834], by Rev. George Perkins 312
William, m. Lois Ann **COLBURN**, of Griswold, June 2, 1839, by Rev. William R. Jewett 223
SPAULDING, Cyril, see under Syral
Ezra M., m. Eunice **OLIN**, Oct. 20, 1822, by Amos Read, Elder 113
Ruth, m. Syral **SPAULDING**, b. of Plainfield, Nov. 9, 1845, by Rev. Cha[rle]s Noble 212
Syral, m. Ruth **SPAULDING**, b. of Plainfield, Nov. 9, 1845, by Rev. Cha[rle]s Noble 212
SPENCER, Alice A., of Griswold, m. Nathan **PRENTICE**, of Groton, June 13, 1822, by Rev. Horatio Waldo 101

Page

SPENCER, (cont.)
Catharine, m. Coddington **BILLINGS**, Sept. 13, 1832, by Rev. S. D. Jewett 286
Charles C., m. Eliza Ann **NORTH[R]UP**, b. of Griswold, Oct. 6, 1846, by Rev. Roswell Whitman 156
Charles R., m. Mary Ann **PRENTICE**, b. of Griswold, Feb. 6, 1822, by Rev. Horatio Waldo 88
Mary Ann, of Griswold, m. Ephraim **WILLIAMS**, of Groton, Dec. 21, 1820, by Rev. Horatio Waldo 61
SPICER, Anne, m. Edward **OLIN**, b. of Griswold, Nov. 17, 1842, by Rev. B. Cook, of Jewett City 95
Betsey Ann, of Jewett City, m. Franklin **FAULKNER**, of Norwich, Aug. 16, 1846, by Tho[ma]s S. Shipman 188
Lucinda, of Preston, m. Joseph **UTLEY**, of Griswold, Dec. 30, 1820, by Rev. John Hyde 59
SPRAGUE, Matilda, of Mass., m. Milo S. **DAVIS**, of Montville, Ct., Oct. 2, 1847, at Jewett City, by Rev. B. Cook, of J[ewett] City 269
STALKER, Daniel, m. Patty M. **BROWN**, Oct. 31, 1834, by Rev. Alfred Gates 164½
STANDISH, Almiraet, d. Molton & Asenath, b. Feb. 2, 1824 102
Almiraetta, of Griswold, m. David D. **WILSON**, of Windham, Mar. 13, 1842, by Rev. N. E. Shailer, of Preston 63
Molton, of Cranston, R.I., m. Asenath **CLARK**, of Griswold, Ct., June 1, 1823, by Welcome A. Browning, J.P. 102
Nathan, m. Mary A. **MORGAN**, b. of Norwich, June 21, 1841, by Rev. William R. Jewett, in Griswold 98
STANTON, Mary. d. Nathan & Mary, b. Nov. 13, 1817 13
Mary, of Griswold, m. Daniel **BROWN**, of Preston, Oct. 7, 1840, by Rev. William R. Jewett 310
Polly, m. Daniel M. **DOUGLASS**, Aug. 19, 1822, by Thomas Stewart, J.P. 110
Robert, s. Nathan & Mary, b. July 30, 1815 13
Sabra, of Griswold, m. Palmer P. **PARTELOW**, of Voluntown, Jan. 1, 1824, by Rev. Horatio Waldo 133
Theophilus F., m. Olive F. **KINNEY**, Apr. 29, 1838, by Nathan Stanton, J.P. 59
STARKWEATHER, Wealthy, m. Rufus **PRENTICE**, Aug. 14, 1823 196
STARR, Fanny, of Griswold, m. Phinehas **HOLDRIDGE**, of Groton, June 26, 1828, by Rev. Seth Bliss, of Jewett City 218
James M., m. Betsey O. **MINER**, b. of Griswold, Aug. 19, 1832, by Rev. George Perkins 295
Vine A., m. Mary **WILCOX**, b. of Griswold, Sept. 25, 1829, by Rev. Seth Bliss 238
STEPHENS, [see also **STEVENS**], Aaron, of Norwich, m. Adeline **MEECH**, of Griswold, Nov. 23, 1841, by Rev. William R. Jewett 113
STETSON, Charles C., of Lisbon, m. Alma S. **MORSE**, of Jewett City, Aug. 19, 1844, by Rev. B. Cook, of Jewett City 275
STEVENS, [see also **STEPHENS**], Alethear, m. John **FRAZIER**, Nov. 10, 1816 26
STEWART, Charles Fannin, s. Thomas, b. Feb. 10, 1814 119
Eliza, m. Nathan **COOK**, Dec. 31, 1812 16
Emma C., of Griswold, m. Stephen A. **DOUGLASS**, of Voluntown, Mar. 18, 1832, by Alexander Stewart, J.P. 282
Hepzibah Buel, d. Thomas, b. Sept. 7, 1818 119
James Munroe, s. Thomas, b. Jan. 10, 1822 119
Joan F., m. John T. **MOTT**, Oct. 2, 1828, by Thomas Stewart, J.P. 224
Thomas Congdon, s. Thomas, b. Feb. 6, 1816 119
STILLMAN, Esther, m. Russell **RIX**, b. of Griswold, Mar. 15, 1844, by Rev. Roswell Whitman 61

Page

STILLMAN, (cont.)
Ezra, m. Eliza **BARROWS**, b. of Jewett City, July 16, 1843, by Rev. B. Cook, of Jewett City 25
STONE, Abby Ann, of Griswold, m. Silas **COLE**, of Foster, R.I., Jan. 1, 1826, by Amos Read, Elder 160
Charles, of Brooklyn, Ct., m. Nancy **BALDWIN**, of Griswold, Ct., [ ], by Rev. William Wright 35
SUMM, James R., of New Berlin, Chenango Co., N.Y., m. Lucy **WILCOX**, of Voluntown, Nov. 8, 1846, by Tho[ma]s S. Shipman 161
SWAN, Nancy E., m. William T. **WILLETT**, b. of Norwich, Mar. 29, 1846, at Jewett City, by Rev. B. Cook, of Jewett City 275
Phebe, of [Griswold], m. John **LILLIBRIDGE**, Jr., of Exeter, R.I., June 4, 1820, by Rev. Levi Walker 53
SWEET, James, m. Sybel **CRUM**, b. of Griswold, Aug. 5, 1827, by Rev. Horatio Waldo 200
TABOR, Constant, m. Sally **GEER**, b. of Griswold, Oct. 8, 1826, by Rev. Horatio Waldo 184
Lucretia G., m. George W. **CHACE**, Apr. 30, 1826, by Rev. Seth Bliss 172
TANNER, Dorcas A., m. James **AUSTIN**, b. of Griswold, Mar. 9, 1845, by Rev. B. Cook, of Jewett City 305
Eliza M., m. W[illia]m **CUMMINS**, b. of Killingly, Dec. 30, 1843, by Rev. Roswell Whitman 223
TEFFT, **TIFT**, Alpha Sprague, s. Sprague & Eliza M., b. Dec. 13, 1841 150
Ann L., d. Nathan & Almira, b. Mar. 26, 1846; d. 253
Betsey, of Griswold, m. James N. **ECCLESTON**, of N. Stonington, July 4, 1844, at Jewett City, by Rev. B. Cook, of Jewett City 224
George D., s. Nathan & Almira, b. Mar. 27, 1843 253
George Johnothan, s. Sprague & Eliza M., b. May 19, 1840 150
Hannah, of Griswold, m. Eason **GARDINER**, of Norwich, Ct., Mar. 16, 1823, by Amos Read, Elder 24
Harriet Elizabeth, d. Sprague & Eliza M., b. Jan. 31, 1845 150
John Kenyon, s. Sprague & Eliza M., b. Apr. 10, 1838 150
Mary C., of Griswold, m. John H. **WILCOX**, of Norwich, [April?] 19, [1847?], by Rev. B. Cook, of J[ewett] City 270
Matilda B., of Griswold, m. Nelson **ROUSE**, of Preston, Sept. 24, 1837, by Rev. William R. Jewett 134
Orra M., d. Nathan & Almira, b. [ ], 1836; d. Apr. 29, 1873 253
Ruth Mary, d. Sprague & Eliza M., b. July 29, 1843 150
William H., s. Nathan & Almira, b. Feb. 21, 1841 253
TENNANT, Allen, of Voluntown, m. Caroline **FRY**, of Plainfield, Aug. 30, 1835, by Erastus Benton 72
TERRY, Harriet, m. William M. **RATHBURN**, b. of Griswold, Nov. 26, 1846, by Rev. Charles Noble 281
TEWKSBURY, [see under **TUOSKSBURY**]
THOMPSON, Isaac W., m. Ann T. **WILCOX**, Mar. 4, 1827, by Thomas Stewart, J.P. 193
Orcelia, m. Asa **DILLABY**, of Noriwch, [ ] 10, [ ], by Cha[rle]s E. Leonard, J.P. 217
THURBER, Allen, of Pittstown, N.Y., m. Archah **CHAPMAN**, of Griswold, June 9, 1835, by Rev. S. D. Jewett 32
TIFFANY, Almira T., of Griswold, m. Lewis W. **BRIGGS**, of Coventry, R.I., Aug. 13, 1844, by Rev. B. Cook, of Jewett City 274
Asia, m. John **LEE**, b. of Griswold, June 29, 1834, by David Avery 313
Hannah, m.l John R. **TRACY**, b. of Griswold, Oct. 2, 1831, by Welcome A. Browning, J.P. 270

Page

TIFFANY, (cont.)
Lydia L., of Griswold, m. Thomas G. **MORSE**, of Dover, N.H., May 16, 1847, at J[ewett] City, by Rev. B. Cook, of J[ewett] City 264
Thomas A., m. Densy **GALLUP**, Nov. 30, 1843, at Hopeville, Griswold, by Rev. B. Cook, of Jewett City 29
TIFT, [see under **TEFFT**]
TILLEY, William, European, m. Betsey **HARVEY**, of Griswold, Oct. 7, 1821, by Amos Read, Elder 78
TILLINGHAST, Amy Ann, m. Charles C. **COREY**, Aug. 18, 1831, by Rev. S. D. Jewett 268
Denison D., of W. Greenwich, R.I., m. Sarah Ann **BRAMAN**, of Griswold, July 3, 1837, by Rev. Levi Nelson 189
Gideon G., of W. Greenwich, R.I., m. Mercy **WALDO**, of Griswold, Jan. 6, 1833, by Rev. Levi Kneeland 290
TILLOTSON, Rhoda, m. Charles **McCOY**, b. of Griswold, Mar. 24, 1834, by Welcome A. Browning, J.P. 307
TINKHAM, Deborah B., of Griswold, m. Rev. Phinehas **CRANDALL**, of Talmouth, Mass., Apr. 9, 1824, by Isaac Jennison, Elder 115
TOURTELLOT, Clarissa, of Griswold, m. Moses **UNDERWOOD**, of Pomfret, Nov. 16, 1820, by Rev. Horatio Waldo 58½
TOWNSEND, Anna, m. Fitch **GEER**, b. of Griswold, Nov. 18, 1819, by Rev. Horatio Waldo 124
TRACY, Albert L., of Lisbon, m. Harriet **BURCH**, of Griswold, Mar. 10, 1825, by Rev. Horatio Waldo 69
Douglass, of Lisbon, m. Sarah **BARNES**, of Preston, Sept. 24, 1834, by Rev. George Perkins 312
John R., m. Hannah **TIFFANY**, b. of Griswold, Oct. 2, 1831, by Welcome A. Browning, J.P. 270
Lucy, m. Israel **BRUMLEY**, Feb. 2, 1795 209
TUCKER, Ann, d. Denison B. & Abiah B., b. Jan. 19, 1832 203
Betsey, d. William & Sally, b. Mar. 12, 1820 4
Charles, s. Stephen & Eunice, b. Apr. 23, 1817 58½
Daniel Morgan, s. W[illia]m & Sally, b. Apr. 9, 1822; d. Jan. 7, 1823 4
Denison B., m. Abiah **BURBANK**, Nov. 8, 1826, by Rev. Reuben S. Hazen, of Agawam & Feeding Hills, W. Springfield 203
Denison Baldwin, s. Stephen & Eunice, b. Oct. 28, 1801 19
Edwin, s. Stephen & Eunice, b. Aug. 13, 1804 19
Edwin, of Plainfield, m. Joann **COGSWELL**, of Griswold, Apr. 13, 1831, by Rev. S. D. Jewett 263
Erastus, s. Stephen & Eunice, b. Aug. 10, 1794 19
Esther, d. Stephen & Eunice, b. Nov. 20, 1806 19
Esther, w. William, d. Oct. 2, 1818 12
Esther M., d. Stephen & Eunice, d. Apr. 17, 1846 58½
Eunice, d. Stephen & Eunice, b. Dec. 22, 1813 19
George, s. William & Sally, b. Feb. 20, 1829 4
Hannah, d. William & Sally, b. Jan. 21, 1827 4
Henry, s. William & Sally, b. Feb. 16, 1815, in Preston 4
Henry, m. Sarah W. **LESTER**, b. of Griswold, Sept. 4, 1837, by Rev. William R. Jewett 233
James Coit, s. Denison B. & Abiah B., b. Feb. 29, 1828 203
John Baldwin, s. Stephen & Eunice, b. Sept. 28, 1811 19
Lucy* D., m. Capt. John **LESTER**, b. of Griswold, Jan. 15, 1822, by Rev. Horatio Waldo. (*Name is Mary in the record of the births of the children.) 87
Lucy Denison, d. Stephen & Eunice, b. Mar. 13, 1796 19

Page

TUCKER, (cont.)
Mary, d. William & Sally, b. Jan. 8, 1818 4
Mary, of Griswold, m. Dwight **JOHNSON**, of New York, Sept. 2, 1844, by Rev. Roswell Whitman 262
Sally, d. Stephen & Eunice, b. Mar. 7, 1809 19
Sarah, d. William & Sally, b. Aug. 11, 1824 4
Sarah B., m. Capt. Moses **LESTER**, b. of Griswold, Sept. 23, 1829, by Rev. Horatio Waldo 235
Stephen, b. Apr. 30, 1768; m. Eunice **BALDWIN**, Jan. 17, 1793 19
Susan, of Griswold, m. Asa **HUTCHENS**, of Thompson, Oct. 28, 1822, by Rev. Horatio Waldo 115
William, S. Stephen & Eunice, b. Dec. 23, 1798 19
William, Jr., m. Sally **MORGAN**, May 5, 1814, by Rev. Horatio Waldo 4
William, d. Nov. 5, 1819 12
William, s. Stephen & Eunice, d. Apr. 13, 1819 58½
William, d. July 11, 1839 4
William, s. Henry & Sarah W., b. July 13, 1839 233
William, m. Happy **WHIPPLE**, Mar. 26, 1843, by Rev. H. Forbush 13
TUOSKSBURY, Pashall N., of Hartland, Vt., m. Eve C. **GOLD**, of [Griswold], Jan. 30, 1837, by Geo[rge] Perkins 196
TURNER, Bushnell, m. Rebecca **PHILLIPS**, b. of Griswold, Nov. 24, 1825, by Rev. Seth Bliss, of Jewett City 158
Hannah R., m. William H. **WISE**, b. residing in Griswold, July 3, 1825, by Amos Read, Elder 139
Lucy, m. Gilbert **GUILE**, b. of Griswold, Dec. 23, 1824, by Levi Meech, Elder 151
TYLER, Abby, m. Frederick **BREWSTER**, b. of Griswold, Nov. 15, 1826, by Rev. Horatio Waldo 186
Ann Mary, d. John, Jr. & Abigail, [B.], b. Dec. 3,1817 11
Charles Coit, s. Elisha & Mary, b. Dec. 30, 1830 246
Charles Wheeler, s. Thomas S. & Dolly, b. Oct. 10, 1828 164
Clarena, d. James & Clarena, d. Feb. 18, 1822 108
Dwight R., m. Eliza C. **TYLER**, b. of Griswold, Dec. 25, 1823, by Rev. Horatio Waldo 132
Dwight R., m. Mary K. **JOHNSON**, Feb. 23, 1846 132
Dwight Ripley, s. Thomas S. & Dolly, b. Dec. 25, 1831 164
Edward Spaulding, s. Thomas S. & Dolly, b. Sept. 13, 1834 164
Elisha, of Griswold, m. Mary **GREEN**, of Plainfield, Mar. 9, 1830, by Rev. Seth Bliss 246
Eliza C., m. Dwight R. **TYLER**, b. of Griswold, Dec. 25, 1823, by Rev. Horatio Waldo 132
Eliza C., w. Dwight R., d. Oct. 12, 1845, ae. 43 y. 132
Elizabeth, m. William **HUNTINGTON**, b. of Griswold, Nov. 6, 1833, by Rev. S. D. Jewett 299
Frances, m. Hezekiah L. **MORGAN**, Dec. 25, 1833, by Rev. S. D. Jewett 187
Frederick. s. F[rederic] W. & Jane E., b. Mar. 25, 1844 288
Harriet, of Griswold, m. Rev. Paul **COUCH**, of W. Newbury, Mass., May 28, 1827, by Rev. Horatio Waldo 199
Harriet, w. Henry C., d. Nov. 24, 1829 123
Harriet, d. Henry C. & Thirzah, b. June 8, 1834 123
Henry, s. Henry C. & Thirzah, b. July 19, 1841 123
Henry C., m. Harriet **HYDE**, b. of Griswold, Mar. 13, 1823, by Rev. Horatio Waldo 123
Henry C., m. Thirzah **MORSE**, Mar. 25, 1828, by Seth Bliss, of Jewett City 123
John, Jr., m. Abigail Belcher **COGSWELL**, Mar. 8, 1815 11

Page

TYLER, (cont.)
John, s. John, Jr. & Abigail B., b. Feb. 6, 1820; d. Dec. 6, 1820 11
John Spaulding, s. Henry C. & Harriet, b. Nov. 16, 1825 123
Joseph Cogswell, s. Thomas S. & Dolly, b. Feb. 9, 1827 164
Josephine, d. F[rederic] W. & Jane E., b. Feb. 11, 1841 288
Lucius, Dr., m. Olive **JOHNSON**, b. of Griswold, Mar. 23, 1824, by Rev. Horatio Waldo 142
Lucretia, of Griswold, m. Charles **COIT**, of Norwich, May 14, 1821, by Rev. Horatio Waldo 68
Lucy Belcher, d. Henry C. & Harriet, b. Feb. 5, 1824 123
Lydia, of Griswold, m. Charles **COIT**, of Chelsea, Jan. 21, 1824, by Rev. John Hyde 134
Mary A., of Griswold, m. Billings **BROWN**, of Preston, Feb. 24, 1825, by Rev. David Austin, of Bozrah 153
Mary Boardman, d. Henry C. & Thirzah, b. Sept. 15, 1831 123
Mary Esther, d. John, Jr. & Abigail B., b. Feb. 5, 1824 11
Mehitable, d. John, Jr. & Abigail B., b. Feb. 1, 1816 11
Moses, Col., d. Apr. 15, 1829 27
Moses, s. Elisha & Mary, b. Aug. 2, 1835 246
Olive, wid., of [Griswold], m. Rev. Gordon **DORRANCE**, of Sunderland, M[as]s., Nov. 21, 1835, by Rev. S. D. Jewett 33
Olive, d. Henry C. & Thirzah, b. Nov. 9, 1839 123
Rowland Green, s. Elisha & Mary, b. Jan. 4, 1832 246
Susannah Green, d. Elisha & Mary, b. Jan. 24, 1834 246
Thomas S., m. Dolly **COGSWELL**, b. of Griswold, Dec. 1, 1824, by Rev. Horatio Waldo 164

UNDERWOOD, Henry, s. Moses & Clarissa, b. Feb. 9, 1822 106
Moses, of Pomfret, m. Clarissa **TOURTELLOT**, of Griswold, Nov. 16, 1820, by Rev. Horatio Waldo 58½
Willard, m. Mary **PERKINS**, b. of Griswold, Apr. 1, 1824, by Rev. Horatio Waldo 144

UTLEY, Abby, m. Charles **WOODWARD**, Dec. 1, 1814 1
Abby, d. Ephraim H. & Betsey [P.], b. Oct. 1, 1818 5
Ephraim H., m. Betsey P. **CHAPMAN**, Feb. 9, 1815, by Rev. Horatio Waldo 5
John C., s. Ephraim H. & Betsey [P.], b. Aug. 13, 1816 5
Joseph, of Griswold, m. Lucinda **SPICER**, of Preston, Dec. 30, 1820, by Rev. John Hyde 59
Peleg, d. June 2, 1823 27
Prudence Ann, m. Nelson **BARBER**, b. of Griswold, June 7, 1834, by Rev. Nathan E. Shailer 213

WADE, Lucretia, m. Samuel H. **CUTLER**, b. of Griswold, Dec. 25, 1825, by Rev. Silas Bliss, of Jewett City 161

WALDO, Dwight, s. Horatio & Frances, b. Nov. 26, 1814 208
Frances, d. Horatio & Frances, b. June 24, 1820 208
Harriet, d. Horatio & Frances, b. May 11, 1822 208
Horatio, m. Frances **WHITNEY**, Oct. 8, 1810 208
John, s. Horatio & Frances, b. Aug. 10, 1811 208
Margaret, d. Horatio & Frances, b. Oct. 28, 1824 208
Mercy, of Griswold, m. Gideon C. **TILLINGHAST**, of W. Greenwich, R.I., Jan. 6, 1833, by Rev. Levi Kneeland 290
Sarah, d. Horatio & Frances, b. June 7, 1818 208

WALKER, Betsey M., m. John H. **PARKER**, b. of Griswold, Nov. 1, 1829, by Seth Bliss, of Jewett City 240

WALLACE, Mary, m. David **FROST**, of Griswold, Jan. 31, 1841, by Charles E. Leonard, J.P. 74

Page

WALLIS, James, of New York, m. Mary Ann **GLASKO**, of Griswold, Dec. 31, 1826, by Levi Meech, Elder 221
WALTON, Alice, d. Daniel & Zerviah, b. Nov. 23, 1780 8
Annes, d. Daniel & Zerviah, b. July 22, 1785 8
Daniel, s. Daniel & Zerviah, b. May 8, 1787 8
Daniel, m. Mary **BLACKMAN**, June 27, 1815, in Canterbury, by Daniel Frost, J.P. 8
Hannah, d. Daniel & Zerviah, b. May 28, 1778 8
Prudence, d. Daniel & Zerviah, b. July 25, 1782 8
Rebeckah, d. Daniel & Zerviah, b. Dec. 1, 1791 8
Sophia, d. Daniel & Zerviah, b. June 1, 1789 8
WAMSLEY, Henrietta, of Griswold, m. Stephen **CONGDON**, of Preston, Mar. 2, 1823, by Rev. Horatio Waldo 99
Martha, m. Thaddeus **MOODEY**, Dec. 10, 1818, by Rev. Horatio Waldo 44
Sarah, of Griswold, m. James **CONGDON**, of Preston, Jan. 23, 1825, by Rev. Horatio Waldo 165
WATSON, Samuel, Jr., m. Eleanor **COREY**, Apr. 26, 1824, by Thomas Stewart, J.P. 100
WEAVER, Alpheas, m. Abby J. **WILLIAMS**, Jan. 19, 1852, at Jewett City, by Rev. Daniel D. Lyon, of Jewett City 118
WEDGE, Bridget, of Canterbury, m. Nathaniel **COGSWELL**, of Preston, May 25, 1757 120
WEEDEN, Ede, wido. of Elijah, d. Sept. 8, 1829 27
Elijah, d. Oct. 29, 1816 27
WETHEY, **WITHEY**, Abby Jane, d. William & Betsey, b. Mar. 5, 1819; d. June 3, 1839 155
Alfred Manning, s. William & Betsey, b. Sept. 25, 1823 155
Elijah, d. Feb. 7, 1816 30
Ezra, s. William & Betsey, b. June 4, 1808 155
Sanford, s. William & Betsey, b. Feb. 23, 1816 155
William, m. Betsey **MANNING**, Apr. 1, 1806 155
WHALEY, Sarah A., m. Eben E. **WILSON**, b. of [Jewett City], Apr. 15, 1848, by Tho[ma]s S. Shipman 40
WHEELER, Ira, of Colchester, m. Adah **SMITH**, of Jewett City, July 13, 1841, by Rev. B. Cook, of Jewett City 169
Mary E., m. Ansel B. **WILLIAMS**, b. of Griswold, Nov. 25, 1847, by Rev. B. Cook, of Jewett City 198
Nancy, m. John **ROSE**, Sept. 8, 1839, by Nathan Stanton, J.P. 126
Samuel W., m. Else **ELLIS**, of Griswold, June 24, 1821, by Rev. Caleb Read 72
WHIPPLE, Charles H., s. Ezra & Ruba, b. Mar. 14, 1830 20
Clark P., s. Ezra & Mary, b. Sept. 26, 1839 242
Daniel D., s. Ezra & Mary, b. Aug. 30, 1841 242
Eliza Diana, d. Ezra & Ruba, b. Dec. 16, 1817 20
Ezra, Jr., m. Mary **JACKSON**, b. of Griswold, Apr. 10, 1836, by Alexander Stewart, Jr., J.P. 242
Ezra A., s. Ezra & Mary, b. Aug. 2, 1838 242
Frances M., d. Ezra & Mary, b. Sept. 6, 1845 242
Happy, m. William **TUCKER**, Mar. 26, 1843, by Rev. H. Forbush 13
Happy Caroline, d. Ezra & Ruba, b. Aug. 17, 1824 20
John Adams, s. Ezra & Ruba, b. Dec. 8, 1821 20
Lucy, d. Ezra & Ruba, b. Mar. 22, 1826 20
Lucy L., of Griswold, m. James **SHAY**, of Plainfield, Aug. 22, 1847, by Rev. John W. Case 129
Mary S., d. Ezra & Mary. b. Dec. 7, 1843 242
Robert Bishop, twin with Ruba Ann, s. Ezra & Ruba, b. Oct. 16, 1815 20
Ruba Ann, twin with Robert Bishop, d. Ezra & Ruba, b. Oct. 16, 1815 20
Sally, m. Cyrus **PARTRIDGE**, Mar. 29, 1820 58

Page

WHIPPLE, (cont.)
Sally, m. Alfred **DAVIS**, May 9, 1824, by Nathan Stanton, J.P. 67
WHITFORD, Samuel, of Griswold, m. Caroline C. **FLETCHER**, of Plainfield, Oct. 17, 1847, by Tho[ma]s S. Shipman 285
WHITING, Avery M., d. July 4, 1836 27
C.S., d. July 19, 1863 27
Charles H., s. Charles S. & Fanny, b. Dec. 2, 1829 159
Charles S., of Lisbon, m. Fanny **JUSTIN**, of Griswold, Nov. 24, 1825, by Amos Read, Elder 159
Edwin W., s. Charles S. & Fanny, b. Jan. 28, 1828 159
James W., d. Sept. 14, 1823 27
Lucy M., d. Charles S. & Fanny, b. Jan. 16, 1832 159
Mary E., d. Charles S. & Fanny, b. Aug. 23, 1826 159
WHITMAN, John, m. Melissa Ann **REYNOLDS**, b. of Canterbury, Sept. 1, 1832, by Elisha Partridge, J.P. 104
Malissa Ann, of Griswold, m. Bennett **GREEN**, of Canterbury, Nov. 24, 1838, by Elisha Partridge, J.P. 157
WHITNEY, Frances, m. Horatio Waldo, Oct. 8, 1810 208
WIGHT, Joseph Kingsbury, s. Daniel & Rosanna, b. Feb. 9, 1824 105
William Ward, s. Daniel & Rosanna, b. Feb. 4, 1822 105
WILBUR, Alice, w. Joseph, d. Mar. 1, 1824 21
Alice Laline, d. Joseph & Alice, b. July 18, 1822 21
Alice Z., m. James A. **PALMER**, b. of Griswold, Feb. 13, 1848, by Rev. Cyrus Miner 277
Elizabeth, of Norwich, m. Samuel **GEER**, of Griswold, Mar. 22, 1821, by Rev. John Sterry, of Norwich
Gustavus Ray, s. Joseph & Alice, b. June 6, 1816; d. Oct. 15, 1823 21
Mary Aletty, d. Joseph & Louisa, b. Jan. 18, 1828 21
Nathan Kimball, s. Joseph & Alice, b. Sept. 24, 1813; d. Sept. 30, 1823 21
Samuel F., m. Lucy A. **BURDICK**, Mar. 29, 1841, by Deac. Comfort D. Fillmore 81
Samuel Fellows, s. Joseph & Alice, b. July 25, 1818 21
Thomas C., m. Eliza P. **NORTHAM**, b. of Griswold, Jan. 26, 1823, by Rev. Horatio Waldo 12
William Norman, s. Joseph & Louisa, b. Nov. 28, 1825 21
WILCOX, Ann T., m. Isaac W. **THOMPSON**, Mar. 4, 1827, by Thomas Stewart, J.P. 193
Calvin, b. Sept. 15, 1845 250
Chester Phillips, s. Henry N. & Welthy, b. May 31, 1816 31
Esther, m. William W. **DOUGLASS**, b. of Griswold, Oct. 26, 1828, by Levi Kneeland 225
Gordon, b. Sept. 20, 1841 250
John H., of Norwich, m. Mary C. **TEFFT**, of Griswold, [April?] 19, [1847?], by Rev. B. Cook, of J[ewett] City 270
Lucy, of Voluntown, m. James R. **SUMM**, of New Berlin, Chenango Co., N.Y., Nov. 8, 1846, by Tho[ma]s S. Shipman 161
Mary, m. Vine A. **STARR**, b. of Griswold, Sept. 25, 1829, by Rev. Seth Bliss 238
Noah, b. Feb. 10, 1837 250
Polly, m. Robert **ROBINSON**, b. of Griswold, Sept. 7, 1820, by Alexander Stewart, Jr., J.P. 56
Reynolds, m. Eliza **POTTER**, b. of Griswold, Feb. 16, 1834, by Welcome A. Browning, J.P. 305
Thomas, of Griswold, m. Salome **RUGG**, of Uxbridge, Mass., Mar. 22, 1836, by Benedict Johnson, Elder 250
William, of W. Greenwich, R.I., m. Irena **LARKIN**, of Griswold, July 15, 1821, by Rev. Horatio Waldo 74
WILKINS, Mary, m. Hiram **SMITH**, b. of Griswold, Aug. 38, 1834, by David Avery 314

GROTON VITAL RECORDS
1704 - 1853

	Vol.	Page
ADAMS, Abby Ann, m. William Jefferson **GRAY**, b. of Groton, Jan. 26, 1824, by Rev. John G. Wightman	1	12
Abigail, [d. Nathan, Jr. & Elizabeth], b. Mar. 1, 1771	1	170
David, b. Mar. 2, 1761	2	23
Elijah, m. [E]unice **LESTER**, Mar. 14, 1771	1	151
Elizabeth, [d. Nathan, Jr. & Elizabeth], b. July 18, 1775	1	170
Esther, [d. James & Mary], b. Aug. 23, 1770	1	167
Eunice, d. [James & Mary], b. May 21, 1768	1	167
George, s. Elijah & [E]unice, b. Dec. 14, 1772	1	151
Hannah, d. Nathaniel & Hannah, b. Sept. 3, 1744	1	152
Hannah, b. Feb. 11, 1771	2	23
Henry, s. James & Mary, b. June 5, 1757	1	167
James, of Stephenstown, N.Y., m. Sarah C. **LESTER**, of Groton, Feb. 11, 1821, by Ralph Hurlbutt, J.P.	1	3
James, Jr., of Stephentown, N.Y., m. Sarah C. **LESTER**, of Groton, Feb. 11, 1821, by Ralph Hurlbutt, J.P.	2	29
James, s. Nathaniel & Hannah, b. Feb. 6, 1732/33	1	152
James, m. Mary **RANDALL**, b. of Groton, Aug. 3, 1756, in Westerly, by Silas Greenman, J.P. Intention of marriage signed by Ebenezer Avery, J.P.	1	167
James, s. [James & Mary], b. Feb. 17, 1759	1	167
James B., of Newport, R.I., m. Julian **WHIPPLE**, of Waterford, Oct. 21, 1821, by Philip Gray, J.P.	1	4
John W., m. Ann Mariah **DICKENSON**, b. of Groton, June 25, 1837, by Rev. Ira R. Steward	1	57
Joseph, twin with Mary, s. Nathaniel & Hannah, b. Aug. 20, 1747	1	152
Josiah, of Stephentown, N.Y., m. Amey **LESTER**, of Groton, Feb. 14, 1833, by Ralph Hurlbutt, J.P.	1	43
Lydia, m. Dudley B. **CRANDALL**, b. of Groton, Jan. 11, 1829, by Ralph Hurlbutt, J.P.	1	29
Mary, twin with Joseph, d. Nathaniel & Hannah, b. Aug. 20, 1747	1	152
Mary, b. June 5, 1759	2	23
Mary, d. [James & Mary], b. Aug. 18, 1761	1	167
Mary, m. Jacob **ALLYN**, b. of Groton, Nov. 7, 1830, by Ralph Hurlbutt, J.P.	1	35
Naomy, b. Aug. 20, 1766	2	23
Nathan, Jr., m. Elizabeth **COMSTOCK**, Jan. 4, 1770	1	170
Nathaniel, b. Mar. 25, 1708/9; m. Hannah **WHEELER**, Jan. 23, 1731/32	1	152
Nathaniel, s. Nathaniel & Hannah, b. June 8, 1739	1	152
Nathaniel, Jr., d. Sept. 6, 1781	1	170
Phebe, b. Dec. 22, 1768	2	23
Prentice, [s. Nathan, Jr. & Elizabeth], b. Feb. 26, 1775 [sic]	1	170

	Vol.	Page
ADAMS, (cont.)		
Priscilla, d. [James & Mary], b. Jan. 28, 1766	1	167
Samuel, b. Jan. 23, 1756	2	23
Sarah, d. Nathaniel & Hannah, b. Nov. 20, 1756	1	152
Sarah, [d. Nathan, Jr. & Elizabeth], b. Jan. 17, 1773	1	170
Simeon, s. Nathaniel & Hannah, b. Jan. 23, 1742/3	1	152
Simeon, b. Jan. 30, 1763	2	23
William, s. Nathaniel & Hannah, b. Nov. 22, 1740	1	152
William, s. [James & Mary], b. Sept. 11, 1763	1	167
William, of Ledyard, m. Hannah **LATHAM**, of Groton, Feb. 5, 1837, by Rev. Roswell Burrows	1	56
Youngs, s. Elijah & [E]unice, b. Aug. 2, 1777	1	151
ADELY, Mary, m. Martin **TILVEST**, b. of Groton, Jan. 9, 1849, by Rev. Simon B. Bailey	1	82
ADGATE, Thomas A., of Montville, m. Lois **PERKINS**, of Groton, Mar. 11, 1835, by Ralph Hurlbutt, J.P.	1	49
ALDEN, Elizabeth, of Duxbury, Mass., m. John **SEABURY**, Dec. 9, 1697	1	103
ALDERMAN, Ann, m. John D. **SMITH**, b. of Stonington, Nov. 21, 1830, by Nathan Daboll, J.P.	1	36
ALEXANDER, Eliza, m. Isaac **LAMB**, b. of Groton, Apr. 3, 1834, by Amos A. Niles, J.P.	1	47
Eliza A., of Groton, m. William T. **ELDREDGE**, of Stonington, Dec. 8, 1845, by Rev. William C. Walker	1	75
Livingstone, s. [Tho[ma]s & Sally], b. Oct. 1, 1803	2	48
Nancy, d. Tho[ma]s & Sally, b. July 4, 1811	2	48
Susan, m. Mason **GUYANT**, b. of Groton, Sept. 18, 1825, by Nathan Daboll, J.P.	1	34
Susanna, d. [Tho[ma]s & Sally], b. May 4, 1800	2	48
Thomas J., m. Mary Ann **MINER**, b. of Groton, July 29, 1830, by Erastus T. Smith, J.P.	1	34
Thomas Jefferson, s. [Tho[ma]s & Sally], b. Apr. 5, 1808	2	48
William, s. Tho[ma]s & Sally, b. Aug. 29, 1797	2	48
ALGER, Hannah, m. Bial **SAMON**, Mar. 28, 1715/16	1	114
ALLEN, [see also **ALLYN**], A.C., m. Eliza M. **LESTER**, b. of Ledyard, Apr. 2, 1854, by Geo[rge] H. Woodward	1	96
Asa, of Hudson, Ohio, m. Amanda D. **DARROW**, of Groton, Jan. 12, 1854, by Rev. Allen Darrow	1	95
Belton, s. Joseph & Mary, b. Oct. 1, 1764	2	5
Elizabeth, m. Jonathan **WILLIAMS**, Jan. 24, 1711	II	369
Elizabeth, m. James **AVERY**, May 28, 1752	2	4
Georgianna J., of Norwich, m. John B. **HALEY**, [s. Henry & Mary Ann]	3	0
Johanna, m. Thomas **PATTEN**, Jr., Oct. 9, 1753	1	157
Joseph, m Mary **BELTON**, b. of Groton, Dec. 30, 1760	2	5
Lydia, m. Jesse **CHAPMAN**, [ ]	3	5
Sarah, m. Abel **SPICER**, b. of Groton, Jan. 14, 1762, by Jacob Johnson	2	7
Sarah, of Groton, m. Albert **ELLSWORTH**, of New London, June 2, 1844, by Rev. Simon B. Bailey	1	71
ALLYN, [see also **ALLEN**], Abigail, d. Robert & Abigail, b. Feb. 2, 1726	1	130
Abigail, d. [Robert & Abigail], b. Feb. 2, 1726/7	1	180
Abigail, d. John & Joanna, b. June 25, 1737	1	142
Abigail, d. [Robert, Jr. & Hannah], b. Jan. 10, 1760	1	167
Abigail, m. Frederick **LARRABEE**, May [ ], 1786	2	80
Albert Munroe, s. [James & Fanny], b. July 28, 1805	2	70

	Vol.	Page
ALLYN, (cont.)		
Alfred, m. Caroline **STODDARD**, b. of Groton, Sept. 4, 1831, by John G. Wightman, Eld.	1	38
Alithea, m. James **ALLYN**, Dec. 17, 1729 ["Avery" in pencil]	1	141
Alithea, d. James & Alethea, b. Apr. 4, 1731	1	141
Alethea, m. Oliver **SPICER**, Aug. 15, 1749	1	165
Alethea, d. [James & Anna], b. Aug. 6, 1776	2	69
Alexander, [s. Christopher & Elizabeth], b. Jan. 2, 1768	2	33
Amos, [s. Ebenezer & Mary], b. Feb. 21, 1748	1	132
Anna, [d. John], b. Nov. 23, 1701	1	111
Anna, d. [James & Anna], b. Nov. 9, 1771	2	69
Anna, b. Nov. 9, 1771; m. Amos A. **NILES**, Mar. 13, 1791	2	92
Anna, [d. Christopher & Elizabeth], b. Mar. 8, 1765	2	33
Anna, w. James, d. Apr. 2, 1814	2	69
Annos, [s. Christopher & Elizabeth], b. Nov. 13, 1776	2	33
Austin, m Lucy **MORGAN**, b. of Groton, Feb. 13, 1824, by Timothy Tuttle	1	12
Benajah Avery, s. James & Fanny, b. Nov. 27, 1796	2	70
Benedam, s. [Robert, Jr. & Hannah], b. Dec. 16, 1761	1	167
Benedam, s. [Robert, Jr. & Hannah], d. Sep. 6, 1781. Killed in the storming of Fort Griswold by the British	1	167
Benjamin, s. John & Joanna, b. Sept. 29, 1732	1	142
Betty, d. John & Joanna, b. Mar. 26, 1753	1	142
Bridget, m. John G. **WIGHTMAN**, July 7, 1817	2	38
Caleb, m. Emily **HALEY**, d. Stephen & Lucy, [ ]	2	79
Caleb, m. Emily **HALLEY**, d. Stephen & Lucy, [ ]	3	0
Caleb J., m. Emily **HALEY**, b. of Groton, Jan. 23, 1831, by John G. Wightman, Eld.	1	36
Carolina, of Groton, m. Seabury **WHITE**, Nov. 3, 1822, by Timothy Tuttle	1	8
Catharine, of Groton, m. John **BACON**, of New Orleans, Sept. 3, 1826, by Timothy Tuttle	1	21
Charles, s. [James & Anna], b. Sept. 28, 1781	2	69
Christopher, [s. Robert & Deborah], b. Apr. 12, 1702; d. Mar. 26, 1703	1	102
Christopher, [s. Robert & Deborah], b. July 21, 1706	1	102
Christopher, m. Elizabeth **BUFF**, Nov. 16, 1757	2	33
Christopher, [s. Christopher & Elizabeth], b. Sept. 23, 1762	2	33
Christopher, Capt., d. May 13, 1776	2	33
Christopher, m. Maria **STODDARD**, Nov. 19, 1820, by Timothy Tuttle	1	2
Clarissa, m. Benjamin **SPICER**, 2d, b. of Groton, Mar. 24, 1822, by Philip Gray, J.P.	1	6
Content, d. John & Joanna, b. Oct. 24, 1743	1	142
Cynthia, d. [Christopher & Elizabeth], b. Jan. 30, 1760	2	33
Daniel, [s. Christopher & Elizabeth], b. Nov. 10, 1774	2	33
Daniel, s. Christopher & Elizabeth, b. Nov. 10, 1775	2	16
David, s. James & Alethea, b. Oct. 23, 1759	1	141
Deborah, [d. Robert & Deborah], b. Nov. 20, 1694	1	102
Deborah, m. Jonathan **LESTER**, Sept. 22, 1724	1	125
Deborah, [d. Ebenezer & Mary], b. Oct. 11, 1730; d. Apr. 19, 1731	1	132
Deborah, d. James & Alethea, b. Feb. 18, 1732/3; d. Jan. [ ], 1733/4	1	141
Deborah, d. James & Alethea, b. Dec. 23, 1735; d. Feb. 23, 1755	1	141
Deborah, d. Samuel & Hannah, b. May 3, 1755	2	10
Ebenezer, m. Mary **THURBER**, Apr. 27, 1726	1	132
Ebenezer, s. Ebenezer & Mary, b. Sept. 6, 1729; d. Nov. 5, 1729	1	132
Ebenezer, [s. Ebenezer & Mary], b. Mar. 28, 1740	1	132

	Vol.	Page
ALLYN, (cont.)		
Ecabod, [s. John], b. Oct. 18, 1711	1	111
Elizabeth, d. [Robert & Deborah], b. Mar. 25, 1691/2	1	102
Elizabeth, twin with James, [d. Robert & Deborah], b. Feb. 29, 1699/00	1	102
Elizabeth, d. [Robert & Abigail], b. Mar. 27, 1731	1	180
Elizabeth, d. James & Alethea, b. Nov. 9, 1749	1	141
Elizabeth, d. Samuel & Hannah, b. Feb. 11, 1753	2	10
Elizabeth, [d. Christopher & Elizabeth], b. Feb. 17, 1770	2	33
Ephraim, s. James & Alethea, b. June 18, 1747	1	141
Ephraim, m. Almira **ARTHUR**, b. of Groton, July 25, 1826, by Ralph Hurlbutt, J.P.	1	21
Esther, d. [Robert, Jr. & Hannah], b. Apr. 7, 1765	1	167
Esther, d. Samuel & Hannah, b. Apr. 19, 1739	2	10
Eunice, d. Samuel & Hannah, b. Mar. 29, 1737	2	10
Fanny, m. Beebe **DENISON**, b. of Groton, Dec. 24, 1820, by Ralph Hurlbutt, J.P.	1	2
Frances William, [s. James & Fanny], b. May 21, 1810	2	70
Frederick, s. [Robert, Jr. & Hannah], b. Apr. 13, 1763; d. Feb. 16, 1794	1	167
Gilbert, m. Matilda **ALLYN**, b. of Groton, June 4, 1820	1	1
Griswold, m. Betsey **CHAPPELL**, b. of Groton, Mar. 4, 1821, by Ralph Hurlbutt, J.P.	1	3
Gurdon, m. Sally S. **BRADFORD**, of Groton, Oct. 13, 1822, by Rodman Niles, J.P.	1	8
Gurdon, m. Mrs. Hannah **RATHBURN**, b. of Groton, Sept. 19, 1842, by Ira R. Steward	1	67
Hannah, d. Samuel & Hannah, b. Nov. 25, 1732	2	10
Hannah, d. James & Alethea, b. Feb. 14, 1755	1	141
Hannah, d. [Robert, Jr. & Hannah], b. Mar. 11, 1758	1	167
Hannah, d. [James & Anna], b. July 7, 1787; d. Sept. 3, 1787	2	69
Hannah, m. John D. **BRADFORD**, b. of Groton, July 21, 1822, by Ralph Hurlbutt, J.P	1	7
Hannah, m. Benjamin F. **GALLUP**, b. of Groton, Dec. 10, 1823, by John G. Wightman	1	11
Hiram, m. Caroline **AVERY**, b. of Groton, Dec. 13, 1835, by John G. Wightman, Elder	1	52
Ichabod, see Ecabod		
Jabez, s. [James & Anna], b. Jan. 12, 1779; d. Sept. 21, 1781	2	69
Jacob, s. [Robert & Abigail], b. Mar. 27, 1743	1	180
Jacob, m. Mary **ADAMS**, b. of Groton, Nov. 7, 1830, by Ralph Hurlbutt, J.P.	1	35
James, twin with Elizabeth, [s. Robert & Deborah], b. Feb. 29, 1699/00	1	102
James, m. Alithea **ALLYN***, Dec. 17, 1729. [*"Avery" in pencil]	1	141
James, s. James & Alethea, b. July 17, 1739	1	141
James, m. Anna **STANTON**, Dec. 15, 1768	2	69
James, s. [James & Anna], b. Oct. 22, 1769	2	69
James, Jr., m. Fanny **AVERY**, b. of Groton, Nov. 30, 1795, by Amos Geer, J.P.	2	70
Jerusha, d. James & Alethea, b. July 5, 1752	1	141
Joanna, m. Thomas **MORGAN**, Jr., b. of Groton, Jan. 4, 1787, by Rev. Park Allyn, of N. Groton	2	46
John, [s. Robert & Deborah], b. Jan. 11, 1695	1	102
John, [s. John], b. Aug. 2, 1706	1	111
John, m. Joanna **MINER**, July 28, 1726	1	142

	Vol.	Page
ALLYN, (cont.)		
John, s. John & Joanna, b. Dec. 24, 1727	1	142
John Stanton, s. [James & Fanny], b. Oct. 21, 1798	2	70
Joseph, s. [Robert & Abigail], b. Feb. 14, 1736/7	1	180
Joseph, s. [Robert, Jr. & Hannah], b. Oct. 1, 1780; d. Jan. 20, 1789, at Aux Cayos, of a fever	1	167
Joseph M., s. Amos & Elizabeth, b. Sept. 19, 1777	2	83
Joseph M., m. Prudence **CHAPPELL**, b. of Groton, Mar. 25, 1827, by Ralph Hurlbutt, J.P.	1	23
Joseph S., s. [James & Anna], b. Jan. 22, 1774	2	69
Joseph S., m. Mary **ROGERS**, b. of Groton, Jan. 11, 1824, by Ralph Hurlbutt, J.P.	1	12
Joshua, [s. John], b. Feb. 14, 1703	1	111
Julia, m. Hyram **PECKHAM**, Feb. 7, 1829, by Philip Gray, J.P.	1	29
Julia, of Groton, m. Luther **KINNEY**, of Griswold, Nov. 18, 1832, by John G. Wightman, Eld.	1	42
Lois, d. James & Alethea, b. Mar. 20, 1737	1	141
Lucretia, d. John & Joanna, b. Nov. 23, 1745	1	142
Lucy, [d. Robert & Deborah], b. Oct. 5, or July 29, 1708 (see Nathan Allyn)	1	102
Lucy, [d. John], b. Sept. 15, 1717	1	111
Lucy, [d. Ebenezer & Mary], b. Feb. 14, 1732	1	132
Lucy, d. Samuel & Hannah, b. Jan. 30, 1748	2	10
Lucy, m. James **AVERY**, 3d, Oct. 12, 1749	2	4
Lucy, m. Edmond **STODDARD**, b. of Groton, May 9, 1830, by Ralph Hurlbutt, J.P.	1	34
Luther, s. [Robert, Jr. & Hannah], b. May 7, 1768; d. Dec. 31, 1769	1	167
Lydia, d. James & Alethea, b. Jan. 15, 1744/5	1	141
Lydia, m. Jesse **CHAPMAN**, b. of Groton, Nov. 27, 1823, by Timothy Tuttle	1	11
Marcy, m. James **AVERY**, Jr., late 3d, b. of Groton, Jan. 13, 1791	2	63
Martha, d. [James & Anna], b. Apr. 17, 1784	2	69
Mary, [d. John], b. Sept. 2, 1708	1	111
Mary, d. Ebenezer & Mary, b. Nov. 26, 1727; d. Jan. 25, 1727	1	132
Mary, d. John & Joanna, b. Mar. 4, 1730	1	142
Mary, [d. Ebenezer & Mary], b. July 4, 1734	1	132
Mary, [d. John & Joanna], b. Sept. 24, 1750	1	142
Mary, m. Thomas **LESTER**, Feb. 28, 1754	1	168
Mary, m. John **MORGAN**, 2d, b. of Groton, Dec. 31, 1820, by John G. Wightman, Elder	1	2
Mary, m. John **MORGAN**, [ ]	3	4
Mary Ann Caroline, d. [James & Fanny], b. Jan. 30, 1802	2	70
Mary Ann Caroline, of Groton, m. Isaac **HEWETT**, of Preston, Nov. 28, 1822, by Philip Gray, J.P.	1	8
Matilda, m. Gilbert **ALLYN**, b. of Groton, June 4, 1820	1	1
Minor, s. John & Joanna, b. Aug. 6, 1748	1	142
Minor, s. Susanna **BAKER**, b. Jan. 18, 1780	2	27
Nathan, [s. Robert & Deborah], b. Oct. 5 or July 29, 1711 (see Lucy **ALLYN**)	1	102
Nathan, s. [Robert & Abigail], b. June 5, 1740	1	180
Nathan, Jr., m. Ann **PERKINS**, b. of Groton, June 10, 1821, by Ralph Hurlbutt, J.P.	1	3
Park, s. [Robert & Abigail], b. June 15, 1733	1	180

	Vol.	Page
ALLYN, (cont.)		
Park, m. Sarah **GALLUP**, b. of Groton, Jan. 19, 1757, by Rev. Jacob Johnson	1	170
Park, s. [Park & Sarah], b. Apr. 6, 1766	1	170
Pacience, [d. John], b. Sept. [ ], 1712	1	111
Persilla, [d. Ebenezer & Mary], b. June 24, 1736	1	132
Phebe, d. John & Joanna, b. Feb. 23, 1735	1	142
Phebe, m. David **AMES**, b. of Groton, Feb. 18, 1754	2	11
Prudence, d. [Robert & Abigail], b. Apr. 9, 1738	1	180
Prudence, d. Samuel & Hannah, b. May 19, 1750	2	10
Prudence, m. Thomas Prentice **GALLUP**, b. of Groton, Jan. 20, 1757, by Rev. Jacob Johnson	1	166
Prudence, b. Mar. 23, 1776; m. Amos **GERE**, Jr., Jan. 5, 1800	2	42
Rebeckah, [d. Ebenezer & Mary], b. May 3, 1738	1	132
Rebecca, d. Ebenezer & Mary Thurber, b. May 3, 1738	1	187
Rebecca, m. Ezekiel **TURNER**, May [ ], 1756	1	187
Rhoda, m. Hyram **PECKHAM**, b. of Groton, Dec. 9, 1824, by Philip Gray, J.P.	1	15
Richard, m. Mary **MASON**, Sept. 23, 1827, by Geo[rge] Foot, V.D.M.	1	24
Rizpah, [s. Christopher & Elizabeth], b. Feb. 19, 1773	2	33
Robert, m. Deborah **AVERY**, of New London, now of Groton, June 29, 1691	1	102
Robert, [s. Robert & Deborah], b. Jan. 25, 1697/8	1	102
Robert, Jr., m. Abigail **AVERY**, May 13, 1725	1	130
Robert, m. Abigail **AVERY**, May 13, 1725	1	180
Robert, s. [Robert & Abigail], b. Sept. 8, 1728	1	180
Robert, Jr., m. Hannah **GALLUP**, b. of Groton, Jan. 23, 1755, by Rev. Jacob Johnson	1	167
Robert, s. [Robert, Jr. & Hannah], b. Nov. 4, 1756	1	167
Roswell, s. [James & Anna], b. July 11, 1789	2	69
Rufus, s. Ebenezer & Mary, b. Aug. 17, 1745	1	132
Rufus, m. Hannah **BILLINGS**, [ ], 1766	2	30
Rufus, m. Hannah **BILLINGS**, Mar. 2, 1766, by Timothy Wightman, Elder	2	28
Rufus, Jr., [s. Rufus & Hannah], b. Jan. 5, 1767	2	30
Russell, [s. Rufus & Hannah], b. Apr. 9, 1776	2	30
Samuel, [s. Robert & Deborah], b. May 26, 1704	1	102
Samuel, m. Hannah **AVERY**, [ ], 1731	2	10
Samuel, s. Samuel & Hannah, b. Nov. 21, 1734	2	10
Samuel G., m. Lydia **SATTERLEE**, June 17, 1821, by Stephen Meech, J.P.	1	3
Sarah, [d. John], b. [ ], 1723	1	111
Sarah, d. James & Alethea, b. Mar. 20, 1741/2	1	141
Sarah, m. Wait **STODDARD**, b. of Groton, Dec. 4, 1791	2	81
Simeon, s. [Robert & Abigail], b. May 27, 1745	1	180
Simeon, m. Easther **STODDARD**, Sept. 1, 1771; d. Sept. 7, 1781	2	15
Stephen, s. Samuel & Hannah, b. May 3, 1741	2	10
Stephen Billings, s. [Rufus & Hannah], b. Feb. 5, 1774	2	30
Susanna, d. John & Joanna, b. Dec. 29, 1739	1	142
Tabitha, d. [Robert, Jr. & Hannah], b. Apr. 24, 1772	1	167
Temperance Ann, of Groton, m. Christopher H. **BRAND**, of Norwich, June 14, 1835, by Ralph Hurlbutt, J.P.	1	50
Thankfull, d. Samuel & Hannah, b. Feb. 14, 1762	2	10
Thomas, s. Ebenezer & Mary, b. June 23, 1742	1	132
Thomas, s. Samuel & Hannah, b. Nov. 27, 1746	2	10

	Vol.	Page
ALLYN, (cont.)		
Timothy, s. [Robert & Abigail], b. June 12, 1748	1	180
Timothy, m. Betsey **HOLDRI[D]GE**, Feb. 7, 1829, by Philip Gray, J.P.	1	29
Tryal, s. Samuel & Hannah, b. Apr. 14, 1744	2	10
Wealthy, d. [Robert, Jr. & Hannah], b. Nov. 9, 1769	1	167
Wealthy, m. Sidney **STODDARD**, b. of Groton, July 12, 1823, by Timothy Tuttle	1	10
William Alexander, s. Tryal & Mary, b. Nov. 24, 1768	2	32
________, - [Rufus & Hannah], b. Sept. 29, 1769	2	30
________, - [Rufus & Hannah], b. Jan. 20, 1772	2	30
AMES, Abigail, d. David & Phebe, b. May 13 1757	2	11
Adam, s. David & Phebe, b. Nov. 2, 1759	2	11
Content, d. David & Phebe, b. Oct. 28, 1764	2	11
David, m. Phebe **ALLYN**, b. of Groton, Feb. 18, 1754	2	11
David, s. David & Phebe, b. July 15, 1770	2	11
Johannah, d. David & Phebe, b. Jan. 17 1761	2	11
Mary, d. David & Phebe, b. Sept. 20, 1768	2	11
Phebe, d. David & Phebe, b. Oct. 9 1755	2	11
Sarah, d. David & Phebe, b. Sept. 13, 1766	2	11
AMIDON, Isaac C., of Rome, N.Y., m. Sally T. **WILBUR**, of Groton, Oct. 25, 1829, by Rev. Roswell Burrows	1	32
AMSBURY, Horatio N., of Stonington, m. Lucy **SHANE**, of Groton, Mar. 9, 1836, by Elias Brown, J.P.	1	53
ANDERSON, Alexander, s. Alexander & Mary, b. Mar. 2, 1732/3	1	143
Polly, of Groton, m. Sylvester **FIELDS**, of East Hampton, Suffolk Co., N.Y., Sept. 4, 1820, by Elisha Avery, J.P.	1	1
ANDREWS, Abigail, [d. Benjamin], b. Mar. 28, 1719	1	109
Augustus D., m. Louisa C. **HAICKES**, b. of Preston, May 6, 1845, by rev. H. R. Knapp	1	74
Benjamin, [s. Benjamin], b. Jan. 19, 1710	1	109
Elisha, s. Samuel, b. June 19, 1765	1	181
George, of West Greenwich, R.I., m. Mary Esther **BARNES**, of Groton, Dec. 16, 1829, by William Williams, J.P.	1	32
Joanna, of N. Stonington, m. Senaca **WILLIAMS**, of Groton, Jan. 2, 1825, by William Williams, J.P.	1	15
John, [s. Benjamin], b. July 30, 1716	1	109
Jonathan, [s. Benjamin], b. Nov. 22, 1721	1	109
Joseph, [s. Benjamin], b. Oct. 24, 1713	1	109
Thomas, [s. Benjamin], b. Mar. 28, 1719	1	109
ANICE, Andrew, s. Andrew & Priscilla, b. Jan. 6, 1778	2	50
John, s. Andrew & Priscilla, b. Jan. 20, 1783	2	50
Lydia, d. Andrew & Priscilla, b. Mar. 20, 1781	2	50
Nancy, d. Andrew & Priscilla, m. Sept. 20, 1784	2	50
Silas, s. Andrew & Priscilla, b. Oct. 27, 1774	2	50
APPLEMAN, Alexander, [s. John & Matilda], b. Feb. 3, 1829	3	17
Benjamin N., [s. John & Matilda], b. May 7, 1821	3	17
Gustavus A., [s. John & Matilda], b. Feb. 23, 1817	3	17
John, s. [John & Matilda], b. Mar. 26, 1812	3	17
Mary Ann, [d. John & Matilda], b. Mar. 20, 1819	3	17
Mary Ann, m. James **PACKER**, b. of Groton, July 8, 1838, by Ira B. Steward	1	59
Matilda, d. [John & Matilda], b. Dec. 2, 1815	3	17

	Vol.	Page
APPLEMAN, (cont.)		
Matilda, of Groton, m. Daniel R. **WILLIAMS**, of Stonington, June 21, 1832, by John G. Wightman, Eld.	1	40
Richard, [s. John & Matilda], b. Mar. 15, 1827	3	17
William Henry, [s. John & Matilda], b. June 1, 1823	3	17
APPLEY, Elnathan, of Canterbury, m. Hannah **STARR**, of Groton, Feb. 6, 1843, by Rev. Jared R. Avery	1	67
ARMSTRONG, Hopestil[l], of Franklin, m. Prudence M. **BAILEY**, of Groton, Jan. 1, 1838, by Rev. John G. Wightman	1	57
ARON, AARON, Hannah, m. Charles **GOLDSMITH**, [Dec. 1, 1854], by Reuben Heath, J.P.	1	97
Reuben, m. Betsey **WAIT**, Apr. 28, 1833, by Geo[rge] Ayer, J.P.	1	43
ARTHUR, Almira, m. Ephraim **ALLYN**, b. of Groton, July 25, 1826, by Ralph Hurlbutt, J.P.	1	21
Betsey, m. William R. **LAMB**, b. of Groton, Jan. 27, 1833, by Nathan Daboll, J.P.	1	42
Bridget, d. Barthalomew & Mary, b. Dec. 14, 1747	1	179
Elisha, s. Bartholomew & Mary, b. Oct. 6, 1764	1	147
Elizabeth, d. Bartholomew & Mary, b. Sept. 29, 1767	1	147
Elles, m. Alfred **BALL**, Dec. 9, 1823, by Rodman Niles, J.P.	1	11
Lucy, m. William **LANE**, b. of New London, Jan. 24, 1836, by John G. Wightman, Elder	1	53
Sanford, m. Betsey **FARSITH**, b. of Groton, Apr. 1, 1821, by Ralph Hurlbutt, J.P.	1	3
ASHBEY, ASHBY, Alfred H., m. Augusta **PACKER**, b. of Groton, Aug. 10, 1825, by John G. Wightman	1	18
Asa, m. Mary Ann **SAWYER**, b. of Noank, Mar. 25, 1850, in Noank, by Rev. William A. Smith	1	88
Aurchia, d. [Prentice & Hannah], b. Aug. 23, 1824	3	11
Aurelia, m. Albert F. **AVERY**, b. of Groton, Dec. 24, 1844, by Rev. Erastus Denison	1	72
Benjamin, m. Hannah **FISH**, b. of Groton, Jan. 6, 1822, by Roswell Burrows, Eld.	1	5
Benjamin, m. Elizabeth **ING[RA]HAM**, b. of Groton, Feb. 4, 1847, by Rev. S. B. Bailey	1	77
Betsey Ann, of Groton, m. Stephen **MURPHY**, of Westerly, R.I., Aug. 5, 1849, by Rev. H. R. Knapp	1	85
Dwight, s. [Ransford & Lucretia], b. Nov. 7, 1829	3	24
Eliza, of Groton, m. Charles **VAN BRUNT**, of Shrewsbury, N.J., Feb. 5, 1853, at Noank, by Rev. James M. Phillips	1	95
Frederick B., of Groton, m. Lydia **ELDREDGE**, of Stonington, June 23, 1826, by Asa Fitch, J.P.	1	20
Harriet, d. Edward, m. Daniel **EDGECOMB**, s. Samuel, b. of Groton, June 2, 1824, by Rev. Roswell Burrows	1	13
Harriet, d. [Moses & Mary], b. May 25, 1827	3	20
Harriet, m. Horace W. **DAVIS**, b. of Groton, Sept. 14, 1845, by Rev. Simon B. Bailey	1	74
Henry, s. Joseph & Mary, b. June 4, 180[ ]	2	19
Henry, s. Joseph & Mary, b. June 4, 1800	2	12
Henry, m. Abby Jane **WOOLF**, b. of Groton, July 8, 1823, by John G. Wightman	1	10
Latham, m. Abby M. **POTTER**, b. of Groton, Jan. 5, 1836, by Ira R. Steward, Eld.	1	53

	Vol.	Page
ASHBEY, **ASBY**, (cont.)		
Margaret, d[Asa & Narcissa], b. June 24, 1829	3	24
Margarette, of Noank, Ct., m. Adrian M. **WILLIAMS**, of N.Y., Sept. 16, 1849, in Noank, by Rev. William S. Smith, of Noank	1	85
Mary E., d. [Asa & Narcissa], b. Jan. 13, 1825	3	24
Mary Elizabeth, of Groton, m. Jared **WILCOX**, of New York, Apr. 16, 1843, by Rev. Erastus Denison	1	68
Mary Ellen, of Groton, m. Levi **LAMB**, Sept. 10, 1843, by Rev. Erastus Denison	1	70
Moses, m. Mary **CHESTER**, b. of Groton, Sept. 25, 1820, by Rev. Roswell Burrows	1	10
Moses, s. [Moses & Mary], b. June 20, 1829	3	20
Moses Austin, s. [Prentice & Hannah], b. Oct. 15, 1826	3	11
Prentice, Capt., m. Priscilla **HALLEY**, b. of Groton, Nov. 18, 1849, by Rev. Nicholas T. Allen	1	87
Ransford, m. Lucretia **RATHBURN**, d. Capt. Elisha, b. of Groton, Aug. 23, 1824, by Rev. Roswell Burrows	1	13
Ransford, Jr., s. [Ransford & Lucretia], b. Jan. 21, 1826	3	24
Sally A., of Groton, m. Denison **LAMB**, of Ledyard, May 3, 1840, by Rev. John G. Wightman	1	62
Sidney, s. [Ransford & Lucretia], b. Sept. 24, 1827	3	24
William, m. Prudence **BURROWS**, b. of Groton, Aug. 10, 1843, by Rev. Charles C. Lewis	1	69
ASHLEY, Asa, m. Narcissa **INGRAHAM**, b. of Groton, Sept. 5, 1821, by Roswell Burrows	1	4
Catharine E., of Groton, m.Joshua L. **HYDE**, of Franklin, Aug. 26, 1832, by Rev. Roswell Burrows	1	41
Lucy P., of Groton, m. Asa **SAWYER**, of Stonington, Aug. 29, 1832, by Rev. Roswell Burrows	1	41
Lydia, of Groton, m. George **CONDALL**, of New London, Oct. 7, 1827, by Roswell Burrows	1	25
Nancy, m. Aaron **MAINE**, b. of Groton, Sept. 24, 1829, by John G. Wightman, Eld.	1	31
Prentice, m. Hannah **MORGAN**, b. of Groton, Nov. 25, 1821, by Rev. John G. Wightman	1	5
Simeon W., m. Hannah **RATHBURN**, b. of Groton, Sept. 9, 1830, by Rev. Erastus Denison	1	35
AVERELL, Eliza A., m. W[illia]m **BROWNING**, May 14, 1826	3	29
Eliza Ann, m. William **BROWNING**, b. of Groton, May 24, 1826, by Ralph Hurlbutt, J.P.	1	20
[*On January 26, 1926, the following entries were copied from a leaf preceding page 1 of Volume 2 of Groton Land Records by Mr. Frank Farnsworth, of Middletown. These entries do not appear in the Arnold copy of Groton Vital Records, now in the Connecticut State Library:*]		
AVERY, Abigail, [d. John & Sarah], b. Dec. 25, 1715	LR2	0
Anna, [d. John & Sarah], b. June 39, 1711; d. Sept. 25, 1720	LR2	0
George, [s. John & Sarah], b. Sept. 2, 1724	LR2	0
John, [s. John & Sarah], m. Sarah **DENISON**, Aug. 23, 1705	LR2	0
John, [s. John & Sarah], b. May 14, 1706	LR2	0
Sarah, [d. John & Sarah], b. Oct. 10, 1713	LR2	0
Thankful, [d. John & Sarah], b. Apr. 15, 1718	LR2	0
AVERY, Aaron, m. Anna **KINNE**, b. of Groton, Feb. 26, 1798	2	58
Aaron, m. Anna **KINNE**, of Groton, Feb. 26, 1798	2	60

	Vol.	Page
AVERY, (cont.)		
Abeele, [s. Jonathan & Elizabeth], b. Sept. 17, 1717	1	120
Abigail, [d. Christopher & Abigail], b. July 16, 1707	1	127
Abigail, w. Christopher, d. Feb. 12, 1713	1	127
Abigail, m. Robert **ALLYN**, Jr., May 13, 1725	1	130
Abigail, m. Robert **ALLYN**, May 13, 1725	1	180
Abigail, d. [Benjamin & Thankfull], b. Dec. 12, 1737	1	182
Abigail, d. [Theophilus & Elizabeth], b. Oct. 11, 1748	2	56
Abigail, d. Ebenezer & Lucy, b. Feb. 24, 1752; d. Oct. 13, 1753	1	130
Abigail, d. James & Elizabeth, b. July 10, 1757	2	4
Abigail, m. Nehemiah **SMITH**, May 3, 1758	1	168
Abigail, d. Christopher & Eunice, b. Feb. 22, 1759	1	148
Abigail, d. William & Mary, b. Aug. 21, 176[ ]	2	4
Abigail, d. W[illia]m, d. July 9, 1788	2	4
Abigail, m. Stanton **SHOLES**, s. Abel & Lucy, b. of Groton, Mar. 14, 1793	2	65
Abigail Fish, d. [Roswell & Martha], b. Sept. 3, 1776	2	35
Abner, [s. Jonathan & Elizabeth], b. May 28, 1712	1	120
Adelia, d. [Nathan & Matilda], b. Mar. 22, 1813	2	86
Addelia Everett, of Groton, m. Benjamin **DURFEY**, of Griswold, Mar. 9, 1830, by Timothy Tuttle	1	33
Adelia, see also Ardelia		
Adeline, d. [Park W. & Clarissa], b. May 11, 1832	3	9
Albert, s. [Nathan & Matilda], b. Jan. 26, 1809	2	86
Albert F., s. [Park W. & Clarissa], b. Feb. 21, 1817; d. Dec. 21, 1890, ae 72	3	9
Albert F., m. Aurelia **ASHBEY**, b. of Groton, Dec. 24, 1844, by Rev. Erastus Denison	1	72
Albert L., s. [John J. & Nancy], b. July 12, 1811	2	54
Alexander Hamilton, s. [Henry & Lucy], b. Aug. 23, 1804	2	81
Alfred, s. [David & Hannah], b. Feb. 2, 1790	2	41
Alfred Anson, s. [Denison & Hannah], b. Sept. 12, 1794	2	85
Alithea, m. James **ALLYN**, Dec. 17, 1729 (First written "Allyn")	1	141
Allyn, m Sally **CHAPMAN**, b. of Groton, June 22, 1828, by Ralph Hurlbutt, J.P.	1	28
Almira, [d. Jonas B. & Esther], b. [ ]	3	2
Amanda, d. [Henry & Lucy], b. July 4, 1802	2	81
Amanda M., m. Urban **AVERY**, b. of Groton, Dec. 10, 1828, by Rev. Roswell Burrows	1	29
Amanda M., of Groton, m. Samuel P. **WHEELER**, of Stonington, Nov. 22, 1838, by Mark Meade, V.D.M.	1	60
Amasa, s. [Ebenezer & Mary], b. Oct. 18, 1801	2	44
Amos, 2d, [s. Amos & Prudence], b. Sept. 14, 1769	2	14
Amos, s. Amos & Prudence, b. Sept. 14, 1769	2	76
Amey, d. Ebenezer & Dorothy, b. Feb. 14, 1724	1	134
Amy, m Jabez **SMITH**, May 26, 1742	1	178
Amy, d. James & Elizabeth, b. May 4, 1761; d. Sept. 14, 1763	2	4
Ann, m. William **SATTERLY**, Sept. 6, 1711	1	136
Ann Maria, m. Benjamin **BURROWS**, of Groton, Oct. 23, 1854, by Rev. Isaac Cheesebrough	1	97
Anna, d. [Thomas & Hannah], b. Oct. 25, 1777	2	28
Anne, d. [Benjamin & Thankfull], b. Jan. 15, 1743/4	1	182
Anson, s. [Daniel & Sibble], b. Feb. 7, 1786	2	39
Ardelia, m. John O. **MINER**, Jr., Sept. 9, 1819	3	6

	Vol.	Page
AVERY, (cont.)		
Ardelia, see also Adelia		
Asa, [s. Edward & Johan[n]ah], b. July 21, 1721	1	111
Asa, m. Lucretia **WILLIAMS**, Dec. 22, 1742	1	178
Asa, s. [David & Hannah], b. Jan. 21, 1786	2	41
Asa Lord, [s. Rufus & Hannah], b. Mar. 1, 1783	2	34
Asa S. m. Betsey **MINER**, b. of Groton, Nov. 27, 1806, by John G. Wightman, Elder	2	78
Austin, s. [David & Hannah], b. Dec. 1, 1794	2	41
Beneiah, s. Edward & Johan[n]ah, b. Oct. 12, 1710	1	111
Benajah, s. [Asa & Lucretia], b. Dec. 15, 1743	1	178
Benajah R., of Salina, N.Y., m. Mary A. **AVERY**, of Groton, Apr. 2, 1840, by Rev. John G. Wightman	1	62
Benjamin, s. [Benjamin & Thankfull], b. Sept. 9, 1735	1	182
Benjamin Gilson, s. [Denison & Hannah], b. May 6, 1804	2	86
Betsey A., of Groton, m. Nehemiah D. **PERRY**, of Colchester, Mar. 16, 1834, by John G. Wightman, Eld.	1	46
Betsey Ann, d. [Latham & Betsey], b. July 4, 1819	3	9
Betsey Ann, of Groton, m. Edmund **FISH**, of New York, Mar. 19, 1838, by Mark Meade	1	58
Billings, s. [Theophilus & Margery], b. Sept. 19, 1802	2	72
Billings, m. Prudence **GEER**, b. of Groton, Sept. 25, 1825, by Timothy Tuttle	1	18
Bridget, b. June 13, 1780; m. Samuel **NILES**, June 24, 1804	2	77
Caleb, had a negro boy Alpheus **SMITH**, b. Jan. 27, 1804	2	61
Caleb, had a negro boy Alpheus **SMITH**, b. Jan. 27, 1804	2	63
Caleb, s. James & Elizabeth, b. Feb. 25, 1760	2	4
Caroline, d. [Park & Clarissa], b. Oct. 12, 1815	3	9
Caroline, m. Hiram **ALLYN**, b. of Groton, Dec. 13, 1835, by John G. Wightman, Elder	1	52
Caroline Maconda (Morgan), w. James D., d. Mar. 22, 1863	3	32
Charles, s. Waitstill & Margaret, b. Oct. 22, 1731	1	138
Charles Eldredge, s. [Ebenezer & Mary], b. Mar. 6, 1794	2	44
Charles G., m. Nancy M. **EDGECOMB**, b. of Groton, Apr. 3, 1842, by Ira R. Steward	1	66
Charles Smith, s. [David & Hannah], b. Feb. 7, 1808	2	67
Christopher, [s. Samuell & Susanna], b. Feb. 10, 1697; d. [ ], 1768, ae. 71 y.	1	121
Christopher, m. Abigail **PARK[E]**, Dec. 19, 1704	1	127
Christopher, [s. Christopher & Abigail], b. Nov. 16, 1709	1	127
Christopher, m. Prudence **WHEELER**, Apr. 1, 1714	1	127
Christopher, m. Mary **LATHAM**, Jan. 25, 1719, by Rev. Ephraim Woodbridge	1	119
Christopher, Jr., m. Mary **LATHAM**, June 25, 1719	1	133
Christopher, Jr., m. [E]unice **PRENTICE**, Sept. 10, 1735	1	146
Christopher, s. Christopher & [E]unice, b. Jan. 22, 1737/8	1	146
Christopher, s. Humphrey & Jerusha, b. May 3, 1739	1	135
Christopher, Capt., d. Jan. 20, 1753, ae 73 y.	1	153
Christopher, s. [George & Eunice], b. Sept. 6, 1760	1	171
Christopher, Col., d. Jan. 17, 1768, ae. 71 y.	1	151
Christopher Lester, s. [Latham & Betsey], b. June 8, 1826	3	9
Christopher Swan, s. [Isaac & Lucy], b. Nov. 25, 1788	2	58
Clara, d. Theophilus & Margery, b. Dec. 23, 1797	2	72

	Vol.	Page
AVERY, (cont.)		
Clarissa, d. [Ebenezer, 2d, & Hannah], b. Mar. 2, 1791; d. June 2, 1791, ae. 3 m.	2	44
Clarissa, m. Park W. **AVERY**, Oct. 24, 1811	3	9
Clarissa, m. Elias **CHAPMAN**, b. of Groton, Aug. 26, 1820, by Timothy Tuttle	1	1
Clarissa, w. Park W., d. Dec. 22, 1867, ae. 75	3	9
Clarissa, [d. Jonas B. & Esther], b. [ ]	3	2
Content, d. [Theophilus & Elizabeth], b. Jan. 24, 1739; d. Nov. 16, 1760	2	56
Cornelia, m. Sanford **MORGAN**, b. of Groton, July 9, 1837, by Ira R. Steward, Elder	1	57
Curtis Lord, s. [David & Hannah], b. June 1, 1810	2	67
Cynthia, [d. Theophilus], b. June 22, 1784	2	56
Cyrus, [s. Ebenezer, Jr. & Phebe], b. July 7, 1779	2	31
Daniel, s. [Benjamin & Thankfull], b. Nov. 14, 1740	1	182
Daniel, s. [Asa & Lucretia], b. Feb. 25, 1758	1	178
Daniel, m. Sibble **PARK[E]**, Apr. 27, 1779	2	39
David, of Groton, m. Lydia **LORD**, of Norwich, June 29, 1763, by Benjamin Throop	2	2
David, d. Sept. 6, 1781	2	2
David, s. [Rufus & Hannah], b. Oct. 9, 1781	2	34
David, m. Hannah **AVERY**, Nov. 12, 1783	2	41
David, s. James & Elizabeth, b. Apr. 3, 1767; d. Mar. 19, 1790	2	4
David, m. Hannah **SMITH**, b. of Groton, Jan. 24, 1804, by John G. Wightman, Elder	2	67
Deborah, of New London, now of Groton, m. Robert ALLYN, June 29, 1691	1	102
Deborah, d. Edward & Johan[n]ah, b. May 6, 1706	1	111
Deborah, m. Nathan **WILLIAMS**, Feb. 17, 1726/7	1	154
Deborah, w. Capt. James, d. Mar. 27, 1729, ae. 77 y.	1	128
Deborah, w. Waitstill, d. Mar. 15, 1729/30	1	138
Deborah, [d. Christopher, Jr. & Mary], b. June 5, 1731	1	133
Deborah, d. [Theophilus & Elizabeth], b. May 27, 1735	2	56
Deborah, d. Benjamin & Thankfull, b. Oct. 24, 1738	1	182
Deborah, d. Ebenezer & Lucy, b. Feb. 1, 1741/2	1	130
Deborah, m. Jasper **LATHAM**, Jr., July 25, 1752	1	163
Deborah, d. [Latham & Betsey], b. Apr. 2, 1830	3	9
Delia, of Groton, m. Benjamin **PEABODY**, Jr., of N. Stonington, Dec. 26, 1824, by John G. Wightman, Eld.	1	15
Delia Ann, of Groton, m. Samuel **WHEELER**, of N. Stonington, Nov. 27, 1827, by Timothy Tuttle	1	25
Denison, s. [Denison & Hannah], b. June 14, 1802	2	86
Desiah, d. [Theophilus & Elizabeth], b. May 15, 1741; d. Apr. 16, 1748	2	56
Dorothy, [d. Ebenezer & Dorothy], b. Jan. 11, 1717	1	123
Dorothy, m. Joseph **MORGAN**, Dec. 4, 1735	1	172
Dudley Bailey, s. [Denison & Hannah], b. June 28, 1806	2	86
Ebenezer, of Groton, m. Dorothy **PARKE**, of Preston, June 16, 1708	1	123
Ebenezer, [s. Ebenezer & Dorothy], b. Apr. 11, 1721	1	123
Ebenezer, Jr., m. Lucy **LATHAM**, June 16, 1726	1	130
Ebenezer, s. Ebenezer & Lucy, b. Mar. 7, 1732/3	1	130
Ebenezer, Jr., m. Phebe **DENISON**, June 11, 1761	2	31
Ebenezer, 4th, [s. Ebenezer, Jr. & Phebe], b. Aug. 8, 1762; m. Mary **MORGAN**, [ ], 1783	2	31

	Vol.	Page
AVERY, (cont.)		
Ebenezer, Lieut., d. Sept. 6, 1781	2	31
Ebenezer, 2d., m. Hannah **MORGAN**, Sept. 25, 1783	2	44
Ebenezer, s. [Ebenezer, 2d & Hannah], b. Apr. 2, 1786	2	44
Ebenezer, 2d, m. Mary **ELDREDGE**, Feb. 17, 1793	2	44
Edward, m. Johan[n]ah **ROSE**, June 3, 1699	1	111
Edward, s. Edward & Johan[n]ah, b. May 22, 1704; d. June 7, 1705	1	111
Edward, s. [Theophilus & Elizabeth, b.] Dec. 23, 1743; d. sometime in 1764 at sea, ae. 21 y.	2	56
Edward, d. Apr. 24, 1759, ae. 84 y.	1	153
Edward, s. [Daniel & Sibble], b. Oct. 27, 1789	2	39
Edwin Miner, s. Elisha & Nancy A., b. Sept. 10, 1815	2	68
Egbert, s. [Ebenezer, 2d, & Hannah], b. July 26, 1789	2	44
Eleazer, s. [James & Elizabeth], b. May 29, 1771	2	4
Elias, s. [Nathan & Matilda], b. Mar. 6, 1805	2	86
Elihu, of Groton, m. Julia M. **BAILEY**, of Groton, Oct. 16, 1848, by Rev. Nicholas T. Allen	1	86
Elijah Murdock, s. [John J. & Nancy], b. Mar. 17, 1798	2	54
Elisha, [s. Ebenezer & Lucy], b. Apr. 6, 1755	1	130
Elisha, m. Mary H. **AVERY**, b. of Groton, Dec. 17, 1801	2	68
Elisha, m. Nancy A. **MINER**, Nov. 18, 1810	2	68
Elisha Simeon, s. Elisha & Mary H., b. Jan. 9, 1806	2	68
Eliza, b. Dec. 1, 1770; m. Sept. 23, 1794	2	48
Eliza, d. [Caleb], b. Aug. 31, 1796	2	63
Eliza, of Groton, m. Denison B. **WILLIAMS**, of Ledyard, Nov. 21, 1850, by Rev. Nicholas T. Allen	1	90
Elizabeth, [d. Jonathan & Elizabeth], b. Jan. 18, 1705	1	120
Elizabeth, [d. James & Elizabeth], b. Jan. 13, 1725/6	1	124
Elizabeth. d. Theophilus & Elizabeth, b. Dec. 22, 1733	2	56
Elizabeth, d. Ebenezer & Lucy, b. Jan. 22, 1747; d. [ ], 1765, ae. 18 y.	1	130
Elizabeth, d. James & Lucy, b. Feb. 15, 1752; d. Feb. 21, 1752	2	4
Elizabeth, d. James & Elizabeth, b. Oct. 19, 1754; d. Apr. 24, 1792	2	4
Elizabeth, [d. Ebenezer, Jr. & Phebe], b. Oct. 28, 1768; m. J. O. **MINER**, [ ], 1785	2	31
Elizabeth, m. John Owen **MINER**, Jan. 21, 1785	2	31
Elizabeth, d. James, of Groton, m. Jacob **AVERY**, s. Jacob & Silvia, Nov. 11, 1787	2	57
Elizabeth, w. Theophilus, d. Aug. 25, 1791, ae. 79 y.	2	56
Elizabeth, of Groton, m. Jesse **WILLIAMS**, Oct. 13, 1802, by Ebenezer Avery, Esq.	3	1
Ellen F., m. E. F. **COATS**, M.D., b. of Groton, Sept. 3, 1848, by Rev. H. R. Knapp	1	84
Ellen N., d. [Park W. & Clarissa], b. Feb. 18, 1834	3	9
Ellsworth, s. [Aaron & Anna], b. Mar. 11, 1801	2	60
Emily, d. [Latham & Betsey], b. Sept. 17, 1821	3	9
Emily, m. David **KNOWLES**, b. of Groton, Oct. 3, 1823, by Caleb Avery, J.P.	1	11
Emily, of Groton, m. Noyes **PALMER**, of Salem, June 26, 1836, by Nathan Daboll, J.P.	1	54
Emily, of Groton, m. Silas Henry **FISH**, of Rochester, N.Y., Mar. 21, 1842, by Rev. Jared R.Avery	1	66
Emily N., d. [James, Jr. & Marcy], b. Nov. 6, 1807	2	63
Erastus, s. [Theophilus], b. Apr. 22, 1787	2	56

	Vol.	Page
AVERY, (cont.)		
Erastus, s. [John J. & Nancy], b. Dec. 8, 1809	2	54
Erastus, m. Mary Elizabeth **DENISON**, b. of Groton, Mar. 20, 1844, by Rev. Jared R. Avery	1	70
Est[h]er, d. Christopher & [E]unice, b. Apr. 14, 1736	1	146
Esther, d. [Asa & Lucretia], b. Feb. 4, 1756	1	178
Esh[h]er, m. Daniel **WILLIAMS**, b. of Groton, Mar. 17, 1758, by William Williams, J.P.	1	169
Eunice, [d. Ebenezer & Dorothy], b. Mar. 2, 1726/7	1	134
Eunice, m. George **AVERY**, b. of Groton, Mar. 29, 1758, by Rev. Jacob Johnson	1	171
Eunice, d. James & Elizabeth, b. Oct. 3, 1765	2	4
Eunice A., of Greenville in Norwich, m. Harlam **HYDE**, of Groton, Nov. 12, 1833, by Timothy Tuttle	1	45
Eunice L., d. [Park W. & Clarissa], b. Mar. 31, 1822	3	9
Eunice L., m. John A. **MORGAN**, Mar. 13, 1846, by Rev. Tho[ma]s J. Greenwood, of New London	1	75
Experience, [d. Jonathan & Elizabeth], b. Nov. 6, 1724	1	120
Fanny, d. [Ebenezer, 2d, & Hannah], b. Apr. 22, 1788	2	44
Fanny, m. James **ALLYN**, Jr., b. of Groton, Nov. 30, 1795, by Amos Gear, J.P.	2	70
Fanny, m. James S. **MITCHELL**, b. of Groton, Mar. 21, 1824, by Timothy Tuttle	1	12
Franklin, [s. Jonas B. & Esther], b. [ ]	3	2
Frederick A., m. Betsey **BELLOWS**, Dec. 29, 1811, by Timothy Tuttle, D.D.	2	88
Freelove, [d. Jonathan & Elizabeth], b. Mar. 16, 1721/2	1	120
Freelove, d. James & Elizabeth, b. May 26, 1764; d. Apr. 25, 1782	2	4
George, m. Eunice **AVERY**, b. of Groton, Mar. 29, 1758, by Rev. Jacob Johnson	1	171
George, s. [George & Eunice], b. Apr. 24, 1759	1	171
George Dolbear, s. William & Mary, b. Aug. 10, 176[ ]	2	4
George Washington, s. [James & Elizabeth], b. Oct. 9, 1776	2	4
Gideon, [s. Edward & Johan[n]ah], b. Jan. 1, 1715	1	111
Gilbert, s. [Thomas & Hannah], b. Jan. 23, 1771; d. Jan. 30, 1772	2	28
Gilbert, s. [Thomas & Hannah], b. Jan. 18, 1775	2	28
Grace, [d. Samuell & Susanna], b. June 2, 1712	1	121
Griswold, s. Ebenezer & Lucy, b. Sept. 25 1739	1	130
Gurdon, s. [Rufus & Hannah], b. Nov. 3, 1786	2	34
Gurdon Latham, s. [Rufus, Jr. & Caroline], b. July 4, 1805	2	91
Hannah, m. Samuel **MORGAN**, Dec. 30, 1708	1	113
Hannah, [d. Edward & Johan[n]ah], b. July 30, 1717	1	111
Hannah, [d. Christopher & Prudence], b. Feb. 10, 1719	1	127
Hannah, d. Ebenezer & Lucy, b. Jan. 16, 1726/7	1	130
Hannah, m. Samuel **ALLYN**, [ ], 1731	2	10
Hannah, [d. Christopher, Jr. & Mary], b. Mar. 19, 1735/6; d. Mar. 5, 1761	1	133
Hannah, m. Thomas **PELTON**, July 9, 1740	1	156
Hannah, m. Benadam **GALLUP**, Jr., Aug. 11, 1740	1	177
Hannah, m. John **PACKER**, Sept. 18, 1746	1	179
Hannah, d. [Nathan & Hannah], b. Feb. 28, 1752	1	178
Hannah, d. Christopher & Mary, d. Mar. 5, 1761, ae. 21 y.	1	153
Hannah, d. William & Mary, b. Feb. 20, 1772	2	4
Hannah, d. [Thomas & Hannah], b. Dec. 13, 1772	2	28

	Vol.	Page
AVERY, (cont.)		
Hannah, m. David **AVERY**, Nov. 12, 1783	2	41
Hannah, w. Ebenezer, 2d, d. Sept. 27, 1792, ae. 29 y. 3 w. 1 d.	2	44
Hannah, d. [Denison & Hannah], b. July 2, 1797	2	86
Hannah, m. Latham T. **AVERY**, b. of Groton, Jan. 1, 1823, by John G. Wightman	1	9
Hannah, d. [Park W. & Clarissa], b. [ ]; d. Nov. 20, 1833, ae. 3 y.	3	9
Hannah Ann, of Groton, m. Giles **WHEELER**, of Stonington, Dec. 4, 1825, by John G. Wightman, Eld.	1	19
Hannah Emmeline, d. David & Hannah, b. Feb. 11, 1806; d. Mar. 11, 1806	2	67
Hannah L., m. Alden **RATHBURN**, b. of Groton, June 13, 1838, by Ira R. Steward	1	59
Hannah M., Mrs., of Groton, m. Charles W. **ELDREDGE**, of Mt. Carmel, Ill., Oct. 1, 1848, by Rev. Jared R. Avery	1	82
Harriet, [d. Amos & Prudence], b. Sept. 21, 1792	2	14
Harriet, d. [Amos & Prudence], b. Sept. 21, 1792	2	76
Henry, [s. Ebenezer, Jr. & Phebe], b. Sept. 2, 1776; m. Lucy **FISH**	2	31
Henry, m. Lucy Morgan **FISH**, b. of Groton, Sept. 20, 1798, by Rev. Aaron Kinne	2	81
Henry Williams, s. [Ebenezer & Mary], b. Oct. 12, 1795	2	44
Hezekiah, [s. Ebenezer & Mary], b. July 20, 1772	2	31
Hiram, m. Louisa Ardelia **AVERY**, b. of Groton, Mar. 8, 1843, by Rev. Erastus Denison	1	68
Humphrey, [s. Samuell & Susanna], b. July 4, 1699	1	121
Humphrey, m. Jerusha **MORGAN**, Feb. 1, 1723/4	1	116
Humphrey, m. Jerusha **MORGAN**, Feb. 5, 1723/4; d. Mar. 28, 1778	1	135
Humphrey, s. Humphrey & Jerusha, b. Mar. 10, 1724/5	1	116
Humphrey, s. Humphrey & Jerusha, b. Mar. 10, 1724/5	1	135
Ichabod, [s. Edward & Johan]n]ah], b. May 7, 1719	1	111
Ichabod, s. [Theophilus], b. May 16, 1789	2	56
Isaac, m. Susanna **ELDERKIN**, Mar. 31, 1742	1	151
Isaac, s. [Nathan & Hannah], b. Aug. 23, 1747	1	178
Isaac, of Groton, m. Lucy **SWAN**, of Stonington, June 11, 1771, in Stonington	2	58
Isaac, 3d, b. Sept. 4, 1774; m. Clarissa **BUTTON**, of Preston, [ ]	2	78
Isaac, Jr., [s. Isaac & Lucy], b. Jan. 14, 1777	2	19
Isaac, s. [Isaac & Lucy], b. Jan. 14, 1778	2	58
Isaac, Jr., of Groton, m. Nabby **WHEELER**, of Stonington, Apr. 27, 1800	2	74
Isaac Wheeler, s. [Isaac, Jr. & Nabby], b. Oct. 14, 1806	2	74
Jabez, [s. Christopher & Prudence], b. Mar. 26, 1717	1	127
Jabez, s. [John & Mary], b. Aug. 12, 1756	1	162
Jabez, [s. Jonas], b. Apr. 4, 1779	2	17
Jacob, [s. Christopher & Prudence], b. Aug. 26, 1721	1	127
Jacob, m. Sylvia **EDY**, June [ ], 1754	1	163
Jacob, s. Jacob & Silvia, b. Apr. 6, 1757	2	57
Jacob, m. Elizabeth **AVERY**, d. James, of Groton, Nov. 11, 1787	2	57
James, s. Edward & Johan[n]ah, b. Oct. 27, 1712; d. Nov. 25, 1715	1	111
James, Jr., m. Elizabeth **SMITH**, Dec. 13, 1719	1	124
James, d. Feb. 22, 1822, ae. 85 y.	2	56
James, s. James & Elizabeth, b. July 27, 1724	1	124
James, Capt., d. Aug. 22, 1728, ae. 82 y.	1	128
James, s. Humphrey & Jerusha, b. Aug. 13, 1733	1	135

	Vol.	Page
AVERY, (cont.)		
James, s. [Theophilus & Elizabeth], b. Feb. 29, 1737; d. Feb. 22, 1822, ae. 85 y.	2	56
James, 3d, m. Lucy **ALLYN**, Oct. 12, 1749	2	4
James, m. Elizabeth **ALLEN**, May 28, 1752	2	4
James, s. James & Elizabeth, b. Apr. 21, 1753; d. Apr. 19, 1777	2	4
James, Jr., late 3d, m. Marcy **ALLYN**, b. of Groton, Jan. 13, 1791	2	63
James, s. [Caleb], b. Jan. 16, 1794	2	63
James A., m. Eunice H. **STEWARD**, b. of Groton, June 11, 1843, by Ira R. Steward	1	69
James Billings, b. Aug. 27, 1826	3	13
James D., m. Caroline M. **MORGAN**, May 26, 1850, at Pequonock Bridge, by Rev. James W. Dennis, of New London	1	89
Jefferson S., s. [Park W. & Clarissa], b. Aug. 14, 1819; d. Aug. 1884	3	9
Jerusha, d. Humphrey & Jerusha, b. June 7, 1735	1	135
Jerusha, m. Russell **BURROWS**, Jan. 28, 1790	2	43
Joannah, m. Mark **STODDARD**, Feb. 13, 1724/3	1	109
Johan[n]ah, d. Edward & Johan[n]ah, b. Nov. 21, 1700	1	111
John, s. Christopher & Abigail, b. Oct. 26, 1705	1	127
John, Jr., m. Mary **DENNIS**, of Stonington, June 13, 1751, by Rev. Nath[anie]l Pells	1	162
John, Jr., d. July 11, 1759	1	162
John, 3d, of Groton, b. Mar. 4, 1769; m. Nancy **MURDOCK**, of Lyme, Jan. 9, 1794	2	47
John, 3d, on Feb. 10, 1799, declared his intention of being known thereafter as John John **AVERY** or John J. **AVERY**	2	54
John, of Griswold, m. Abigail **WILLIAMS**, of Groton, Dec. 9, 1824, by Timothy Tuttle	1	14
John D., s. [Park W. & Clarissa], b. Oct. 22, 1820	3	9
John E., s. [Park W. & Clarissa], b. Feb. [ ], 1828; d. Sept. [ ], 1886	3	9
Jonas B., m. Esther **DENISON**, July 24, 1791	3	2
Jonathan, [s. Samuell & Susanna], b. Jan. 18, 1689	1	121
Jonathan, m. Elizabeth **BILL**, Apr. 11, 1703	1	120
Jonathan, s. Jonathan & Elizabeth, b. Dec. 30, 1703	1	130
Johnathan, Jr., m. Mary **LATHAM**, Dec. 12, 1734	1	135
Jonathan, s. [Ebenezer, 2d, & Hannah], b. July 13, 1792; d. Sept. 16, 1792, ae. 9m. 2d.	2	44
Julia, d. [Latham & Betsey], b. May 9, 1828	3	9
Julia, [d. Jonas B. & Esther], b. [ ]	3	2
Julia E., of Groton, m. Moses R. **AVERY**, of Syracuse, N.Y., Feb. 5, 1849, by Rev. Nicholas T. Allen	1	86
Julia Stoddard, d. Elisha & Nancy A., b. Feb. 11, 1820	2	68
Katherine, d. Ebenezer & Lucy, b. June 9, 1737	1	130
Lamira, d. Henry & Lucy, b. May 3, 1800	2	81
Latham, s. Ebenezer & Lucy, b. Apr. 15, 1735	1	130
Latham, m. Betsey **LESTER**, July 7, 1816	3	9
Latham Burrows, s. [Latham & Betsey], b. Sept. 5, 1817	3	9
Latham T., m. Hannah **AVERY**, b. of Groton, Jan. 1, 1823, by John G. Wightman	1	9
Lauriston, s. [Park W. & Clarissa], b. Jan. 12, 1813; d. June 6, 1836	3	9
Lois L., of Groton, m. Judson D. **FISH**, of Halifax, Vt., Nov. 26, 1848, by Rev. Nicholas T. Allen	1	86

	Vol.	Page
AVERY, (cont.)		
Louisa Ardelia, m. Hiram **AVERY**, b. of Groton, Mar. 8, 1843, by Rev. Erastus Denison	1	68
Lucretia, d. [Asa & Lucretia], b. Oct. 29, 1748	1	178
Lucy, [d. Samuell & Susanna], b. Apr. 17, 1703	1	121
Lucy, [d. Jonathan & Elizabeth], b. Mar. 20, 1709	1	120
Lucy, [d. Ebenezer & Dorothy], b. Oct. 14, 1719; d. Jan. 9, 1719/20	1	123
Lucy, [d. Christopher, Jr. & Mary], b. Apr. 13, 1722; d. Aug. 21, 1754	1	133
Lucy, d. Ebenezer & Lucy, b. Jan. 27, 1728/9	1	130
Lucy, d. James & Lucy, b. July 12, 1750; d. Feb. 22, 1752	2	4
Lucy, w. James, 3d, d. Feb. 19, 1752	2	4
Lucy, d. James & Elizabeth, b. Nov. 19, 1763; d. Sept. 30, 1764	2	4
Lucy, d. [Ebenezer, Jr. & Phebe], b. Apr. 24, 1766; m. William **MORGAN**, [ ], 1784	2	31
Lucy, d. Isaac & Lucy, b. Jan. 18, 1773, in Stonington	2	58
Lucy, m. William **MORGAN**, Jan. 1, 1784	2	49
Lucy, d. [Ebenezer, 2d, & Hannah], b. June 11, 1784	2	44
Lucy, d. [Thomas & Hannah], b. July 3, 1784	2	28
Lucy, d. [Theophilus], b. Oct. 30, 1794	2	56
Lucy, m. Albert **EDGECOMB**, b. of Groton, Feb. 20, 1822, by John G. Wightman	1	6
Lucy, m. Albert **EDGECOMB**, Feb. 20, 1822	3	4
Lucy, m. John O. **MINER**, 2d, b. of Groton, June 13, 1841, by Ira R. Steward	1	64
Lucy, d. [Park W. & Clarissa], b. [ ]; d. Nov. 26, 1851	3	9
Lucy A., m. Hubbard D. **MORGAN**, b. of Groton, Aug. 7, 1844, by Rev. Erastus Denison	1	71
Lucy Ann, of Groton, m. Lodowick H. **EDWARDS**, of S. Hampton, L.I., Jan. 1, 1845, by Rev. Cyrus Miner	1	72
Lucy Ann, d. [Isaac, Jr. & Nabby], b. May 7, 1804, at Woodstock	2	74
Lucy Ann, d. Elijah & Lucy, b. Jan. 8, 1807	2	48
Lucy S., of Groton, m. George **EVANS**, of N.Y. City, Jan. 2, 1837, by Timothy Tuttle	1	56
Luke William, s. [Rufus, Jr. & Caroline], b. Dec. 2, 1810	2	91
Luke W[illia]m, m. Hannah M. **MITCHELL**, b. of Groton, Sept. 12, 1838, by Rev. Mark Meade	1	60
Luther, s. [Jacob & Elizabeth], b. Dec. 4, 1795	2	57
Lydia, d. [Rufus & Hannah], b. Sept. 24, 1791	2	34
Lydia, d. [Theophilus], b. Oct. 15, 1791	2	56
Lydia Fish, twin with Martha Fish, [d. Roswell & Martha], b. Oct. 2, 1771	2	35
Margaret, m. William **MORGAN**, July 1, 1696	1	117
Margaret, [d. Christopher, Jr. & Mary], b. Mar. 12, 1738/9	1	133
Margaret, m. Daniel **LESTER**, Jan. 14, 1760	1	160
Margaret, [d. Jonas], b. Feb. 27, 175	2	17
Margaret H., of Groton, m. Christopher **WILLIAMS**, of Taunton, Mass., July 9, 1835, by Timothy Tuttle	1	51
Maria, d. John J. & Nancy, b. Jan. 26, 1796	2	54
Maria, m. Prentice P. **SMITH**, b. of Groton, Dec. 1, 1814, by Daniel Eldredge, J.P.	2	94
Martha, of Groton, m. Nathan **NILES**, of Stonington, July 19, 1820, by Rev. John G. Wightman	1	1
Martha Fish, twin with Lydia Fish, [d. Roswell & Martha], b. Oct. 2, 1771	2	35

	Vol.	Page
AVERY, (cont.)		
Marvin B., of Springfield, Mass., m. Mary L. **AVERY**, of Groton, Mar. 20, 1828, by Timothy Tuttle	1	27
Marvin Steward, s. [David & Hannah], b. Apr. 22, 1812	2	67
Mary, [d. Samuell & Susanna], b. Jan. 10, 1695; d. May [ ], 1739	1	121
Mary, [d. Ebenezer & Dorothy], b. Apr. 1,1714	1	123
Mary, m. William **MORGAN**, July 3, 1716	1	131
Mary, m. William **WALSWORTH**, Jan. 16, 1720, by Rev. Ephraim Woodbridge	1	119
Mary, [d. Edward & Johan[n]ah], b. Nov. 3, 1723	1	111
Mary, [d. Christopher & Mary], b. Feb. 6, 1727	1	119
Mary, [d. Christopher, Jr. & Mary], b. Feb. 6, 1727; d. Aug. 22, 1727	1	133
Mary, d. Ebenezer & Lucy, b. Nov. 30, 1730	1	130
Mary, m. Josiah **HARRIS**, Mar. 11, 1730/1	1	144
Mary, d. Waitstill & Margaret, b. Nov. 6, 1733	1	138
Mary, m. Paul **PELTON**, Aug. 20, 1743	1	173
Mary, [d. Christopher, Jr. & Mary], b. Nov. 1, 1744; d. Aug. 10, 1754	1	133
Mary, m. Youngs **LEDYARD**, Dec. 8, 1748	2	29
Mary, d. John & Mary, b. June 21, 1753	1	162
Mary, w. Christopher, d. Aug. 14, 1754, ae. 56 y.	1	133
Mary, d. William & Mary, b. Nov. 23, 176[ ]	2	4
Mary, w. William, d. Oct. 4, 1774	2	4
Mary, d. [Isaac & Lucy], b. July 18, 1780	2	58
Mary, m. Timothy **WIGHTMAN**, Jr., Apr. 17, 1783	2	39
Mary, d. [Thomas & Hannah], b. June 26, 1786	2	28
Mary, d. [Jacob & Elizabeth], b. Apr. 2, 1799	2	57
Mary, of Groton, m. Peleg Spicer **TIFT**, of R.I., Dec. 7, 1831, by John Brewster, J.P.	1	38
Mary A., of Groton, m. Benajah R. **AVERY**, of Salina, N.Y., Apr. 2, 1840, by Rev. John G. Wightman	1	62
Mary Angelina, d. Elisha & Nancy, b. Jan. 8, 1812	2	68
Mary E., m. Nathan F. **DENISON**, b. of Groton, Dec. 25, 1823, by Ebenezer Avery, Jr., J.P.	1	12
Mary H., m. Elisha **AVERY**, b. of Groton, Dec. 17, 1801	2	68
Mary H., d. Apr. 14, 1810	2	68
Mary Hannah, d. [Nathan & Matilda], b. Apr. 24, 1811	2	86
Mary Jane, d. [Nathan & Matilda], b. Feb. 12, 1824	3	9
Mary L, of Groton, m. Marvin B. **AVERY**, of Springfield, Mass., Mar. 20, 1828, by Timothy Tuttle	1	27
Mary Latham, b. Feb. 24, 1808	2	34
Mary M., m. William **LATHAM**, b. of Groton, Apr. 24, 1836, by Rev. Ira R. Steward	1	54
Matilda, m. Ira R. **STEWARD**, b. of Groton, Feb. 4, 1834, by Rev. Roswell Burrows	1	46
Matilda Fish, d. [Roswell & Martha], b. Aug. 8, 1780	2	35
Mercy, [d. Jonathan & Elizabeth], b. Dec. 3, 1707	1	120
Moses, s. [Daniel & Sibble], b. Aug. 17, 1779	2	39
Moses Fish, s. [Roswell & Martha], b. Aug. 10, 1773	2	35
Moses R., of Syracuse, N.Y., m. Julia E. **AVERY**, of Groton, Feb. 5, 1849, by Rev. Nicholas T. Allen	1	86
Nabby, d. [Isaac, Jr. & Nabby], b. June 6, 1801, at Woodstock	2	74
Nancy, d. [Aaron & Anna], b. Oct. 9, 1799	2	58
Nancy, d. [Aaron & Anna], b. Oct. 9, 1799	2	60

	Vol.	Page
AVERY, (cont.)		
Nancy, d. Elisha & Nancy A., b. Aug. 7, 1813	2	68
Nancy, m. Robert Austin **AVERY**, b. of Groton, Oct. 6, 1822, by Caleb Avery, J.P.	1	7
Nancy, [d. Jonas B. & Esther], b. [ ]	3	2
Nathan, [s. Samuell & Susanna], b. Jan. 30, 1703	1	121
Nathan, [s. Christopher & Abigail], b. Mar. 10, 1712	1	127
Nathan, m. Hannah **STODDARD**, Mar. 27, 1746	1	178
Nathan, s. [Nathan & Hannah], b. Dec. 21, 1749	1	178
Nathan, s. Isaac & Lucy, b. Sept. 21, 1775	2	19
Nathan, s. [Isaac & Lucy], b. Sept. 21, 1775	2	58
Nathan, 2d, m. Matilda **BABCOCK**, b. of Groton, Dec. 16, 1801, by Amos Geer, J.P.	2	86
Nathan Smith, s. Nathan & Matilda, b. Apr. 8, 1803	2	86
Oliver, s. Christopher & Eunice, b. Feb. 8, 1757	1	146
Oliver, s. David & Hannah, b. Sept. 29,1784	2	41
Orin Williams, s. Elisha & Nancy A., b. Apr. 6,1818	2	68
Palmer, s. Humphrey & Jerusha, b. Apr. 3, 1737	1	135
Parke, [s. Ebenezer & Dorothy], b. Dec. 9, 1710	1	123
Park W., m. Clarissa **AVERY**, Oct. 24, 1811	3	9
Park W., d. Dec. 10, 1866, ae. 78	3	9
Peyton Randolph, s. [Theophilus], b. Sept. 12, 1797	2	56
Phebe, m. Nicholas **MORGAN**, b. of Groton, Mar. 1, 1790	2	67
Phebe, d. [Isaac & Lucy], b. Feb. 18, 1783; d. Sept. 12, 1795, ae. 12 y. 6 m. 24 d.	2	58
Phebe, d. [Denison & Hannah], b. Jan. 29, 1799	2	85
Phebe, d. [Nathan & Matilda], b. Sept. 5, 1806	2	86
Phebe, of Groton, m. Youngs **MORGAN**, of Cranston, R.I., May 3, 1835, by Rev. Roswell Burrows	1	50
Phebe Ann, m. James **BENHAM**, b. of Groton, Mar. 28, 1841, by Ira R. Steward	1	64
Polly, m. Sanford **STODDARD**, b. of Groton, Feb. 22, 1804, by Amos Geer, J.P.	2	85
Prentice, [s. Christopher & [E]unice], b. Feb. 10, 1755. (Entry written in pencil)	1	146
Prentice. s. Christopher, Jr. & Eunice, b. Feb. 10, 1755	1	146
Prentice. s [Daniel & Sibble], b. July 19, 1781	2	39
Prentice P., s. [Park W. & Clarissa], b. Jan. 6, 1836; d. Aug. 19, 1884, ae. 48 y.	3	9
Priscilla, d. Christopher & Prudence, b. Apr. 29, 1715	1	127
Priscilla, d. [Jacob & Elizabeth], b. July 17, 1793	2	57
Priscilla, m. Enoch **LAMB**, b. of Groton, Mar. 26, 1818, by Rev. John G. Wightman	2	90
Prudence, m. Joseph **MORGAN**, Jr., Dec. 10, 17[ ], by Rev. Jacob Johnson	2	18
Prudence, d. Jacob & Elizabeth, b. Aug. 26, 1788	2	57
Rachel, d. Ebenezer & Lucy, b. Sept. 8, 1745	1	130
Rachel, m. Charles **ELDREDGE**, Jr., b. of Groton, Sept. 13, 1764, by Rev. Jonathan Barber	2	33
Rachel, w. Col. Ebenezer, d. Feb. 5, 1791	1	131
Rebeckah, [d. Christopher, Jr. & Mary], b. Dec. 24, 1741	1	133
Rhoda Emeline, d. [Denison & Hannah], b. June 22, 1809	2	86
Robert, s. James & Elizabeth, b. Jan. 27, 1756; d. Aug. 27, 1780	2	4

	Vol.	Page
AVERY, (cont.)		
Robert Austin, s. [Caleb], b. Aug. 3, 1803	2	63
Robert Austin, m. Nancy **AVERY**, b. of Groton, Oct. 6, 1822, by Caleb Avery, J.P.	1	7
Robert P., m. Hannah B. **PACKER**, b. of Groton, Sept. 22, 1841, by Ira R. Steward	1	65
Rosannah, [d. Christopher, Jr. & Mary], b. Oct. 14, 1728	1	133
Roswell, m. Martha **FISH**, Dec. 13, 1770, by Timothy Wightman, Elder	2	35
Roswell, d. Dec. 2, 1781	2	35
Rufus, s. James & Elizabeth, b. Nov. 16, 1758	2	4
Rufus, m. Hannah **LORD**, Mar. 1, 1781	2	34
Rufus, s. [Rufus & Hannah], b. Mar. 7, 1785	2	34
Rufus, Jr., m. Caroline **LATHAM**, Sept. 3, 1804	2	91
Russell, s. [Thomas & Hannah], b. July 18, 1769	2	28
Sabra, d. [Thomas & Hannah], b. Sept. 10, 1779	2	28
Sabra, b. Sept. 10, 1779; m. Vine **STODDARD**, Jr., June 11, 1801	3	10
Sabra, d. [James, Jr. & March], b. Jan. 30, 1796	2	63
Sabra, m. Paul F. **NILES**, Oct. 18, 1798, by Amos Geer, J.P.	2	85
Sabra E., of Groton, m. Joseph **MINDER**, 2d, of Stonington, Nov. 10, 1831, by John G. Wightman, Eld.	1	38
Sallacia, d. [James, Jr. & Marcy], b. Mar. 4, 1800	2	63
Sally, d. [Caleb], b. June 25, 1790	2	63
Sally, m Elisha **SATTERLEE**, b. of Groton, Apr. 3, 1796	2	82
Sally, m. Amos **LESTER**, Jr., b. of Groton, Jan. 18, 1801, by Amos Geer, J.P.	2	72
Sally, m. Thomas **HAMMOND**, May 8, 1814	2	82
Samuell, b. Aug. 14, 1664; d. May 1, 1723 (noted in pencil)	1	121
Samuell, m. Susanna **PALINS**, Oct. 27, 1686	1	121
Samuell, s. Sam[ue]ll & Susan[n]a, b. Aug. 11, 1687; d. Aug. 7, 1714	1	121
Samuell, [s. Jonathan & Elizabeth], b. July 7, 1715	1	120
Samuell, [s. Christopher & Mary], b. Mar. 1, 1719/20	1	119
Samuel, [s. Christopher, Jr. & Mary], b. Mar. 1, 1720; d. Feb. 13, 1748/9	1	133
Samuel, Capt., d. May 1, 1723, ae. 59 y.	1	128
Samuel, s. Humphrey & Jerusha, b. Oct. 1, 1731	1	135
Samuel, s. Christopher & [E]unice, b. Nov. 15, 1752	1	146
Samuel, s. William & Mary, b. May 12, 1774	2	4
Samuel, [s. Theophilus], b. July 2, 1781	2	56
Samuel Prentice, s. [Thomas & Hannah], b. Nov. 9, 1793	2	28
Sarah, [d. Christopher, Jr. & Mary], b. Feb. 23, 1733/4; d. Aug. 2, 1759	1	133
Sarah, d. [Benjamin & Thankfull], b. July 29, 1742	1	182
Sarah, d. [Theophilus & Elizabeth], b. Dec. 2, 1750	2	56
Sarah, d. Christopher & Mary, d. Aug. 2, 1759, ae. 25 y.	1	153
Sarah, d. Christopher & Eunice, b. Aug. 7, 1761	1	146
Sarah, d. William & Hannah, b. Jan. 16, 1776	2	23
Sarah Augusta, of Groton, m. Joseph Aborn **SMITH**, of New London, June 24, 1832, by John G. Wightman, Elder	1	40
Sarah S., m. Robert A. **MORGAN**, b. of Groton, June 7, 1842, by Rev. Jared R. Avery	1	66
Sarah Sands, d. John & Sally D., b. July 13, 1820	3	1
Sidney, s. [Ebenezer & Mary], b. Mar. 23, 1800	2	44
Simeon, m. Sarah **NILES**, Oct. 25, 1750	1	162
Simeon, s. Simeon & Sarah, b. July 1, 1751	1	162
Solomon, s. Humphrey & Jerusha, b. July [ ], 1729; d. Aug, [ ], 1728	1	116

	Vol.	Page
AVERY, (cont.)		
Solomon, s. Humphrey & Jerusha, b. July 17, 1728; d. Aug. [ ], 1728	1	135
Solomon, s. [Jacob & Elizabeth], b. May 31, 1792; d. Sept. 31, 1792	2	57
Solon C., of Rochester, N.Y., m. Susan A. **COOK**, of Groton, Aug. 11, 1845, by Rev. Jared R. Avery	1	73
Sophia. d. [Davis & Hannah], b. Nov. 2, 1788	2	41
Stephen, s. [Nathan & Hannah], b. Jan. 13, 1756	1	178
Susannah, m. Ralph **STODDARD**, Jr., Apr. 3, 1746	1	184
Susanna, wid. of Capt. Samuel, d. Oct. 9, 1747, ae. 82 y.	1	152
Susanna, m. Oliver **WOODBRIDGE**, Dec. 28, 1749	1	161
Susan[na] (Palins), b. [ ]; d. Oct. 9, 1747, ae. 82 y. (Noted in pencil)	1	121
Sylvia, d. Jacob & Elizabeth, b. Mar. 16, 1789	2	57
Temperance, [d. Jonathan & Elizabeth], b. Feb. 3, 1719/20	1	120
Temperance, m. John **HEATH**, Sept. 29, 1743	1	184
Temperance, m. William **MORGAN**, July 4, 1744	1	170
Theophilus, s. Edward & Johan[n]ah, b. Sept. 6, 1708	1	111
Theophilus, of Groton, m. Elizabeth **BILLINGS**, of Preston, July 16, 1733, by John Brown, J.P.	2	56
Theophilus, s. [Theophilus & Elizabeth], b. June 22, 1753	2	56
Theophilus, 3d, m. Margery **NEWTON**, b. of Groton, Mar. 26, 1797, by Amos Geer, J.P.	2	72
Theophilus, d.Sept. 30, 1799, ae. 92 y.	2	56
Thomas, d. Edward & Johan[n]ah, b. June 15, 1702; d. May 3, 1703	1	111
Thomas, m. Hannah **SMITH**, July 7, 1768	2	28
Thomas, s. [Thomas & Hannah], b. Jan. 1, 1782	2	28
Urban, m. Amanda M. **AVERY**, b. of Groton, Dec. 10, 1828, by Rev. Roswell Burrows	1	29
Urban, m. Mary Ann **STODDARD**, b. of Groton, Jan. 5, 1836, by Ira R. Steward, Eld.	1	53
Waitestill, [s. Samuell & Susanna], b. Mar. 27, 1708	1	121
Waitstill, m. Deborah **WILLIAMS**, Sept. 18, 1729	1	138
Washington, m. Mary **MOXLEY**, b. of Groton, Nov. 26, 1829, by Ralph Hurlbutt, J.P.	1	32
Welthy, d. [Isaac & Lucy], b. Sept. 19, 1785; d. May 12, 1795, ae. 9 y. 8 m. 23 d.	2	58
William, [s. Samuell & Susanna], b. Aug. 25, 1692; d. Feb. 20, 1718	1	121
William, [s. Christopher & Mary], b. Nov. 5, 1724	1	119
William, [s. Christopher, Jr. & Mary], b. Nov. 5, 1724; d. May 4, 1757	1	133
W[illia]m, s. Humphrey & Jerusha, b. Sept. 3, 1726	1	116
William, s. Humphrey & Jerusha, b. Sept. 13, 1726	1	135
William, s. [Theophilus & Elizabeth], b. May 7, 1746; d. Jan. 28, 1773, at sea	2	56
William, of Groton, m. Mary **DOLBEAR**, of New London, Sept. 16, 176[ ]	2	4
William, m. Hannah **WALLSWORTH**, Mar. 16, 1775	2	23
William, Jr., m. Eunice **MORGAN**, b. of Groton, Jan. 31, 1830, by John G. Wightman, Eld.	1	33
William Billings, s. [James, Jr. & Marcy], b. Feb. 21, 1793	2	63
W[illia]m P., s. [Park W. & Clarissa], b. Nov. 12, 1812; d. Sept. 20, 1835, ae. 18 [sic]. Drowned.	3	9
William Wheeler, s. [Isaac & Lucy], b. June 20, 1791	2	58
Youngs, m. Maria L. **HALEY**, b. of Groton, Dec. 12, 1847, by Rev. S. B. Bailey	1	80

	Vol.	Page
AVERY, (cont.)		
Youngs, s. [Park W. & Clarissa], b. [ ]; d. Apr. 22, 1870	3	9
Zip[p]orah, d. [Asa & Lucretia], b. May 22, 1746	1	178
________, m. Charles **HALEY**, s. Caleb, Jr. & Sally, [ ]	3	0
AYER, AYRE, AYERS, Elisha, of Northampton, Mass., m. Sarah **WILLIAMS**, of Groton, Feb. 10, 1822, by William Williams, J.P.	1	6
Peter, of Preston, m. Mary **BAILEY**, of Groton, July 23, 1749	1	185
Peter, of Preston, m. Mary **BA[I]LEY**, of Groton, July 23, 1749	2	95
William, of Preston, m. Mrs. Dorothy **NILES**, of Groton, Nov. 10, 1840, by Ira R. Steward	1	64
BABCOCK, Abby E., of Groton, m. Abel **HINCKLEY**, of Stonington, May 5, 1836, by John G. Wightman, Elder	1	53
Abby Eliza, d. [Stanton P. & Lucy], b. Sept. 22, 1817	3	34
Ann, of Groton, m. Joseph **HOXEY**, of Richmond, R.I., Mar. 6, 1836, by Joseph Durfey, J.P.	1	53
Betsey, d. [Amos & Marcy], b. Nov. 30, 1804	2	58
Ceaser, of S. Kingstown, R.I., m. Phillis **FREEMAN**, of Groton, Nov. 21, 1830, by Ralph Hurlbutt, J.P.	1	36
Charlotte, m. John **STARK**, b. of Groton, June 19, 1803, by John G. Wightman, Eld.	2	71
Clarissa, m. Eli **EDG[E]COMB**, b. of Groton, July 30, 1843, by Rev. Erastus Denison	1	69
Edwin, s. [Stanton P. & Lucy], b. Nov. 20, 1822	3	34
Eliza, d. [Stanton P. & Lucy], b. Jan. 11, 1815; d. Apr. 19, 1817	3	34
Frances, of Groton, m. Daniel **MORGAN**, of Unidilly, N.Y., Apr. 29, 1832, by John G. Wightman, Eld.	1	40
Frances Harriet, d. [Stanton P. & Lucy], b. Dec. 21, 1805	3	34
George, s. Amos & Marcy, b. Oct. 15, 1795	2	58
George, m. Nancy **REEVE**, Mar. 15, 1818	2	83
James, m. Margaret **GERE**, b. of Groton, Jan. 31, 1779	2	51
John D., m. Harriet D. **BENTLEY**, b. of N. Stonington, Jan. 5, 1843, by Rev. Erastus Denison	1	67
John P., s. [Stanton P. & Lucy], b. May 24, 1802	3	34
John Prentice, s. John P[rentice], b. May 22, 1781	1	170
John Prentice, d. Sept. 6, 1781	1	170
Lucy Ann, d. [Stanton P. & Lucy], b. Nov. 2, 1803	3	34
Lucy Ann, of Groton, m. Peleg **PENDLETON**, of Norwich, N.Y., Sept. 19, 1824, by Rev. John G. Wightman	1	14
Mary, d. [Stanton P. & Lucy], b. Dec. 5, 1807	3	34
Mary, m. Hadley **FISH**, b. of Groton, Aug. 27, 1826, by John G. Wightman, Eld.	1	21
Matilda, d. [James & Margaret], b. Nov. 1, 1779	2	51
Matilda, m. Nathan **AVERY**, 2d, b. of Groton, Dec. 16, 1801, by Amos Geer, J.P.	2	86
Rebecca, m. George **LATHAM**, Nov. 12, 1795	2	71
Stanton P., m. Lucy GRAY, Aug. 30, 1801	3	34
BACON, John, of New Orleans, m. Catharine **ALLYN**, of Groton, Sept. 3, 1826, by Timothy Tuttle	1	21
BAGLEY, BAGSLEY, James, s. Thomas & Ruth, b. June 7, 1706	1	117
Jerediah, s. Thomas & Ruth, b. Apr. 23, 1708	1	117
William R., of St. Helena, m. Hannah **REED**, of Groton, Aug. 23, 1840, by Rev. John G. Wightman	1	63

	Vol.	Page
BAILEY, BAILY, BALEY, Abel, s. Joseph & Mary, b. July 2, 1736	1	148
Almira, of Groton, m. John **RATHBUN**, of New London, Apr. 19, 1846, by Rev. Simon B. Bailey	1	75
Amie, d. James & Bridgett, b. June 26, 1738	1	126
Anna, d. thaddeus & Lois, b. Mar. 31, 1764	2	22
Anna, m. Isaac C. **ROGERS**, b. of Groton, Oct. 12, 1829, by Ralph Hurlbutt, J.P.	1	32
Anna, m. Jedadiah **BAILEY**, [ ]	1	172
Asa, s. [Thomas, Jr. & Huldah], b. Apr. 27, 1740	1	174
Avery, s. Joseph & Hannah, b. Jan. 2, 1777	2	17
Avery, m. Phebe **MORGAN**, Feb. 22, 1807, by John G. Wightman, Elder	2	80
Avery E., of New London, m. Rebecca Ann **LESTER**, of Groton, Mar. 18, 1832, by Ralph Hurlbutt, J.P.	1	39
Azubah, d. [Obadiah, Jr. & Azubah], b. Jan. 29, 1758	1	174
Benjamin, s. Joseph & Mary, b. Oct. 25, 1721	1	148
Bridgett, d. James & Bridgett, b. Aug. 19, 1735	1	126
Caroline A., m. Charles S. **WHITTEMORE**, Apr. 30, 1844, by Rev. Simon B. Bailey	1	71
Caroline Delight, m. Aaron **CULVER**, [ ], 1801/2	1	192
Content, s. [Jedadiah & Anna], b. Oct. 1, 1745	1	172
Dan G., m. Mrs. Wealthy Ann **RATHBURN**, b. of Groton, Nov. 28, 1833, by Rev. Erastus Denison	1	45
Daniel, [s. Joseph & Mary], b. Mar. 7, 1727/8	1	121
David, s. Joseph & Mary, b. Mar. 7, 1727/8	1	148
Deborah, d. Obadiah & Elizabeth, b. Sept. 24, 1724	1	122
Deborah, m. Jonathan **FORESITH**, May 10, 1743	1	160
Delight Keren, d. [Jedadiah & Anna], b. Apr. 13, 1741	1	172
Dorothy, d. [Obadiah, Jr. & Azubah], b. Mar. 1, 1763	1	174
Dudley, s. Elijah & Elizabeth, b. July 21, 1763	2	1
Dudley, m. Eliza M. **MITCHELL**, b. of Groton, Aug. 14, 1842, by Nathan Daboll, J.P.	1	66
Elijah, s. James & Bridgett, b. Aug. 19, 1722	1	126
Elijah, m. Mary **LESTER**, Feb. 1, 1750	2	1
Elijah, s. Elijah & Mary, b. Sept. 15, 1758	2	1
Elijah, m. Elizabeth **HEATH**, Mar. 25, 1762	2	1
Elijah, s. Thad[deus] & Lois, b. Jan. 27, 1767	2	22
Elisha M., m. Frances M. **BAKER**, b. of Groton, Mar. 21, 1742, by Rev. Jared R. Avery	1	66
Elizabeth, m. John **FOX**, Dec. 25, 1707	1	110
Elizabeth, d. John & Elizabeth, b. July 31, 1715	1	108
Elizabeth, d. Obadiah & Elizabeth, b. Sept. 27, 1722	1	122
Elizabeth, d. Elijah & Mary, b. Feb. 10, 1756	2	1
Elizabeth, d. [Obadiah, Jr. & Azubah], b. Sept. 19, 1760	1	174
Easther, d. James & Mary, b. Oct. 10, 1735	1	144
Esh[h]er, m. Christopher **LESTER**, Jr., b. of Groton, Oct. 23, 1825, by John G. Wightman, Eld.	1	19
Eunice, d. Thad[deus] & Lois, b. Nov. 16, 1768	2	22
Eveline, of Groton, m. Dudley **BRAND**, of Westerly, R.I., Apr. 24, 1836, by Nathan Daboll, J.P.	1	53
Experience, m. David **WILLIAMS**, June 18, 1721	1	124
Experience, [d. Obadiah & Elizabeth], b. May 23, 1734	1	122
Ezra, m. Mrs. Prudence **DUNHAM**, b. of Groton, Nov. 11, 1849, by Rev. W[illia]m C. Walker	1	86

	Vol.	Page
BAILEY, BAILY, BALEY, (cont.)		
Ezra G., m. Jane E. **TURNER**, b. of Groton, Apr. 30, 1837, by John G. Wightman, Elder	1	56
Francina, m. Russell **PERKINS**, Jr., b. of Groton, Mar. 13, 1828, by Ralph Hurlbutt, J.P.	1	27
Frank, of Morgan, Ohio, m. Rebecca **LATHAM**, of Groton, Sept. 21, 1825, by John G. Wightman, Eld.	1	18
Frederick. s. Thaddeus & Lois, b. Oct. 23, 1765	2	22
Freelove, b. Dec. 16, 1774; m. Rodman **NILES**, Nov. 15, 1797	2	75
Gilbert S., m. Mary D. **PACKER**, b. of Groton, Apr. 16, 1851, by Rev. Simon B. Bailey	1	91
Giles, m. Dolly **REED**, b. of Groton, Oct. 21, 1821, by Rev. John G. Wightman	1	4
Giles, m. Meribah **MERRITT**, b. of Groton, June 27, 1824, by Ralph Hurlbutt, J.P.	1	13
Hannah, m. Jonathan **CHAPMAN**, Dec. 26, 1723	1	132
Hannah, m. Joshua **CHAPMAN**, b. of Groton, Dec. 13, 1805, by Amos Geer, J.P.	2	75
Hannah W., m. Jasper **LATHAM**, b. of Groton, June 14, 1836, by John G. Wightman, Elder	1	54
Henry, m. Susannah **FRANKLIN**, b. of Groton, Jan. 27, 1822, by Roswell Burrows, Elder	1	6
Isaac, m. Hannah **LESTER**, b. of Groton, June 15, 1828, by Timothy Tuttle	1	27
Jabez, s. [Obadiah, Jr. & Azubah], b. Sept. 3, 1748	1	174
James, m. Bridgett **STANTON**, Feb. 8, 1721	1	126
James, Jr., m. Mary **SAMSON**, Oct. 20, 1730	1	144
Jane, w. Thomas, d. Apr. 17, 1753	1	153
Jedadiah, m. Anna **BAILEY**, [ ]	1	172
Jesse, [s. Obadiah & Elizabeth], b. Jan. 23, 1736/7	1	122
Joanna, of New London, m. Braddock **CHESTER**, of Groton, Apr. 14, 1829, by John G. Wightman, Eld.	1	30
John, m. Elizabeth **STALLIN**, Dec. 25, 1713	1	108
John, m Elizabeth **LEE**, July 2, 1722	1	110
John, s. John & Elizabeth, b. Oct. 25, 1722	1	108
Jonathan, [s. Joseph & Mary], b. Feb. 4, 1725/6	1	121
Jonathan, s. Joseph & Mary, b. Feb. 4, 1725/6	1	148
Joseph, m. Mary **CHAPMAN**, Feb. 20, 1718	1	121
Joseph, Jr., m. Mary **CHAPMAN**, Feb. 20, 1718/19	1	148
Joseph, [s. Joseph & Mary], b. Nov. 19, 1723	1	121
Joseph, s. Joseph & Mary, b. Nov. 19, 1723	1	148
Joseph, s. [Jedadiah & Anna], b. Oct. 10, 1748	1	172
Joshua, s. Elijah & Elizabeth, b. July 29, 1766	2	1
Julia Ann, m. Capt. Henry **HALLETT**, b. of Groton, Apr. 29, 1833, by William Williams, J.P.	1	44
Julia M., of Groton, m. Elihu **AVERY**, of Groton, Oct. 16, 1848, by Rev. Nicholas T. Allen	1	86
Lodowich, s. Obadiah & Esther, b. Sept. 14, 1785	2	3
Lucy, d. Thomas & Jane, b. May 10, 1712	1	119
Lucy, m. Thomas **STANTON**, Mar. 12, 1731/32	1	145
Lucy Ann, of Groton, m. Dudley **BROWN**, of Stonington, Apr. 28, 1833, by Nathan Daboll, J.P.	1	43

	Vol.	Page
BAILEY, BAILY, BALEY, (cont.)		
Lyman, m. Betsey E. **IRISH**, b. of N. Stonington, Dec. 24, 1827, by Rev. Asher Miner	1	33
Malinda, m. Avery **GALLUP**, b. of Groton, Nov. 21, 1822, by Timothy Tuttle	1	8
Malinda, m. Avery **GALLUP**, b. of Groton, Nov. 21, 1822, by Rev. Timothy Tuttle	3	12
Martha J., of Groton, m. Erastus **HALL**, of Coventry, Dec. 25, 1834, by Ralph Hurlbutt, J.P.	1	48
Mary, m. William **BAILEY**, Sept. 20, 1716	1	118
Mary, [d. Thomas & Jane], b. June 2, 1721	1	119
Mary, d. Joseph & Mary, b. Mar. 20, 1737/8	1	148
Mary, of Groton, m. Peter **AYER**, of Preston, July 23, 1749	1	185
Mary, of Groton, m. Peter **AYRE**, of Preston, July 23, 1749	2	95
Mary, d. Elijah & Mary, b. Sept. 12, 1753	2	1
Mary, w. Elijah, d. Sept. 14, 1761	2	1
Mary, m. Samuel **LESTER**, Jr., Nov. 27, 1777	2	36
Michael, twin with R[h]oda, [s. Obadiah & Elizabeth], b. Aug. 23, 1739	1	122
Michael, d. [sic] [Obadiah, Jr. & Azubah], b. June 19, 1765	1	174
Noah, s. [Jedadiah & Anna], b. June 20, 1743	1	172
Obadiah, m. Elizabeth **WILLIAMS**, July 10, 1718	1	122
Obadiah, s. Obadiah & Elizabeth, b. Dec. 24, 1728	1	122
Obadiah, Jr., m. Azubah **RODGERS**, Dec. 9, 1747	1	174
Obadiah, s. [Obadiah, Jr. & Azubah], b. Aug. 12, 1750	1	174
Orlando, m. Deborah **LATHAM**, b. of Groton, Dec. 23, 1827, by John G. Wightman, Eld.	1	26
Pethual, s. [Jedadiah & Anna], b. Apr. 13, 1739	1	172
Pres[erve]d, [s. Joseph & Mary], b. Oct. 25, 1721	1	121
Priscilla, d. John & Elizabeth, b. Aug. 4, 1717	1	108
Prudence M., of Groton, m. Hopestil[l] **ARMSTRONG**, Jan. 1, 1838, by Rev. John G. Wightman	1	57
Ransford, s. Elijah & Elizabeth, b. Dec. 20, 1769	2	1
R[h]oda, twin with Michael [s. Obadiah & Elizabeth], b. Aug. 23, 1739	1	122
Rhoda, d. [Obadiah, Jr. & Azubah], b. Jan. 23, 1768	1	174
Russell, m. Abby **PARKS**, b. of Groton, Aug. 29, 1852, by Nicholas T. Allen, Minister	1	94
Ruth, d. James & Mary, b. Sept. 3, 1731	1	144
Ruth, s. James & Mary, b. Apr. 29, 1738	1	144
Ruth, m. W[illia]m **STEEL**, [ ]	1	114
Sarah, m. John **PERKINS**, Aug. 26, 1711	1	120
Sarah, 2d, w. of Thomas, d. Mar. 4, 1762	1	153
Silas P., m. Eunice **CULVER**, b. of Groton, June 6, 1831, by Ralph Hurlbutt, J.P.	1	37
Simeon, s. [Obadiah, Jr. & Azubah], b. Jan. 17, 1754	1	174
Simeon A., Jr., m. Emeline **LATHAM**, b. of Ledyard, Apr. 24, 1838, by Rev. John G. Wightman	1	58
Simon B., m. Emeline **HETH**, b. of Groton, Dec. 10, 1828, by Rev. N. S. Spa]u]lding	1	29
Temperance, d. Obadiah & Elizabeth, b. June 20, 1719	1	122
Temperance, m. Hutchinson **SHOLES**, May 28, 1741	1	174
Temperance, d. [Obadiah, Jr. & Azubah], b. Feb. 17, 1745	1	174
Thaddeus, s. [Jedadiah & Anna], b. May 22, 1737	1	172

	Vol.	Page
BAILEY, BAILY, BALEY, (cont.)		
Thaddeus, m. Lois **MORGAN**, b. of Groton, Dec. 30, 1762, by Jacob Johnson, Minister	2	22
Thaddeus, s. Thad[deus] & Lois, b. Sept. 8, 1770	2	22
Thomas, m. Jane **WILLEA**, June 13, 1711	1	119
Thomas, [s. Thomas & Jane], b. Mar. 13, 1716	1	119
Thomas, Jr., m. Huldah **STANTON**, Apr. 13, 1739	1	174
Thomas, s. Elijah & Mary, b. June 17, 1751	2	1
Thomas M., m. Nancy A. **CLARK**, b. of Groton, Apr. 18, 1837, by John G. Wightman, Elder	1	56
Titus, s. James & Mary, b. Oct. 2, 1733	1	144
Vine, s. [Obadiah, Jr. & Azubah], b. Nov. 15, 1771	1	174
William, m. Mary **BAILEY**, Sept. 20, 1716	1	118
William, m. Martha **WILLIAMS**, Dec. 24, 1796	2	82
Zilpha, d. Elijah & Mary, b. Sept. 9, 1760; d. Jan. 28, 1762	2	1
BAIRD, Alexander, m. Margaret Ellen **MURPHY**, b. of [Groton], Mar. 30, 1851, by W. Munger	1	92
BAKER, Amy, d. [Samuel & Jerusha], b. Jan. 9, 1739/40	1	177
Andrew, s. [Samuel & Jerusha], b. Sept. 18, 1738	1	177
Andrew, s. [Samuel & Jerusha], b. Mar. 22, 1756	1	177
Anna, m. Moses **HILL**, b. of Groton, Aug. 13, 1838, by Rev. John G. Wightman	1	59
Charlotte A., of Groton, m. Nathan **GARDINER**, of New London, Aug. 19, 1850, by Rev. Jared R. Avery	1	89
Daniel, s. [Samuel & Jerusha], b. Feb. 26, 1745/6	1	177
Elizabeth, d. [Samuel & Jerusha], b. May 5, 1748	1	177
Emily, m. Mark S. **BAKER**, June 1, 1849, by Rev. Jared R. Avery	1	83
Eunice, d. [Samuel & Jerusha], b. June 14, 1758	1	177
Eunice, m. Daniel **THOMAS**, b. of Groton, Jan. 11, 1781	2	54
Frances, M., m. Elisha M. **BAILEY**, b. of Groton, Mar. 21, 1842, by Rev. Jared R. Avery	1	66
Harlam, m. Frances **RATHBUN**, b. of Noank, Dec. 23, 1849, by Rev. William A. Smith, in Noank	1	87
Jerusha, of Groton, m. Daniel C. **HAVENS**, of Lyme, Sept. 17, 1832, by Nathan Daboll, J.P.	1	41
John, Jr., m. Katharine **HILL**, b. of Groton, June 15, 1831, by Nathan Daboll, J.P.	1	37
John, s. Peter, m. Hannah C. **SPENCER**, b. of Groton, July 3, 1836, by Rev. Roswell Burrows	1	54
John C., of Griswold, m. Clarissa **WILLIAMS**, of Groton, Mar. 9, 1821, by William Williams, J.P.	1	3
Julia, m. John **PALMER**, Jr., b. of Groton, Jan. 1, 1840, by Ira R. Steward	1	63
Julia A., of Groton, m. Hubbard **CHESTER**, of Groton, Apr. 4, 1849, by Rev. Nicholas T. Allen	1	86
Leonord C., m. Cynthia M. **CHAPMAN**, d. of William, b. of Groton, Feb. 16, 1845, by Belton A. Copp, J.P.	1	72
Lorenzo, m. Elizabeth **FENNER**, b. of Groton, Mar. 24, 1836, by Joseph Durfey, J.P.	1	53
Lorenzo D., m. Eliza A. **MORGAN**, b. of Groton, July 18, 1848, by Rev. Jared R. Avery	1	81
Lucy Ann, of Groton, m. George **NORMAN**, of Stonington, Dec. 10, 1850, at Noank, by Rev. James M. Phillips	1	90
Lydia, d. [Samuel & Jerusha], b. July 13, 1742	1	177

	Vol.	Page
BAKER, (cont.)		
Lydia, m. Nathaniel **ROACH**, June 4, 1761	2	17
Mark S., m. Emily **BAKER**, June 3, 1849, by Rev. Jared R. Avery	1	83
Mary H., of Pembroke, Mass., m. William M. **RIDENT**, of Quincy, Mass., July 22, 1838, by Rev. Nathan Paine	1	60
Nancy M., m. David A. **CLARK**, June 8, 1851, by Geo[rge] A. Woodward	1	91
Peter, m. Elizabeth **DEWEY**, b. of Groton, May 12, 1839, by Ira R. Steward	1	60
Peter, Jr., m. Caroline **PACKER**, b. of Groton, Sept. 25, 1842, by Ira R. Steward	1	67
Prudence M., m. James R. **DAVIS**, b. of Groton, Nov. 1, 1843, by Ira R. Steward	1	70
Richard P., m. Mary Jane **CHESTER**, b. of Groton, Sept. 30, 1849, by Rev. Jared R. Avery	1	85
Samuel, m. Jerusha **DAVIS**, Dec. 8, 1733	1	177
Samuel, s. [Samuel & Jerusha], b. July 27, 1750	1	177
Sarah, m. Andrew **DAVIS**, Dec. 9, 1707	1	107
Sarah, d. [Samuel & Jerusha], b. Feb. 16, 1754	1	177
Sarah, m. Jabez **SHOLES**, b. of Groton, June 5, 1791	2	62
Sarah had s. James **STARKWEATHER**, b. May 6, 1801	2	62
Susanna had s Minor **ALLYN**, b. Jan. 18, 1780	2	27
William, m. Almira **CHIPMAN**, b. of Groton, May 30, 1830, by Rev. John G. Wightman	1	34
BALDWIN, Ebenezer, of Yonkers, N.Y., m. Lydia P. **WILLIAMS**, of Groton, Dec. 29, 1847, by Rev. Nicho[la]s T. Allen	1	80
Erastus, m. Mary **REID**, b. of Groton, Jan. 28, 1821, by Ralph Hurlbutt, J.P.	1	3
Martha A., of Groton, m. Benjamin G. **HULL**, of Norwich, Oct. 16, 1848, by Rev. Nicholas T. Allen	1	86
Martha Ann, of Groton, m. Frederick **BRADLEY**, Jr., of Stockbridge, Mass., Oct. 2, 1827, by Nathan Daboll, J.P.	1	24
Mary E., m. ________ **BALDWIN**, b. of Groton, June 4, 1854, by Rev. Isaac Chees[e]brough	1	96
Mary H., of Groton, m. Collins **WARDEN**, of Richmond, Mass., Oct. 9, 1846, by Rev. Jared R. Avery	1	76
Mary M., m. Charles **LARAY**, Mar. 9, 1845, at Amos Baldwin's house, by Rev. R. Russell	1	73
________, m. Mary E. **BALDWIN**, b. of Groton, June 4, 1854, by Rev. Isaac Chees[e]brough	1	96
BALL, Abby, of Groton, m. Peleg **BILLINGS**, of Griswold, Nov. 4, 1821, by Ralph Hurlbutt, J.P.	1	4
Alfred, m. Elles **ARTHUR**, Dec. 9, 1823, by Rodman Niles, J.P.	1	11
Lucy, of Groton, m. Alfred **KEENEY**, of Griswold, Mar. 12, 1826, by Ralph Hurlbutt, J.P.	1	20
Sally, of Groton, m. James **BELDEN**, of Norwich, Feb. 14, 1836, by Ralph Hurlbutt, J.P.	1	53
BANAHAM, Solomon, s. John, b. Feb. 21, 1808	2	82
BARBER, Adelaide, d. Noyes & Catharine, b. Sept. 27, 1802	2	83
Adelaide, [d. Noyes & Catharine], d. Nov. 15, 1804	2	83
Betsey Ann, d. [Noyes & Catharine], b. Nov. 27, 1809	2	83
Betsey Ann, of Groton, m. Belton A. **COPP**, Aug. 15, 1833, by Timothy Tuttle	1	44
Bettey, d. [John & Elizabeth], b. May 12, 1771	2	53
Catharine, w. Noyes, d. Dec. 4, 1813, ae. 33y. 2 m. 13 d.	2	83
David White, s. [John & Elizabeth], b. Sept. 20, 1778	2	53

	Vol.	Page
BARBER, (cont.)		
Edwin, s. [John & Elizabeth], b. May 6, 1793	2	53
Edwin N., s. [Noyes & Catharine], b. Nov. 28, 1806	2	83
Eliza D., of Groton, m. Gilbert A. **SMITH**, of Springfield, Mass., June 8, 1823, by Timothy Tuttle	1	9
Ellen, of Groton, m. Robert A. **MANWARING**, of Greenville, May 15, 1845, by Rev. Jared R. Avery	1	73
Henrietta, d. [Noyes & Catharine], b. Dec. 14, 1803	2	83
Henrietta C., of Groton, m. Edwin **CHESTER**, July 16, 1823, by Timothy Tuttle	1	10
John, m. Elizabeth **DENISON**, b. of Groton, Nov. [ ], 1770	2	53
John, s. [John & Elizabeth], b. Aug. 25, 1783	2	53
Julia Maria, d. [Noyes & Mary], b. Sept. 11, 1818	2	83
Mary E., of Groton, m. Rev. A. L. **WHITMAN**, of Greenville, Apr. 26, 1843, by Rev. J. R. Avery	1	68
Mary Elizabeth, d. [Noyes & Mary], b. Feb. 5, 1817	2	83
Nancy, d. [John & Elizabeth], b. Aug. 29, 1785	2	53
Noyes, s. [John & Elizabeth], b. Apr. 28, 1781	2	53
Noyes, b. Apr. 28, 1781; m. Catharine **BURDICK**, Dec. 13, 1801	2	83
Noyes, m. Mary (Chester) **SMITH**, Aug. 11, 1814	2	83
Noyes Chester, s. [Noyes & Mary], b. May 23, 1815	2	83
Orlando N., s. [Noyes & Catharine], b. Aug. 28, 1805; d. Oct. 23, 1806	2	83
Rebecca, d. [John & Elizabeth], b. Mar. 6, 1789	2	53
Sarah, d. [John & Elizabeth], b. Nov. 6, 1773	2	53
Thomas, s. [John & Elizabeth], b. Mar. 11, 1776	2	53
BARKER, Hannah, m. Silas **DEAN**, Nov. 21, 1734	1	172
BARNES, BARNS, Abigail, d. [Nehemiah & Esther], b. Jan. 3, 1755	1	171
Abigail, m. James **BROWN**, Oct. 8, 1772	2	51
Amos, [twin with Nathan?, s. Ezra & Unice], b. May 10, 1778	1	173
Asa, [s. Ezra & Unice], b. Mar. 26, 1769	1	173
Asa, of Preston, m. Nancy **GALLUP**, of Groton, Mar. 15, 1829, by John G. Wightman, Eld.	1	30
Betsey, m. Avery **BILL**, b. of Groton, Dec. 10, 1820, by Rev. John G. Wightman	1	2
Elias, s. Nehemiah & Sarah, b. Jan. 10, 1735/6	1	140
Esther, d. [Nehemiah & Esther], b. Nov. 24, 1757	1	171
Eunice, of Groton, m. Albert S. **HOLMES**, of Norwich, Chenango Co., N.Y., Jan. 7, 1833, by William Williams, J.P.	1	42
Ezra, twin with Nehemiah, s. Matthew & Sarah, b. Sept. 10, 1730	1	140
Ezra, m. [E]unice **MORGAN**, Apr. 17, 1754	1	173
Ezra, [s. Ezra & [E]unice], b. May 25, 1767	1	173
Hannah, [d. Ezra & [E]unice], b. Jan. 20, 1762	1	173
Lucy, [d. Matthew & Sarah], b. Sept. 20, 1732	1	140
Lucy, [d. Ezra & [E]unice], b. Mar. 27, 1764	1	173
Lydia A., of Ledyard, m. Peter **WILLIAMS**, of Groton, July 15, 1849, by Rev. Jared R. Avery	1	85
Mary, [d. Ezra & [E]unice], b. Mar. 25, 1773	1	173
Mary Esther, of Groton, m. George **ANDREWS**, of West Greenwich, R.I., Dec. 16, 1829, by William Williams, J.P.	1	32
Nancy, m. John **MAINE**, b. of Groton, Feb. 1, 1835, by W[illia]m M. Williams, J.P.	1	49
Nathan, [twin with Amos(?), s. Ezra & [E]unice], b. May 10, 1778	1	173
Nehemiah, twin with Ezra, s. Matthew & Sarah, b. Sept. 10, 1730	1	140

	Vol.	Page
BARNES, BARNS, (cont.),		
Nehemiah, m. Esther **LAMB**, Mar. 22, 1752	1	171
Nehemiah, s. [Nehemiah & Esther], b. Feb. 24, 1761	1	171
Phebe, [d. Ezra & [E]unice], b. Apr. 13, 1776	1	173
Prudence, [d. Ezra & [E]unice], b. Nov. 19, 1763	1	173
Sarah, [d. Ezra & [E]unice], b. Sept. 13, 1765	1	173
Sarah, [d. Ezra & [E]unice], b. Mar. 31, 1771	1	173
BARNETT, Richard, m. Sally **HALLEY**, d. Stephen & Lucy, 2-11-1835	3	0
BARROWS, Lucy L., of Groton, m. Alexander **STUART**, Jr., of Griswold, Feb. 22, 1821, by Rev. Roswell Burrows	1	3
William, of Mansfield, m. Betsey **WILLIAMS**, of Groton, May 11, 1823, by Philip Gray, J.P.	1	9
BATTEY, BATTY, Susan, of Groton, m. Hamilton **MORGAN**, of Ledyard, May 26, 1842, by Rev. Erastus Denison	1	66
William G., of Porterville, in Groton, m. Charlotte A. **DENISON**, of Porterville, in Groton, Feb. 20, 1844, by Rev. W[illia]m S. Simmons, Jr.	1	70
BEARS, Orlando H., of Sag Harbour, L.I., m. Mary G. **WHIPPLE**, of Groton, Nov. 4, 1838, by Mark Meade, V.D.M.	1	60
BECKWITH, Amanda, of Groton, m. Leonord **CROCKER**, of Waterford, Feb. 24, 1828, by Rev. John G. Wightman	1	27
Caleb, of Waterford, m. Mrs. Ann **SMITH**, of Groton, Nov. 30, 1848, by Rev. Jared R. Avery	1	83
Mary A., of Waterford, m. Thomas **HEWLET**, of Groton, Feb. 2, 1841, by Rev. Jared R. Avery	1	64
Nancy C., of Salem, m. Allyn **TURNER**, of Groton, Oct. 27, 1833, by Ralph Hurlbutt, J.P.	1	45
Oliver, of Norwich, m. Bethana **HEATH**, of Groton, Nov. 27, 1836, by John G. Wightman, Elder	1	55
BEDENT, Harriet, of Ledyard, m. Joshua **CONGDON**, of Montville, Mar. 26, 1838, by Rev. John G. Wightman	1	58
BEEBE, Adon, of Waterford, m. Betsey **MURPHEY**, of Groton, May 10, 1829, by Roswell Fish, J.P.	1	31
Elizabeth, of Groton, m. James R. **MITCHELL**, of New London, Jan. 29, 1837, by John G. Wightman, Elder	1	56
Emeline, of Groton, m. Sands H. **FISH**, Mar. 14, 1850, by Rev. H. R. Knapp	1	88
Ezra E., m. Harriet E. **FISH**, b. of Groton, Sept. 20, 1842, by Rev. Erastus Denison	1	67
Frank, m. Eliza A. **MURPHY**, b. of Groton, Aug. 10, 1848, by Rev. H. R. Knapp	1	84
Henry G., of Waterford, m. Hannah P. **MURPHEY**, of Groton, Aug. 30, 1835, by Asa Fish, J.P.	1	51
James, of Norwich, m. Prudence Ann **LAMB**, of Groton, Dec. 20, 1829, by Philip Gray, J.P.	1	32
Mary (or Sally) Ann, m. Alden **FISH**, b. of Groton, Mar. 15, 1843, by Ira R. Steward	1	68
Silas, m. Mrs. Prudence **MORGAN**, b. of Groton, Jan. 15, 1849, by Rev. H. R. Knapp	1	84
BELDEN, James, of Norwich, m. Sally **BALL**, of Groton, Feb. 14, 1836, by Ralph Hurlbutt, J.P.	1	53
BELLOWS, Betsey, m. Frederick A. **AVERY**, Dec. 29, 1811, by Timothy Tuttle, D.D.	2	88

	Vol.	Page
BELLOWS, (cont.)		
Damares, d. Nathaniel & Dorcas, b. Sept. 17, 1707	1	110
Dorcas, twin with Hannah, d. Nath[anie]l [& Dorcas], b. Oct. 18, 1722	1	110
Elizabeth, d. Nathaniel & Sarah, b. Aug. 16, 1794	2	49
Hannah, twin with Dorcas, d. Nath[anie]l [& Dorcas], b. Oct. 18, 1722	1	110
Johanah, d. Nathaniel & Dorcas, b. Mar. 24, 1711/12	1	110
John, s. Nathaniel & Dorcas, b. Sept. 13, 1705	1	110
John, s. John & Mary, b. Feb. 29, 1727/8	1	135
Lucretia, b. Sept. 2, 1763; m. Daniel **STODDARD**, Jan. 1, 1784	2	90
Margaret, d. Nathaniel & Dorcas, b. Jan. 5, 1718	1	110
Nathaniel, m. Dorcas **ROSE**, Nov. 15, 1704	1	110
Nathaniel, d. Jan. 24, 1814	2	72
Thomas, s. Nathaniel & Dorcas, b. Feb. 24, 1713/4	1	110
Zeruiah, d. Nathaniel & Dorcas, b. Oct. 30, 1709	1	110
BELTON, James, m. Tabitha **NILES**, Apr. 3, 1740	1	151
Jonas, m. Mary **MORGAN**, Aug. 7, 1737	1	151
Mary, m. Joseph **ALLEN**, b. of Groton, Dec. 30, 1760	2	5
BEMAN, Frederick C., m. Mary M. **RUSSELL**, Aug. 9, 1846, by Rev. R. Russell	1	76
BENHAM, Amos, m. Phebe **HEWLET**, b. of Groton, Sept. 7, 1828, by Nathan Daboll, J.P.	1	28
Elizabeth, m. Giles **PERKINS**, Dec. 26, 1821, by Rufus Smith, J.P.	1	5
James, m. Phebe Ann **AVERY**, b. of Groton, Mar. 28, 1841, by Ira R. Steward	1	64
John, Jr., m. Diana **PERKINS**, b. of Groton, Aug. 19, 1827, by Nathan Daboll, J.P.	1	24
Mary Ann, m. Peter **HEWLET**, b. of Groton, Apr. 18, 1841, by Ira R. Steward	1	64
Sarah A., m. Edward C. **KENYON**, b. of Groton, June 4, 1854, by Rev. Isaac Cheesebrough	1	96
Solomon, m. Sarah **STORY**, b. of Groton, Sept. 4, 1831, by Nathan Daboll, J.P.	1	38
William H., m. Sally A. **EDGECOMB**, b. of Groton, July 14, 1839, by Ira R. Steward	1	61
BENJAMIN, Seba, of Preston, m. Wid. Phebe **MITCHELL**, of Groton, Aug. 31, 1845, by W[illi]m C. Walker	1	74
Seba, of Preston, m. Phebe MITCHELL, of Groton, Aug. 31, 1845, by Rev. William C. Walker	1	75
BENNETT, BENNET, BENET, Elisha, of Stonington, m. Mrs. Nancy **WATROUS**, of Groton, [ ], by Rev. Roswell Burrows. Recorded July 25, 1831	1	37
James, of Penn., m. Mary Ann **HOWLAND**, of Groton, Sept. 28, 1828, by Roswell Fish, J.P.	1	28
Marinda, m. Rhodes **BURROWS**, b. of Groton, June 21, 1840, by Charles Bennett, J.P.	1	63
Oliver S., m. Adelia E. **PERKINS**, b. of Groton, Sept. 29, 1839, by Charles Bennett, J.P.	1	61
Reuben, m. Phebe A. **CHESEBRO[UGH]**, of Stonington, July 9, 1848, by Rev. H. R. Knapp	1	84
Susannah, m. David **CHURCH**, Mar. 16, 1728	1	139
Terry, of Stonington, m. Amanda **MORGAN**, of Groton, Oct. 18, 1846, by Rev. Simon B. Bailey	1	76

	Vol.	Page
BENNETT, BENNET, BENET, (cont.)		
Thomas, of New London, m. Anna **RE[Y]NOLDS**, of Preston, Oct. 29, 1713, by Salmon Treat	1	109
BENTLEY, David N., Rev., m. Betsey **CALLAGHAN**, b. of Norwich, July 31, 1854, at Mystic River Village, by Rev. Ebenezer Blake	1	96
Harriet D., m. John D. **BABCOCK**, b. of N. Stonington, Jan. 5, 1843, by Rev. Erastus Denison	1	67
Joseph C., m. Lucy A. **WILLIAMS**, b. of Groton, Nov. 19, 1835, by W[illia]m M. Williams, J.P.	1	52
W[illia]m, m. Delia **BROWN**, b. of Groton, Oct. 26, 1842, by Ira R. Steward	1	67
BENTON, Emeline, m. Anson **NILES**, b. of Groton, Apr. 12, 1832, by Nathan Daboll, J.P.	1	39
BERRY, John H., of Plattsburgh, N.Y., m. Lucy Ann **DOUGLASS**, of Groton, June 4, 1848, by Nathan Daball, J.P.	1	81
BETHWICK, Lucy Ann, m. Aaron E. **MITCHELL**, b. of Groton, Nov. 24, 1831, by Ralph Hurlbutt, J.P.	1	38
BIBBER, Emerson, m. Mary Ann **YORK**, b. of Groton, July 18, 1852, at Noank, by Rev. James M. Phillips	1	94
BILL, Avery, m. Betsey **BARN[E]S**, b. of Groton, Dec. 20, 1820, by Rev. John G. Wightman	1	2
Benjamin, s. Phillip & Mary, b. Aug. 6, 1708	1	114
Benjamin, m. Amey **BOLLES**, May 8, 1791, by Rev. Park Allyn	2	68
Betsey, of Groton, m. John **DARER**, of Otis, Mass., Oct. 5, 1825, by John G. Wightman, Eld.	1	19
David, s. Phineas & Lucy, b. July 15, 1787	2	17
Deborah, of Groton, m. James **FERBS**, of Mass., Oct. 11, 1828, by Nathan Daboll, J.P.	1	28
Desire, m. Charles **ELDREDGE**, b. of Groton, July 16, 1820, by Rev. John G. Wightman	1	1
Elizabeth, m. Jonathan **AVERY**, Apr. 11, 1703	1	120
Eunice, m. William **PERKINS**, b. of Groton, July 25, 1830, by Ralph Hurlbutt, J.P.	1	34
Fanny, m. Peter L. **HURLBUTT**, b. of Groton, Feb. 3, 1822, by Ralph Hurlbutt, J.P.	1	6
Gurdon, Jr., of Ledyard, m. Emelia Amanda **DENISON**, of Groton, May 12, 1853, by Rev. Erastus Denison	1	95
Hannah, m. Sam[ue]ll **LESTER**, Nov. 5, 1707	1	122
Hannah, m. Edward **SPICER**, Oct. 17, 1743	1	184
Jacob, [s. Joseph & Bethiah], b. Feb. 8, 1723	1	117
Joseph, m. Bethiah **PACKER**, Nov. [ ], 1716	1	117
Joseph, [s. Joseph & Bethiah], b. Aug. 26, 1720	1	117
Lodowick, s. Benajah & Content, b. Oct. 9, 1784; m. Betsey **GEER**, b. of Groton, Oct. 20, 1805, by Amos Geer, J.P.	2	73
Mary, m. Albert **EDGECOMB**, Aug. 29, 1819	3	4
Phillip, [s. Joseph & Bethiah], b. Oct. 22, 1717	1	117
Richard, s. Benjamin & Sarah, b. June 28, 1776	2	8
Sabra, m. Joshua **SMITH**, b. of Groton, Oct. 9, 1786, by Elder Park Allyn	2	67
Thomas, s. Sergt. Phillip & Mary, b. Sept. 26, 1705	1	114
BILLINGS, Andrew, s. [Stephen & Bridget], b. Aug. 3, 1760	1	179
Andrew, [s. Stephen & Bridget(?)], d. Sept. 6, 1781	1	179
Anna, m. Christopher M. **GALLUP**, b. of Groton, June 5, 1833, by John G. Wightman, Eld.	1	43

	Vol.	Page
BILLINGS, (cont.)		
Bridget, d. Stephen & Bridget, b. Feb. 15, 1754	1	179
Bridget, w. Stephen, d. Aug. 15, 1762	1	179
Bridget, m. Youngs **LEDYARD**, June 24, 1773	2	6
Cynthia, m. William **MORGAN**, b. of Groton, Feb. 20, 1836, by Timothy Tuttle	1	53
Elizabeth, of Preston, m. Theophilus **AVERY**, of Groton, July 16, 1733, by John Brown, J.P.	2	56
Elizabeth, d. [Stephen & Mary], b. Aug. 14, 1766	1	179
Esther, m. Asahel **FISH**, Oct. 2, 1755	1	165
Eunice Williams, d. [Stephen & Bridget], b. Aug. 6, 1762; d. Aug. 28, 1762	1	179
Hannah, m. Rufus **ALLYN**, [ ], 1766	2	30
Hannah, m. Rufus **ALLYN**, Mar. 2, 1766, by Timothy Wightman, Elder	2	28
Hannah Adelia, of Groton, m. Alexander **PALMER**, of Stonington, Jan. 26, 1831, by Timothy Tuttle	1	36
Henry, of Waterford, m. Polly **STODDARD**, of Groton, Nov. 9, 1806, by Amos Geer, J.P.	2	81
Increase, m. Sarah **STODDARD**, July 26, 1751, by Ebenezer Punderson, Missionary	1	175
Isaac, s. Henry & Polly, b. Dec. 28, 1807	2	81
Katharine, d. [Stephen & Bridget], b. May 5, 1758	1	179
Lucy, of Groton, m. Robert **STODDARD**, Jr., June 18, 1752	2	27
Mary, w. Stephen, d. Mar. 7, 1787, ae. 54 y.	1	179
Peleg, of Griswold, m. Abby **BALL**, of Groton, Nov. 4, 1821, by Ralph Hurlbutt, J.P.	1	4
Stephen, m. Mary **LEDYARD**, Dec. 12, 1765	1	179
Stephen, m. Martha **DENISON**, Apr. 9, 1789	1	179
Tabitha, m. Ichabod **STODDARD**, b. of Groton, May 10, 1767, by Jacob Johnson, Elder	2	6
BINKS, John, m. Julia **DENNIS**, b. of Groton, Dec. 14, 1845, by Elisha Morgan, J.P.	1	74
John, m. Sally **REED**, b. now residing in Groton, June 13, 1847, by Nathan Daboll, J.P.	1	79
BIRCH, [see also **BURCH**], Coddington, m. Betsey **BURROWS**, b. of Groton, [Dec.(?)] 9, 1821, by John G. Wightman	1	5
Zeruiah, m. John **NEWBER[R]Y**, Jr., Nov. 26, 1739	1	146
BLACKSTONE, Richard, of S. Atlantic Ocean, m. Phebe **REED**, of Groton, June 28, 1838, by Rev. John G. Wightman	1	59
BOARDMAN, Mary, m. Henry **WILLIAMS**, Jr., Oct. 12, 174[ ]	2	9
BOLLES, Amey, m. Benjamin **BILL**, May 8, 1791, by Rev. Park Allyn	2	68
Dianna, m. Daniel **WILLIAMS**, b. of Groton, May 29, 1825, by Ralph Hurlbutt, J.P.	1	17
John C., M.D., of Montville, m. Eunice **BUDDINGTON**, of Ledyard, Feb. 7, 1843, by Rev. Jared R. Avery	1	67
Joseph, of New London, m. Nancy **FELLOWS**, of Groton, Nov. 8, 1827, by Asa Fitch, J.P.	1	25
Joseph, m. Sally **STERRY**, b. of Montville, Feb. 3, 1830, by Philip Gray, J.P.	1	33
Lucinda, of Waterford, m. Newman **NEWBURY**, of Groton, Aug. 23, 1835, by Joseph Durfey, J.P.	1	51
Margaret, m. Ralph **HURLBUTT**, Jan. 27, 1833, by Ralph Hurlbutt, J.P.	1	42
BOWEN, Aaron, m. Nancy **BRICE**, Dec. 15, 1822, by John Brewster, J.P.	1	8

	Vol.	Page
BOYDEN, John, of Guilford, Vt., m. Eunice **FISH**, of Groton, Apr. 30, 1824, by Rev. Roswell Burrows	1	13
BOYNTON, James L., of Portland, Me., m. Ellen **DANIELS**, of Groton, Apr. 22, 1838, by Joseph Durfey, J.P.	1	58
BRADFORD, John D., m. Hannah **ALLYN**, b. of Groton, July 21, 1822, by Ralph Hurlbutt, J.P.	1	7
Sally S., of Groton, m. Gurdon **ALLYN**, Oct. 13, 1822, by Rodman Niles, J.P.	1	8
BRADLEY, Frederick, Jr., of Stockbridge, Mass., m. Martha Ann **BALDWIN**, of Groton, Oct. 2, 1827, by Nathan Daboll, J.P.	1	24
BRAMAN, Allen T., m. Elmira **REYNOLDS**, b. of Groton, Aug. [ ], 1837, by John G. Wightman, Elder	1	56
Cynthia, of Groton, m. Leonord **LOVEL[L]**, of Waterford, May 29, 1825, by Nathan Daball, J.P.	1	16
Erastus D., of Groton, m. Mary **GAVIT[T]**, of Norwich, May 5, 1833, by Rev. Roswell Burrows	1	43
Fanny, m. Albert **MA[Y]NARD**, b. of Groton, Oct. 27, 1850, by Rev. Jared R. Avery	1	90
Lucy A., m. Prentice A. **PARK[E]**, b. of Groton, Aug. 13, 1834, by John G. Wightman, Elder	1	47
Mary, of Groton, m. Charles **LOVEL[L]**, of Waterford, Apr. 23, 1826, by Roswell Fish, J.P.	1	20
Mary A., m. John A. **MERRITT**, b. of Groton, Dec. 8, 1850, by Rev. Nicholas T. Allen	1	90
Mary E., of Groton, m. Henry **MANDEVILLE**, of N.Y., Mar. 7, 1848, by Rev. H. R. Knapp	1	84
Oliver, m. Abby C. **PARKS**, b. of Groton, July 28, 1833, by John G. Wightman, Eld.	1	44
Seabury, m. Anna **RENHAM**, b. of Groton, Jan. 11, 1852, by Rev. Nicholas T. Allen	1	93
BRANCH, Mary Anny, d. Elisha & Mary, b. Feb. 8, 1815	2	87
BRAND, Christopher H., of Norwich, m. Temperance Ann **ALLYN**, of Groton, June 14, 1835, by Ralph Hurlbutt, J.P.	1	50
Dudley, of Westerly, R.I., m. Eveline **BAILEY**, of Groton, Apr. 24, 1836, by Nathan Daboll, J.P.	1	53
Ellen, of Groton, m. Thomas E. **DWYER**, of New London, Nov. 28, 1850, by Rev. Jared R. Avery	1	90
Nathaniel, m. Ellen **DENHAM**, b. of Groton, Jan. 5, 1846, by Nathan Daboll, J.P.	1	75
BRAY, William S., of New Foundland, m. Frances L. **PACKER**, of Groton, July 4, 1838, by I. R. Steward. Intention dated July 1, 1838.	1	59
BRAYMAN, Erastus D., s. [John & Polly], b. June 21, 1808	3	10
John, m. Polly **PARK**, Aug. 1, 1821	3	10
Oliver T., s. [John & Polly], b. Feb. 2, 1810	3	10
BRAYTON, James W., of Providence, R.I., m. Lucy **PENDLETON**, of Groton, Oct. 2, 1836, by John G. Wightman, Elder	1	55
BREACHER, J. H., of Florida, m. A. D. **NILES**, of Groton, Aug. 24, 1842, by Rev. B. F. Hedden	1	67
BREAKER, John W., of Camden, S.C., m. Lucy Ann **NILES**, of Groton, May 24, 1837, by John G. Wightman, Elder	1	56
BREED, Jesse, of Litchfield, m. Hannah T. **RANDALL**, of Stonington, July 3, 1825, by Timothy Tuttle	1	17

	Vol.	Page
BREED, (cont.)		
Lucy A., of Mass., m. George J. **CARTER**, of R.I., Mar. 15, 1846, by Rev. William C. Walker	1	75
Sally, of Groton, m. William **PENDLETON**, of Stonington, June 7, 1821, by Rev. Roswell Burrows	1	3
William H., m. Mary E. **WASHINGTON**, of Portersville, Groton, Aug. 17, 1845, by Rev. H. R. Knapp	1	74
BRERETON, Joseph, Capt., of Manchester, England, m. Abby Jane **WELSH**, of Groton, July 18, 1847, by Rev. Erastus Denison	1	79
BREWSTER, Clarissa, of Waterville, N.Y., m. Rev. Ashbel **STEELE**, of Waterbury, Ct., June 28, 1825, in St. James Church, by Rev. S. B. Paddock, of Norwich.	1	17
Edwin, s. John & Polly, b. Feb. 12, 1823; d. July 7, 1823	3	8
Eliza, of Groton, m. Elisha A. **CRARY**, of Preston, Jan. 29, 1828, by Timothy Tuttle	1	26
Franklin, of Norwich, m. Almira **STODDARD**, of Groton, Nov. 29, 1832, by Timothy Tuttle	1	42
Lovisa, m. William S. **GEER**, Feb. 14, 1816, at Franklin, by Rev. David Austen, of Franklin	2	89
Nathan, m. Nancy **BROWN**, b. of Groton, May 18, 1828, by William Williams, J.P.	1	27
BRIA, Allice, m. Winthrop **SAWYER**, b. of Groton, Aug. 5, 1821, by Rev. Roswell Burrows	1	3
BRICE, Henry, s. Robert **BRICE** & Martha **GARD**, b. Mar. 4, 1796	2	10
Nancy, m. Aaron **BOWEN**, Dec. 15, 1822, by John Brewster, J.P.	1	8
BRICK, George C., m. Amanda M. **STRONG**, b. of Groton, Jan. 8, 1853, by Rev. Nicholas T. Allen	1	94
BRIEN, [see also **O'BRIEN**], Henry, s. Robert & Mary, b. Mar. 4, 1775	2	10
BRIGGS, Aaron, m. Grace **SPENCER**, b. of Stonington, Aug. 30, 1835, by Joseph Durfey, J.P.	1	51
Charles, of Pembroke, N.Y., m. Nancy B. **SAWYER**, of Portersville, Groton, Aug. 13, 1845, by Rev. H. R. Knapp	1	74
Lydia Ann, of Groton, m. Nathan S. **WEAVER**, of Stonington, May 17, 1835, by John G. Wightman, Elder	1	50
William Henry, of New London, m. Mary **COMSTOCK**, of Groton, July 4, 1846, by Belton A. Copp, J.P.	1	76
BRIGHTMAN, Abby, d. [Latham & Abby], b. Nov. 17, 1816	3	21
Elizabeth, m. Conrad **KELCIN**, July 27, 1843, by Henry W. Avery, J.P.	1	69
George Washington, s. [Latham & Abby], b. June 11, 1829	3	21
Henry, s. [Latham & Abby], b. Sept. 27, 1814	3	21
Joanna, m. [A]Eneas **DAY**, Nov. 25, 1841, by Henry W. Avery, J.P.	1	65
Joseph Warren, s. [Latham & Abby], b. Feb. 21, 1827	3	21
Latham, s. [Latham & Abby], b. June 21, 1818	3	21
Lucy Ann, d. [Latham & Abby], b. Apr. 12, 1825	3	21
Mary, of Stonington, m. George W. **TAYLOR**, of Groton, Dec. 23, 1832, by John G. Wightman, Eld.	1	42
BRISTOL, Reuben, of Cheshire, m. Mary E. **FISH**, of Groton, Sept. 27, 1849, by Rev. Jabez S. Swan	1	87
BROOKS, Thomas, of Waterford, m. Susan **PACKER**, of Groton, July 3, 1836, by Rev. John G. Wightman	1	54
Thomas W., of Waterford, m. Marybe **TAYLOR**, of Groton, Apr. 28,1828, by N. S. Spaulding	1	27
BROWN, Abigail, d. [James & Abigail], b. Jan. 25, 1778	2	51

	Vol.	Page
BROWN, (cont.)		
Almira, m. Patrick **HOOKS**, b. of Groton, Feb. 27, 1831, by William M. Williams	1	37
Ann, [d. Gershom & Ann], b. Apr. 7, 1723	1	129
Anna, m. Richard **WILLIAMS**, Nov. 6, 1745	1	177
Ardelia, d. [Benjamin & Mary], b. Aug. 11, 1822	3	25
Avery, m. Anniss **HOLDREDGE**, b. of Groton, July 21, 1833, by John Spicer, J.P.	1	44
Benjamin, m. Mary A. **MIDDLETON**, b. of Groton, Dec. 30, 1821, by Roswell Burrows, Elder	1	5
Benjamin A., of Stonington, m. Julia **CRUMB**, of Groton, Jan. 5, 1851, by Rev. James Squier	1	91
Benjamin Warren, s. [Benjamin & Mary], b. May 19 1825	3	25
Benjamin Washington, s. Robert J. L. & Amy, b. Aug. 7, 1817	2	5
Christopher, s. [John & Rachel], b. Feb. 27, 1748	1	168
Christopher, m. Betsey **SPICER**, b. of Groton, Dec. 10, 1824, by Robert Avery, J.P.	1	14
Comfort, [s. Nathaniel & Anna], b. Oct. 11, 1718	1	118
Comfort William, m. Lydia Maria **FISH**, b. of Groton, June 5, 1831, by Rev. Roswell Burrows	1	37
Comstock, s. [John & Rachel], b. May 15, 1754	1	168
Cyrus, s. [James & Abigail], b. Oct. 12, 1783	2	51
Daniel, s. [John & Rachel], b. May 15, 1754	1	168
Delia, m. W[illia]m **BENTLEY**, b. of Groton, Oct. 26, 1842, by Ira R. Steward	1	67
Desire, d. [James & Abigail], b. Oct. 11, 1796	2	51
Dudley, of Stonington, m. Lucy Ann **BAILEY**, of Groton, Apr. 28, 1833, by Nathan Daboll, J.P.	1	43
Eleazer, s. [James & Abigail], b. July 16, 1780; d. July 19, 1785	2	51
Eleazer, s. [James & Abigail], b. Mar. 31, 1791	2	51
Elijah, s. Elijah & [E]unice, b. May 1, 1778	2	27
Elijah, m. [E]unice **MORGAN**, [ ]	2	27
Eliza, of Groton, m. John **LATHAM**, of Lebanon, Feb. 17, 1833, by John G. Wightman, Eld.	1	43
Elizabeth, m. Nehemiah **GALLUP**, Jan. 28, 1784 (1783?)	2	46
[E]unice, d. Elijah, b. Dec. 14, 1768	1	172
[E]unice, d. Elijah & [E]unice, b. Dec. 15, 1768	2	27
Eunice had s. Gardiner **PACKER**, b. July 15, 1798	2	61
Gershom, m. Ann **FOOT**, July 8, 1714	1	129
Gershom, [s. Gershom & Ann], b. May 8, 1717	1	129
Harriet, m. Alva **SAWYER**, Aug. 29, 1850, by Rev. W. Munger	1	89
Harriet N., of Groton, m. Nathan S. **HOLLOWAY**, of Stonington, May 15, 1842, by Rev. B. F. Hedden	1	66
Humphr[e]y, m. Mary **FANNING**, b. of Groton, Dec. 5, 1750, by William Williams, J.P.	1	176
James, s. Comfort & Temperance, b. Apr. 22, 1751; m. Abigail **BARNES**, Oct. 8, 1772	2	51
James, Jr., s. [James & Abigail], b. Dec. 18, 1773	2	51
John, m. Rachel **COMSTOCK**, Oct. [ ], 1740	1	168
John, s. [John & Rachel], b. Dec. 15, 1743	1	168
John, s. John & Experience, b. Mar. 13, 1797	2	54
Joseph, [s. Gershom & Ann], b. Mar. 7, 1719	1	129
Joseph, [s. Nathaniel & Anna], b. Nov. 16, 1720; d. Dec. 25, 1720	1	118

	Vol.	Page
BROWN, (cont.)		
Kingsland, s. [John & Rachel], b. Jan. 12, 1746	1	168
Lois, of Groton, m. John C. **DAVIS**, of Westerly, R.I., Jan. 20, 1822, by Rev. John G. Wightman	1	6
Louisa, m. Thomas **MAIN**, of N. Stonington, Apr. 20, 1806	2	94
Lucy T., of Groton, m. William **MORTON**, of Rochester, Oct. 22, 1846, by Rev. S. B. Bailey	1	77
Mary, d. Gershom & Ann, b. Sept. 16, 1715	1	129
Mary, m. William Johnson **BROWN**, b. of Groton, July 3, 1825, by Robert Avery, J.P.	1	17
Mary A., m. Thomas **RYAN**, b. residing in Groton, Apr. 30, 1838, by Nathan Daboll, J.P.	1	58
Mary Ann, m. Giles **WILLIAMS**, b. of Stonington, Aug. 5, 1833, by John G. Wightman, Eld.	1	44
Mary Elizabeth, d. Robert J. L. & Amy, b. June 6, 1820	2	5
Mary Ellen, d. [Benjamin & Mary], b. July 30, 1829	3	25
Mercy, Mrs., m. Nehemiah **GALLUP**, b. of Groton, Oct. 11, 1827, by William Williams, J.P.	1	25
Nancy, m. Nathan **BREWSTER**, b. of Groton, May 18, 1828, by William Williams, J.P.	1	27
Nathaniel, m. Anna **HAINS**, July 11, 1715, by Rev. Woodbridge	1	118
Nathaniel, s. Nathaniel & Anna, b. June 6, 1716	1	118
Nathaniel, 4th, m. Rhuhamah **HOLDREDGE**, b. of Groton, Jan. 2, 1803, by Amos Gere, J.P.	2	64
Nehemiah, s. [James & Abigail], b. Feb. 17, 1776	2	51
Orlando, s. [Benjamin & Mary], b. Apr. 13, 1827	3	25
Pardon T., m. Prudence **SPICER**, b. of Groton, July 31, 1842, by Ira R. Steward	1	66
Patty, of Stonington, m. John **SMITH**, of Groton, June 13, 1792, by Eleazer Brown, Elder	2	43
Peter, [s. Gershom & Ann], b. Mar. 15, 1721	1	129
Phebe, of Groton, m. Joseph **CASWELL**, of N. Stonington, Dec. 1, 1822, by Paris Hewitt, J.P.	1	9
Rachel, d. [John & Rachel], b. May 28, 1741	1	168
Rhoda E., of N. Stonington, m. Saunders **YORK**, of Hopkinton, R.I., Oct. 25, 1847, by Rev. Erastus Denison	1	79
Roswell, m. Catharine W. **CHESEBRO[UGH]**, b. of Groton, Mar. 17, 1844, by Rev. Erastus Denison	1	71
Roxany, m. John **BURROWS**, 2d, b. of Groton, Aug. 23, 1821, by Rev. Roswell Burrows	1	4
Sabra, of Groton, m. Jeremiah **WILCOX**, of Stonington, Dec. 11, 1831, by Robert S. Avery, J.P.	1	39
Sally, m. William **MAIN**, b. of Groton, Dec. 25, 1834, by Oliver Hewitt, J.P.	1	49
Sally Ann, of Groton, m. Silas **DEWEY**, of Lebanon, Oct. 20, 1828, by Rev. Roswell Burrows	1	29
Sarah E., of Groton, m. John Henry **JONES**, of N.Y., Sept. 3, 1848, by David Avery, Elder	1	82
Sarah S., m. Thomas W. **LAMPHEAR**, b. of Groton, Mar. 26, 1843, by Rev. Benjamin C. Phelps, of Mystic	1	68
W[illia]m, m. Nancy M. **HILL**, b. of Groton, May 11, 1848, by Rev. H. R. Knapp	1	84
William Johnson, m. Mary **BROWN**, b. of Groton, July 3, 1825, by Robert Avery, J.P.	1	17

	Vol.	Page
BROWNING, Abby Eliza, [d. William & Eliza A.], b. May 1, 1827	2	29
Catharine Augusta, [d. William & Eliza A.], b. Jan. 4, 1833	3	29
W[illia]m, m. Eliza A. **AVERELL**, May 14, 1826	3	29
William, m. Eliza Ann **AVERELL**, b. of Groton, May 24, 1826, by Ralph Hurlbutt, J.P.	1	20
William Franklin, [s. William & Eliza A.], b. July 23, 1830	2	29
BRUSH, Thomas, of Jamaica, L.I., m. Hannah P. **FISH**, of Groton, Oct. 24, 1843, by Ira R. Steward	1	70
BUCKLEY, Julia A., m. Albert F. **SMITH**, b. of Groton, Dec. 24, 1837, by Rev. John G. Wightman	1	57
BUDDINGTON, BUDINGTON, Adeline, m. Edwin **WHITE**, b. of Groton, Aug. 29, 1836, by Joseph Durfey, J.P.	1	55
Charles E., m. Louisa J. **HOLDREDGE**, b. of Groton, Jan. 1, 1854, by Geo[rge] H. Woodward	1	95
Edward, s. Walter & Johan[n]a, b. Sept. 16, 1708	1	113
Esh[h]er H., of Groton, m. John H. **WHEELER**, of Stonington, Nov. 22, 1821, by Caleb Avery, J.P.	1	5
Eunice, of Ledyard, m. John C. **BOLLES**, M.D., of Montville, Feb. 7, 1843, by Rev. Jared R. Avery	1	67
Joshua E., m. Delia Ann **MERRIT[T]**, b. of Groton, Aug. 4, 1839, by Rev. John G. Wightman	1	61
Julia, m. Giles **MORGAN**, b. of New London, Nov. 9,1826, by Rev. Ward Stafford, of New York	3	13
Leflet, s. Wallter & Johan[n]a, b. Mar. 4, 1710/11	1	113
Martha, of Groton, m. Albert S. **CHASE**, of Shelter Island, Aug. 21, 1842, by Rev. Erastus Denison	1	67
Martha Louisa, of Groton, m. Abraham **TOURTELETT**, of Dudley, Mass., Oct. 20, 1825, by Caleb Avery, J.P.	1	19
Ozias, s. Wallter & Johan[n]a, b. Dec. 7, 1712	1	113
Sidney O., of Groton, m. Sarah H. **KNOWLES**, of Groton, Feb. 7, 1850, by Rev. Nicholas T. Allen	1	87
Stephen, m. Caroline M. **RANDALL**, b. of Groton, Aug. 13, 1843, by Timothy Tuttle	1	69
Wallter, s. Wallter & Johan[n]a, b. Aug. 12, 1704	1	113
Waterman Z., m. Nancy M. **JEFFREY**, b. of Groton, Sept. 13, 1835, by Timothy Tuttle	1	51
BUFF, Elizabeth, m. Christopher **ALLYN**, Nov. 16, 1757	2	33
Mary, m. Samuel **DABOLL**, Nov. 3, 1742	2	25
BULKLEY, Anne, d. Lucy **WOOD**, b. Mar. 9, 1734	2	10
BURCH, [see also **BIRCH**], Coddington, m. Betsey **BURROWS**, [ ]	3	0
BURDICK, Caleb, of Plainfield, Ct., m. Sarah A. **DENISON**, of Groton, [Oct.] 23, [1853], by Rev. James M. Phillips	1	95
Catharine, b. Sept. 21, 1780, at Charlestown, R.I., m. Noyes **BARBER**, Dec. 13, 1801, at Groton	2	83
George F., of Norwich, m. Sabra Emeline **STRONG**, of Groton, Mar. 30, 1847, by Rev. Jared R. Avery	1	78
James P., of Westerly, R.I., m. Lucinda **MA[Y]NARD**, of Groton, Dec. 8, 1833, by John Brewster, J.P.	1	46
Staunton, of Hopkinton, R.I., m. Esther **HALL**, of Groton, Mar. 20, 1831, by Rev. Erastus Denison	1	37
BURNETT, BURNET, Richard, m. Sally G. **HALEY**, b. of Groton, Feb. 11, 1835, by John G. Wightman, Elder	1	49
Richard, m. Sally **HALEY**, d. Stephen & Lucy, [ ]	2	79

	Vol.	Page
BURROWS, Abigail, d. John & Lydia, b. July 19, 1712	1	115
Abigail, d. [John, Jr. & Desire], b. Mar. 7, 1742/3	1	176
Albert C., m. Betsey Ann **HALEY**, [d. Henry & Mary Ann], May 27, 1860	3	0
Almira J., of Groton, m. James W. **MILLER**, of New London, June 3, 1851, by Rev. Nicholas T. Allen	1	91
Ambrose H., s. [Ambrose H. & Ann], b. June 29, 1813	3	23
Ambrose H., m. Lucy E. **LATHAM**, b. of Groton, Sept. 3, 1837, by Nehemiah B. Cooke	1	57
Amos, s. John & Lydia, b. Aug. 6, 1714	1	115
Austin, m. Almira **HILL**, b. of Groton, May 21, 1826, by Nathan Daboll, J.P.	1	20
Benjamin, Jr., m. Sarah A. **HAMMOND**, b. of Groton, July 25, 1838, by Ira R. Steward	1	59
Benjamin, m. Mrs. Lucy C. **PERKINS**, b. of Groton, Nov. 10, 1844, by Rev. Simon B. Bailey	1	72
Benjamin, of Groton, m. Ann Maria **AVERY**, Oct. 23, 1854, by Rev. Isaac Cheesebrough	1	97
Betsey, m. Coddington **BIRCH**, b. of Groton, [Dec. (?)] 9, 1821, by John G. Wightman	1	5
Betsey, m. John **WILBUR**, b. of Groton, Aug. 1, 1829, by Roswell Fish, J.P.	1	31
Betsey, m. Coddington **BURCH**, [ ]	3	0
Burton, s. [Ambrose H. & Ann], b. Sept. 14, 1806	3	23
Caleb, m. Julia Ann **LEEDS**, b. of Groton, June 10, 1821, by John G. Wightman, Elder	1	3
Caleb, m. Julia **LEEDS**, [ ]	3	0
Caleb O., of Ledyard, m. Eliza J. **SMITH**, of Groton, July 23, 1845, by Rev. Erastus Denison	1	74
Calvin, m. Catharine **GATES**, b. of Groton, Apr. 11, 1843, by Ira R. Steward	1	68
Caroline E., m. Henry **DENISON**, b. of Groton, Aug. 29, 1841, by Benjamin C. Phelps	1	65
Charles, m. Emily **WHEELER**, [ ]	3	0
Charles C., s. [Guy E. & Fanny], b. Mar. 13, 1827	3	17
Charles H., m. Mary J. **DAVIS**, b. of Groton, Jan. 28, 1847, by Rev. Erastus Denison	1	77
Charles Henry, s. [Jonathan & Sarah], b. Nov. 21, 1823	3	22
Daniel, m. Wid. Abigail **PARKS**, b. of Groton, Jan. 23, 1825, by Roswell Fish, J.P.	1	16
Daniel E., s. [Guy E. & Fanny], b. Sept. 22, 1821	3	17
Desire, d. [John, Jr. & Desire], b. Mar. 11, 1738	1	176
Diana, of Groton, m. Silas B. **DENISON**, of Stonington, Aug. 20, 1836, by Rev. Erastus Denison	1	55
Edmund F., [s. Guy E. & Fanny], b. Apr. 11, 1829	3	17
Elam, s. John & Hannah, b. Sept. 6, 1769	2	8
Elias Rogers, s. [Jonathan & Sarah], b. July 17, 1828	3	22
Elisha, s. [Hubburd & Mary], b. Nov. 27, 1744	1	164
Emma J., m. Thomas E. **PARKER**, b. of Groton, July 4, 1849, by Rev. Simon B. Bailey	1	83
Enock, of Stonington, m. Caroline Hope **KING**, of Groton, Dec. 28, 1826, by Rev. Roswell Burrows	1	22
Esther, d. [Hubburd & Mary], b. Sept. 28, 1731	1	164

	Vol.	Page
BURROWS, (cont.)		
Eunice, m. Elam **ELDREDGE**, b. of Groton, Aug. 12, 1821, by Roswell Fish, J.P.	1	3
Eunice E., of Groton, m. Isaac W. **DENISON**, of Stonington, May 10, 1843, by Rev. Erastus Denison	1	68
Fanny, m. Ledyard **PARK[E]**, Sept. 23, 1838, by Rev. John G. Wightman	1	59
Fanny S., d. [Guy E. & Fanny], b. July 17, 1815	3	17
Frances, m. Hezekiah **PARK[E]**, b. of Groton, July 2, 1837, by John G. Wightman, Elder	1	57
Frances, m. Frederick D. **CLIFT**, b. of Groton, July 11, 1837, by John G. Wightman, Elder	1	57
Frances, m. Horace **CLIFT**, b. of Groton, Oct. 25, 1848, by Rev. Simon B. Bailey	1	81
Frances S., m. John **LEWEY**, b. of Groton, Dec. 8, 1839, by Ira R. Steward	1	62
Frances Sarah, d. [Jonathan & Sarah], b. Sept. 21, 1820	3	22
George, s. Paul & Catharine, b. Oct. 15, 1795	2	12
George S., s. [Guy E. & Fanny], b. Mar. 20, 1812	3	17
Han[n]ah, d. John & Lydia, b. Jan. 23, 1709	1	11
Hannah, d. [Hubburd & Mary], b. Nov. 21, 1733	1	164
Hannah, m. Franklin **GALLUP**, b. of Groton, Aug. 18, 1834, by Rev. Ira R. Steward	1	47
Hub[b]ard, s. John & Lydia, b. Feb. 10, 1707; d. Aug. 2, 1795	1	115
Hubbard, s. [Hubburd & Mary], b. June 26, 1739	1	164
Hubburd, m. Mary **DENISON**, [ ]	1	164
Hubbard, m. Amy **MARTIN**, [ ]; m. Mary Esther **WHEELER**	3	0
James, s. [John, Jr. & Desire], b. Apr. 11, 1740	1	176
Jerusha Avery, d. [Russell & Jerusha], b. June 24, 1795	2	43
John, m. Lydia **HUB[B]ARD**, Oct. 14, 1700	1	115
John, s. John & Lydia, b. Nov. 14, 1701	1	115
John, Jr., m. Desire **PACKER**, July 1, 1731	1	176
John, s. [John, Jr. & Desire], b. Oct. 9, 1734	1	176
John, 2d, m. Roxany **BROWN**, b. of Groton, Aug. 23, 1821, by Rev. Roswell Burrows	1	4
John Baldwin, m. Betsey **HALEY**	3	0
John Baldwin, m. Betsey **HALEY**, d. Caleb & Mary, [ ]	3	0
John Calvin, m. Mary A. **NILES**, Oct. 7, 1838, by Rev. John G. Wightman	1	60
John S., m. Caroline **NILES**, b. of Groton, Aug. 10, 1831, by John G. Wightman, Eld.	1	38
John S., m. Cylora A. **WELLS**, [ ]	3	0
Jonathan, s. [Hubburd & Mary], b. May 13, 1752	1	164
Joseph, m. Mrs. Mary **HILL**, b. of Groton, May 29, 1836, by Rev. Roswell Burrows	1	54
Joseph, s. [John, Jr. & Desire], b. Aug. 28, 1736	1	176
Julia Ann, of Groton, m. Albert G. **SMITH**, of Rochester, N.Y., May 12, 1830, by Rev. Roswell Burrows	1	34
Katharine, m. Charles **WOLF**, b. of Groton, June 12, 1833, by John G. Wightman, Eld.	1	44
Latham Avery, s. [Russell & Jerusha], b. Aug. 30, 1792	2	43
Lemuel, s. Samuel & Marcy, b. Jan. 13, 1709	1	110
Lemuel, Capt., m. Experience **WOODWARD**, Aug. 12, 1832, by Rev. Erastus Denison	1	40
Lorenzo, s. [Roswell & Jerusha], b. Mar. 15, 1805	2	43

	Vol.	Page
BURROWS, (cont.)		
Lorenzo, of Albecum, Orleans Co., N.Y., m. Louisa **LORD**, of Groton, May 11, 1830, by Rev. Roswell Burrows	1	34
Lucretia, d. [John, Jr. & Desire], b. Mar. 20, 1748	1	176
Lucy, m. William **ELDREDGE**, b. of Groton, Aug. 28, 1839, by Ira R. Steward	1	61
Lucy A., d. [Guy E. & Fanny], b. Jan. 18, 1819	3	17
Lucy E., Mrs., of Groton, m. Rev. D. M. **MILLER**, Mar. 5, 1848, by Rev. H. R. Knapp	1	84
Lucy Latham, d. [Roswell & Jerusha], b. Jan. 19, 1801	2	43
Lura, m. Joseph L. **DENISON**, b. of Groton, Feb. 27, 1845, by Rev. Erastus Denison	1	72
Lydia, d. John & Lydia, b. Apr. 19, 1703	1	115
Lydia, d. [John, Jr. & Desire], b. Jan. 20, 1743/4	1	176
Mary, d. John & Lydia, b. Nov. 4, 1704	1	115
Mary, d. [John, Jr. & Desire], b. June 17, 1732	1	176
Mary, d. [Hubburd & Mary], b. Oct. 7, 1749	1	164
Mary, m. David **SCOTT**, Apr. 23, 1848, by Rev. H. R. Knapp	1	84
Mary A., m. George W. **MORGAN**, b. of Groton, Feb. 18, 1849, by Rev. S. B. Bailey	1	82
Mary Ann, d. [Guy E. & Fanny], b. Sept. 24, 1824	3	17
Mary Ann, m. Henry **HALEY**, b. of Groton, June 15, 1834, by John G. Wightman	1	47
Mary Ann, m. Henry **HALEY**, June 15, 1834	3	0
Mary Ann, m. Henry **HALEY**, [ ]	3	0
Mary C., m. John D. **DENISON**, May 10, 1853, by J. W. Holman	1	95
Mary Esther, d. Roswell & Jerusha, b. Apr. 7, 1809	2	43
Nancy, m. George **WOODWARD**, b. of Groton, Aug. 25, 1830, by Rev. John G. Wightman	1	34
Nancy, m. Richard **POTTER**, b. of Groton, Sept. 19, 1830, by Rev. Erastus Denison	1	35
Nathan, s. [John, Jr. & Desire], b. May 17, 1746	1	176
Phebe, d. [John, Jr. & Desire], b. Mar. 29, 1750	1	176
Phebe H., of Groton, m. Albert B. **LAMB**, of New London, Mar. 7, 1850, by Rev. H. R. Knapp	1	88
Phebe T., of Groton, m. Isaac D. **MINER**, of Stonington, Apr. 28, 1833, by Rev. Erastus Denison	1	43
Polly, m. Elias **MINER**, b. of Groton, Jan. 28, 1827, by Nathan Daboll, J.P.	1	23
Priscilla A., m. Simeon **HALEY**, b. of Groton, Apr. 16, 1837, by John G. Wightman, Elder	1	56
Prescilla A., m. Simeon **HALLY**	3	0
Prudence, d. [Jonathan & Sarah], b. Dec. 14, 1825	3	22
Prudence, m. William **ASHBEY**, b. of Groton, Aug. 10, 1843, by Rev. Charles C. Lewis	1	69
Prudence, unmarried [ ]	3	0
Rhodes, m. Marinda **BENNETT**, b. of Groton, June 21, 1840, by Charles Bennett, J.P.	1	63
Robert, m. Mary **CULLVER**, Aug. 6, 1712	1	125
Roswell S., m. Mary Ann **RANDALL**, b. of Groton, Jan. 16, 1822, by Roswell Burrows, Elder	1	6
Roswell S., m. Clarissa **EDG[E]COMB**, b. of Groton, Oct. 13, 1844, by Rev. Augustus Bolles	1	72
Roswell Smith, s. [Roswell & Jerusha], b. Feb. 22, 1798	2	43

	Vol.	Page
BURROWS, (cont.)		
Rufus C., m. Frances L. **SISSON**, July 1, 1850, at Porterville, by Rev. W. Munger	1	89
Russell, m. Jerusha **AVERY**, Jan. 28, 1790	2	43
Sally, m. Charles **STARK**, [ ]	3	0
Sally, m. Caleb **HALEY**, s. Caleb & Mary, [ ]	3	0
Samuel, m. Marcy **CHESTER**, Nov. 21, 1706	1	110
Samuel, s. Samuel & Marcy, b. Jan. 11, 1707/8	1	110
Sarah, d. [Hubburd & Mary], b. Aug. 16, 1747	1	164
Sarah A., of Rochester, N.Y., m. William R. **CROMWELL**, of Groton, May 29, 1850, by Rev. Nicholas T. Allen	1	88
Sarah Ann, m. Nathan **NOYES**, Jr., Mar. 18, 1830, by Erastus Denison, Minister	1	33
Sarah E., m. Franklin **GALLUP**, b. of Groton, Apr. 9, 1843, by Ira R. Steward	1	68
Seth W., m. Ann C. **PARK[E]**, b. of Groton, Jan. 27, 1849, by Rev. H. R. Knapp	1	84
Silame, d. [Silas & Hannah], b. June 20, 1741	1	180
Silas, s. John & Lydia, b. Oct. 4, 1710	1	115
Silas, of Groton, m. Hannah **GORE**, of Preston, July 17, 1740	1	180
Silas, s. Paul & Katharine, b. July 24, 1782	2	34
Stephen, lost at sea	3	0
Waitey L., unmarried	3	0
William, s. [Jonathan & Sarah], b. Nov. 13, 1818	3	22
W[illia]m, m. Eliza **DAVIS**, b. of Groton, Dec. 13, 1840, by Ira R. Steward	1	64
William T., m. Almira W. **SMITH**, b. of Groton, July 4, 1833, by Ira R. Steward, Eld.	1	44
BUSTON, James, s. Sam[ue]ll & Mary, b. Jan. 19, 1708	1	117
Mary, d. Sam[ue]ll & Mary, b. Apr. 11, 1711	1	117
Samuell, m. Mary **DAVIS**, Apr. 15, 1706	1	117
Simeon, s. Sam[ue]ll & Mary, b. Apr. 22, 1716	1	117
BUTTOLPH, Jonathan, [s. Joseph & Hannah], b. Dec. 27, 1721	II	369
Joseph, m. Hannah **STARR**, Mar. 17, 1719	II	369
Mary, d. Joseph & Hannah, b. July 3, 1720	II	369
William, [s. Joseph & Hannah], b. Nov. 11, 1723	II	369
BUTTON, Abigail, [d. Asa & Abigail], b. July 16, 1783; d. Dec. 1, 1868	1	192
Asa, s. Jedediah, of Groton, m. Abigail **CULVER**, d. Joseph, of Groton, May 29, 1770	1	192
Asa, Jr., [s. Asa & Abigail], b. Apr. 8, 1781; d. Jan. 3, 1795	1	192
Asa, b. May 13, 1745; d. June 2, 1826	1	192
Cynthia, [d. Asa & Abigail], b. Feb. 7, 1771	1	192
Hannah, [d. Asa & Abigail], b. Apr. 25, 1775	1	192
Joseph, [s. Asa & Abigail], b. Feb. 3, 1773	1	192
Polly, [d. Asa & Abigail], b. Jan. 20, 1778	1	192
Zeruiah, m. Daniel **LAMB**, Oct. 5, 1727	1	192
CAFLON, Osmond P., m. Julia A. **MORGAN**, Nov. 6, 1833, by Joseph Durfey, J.P.	1	45
CALLAGHAN, Betsey, m. Rev. David N. **BENTLEY**, b. of Norwich, July 31, 1854, at Mystic River Village, by Rev. Ebenezer Blake	1	96
CAMPBELL, CAMPBEL, Agness, d. Daniel & Elizabeth, b. Feb. 21, 1774	1	157
Elizabeth, d. [Daniel & Elizabeth], b. Sept. [ ], 1775	1	158
Jennet, of Voluntown, m. Joseph **WHIPPLE**, of Groton, Dec. 10, 1772	2	1

	Vol.	Page
CAPRON, CAPORN, Clarissa G., of Preston, m. Joseph T. **TUTTLE**, of Groton, Sept. 5, 1830, by W[illia]m M. Williams, J.P.	1	35
Elizabeth, m. Thomas **FANNING**, July 26, 1744	1	182
Giles, s. [Walter & Hannah], b. Mar. 22, 1747/8	1	179
James, s. [Walter & Hannah], b. Apr. 14, 1746	1	179
Sabra, d. Giles & Lucy, b. Aug. 16, 1769	2	12
Sabra, m. Nathan **MORGAN**, Nov. 27, 1788	2	88
Samuel, s. Walter, b. Sept. 30, 1723	1	106
Sibel, d. Giles [& Lucy], b. Feb. 25, 1771	2	12
Sibell, of Preston, m. Gurdon **GALLUP**, of Groton, Feb. 15, 1795, by Elias Brown, J.P.	2	77
Simeon, s. [Walter & Hannah], b. Mar. 29, 1750	1	179
Walter, m. Hannah **WENTWORTH**, Oct. 28, 1739	1	179
CARD, Ruth, m. Samuel **WHIPPLE**, Nov. 15, 1720	1	124
CARPENTER, Mary, d. Jeremiah & Abigail, b. Aug. 5, 1732	1	135
CARTER, George J., of R.I., m. Lucy A. **BREED**, of Mass., Mar. 15, 1846, by Rev. William C. Walker	1	75
CASWELL, Joseph, of N. Stonington, m. Phebe **BROWN**, of Groton, Dec. 1, 1822, by Paris Hewitt, J.P.	1	9
CASWINE, David, m. Esther **DAVIS**, b. of Groton, May 14, 1826, by Robert S. Avery, J.P.	1	20
CHAFFE, W[illia]m O., m. Louisa H. **MUNGER**, June 19, 1850, at Porterville, by Rev. W. Munger	1	89
CHAMPLAIN, Abby, [d. John & Sally], b. Mar. 7, 1809	3	6
Clarissa, [d. John & Sally], b. Feb. 17, 1807	3	6
Isaac S., [s. John & Sally], b. Dec. 17, 1810	3	6
John J., [s. John & Sally], b. Mar. 21, 1803	3	6
Mary Ann , [d. John & Sally], b. Sept. 7, 1814	3	6
Oliver, of Preston, m. Lydia **STANTON**, of Groton, Oct. 12, 1823, by Jona[than] Brewster, J.P.	1	10
Oliver W., [s. John & Sally], b. Feb. 2, 1805	3	6
Thomas A., [s. John & Sally], b. July 18, 1816	3	6
Thomas W., [s. John & Sally], b. Sept. 9, 1817	3	6
William M., [s. John & Sally], b. Dec. 18, 1812	3	6
CHAPMAN, Abel, s. Joshua & Sarah, b. Dec. 11, 1759	2	17
Abel A., s. [Avery & Welthian], b. Oct. 11, 1805	2	73
Abiah, m. Zephaniah **WATROUS**, b. living in Groton, [ ], by Zephaniah Watrous. Recorded Oct. 15, 1827	1	25
Amos, [s. William & Mary], b. May 18 1721	1	108
Amos, s. William & Mary, b. May 18, 1721	1	155
Amos, s. Joshua & Sarah, b. Oct. 26, 1761	2	17
Amos, m. Rispah **HURLBUTT**, Feb. 26, 1786	2	44
Anna, d. [Joseph & Anna], b. Feb. 13, 1757	1	161
Avery, [s. Joshua & Sarah], b. Nov. 2, 1781	2	17
Avery, m. Welthian **THOMAS**, b. of Groton, Nov. 20, 1804, by Amos Geer, J.P.	2	73
Barnabas, s. [Thomas & Abigail], b. Feb. 4, 1723; d. Mar. 6, 1723	1	126
Betsey, m. Nathan **LAMB**, b. of Groton, Oct. 14, 1821, by Rev. Levi Nelson, of Lisbon	1	4
Caleb, s. William & Mary, b. Dec. 19, 1735	1	155
Caleb, m. Freelove **LAMB**, b. of Groton, May 4, 1760, by Timothy Wightman, Elder	2	26
Caleb, Jr., s. [Caleb & Freelove], b. Jan. 2, 1763	2	26

	Vol.	Page
CHAPMAN, (cont.)		
Caroline B., of Groton, m. Reuben P. **SMITH**, of Waterford, Aug. 12, 1827, at the dwelling of Noah Chapman, by Rev. Reuben Palmer	1	24
Christopher, of Bozrah, m. Clementine **STEDMAN**, of Groton, Feb. 20, 1833, by Nathan Daboll, J.P.	1	42
Cynthia M., d. of William, m. Leonord C. **BAKER**, b. of Groton, Feb. 16, 1845, by Belton A. Copp, J.P.	1	72
David, s. William & Mary, b. [ ], 1719	1	108
David, s. William & Mary, b. Apr. 3, 1719	1	155
Eber, s. [Joseph & Anna], b. May 16, 1770	1	161
Elias, m. Clarissa **AVERY**, b. of Groton, Aug. 26, 1820, by Timothy Tuttle	1	1
Elizabeth H., of Groton, m. William A. **SPICER**, Oct. 31, 1852, by Rev. Nicholas T. Allen	1	94
Elizabeth M., m. Russell **FISH**, Sept. 20, 1838, by Rev. John G. Wightman	1	59
Elie, s. [Joseph & Anna], b. Oct. 20, 1759	1	161
Ephraim A., [s. Jesse & Lydia], b. Apr. 9, 1835	3	5
Est[h]er, d. [Joseph & Anna], b. Feb. 6, 1764	1	161
Esther, m. Russell **FISH**, b. of Groton, July 16, 1836, by Ralph Hurlbutt, J.P.	1	54
Eunice, d. Joshua & Sarah, b. May 8, 1768	2	17
Eunice, m. Ephraim **WALEY**, June 16, 1793	2	43
Eunice, m. William **CRUMB**, b. of Groton, Oct. 10, 1832, by John G. Wightman, Eld.	1	41
Eunice, of Groton, m. Levi **STANDISH**, of Preston, Aug. 4, 1834, by John Brewster, J.P.	1	48
Ezra, s. William & Mary, b. Mar. 15, 1737/8	1	155
Francina, m. Isaac **SPICER**, of Preston, Feb. 25, 1827, by Zelotes Fuller, Minister	1	23
Grace, [d. Jonathan & Hannah], b. Sept. 5, 1729	1	132
Hannah, m. Ephraim **SMITH**, Apr. 12, 1722	1	102
Hannah, d. Jonathan & Hannah, b. Oct. 11, 1725	1	132
Hannah, d. Joshua & Sarah, b. Aug. 7, 1770	2	17
Ira H., [s. Jesse & Lydia], b. [ ]	3	5
Isaac, s. William & Mary, b. Dec. 18, 1740	1	155
Isaac A., [s. Jesse & Lydia], b. [ ]	3	5
Jesse, m. Lydia **ALLYN**, b. of Groton, Nov. 27, 1823, by Timothy Tuttle	1	11
Jesse, m. Lydia **ALLEN**	3	5
John, s. Thomas & Abigail, b. June 27, 1716	1	126
John, s. Levy & Elizabeth, b. Apr. 10, 1775	2	8
John, Jr., m. Nancy **MIERS**, b. of Groton, Mar. 1, 1835, by W[illia]m M. Williams, J.P.	1	50
Jonathan, m. Hannah **BA[I]LEY**, Dec. 26, 1723	1	132
Jonathan, [s. Jonathan & Hannah], b. Nov. 2, 1727	1	132
Joseph, [s. William & Mary], b. May 2, 1731	1	108
Joseph, s. William & Mary, b. May 2, 1731	1	155
Joseph, s. Joseph & Anna, b. Dec. 18, 1753	1	161
Joshua, [s. William & Mary], b. Mar. 22, 1723	1	108
Joshua, s. William & Mary, b. Mar. 22, 1733	1	155
Joshua*, m. Sarah **LEF[F]INGWELL**, b. of Groton, Oct. 18, 1748, by Rev. Jacob Johnson (*First written "Joseph". Changed by L.B.B.)	2	17
Joshua, [s. Joshua & Sarah], b. Feb. 5, 1776	2	17
Joshua, of Groton, m. Jemima **STEAD**, of Swanzey, Jan. 27, 1783, in Swanzey, by Russell Mason, J.P.	2	2

	Vol.	Page
CHAPMAN, (cont.)		
Joshua, m. Hannah **BAILEY**, b. of Groton, Dec. 13, 1805, by Amos Geer, J.P.	2	75
Kezia, [d. William & Mary], b. May 31, 1726	1	108
Keziah, d. William & Mary, b. May 31, 1726	1	155
Letilia F., m. Christopher G. **RODMAN**, b. of Preston, Sept. 24, 1833, by John Brewster, J.P.	1	45
Levi, 2d, m. Loanna **LAMB**, b. of Groton, Dec. 2, 1827, by W[illia]m Williams, J.P.	1	26
Lucy, d. Joshua & Sarah, b. Jan. 31, 1766	2	17
Lucy, m. Ebenezer **GERE**, Apr. 27, 1786	2	42
Mary, m. Joseph **BAILEY**, Feb. 20, 1718	1	121
Mary, m. Joseph **BA[I]LEY**, Jr., Feb. 20, 1718/19	1	148
Mary, [d. William & Mary], b. Oct. 13, 1723	1	108
Mary, d. William & Mary, b. Oct. 13, 1723	1	155
Mary, [d. Jonathan & Hannah], b. Oct. 3, 1733	1	132
Mary, m. John **SPICER**, Oct. 25, 1744	1	181
Mary, d. [Joseph & Anna], b. June 9, 1766	1	161
Mary, m. Amos **HEATH**, b. of Groton, Apr. 10, 1815	3	14
Mary A., of Lee, Mass., m. William L. **CULVER**, of Tyringham, Feb. 9, 1833	1	191
Mary S., of Groton, m. Roswell **SMITH**, of Waterford, Oct. 13, 1826, by John G. Wightman, Eld.	1	19
Mercy, m. Thomas **MULKEY**, Jr., b. of Groton, Feb. 9, 1823, by John Brewster, J.P.	1	9
Nathan, m. Mary **WATROUS**, b. of Groton, Mar. 1, 1829, by Zephaniah Watrous	1	30
Nathaniel, s. [Joseph & Anna], b. Feb. 4, 1762	1	161
Ori, m. Content **WHIPPLE**, Aug. 24, 1834, by Zephaniah Watrous	1	47
Perez, m. Caroline **PALMER**, b. of Groton, Oct. 28, 1835, by Rev. Roswell Burrows	1	52
Prudence M., m. Lorenzo D. **PERKINS**, b. of Groton, May 11, 1852, by Rev. Nicholas T. Allen	1	93
Robert, s. Levy & Elizabeth, b. Feb. 1, 1784	2	8
Rufus, s. [Joseph & Anna], b. May 14, 1773	1	161
Ruth, d. [Joseph & Anna], b. May 14, 1773	1	161
Sally, m. Allyn **AVERY**, b. of Groton, June 22, 1828, by Ralph Hurlbutt, J.P.	1	28
Samuel, s. [Thomas & Abigail], b. Mar. 22, 1720	1	126
Samuel, m. Annass **LESTER**, b. of Groton, Nov. 13, 1814, by W[illia]m Robinson, J.P., in Stonington	2	80
Samuel, m. Abiah **CHROUGH**, b. living in Groton, Oct. 14, 1827, by Zephaniah Watrous	1	25
Sarah, d. Thomas & Abigail, b. July 7, 1718	1	126
Sarah, d. Joshua & Sarah, b. Dec. 18, 1763	2	17
Sarah, d. [Amos & Rispah], b. May 25, 1787	2	44
Seth, s. [Thomas & Abigail], b. July 12, 1724; d. July 29, 1724	1	126
Sibel, of Groton, m. Giles **STAPLINGS**, of Salem, Jan. 27, 1833, by W[illia]m M. Williams, J.P.	1	42
Simeon, m. Ursula M. **ROGERS**, b. of Groton, Mar. 14, 1824, by Timothy Tutle	1	12
Solomon, m. Eliza **HAZEN**, b. of Groton, Nov. 2, 1823, by John Brewster, J.P.	1	11

	Vol.	Page
CHAPMAN, (cont.)		
Theophilus Avery, s. Elias & Clara, b. May 12, 1821	3	3
We[a]lthy, [d. Joshua & Sarah], b. Sept. 22, 1778	2	17
William, m. Mercy **STODDARD**, Jan. 8, 1718	1	108
William, m. Mary **STOD[D]ARDS**, Jan. 8, 1718/19	1	155
William, [s. William & Mary], b. Aug. 29, 1728	1	108
William, s. William & Mary, b. Aug. 29, 1728	1	155
Zip[p]orah, [d. Joshua & Sarah], b. Jan. 25, 1773	2	17
CHAPPELL, **CHAPEL**, Betsey, m. Griswold **ALLYN**, b. of Groton, Mar. 4, 1821, by Ralph Hurlbutt, J.P.	1	3
Edward, m. Mrs. Sophia **SLATE**, Feb. 25, 1839, by Rev. John G. Wightman	1	60
Joseph, s. Samuel & Dorothy, b. Nov. 22, 1740	1	147
Polly, m. James **NOYES**, b. of Groton, Dec. 2, 1827, by Rodman Niles, J.P.	1	26
Prudence, m. Joseph M. **ALLYN**, b. of Groton, Mar. 25, 1827, by Ralph Hurlbutt, J.P.	1	23
Sally, m. Elisha **LAMB**, b. of Groton, Mar. 25, 1827, by Ralph Hurlbutt, J.P.	1	23
Samuel, s. Samuel & Dorothy, b. Nov. 14, 1733	1	147
Samuel, m. Dorothy **YEAMAN**, Dec. 3, 1737	1	147
Sarah, m. Thomas **ROATH**, Feb. 26, 1719	1	129
CHASE, Albert S., of Shelter Island, m. Martha **BUD[D]INGTON**, of Groton, Aug. 21, 1842, by Rev. Erastus Denison	1	67
CHEATS, Mary Angeline, of Groton, m. Daniel **HULL**, of S. Kingston, R.I., Jan. 16, 1848, by Rev. Erastus Denison	1	80
Prudence, of Groton, m. Henry **HENDERSON**, of Stonington, Mar. 6, 1825, by Nathan Daball, J.P.	1	16
CHESEBROUGH, **CHESEBRO**, **CHEESEBOROUGH**, **CHEESEBROUGH**		
Almira, of Groton, m. George W. **DENISON**, of Stonington, Aug. 19, 1838, by Ira. R. Steward	1	59
Amos, of Stonington, m. Eunice D. **GATES**, of Groton, Sept. 24, 1851, by Rev. Franklin A. Slater	1	92
Andrew, m. Betsey **LEWIS**, b. of Stonington, Mar. 21, 1838, by Rev. John G. Wightman	1	58
Andrew, of Groton, m. Nancy **WILCOX**, of Stonington, July 14, 1847, by Rev. H. R. Knapp	1	83
Catharine W., m. Roswell **BROWN**, b. of Groton, Mar. 17, 1844, by Rev. Erastus Denison	1	71
Charles H., of Stonington, m. Prudence **POTTER**, of Groton, Oct. 19, 1844, by Rev. Simon B. Bailey	1	72
Daniel, Jr., m. Zerviah **PACKER**, b. of Groton, Sept. 17, 1820, by Rev. John G. Wightman	1	2
Dudley E., m. Idutha **WILCOX**, of Stonington, Dec. 7, 1848, by Rev. H. R. Knapp	1	84
Edmund, of Stonington, m. Nancy **CLIFT**, of Groton, Sept. 30, 1840, by Rev. Erastus Denison	1	63
Elihu, m. Mary Ann **WILBUR**, b. of Groton, Nov. 13, 1842, by Ira. R. Steward	1	67
Eliza, of Groton, m. Frederick **STORER**, of Mansfield, Apr. 29, 1822, by Rev. John G. Wightman	1	6
Johnathan, of Stonington, m. Mrs. Sally **YEOMAN**, of Groton, Nov. 9, 1849, by Henry W. Avery, J.P.	1	86
Phebe A., of Stonington, m. Reuben **BENNET[T]**, July 9, 1848, by Rev. H. R. Knapp	1	84
Prudence, m. John **STANTON**, Feb. 27, 1736/7	1	181

	Vol.	Page
CHESEBROUGH, CHESEBRO, CHEESEBOROUGH, CHEESEBROUGH, (cont.)		
Sarah, m. James **GEER**, Nov. 27, 1739	1	179
CHESTER, Adelia P., m. George W. **CHIPMAN**, b. of Groton, June 15, 1845, by Rev. Simon B. Bailey	1	73
Adeline, d. [Charles & Elizabeth], b. June 22, 1825	3	22
Albert, s. [Nathan & Abigail], b. Mar. 29, 1811	3	23
Albert, m. Maria **ING[RA]HAM**, b. of Groton, Oct. 6, 1833, by Rev. Ira R. Stewart	1	45
Amanda Malvina, d. [Benjamin & Caroline], b. July 18 1831	3	26
Amos Morgan, s. [Benjamin & Caroline], b. Mar. 27, 1833	3	26
Ann Maria, m. Reuben **KELLEY**, b. of Groton, May 20, 1844, by Rev. Jared R. Avery	1	71
Asa P., m. Mary A. **MORGAN**, b. of Groton, July 29, 1832, by Rev. Roswell Burrows	1	40
Asa Packer, twin with Eldredge, [s. Nathan & Abigail], b. Aug. 30, 1804	3	23
Benajah, s. John & Mary, b. [ ]	1	108
Benjamin, Capt., m. Caroline **MORGAN**, b. of Groton, Dec. 25, 1828, by Rev. Roswell Burrows	1	29
Braddock, of Groton, m. Joanna **BAILEY**, of New London, Apr. 14, 1829, by John G. Wightman, Eld.	1	30
Catharine, d. John & Mary, b. June 20, 1736	1	108
Charles, s. [Nathan & Abigail], b. Feb. 25, 1793	3	23
Charles, m. Betsey **WILBUR**, b. of Groton, Sept. 9, 1821, by John G. Wightman, Elder	1	4
Charles W., m. Mary Ann **WILLIAMS**, b. of Groton, July 15, 1849, by Rev. Jared R. Avery	1	85
Daniel, s. [Nathan & Abigail], b. Apr. 20, 1803	3	23
Edwin, m. Henrietta C. **BARBER**, of Groton, July 16, 1823, by Timothy Tuttle	1	10
Edwin B., m. Nancy **FENNER**, May 1, 1845, at Rev. R. Russell's house, by Rev. R. Russell	1	73
Elbridge, m. Lucy **CHIPMAN**, Sept. 7, 1826, by John G. Wightman, Eld.	1	21
Eldredge, twin with Asa Packer, [s. Nathan & Abigail], b. Aug. 30, 1804	3	23
Eldredge P., m. Mary A. **CHESTER**, b. of Groton, Apr. 13, 1831, by Rev. Roswell Burrows	1	37
Elijah, s. [Nathan & Abigail], b. Jan. 14, 1797	3	23
Eliza, m. Henry **SMITH**, b. of Groton, June 29, 1828, by Nathan Daboll, J.P.	1	28
Ellen Caroline, d. [Benjamin & Caroline], b. July 21, 1835	3	26
Emily, d. [Nathan & Abigail], b. Nov. 18, 1800	3	23
Emily, m. Francis **INGHAM**, Sept. 11, 1825, by John G. Wightman, Eld.	1	18
Eunice W., m. William P. **MORGAN**, b. of Groton, Apr. 14, 1831, by Rev. Roswell Burrows	1	37
Fanny, m. Thomas **CHESTER**, b. of Groton, Mar. 31, 1830, by Timothy Tuttle	1	33
Hubbard, m. Adaline **CROMWELL**, b. of Groton, Jan. 21, 1831, by Rev. Erastus Denison	1	36
Hubbard, of Groton, m. Julia A. **BAKER**, of Groton, Apr. 4, 1849, by Rev. Nicholas T. Allen	1	86
James, s. John & Mary, b. Mar. 4, 1727	1	108
James, m. Thankfull **PACKER**, Oct. 17, 1750	1	182
James, s. [James & Thankfull], b. July 18, 1751	1	182
John, m. Mary **STARR**, Nov. 1, 1716	1	108
John, s. John & Mary, b. Sept. 9, 1717	1	108

	Vol.	Page
CHESTER, (cont.)		
John, m. Sarah **REED**, b. of Groton, Aug. 17, 1829, by Joseph Durfey, J.P.	1	31
Joseph, s. John & Mary, b. Mar. 6, 1730	1	108
Julia, m. Willis **CLARK**, b. of Groton, Aug. 18, 1839, by Rev. Jared R. Avery	1	61
Levi, s. John & Mary, b. July 25, 1739	1	108
Marcy, m. Samuel **BURROWS**, Nov. 21, 1706	1	110
Mary, b. Nov. 19, 1780	2	83
Mary, m. Moses **ASHBY**, b. of Groton, Sept. 25, 1820, by Rev. Roswell Burrows	1	10
Mary, m. Oliver **PERKINS**, b. of Groton, Dec. 3, 1832, by Nathan Daboll, J.P.	1	41
Mary A., m. Eldredge P. **CHESTER**, b. of Groton, Apr. 13, 1831, by Rev. Roswell Burrows	1	37
Mary Jane, m. Richard P. **BAKER**, b. of Groton, Sept. 30, 1849, by Rev. Jared R. Avery	1	85
Nathan, s. [Nathan & Abigail], b. May 16, 1795	3	23
Nicholas Starr, s. [Benjamin & Caroline], b. Oct. 3, 1829	3	26
Simeon, s. John & Mary, b. Mar. 20, 1733	1	108
Simeon, Jr., m. Eveline **FISH**, b. of Groton, Aug. 21, 1823, by Roswell Burrows, Min.	1	10
Susan E., of Groton, m. Charles **GILBERT**, of Stonington, Jan. 30, 1854, by G. H. Woodward	1	96
Thomas, m. Fanny **CHESTER**, b. of Groton, Mar. 31, 1830, by Timothy Tuttle	1	33
Thomas, s. John & Mary, b. [ ]	1	108
William E., m. Henrietta **RATHBURN**, b. of Groton, July 10, 1831, by Rev. Roswell Burrows	1	37
William E., m. Desire **RATHBURN**, b. of Groton, Mar. 23, 1842, by Caleb M. Williams, J.P.	1	66
William Pitt, s. [Benjamin & Caroline], b. Mar. 27, 1838	3	26
William Wilbur, s. [Charles & Elizabeth], b. July 22, 1822	3	22
CHIPMAN, Abby, of Groton, m. George **GRINMON**, of Hopkinton, R.I., Feb. 10, 1828, by N. S. Spalding	1	27
Almira, m. William **BAKER**, b. of Groton, May 30, 1830, by Rev. John G. Wightman	1	34
Caroline E., m. W[illia]m E. **WILCOX**, b. of Groton, Sept. 1, 1840, by Rev. John G. Wightman	1	63
Catharine, of Groton, m. Ezra Moore **KEENEY**, of Montville, Jan. 25, 1835, by John G. Wightman, Elder	1	48
Elisha, m. Sally **GUARD**, b. of Groton, May 17, 1829, by Rev. John G. Wightman	1	31
Eliza, m. Thomas FRANKLIN, b. of Groton, Sept. 10, 1826, by Rev. Roswell Burrows	1	22
Eliza Ann, d. [Perez & Dorcas], b. Jan. 14, 1808	3	25
Elvira, m. Holdthrop **PARK[E]**, b. of Groton, May 20, 1836, by Roswell Fish, J.P.	1	54
George W., s. [Perez & Dorcas], b. July 16, 1816	3	25
George W., m. Adelia P. **CHESTER**, b. of Groton, June 15, 1845, by Rev. Simon B. Bailey	1	73
Hannah, m. James **WHEELER**, b. of Groton, Oct. 18, 1829, by Roswell Fish, J.P.	1	33
Harriet, widow of Joseph, m. Charles **FENNER**, Nov. 6, 1814	3	33

	Vol.	Page
CHIPMAN, (cont.)		
Lucy, m. Elbridge **CHESTER**, Sept. 7, 1826, by John G. Wightman, Eld.	1	21
Mary, m. Luther **RATHBURN**, b. of Groton, July 3, 1836, by Rev. Ira R. Steward	1	54
Perez, s. [Perez & Dorcas], b. Dec. 4, 1813	3	25
Perez, of Groton, m. Lydia **SHAW**, of Stonington, Feb. 16, 1840, in Stonington, by Ira R. Steward	1	62
Prudence, m. Calvin **CROMWELL**, b. of Groton, Aug. 25, 1822, by Caleb Avery, J.P.	1	7
Sally Louisa, m. Peter **SHERD**, June 24, 1831, by Joseph Durfey, J.P.	1	37
Samuel, m. Phebe TIFT, b. of Groton, Aug. 30(?), 1821, by Rev. Roswell Burrows	1	4
Sarah, m. Daniel **ELDREDGE**, Nov. 17, 1739	1	185
Sarah, m. Daniel **ELDREDGE**, Nov. 17, 1739	2	96
Thomas Franklin, s. [Thomas & Eliza], b. Sept. 24, 1828	3	25
CHRISTIE, Jonathan L., m. Eunice **HAMBLETON**, b. of Groton, Oct. 14, 1823, by Ralph Hurlbutt, J.P.	1	10
CHURCH, David, m. Susannah **BENNET**, Mar. 16, 1728	1	139
[E]unice, d. David & Susanna, b. Aug. 8, 1729	1	139
John, s. David & Susanna, b. May 15, 1731	1	139
Joseph, s. Joseph & Sarah, b. Mar. 4, 1719	1	128
Noah Whipple, b. Mar. 8, 1774	2	6
Simeon, of Montville, m. Eliza J. **LAMB**, of Groton, May 25, 1851, by Rev. Nicholas T. Allen	1	91
Stephen, m. Nancy **HEWITT**, b. of Groton, Oct. 1, 1854, by Rev. Ebenezer Blake	1	96
CLAPP, Mary B., of Groton, m. Ezekiel L. **MEECH**, of Lisbon, Apr. 18, 1832, by Ralph Hurlbutt, J.P.	1	39
CLARK, CLARKE, Abby M., m. Youngs **MORGAN**, b. of Groton, Apr. 26, 1835, by Ira R. Steward	1	50
Benjamin P., of Greenport, L.I., m. Elizabeth **COBB**, of Groton, Oct. 4, 1843, by Ira R. Steward	1	70
Daniel, of Con[e]y Island, N.Y., m. Sarah **WILBUR**, of Groton, May 28, 1848, by David Avery, Elder	1	81
David A., m. Nancy M. **BAKER**, June 8, 1851, by Geo[rge] A. Woodward	1	91
David G., m. Phebe E. **PARK[E]**, Sept. 17, 1850, at Porterville, by Rev. W. Munger	1	89
Denison Smith, [s. Jonathan & Sally D.], b. Aug. 27, 1807	3	1
Eliza Ann, m. Youngs **MORGAN**, b. of Groton, Apr. 2, 1837, by Ira R. Steward	1	56
Frances Smith, [s. Jonathan & Sally D.], b. Oct. 13, 1811	3	1
George B., of Salem Ct., m. Mary Esther **CLIFT**, of Groton, Sept. 25, 1853, by Rev. S. W. Coggeshall	1	95
George Washington, s. Jonathan & Sally D., b. June 26, 1804	3	1
James Madison, [s. Jonathan & Sally D.], b. May 21, 1814	3	1
Jesse Smith, [s. Jonathan & Sally D.], b. Oct. 10, 1809	3	1
Jonathan Gilson, s. Jonathan & Sally D., b. Mar. 30, 1802	3	1
Joseph R., now residing in Stonington, m. Emily **MURPHEY**, of Groton, Feb. 7, 1841, by Nathan Daboll, J.P.	1	64
Lucinda E., d. William & Charlotte, b. Dec. 23, 1817	3	27
Mary, m. John **WILLIT**, Nov. 19, 1719	1	125
Mary A., m. William F. **FAIRBANKS**, b. of Groton, Jan. 1, 1851, by Rev. Franklin A. Slater	1	91

	Vol.	Page
CLARK, CLARKE, (cont.)		
Mary Angeline, m. Ephraim **MARSTON**, b. of Groton, Aug. 11, 1850, by Rev. James Squier	1	90
Mercy, m. John Gano **WIGHTMAN**, Jan. 22, 1789	2	38
Nancy A., m. Thomas M. **BAILEY**, b. of Groton, Apr. 18, 1837, by John G. Wightman, Elder	1	56
Nancy Avery, twin with Peter Avery, [d. Jonathan & Sally D.], b. July 1, 1818	3	1
Orlando, m. Caroline **FISH**, of Groton, Aug. 16, 1829, by Rev. Roswell Burrows	1	31
Peter Avery, twin with Nancy Avery, [s. Jonathan & Sally D.], b. July 1, 1818	3	1
Samuel, m. Lucretia **CUTLER**, b. of Stonington, Apr. 5, 1847, by Rev. Simon B. Bailey	1	78
Sarah, m. John **STEBBINS**, b. of Waterford, Oct. 8, 1853, by Rev. William A. Smith	1	95
Sarah, m. John **STEB[B]INS**, b. of Waterford, Oct. 8, 1853, by Rev. William A. Smith	3	35
Sarah N., of Charlestown, R.I., m. James S. **PARKS**, of Groton, May 17, 1840, by Ira R. Steward	1	63
Wealthy, of Groton, m. Nathaniel **STILLMAN**, of New London, Feb. 10, 1822, by Ralph Hurlbutt, J.P.	1	6
William, b. Sept. 4, 1784	3	27
William F., of Stonington, m. Sophroney R. **WILLEY**, of New Shoram, R.I., May 27, 1832, by John G. Wightman, Eld.	1	40
Willis, of Providence, R.I., m. Mary C. **ROBERTSON**, of New London, Mar. 28, 1832, by Rev. Abel McEwen, of New London	1	39
Willis, m. Julia **CHESTER**, b. of Groton, Aug. 18, 1839, by Rev. Jared R. Avery	1	61
CLEVERLY, Ebenezer, m. Nancy **POTTER**, b. of Groton, Nov. 15, 1846, by Nathan Daboll, J.P.	1	77
CLIFT, Amos, m. Charity **MORGAN**, b. of Groton, Jan. 29, 1829, by Timothy Tuttle	1	29
Amos, s. Amos & Charity, b. May 15, 1830	3	33
Frederick D., m. Frances **BURROWS**, b. of Groton, July 11, 1837, by John G. Wightman, Elder	1	57
Horace, s. [Amos & Charity], b. May 27, 1840	3	33
Horace, m. Frances **BURROWS**, b. of Groton, Oct. 25, 1848, by Rev. Simon B. Bailey	1	81
Isaac D., m. Elizabeth J. **TEFT**, b. of Groton, Oct. 5, 1853, by Rev. Walter R. Seny, of Mystic Bridge	1	96
Lemuel, s. Amos & Charity, b. Nov. 30, 1833	3	33
Lydia Holmes, d. [Amos & Charity], b. Feb. 4, 1836	3	33
Mary Esther, of Groton, m. George B. **CLARK**, of Salem, Ct., Sept. 25, 1853, by Rev. S. W. Coggeshall	1	95
Nancy, of Groton, m. Edmund **CHESEBRO[UGH]**, of Stonington, Sept. 30, 1840, by Rev. Erastus Denison	1	63
William, of Stonington, m. Bridget **FISH**, of Groton, June 18, 1833, by John G. Wightman, Eld.	1	44
COATS, E. F., M.D., m. Ellen F. **AVERY**, b. of Groton, Sept. 3, 1848, by Rev. H. R. Knapp	1	84
Lucy, m. James **FORSYTH**, Feb. 16, 1804	2	71
COBB, Abigail, [d. Gideon], b. Jan. 19, 1720	1	107

	Vol.	Page
COBB, (cont.)		
Elizabeth, of Groton, m. Benjamin P. **CLARK**, of Greenport, L.I., Oct. 4, 1843, by Ira R. Steward	1	70
Elkanah, [s. Gideon], b. Aug. 20, 1723	1	107
Gideon, [s. Gideon], b. July 8, 1718	1	107
Grace, of New London, m. James **POTTER**, of Groton, July 12, 1835, by John G. Wightman, Elder	1	51
Grace, Mrs., m. James **POTTER**, b. of Groton, Feb. 24, 1842, by Caleb M. Williams, J.P.	1	65
Sarah, m. John **MORGAN**, Jr., Apr. 17, 1728	1	180
COLLINS, George M., m. Ann C. **NORTH[R]UP**, b. of Providence, R.I., Aug. 20, 1848, by Rev. Nicholas T. Allen	1	81
Joseph, of Stonington, m. Lucy Ann **MORGAN**, of [Groton], Nov. 27, 1850, by W. Munger	1	92
Thomas B., of Stonington, m. Frances **MORGAN**, of Groton, May 27, 1844, by Rev. Simon B. Bailey	1	71
COLVER, COLLVER, [see also **CULVER**], Amanda, of Groton, m. Charles A. **SMITH**, of Ledyard, Mar. 31, 1842, by Rev. Erastus Denison	1	66
Amy, m. Elijah **NEWTON**, b. of Groton, Apr. 4, 1756, by Rev. Jacob Johnson	1	169
Andrew, s. [Peter & Chloe], b. June 15, 1771	1	176
Anstis, d. [Peter & Chloe], b. Apr. 15, 1764	1	176
Daniel, [s. Joseph & Mary], b. Oct. 2, 1714	1	125
Ephraim, s. Ephraim & Mary, b. May 16, 1692, in New London now Groton	1	118
Est[h]er, d. Joseph & Mary, b. Feb. 2, 1708	1	125
Freelove, m. William **CROUCH**, Nov. 8, 1737	1	149
Hannah, d. [Joseph & Mary], b. Apr. 8, 1787	2	29
Jabez, s. John & Freelove, b. June 19, 1739	1	127
James, s. [Peter & Chloe], b. Apr. 23, 1774	1	176
Joseph, m. Mary **STARK**, Jan. 29, 1707	1	125
Joseph, [s. Joseph & Mary], b. Dec. 30, 1712	1	125
Joseph, m. Mary **WILLIAMS**, Nov. 17, 1782	2	29
Joseph, s. [Joseph & Mary], b. Feb. 21, 1792	2	29
Mary, m. John **STANTON**, Feb. 12, 1725	1	183
Mary, d. [Joseph & Mary], b. July 7, 1789	2	29
Peter, m. Chloe **DAVIS**, Nov. [ ]	1	176
Philena, d. Timothy & Mary, b. Mar. 30, 1734	1	140
Rhoda, m. Austin D. (or S.?) **STARR**, b. of Groton, Dec. 30, 1844, by Rev. Erastus Denison	1	72
Sarah, [d. Joseph & Mary], b. May 24, 1710	1	125
Sarah, d. [Peter & Chloe], b. Apr. 14, 1766	1	176
Thankful, d. Timothy & Mary, b. Aug. 16, 1727	1	140
Timothy, m. Mary **LAMB**, Jan. 11, 1726/7	1	140
COMIT, Mary, of N.Y., m. Albert G. **WOLF**, of Groton, Sept. 6, 1835, by Ira R. Steward	1	51
COMSTOCK, Amos, of Montville, m. Nancy **LESTER**, of Groton, Jan. 1, 1832, by Ralph Hurlbutt, J.P.	1	39
Elizabeth, m. Nathan **ADAMS**, Jr., Jan. 4, 1770	1	170
Henry, s. Simeon & Mary, b. Sept. 20, 1789	2	17
Mary, m. Edward **WALSWORTH**, Jr., b. of Groton, Apr. 24, 1825, by Rev. Roswell Burrows	1	16

	Vol.	Page
COMSTOCK, (cont.)		
Mary, of Groton, m. William Henry **BRIGGS**, of New London, July 4, 1846, by Belton A. Copp, J.P.	1	76
Rachel, m. John **BROWN**, Oct. [ ], 1740	1	168
William, m. Betsey **GARD**, b. of Groton, July 25, 1803, by Rev. Silas Barrows	2	77
CONDALL, George, of New London, m. Lydia **ASHLEY**, of Groton, Oct. 7, 1827, by Roswell Burrows	1	25
CONGDON, Daniel, of Norwich, m. Eliza **STODDARD**, of Groton, Mar. 29, 1829, by John Brewster, J.P.	1	30
Joshua, of Montville, m. Harriet **BEDENT**, of Ledyard, Mar. 26, 1838, by Rev. John G. Wightman	1	58
Sally, of Groton, m. James **STRICKLAND**, of Waterford, Nov. 29, 1840, by Nathan Daboll, J.P.	1	64
CONKLING, Phebe, of Long Island, m. Samuel **ELDREDGE**, of Groton, Jan. 17, 1788	2	32
CONNELL, Daniel, of Norwich, m. Betsey Ann **GUIANT**, of Groton, July 12, 1846, by Rev. Erastus Denison	1	76
COOK, COOKE, Christa, m. Asa **GORE**, b. of Preston, Mar. 13, 1831, by William Williams, J.P.	1	37
John, m. Sarah **SPRINGER**, Dec. 22, 1703	1	120
John, [s. John & Sarah], b. Jan. 9, 1711	1	120
Marg[a]ret, m. William **WILLIAMS**, Jr., Nov. 10,1736	1	155
Samuel, of Griswold, m. Abby **CRARY**, of Groton, Nov. 14, 1822, by John G. Wightman, Clerk	1	8
Sarah, [d. John & Sarah], b. Sept. 28, 1707	1	120
Susan A., of Groton, m. Solon C. **AVERY**, of Rochester, N.Y., Aug. 11, 1845, by Rev. Jared R. Avery	1	73
William, [s. John & Sarah], b. Nov. 23, 1715	1	120
COOMES, Mary, (his second wife), m. Moses **CULVER**, Mar. 24, 1851	1	188
COPP, Belton A., m. Betsey Ann **BARBER**, of Groton, Aug. 15, 1833, by Timothy Tuttle	1	44
Catharine Burdick, d. [Belton A. & Betsey Ann], b. Aug. 27, 1842	3	30
Daniel Noyes, s. B[elton] A. & B[etsey] A[nn], b. Mar. 3, 1838	3	30
Ellen B., d. Belton A. & Betsey Ann, b. July 20, 1834	3	30
George Denison, s. [Belton A. & Betsey Ann], b. Aug. 17, 1845	3	30
John Joseph, s. [Belton A. & Betsey Ann], b. June 28, 1840	3	30
Sarah Maria, d. B[elton] A. & B[etsey] A[nn], b. May 29, 1837	3	30
CORNISH, Aaron, s. [Joseph & Phebe], b. Mar. 1, 1767	1	163
Daniel, s. [Joseph & Phebe], b. Mar. 10, 1769	1	163
Elisha, s. [Joseph & Phebe], b. Feb. 24, 1771	1	163
Joseph, s. Joseph & Phebe, b. July 14, 1765	1	163
COST, Peter, m. Emily **DENHAM**, b. of Groton, [June] 22, 1854, by Geo[rge] H. Woodward	1	96
COTTRELL, COTERAL, Hannah, of Groton, m. Robert **SUTTON**, of the town of Maraland, June 6, 1830, by John G. Wightman, Eld.	1	34
Phebe H., m. Sullivan **FAGINS**, May 3, 1835, by W[illia]m M. Williams, J.P.	1	50
CRANDALL, Catharine, m. Luther **DRISCOLL**, b. of Groton, Jan. 7, 1821, by Ralph Hurlbutt, J.P.	1	2
Dudley B., m. Lydia **ADAMS**, b. of Groton, Jan. 11, 1829, by Ralph Hurlbutt, J.P.	1	29

	Vol.	Page
CRANDALL, (cont.)		
Harriet A., m. Henry A. **CROMWELL**, b. of Groton, May 29, 1850, by Rev. Nicholas T. Allen	1	88
Joseph, Jr., m. Deborah **WILCOX**, b. of Groton, Sept. 3, 1826, by William Williams, J.P.	1	21
Lucy, m. W[illia]m H. **CRANDALL**, b. of Stonington, Dec. 27, 1846, by Rev. W[illia]m C. Walker	1	77
Mary, m. Jefferson **LAMB**, b. of Groton, Sept. 28, 1823, by William Williams, J.P.	1	10
W[illia]m H., m. Lucy **CRANDALL**, b. of Stonington, Dec. 27, 1846, by Rev. W[illia]m C. Walker	1	77
CRANSON, W[illia]m S., of Norwich, m. Eunice **HEMPSTEAD**, of Stonington, Mar. 17, 1850, by Rev. W[illia]m C. Walker	1	87
CRARY, Isaac, s. Isaac & Mary, b. Feb. [7, 1777]		
Mary, d. Isaac & Mary, b. Feb. [26, 1779]		
Above dates supplied by Judge S. O. Prentice.		
CRARY, Abby, of Groton, m. Samuel **COOK**, of Griswold, Nov. 14, 1822, by\ John G. Wightman, Clerk	1	8
Albert G., s. [Jesse & Catharine], b. Aug. 7, 1815	3	25
Ann, [d. Peter & Ann], b. Nov. 29, 1713	II	368
Daniel, s. [Isaac & Mary], b. Jan. 23, 1790	2	29
Dorothy, d. Nathan & Dorothy, b. Mar. 26, 1759	1	161
Dorothy, d. Nathan & Dorothy, b. Mar. 26, 1759	1	165
Edward Parker, s. [Isaac & Mary], b. July 24, 1787	2	29
Elisha A., of Preston, m. Eliza **BREWSTER**, of Groton, Jan. 29, 1828, by Timothy Tuttle	1	26
[E]unis, [d. Peter & Ann], b. Aug. 26, 1719	II	368
George B., s. [Jesse & Catharine], b. Mar. 13, 1822	3	25
George B., m. Catharine **LATHAM**, b. of Groton, Aug. 6, 1843, by Rev. Erastus Denison	1	69
Hannah, [d. Nathan & Dorothy], b. Nov. 1, 1761	1	161
Hannah, d. [Isaac & Mary], b. Sept. 23, 1794	2	29
Humphrey, [s. Peter & Ann], b. Sept. 7, 1721	II	368
Isaac, m. Mary **GALLUP**, of Groton, Nov. 12, 1775	2	29
Isaac, s. Isaac & Mary, b. Feb. [ ]	2	29
Jesse, s. Nathan & Ruth, b. Apr. 1, 1789	1	161
Jesse, s. Nathan & Ruth, b. Apr. 1, 1789	2	34
Joseph, s. [Isaac & Mary], b. Jan. 28, 1781	2	29
Lucy, [d. Peter & Ann], b. Dec. 29, 1715	II	368
Mary, d. Isaac & Mary, b. Feb. 2, [ ]	2	29
Nancy, b. Nov. 30, 1780; m. Elisha **HALEY**, [ ]; d. Sept. 11, 1860	3	0
Nancy, m. Elisha **HALEY**, s. Caleb & Mary, July 24, 1803	3	0
Nathan, [s. Peter & Ann], b. Oct. 7, 1717	II	368
Nathan, s. [Isaac & Mary], b. Feb. 11, 1784	2	29
Peter, m. Ann **CULVER**, Jan. 11, 1709/10	II	368
Peter, s. Peter & Ann, b. Jan. 6, 1710/11	II	368
Sarah, [d. Nathan & Ruth], b. May 25, 1793	1	161
Temperance, [d. Peter & Ann], b. Nov. 2, 1723	II	368
Thomas, [s. Peter & Ann], b. Feb. 2, 1711/12	II	368
William, s. [Isaac & Mary], b. June 22, 1792	2	29
CROCKER, Elizabeth, m. William **SWADDLE**, Jan. 22, 1718	1	113
Leonord, of Waterford, m. Amanda **BECKWITH**, of Groton, Feb. 24, 1828, by Rev. John G. Wightman	1	27

	Vol.	Page
CROMWELL, CROWNWELL, Adaline, m. Hubbard **CHESTER**, b. of Groton, Jan. 21, 1831, by Rev. Erastus Denison	1	36
Calvin, m. Prudence **CHIPMAN**, b. of Groton, Aug. 25, 1822, by Caleb Avery, J.P.	1	7
Calvin, m. Charlotte M. **CURRY**, b. of Groton, Oct. 17, 1852, by Rev. J. Cady	1	95
Esther, m. John **PERKINS**, b. of Groton, Dec. 5, 1821, by Rufus Smith, J.P.	1	5
Frances, m. Phinehas **PERKINS**, Jr., b. of Groton, July 3, 1825, by John G. Wightman	1	17
Hannah E., of Groton, m. Charles P. **SAVANEY**, Jan. 18, 1849, by Rev. H. R. Knapp	1	84
Henry A., of Groton, m. Harriet A. **CRANDALL**, of Groton, May 29, 1850, by Rev. Nicholas T. Allen	1	88
Nancy, m. Thomas **WHITE**, b. of Groton, July 1, 1826, by Nathan Daboll, J.P.	1	21
William R., of Groton, m. Sarah A. **BURROWS**, of Rochester, N.Y., May 29, 1850, by Rev. Nicholas T. Allen	1	88
CROSSMAN, Ann Maria, m. James D. **PARK[E]**, b. of Groton, Aug. 2, 1854, by Rev. S. W. Coggeshall, of Mystic Bridge	1	96
CROUCH, CHROUCH, CHOUCH, CHROUGH, CROUGH,		
Abiah, m. Samuel **CHAPMAN**, b. living in Groton, Oct. 14, 1827, by Zephaniah Watrous	1	25
Abigail, [d. Christopher & Ruth], b. Dec. 30, 1718	1	119
Anna, m. Jabez **CROUCH**, b. of Groton, Oct. 9, 1831, by Zephaniah Watrous	1	38
Christopher, s. William & Desire, b. June 15, 1734	1	149
Daniel, m. Nancy **WATROUS**, b. living in Groton, Sept. 2, 1827, by Zephaniah Watrous	1	24
David, s. William & Desire, b. Nov. 11, 1736	1	149
David, m. Elizabeth **WHIPPLE**, Jan. 26, 1834, by Zephaniah Watrous	1	46
Deborah, d. William & Desire, b. Mar. 25, 1732	1	149
Desire, w. William, d. May 18, 1737	1	149
Hannah, m. Joel **CHROUCH**, b. of Groton, Aug. 24, 1834, by Zephaniah Watrous	1	47
Jabez, m. Anna **CROUCH**, b. of Groton, Oct. 9, 1831, by Zephaniah Watrous	1	38
Joel, m. Hannah **CHROUCH**, b. of Groton, Aug. 24, 1834, by Zephaniah Watrous	1	47
John, m. Rachal **WATROUS**, b. of Groton, July 29, 1821, by Zephaniah Watrous	1	4
John, Jr., m. Eunice **WHIPPLE**, b. of Groton, Dec. 30, 1826, by Zephaniah Watrous	1	23
Mary, [d. Christopher & Ruth], b. Sept. 17, 1716	1	119
Mary, m. Caleb **WILLIS**, b. of Groton, Oct. 29, 1821, by Zephaniah Watrous	1	4
Mary, m. Silas **WATROUS**, Sept. 14, 1823, by Zephaniah Watrous	1	10
Mary, m. Henry **WATROUS**, Jr., b. of Ledyard, Nov. 29, 1848, by Nathan Daball, J.P.	1	82
Richard, s. Christopher & Ruth, b. Apr. 5, 1712	1	119
Ruth, [d. Christopher & Ruth], b. July 9, 1721	1	119
William, brother of Christopher, b. May 25, 1707	1	119
William, m. Desire **WILLIAMS**, Sept. 8, 1731	1	149

	Vol.	Page
CROUCH, CHROUCH, CHOUCH, CHROUGH, CROUGH, (cont.)		
William, m. Freelove **COLLVER**, Nov. 8, 1737	1	149
William, s. William & Freelove, b. Aug. 3, 1739	1	149
Zachariah, m. Delight **WATROUS**, b. of Groton, Apr. 20, 1834, by Zephaniah Watrous	1	47
CRUMB, Eliza, m. Charles G. **HEMPSTEAD**, b. of Groton, Apr. 29, 1838, by Rev. John G. Wightman	1	58
Eunice, m. Dexter **IRONS**, b. of Groton, Mar. 1, 1829, by Rev. N. S. Spaulding	1	30
Joseph, of Groton, m. Harriet **PHELPS**, of Stonington, Apr. 29, 1838, by Rev. John G. Wightman	1	58
Julia, of Groton, m. Benjamin A. **BROWN**, of Stonington, Jan. 5, 1851, by Rev. James Squier	1	91
William, m. Eunice **CHAPMAN**, b. of Groton, Oct. 10, 1832, by John G. Wightman, Eld.	1	41
CULVER, CULLVER, [see also **COLVER**], Aaron, s. [Moses & Lucy], b. [ ], 1777	1	187
Aaron, m. Caroline Delight **BAILEY**, [ ], 1801/2	1	192
Aaron Austin, [s. Aaron & Caroline Delight], b. [ ], 1807	1	192
Abigail, d. Joseph, of Groton, m. Asa **BUTTON**, s. Jedediah, of Groton, May 29, 1770	1	192
Abigail, m. Thomas **STODDARD**, b. of Groton, May 3, 1772	2	16
Abigail, b. Feb. 16, 1747; d. Oct. 13, 1824	1	192
Albert D., m. Betsey Ann **RANDALL**, b. of Groton, Apr. 14, 1844, by Rev. Erastus Denison	1	71
Allen F., [s. Aaron & Caroline Delight], b. [ ], 1805	1	192
Amy, d. [Moses & Susanna], b. [ ], 1743	1	186
Amy, m. Elijah **NEWTON**, Apr. 4, 1756	1	165
Amy Delight, [d. Aaron & Caroline Delight], b. [ ]	1	192
Ann, m. Peter **CRARY**, Jan. 11, 1709/10	II	368
Anna, d. [Moses & Lucy], b. Dec. 13, 1782	1	187
Anna, m. Henry **TRANCHARD**, Nov. 9, 1807	1	189
Anna M., [d. Moses & Hannah], b. May 10, 1820, at Tyringham, Mass.	1	188
Betsey, (born Elizabeth), d. Moses & Lucy Turner, m. Daniel **WILCOX**, Jr., Sept. 13, 1812, at Preston	1	188
Caleb, s. [Moses & Lucy], b. [ ], 1788	1	187
Caleb, m. Lydia **MORGAN**, b. of Groton, Aug. 6, 1820, by Timothy Tuttle	1	1
Caleb, m. Lydia **MORGAN**, Aug. 6, 1820	1	189
Caleb B., [s. Moses & Hannah], b. Feb. 16, 1818, at Preston	1	188
Daniel, [s. Joseph & Mary], b. Oct. 2, 1714	1	186
Desier, d. [Moses & Susanna], b. [ ], 1739	1	186
Desire, d. [Moses & Lucy], b. [ ], 1778	1	187
Eliza Turner, [d. Aaron & Caroline Delight], b. [ ], 1822	1	192
Elizabeth, called Betsey, d. [Moses & Lucy], b. Mar. 29, 1793	1	187
Esther, [d. Joseph & Mary], b. Feb. 2, 1708	1	186
Esther, m. John **WATROUS**, 28 of the 12th mo., 1719/20, by Peter Crandall, Justice	1	121
Eunice, d. [Moses & Susanna], b. [ ], 1745	1	186
Eunice. d. [Moses & Lucy], b. [ ], 1781	1	187
Eunice, of Groton, m. Ezekiel **MAXSON**, of Hopkinton, R.I., Dec. 9, 1813; d. Feb. 12, 1867	1	189
Eunice, m. Silas P. **BAILEY**, b. of Groton, June 6, 1831, by Ralph Hurlbutt, J.P.	1	37

	Vol.	Page
CULVER, CULLVER, (cont.)		
Frederick D., [s. Moses & Hannah], b. Aug. 1, 1828	1	188
George B., [s. Moses & Hannah], b. Oct. 1, 1822, at Tyringham, Mass.	1	188
Hannah, m. Stephen **STARK**, Feb. 15, 1708	1	125
Hannah, m. Daniel **LAMB**, Oct. 11, 1807	3	11
Hannah, [d. Moses & Hannah], b. Jan. 16, 1809	1	188
Hannah (Newton), s. Moses, d. Nov. 13, 1849, ae. 62 y.	1	188
Hepsabath, s. [Moses & Susanna], b. [ ], 1749	1	186
James H., [s. Moses & Hannah], b. July 1, 1825	1	188
Jemima, [d. Jonathan & Sarah], b. Jan. 1, 1726	1	125
Jonathan, m. Sarah **LAMB**, July 19, 1722	1	125
Joseph, m. Mary **STARR***, Jan. 29, 1707 [*Should be "Slack"]	1	186
Joseph, Jr., [s. Joseph & Mary], b. Sept. 11, 1711	1	187
Joseph, Jr., m. Salinda **LAMB**, b. of Groton, June 30, 1816, by John G. Wightman	3	5
Joseph, Jr., m. Pamela **LAMB**, Mar. 10, 1822, by Rev. John G. Wightman	1	6
Joseph, Jr., m. Parmelia **LAMB**, Mar. 10, 1822	3	5
Joseph Edwin, s. Joseph & Parmelia, b. Feb. 9, 1823	3	5
Lois, d. Jonathan & Sarah, b. May 6, 1723	1	125
Lucy, d. [Moses & Lucy], b. May 29, 1780	1	187
Lucy, w. Moses, d. Feb. 2, 1831, at Lee, Mass., ae. 73 y.	1	187
Mary, m. Robert **BURROWS**, Aug. 6, 1712	1	125
Mary, d. [Moses & Susanna], b. [ ], 1737	1	186
Mary, m. Moses **CULVER**, [ ], 1759	1	186
Mary, of Groton, m. George **WOODBURN**, of Stonington, July 22, 1759, by Timothy Wightman, Elder	1	189
Mary Ann, [d. Aaron & Caroline Delight], b. [ ], 1803	1	192
Mary Ann, m. Jonathan **ROGERS**, b. of Groton, Jan. 16, 1825, by John Brewster, J.P.	1	16
Moses, [s. Joseph & Mary], b. Dec. 30, 1712; m. Mary **CULVER**, [ ], 1759; d. July [ ], 1770	1	186
Moses, of Groton, m. Susanna [ ], 1735	1	186
Moses, s. [Moses & Susanna], b. Apr. 11, 1747; d. Sept. [ ], 1795	1	186
Moses, m. Lucy **TURNER**, [ ], 1775/6	1	187
Moses, s. [Moses & Lucy], b. [ ], 1786	1	187
Moses, d. Sept. [ ], 1795, ae. 48 y.	1	187
Moses, m. Hannah **NEWTON**, Jan. 22, 1808	1	188
Moses, m. Mary **COOMES** (his second wife), Mar. 24, 1851	1	188
Moses, s. Moses & Lucy, d. Mar. 8, 1853, ae. 77 y., in Tyringham, Mass.	1	191
Moses, d. Mar. 9, 1863, ae. 76 y.	1	188
Moses Edmund, [s. Moses & Hannah], b. July 5, 1812, at Preston	1	188
Nancy, of Groton, m. John **THURSTON**, of Boxford, Mass., May 10, 1835, by John G. Wightman, Elder	1	50
Nathan Lorin, [s. Aaron & Caroline Delight], b. [ ]	1	192
Sabra, d. [Moses & Lucy], b. [ ], 1790	1	187
Salinda, w. Joseph, Jr., d. May 12, 1821	3	5
Sally Gallup, [d. Aaron & Caroline Delight], b. Aug. 24, 1817	1	192
Samuel Whitman, s. [Joseph & Parmelia], b. Sept. 4, 1825	3	5
Sanford, [s. Moses & Hannah], b. May 17, 1816, at Preston	1	188
Sarah, [d. Joseph & Mary], b. May 24, 1710	1	186
Susanna, d. [Moses & Susanna], b. [ ], 1741	1	186
William L., of Tyringham, m. Mary A. **CHAPMAN**, of Lee, Mass., Feb. 9, 1833	1	191

	Vol.	Page
CULVER, CULLVER, (cont.)		
William Lothrop, [s. Moses & Hannah], b. Apr. 22, 1811	1	188
CUNNINGHAM, CONINGHAM*, Andrew, s. Samuel & Abial, b. Nov. 28, 1727 (*also written Kinicum)	1	173
Archible, s. [Samuel & Abial], b. May 2, 1734	1	173
Elizabeth, d. [Samuel & Abial], b. Sept. 13, 1729	1	173
Mary, m. JohN **WILLSON**, Sept. 3, 1730	1	146
Obadiah, s. [Samuel & Abial], b. Aug. 25, 1736	1	173
Samuel, s. [Samuel & Abial], b. Oct. 2, 1731	1	173
Samuel, m. Abial **ROBINSON**, May 8, 1755 (Changed to 1725 by L.B.B.)	1	172
CURRY, Charlotte M., m. Calvin **CROMWELL**, b. of Groton, Oct. 17, 1852, by Rev. J. Cady	1	95
CUTLER, Lucretia, m. Samuel **CLARK**, b. of Stonington, Apr. 5, 1847, by Rev. Simon B. Bailey	1	78
DABOLL, DABALL, Benjamin, of Stephentown, N.Y., m. Prudence **MOSELEY**, of Groton, July 15, 1827, by Nathan Daboll, J.P.	1	24
Betsey M., m. George A. **PERKINS**, b. of Groton, June 30, 1839, by Rev. John G. Wightman	1	61
Betsey Moxley, [d. Nathan, Jr. & Elizabeth], b. May 21, 1809	3	3
Celedon Leeds, twin with Eliza Diadama, [d. Nathan, Jr. & Elizabeth], b. July 21, 1818	3	3
Charlotte N., m. Whitman **WILBUR**, b. of Groton, July 10, 1844, by Rev. Simon B. Bailey	1	71
David A., m. Esther B. Wightman, June 27, 1839, by Rev. John G. Wightman	1	61
David Austin, [S. Nathan, Jr. & Elizabeth], b. May 11, 1813	3	3
Diademia, b. Sept. 15, 1783; m. George **GERE**, Dec. 14, 1809	3	7
Eliza D., of Groton, m. George N. **WRIGHT**, of Montville, Aug. 18, 1840, by Rev. Erastus Denison	1	63
Eliza Diadama, twin with Celedon Leeds, [d. Nathan, Jr. & Elizabeth], b. July 21, 1818	3	3
Elizabeth, m. Nathan **DABOLL**, Jr., b. of Groton, Nov. 13, 1804, by Lemuel Tyler, Clerk	3	3
Elizabeth, m. Nathan O. **ING[RA]HAM**, b. of Groton, Aug. 8, 1838, by Ira R. Steward	1	59
George L., m. Betsey F. **SMITH**, b. of Groton, May 26, 1839, by Rev. John G. Wightman	1	60
George Lathrop, [s. Nathan, Jr. & Elizabeth], b. May 8, 1815	3	3
Hannah, [d. Samuel & Mary], b. May 29, 1755	2	25
John, m. Lucy E. **FITCH**, b. of Groton, Feb. 26, 1849, by Rev. S. B. Bailey	1	82
John, s. John & Abiah, b. Feb. 13, 1751	1	131
John, s. Nathan & Anna, b. Mar. 24, 1755	1	131
Jonathan, [s. Samuel & Mary], b. Oct. 30, 1752	2	25
Lorenzo, [s. Nathan, Jr. & Elizabeth], b. Aug. 25, 1805; d. [Apr.(?)] 6, 1807	3	3
Lucretia, [d. Samuel & Mary], b. May 2, 1743	2	25
Lucy, of Groton, m. Clark **LEWIS**, of N. Stonington, Feb. [ ], 1830, by Nathan Daboll, J.P.	1	33
Mary, [d. Samuel & Mary], b. May 25, 1750	2	25
Nancy, m. Charles **MURPHY**, b. of Groton, Feb. 11, 1847, by Rev. S. B. Bailey	1	77
Nathan, Jr., m. Elizabeth **DABOLL**, b. of Groton, Nov. 13, 1804, by Lemuel Tyler, Clerk	3	3
Nathan Madison, [s. Nathan, Jr. & Elizabeth], b. Apr. 22, 1811	3	3

	Vol.	Page
DABOLL, DABALL, (cont.)		
Prudence, [s. Samuel & Mary], b. Mar. 3, 1745	2	25
Samuel, m. Mary **BUFF**, Nov. 3, 1742	2	25
Samuel, [s. Samuel & Mary], b. Feb. 7, 1748	2	25
William V., m. Mrs. Caroline C. **SMITH**, b. of Groton, Feb. 2, 1835, by Rev. Ira R. Steward	1	49
DANIELS, Amy, m. Peter **WILLIAMS**, Jr., b. of Groton, Nov. 21, 1821, by Caleb Avery, J.P.	1	5
Bradley, m. Clarinda **LEEDS**, b. of Groton, June 29, 1828, by Nathan Daboll, J.P.	1	28
Ellen, of Groton, m. James L. **BOYNTON**, of Portland, Me., Apr. 22, 1838, by Joseph Durfey, J.P.	1	58
Frederick, m. Hannah **WHITE**, b. of Groton, May 10, 1829, by John G. Wightman, Eld.	1	30
Gurdon, m. Nancy **WOODWARD**, b. of Groton, Sept. 1, 1850, by Rev. William C. Walker	1	90
Henry, of New London, m. Sally **GUYANT**, of Groton, Dec. 9, 1824, by Nathan Daboll, J.P.	1	14
Lydia, of Groton, m. Jeremiah **POTTS**, of New London, Apr. 7, 1834, by John G. Wightman, Eld.	1	46
Sarah, b. Oct. 9, 1759; m. Thomas **HALLET**, Dec. 4, 1783	2	70
DARROW, DARER, Amanda, D., of Groton, m. Asa **ALLEN**, of Hudson, Ohio, Jan. 12, 1854, by Rev. Allen Darrow	1	95
Ichabod, s. Lemuel & Preserved, b. Aug. 11, 1752	2	9
John, of Canaan, m. Polly **MALISON**, of Groton, Dec. 9, 1821, by Timothy Tuttle	1	5
John, of Otis, Mass., m. Betsey **BILL**, of Groton, Oct. 5, 1825, by John G. Wightman, Eld.	1	19
Lemuel, m. Preserved **RANDALL**, Sept. 19, 1751	2	9
DART, Eunice A., of Groton, m. Anson G. **PERKINS**, of Groton, July 1, 1849, by Rev. Nicholas T. Allen	1	86
Sarah A., m. John E. **PERKINS**, b. of Groton, May 29, 1850, by Rev. Nicholas T. Allen	1	88
DAVIS, Aaron*, [s. Jeptha & Amy], b. Mar. 15, 1802 (*Anson)	2	27
Amanda M., d. Comfort & Fanny, b. Aug. 23, 1838	3	34
Andrew, m. Sarah **BAKER**, Dec. 9, 1707	1	107
Andrew, s. Andrew & Sarah, b. Aug. 14, 1709	1	107
Andrew, Jr., m. Marian **LAMPHERE**, June 12, 1735	1	183
Andrew, s. [Andrew, Jr. & Marian], b. Jan. 13, 1740	1	183
Anna, [d. Andrew & Sarah], b. July 22, 1717	1	107
Anna, [d. Comfort & Anna], b. Apr. 3, 1721	1	113
Anna, d. [Andrew, Jr. & Marian], b. Feb. 25, 1745/6	1	183
Anson, m. Abby **MINER**, b. of Groton, Sept. 21, 1826, by Nathan Daboll, J.P.	1	22
Benajah, s. Comfort & Anna, b. Oct. 23, 1711	1	113
Charles, m. Eliza **SMITH**, b. of Groton, Feb. 9, 1834, by Joseph Durfey, J.P.	1	46
Charles H., of Westerly, m. Julia Ann **THOMPSON**, of N. Stonington, July 23, 1842, by Ira R. Steward	1	67
Chloe, m. Peter **COLVER**, Nov. [ ]	1	176
Clohe, d. [Andrew, Jr. & Marian], b. July 2, 1738	1	183
Chloe, had s. John **HEMINGER**, b. July 13, 1761	1	181
Comfort, m. Anna **SWADLE**, July 18, 1708	1	113

	Vol.	Page
DAVIS, (cont.)		
Comfort, m. Mrs. Fanny **SMITH**, b. of Groton, Feb. 13, 1825, by Amos A. Niles, J.P.	1	16
Daniel, m. Mary A. HEATH, b. of Groton, Apr. 9, 1837, by Rev. Mark Meade	1	56
Dayton, m. Sally Ann **GAVIT[T]**, b. of Stonington, June 10, 1838, by Rev. John G. Wightman	1	58
Deborah, m. Nathaniel **WILLIAMS**, Dec. 9, 1717, by Justice Chesebrough. Witnesses: Samuel Buston, Robert Davis.	1	118
Ebenezer, s. [Andrew, Jr. & Marian], b. Jan. 19, 1743/4	1	183
Eliza, m. W[illia]m **BURROWS**, b. of Groton, Dec. 13, 1840, by Ira R. Steward	1	64
Elizabeth, d. Comfort & Anna, b. Oct. 13, 1709	1	113
Enos, of Preston, m. Lois **PERKINS**, of Groton, June 22, 1826, by Ralph Hurlbutt, J.P.	1	20
Esther, m. David **CASWINE**, b. of Groton, May 14, 1826, by Robert S. Avery, J.P.	1	20
Hannah, [d. Samuel & Margaret], b. Feb. 13, 1720; d. May 17, 1721	1	127
Hannah, d. [Andrew, Jr. & Marian], b. Sept. 3, 1749	1	183
Hannah, [d. Jeptha & Amy], b. Apr. 2, 1804	2	27
Hannah, m. John **GUINANT**, b. of Groton, July 23, 1820, by Roswell Fish, J.P.	1	1
Henry, m. Frances **WILBUR**, b. of Groton, May 4, 1848, by David Avery, Elder	1	81
Horace W., m. Harriet **ASHBEY**, b. of Groton, Sept. 14, 1845, by Rev. Simon B. Bailey	1	74
Ichabod, m. Elizabeth **WHIPPLE**, b. of Groton, Aug. 27, 1820, by Amos Watrous	1	1
James R., m. Prudence M. **BAKER**, b. of Groton, Nov. 1, 1843, by Ira R. Steward	1	70
Jemima, [d. Andrew & Sarah], b. Sept. 25, 1719	1	107
Jerusha, [d. Andrew & Sarah], b. Aug. 13, 1715	1	107
Jerusha, m. Samuel **BAKER**, Dec. 8, 1733	1	177
John C., of Westerly, R.I., m. Lois **BROWN**, of Groton, Jan. 20, 1822, by Rev. John G. Wightman	1	6
Joshua, [s. Andrew & Sarah], b. Aug. 4, 1711	1	107
Josiah, s. Comfort, b. Aug. 2, 1817; d. Aug. 23, 1818	3	34
Lois M., m. William S. **FISH**, b. of Groton, Oct. 8, [1853], by Rev. James M. Phillips	1	95
Lucy, [d. Samuel & Margaret], b. June 15, 1724	1	127
Lucy, [d. Jeptha & Amy], b. May 30, 1800	2	27
Lydia, m. Luke **PERKINS**, Jr., Dec. 12, 1715	1	116
Margaret, [d. Samuel & Margaret], b. Aug. 4, 1722; d. May 26, 1725	1	127
Margaret, s. Samuel, d. Aug. 15, 1724	1	127
Mary, m. Samuel **BUSTON**, Apr. 15, 1706	1	117
Mary J., m. Charles H. **BURROWS**, b. of Groton, Jan. 28, 1847, by Rev. Erastus Denison	1	77
Sally, m. W[illia]m W. **SMITH**, b. of Groton, May 16, 1841, by Rev. Jared R. Avery	1	64
Samuel, m. Margaret **MORGAN**, Jan. 29, 1718/9	1	127
Samuel, s. Samuel & Margaret, b. Nov. 2, 1719; d. Feb 17, 1719/20	1	127
Samuel, d. Feb. 15, 1733/4	1	139
Sarah, [d. Andrew & Sarah], b. June 21, 1713	1	107

	Vol.	Page
DAVIS, (cont.)		
Sarah, d. [Andrew, Jr. & Marian], b. May 14, 1736	1	183
Sarah, m. Ebenezer **PERKINS**, July 20, 1749	1	183
Silence, d. Comfort & Anna, b. June 9, 1716	1	113
Solomon, s. Comfort & Anna, b. Jan. 16, 1713	1	113
William, s. [Andrew, Jr. & Marian], b. Aug. 13, 1747	1	183
DAY, [A]Eneas, m. Joanna **BRIGHTMAN**, Nov. 25, 1841, by Henry W. Avery, J.P.	1	65
DEAN, **DEEN**, Anna, d. John, b. May 27, 1722*; d. May 29, 1723 (*The note "Should be 1711" follows)	1	101
Anna, d. John & Lydia, b. May 27, 1711; d. May 29, 1723	1	113
Anna, [d. John & Lydia], b. May 27, 1711; d. May 29, 1723	1	130
Barnabas, s. John & Lydia, b. Jan. 31, 1723/4	1	113
Barnabas, [s. John & Lydia], b. Jan. 31, 1724/5; d. Dec. 9, 1726	1	130
Barnabas, s. [Silas & Hannah], b. July 29, 1743	1	172
Barzillai, s. John & Lydia, b. Dec. 28, 1714	1	113
Barzilla, [s. John & Lydia], b. Dec. 28, 1714	1	130
Barzillai, s. [Silas & Hannah], b. Sept. 20,1746	1	172
Charles H., of N. Stonington, m. Lydia W. **GRAY**, of Groton, Jan. 20, 1828, by William Williams, J.P.	1	26
Hannah, s. [Silas & Hannah], b. June 11, 1754	1	172
James, s. [John & Sarah], b. Aug. 20, 1748	1	181
Jesse, s. [Silas & Hannah], b. Apr. 2, 1736; d. Jan. 20, 1736/7	1	172
Jesse, s. [Silas & Hannah], b. July 12, 1740	1	172
John, s. John & Lydia, b. May 27, 1713	1	113
John, s. John & Lydia, b. May 27, 1713	1	130
John, m. Sarah **DOUGLASS**, Dec. 21, 1738	1	181
John, s. [John & Sarah], b. Mar. 4, 1741/2	1	181
John, s. [Silas & Hannah], b. Apr. 11, 1759	1	172
Jonathan, s. [John & Sarah], b. Dec. 20, 1744	1	181
Lydia, d. John & Lydia, b. Apr. 10, 1721	1	113
Lydia, [d. John & Lydia], b. Apr. 16, 1721; d. Dec. 12, 1726	1	130
Lydia. w. Ensign John, d. Jan. 15, 1737	1	129
Lydia, d. [John & Sarah], b. Apr. 6, 1740	1	181
Samuel, s. [John & Sarah], b. Sept. 2, 1743	1	181
Sarah, d. [John & Sarah], b. Oct. 12, 1746	1	181
Silas, m. Hannah **BARKER**, Nov. 21, 1734	1	172
Silas, s. Silas [& Hannah], b. Dec. 24, 1737	1	172
Simeon, s. [Silas & Hannah], b. Apr. 22, 1750	1	172
DECKER, Phebe, m. Albert **HALLEY**, [s. Stephen & Lucy], [ ]	3	0
DENHAM, Ellen, m. Nathaniel **BRAND**, b. of Groton, Jan. 5, 1846, by Nathan Daboll, J.P.	1	75
Emily, m. Peter **COST**, b. of Groton, [June] 22, 1854, by Geo[rge] H. Woodward	1	96
Mary Ann, of Groton, m. John **JORDAN**, of N.Y., Apr. 25, 1847, by Nathan Daboll, J.P.	1	78
DENISON, Abby Ann, m. Joseph **GALLUP**, b. of Groton, Nov. 2, 1826, by John G. Wightman, Eld.	1	22
Abby C., of Groton, m. William B. **NOYES**, of Stonington, Aug. 23, 1848, by Rev. Erastus Denison, of Waterford	1	81
Albert, of Stonington, m. Margaret **HEATH**, of Groton, Mar. 15, 1829, by Nathan Daboll, J.P.	1	30

	Vol.	Page
DENISON, (cont.)		
Allyn P., of Stonington, m. Eliza **PARKES**, of Groton, Dec. 9, 1832, by Nathan Daboll, J.P.	1	42
Andrew, of Stonington, m. Polly **MIDDLETON**, of Groton, Nov. 14, 1836, by Rev. Roswell Burrows	1	55
Baradel, m. Ezekiel **TURNER**, May 11, 1729	1	144
Beebe, m. Fanny **ALLYN**, b. of Groton, Dec. 24, 1820, by Ralph Hurlbutt, J.P.	1	2
Caroline E., of Groton, m. John B. **GOULD**, of Hull, Mass., Apr. 21, 1847, by Rev. H. F. Kenney	1	78
Charlotte A., m. William G. **BATTY**, b. of Porterville, in Groton, Feb. 20, 1844, by Rev. W[illia]m S. Simmons, Jr.	1	70
Delia Ann, m. Daniel **LATHAM**, b. of Groton, Sept. 10, 1826, by John G. Wightman, Eld.	1	21
Desire, m. Jabez **SMITH**, Nov. 11, 1736	1	178
Elisha W., of Stonington, m. Fanny **HICKS**, of Groton, June 5, 1820, by Rev. John G. Wightman	1	1
Elizabeth, m. John **BARBER**, b. of Groton, Nov. [ ], 1770	2	53
Emelia Amanda, of Groton, m. Gurdon **BILL**, Jr., of Ledyard, May 12, 1853, by Rev. Erastus Denison	1	95
Erastus, m. Prudence **SPICER**, b. of Groton, June 25, 1815, by John G. Wightman, Elder	2	87
Esther, m. Isaac **SMITH**, Nov. 4, 1729	1	138
Esther, m. Jonas B. **AVERY**, July 24, 1791	3	2
Eunice, m. Gilbert **SMITH**, Aug. 2, 1764	2	37
Eunice C., of Groton, m. Henry P. **HEWITT**, of Waterford, Aug. 26, 1849, by Rev. W. C. Walker	1	86
Frances J., of Groton, m. Robert **GREEN**, Aug. 6, 1843, by Rev. Erastus Denison	1	69
George W., of Stonington, m. Almira **CHESEBRO[UGH]**, of Groton, Aug. 19, 1838, by Ira R. Steward	1	59
Hannah F., of Groton, m. Hiram C. **HOLMES**, of Stonington, Jan. 30, 1830, by Rev. Jared R. Avery	1	87
Henry, m. Caroline E. **BURROWS**, b. of Groton, Aug. 29, 1841, by Benjamin C. Phelps	1	65
Isaac, of Stonington, m. Levina **FISH**, of Groton, Feb. 18, 1817, by John G. Wightman	3	11
Isaac W., of Stonington, m. Eunice E. **BURROWS**, of Groton, May 10, 1843, by Rev. Erastus Denison	1	68
John D., m. Mary C. **BURROWS**, May 10, 1853, by J. W. Holman	1	95
Joseph L, m. Lura **BURROWS**, b. of Groton, Feb. 27, 1845, by Rev. Erastus Denison	1	72
Joseph S., of Stonington, m. Sarah **GALLUP**, of Groton, Sept. 5, 1822, by Philip Gray, J.P.	1	8
Martha, m. Stephen **BILLINGS**, Apr. 9, 1789	1	179
Mary, m. Nathan **SMITH**, Dec. 5, 1723	1	107
Mary, m. Hubburd **BURROWS**, [ ]	1	164
Mary Elizabeth, m. Erastus **AVERY**, b. of Groton, Mar. 20, 1844, by Rev. Jared R. Avery	1	70
Nancy, of Stonington, m. Zebadiah **GATES**, of Groton, June 7, 1820, by Rev. Ira Hart, of Stonington	1	1
Nathan F., m. Mary E. **AVERY**, b. of Groton, Dec. 25, 1823, by Ebenezer Avery, Jr., J.P.	1	12

	Vol.	Page
DENISON, (cont.)		
Noyes P., m. Harriet L. **SMITH**, b. of Groton, Dec. 9, 1830, by Timothy Tuttle	1	36
Phebe, m. Ebenezer **AVERY**, Jr., June 11, 1761	2	31
Sarah, w. Joseph S., d. Sept. 13, 1822	1	8
Sarah A., of Groton, m. Caleb **BURDICK**, of Plainfield, Ct., [Oct.] 23, [1853], by Rev. James M. Phillips	1	95
Silas B., of Stonington, m. Diana **BURROWS**, of Groton, Aug. 20, 1836, by Rev. Erastus Denison	1	55
William W. of Stonington, m. Sally **HOWELL**, of Groton, Sept. 16, 1827, by Rev. John G. Wightman	1	24
*Sarah, m. John **AVERY**, Aug. 23, 1705	LR2	0
DENNIS, Julia, m. John **BINKS**, b. of Groton, Dec. 14, 1845, by Elisha Morgan, J.P.	1	74
Mary, of Stonington, m. John **AVERY**, Jr., June 13, 1751, by Rev. Nath[anie]l Pells	1	162
DERBY, Mary, d. Samuel & Mary, b. June 27, 1744	1	136
DEVEROW, Ann Elizabeth, of Groton, m. William **MILLER**, of New London, Nov. 8, 1825, by Caleb Avery, J.P.	1	19
DEWEY, Abigail, m. Henry **LAMB**, b. of Groton, Nov. 21, 1824, by John G. Wightman, Eld.	1	14
Benjamin C., m. Amanda **HOLDREDGE**, b. of Groton, Apr. 5, 1847, by Rev. H. R. Knapp	1	83
Elizabeth, m. Peter **BAKER**, b. of Groton, May 12, 1839, by Ira R. Steward	1	60
Naomi, of Groton, m. Richard **PARK[E]**, of Island of Wight, G.B., July 4, 1838, by Rev. John G. Wightman	1	59
Reuben B., of N. Stonington, m. Sally M. **WHITNEY**, of Groton, Mar. 22, 1825, by William Williams, J.P.	1	16
Silas, of Lebanon, m. Sally Ann **BROWN**, of Groton, Oct. 20, 1828, by Rev. Roswell Burrows	1	29
William G., m. Jane **STODDARD**, b. of Groton, June 28, 1829, by John G. Wightman, Eld.	1	31
DeWOLF, Eldredge, s. Anthony & Mary, b. June 21, 1797	2	91
DICKENSON, Ann Mariah, m. John W. **ADAMS**, b. of Groton, June 25, 1837, by Rev. Ira R. Steward	1	57
DILL, Lois, m. John **SHOLES**, b. of Groton, May 12, 1764	2	62
DODGE, David, m. Rebeckah **YEOMANS**, May 15, 1717	1	119
David, [s. David & Rebeckah], b. July 15, 1719	1	119
Eunice, of Stonington, m. John **SCHRIDER**, of New York, Dec. 8, 1839, by Rev. John G. Wightman	1	62
DOLBEAR, Mary, of New London, m. William **AVERY**, of Groton, Sept. 16, 176[ ]	2	4
DORE, Eleoner, m. John **POOLER**, Feb. 20, 1707	1	116
DOUGLASS, James W., m. Eliza J. **RATHBONE**, b. of Groton, June 4, 1848, by Nathan Daball, J.P.	1	80
Lucy Ann, of Groton, m. John H. **BERRY**, of Plattsburgh, N.Y., June 4, 1848, by Nathan Daball, J.P.	1	81
Margary, m. Charles H. **MURPHEY**, b. of Douglass(?)*, Apr. 17, 1829, by Asa Fish, J.P. (*Probably Groton)	1	30
Mary, of Stonington, m. Nelson **LAMB**, of Groton, Mar. 19, 1851, by James C. LAMB, J.P.	1	91

	Vol.	Page
DOUGLASS, (cont.)		
Rachel, m. [A]Eneas H. **MURPHEY**, Feb. 17, 1833, by Rev. Erastus Denison	1	43
Sarah, m. John **DEAN**, Dec. 21, 1738	1	181
William, Jr., m. Martha **PARK[E]**, b. of Groton, May 21, 1826, by Roswell Fish, J.P.	1	20
William, of Maine, m. W[i]d. Lucy **PARK**, of Groton, Nov. 16, 1826, by Roswell Fish, J.P.	1	22
DOWNING, Christopher, [s. John], b. Apr. 28, 1719	1	127
Elizabeth, d. Jonathan & Mary, b. Apr. 9, 1705	1	131
Elizabeth, m. La[w]rence **STOGERS**, June 19, 1718	1	110
Jedediah, [s. John], b. Aug. 23, 1725	1	127
John, [s. John], b. Apr. 5, 1717	1	127
Jonathan, s. Jonathan & Mary, b. Sept. 11, 1703	1	131
Joseph, [s. John], b. July 31, 1723	1	127
Mary, d. Jonathan & Mary, b. May 15, 1699	1	131
Nathaniel, [s. John], b. May 22, 1721	1	127
DOWNS, Eliza W., of New York, m. Jabez **PENDLETON**, of Westerly, R.I., Nov. 10, 1822, by Elisha Avery, J.P.	1	8
DRAPER, Hannah, d. [William & Mary], b. Jan. 2, 1745/6	1	184
Thomas, s. William & Mary, b. Sept. 16, 1744	1	184
DRISCOLL, Luther, m. Catharine **CRANDALL**, b. of Groton, Jan. 7, 1821, by Ralph Hurlbutt, J.P.	1	2
DUDLEY, Alviah H., s. [Lyman & Asenath M.], b. Aug. 22, 1829	3	16
Lucretia, of Groton, m. Capt. Thomas **WILLIAMS**, of Stonington, Dec. 24, 1826, by John G. Wightman, Eld.	1	23
Mary M., d. [Lyman & Asenath M.], b. Aug. 22, 1829	3	16
Mary M., m. Capt. Elihu **SPICER**, Jr., b. of Groton, Jan. 21, 1852, by Rev. Franklin A. Slater	1	93
DUNBAR, Anna, [d. Thomas & Anna], b. Mar. 28, 1711	1	103
Elizabeth, [d. Thomas & Anna], b. May 19, 1712	1	103
Eunice, [d. Thomas & Anna], b. Sept. 4, 1717	1	103
Gurdon, m. Ann E. **SMITH**, b. of Groton, Apr. 23, 1854, by Rev. Isaac Cheesebrough	1	96
James, [s. Thomas & Anna], b. Aug. 17, 1707	1	103
Jemima, [s. Thomas & Anna], b. Mar. 20, 1725	1	103
Mary, [d. Thomas & Anna], b. July 8, 1704	1	103
Thomas, m. Anna **NICHOLS**, Apr. 21, 1703	1	103
Thomas, [s. Thomas & Anna], b. Apr. 10, 1709	1	103
DUNHAM, Dorcas, of Charleston, S.C., m. Greenman **GERE**, of Groton, Mar. 14, 1799	2	42
John, of Stonington, m. Prudence **PARK**, of Groton, June 6, 1825, by Roswell Fish, J.P.	1	17
Prudence, Mrs., m. Ezra **BAILEY**, b. of Groton, Nov. 11, 1849, by Rev. W[illia]m C. Walker	1	86
DURFEY, Benjamin, of Griswold, m. Addelia Everett AVERY, of Groton, Mar. 9, 1830, by Timothy Tuttle	1	33
Elizabeth, W. Dr. Joseph, d. Mar. 21, 1834	3	30
DWYER, Thomas E., of New London, m. Ellen **BRAND**, of Groton, Nov. 28, 1850, by Rev. Jared R. Avery	1	90
EAGLETON, Phebe, of Stonington, m. Thomas **WELLS**, of Groton, Mar. 21, 1782, in Stonington, by Eleazer Brown, Elder	2	22
EDGECOMB, EDGCOMB, Albert, m. Mary **BILL**, Aug. 29, 1819	3	4

	Vol.	Page
EDGECOMB, EDGCOMB, (cont.)		
Albert, m. Lucy **AVERY**, b. of Groton, Feb. 20, 1822, by John G. Wightman	1	6
Albert, m. Lucy **AVERY**, Feb. 20, 1822	3	4
Albert, m. Clarissa H. **FISH**, b. of Groton, May 21, 1826, by John G. Wightman, Eld.	1	20
Asa Parke, s. [David & Desire], b. Oct. 10, 1795	2	79
Avery, s. [David & Desire], b. Dec. 28, 1790	2	79
Betsey, d. [David & Desire], b. Apr. 29, 1793; d. May 27, 1827	2	79
Bridget, of Groton, m. Horace **TRUMAN**, of Norwich, Aug. 1, 1847, by Rev. Nicholas T. Allen	1	79
Clarissa, m. Roswell S. **BURROWS**, b. of Groton, Oct. 13, 1844, by Rev. Augustus Bolles	1	72
Daniel, s. Samuel, m. Harriet **ASHBEY**, d. Edward, b. of Groton, June 2, 1824, by Rev. Roswell Burrows	1	13
Daniel Webster, [s. Daniel D. & Esther], b. Aug. 23, 1840	3	16
David, m. Desire **PARK[E]**, b. of Groton, Mar. 29, 1781, by Jonathan Brewster, J.P.	2	79
David, s. [David & Desire], b. Aug. 3, 1786	2	79
David, s. Asa P., b. Mar. 21, 1828	3	14
David, Sr., d. [ ]	2	79
Deborah, d. [David & Desire], b. Jan. 22, 1784	2	79
Deborah, d. [David & Desire], d. June 22, 1800	2	79
Desire, w. David, Sr., d. Sept. 6, 1826	2	79
Dorothy, d. [David & Desire], b. Feb. 19, 1782	2	79
Edmund, [s. Daniel D. & Esther], b. Feb. 24, 1844	3	16
Eli, m. Clarissa **BABCOCK**, b. of Groton, July 30, 1843, by Rev. Erastus Denison	1	69
Elizabeth F., of Groton, m. Cyrus **HEWIT[T]**, of New London, June 19, 1847, by Rev. Nicholas T. Allen	1	78
Emily, d. [Daniel D. & Esther], b. July 11, 1832	3	16
Esther, m. Henry **REYNOLDS**, b. of Groton, Sept. 4, 1827, by John G. Wightman, Eld.	1	24
Gilbert, s. Daniel D. & Esther, b. Oct. 11, 1830	3	16
Gilbert, [s. Daniel D. & Esther], d. June 24, 1843	3	16
Harriet, w. Daniel D., d. May 9, 1826	3	16
Harriet, d. Daniel D. & Esther, b. Sept. 7, 1828	3	16
Harriet, m. Sanford **MORGAN**, b. of Groton, Dec. 14, 1828, by John G. Wightman, Eld.	1	29
Henry R., m. Caroline A. **GETCHELL**, of New London, Oct. 2, 1852, by Rev. Nicholas T. Allen	1	94
John, m. Abby **GATES**, b. of Groton, Aug. 1, 1826, by Rev. Roswell Burrows	1	21
Jonathan, s. [David & Desire], b. Aug. 24, 1788	2	79
Julia A., m. Silas W. **FISH**, May 8, 1850, by Rev. W. Munger	1	89
Julia Catharine, d. [Albert & Lucy], b. Jan. 23, 1825	3	4
Lucy C., of Groton, m. James A. **STODDARD**, of Ledyard, Sept. 6, 1846, by Rev. H. R. Knapp	1	83
Lyman, s. [David & Desire], b. Feb. 27, 1798; d. Mar. 27, 1805	2	79
Malvina, d. Daniel D. & Harriet, b. Mar. 6, 1825	3	16
Mary, w. Albert, d. Dec. 22, 1820	3	4
Mary, w. Asa P., d. Jan. 10, 1829	3	14

	Vol.	Page
EDGECOMB, EDGCOMB, (cont.)		
Mary A., of Groton, m. Albert **MOXLEY**, of Ledyard, Feb. 5, 1839, by Ira R. Steward	1	60
Mary Abby, m. William B. **SMITH**, b. of Groton, June 1, 1851, in Porterville, by Rev. A. F. Slater	1	91
Mary Adelia, [d. Albert & Mary], b. June 25, 1820	3	4
Mary Ann, d. Daniel D., b. Jan. 29, 1836	3	16
Nancy M., m. Charles G. **AVERY**, b. of Groton, Apr. 3, 1842, by Ira R. Steward	1	66
Nathan S., of N. Stonington, m. July E. **WILLIAMS**, of Groton, Dec. 9, 1824, by William Williams, J.P.	1	14
Sally A., m. William H. **BENHAM**, b. of Groton, July 14, 1839, by Ira R. Steward	1	61
William Cary, [s. Daniel D. & Esther], b. Aug. 14, 1845	3	16
EDWARDS, Bildad, s. Daniel & Mary, b. Dec. 31, 1752	1	162
Lodowick H., of S. Hampton, L.I., m. Lucy A. **AVERY**, of Groton, Jan. 1, 1845, by Rev. Cyrus Miner	1	72
EDY, Sylva, m. Jacob **AVERY**, June [ ], 1754	1	163
ELDERKIN, Ahira, of Lebanon, m. Roxelany **ELDERKIN**, of Groton, Oct. 22, 1783, in N. Groton, by Rev. Parke Allyn	2	33
Erastus, b. Sept. 18, 1784	2	29
Nancy, b. Aug. 15, 1786	2	29
Roxelany, of Groton, m. Ahira **ELDERKIN**, of Lebanon, Oct. 22, 1783, in N. Groton, by Rev. Parke Allyn	2	33
Susanna, m. Isaac **AVERY**, Mar. 31, 1742	1	151
ELDREDGE, Abel, m. Sabrina **PACKER**, b. of Groton, Sept. 7, 1820, by Roswell Fish, J.P.	1	2
Abigail, d. Daniel & Abigail, b. May 20, 1712	1	122
Abigail, m. Ichabod Packer, Oct. 30, 1729	1	139
Abigail, d. [Thomas & Abigail], b. Mar. 24, 1731	1	145
Abigail, d. [Daniel & Sarah], b. May 3, 1745	1	185
Abigail, d. Daniel & Sarah, b. May 3, 1745	2	96
Abigail, d. [Charles & Mary], b. May 11, 1761	1	185
Abigail, d. [Charles & Mary], b. May 11, 1761	2	96
Amos, s. [Daniel & Sarah], b. Dec. 29, 1747	1	185
Amos, s. [Daniel & Sarah], b. Dec. 29, 1747	2	96
Amos, m. Mary **LESTER**, b. of Groton, Feb. 11, 1821, by Ralph Hurlbutt, J.P.	2	29
Betsey, d. [Samuel & Mary], b. May 19, 1782	2	32
Catherine, d. [Charles & Mary], b. Nov. 7, 1754	1	185
Catherine, d. [Charles & Mary], b. Nov. 7, 1754	2	96
Catherine, d. [Charles, Jr. & Gloriana], b. Sept. 22, 1779; d. Aug. 11, 1780	2	33
Caty, d. [Samuel & Mary], b. Dec. 17, 1786	2	32
Charles, s. Daniel & Abigail, b. Nov. 14, 1720; d. Aug. 21, 1795	1	122
Charles, m. Mary **STARR**, Apr. 23, 1741	2	96
Charles, m. Mary **STARR**, Apr. 23, 1741	1	185
Charles, s. [Charles & Mary], b. Aug. 28, 1743	1	185
Charles, s. Charles & Mary, b. Aug. 28, 1743	2	96
Charles, Jr., m. Rachel **AVERY**, b. of Groton, Sept. 13, 1764, by Rev. Jonathan Barber	2	33
Charles, s. [Charles, Jr. & Rachel], b. June 7, 1765	2	33
Charles, Jr., of Groton, m. Gloriana **HAVENS**, of Shelter Island, June 21, 1778, by Rev. Aaron Kinne	2	33

	Vol.	Page
ELDREDGE, (cont.)		
Charles, Jr., had negro boy Nero, b. Dec. 5, 1790	2	33
Charles, s. [Samuel & Phebe], b. Nov. 7, 1795	2	32
Charles, [Jr.], d. Nov. 27, 1798, ae. 55 y.	2	33
Charles, m. Desire **BILL**, b. of Groton, July 16, 1820, by Rev. John G. Wightman	1	1
Charles, m. Bridget **HEM[P]STEAD**, b. of Groton, May 28, 1827, by Roswell Fish, J.P.	1	26
Charles W., of Mt. Carmel, Ill., m. Mrs. Hannah M. **AVERY**, of Groton, Oct. 1, 1848, by Rev. Jared R. Avery	1	82
Charlotte, d. [Samuel & Mary], b. Oct. 20, 1784	2	32
Daniel, m. Abigail **FISH**, June 26, 1711, by Rev. Ephraim Woodbridge	1	122
Daniel, s. Daniel & Abigail, b. June 13, 1718	1	122
Daniel, m. Sarah **CHIPMAN**, Nov. 17, 1739	1	185
Daniel, m. Sarah **CHIPMAN**, Nov. 17, 1739	2	96
Daniel, s. [Daniel & Sarah], b. Oct. 13, 1740	1	185
Daniel, s. Daniel & Sarah, b. Oct. 13, 1740	2	96
Daniel, d. Oct. 5, 1748	1	185
Daniel, d. Oct. 5, 1748	2	96
Daniel, s. [Charles & Mary], b. Dec. 24, 1758; d. Nov. 18, 1781	1	185
Daniel, s. [Charles & Mary], b. Dec. 24, 1758; d. Nov. 18, 1781	2	96
Daniel, d. Sept. 3, 1789	2	3
David, s. [Charles, Jr. & Rachel], b. Oct. 23, 1772; d. Oct. 14, 1778	2	33
Delight, m. George **PACKER**, b. of Groton, July 17, 1820, by Rev. John G. Wightman	1	1
Elam, m. Eunice **BURROWS**, b. of Groton, Aug. 12, 1821, by Roswell Fish, J.P.	1	3
Elam, m. Hannah **FITCH**, b. of Groton, June 10, 1827, by Roswell Burrows	1	23
Elizabeth, d. [Charles & Mary], b. Dec. 10, 1756	1	185
Elizabeth, d. [Charles & Mary], b. Dec. 10, 1756	2	96
Emily, m. John **HEATH**, b. of Groton, Aug. 4, 1840, by Rev. John W. Case	1	63
Fanny, d. [Charles & Mary], b. Apr. 16, 1766	1	185
Fanny, d. [Charles & Mary], b. Apr. 16, 1766	2	96
Fanny, m. Zabdial **ROGERS**, Feb. 27, 1791	2	35
Freelove, d. Thomas & Abigail, b. Feb. 12, 1728/9	1	145
George, Jr., m. Phebe **SAWYER**, b. of Groton, Sept. 6, 1825, by Asa Fitch, J.P.	1	18
Gloriana, w. Charles [Jr.], d. Oct. 14, 1823, ae. 76 y.	2	33
Hannah, d. [Elam & Hannah], b. Mar. 3, 1829	3	15
Hannah, m. W[illia]m H. **LATHAM**, b. of Groton, July 23, 1849, by Rev. H. R. Knapp	1	85
James, s. [Charles & Mary], b. May 30, 1745	1	185
James, s. Charles & Mary, b. May 30, 1745	2	96
John, s. [Daniel & Sarah], b. Dec. 13, 1742	1	185
John, s. Daniel & Sarah, b. Dec. 13, 1742	2	96
John Burrows, s. [Elam & Hannah], b. Feb. 3, 1830	3	15
Jonathan, s. [Charles & Mary], b. Nov. 17, 1752	1	185
Jonathan, s. [Charles & Mary], b. Nov. 17, 1752	2	96
Joseph, s. [Charles & Mary], b. Nov. 28, 1763	1	185
Joseph, s. [Charles & Mary], b. Nov. 28, 1763	2	96
Joseph Conkling, s. [Samuel & Phebe], b. Nov. 2, 1791	2	32
Lydia, of Stonington, m. Frederick B. **ASHBEY**, of Groton, June 23, 1826, by Asa Fitch, J.P.	1	20

	Vol.	Page
ELDREDGE, (cont.)		
Mary, d. [Thomas & Abigail], b. Dec. 9, 1735	1	145
Mary, d. [Charles & Mary], b. Mar. 21, 1746	1	185
Mary, d. Charles & Mary, b. Mar. 21, 1746	2	96
Mary, d. [Charles, Jr. & Rachel], b. Sept. 25, 1767	2	33
Mary, w. Samuel, d. Jan. 26, 1787	2	32
Mary, w. Charles, d. May 19, 1779	1	185
Mary, w. Charles, d. May 19, 1779 (The name is "Stanton"in the copy)	2	96
Mary, m. Ebenezer **AVERY**, 2d, Feb. 17, 1793	2	44
Mary, of Groton, m. Joseph W. **RICE**, of Stonington, Aug. 5, 1804, by Rev. Christ[opher] Avery	2	68
Nathaniel Thompson, s. [Samuel & Phebe], b. Oct. 22, 1793	2	32
Phebe, d. [Samuel & Phebe], b. Oct. 29, 1789	2	32
Polly, [d. Samuel & Mary], b. Oct. 12, 1780	2	32
Rachel, d. [Charles, Jr. & Rachel], b. Aug. 25, 1777; d. Sept. 4, 1777	2	33
Rachel, w. Charles, Jr., d. Aug. 31, 1777	2	33
Samuel, s. [Charles & Mary], b. Nov. 27, 1750	1	185
Samuel, s. Charles & Mary, b. Nov. 27, 1750	2	96
Samuel, b. Nov. 27, 1750; m. Mary **TURNER**, Dec. 17, 1771	2	32
Samuel, s. Samuel & Mary, b. Apr. 22, 1773	2	32
Samuel, of Groton, m. Phebe **CONKLING**, of Long Island, Jan. 17, 1788	2	32
Saviah, d. [Samuel & Mary], b. Aug. 4, 1775	2	32
Thomas, s. [Thomas & Abigail], b. June 28, 1733	1	145
William, s. [Charles, Jr. & Rachel], b. Dec. 14, 1769	2	33
William, b. Dec. 14, 1769; m. Eliza **AVERY**, Sept. 23, 1794	2	48
William, m. Lucy **BURROWS**, b. of Groton, Aug. 28, 1839, by Ira R. Steward	1	61
William Pitt, s. [Samuel & Mary], b. July 5, 1778	2	32
William T., of Stonington, m. Eliza A. **ALEXANDER**, of Groton, Dec. 8, 1845, by Rev. William C. Walker	1	75
Zerviah, d. Daniel & Abigail, b. Oct. 6, 1715; d. May 7, 1795	1	122
Zerviah, d. [Charles & Mary], b. Feb. 7, 1748/9; d. Mar. 13, 1766, then Zerviah **STANTON**	1	185
Zerviah, d. Charles & Mary, b. Feb. 7, 1748/9	2	96
ELLIS, Elizabeth, m. Williams **GILES**, June 25, 1768	1	183
ELLISON, Benjamin, m. Aliss Abby **FITCH**, resident in Groton, July 28, 1825, by Asa Fish, J.P.	1	17
ELLS, James, of Harpersfield, N.Y., m. Fanny **LEDYARD**, of Groton, Apr. 19, 1825, by John G. Wightman, Elder	1	16
ELLSWORTH, Albert, of New London, m. Sarah **ALLEN**, of Groton, June 2, 1844, by Rev. Simon B. Bailey	1	71
ENOS, John, m. Mary **MORGAN**, b. of Groton, Sept. 24, 1795	2	65
John, s. [John & Mary], b. June 20, 1802	2	65
Joshua, s. [John & Mary], b. July 16, 1796	2	65
Paulina, d. [John & Mary], b. July 10, 1800; d. May 13, 1802	2	65
Phebe, d. [John & Mary], b. Aug. 17, 1798	2	65
ETH[E]RIDGE, Amos, m. Mary **LESTER**, b. of Groton, Feb. 11, 1821, by Ralph Hurlbutt, J.P.	1	3
EVANS, George, of N.Y. City, m. Lucy S. **AVERY**, of Groton, Jan. 2, 1837, by Timothy Tuttle	1	56
FAGINS, FAGENS, Lucy, of N. Stonington, m. Peter **GEORGE**, of Groton, May 2, 1832, by Philip Gray, J.P.	1	40

	Vol.	Page
FAGINS, FAGENS, (cont.)		
Sullivan, m. Phebe H. **COTERAL**, May 3, 1835, by W[illia]m M. Williams, J.P.	1	50
FAIRBANKS, William F., m. Mary A. **CLARK**, b. of Groton, Jan. 1, 1851, by Rev. Franklin A. Slater	1	91
FAIRBROTHER, Isaac N., of Providence, R.I., m. Emily D. **LAMB**, of Groton, July 7, 1839, by Rev. John G. Wightman	1	61
FANNING, Abigail, d. John & Abigail, b. Mar. 26, 1741	1	163
Ann, [d. Jonathan & Elizabeth], b. July 1, 1729	1	137
Charles, s. [Thomas & Elizabeth], b. Dec. 16, 1749	1	182
David, [s. Jonathan & Elizabeth], b. Mar. 2, 1727	1	137
Deborah, d. [John & Abigail], b. Mar. 9, 1745	1	163
Edmond, s. [Edward & Hannah], b. Sept. 1, 1730	1	181
Elisha, s. [Thomas & Elizabeth], b. June 18, 1765	1	182
Elkany, s. [Thomas & Elizabeth], b. Oct. 17, 1762	1	182
Emeline, of Groton, m. Lyman **SMITH**, of Montville, Jan. 25, 1829, by William Williams, J.P.	1	30
Eunice, d. [George], b. Apr. 7, 1771	2	20
Frederick, s. [Thomas & Elizabeth], b. Feb. 11,1760	1	182
Hannah, [d. Jonathan & Elizabeth], b. Sept. 20, 1736	1	137
Hope, d. [Thomas & Elizabeth], b. Aug. 14, 1757	1	182
Isaac, m. Betsey **LATHAM**, Jan. 24, 1836, by W[illia]m M. Williams, J.P.	1	53
James, s. [George], b. July 5, 1772	2	20
John, s. [John & Abigail], b. Nov. 9, 1746	1	163
Joshua, s. [John & Abigail], b. Sept. 6, 1748	1	163
Katherine, d. [Thomas & Elizabeth], b. June 9, 1745; d. Mar. 9, 1755	1	182
Keturah, d. [George], b. Aug. 4, 1776	2	20
Lois, d. Jonathan, Jr. & Mary, b. May 25, 1743	1	154
Margaret, d. Jonathan & Elizabeth, b. Nov. 23, 1724	1	137
Mary, [d. Jonathan & Elizabeth], b. June 5, 1731	1	137
Mary, m. Humphr[e]y **BROWN**, b. of Groton, Dec. 5, 1750, by William Williams, J.P.	1	176
Phinehas, s. Jona[than, Jr.] & Mary, b. Nov. 16 1743	1	154
Prudence, d. [Thomas & Elizabeth], b. Apr. 28, 1752	1	182
Rufus L., m. Mary L. **WILLIAMS**, b. of Groton, Dec. 12, 1830, by W[illia]m M. Williams, J.P.	1	36
Sarah, [d. John & Abigail], b. Mar. 18, 1743	1	163
Simeon, s. [John & Abigail], b. Oct. 21, 1750	1	163
Thankful, d. [John & Abigail], b. Aug. 19, 1752	1	163
Thomas, s. Jonathan, Jr. & Mary, b. Nov. 14, 1741	1	154
Thomas, m. Elizabeth **CAPRON**, July 26, 1744	1	182
Thomas, s. [Thomas & Elizabeth], b. May 22, 1755	1	182
Thomas, Capt., d. Dec. 15, 1787	1	182
William, s. Edward & Hannah, b. Dec. 23, 1715	1	181
William, m. Anna **MINER**, Mar. 17, 1737	1	181
FARSEE, FORESEE, FEARSHEE, FEARSEE [see also **FORSYTH**],		
Abigail, [d. James & Hannah], b. Jan. 4, 1723/4	1	115
Amey, [d. James & Hannah], b. Nov. 30, 1733	1	115
Amey, d. James & Mary, b. Feb. 27, 1735/6	1	172
Andrew, [s. James & Hannah], b. June 28, 1730	1	115
Caleb, s. James, Jr. & Mary, b. Oct. 21, 1733	1	172
Elizabeth, d. James & Hannah, b. Jan. 12, 1709	1	115
Gilbert, [s. James & Hannah], b. Feb. 13, 1716	1	115

	Vol.	Page
FARSEE, FORESEE, FEARSHEE, FEARSEE, (cont.)		
Hannah, [d. James & Hannah], b. Feb. 12, 1713	1	115
James, m. Hannah **LESTER**, Sept. 9, 1708	1	115
James, [s. James & Hannah], b. July 12, 1711	1	115
Jonathan, [s. James & Hannah], b. May 14, 1720	1	115
Mary, [d. James & Hannah], b. Apr. 28, 1722	1	115
Nathan, [s. James & Hannah], b. Dec. 28, 1727	1	115
Sarah, [d. James & Hannah], b. Oct. 26, 1725	1	115
Timothy, [s. James & Hannah], b. Mar. 15, 1718	1	115
FELLOWS, John, m. Mary Ann **SHAW**, b. of Groton, Feb. 10, 1830, by Nathan Daboll, J.P.	1	33
Nancy, of Groton, m. Joseph **BOLLES**, of New London, Nov. 8, 1827, by Asa Fitch, J.P.	1	25
FENNER, Charles, m. Harriet **CHIPMAN**, widow of Joseph, Nov. 6, 1814	3	33
Charles L., m. Elizabeth **GALLUP**, b. of Groton, Oct. 11, 1849, by Rev. Jared R. Avery	1	85
Charles Lafayette, s. [Charles & Harriet], b. Feb. 5, 1825	3	33
Elizabeth, d. [Charles & Harriet], b. June 27, 1817	3	33
Elizabeth, m. Lorenzo **BAKER**, b. of Groton, Mar. 24, 1836, by Joseph Durfey, J.P.	1	53
James Munroe, s. [Charles & Harriet], b. June 15, 1820	3	33
Marcus, s. [Charles & Harriet], b. Jan. 6, 1830	3	33
Mary Louisa, d. [Charles & Harriet], b. June 22, 1822	3	33
Nancy, d. [Charles & Harriet], b. July 6, 1827	3	33
Nancy, m. Edwin B. **CHESTER**, May 1, 1845, at Rev. R. Russell's house, by Rev. R. Russell	1	73
William Henry, s. [Charles & Harriet], b. Aug. 17, 1815	3	33
FERBS, James, of Mass., m. Deborah **BILL**, of Groton, Oct. 11, 1828, by Nathan Daboll, J.P.	1	28
FERGO, FARGO, Lucy Ann, b. Jan. 31, 1816	2	40
Lyman, s. [Thomas & Sarah], b. Oct. 11, 1790	2	48
Polly, d. [Thomas & Sarah], b. Feb. 1, 1795	2	48
Thomas, m. Sarah **WOODBRIDGE**, Jan. 4, 1790	2	48
FERRIS, James P., m. Melissa B. **WILBUR**, b. of Groton, Apr. 22, 1849, by Rev. Simon B. Bailey	1	83
FIELDS, Sylvester, of East Hampton, Suffolk Co., N.Y., m. Polly **ANDERSON**, of Groton, Sept. 4, 1820, by Elisha Avery, J.P.	1	1
FISH, [see also **FISK**], Abby Ellen, d. [Joseph & Betsey], b. Feb. 1, 1829	3	27
Abel, s. [George & Sarah], b. May 26, 1789	2	87
Abigail, m. Daniel **ELDREDGE**, June 26, 1711, by Rev. Ephraim Woodbridge	1	122
Abigail, d. Nathan & Mary (**BURROWS**), m. Capt. Jonathan FISH, Dec. 3, 1747	2	16
Abigail, [d. Nathan], b. May 21, 1760	2	16
Albert, m. Frances E. **FITCH**, b. of Groton, Oct. 25, 1842, by Ira R. Steward	1	67
Aldin, s. [Sands & Bridget], b. Aug. 7, 1808	2	55
Alden, m. Mary (or Sally) Ann **BEEBE**, b. of Groton, Mar. 15, 1843, by Ira R. Steward	1	68
Amos A., of N.Y. City, m. Emily **HAVENS**, of Groton, May 12, 1847, by Rev. Erastus Denison	1	78
Amos Avery, s. [Roswell & Isabel], b. Aug. 19, 1807	2	53
Anna, [d. Nathan], b. Aug. 26, 1776	2	12

	Vol.	Page
FISH, (cont.)		
Arsena, d. [Thomas & Lucy], b. Mar. 30, 1795	2	31
Asa, s. Sands & Bridget, b. July 17, 1790	2	55
Asahel, m. Esther **BILLINGS**, Oct. 2, 1755	1	165
Benjamin S., m. Lavinia A. **MORGAN**, b. of Groton, Apr. 1, 1846, by Rev. Erastus Denison	1	75
Betsey, m. Erastus **TURNER**, b. of Ledyard, June 25, 1849, by Rev. W. C. Walker	1	86
Bridget, d. [Sands & Bridget], b. Aug. 21, 1811	2	55
Bridget, of Groton, m. William **CLIFT**, of Stonington, June 18, 1833, by John G. Wightman, Eld.	1	44
Caroline, d. [Thomas & Lucy], b. Mar. 24, 1793	2	31
Caroline, of Groton, m. Orlando **CLARKE**, Aug. 16, 1829, by Rev. Roswell Burrows	1	31
Catharine, m. Russell **LATHAM**, b. of [ ], Oct. 29, 1848, by Caleb M. Williams, J.P.	1	81
Charles, s. [Sands & Bridget], b. Feb. 3, 1801	2	55
Clarissa, d. [George & Sarah], b. Apr. 11, 1792	2	87
Clarissa H., m. Albert **EDGECOMB**, b. of Groton, May 21, 1826, by John G. Wightman, Eld.	1	20
Content, m. Joseph **HOLDREDGE**, Jan. 29, 1795	2	50
Cynthia, [d. Nathan], b. Sept. 21, 1770	2	12
Cynthia, m. Benadam **GALLUP**, Jr., Oct. 14, 1792	2	84
Edmund, [s. Nathan], b. Feb. 5, 1772	2	12
Edmund, s. [Roswell & Isabel], b. Jan. 26, 1805	2	53
Edmund, of New York, m. Betsey Ann **AVERY**, of Groton, Mar. 19, 1838, by Mark Meade	1	58
Elisha, [s. Moses & Martha], b. Feb. 7, 1720	1	121
Elisha, [s. Thomas & Lucy], b. Dec. 4, 1782	2	31
Eliza, m. Roswell **PACKER**, b. of Groton, Dec. 20, 1820, by John O. Miner, J.P.	1	2
Elizabeth, d. [George & Sarah], b. July 9, 1796	2	87
Erastus, m. Catharine **ING[RA]HAM**, b. of Groton, Dec. 4, 1846, by Rev. S. B. Bailey	1	77
Eunice, d. [Asahel & Esther], b. Mar. 15, 1756	1	165
Eunice, [d. Jonathan & Abigail], b. July 18, 1765; m. [ ], Daniel **ASHCRAFT**	2	16
Eunice, [d. Thomas & Lucy], b. Dec. 13, 1784	2	31
Eunice, of Groton, m. John **BOYDEN**, of Guilford, Vt., Apr. 30, 1824, by Rev. Roswell Burrows	1	13
Eveline, m. Simeon **CHESTER**, Jr., b. of Groton, Aug.21, 1823, by Roswell Burrows, Min.	1	10
Fred R., s. Simeon & [Eliza **RANDALL**], b. Nov. 20, 1832	3	15
George, [s. Jonathan & Abigail], b. Mar. 20, 1763; m. [ ], Sarah **HINCKLEY**	2	16
George, m. Sarah **HINCKLEY**, Jan. 20, 1785	2	87
George, s. [George & Sarah], b. Apr. 8, 1798	2	87
George T., of New London, m. Hannah E. **WILLIAMS**, of Groton, May 11, 1846, by Rev. Jared R. Avery	1	76
Hadlai, s. [George & Sarah], b. Mar. 21, 1804	2	87
Hadley, m. Mary **BABCOCK**, b. of Groton, Aug. 27, 1826, by John G. Wightman, Eld.	1	21
Hannah, [d. Nathan], b. Aug. 3, 1764	2	12

	Vol.	Page
FISH, (cont.)		
Hannah, d. [Thomas & Lucy], b. May 2, 1791	2	31
Hannah, d. [Sands & Bridget], b. Mar. 10, 1792	2	55
Hannah, of Colchester, m. Holloway **LATHAM**, of Groton, Jan. 22, 1815, by Amasa Loomis, Jr.	1	14
Hannah, m. Benjamin **ASHBY**, b. of Groton, Jan. 6, 1822, by Roswell Burrows, Eld.	1	5
Hannah E., of Groton, m. Hiram **PECKHAM**, of Ledyard, Nov. 13, 1853, at Noank, by Rev. James M. Phillips	1	95
Hannah P., of Groton, m. Thomas **BRUSH**, of Jamaica, L.I., Oct. 24, 1843, by Ira R. Steward	1	70
Harriet E., m. Ezra E. **BEEBE**, b. of Groton, Sept. 20, 1842, by Rev. Erastus Denison	1	67
Hobart, s. [George & Sarah], b. May 8, 1802	2	87
Horatio N., m. Lydia **MORGAN**, Aug. 29, 1824, by Rev. Roswell Burrows	1	13
Horatio Nelson, s. [George & Sarah], b. June 18, 1800	2	87
Jabez, s. [Thomas & Jemima], b. July 10, 1747	1	180
Jane, m. Timothy **WIGHTMAN**, June 1, 1743	1	175
Jasper S., m. Jane Ann **MORGAN**, b. of Groton, Sept. 14, 1843, by Ira R. Steward	1	70
Jemima, d. [Thomas & Jemima], b. Oct. 4, 1748	1	180
Jemima, [d. Jonathan & Abigail], b. Oct. 31, 1767; m. [ ], Joshua **MORGAN**; m. [ ], Daniel **BILL**	2	16
Jemima, d. [Thomas & Lucy], b. Dec. 14, 1786	2	31
John, 2d, m. Susan Angeline **WALSWORTH**, b. of Groton, Sept. 8, 1833, by John G. Wightman, Eld.	1	45
Jonathan, Capt., m. Abigail **FISH**, d. Nathan & Mary Burrows FISH, Dec. 3, 1747	2	16
Jonathan, [s. Jonathan & Abigail], b. June 16, 1770	2	16
Joseph, m. Betsey **RATHBURN**, b. of Groton, Sept. 29, 1824, by Gideon B. Perry, Minister	1	15
Judson D., of Halifax, Vt., m. Lois L. **AVERY**, of Groton, Nov. 26, 1848, by Rev. Nicholas T. Allen	1	86
Katharine, d. Nathan, b. Aug. 24, 175[ ]	2	12
Katharine Mary, d. [Roswell & Isabel], b. Jan. 20, 1803	2	53
Katharine (**NILES**), w. Nathan, d. Jan. [ ], 1759	2	12
Levina, of Groton, m. Isaac **DENISON**, of Stonington, Feb. 18, 1817, by John G. Wightman	3	11
Levinia, d. [Sands & Bridget], b. Oct. 1, 1794	2	55
Lucy, d. [Roswell & Isabel], b. Sept. 17, 1810	2	53
Lucy, of Conn., m. Jonas **STAFFORD**, of New York, Aug. 12, 1841, by Rev. Erastus Denison	1	65
Lucy, m. Joshua **PACKER**, b. of Groton, Sept. 27, 1842, by Ira R. Steward	1	67
Lucy Morgan, [d. Thomas & Lucy], b. Jan. 26, 1780	2	31
Lucy Morgan, m. Henry **AVERY**, b. of Groton, Sept. 20, 1798, by Rev. Aaron Kinne	2	81
Lydia, [d. Jonathan & Abigail], b. Mar. 20, 1761; m. [ ], Ebenezer **FISH**	2	16
Lydia Maria, m. Comfort William **BROWN**, b. of Groton, June 5, 1831, by Rev. Roswell Burrows	1	37
Margaret Eliza, d. [Roswell & Isabel], b. Mar. 5, 1813	2	53
Martha, [d. Jonathan & Abigail], b. Apr. 1, 1753; m. [ ], Roswell **AVERY**	2	16

	Vol.	Page
FISH, (cont.)		
Martha, m. Roswell **AVERY**, Dec. 13, 1770, by Timothy Wightman, Elder	2	35
Mary, [d. Jonathan & Abigail], b. Apr. 18, 1749; m. [ ], Joseph **FISH**	2	16
Mary, [d. Nathan], b. Nov. 3, 1765	2	12
Mary, of Groton, m. Christopher **LESTER**, Apr. 10, 1791	2	60
Mary, d. [George & Sarah], b. May 13, 1794	2	87
Mary, Mrs., m. Joseph A. **LAMB**, b. of Groton, Sept. 1, 1839, by Rev. John G. Wightman	1	61
Mary Anna, d. [Thomas & Lucy], b. Jan. 11, 1789	2	31
Mary E., of Groton, m. Reuben **BRISTOL**, of Cheshire, Sept. 27, 1849, by Rev. Jabez S. Swan	1	87
Mehetable, [d. Jonathan & Abigail], b. Mar. 18,1756; m. [ ], Jesse **MORGAN**	2	16
Moses, m. Martha **WILLIAMS**, Nov. 5, 1713	1	121
Moses, [s. Moses & Martha], b. Oct. 20, 1714	1	121
Nathan, m. Katharine **NILES**, Oct 13, 1748	2	12
Nathan, s. Nathan, b. Mar. 3, 1749	2	12
Nathan, m. Katharine **HOLMES**, July 24, 1759	2	12
Nathan, s. Charles, b. June 7, 1823	2	87
Nathan Austin, s. [Roswell & Isabel], b. July 10, 1815	2	53
Nathan G., m. Emeline F. **MINER**, b. of Groton, Jan. 9, 1833, by Timothy Tuttle	1	42
Nathan S., s. Simeon & [Eliza **RANDALL**], b. Apr. 11, 1829	3	15
Nathan S., m. Penette E. **MORGAN**, b. of Groton, Mar. 24, 1850, by Rev. J. R. Avery	1	88
Phebe Williston, m. Joseph Ellery **WOODWORTH**, b. of Groton, July 14, 1822, by Timothy Tuttle	1	7
Rawzell, [s. Nathan], b. Mar. 5, 1769	2	12
Roswell, m. Isabel **PHELPS**, Feb. 2, 1797	2	53
Roswell Phelps, s. [Roswell & Isabel], b. Aug. 20, 1798	2	53
Russell, m. Esther **CHAPMAN**, b. of Groton, July 16, 1836, by Ralph Hurlbutt, J.P.	1	54
Russell, m. Elizabeth M. **CHAPMAN**, Sept. 20, 1838, by Rev. John G. Wightman	1	59
Samuel, [s. Nathan], b. July 17, 1751	2	12
Samuel, Jr., of Groton, m. Prudence **SMITH**, of Lyme, Nov. 5, 1820, by Roswell Burrows, Elder	1	2
Samuel Merrick, s. [Roswell & Isabel], b. July 8, 1800	2	53
Sands, [s. Nathan], b. Oct. 14, 1762	2	12
Sands, m. Bridget **GALLUP**, June 18, 1789	2	55
Sands, s. [Sands & Bridget], b. Feb. 27, 1799	2	55
Sands H., m. Emeline **BEEBE**, of Groton, Mar. 14, 1850, by Rev. H. R. Knapp	1	88
Sarah, [d. Nathan], b. July 1, 1761	2	12
Sarah, d. George & Sarah, b. Oct. 24, 1785	2	87
Sarah, m. Josiah **GALLUP**, Nov. 4, 1787	2	45
Silas, [s. Nathan], b. Aug. 9, 1767	2	12
Silas, of Stonington, m. Mary D. **STODDARD**, of Groton, Apr. 10, 1851, by Rev. Nehemiah B. Cooke, of Stonington	1	91
Silas Henry, s. [Roswell & Isabel], b. May 26, 1818	2	53
Silas Henry, of Rochester, N.Y., m. Emily **AVERY**, of Groton, Mar. 21, 1842, by Rev. Jared R. Avery	1	66
Silas W., m. Julia A. **EDGECOMB**, May 8, 1850, by Rev. W. Munger	1	89

	Vol.	Page
FISH, (cont.)		
Simeon, s. Nathan, b. Mar. 24, 1756; d. Feb. 16, 1757	2	12
Simeon, s. [Sands & Bridget], b. Jan. 18, 1797	2	55
Simeon, m. Eliza **RANDALL**, Oct. 15, 1823, by Roswell Burrows, Min.	1	10
Sprague, b. Mar. 10, 1768; m. Nabby **PARK[E]**, June 16, 1789	2	40
Thomas, [s. Moses & Martha], b. Aug. 18, 1716	1	121
Thomas, m. Jemima **MORGAN**, Aug. 25, 1743	1	180
Thomas, s. [Thomas & Jemima], b. Jan. 18, 1750/51	1	180
Thomas, m. Lucy **MORGAN**, d. Solomon, Nov. 12, 1778, by Rev. Aaron Kenne	2	31
William R., s. Simon & Eliza **RANDALL**, b. July 13, 1824	3	15
William S., m. Lois M. **DAVIS**, b. of Groton, Oct. 8, [1853], by Rev. James M. Phillips	1	95
FISHER, Donald, of Norwich, m. Catharine **SARLES (SEARLES?)**, of Groton, Nov. 24, 1827, by Elisha Brewster, J.P.	1	26
FISK, [see also **FISH**], John W., of Groton, m. Malinda B. **LATHAM**, of Groton, Oct. 25, 1849, by Rev. Nicholas T. Allen	1	87
FITCH, Abby, d. [Josephus & Phebe], b. Aug. 31, 1808	3	19
Aliss Abby, resident in Groton, m. Benjamin **ELLISON**, July 28, 1825, by Asa Fish, J.P.	1	17
Betsey, d. [Josephus & Phebe], b. Feb. 13, 1812	3	19
Clarissa, d. [Josephus & Phebe], b. Aug. 16, 1814	3	19
Clarissa, of Groton, m. Benjamin F. **HEDDEN**, of Stonington, Aug. 21, 1836, by Rev. Roswell Burrows	1	55
Edward, s. [Josephus & Phebe], b. June 16, 1798	3	19
Elisha, s. Pelatiah & Elizabeth, b. Apr. 30, 1756	1	166
Elisha, m. Mary **PEABODY**, b. of Groton, Nov. 3, 1822, by Rev. Roswell Burrows	1	8
Elisha, s. [Elisha & Mary], b. July 2, 1823	3	17
Elisha, m. Ann Maria **WILBUR**, Dec. 2, 1849, in Noank, by Rev. H. R. Knapp	1	88
Eliza, m. Jonathan **REYNOLDS**, Jr., b. of Groton, Nov. 3, 1833, by Rev. Ira R. Steward	1	45
Fanny, m. Ezra S. **SPENCER**, b. of Groton, Dec. 26, 1836, by Rev. Roswell Burrows	1	55
Frances E., m. Albert **FISH**, b. of Groton, Oct. 25, 1842, by Ira R. Steward	1	67
Frederick, s. [Elisha & Mary], b. Apr. 2, 1827	3	17
Hannah, m. Elam **ELDREDGE**, b. of Groton, June 10, 1827, by Roswell Burrows	1	23
Hannah, m. John **PRAY**, b. of Groton, Aug. 20, 1848, by Rev. Simon B. Bailey	1	81
Harriet P., m. Ray S. **WILBUR**, b. of Groton, Apr. 28, 1850, by Rev. N. E. Shailer	1	88
Josephus, 2d, m. Charlotte **PACKER**, of Groton, May 19, 1822, by Roswell Burrows	1	7
Latham, m. Eliza **WILBUR**, b. of Groton, July 17, 1836, by Rev. Ira R. Steward	1	55
Lucy, of Windham, m. Robert **GEER**, of Groton, Nov. 4, 1767, by Rev. Stephen White, of Windham	2	15
Lucy, m. Calvin **WILBUR**, b. of Groton, Sept. 30, 1835, by Ira R. Steward	1	52
Lucy E., m. John **DABALL**, b. of Groton, Feb. 26, 1849, by Rev. S. B. Bailey	1	82
Lucy Elizabeth, d. [Elisha & Mary], b. Apr. 3, 1829	3	17

	Vol.	Page
FITCH, (cont.)		
Lurene, d. Pelatiah & Elizabeth, b. Oct. 4, 1748	1	166
Mary, of Colchester, m. George **LAMPHERE**, of Groton, Mar. 1, 1758, by Rev. Ichabod Allyn, of Colchester	1	169
Mary, d. [Josephus & Phebe], b. Nov. 24, 1802	3	19
Mary, m. James **WILBUR**, 2d, b. of Groton, Sept. 8, 1822, by Roswell Burrows	1	7
Polly, m. Mason R. **PACKER**, b. of Groton, July 6, 1825, by John G. Wightman, Elder	1	17
Prudence, d. [Josephus & Phebe], b. Nov. 15, 1799	3	19
Prudence, m. Eldredge D. **WOLFE**, b. of Groton, Aug. 2, 1824, by Rev. Roswell Burrows	1	13
W[illia]m, m. Elizabeth **PECKHAM**, b. of Groton, July 20, 1851, by Rev. James M. Phillips, of Noank	1	92
________, s. Chester, b. Oct. 10, 1800	2	16
FLINN, Catharine, m. W[illia]m **LITTLE**, Apr. 23, 1850, at Porterville, by Rev. W. Munger	1	89
FLOID, William, s. William & Hannah, b. Mar. 9, 1728	1	136
FOOT, Ann, m. Gershom BROWN, July 8, 1714	1	129
FORSYTH, FORESITH, FORSITH, [see also **FARSEE**], Andrew, twin with Jesse, s. Jonathan & Deborah, b. Apr. 10, 1757	1	160
Anna, d. Jonathan & Deborah, b. Sept. 2, 1747	1	160
Betsey, m. Sanford **ARTHUR**, b. of Groton, Apr. 1, 1821, by Ralph Hurlbutt, J.P.	1	3
Charles, s. Jonathan & Deborah, b. Jan. 2, 1755	1	160
Deborah, w. Jonathan, d. June 23, 1761	1	160
Elizabeth, d. Jonathan & Deborah, b. Apr. 10, 1750	1	160
James, m. Lucy **COATS**, Feb. 16, 1804	2	71
Jesse, twin with Andrew, s. Jonathan & Deborah, b. Apr. 10, 1757	1	160
John, m. Susan **LESTER**, b. of Groton, Jan. 1, 1832, by Ralph Hurlbutt, J.P.	1	39
John A., of New London, m. Emeline **POTTER**, of Groton (Noank), Oct. 2, 1850, at Noank, by Rev. W[illia]m A. Smith	1	90
Jonathan, m. Deborah **BA[I]LEY**, May 10, 1743	1	160
Jonathan, s. Jonathan & Deborah, b. May 18, 1745	1	160
Lucy, d. [James & Lucy], b. Dec. 24, 1804	2	71
FOWLER, Gilbert, of New London, m. Serena **SPENCER**, of Groton, Sept. 6, 1835, by Ira R. Steward	1	52
Harris, of New London, m. Mary Ann **SPENCER**, of Groton, Apr. 17, 1838, by Ira R. Steward	1	58
Harris, m. Fanny F. **SPENCER**, b. of Groton, May 30, 1847, by Rev. Simon B. Bailey	1	78
FOX, Abigail, d. Isaac & Hannah, b. Mar. 6, 1710	1	110
Abigail, twin with Zeruiah, [d. John & Elizabeth], b. Mar. 29, 1726	1	110
Elizabeth, d. John & Elizabeth, b. Nov. 24, 1708	1	110
Experience, twin with James, [d. John & Elizabeth], b. Apr. 7, 1719	1	110
Hannah, d. Isaac & Hannah, b. Mar. 4, 1712	1	110
Isaac, m. Hannah **STARK**, Apr. 21, 1707	1	110
James, twin with Experience, [s. John & Elizabeth], b. Apr. 7, 1719	1	110
John, m. Elizabeth **BAILEY**, Dec. 25, 1707	1	110
John, s. John & Elizabeth, b. Jan. 15, 1710/11	1	110
Joseph, [s. John & Elizabeth], b. June 29, 1723	1	110
Lydia, d. John & Elizabeth, b. Dec. 31, 1714	1	110
Mary, d. Samuel & Mary, b. Oct. 17, 1722	1	139

	Vol.	Page
FOX, (cont.)		
Sarah, [d. Isaac & Hannah], b. Nov. 6, 1714	1	110
William, [s. John & Elizabeth], b. May 2, 1721	1	110
Zeruiah, twin with Abigail, [d. John & Elizabeth], b. Mar. 29, 1726	1	110
FRANKLIN, Dianah, of Groton, m. Albert **SHERLEY**, of Stonington, Feb. 18, 1838, by Caleb M. Williams, J.P.	1	57
Susannah, m. Henry **BAILEY**, b. of Groton, Jan. 27, 1822, by Roswell Burrows, Elder	1	6
Thomas, m. Eliza **CHIPMAN**, b. of Groton, Sept. 10, 1826, by Rev. Roswell Burrows	1	22
FREEMAN, Betsey, m. Frank **RANDALL**, Sept. 28, 1851, by Rev. Reuben Palmer	1	92
George, of Groton, m. Eliza **ROATH**, of Stonington, Jan. 27, 1850, by Nathan Daboll, J.P.	1	87
Peter M., m. Mary A. **HEWLETT**, Sept. 1, 1833, by Joseph Durfey, J.P.	1	44
Phillis, of Groton, m. Ceaser **BABCOCK**, of S. Kingstown, R.I., Nov. 21, 1830, by Ralph Hurlbutt, J.P.	1	36
Sarah, of Stonington, m. Elias **LIRRAS**, of Groton, May 29, 1828, by Rev. N. S. Spaulding, of Stonington	1	28
FULLER, Aaron C., m. Eunice A. **AVERY**, b. of Groton, Nov. 24, 1851, by Rev. Nicholas T. Allen	1	93
GALLUP, Alfred, s. [Henry, Jr. & Desire], b. Mar. 28, 1798	2	47
Alfred, m. Eliza W. **HEWIT[T]**, b. of Groton, Oct. 19, 1823, by William Williams, J.P.	1	11
Andrew, s. Henry & Hannah, b. June 26, 1761	2	10
Andrew, of Groton, m. Nancy **WHELDON**, of Stonington, Dec. 16, 1792, by Rev. Valentine W. Rathburn	2	46
Andrew Henry, s. [Andrew & Nancy], b. Mar. 29, 1811	2	46
Anna, d. [Capt. Isaac & Anne], b. Sept. 3, 1787	2	36
Anna, d. [Henry, Jr. & Desire], b. Mar. 26, 1805	2	47
Anna, m. David **GEER**, Jr., b. of Groton, Jan. 11, 1810, by Isaac Gallup, J.P.	2	82
Anna, m. Seth **WILLIAMS**, b. of Groton, Jan. 30, 1825, by Timothy Tuttle	1	16
Anna, d. Avery & Mary, b. July 13, 1835	3	12
Annice J., d. [Peter A. & Rebecca T.], b. July 9, 1824	3	5
Asa Lyman, s. [Andrew & Nancy], b. Feb. 21, 1814	2	46
Asa S., s. Christopher & Patty, b. Dec. 17, 1792; d. Jan. 31, 1800	2	66
Austin, s. [Benadam & Cynthia], b. Feb. 24, 1796	2	84
Austin, [s. Benadam & Cynthia], d. June 19, 1805	2	84
Avery, s. [Capt. Isaac & Anne], b. Apr. 6, 1796	2	36
Avery, m. Malinda **BAILEY**, b. of Groton, Nov. 21, 1822, by Timothy Tuttle	1	8
Avery, m. Malinda **BAILEY**, b. of Groton, Nov. 21, 1822, by Rev. Timothy Tuttle	3	12
Avery, m. Mary **HALEY**, b. of Groton, Mar. 13, 1834, by John G. Wightman, Eld.	1	46
Avery, Dea., m. Mary **HALLEY**, d. Stephen & Lucy, 3-13-1834	3	0
Avery, m. Mary **HALEY**, Mar. 13, 1834	3	12
Benedam, s. Benedam & Eunice, b. Oct. 26, 1716	1	118
Benadam, Jr., m. Hannah **AVERY**, Aug. 11, 1740	1	177
Benadam, s. Benadam, Jr. [& Hannah], b. June 29, 1741	1	177
Benadam, Col., had negro girl Lydia, b. Oct. 27, 1788	1	177
Benadam, Jr., m. Cynthia **FISH**, Oct. 14, 1792	2	84
Benadam, Col., d. Mar. 29, 1800	1	177

	Vol.	Page
GALLUP, (cont.)		
Benadam, s. [Benadam & Cynthia], b. June 3, 1804	2	84
Benjamin F., m. Hannah **ALLYN**, b. of Groton, Dec. 10, 1823, by John G. Wightman	1	11
Benjamin Franklin, s. [Josiah & Polly], b. Aug. 1,1 797	2	45
Betsey, d. Christ[ophe]r & Patty, b. Jan. 21, 1795	2	66
Bridget, m. Sands **FISH**, June 18, 1789	2	55
Caroline Wood, d. James & Abigail, b. June 19, 1821	3	4
Cecelia, d. [Lodowick & Peggy], b. Nov. 7, 1804	2	69
Charles, s. Oliver & Freelove, b. Apr. 12, 1759	1	161
Charles, m. Olive **MORGAN**, b. of Groton, Feb. 7, 1821, by Timothy Tuttle	1	3
Charles Randall, s. [Josiah & Polly], b. July 3, 1795	2	45
Christopher, of Groton, m. Patty **PRENTICE**, of Stonington, Apr. 13, 1792, by Jona[tha]n Palmer, Jr., J.P.	2	66
Christopher M., m. Anna **BILLINGS**, b. of Groton, June 5, 1833, by John G. Wightman, Eld.	1	43
Christopher Milton, [s. Christopher & Patty], b. Nov. 23, 1809	2	66
Cynthia, d. [Benadam & Cynthia], b. Aug. 14, 1806	2	84
Cinthia, of Groton, m. Richard **WHEELER**, of Stonington, Nov. 23, 1824, by John G. Wightman, Eld.	1	14
Desire Ann, m. Elisha Jefferson **HEWITT**, b. of Groton, Nov. 27, 1823, by William Williams, J.P.	1	11
Ebenezer, s. [Nathan & Sarah], b. Feb. 8, 1757	1	170
Ebenezer, m. Lavinia **STANTON**, b. of Groton, Apr. 27, 1823, by William Williams, J.P.	1	9
Ebenezer, m. Angelina **STANTON**, b. of Groton, Dec. 10, 1826, by William Williams, J.P.	1	22
Elias, s. [Capt. Isaac & Anne], b. Apr. 14, 1798	2	36
Elisha, s. [Nehemiah & Elizabeth], b. June 22, 1792	2	46
Elisha, s. [Capt. Isaac & Anne], b. Dec. 12, 1803	2	36
Eliza, d. Peter A. & Rebecca T., b. Dec. 16, 1820	3	5
Elizabeth, d. [Nehemiah & Elizabeth], b. Nov. 10, 1783	2	46
Elizabeth, d. [Avery & Malinda], b. Oct. 8, 1828	3	12
Elizabeth, m. Charles L. **FENNER**, b. of Groton, Oct. 11, 1848, by Rev. Jared R. Avery	1	85
Emeline, d. [Isaac & Prudence], b. Feb. 27, 1818	3	28
Erastus, s. [Capt. Isaac & Anne], b. July 31, 1800	2	36
Erastus, m. Eunice **WILLIAMS**, b. of Groton, Oct. 2, 1823, by Timothy Tuttle	1	10
Esther, d. Benedam & Eunice, b. Feb. 24, 1718	1	119
Easther, d. [Benadam, Jr. & Hannah], b. Dec. 9, 1746	1	177
Esther, d. [Joseph & Mary], b. Apr. 14, 1769	1	166
[E]unis, twin with Lois, d. Benedam & Eunice, b. May 29, 1721	1	119
Eunice, d. Henry & Hannah, b. Aug. 7, 1755	2	10
Eunice, d. [Andrew & Nancy], b. Jan. 16, 1794	2	46
Eunice, of Groton, m. Benjamin **ROUSE**, of Stonington, Mar. 16, 1823, by William Williams, J.P.	1	9
Fanny Maria, of Groton, m. Giles **WILLIAMS**, of Pomfret, Sept. 16, 1833, by Rev. Jared R. Avery	1	45
Franklin, [s. Gurdon & Sibell], b. Aug. 18, 1812	2	77
Franklin, m. Hannah **BURROWS**, b. of Groton, Aug. 18, 1834, by Rev. Ira R. Steward	1	47

	Vol.	Page
GALLUP, (cont.)		
Franklin, m. Sarah E. **BURROWS**, b. of Groton, Apr. 9, 1843, by Ira R. Steward	1	68
Frederick, s. [Gurdon & Sibell], b. May 29, 1801	2	77
Gardiner, s. [Joseph & Mary], b. Mar. 5, 1765	1	166
Gilbert, s. Oliver & Freelove, b. May 2, 1761	1	161
Giles, s. [Gurdon & Sibell], b. May 17, 1805	2	77
Grace, d. [Gurdon & Sibell], b. Oct. 10, 1799	2	77
Grace, m. Ebenezer **ROGERS**, b. of Groton, Jan. 8, 1824, by Rev. Roswell Burrows	1	12
Gurdon, s. [Joseph & Mary], b. Dec. 18, 1771	1	166
Gurdon, of Groton, m. Sibell **CAPRON**, of Preston, Feb. 15, 1795, by Elias Brown, J.P.	2	77
Gurdon, s. [Gurdon & Sibell], b. May 16, 1798	2	77
Hallett, s. [William & Judith], b. Jan. 1, 1756	1	167
Hannah, d. [Benadam, Jr. & Hannah], b. Nov. 4, 1744	1	177
Hannah, m. Robert **ALLYN**, Jr., b. of Groton, Jan. 23, 1755, by Rev. Jacob Johnson	1	167
Hannah, d. Henry & Hannah, b. Dec. 29, 1764	2	10
Hannah, w. Col. Benadam, d. July 28, 1799	1	177
Hannah, d. [Josiah & Polly], b. Nov. 21, 1801	2	45
Harriet, d. [Andrew & Nancy], b. Sept. 20, 1798	2	46
Harriet, d. James & Abigail, b. Aug. 10, 1835	3	32
Henry, [s. Benedam & Eunice], b. Oct. 5, 1725	1	119
Henry, of Groton, m. Hannah **MASON**, of Stonington, Oct. 4, 1750, by Ebenezer Rossiter	2	10
Henry, s. Henry & Hannah, b. Oct. 17, 1758	2	10
Henry, Jr., m. Desire **STANTON**, b. of Groton, Nov. 17, 1793, by Christ[ophe]r Avery, Elder	2	47
Isaac, s. [Benadam, Jr. & Hannah], b. Dec. 22, 1742	1	177
Isaac, Capt., m. Anne **SMITH**, b. of Groton, Oct. 5, 1786, by Benedam Gallup, J.P.	2	36
Isaac, s. [Capt. Isaac & Anne], b. Jan. 21, 1789	2	36
Isaac, Jr., m. Prudence **GEER**, b. of Groton, Mar. 12, 1812, by Isaac Gallup, J.P.	2	85
Isaac, 3d, s. [Isaac & Prudence], b. Nov. 13, 1820	3	28
Jabez, s. [Capt. Isaac & Anne], b. Aug. 23, 1794	2	36
Jacob, m. Sarah **WILLIAMS**, b. of Groton, Oct. 15, 1829, by Timothy Tuttle	1	31
James, s. [Benadam, Jr. & Hannah], b. May 1, 1749	1	177
James, s. [Benadam & Cynthia], b. Nov. 25, 1793	2	84
James, 2d, m. Abigail **SPICER**, b. of Groton, June 5, 1820, by John G. Wightman	1	1
James, s. James & Abigail, b. Aug. 8, 1838	3	32
James M., s. [Peter A. & Rebecca T.], b. Oct. 28, 1822	3	5
Jared, s. Henry & Hannah, b. Nov. 22, 1767	2	10
Jesse, s. [Benadam, Jr. & Hannah], b. Feb. 2, 1751	1	177
Jesse, s. Jesse & Katharine, b. Oct. 21, 1782	2	28
John, s. [Benadam, Jr. & Hannah], b. Jan. 13, 1753	1	177
John, s. [Joseph & Mary], b. July 17, 1758	1	166
John, s. [Benadam & Cynthia], b. Mar. 6, 1809	2	84
John Stanton, s. [Nehemiah & Elizabeth], b. Apr. 5, 1787	2	46
Jonathan, s. [Joseph & Mary], b. Nov. 23, 1766	1	166

	Vol.	Page
GALLUP, (cont.)		
Joseph, m. Mary **GARDINER**, May 18, 1749	1	166
Joseph, m. Mary **GARDINER**, May 18, 1749	2	9
Joseph, s. [Joseph & Mary], b. Mar. 21, 1750; d. Feb. 11, 1753	1	166
Joseph, s. [Joseph & Mary], b. Sept. 26, 1754	1	166
Joseph, s. [Gurdon & Sibell], b. May 2, 1803	2	9
Joseph, m. Abby Ann **DENISON**, b. of Groton, Nov. 2, 1826, by John G. Wightman, Eld.	1	22
Josiah, m. Sarah **FISH**, Nov. 4, 1787	2	45
Josiah, m. Polly **RANDALL**, Nov. 11, 1792	2	45
Josiah, Jr., s. Josiah & Polly, b. Aug. 30, 1793	2	45
Julian, d. [Christopher & Patty], b. July 26, 1807	2	66
Julia, d. [Isaac & Prudence], b. Apr. 4, 1823	3	28
Julia Ann, of Groton, m. Joseph S. **WILLIAMS**, of Stonington, Dec. 9, 1824, by Timothy Tuttle	1	14
July Ann, d. [Peter A. & Rebecca T.], b. Oct. 2, 1832	3	5
Lavinia S., m. Charles H. **STANTON**, b. of Ledyard, Nov. 28, 1847, by Rev. Erastus Denison	1	80
Lodowick, of Groton, m. Peggy **PHELPS**, of West Springfield, Mass., Feb. 28, 1799	2	69
Lois, twin with [E]unis, d. Benedam & Eunice, b. May 29, 1721	1	119
Lucretia, d. Joseph & Mary, b. Aug. 15, 1760	1	166
Lucy, d. Gurdon & Sibell, b. Nov. 5, 1796	2	77
Lucy, d. [Lodowick & Peggy], b. May 11, 1801	2	69
Lucy, b. [ ]; m. Stephen **HALEY**, Dec. 1, 1803	2	79
Lucy, m. Stephen **HALEY**, Dec. 1, 1803	3	0
Lucy, m. Stephen **HALEY**, s. Caleb & Mary, [ ]	3	0
Lydia, d. [William & Judith], b. Feb. 14, 1754	1	167
Mary, d. Oliver & Freelove, b. Apr. 27, 1763	1	161
Mary, of Groton, m. Isaac **CRARY**, Nov. 12, 1775	2	29
Mary, d. [Benadam & Cynthia], b. Mar. 4, 1800	2	84
Mary, of Groton, m. Lyman **LATHAM**, of Preston, Nov. 4, 1829, by Rev. Roswell Burrows	1	32
Mary Ann, d. [Josiah & Polly], b. Aug. 30, 1799	2	45
Mary Ann, d. [Isaac & Prudence], b. Dec. 10, 1812	3	28
Mary Esther, d. James & Abigail, b. Apr. 4, 1829	3	4
Nancy, d. [Andrew & Nancy], b. Oct. 15, 1795	2	46
Nancy, of Groton, m. Asa **BARNES**, of Preston, Mar. 15, 1829, by John G. Wightman, Eld.	1	30
Nathan, m. Sarah **GIDEON**, May 25, 1749	1	170
Nathan, s. [Nathan & Sarah], b. Nov. 14, 1754	1	170
Nathan, s. [Lodowick & Peggy], b. Jan. 24, 1803	2	69
Nathan S., s. [Peter A. & Rebecca T.], b. Sept, 13, 1829	3	5
Nehemiah, s. Henry & Hannah, b. June 19, 1751	2	10
Nehemiah, m. Elizabeth **BROWN**, Jan. 28, 1784* (*1783?)	2	46
Nehemiah, m. Mrs. Mercy **BROWN**, b. of Groton, Oct. 11, 1827, by William Williams, J.P.	1	25
Nehemiah Mason, s. [Nehemiah & Elizabeth], b. Feb. 12, 1785	2	46
Oliver, s. Oliver & Freelove, b. June 26, 1754	1	161
Orendia, d. [Nehemiah & Elizabeth], b. Mar. 8, 1790	2	46
Palmer, s. [Benadam & Cynthia], b. June 14, 1802	2	84
Pattey, d. [Christopher & Patty], b. Sept. 26, 1796	2	66

	Vol.	Page
GALLUP, (cont.)		
Peter A., m. Rebecca T. **MORGAN**, b. of Groton, Apr. 9, 1820, by Roswell Fish, J.P.	3	5
Phebe, of Stonington, m. John **GARDINER**, of Groton, Dec. 18, 1760	2	2
Phebe, d. [Joseph & Mary], b. Apr. 10, 1762	1	166
Prentice, s. [Thomas Prentice & Prudence], b. Apr. 23, 1759	1	166
Prudence, d. [Benadam, Jr. & Hannah], b. Jan. 30, 1755	1	177
Prudence Almira, d. [Isaac & Prudence], b. Mar. 4, 1815	3	28
Prudence D., m. Isaac D. **GATES**, b. of Groton, Sept. 24, 1851, at Mystic River, by Rev. Franklin A. Slater	1	92
Ray Denison, s. [Peter A. & Rebecca T.], b. Aug. 29, 1834	3	5
Roswell, s. [Benadam & Cynthia], b. Mar. 11, 1798	2	84
Roswell, s. [Benadam & Cynthia], d. July 24, 1817	2	84
Russell, s. [Capt. Isaac & Anne], b. Apr. 11, 1791	2	36
Sabrina, m. Caleb M. **WILLIAMS**, b. of Groton, Nov. 22, 1829, by John G. Wightman, Eld.	1	32
Sally, d. [Christopher & Patty], b. July 3, 1798; d. Mar. 29, 1800	2	66
Sally, d. [Christopher & Patty], b. Aug. 9, 1800; d. Mar. 17, 1805	2	66
Samuel, of N.Y. State, m. Patty **PALMER**, of Groton, Dec. 2, 1821, by Roswell Burrows	1	5
Sarah, d. [Nathan & Sarah], b. Dec. 29, 1751	1	170
Sarah, d. [Joseph & Mary], b. Nov. 10, 1752	1	166
Sarah, d. Joseph & Mary, b. Nov. 10, 1752	2	9
Sarah, m. Park **ALLYN**, b. of Groton, Jan. 19, 1757, by Rev. Jacob Johnson	1	170
Sarah, s. Josiah, d. Feb. 11, 1791	2	45
Sarah, d. [Capt. Isaac & Anne], b. Nov. 9, 1792	2	36
Sarah, d. [Andrew & Nancy], b. July 27, 1804	2	46
Sarah, of Groton, m. Joseph S. **DENISON**, of Stonington, Sept. 5, 1822, by Philip Gray, J.P.	1	8
Shubael, s. [Capt. Isaac & Anne], b. Mar. 6, 1802	2	36
Sophia, d. [Benadam & Cynthia], b. June 16, 1812	2	84
Sophia, of Groton, m. William E. **SMITH**, of Stonington, Aug. 10, 1834, by John G. Wightman, Elder	1	47
Susanna, m. Nathan **LESTER**, b. of Groton, Apr. 24, 1796	2	64
Thomas, s. Oliver & Freelove, b. Apr. 17, 1756	1	161
Thomas, s. [Thomas Prentice & Prudence], b. Jan. 14, 1758	1	166
Thomas Prentice, m. Prudence **ALLYN**, b. of Groton, Jan. 20, 1757, by Rev. Jacob Johnson	1	166
William, [s. Benedam & Eunice], b. July 4, 1723	1	119
William, of Groton, m. Judith **REED**, of Norwich, June 9, 1752, in Norwich, by Rev. Jabez White	1	167
William Avery, s. [Avery & Malinda], b. June 9, 1826	3	12
GARD, GUARD, Bethany, m. Charles **GARD**, b. of Groton, Aug. 13, 1824, by John G. Wightman	1	13
Betsey, m. William **COMSTOCK**, b. of Groton, July 25, 1803, by Rev. Silas Barrows	2	77
Caroline, of Groton, m. Noyes **PERKINS**, of Stephenstown, N.Y., Jan. 20, 1822, by Rufus Smith, J.P.	1	6
Charles, m. Bethany **GARD**, b. of Groton, Aug. 13, 1824, by John G. Wightman	1	13
Jenette, of Groton, m. Amasa **ROCKWELL**, of Mass., July 20, 1826, by Nathan Daboll, J.P.	1	21

	Vol.	Page
GARD, GUARD, (cont.)		
Lucy, of Groton, m. Isaac B. **PECOR**, of Bridgeport, Feb. 1, 1835, by Rev. Ira R. Steward	1	49
Martha, had s. Henry **BRICE**, b. Mar. 4, 1796. Father Robert BRICE.	2	10
Phebe, m. Asa **PERKINS**, b. of Groton, Jan. 29, 1822, by Ralph Hurlbutt, J.P.	1	6
Sally, m. Elisha **CHIPMAN**, b. of Groton, May 17, 1829, by Rev. John G. Wightman	1	31
GARDINER, Abigail, of Westerly, R.I., m. David **PALMER**, of Groton, Nov. 25, 1773, by Joseph Parke, Clerk	2	20
[E]unice, d. John & Phebe, b. May 14, 1766	2	2
Johns, Joseph & Sarah, b. Sept. 21, 1732	1	162
John, of Groton, m. Phebe **GALLY**, of Stonington, Dec. 18, 1760	2	2
John, s. John & Phebe, b. Jan. 18, 1771	2	2
Lucy, d. John & Phebe, b. Apr. 30, 1776	2	2
Mary, d. Joseph & Sarah, b. Aug. 30, 1730	1	162
Mary, m. Joseph **GALLUP**, May 18, 1749	1	166
Mary, m. Joseph **GALLUP**, May 18, 1749	2	9
Mary, d. John & Phebe, b. Apr. 11, 1764	2	2
Nathan, of New London, m. Charlotte A. **BAKER**, of Groton, Aug. 19, 1850, by Rev. Jared R. Avery	1	89
Paris, [s. John & Phebe], b. Aug. 20, 1773	2	2
Peregrine, s. Jonathan & Eunice, b. Aug. 30, 1792	2	21
William, s. Joseph & Sarah, b. Sept. 5, 1741	1	162
GARO, Anne, m. Daniel **TILER**, May 28, 1700	1	105
GARSIDE, Samuel, of Stonington, m. Mary A. **OBRIEN**, of Groton, Oct. 11, 1832, by John G. Wightman, Eld.	1	41
GATES, Abby, m. John **EDGECOMB**, b. of Groton, Aug. 1, 1826, by Rev. Roswell Burrows	1	21
Abigail, d. Zeb[adiah] & Sarah, b. Feb. 5, 1762	2	8
Anna, d. Zeb[adiah] & Sarah, b. May 24, 1757	2	8
Catharine, d. [John], b. July 27, 1773	2	7
Catharine, m. Calvin **BURROWS**, b. of Groton, Apr. 11, 1843, by Ira R. Steward	1	68
Charles H., m. Jane E. **LATHAM**, b. of Groton, Aug. 21, 1851, by Rev. Nicholas T. Allen	1	92
Clarreysea, d. [John], b. Apr. 11, 1780	2	7
David, s. Zebadiah & Sarah, b. Feb. 4, 1749	2	8
Easter, d. Zeb[adiah] & Sarah, b. Nov. 15, 175[ ]	2	8
Elisha, s. Zeb[adiah] & Sarah, b. Feb. 28, 1768	2	8
Esther, of Groton, m. William **NILES**, of Stonington, Sept. 25, 1828, by John G. Wightman, Eld.	1	28
Eunice, d. [John], b. Sept. 18, 1768	2	7
Eunice D., of Groton, m. Amos **CHESEBROUGH**, of Stonington, Sept. 24, 1851, by Rev. Franklin A. Slater	1	92
Hannah, d. [John], b. Oct. 18, 1775	2	7
Henry, s. [John], b. Nov. 21, 1787	2	7
Henry A., of N. Stonington, m. Jane L. **LAMB**, of Groton, June 14, 1835, by W[illia]m M. Williams, J.P.	1	51
Isaac D., m. Prudence D. **GALLUP**, b. of Groton, Sept. 24, 1851, at Mystic River, by Rev. Franklin A. Slater	1	92
John, s. [John], b. July 6, 1771; d. Dec. 9, 1772	2	7
John, s. Zeb[dia]h & Sarah, b. Dec. 13, 174[ ]	2	8

	Vol.	Page
GATES, (cont.)		
Mary, d. [Zeba[dia]h & Sarah, b. Aug. 8, 174[ ]	2	8
Mary, d. Zeba[diah] & Sarah, b. Sept. 1, 1759	2	8
Moses, s. [John], b. Nov. 27, 1783; d. Jan. 5, 1784	2	7
Peter, s. Zeb[adiah] & Sarah, b. Feb. 15, 175[ ]	2	8
Phebe, d. [John], b. mar. 23, 1778	2	7
Sarah, twin with Zebadiah, d. Zebadiah & Sarah, b. Feb. 3, 1751	2	8
Sarah, d. [John], b. Nov. 9, 1782; d. Jan. 9, 1783	2	7
Sophi, d. [John], b. Mar. 19, 1785	2	7
Warren, s. Zeb[adiah] & Sarah, b. Aug. 17, 1765	2	8
Zebadiah, m. Sarah **WOODMANSEY**, Nov. 9, 1742	2	8
Zebadiah, twin with Sarah, s. Zebadiah & Sarah, b. Feb. 3, 1751	2	8
Zebadiah, of Groton, m. Nancy **DENISON**, of Stonington, June 7, 1820, by Rev. Ira Hart, of Stonington	1	1
GAVITT, **GAVIT**, Almira, m. Alfred **REYNOLDS**, of Groton, July 5, 1829, by John G. Wightman, Eld.	1	31
Mary, of Norwich, m. Erastus D. **BRAMAN**, of Groton, May 5, 1833, by Rev. Roswell Burrows	1	43
Patty, of Westerly, R.I., m. Abel **MAINE**, of Groton, Mar. 9, 1828, by Geo[rge] Ayer, J.P.	1	27
Sally Ann, m. Dayton **DAVIS**, b. of Stonington, June 10, 1838, by Rev. John G. Wightman	1	58
GEORGE, Peter, of Groton, m. Lucy **FAGENS**, of N. Stonington, May 2, 1832, by Philip Gray, J.P.	1	40
GERE, **GEER**, **GEERE**, Abby, d. [James & Sally], b. Dec. 20, 1820	3	10
Abel, s. [Ebenezer & Lucy], b. Feb. 19, 1787	2	42
Abigail, d. [Amos & Mary], b. Aug. 28, 1766	2	42
Abigail, d. [Robert, 3d, & Cassandra], b. Oct. 12, 1783; d. Feb. 26, 1789	2	42
Abigail, w. Robert, d. Feb. 2, 1790	2	35
Abigail, m. Nehemiah **SMITH**, Jr., b. of Groton, Dec. 9, 1792, by A. Gere, J.P.	2	49
Alice, [d. Robert & Lucy], b. Apr. 26, 1781	2	15
Amos, s. Robert & Abigail, b. Feb. 19, 1740	1	145
Amos, s. [Amos & Mary], b. Oct. 7, 1772	2	42
Amos, s. [Robert, 3d & Cassandra], b. Apr. 13, 1790; d. Feb. 28, 1791	2	42
Amos, Jr., m. Prudence **ALLYN**, Jan. 5, 1800	2	42
Amos, s. [Amos, Jr. & Prudence], b. Nov. 10, 1800	2	42
Amos, of Goshen, m. Eunice **MORGAN**, of Groton, Apr. 11, 1824, by Timothy Tuttle	1	12
Amos, s. [Ebenezer & Lucy], b. [ ]	2	42
Anna, d. [David & Mary], b. Aug. 12, 1794	2	64
Asseneth Williams, d. Isaac W. & Asseneth, b. May 26, 1826	3	14
Benjamin, [s. Isaac], b. Oct. 22, 1716	1	126
Benjamin, 2d, of Groton, m. Susanna **WHITMARSH**, of Dighton, Mass., Sept. 12, 1779, by Rufus Allyn, Elder	2	30
Betsey, d. [Amos & Mary], b. June 12, 1781	2	42
Betsey, m. Lodowick **BILL**, b. of Groton, Oct. 20, 1805, by Amos Geer, J.P.	2	73
Charles, s. Ebenezer & Prudence, b. July 6, 1748	1	154
Charles, [s. Robert & Lucy], b. July 19, 1776	2	15
Charles, s. [David & Mary], b. Aug. 19, 1803	2	64
Charlotte F., m. Erastus H. **LATHAM**, b. of Groton, Feb. 7, 1830, by Timothy Tuttle	1	33
Clarina, d. Rich[ar]d & Hannah, b. May 23, 1785	2	50

	Vol.	Page
GERE, GEER, GEERE, (cont.)		
Cyrus, s. [David & Mary], b. Apr. 1, 1792	2	64
Darius, s. [Benjamin & Susanna], b. July 18, 1786	2	30
David, s. Ebenezer & Prudence, b. June 18, 1756	1	154
David, of Groton, m. Mary **STANTON**, of Stonington, May 17, 1781, by Rev. Nath[anie]l [ ]ells	2	64
David, s. [David & Mary], b. Jan. 20, 1784	2	64
David, Jr., m. Anna **GALLUP**, b. of Groton, Jan. 11, 1810, by Isaac Gallup, J.P.	2	82
Dorothy, d. David & Mary, b. Apr. 22, 1782	2	64
Ebenezer, [s. Robert & Martha], b. Apr. 1, 1710	1	103
Ebenezer, m. Prudence **WHEELER**, Jan. 2, 1734/5	1	154
Ebenezer, s. Ebenezer & Prudence, b. June 30, 1737	1	154
Ebenezer, s. [Amos & Mary], b. Oct. 28, 1764	2	42
Ebenezer, [s. Robert & Lucy], b. Feb. 8, 1779	2	15
Ebenezer, m. Lucy **CHAPMAN**, Apr. 27, 1786	2	42
Ebenezer, s. [Ebenezer & Lucy], b. Apr. 13, 1789	2	42
Eliza, d. [Amos & Prudence], b. Jan. 19, 1809	2	42
Erastus, twin with Fanny, s. Rich[ar]d & Hannah, b. Jan. 14, 1789	2	50
Eunice, [d. Robert & Lucy], b. June 20, 1771	2	15
Fanny, twin with Erastus, d. Rich[ar]d & Hannah, b. Jan. 14, 1789	2	50
George, b. May 2, 1783; m. Diademia **DABOLL**, Dec. 14, 1809	3	7
Gilbert, s. Rich[ar]d & Hannah, b. Sept. 7, 1795	2	50
Gilbert, s. [Greenman & Dorcas], b. Apr. 8, 1801	2	42
Greenman, s. [Amos & Mary], b. Oct. 2, 1768	2	42
Greenman, of Groton, m. Dorcas **DUNHAM**, of Charleston, S.C., Mar. 14, 1799	2	42
Hannah, d. Benjamin & Susanna, b. Sept. 20, 1780	2	30
Isaac, [s. Isaac], b. Apr. 27, 1709	1	126
Isaac, s. [Isaac, Jr. & Martha], b. Feb. 23, 1740/1	1	181
Isaac, Jr., m. Martha **MORGAN**, May 1, 1741[sic]	1	181
Isaac W., Capt., m. Asenith **WILLIAMS**, b. of Groton, Jan. 9, 1825, by Park Williams, J.P.	1	15
Isaac W., Capt., m. Asseneth **WILLIAMS**, b. of Groton, Jan. 9, 1825, by Park Williams, J.P.	3	14
Isaac Wheeler, s. [David & Mary], b. June 1, 1801	2	64
Jabez, s. [Ebenezer & Lucy], b. May 23, 1794	2	42
James, [s. Robert & Martha], b. Dec. 7, 1713	1	103
James, m. Zipporah **WILLIAMS**, Mar. 24, 1736/7	1	179
James, m. Sarah **CHESEBROUGH**, Nov. 27, 1739	1	179
James, s. [James & Sarah], b. Feb. 17, 1747/8	1	179
James, b. Oct. 31, 1783; m. Sally **LEWIS**, Jan. 20, 1808	3	10
James, s. [Ebenezer & Lucy], b. Jan. 1, 1801	2	42
James Lewis, s. [James & Sally], b. Nov. 8, 1808	3	10
Job, s. Benjamin & Susanna, b. May 6, 1783	2	30
John, s. Ebenezer & Prudence, b. Feb. 24, 1745/6	1	154
John O., of Groton, m. Almira **PENDLETON**, residing in Groton, May 11, 1826, by Rev. Gideon B. Perry, of Stonington	1	20
John Wheeler, s. Ebenezer & Prudence, b. Mar. 8, 1753	1	154
Joseph, s. [David & Mary], b. Feb. 16, 1790	2	64
Joseph, of Groton, m. Lura **WITTER**, of Preston, Feb. 21, 1816, by Rev. John Hyde	2	89
Livia, d. [Ebenezer & Lucy], b. May 6, 1791	2	42

	Vol.	Page
GERE, GEER, GEERE, (cont.)		
Lucinda, [d. Robert & Lucy], b. June 27, 1774	2	15
Lucinda Ann, of Groton, m. Noyes **HOLMES**, of N. Stonington, June 18, 1815	3	14
Lucy, [d. Isaac], b. Apr. 1, 1718	1	126
Lucy, d. [James & Sarah], b. May 16, 1745	1	179
Lucy D., d. [George & Diademia], b. Sept. 22, 1810	3	7
Lucy D., m. William **MOXLEY**, Feb. 28, 1830	3	28
Luther, Jr., m. Abby Amelia **HEM[P]STEAD**, b. of Groton, Oct. 30, 1836, by Nathan Daboll, J.P.	1	55
Lydia, d. [James & Sarah], b. Nov. 10, 1742	1	179
Lydia D., m. William **MOXLEY**, b. of Groton, Feb. 28, 1830, by Nathan Daboll, J.P.	1	33
Margaret, d. [Amos & Mary], b. Jan. 26, 1775	2	42
Margaret, m. James **BABCOCK**, b. of Groton, Jan. 31, 1779	2	51
Margaret, d. [Amos & Mary], d. Feb. 14, 1787	2	42
Martha, [d. Robert & Martha], b. Mar. 18, 1704	1	103
Martha, [d. Isaac], b. June 30, 1710	1	126
Martha, m. Jacob **PARK[E]**, July 18, 1723	1	144
Martha, w. Robert, d. Sept. 18, 1741	1	152
Martha, d. Ebenezer & Prudence, b. Dec. 18, 1741	1	154
Martha, m. Benjamin **GILES**, Apr. 29, 1742	1	182
Mary, m. Zech[a]riah **MANER**, Sept. 23, 1697	1	106
Mary, [d. Robert & Martha], b. May 14, 1701	1	103
Mary, m. Jonathan **POTTS**, Nov. 10, 1713	1	109
Mary, [d. Isaac], b. July 12, 1720	1	126
Mary, m. John **SPICER**, Oct. 22, 1720	1	102
Mary, d. Ebenezer & Prudence, b. Sept. 24, 1739	1	154
Mary, d. [Amos & Mary], b. Nov. 16, 1762	2	42
Matilda, d. [Richard & Hannah], b. Apr. 5, 1798	2	50
Mollie, d. [James & Sarah], b. Aug. 30, 1740	1	179
Nancy, of Groton, m. Samuel **GEER**, of Griswold, Oct. 5, 1820, by Timothy Tuttle	1	2
Nathan, s. [Isaac, Jr. & Martha], b. Feb. 25, 1742/3	1	181
Nathan, Jr., of Griswold, m. Priscilla L. **STODDARD**, of Groton, Feb. 5, 1824, by Timothy Tuttle	1	12
Nathaniel Bellows, s. [James & Sally], b. Jan. 31, 1810	3	10
Polly, d. Rich[ar]d & Hannah, b. Apr. 2, 1793	2	50
Prudence, d. Ebenezer & Prudence, b. Dec. 2, 1735	1	154
Prudence, m. Ebenezer **PUNDERSON**, Sept. 21, 1757	1	171
Prudence, [d. Robert & Lucy], b. Oct., 13, 1768	2	15
Prudence, d. [David & Mary], b. Mar. 30, 1788	2	64
Prudence, d. [Amos, Jr. & Prudence], b. Oct. 28, 1802	2	42
Prudence, m. Isaac **GALLUP**, Jr., b. of Groton, Mar. 12, 1812, by Isaac Gallup, J.P.	2	85
Prudence, m. Billings **AVERY**, b. of Groton, Sept. 25, 1825, by Timothy Tuttle	1	18
Richard, s. Ebenezer & Prudence, b. July 11, 1750	1	154
Robert, m. Martha **TILER**, Apr. 3, 1700	1	103
Robert, [s. Robert & Martha], b. Apr. 5, 1707; d. Jan. 1, 1801	1	103
Robert, Jr., m. Abigail **GREENMAN**, Aug. 29, 1733	1	145
Robert, s. Robert & Abigail, b. June 20, 1734	1	145
Robert, d. Nov. 20, 1742	1	152

	Vol.	Page
GERE, GEER, GEERE, (cont.)		
Robert, s. Robert & Abigail, d. Dec. 3, 1742, ae. 9 y.	1	145
Robert, Jr., d. Dec. 3, 1742, ae. 9 y.	1	152
Robert, s. Ebenezer & Prudence, b. Feb. 18, 1743/4	1	154
Robert, s. Amos & Mary, b. Mar. 28, 1761	2	41
Robert, of Groton, m. Lucy **FITCH**, of Windham, Nov. 4, 1767, by Rev. Stephen White, of Windham	2	15
Robert had following slaves: Nero, s. Cato & Chloe, b. May 16, 1771: Elas, s. Cato & Chloe, b. Nov. 11, 1775: Nancy, d. Cato & Chloe, b. Mar. 21, 1778	2	51
Robert had following slaves: York, s. [Cato & Chloe], b. Sept. 23, 1780: Milla, d. [Cato & Chloe], b. Mar. 12,1783: Cate, d. [Cato & Chloe], b. Apr. 28, 1785; Sam, s. [Cato & Chloe], b. July 1, 1787	2	51
Robert, 3d, m. Cassandra **STANTON**, b. of Groton, Dec. 5, 1782, by Amos Geer, J.P.	2	42
Robert, s. [Robert, 3d & Cassandra], b. Sept. 30, 1785	2	42
Robert had negro woman Chloe who d. Apr. 11, 1788; Cato, husband of Chloe, d. Aug. 5, 1791	2	35
Robert, s. [David & Mary], b. Nov. 20, 1796	2	64
Robert, d. Jan. 1, 1801	2	35
Robert Allyn, s. Amos & Prudence, b. Oct. 25, 1806	2	42
Roxellana, d. Richard & Hannah, b. Jan. 7, 1782	2	50
Ruth, d. [Amos & Mary], b. Sept. 12, 1770	2	42
Sally Maria, d. [James & Sally], b. Dec. 16, 1813	3	10
Samuel, s. [James & Sarah], b. Dec. 13, 1750	1	179
Samuel, s. Gurdon & Sarah, b. Nov. 25, 1784	2	17
Samuel, m. Polly **LATHAM**, b. of Groton, July 10, 1804, by Amos Geer, J.P.	2	68
Samuel, of Griswold, m. Nancy **GEER**, of Groton, Oct. 5, 1820, by Timothy Tuttle	1	2
Sarah, [d. Isaac], b. Nov. 12, 1714	1	126
Sarah, d. [Amos & Mary], b. Apr. 26, 1777	2	42
Seth, s. [Benjamin & Susanna], b. July 22, 1784	2	30
Shubael, s. [Amos, Jr. & Prudence], b. Aug. 20, 1804	2	42
Shubael, m. Mary **WILBUR**, b. of Groton, Aug. 5, 1827, by Rev. Roswell Burrows	1	24
Solomon, s. Jacob, b. Mar. 2, 1767	2	28
Thomas, m. Hannah **WHIPPLE**, b. of Groton, Oct. 7, 1821, by Zephaniah Watrous	1	4
Thomas, m. Thankful **WHIPPLE**, b. of Groton, Dec. 11, 1825, by Nathan Daboll, J.P.	1	19
William S., m. Lovisa **BREWSTER**, Feb. 14, 1816, at Franklin, by Rev. David Austin, of Franklin	2	89
William Stanton, s. [David & Mary], b. Oct. 28, 1785	2	64
Zeporah, d. Jeremiah, b. Aug. [ ], 1715	1	131
Ziporah, d. James & Zipporah, b. Mar. 18, 1738/9	1	179
______, s. [James & Sally], b. Dec. 22, [1816]; d. Dec. 24, 1816	3	10
GEORGE, Peter, of Groton, m. Lucy **FOGENS**, of N. Stonington, May 2, 1832, by Philip Gray, J.P.	1	40
GETCHELL, Caroline A., of New London, m. Henry R. **EDGECOMB**, Oct. 2, 1852, by Rev. Nicholas T. Allen	1	94
Clarissa, of Ledyard, m. Simeon A. **GRAY**, of Groton, June 17, 1849, by Ella Dunham, Elder	1	83

	Vol.	Page
GIDDINGS, Gurdon, of Stonington, m. Louisa **NILES**, of Groton, Mar. 4, 1838, by Rev. Erstus Denison	1	58
GIDEON, Sarah, m. Nathan **GALLUP**, May 25, 1749	1	170
GIFFORD, Hannah, of Norwich, m. Samuel **LESTER**, Jr., Dec. 4, 1782, by Nath[anie]l Waterman, Jr., J.P., of Norwich	2	36
GILBERT, Charles, of Stonington, m. Susan E. **CHESTER**, of Groton, Jan. 30, 1854, by G. H. Woodward	1	96
GILES, Abby, of New York, m. Martin **THOMPSON**, of Groton, Aug. 30, 1834, by Nathan Daboll, J.P.	1	47
Anna, [d. Thomas & Bathsheba], b. Sept. 24, 1770	2	13
Bathsheba, [d. Thomas & Bathsheba], b. Nov. 18, 1775	2	13
Bathsheba, m. John **STANTON**, [ ]	3	32
Benjamin, m. Martha **GEER**, Apr. 29, 1742	1	182
Benj[ami]n, [s. Thomas & Bathsheba], b. Jan. 17, 1778	2	13
Daniel, [s. Thomas & Bathsheba], b. Jan. 26, 1774	2	13
Elizabeth, [d. William & Elizabeth], b. Mar. 25, 1769	1	183
Friend Charles, [s. William & Elizabeth], b. Jan. 30, 1775	1	183
Hannah, d. [Benjamin & Martha], b. Sept. 30, 1747	1	182
John, [s. Thomas & Bathsheba], b. Apr. 5,1 780	2	13
Margaret, [d. William & Elizabeth], b. Jan. 8, 1773	1	183
Mary, d. [Benjamin & Martha], b. Nov. 1, 1745	1	182
Polly, [d. William & Elizabeth], b. Jan. 10, 1771	1	183
Thomas, Ensign, m. Bathsheba **HAYNES**, May 4, 1769	2	13
Thomas, [s. Thomas & Bathsheba], b. May 13, 1772	2	13
William, s. [Benjamin & Martha], b. June 24, 1744	1	182
William, m. Elizabeth **ELLIS**, June 25, 1768	1	183
GILLSON, James D., of Worcester, Mass., m. Fanny C. **SPAULDING**, of Groton, May 4, 1835, by Ira D. Steward	1	50
GLASSENDER, William, of Groton, m. Julia Ann **SHALER**, of Colchester, Aug. 24, 1850, by Rev. Jared R. Avery	1	89
GODDARD, Hannah, m. Edward **JEFFREY**, Jr., Aug. 25, 1799, at Newport, R.I.	2	86
Mary Katharine, d. Giles & Sarah, b. June 16, 1738	1	151
GOLDSMITH, Charles, m. Hannah **ARON**, [Dec. 1, 1854], by Reuben Heath, J.P.	1	97
GOOD, Edward Latham, s. [William & Abigail], b. July 8, 1788, on Groton Bank	2	23
William, m. Abigail **LATHAM**, June 24, 1787	2	23
GORE, Asa, m. Christa **COOK**, b. of Preston, Mar. 13, 1831, by William Williams, J.P.	1	37
Hannah, of Preston, m. Silas **BURROWS**, of Groton, July 17, 1740	1	180
GOULD, John B., of Hull, Mass., m. Caroline E. **DENISON**, of Groton, Apr. 21, 1847, by Rev. H. F. Kenney	1	78
GRAD, John, M.D., m. Eunice* **PACKER**, b. of Groton, Jan. 6, 1848, by Rev. H. R. Knapp (*Written in pencil "Emma, d. of Mason P.")	1	83
GRANT, William N., m. Peace C. **LEEDS**, b. of Groton, May 10, 1837, by Ira R. Steward	1	56
GRAY, Abby Ann, d. [Elijah Perkins & Abigail], b. May 2, 1808	2	76
Asa, m. Lusana **PROSSER**, b. of Groton, Feb. 15, 1821, by Stephen Billings, J.P.	1	3
Austin, m. Betsey F. **SMITH**, Jan. 5, 1834, by W[illia]m M. Williams, J.P.	1	46
Benjamin, s. Phillip & Mary, b. Dec. 1, 1740	1	149
Caroline, d. [Elijah Perkins & Abigail], b. Aug. 13, 1805	2	76
Charlotte, m. Russell **PERKINS**, Jr., b. of Groton, Apr. 2, 1848, by Rev. Jared R. Avery	1	80

	Vol.	Page
GRAY, (cont.)		
Elijah, s. Phillip & Mary, b. Aug. 16, 1745	1	149
Elijah Perkins, b. Aug. 17, 1771; m. Abigail **HILLIARD**, Mar. 24, 1796	2	76
Ezekiel, s. Phillip & Mary, b. Apr. 14, 1743	1	149
Ezekiel, s. [Elijah Perkins & Abigail], b. May 23,1798	2	76
Ezekiel, of Montville, m. Hannah **PERKINS**, of Groton, Mar. 29, 1829, by Philip Gray, J.P.	1	30
Hezekiah, of New York, m. Eunice **LATHAM**, of Groton, Oct. 21, 1822, by Rev. Roswell Burrows	1	7
Hilliard, s. [Elijah Perkins & Abigail], b. Feb. 9, 1813	2	76
Jonathan, s. [Elijah Perkins & Abigail], b. Feb. 26, 1811	2	76
Lucy, m. Stanton P. **BABCOCK**, Aug. 30, 1801	3	34
Lucy A., of Preston, m. Albert A. **LATHAM**, Dec. 7, 1848, by Rev. H. R. Knapp	1	84
Lydia W., of Groton, m. Charles H. **DEAN**, of N. Stonington, Jan. 20, 1828, by William Williams, J.P.	1	26
Phebe, d. [Elijah Perkins & Abigail], b. May 13, 1803	2	76
Phillip, m. Mary **KILLIAM**, Nov. 24, 1737	1	149
Phillip, s. Phillip & Mary, b. Dec. 29, 1738	1	149
Phillip, 2d, of Groton, m. Sabra **STANTON**, of Groton, but residing in Preston, Feb. 9, 1797	2	61
Phillip, 2d, m. Sarah **MORGAN**, b. of Groton, Dec. 24, 1801	2	61
Sabra, w. of Phillip, 2d, d. June 5, 1800	2	61
Sabra, m. James B. **WILLIAMS**, b. of Groton, May 25, 1823, by William Williams, J.P.	1	9
Sally, d. [Elijah Perkins & Abigail], b. Nov. 16, 1800	2	76
Simeon A., of Groton, m. Clarissa **GETCHELL**, of Ledyard, June 17, 1849, by Ella Dunham, Elder	1	83
Thomas B., m. Amanda **WILLIAMS**, b. of Groton, Nov. 2, 1823, by William Williams, J.P.	1	11
William Jefferson, m. Abby Ann **ADAMS**, b. of Groton, Jan. 26, 1824, by Rev. John G. Wightman	1	12
GREEN, Robert, m. Frances J. **DENISON**, of Groton, Aug. 6, 1843, by Rev. Erastus Denison	1	69
William, of Pitcher, N.Y., m. Sally L. **STODDARD**, of Groton, Oct. 13, 1833, by Timothy Tuttle	1	45
GREENMAN, Abigail, m. Robert **GEER**, Jr., Aug. 29, 1733	1	145
GREER, Martha, m. Jacob **STARK**, July 18, 1728	1	114
GRIFFIN, Ann, m. George **HARRISON**, b. of Groton, May 10, 1835, by John G. Wightman, Elder	1	50
Mary L., m. Thomas **PARK[E]**, b. of Groton, Sept. 29, 1845, by Rev. S. B. Bailey	1	74
GRINMON, George, of Hopkinton, R.I., m. Abby **CHIPMAN**, of Groton, Feb. 10, 1828, by N. S. Spalding	1	27
GRINNELL, Hannah W., of New Bedford, Mass., m. Jesse B. **LAMPHERE**, of Groton, July 4, 1850, by Rev. Erastus Denison	1	89
GRISWOLD, Frances A., of New London, m. Jane **MAYRATH**, of Groton, Aug. 19, 1849, by Rev. Nicholas T. Allen	1	87
GRUMBY, Freelove, m. Calvin S. **WILCOX**, b. of Groton, Jan. 27, 1851, by Rev. James M. Phillips	1	91
GUYANT, GUIANT, GUINANT, Betsey Ann, of Groton, m. Daniel **CONNELL**, of Norwich, July 12, 1846, by Rev. Erastus Denison	1	76

	Vol.	Page
GUYANT, GUIANT, GUINANT, (cont.)		
Frances M., m. Francis W. **PIERCE**, b. of Groton, Jan. 26, 1851, by Rev. F. A. Slater	1	91
Frances Mary, [d. Luke M. & Susan], b. Apr. 26, 1831	3	29
John, m. Hannah **DAVIS**, b. of Groton, July 23, 1820, by Roswell Fish, J.P.	1	1
Julia, of Groton, m. Sanford **LAMB**, of Ledyard, Jan. 26, 1840, by Rev. John G. Wightman	1	62
Luke William, [s. Luke M. & Susan], b. Nov. 30, 1828	3	29
Mary, m. Richard **HEWLET**, b. of Groton, Mar. 18, 1835, by John G. Wightman, Eld.	1	49
Mason, m. Susan **ALEXANDER**, b. of Groton, Sept. 18, 1825, by Nathan Daboll, J.P.	1	18
Phebe Esther, [d. Luke M. & Susan], b. July 23, 1826	3	29
Sally, of Groton, m. Henry **DANIELS**, of New London, Dec. 9, 1824, by Nathan Daball, J.P.	1	14
HADLEY, W[illia]m Parkinson, m. Mary Ann **PUTNAM**, b. of Groton, Apr. 20, 1845, by Rev. Erastus Denison	1	72
HAINS, [see also **HAYNES**], Anna, m. Nathaniel **BROWN**, July 11, 1715, by Rev. Woodbridge	1	118
HAKES, HAICKES, Elihu, Jr., of Preston, m. Mary **LEEDS**, of Groton, Sept. 14, 1829, by John G. Wightman, Eld.	1	31
Isaac W., of N. Stonington, m. Lois **WEST**, of Lee, Mass., Oct. 1, 1827, by Ralph Hurlbutt, J.P.	1	25
Louisa C., m. Augustus D. **ANDREWS**, b. of Preston, May 6, 1845, by Rev. H. R. Knapp	1	74
HALEY, HALLEY, Abby Ann, m. W[illia]m F. **MITCHELL**, b. of Groton, Apr. 21, 1839, by Rev. John G. Wightman	1	60
Abby Ann, b. May 28, 1814; m. W[illia]m F. **MITCHELL**, Apr. 21, 1839	3	0
Albert, s. [Stephen & Lucy], b. Mar. 25, 1806	2	79
Albert, [s. Stephen & Lucy], b. Mar. 25, 1806; m. Phebe **DECKER**	3	0
Austin, b. May 11, 1810; unmarried	3	0
Betsey, [d. Caleb & Mary], b. [ ], 17[ ]; m. John Baldwin **BURROWS**	3	0
Betsey, [d. Caleb & Helen], b. [ ]; m. John Baldwin **BURROWS**	2	78
Betsey, m. John Baldwin **BURROWS**	3	0
Betsey Ann, [d. Henry & Mary Ann], b. Mar. 17, 1838; m. Albert C. **BURROWS**, May 27, 1860	3	0
Caleb, [s. Caleb & Mary], b. [ ], 17[ ]; m. Sally **BURROWS**	3	0
Caleb, [s. Caleb & Helen], b. [ ]; m. Sally **BURROWS**	2	78
Caleb, m. Mary **HOLMES**, [ ]	3	0
Charles, [s. Caleb, Jr. & Sally], b. [ ]; 18[ ]; m. [ ] **AVERY**	3	0
Cordelia, [d. Stephen & Lucy], b. [ ]; m. Nelson **HALEY**	2	79
Cordelia, m. Nelson **HALEY**, s. Caleb, Jr. & Sally, [ ]	3	0
Cornelia, m. Nelson **HALEY**, b. of Groton, Nov. 27, 1834, by John G. Wightman, Elder	1	48
Cornelia, [d. Stephen & Lucy], b. [ ]; m. Nelson **HALEY**	3	0
Dudley, s. [Stephen & Lucy], m. Rebec[c]a **VORES**, [ ]	2	79
Dudley, [s. Stephen & Lucy], m. Rebecca **VORHIS**	3	0
Elisha, [s. Caleb & Mary], b. Jan. 21, 1776; m. Nancy **CRARY**, July 24, 1803	3	0
Elisha, [s. Caleb & Helen], b. [ ]; m. Nancy **CRARY**	2	78
Elisha, m. Nancy **CRARY**, [ ]; d. Jan. 22, 1860	3	0
Eliza, b. Nov. 13, 1818; m. R. W. **SMITH**, Nov. 23, 1838	3	0

	Vol.	Page
HALEY, HALLEY, (cont.)		
Eliza, m. Richard William **SMITH**, b. of Groton, Nov. 23, 1838, by Rev. John G. Wightman	1	60
Emily, m. Caleb J. **ALLYN**, b. of Groton, Jan. 23, 1831, by John G. Wightman, Eld.	1	36
Emily, d. [Stephen & Lucy], m. Caleb **ALLYN**	3	0
Giles, b. Sept. 24, 1805; m. Prudence **WHEELER**, [ ], in Stonington	3	0
Hannah, m. Seabury **THOMAS**, b. of Groton, Sept. 18, 1825, by John G. Wightman, Eld.	1	18
Hannah, d. [Caleb, Jr. & Sally], b. [ ], 18[ ]; m. Sebra(?) **THOMAS**	3	0
Hannah Avery, m. Seabury **THOMAS**, Sept. 18, 1825	2	54
Henry, b. May 11, 1804; m. Mary Ann **BURROWS**, June 15, 1834	3	0
Henry, m. Mary Ann **BURROWS**, b. of Groton, June 15, 1834, by John G. Wightman, Elder	1	47
Jabez D., m. Priscilla **MORGAN**, of Groton, Jan. 1, 1823, by John G. Wightman [Elder]	1	9
John B., [s. Henry & Mary Ann], b. July 1, 1843; m. Georgianna J. **ALLEN**, of Norwich	3	0
Joshua, Jr., of Stonington, m. Matilda **WILLIAMS**, of Groton, Jan. 1, 1851, by Rev. Jared R. Avery	1	90
Lucy, d. [Stephen & Lucy, b.]; d. unmarried	2	79
Lucy, [d. Stephen & Lucy], b. [ ]; unmarried	3	0
Margaret, of Groton, m. James **ROSS**, of Ledyard, June 2, 1840, by Rev. John G. Wightman	1	63
Maria L., m. Youngs **AVERY**, b. of Groton, Dec. 12, 1847, by Rev. S. B. Bailey	1	80
Mary, d. [Stephen & Lucy], b. Sept. 1, 1804	2	79
Mary, [d. Stephen & Lucy], b. Sept. 1, 1804; m. Dea. Avery **GALLUP**, 3-13-1834	3	0
Mary, m. Avery **GALLUP**, b. of Groton, Mar. 13, 1834, by John G. Wightman, Eld.	1	46
Mary, m. Avery **GALLUP**, Mar. 13, 1834	3	12
Nelson, m. Cornelia **HALEY**, b. of Groton, Nov. 27, 1834, by John G. Wightman, Elder	1	48
Nelson, [s. Caleb, Jr. & Sally], b. [ ], 18[ ], m. Cordelia **HALLY**	3	0
Nelson, m. Cordelia **HALEY**, d. Stephen & Lucy, [ ]	2	79
Nelson, m. Cornelia, **HALLEY**, [d. Stephen & Lucy,]	3	0
Priscilla, m. Capt. Prentice **ASHBEY**, b. of Groton, Nov. 18, 1849, by Rev. Nicholas T. Allen	1	87
Sally, d. [Stephen & Lucy], m. Richard **BURNETT**	2	79
Sally, [d. Caleb, Jr. & Sally], b. [ ]; m. [ ] **SMITH**	3	0
Sally, [d. Stephen & Lucy], b. [ ]; m. Richard **BARNETT**, 2-11-1835	3	0
Sally G., m. Richard **BURNET[T]**, b. of Groton, Feb. 11, 1835, by John G. Wightman, Elder	1	49
Simeon, m. Priscilla A. **BURROWS**, b. of Groton, Apr. 16, 1837, by John G. Wightman, Elder	1	56
Simeon, m. Prescilla A. **BURROWS**	3	0
Stephen, [s. Caleb & Helen], b. July 5, 1772; m. Lucy **GALLUP**	2	78
Stephen, b. July 5, 1772; m. Lucy **GALLUP**, Dec. 1, 1803	2	79
Stephen, [s. Caleb & Mary], b. July 5, 1772; m. Lucy **GALLUP**	3	0
Stephen, m. Lucy **GALLUP**, Dec. 1, 1803	3	0
Stephen, s. [Stephen & Lucy], b. [ ]	2	79
Stephen, [s. Stephen & Lucy], b. [ ]; unmarried	3	0

	Vol.	Page
HALEY, HALLEY, (cont.)		
Virginia, [d. Henry & Mary Ann], b. Aug. 22, 1733; m. Nelson **MORGAN**, June 28, 1855	3	0
Warren, s. [Stephen & Lucy], b. [ ]	2	79
Warren, [s. Stephen & Lucy], b. [ ]; unmarried	3	0
HALL, Erastus, of Coventry, m. Martha J. **BAILEY**, of Groton, Dec. 25, 1834, by Ralph Hurlbutt, J.P.	1	48
Esther, of Groton, m. Staunton **BURDICK**, of Hopkinton, R.I., Mar. 20, 1831, by Rev. Erastus Denison	1	37
Gurdon, of Westerly, R.I., m. Mary A. **WILCOX**, of Groton, Aug. 2, [1853], by Rev. James M. Phillips	1	95
Lydia, m. Thomas B. **MAINE**, b. of Groton, Nov. 15, 1835, by John G. Wightman, Elder	1	52
Mary, m. Luke **HOPKINS**, b. of Charlestown, R.I., Aug. 22, 1847, at Porterville, by Rev. Amos A. Watrous, of Lyme	1	79
HALLAHAN, Grace, now residing in Stonington, m. Henry **SEWALL**, Jr., Sept. 16, 1834, by Rev. John G. Wightman	1	48
HALLAM, Almira, of Groton, m. James **PARKER**, of S. America, Apr. 16, 1834, by Rev. Ira R. Steward	1	46
Henry, m. Philena **LIMAS**, Apr. 1, 1833, by John G. Wightman, Eld.	1	43
Prudence, m. Joseph **HITCHCOCK**, b. of Stonington, May 13, 1838, by Rev. John G. Wightman	1	58
HALLET, Betsey, d. [Thomas & Sarah], b. June 26, 1801	2	70
Betsey, of Groton, m. Charles **SPENCER**, of Griswold, Mar. 14, 1830, by William Williams, J.P.	1	34
Catharine, 2d, d. [Thomas & Sarah], b. June 26, 1793	2	70
Catherine, d. [Thomas & Sarah], b. May 16, 1788; d. Feb. 16, 1794	2	70
Emelia, d. [Thomas & Sarah], b. June 6, 1795	2	70
Hannah, d. [Thomas & Sarah], b. Mar. 15, 1786	2	70
Henry, s. [Thomas & Sarah], b. July 24, 1799	2	70
Henry, Capt. m. Julia Ann **BAILEY**, b. of Groton, Apr. 29, 1833, by William Williams, J.P.	1	44
Samuel, s. [Thomas & Sarah], b. Aug. 6, 1790	2	70
Sarah, w. Thomas, d. Nov. 22, 1804	2	70
Thomas, b. Feb. 12, 1760; m. Sarah **DANIELS**, Dec. 4, 1783	2	70
William, s. Thomas & Sarah, b. July 18, 1784	2	70
HALLOWAY, Alfred P., m. Mary S. **STARR**, b. of Groton, Feb. 22, 1852, by Rev. N. T. Allen	1	93
HAMBLETON, Eunice, m. Jonathan L. **CHRISTIE**, b. of Groton, Oct. 14, 1823, by Ralph Hurlbutt, J.P.	1	10
HAMMOND, Sarah A., m. Benjamin **BURROWS**, Jr., b. of Groton, July 25, 1838, by Ira R. Steward	1	59
Thomas, m. Sally **AVERY**, May 8, 1814	2	82
HANCOCK, Charles, of Stonington, m. Almyra **HEMPSTEAD**, of Groton, Jan. 3, 1847, by Rev. W[illia]m C. Walker	1	77
W[illia]m Edwin, m. Mary Ellen **HEMPSTEAD**, b. of Groton, Mar. 3, 1841, by Rev. Erastus Denison	1	64
HARDEN, Jemima, m. Jonathan **SMITH**, Jr., Aug. 6, 1747	1	141
HARRINGTON, Isaac, s. Isaac & Lucy, b. Mar. 12, 1749/50	1	145
Prudence, [s. Isaac & Lucy], b. Apr. 12, 1754	1	145
Timothy, [s. Isaac & Lucy], b. Apr. 18, 1752	1	145
HARRIS, Elizabeth, m. Nehemiah **SMITH**, Sept. 9, 1724	1	128

	Vol.	Page
HARRIS, (cont.)		
Griswold, of New London, m. Mrs. Betsey **PITCHER**, of Groton, May 31, 1820, by Thomas Avery, J.P.	1	1
Joshua, s. Josiah & Mary, b. Dec. 31, 1731	1	144
Josiah, m. Mary **AVERY**, Mar. 11, 1730/1	1	144
Russell, of R.I., m. Lucy **SMITH**, of Groton, Oct. 11, 1835, by Rev. Ira R. Steward	1	52
Thomas Jefferson, s. Dr. Benjamin, b. July 19, 1802	2	10
HARRISON, George, m. Ann **GRIFFIN**, b. of Groton, May 10, 1835, by John G. Wightman, Elder	1	50
Julia, of Groton, m. Robert **KELLEY**, of New London, Aug. 13, 1843, by Rev. Charles C. Lewis	1	69
Prudence, m. Dudley **PARK[E]**, b. of Groton, Dec. 20, 1846, by Rev. H. R. Knapp	1	83
Sarah, m. Gilbert **PARKS**, Jr., b. of Groton, Aug. 4, 1842, by Rev. Ira R. Steward	1	66
HARTLEY, Thomas, m. Susannah **REYNOLDS**, Oct. 24, 1830, by Rev. Erastus Denison	1	35
HARVEY, Sarah, m. Ebenezer NORTON, July 22, 1736	1	183
HAVENS, Catharine, m. Thomas **MUMFORD**, Jr., Dec. 7, 1752	1	162
Daniel C., of Lyme, m. Jerusha **BAKER**, of Groton, Sept. 17, 1832, by Nathan Daboll, J.P.	1	41
Elizabeth A., of Lyme, m. George A. **HAYNES**, of New London, July 11, 1852, at Noank, by Rev. James M. Phillips	1	94
Emily, of Groton, m. Amos A. **FISH**, of N.Y. City, May 12, 1847, by Rev. Erastus Denison	1	78
Fernando Cortez, of New London, m. Hannah **HEATH**, of Groton, June 30, 1835, by Timothy Tuttle	1	51
Francina, of Groton, m. Matthew **STILLMAN**, of Westerly, R.I., Aug. 1, 1832, by John G. Wightman, Elder	1	40
Gloriana, of Shelter Island, m. Charles **ELDREDGE**, Jr., of Groton, June 21, 1778, by Rev. Aaron Kinne	2	33
Hannah, of Groton, m. Samuel **WHEELER**, of Stonington, May 1, 1845, by Elias Brown, J.P.	1	73
Lavina, of Groton, m. Enock **MURDOCK**, of Westbrook, Dec. 14, 1845, by Rev. Erastus Denison	1	75
HAYDEN, see under **HEYDEN**		
HAYNES, [see also **HAINS**], Bathsheba, m. Ensign Thomas **GILES**, May 4, 1769	2	13
Caleb, [s. Josiah & Elizabeth], b. Feb. 2, 1702/3	1	102
Comfort, [s. Josiah & Elizabeth], b. Aug. 2, 1711	1	102
George A., of New London, m. Elizabeth A. **HAVENS**, of Lyme, July 11, 1852, at Noank, by Rev. James M. Phillips	1	94
Josiah, m. Elizabeth **LOMBARD**, Mar. 3, 1693	1	102
Kezia, [d. Josiah & Elizabeth], b. June 7, 1705	1	102
HAZARD, Silas, of Stonington, m. Delacy **WILLIAMS**, of Groton, Dec. 10, 1823, by Rufus Smith, J.P.	1	10
HAZEN, Eliza, m. Solomon CHAPMAN, b. of Groton, Nov. 2, 1823, by John Brewster, J.P.	1	11
HEATH, Abigail, d. Joseph & Dorithy, b. Feb. 13, 1720	1	114
Abigail, m. Samuel **MORGAN**, Sept. 30, 1741	1	165
Abigail, d. [John & Temperance], b. May 2, 1746	1	184

	Vol.	Page
HEATH, (cont.)		
Adelia A., of Groton, m. Andrew D. **KING**, of Norwich, Mar. 3, 1844, by Rev. Cha[rle]s C. Lewis	1	70
Amos, m. Mary **CHAPMAN**, b. of Groton, Apr. 10, 1815	3	14
Asa, m. Mrs. Content **LAMB**, Oct. 27, 1850, by Henry W. Avery, J.P.	1	90
Avery, s. [John & Temperance], b. Nov. 23, 1750	1	184
Bethana, of Groton, m. Oliver **BECKWITH**, of Norwich, Nov. 27, 1836, by John G. Wightman, Elder	1	55
Betsey A., m. Charles A. **SMITH**, b. of Groton, Sept. 7, 1851, by Rev. Nicholas T. Allen	1	92
Charles, m. Betsey **PERKINS**, b. of Groton, Aug. 28, 1836, by Nathan Daboll, J.P.	1	55
Cordelia, m. Elisha **WATROUS**, b. of Groton, June 7, 1840, by Rev. John W. Case	1	63
Dorothy, w. Joseph, d. Oct. 24, 1734	1	153
Dorothy, d. [John & Temperance], b. June 10,1744	1	184
Dorothy, w. Joseph, d. Oct. 24, 1754	1	153
Elizabeth, m. Elijah **BAILEY**, Mar. 25, 1762	2	1
Emeline M., of Groton, m. Roswell E. **MAYNARD**, of Norwich, May 10, 1846, by Rev. W. C. Walker	1	76
Exeline, m. Simon B. **BAILEY**, b. of Groton, Dec. 10, 1828, by Rev. N. S. Spa[u]lding	1	29
Frances Louisa, m. Huntington **WARD**, b. of Norwich, Sept. 28, 1853, by Rev. S. W. Coggeshall	1	95
Gilbert, m. Martha **WATROUS**, b. of Groton, Aug. 8, 1846, by Rev. W. C. Walker	1	76
Hannah, of Groton, m. Fernando Cortez **HAVENS**, of New London, June 30, 1835, by Timothy Tuttle	1	51
Hannah, d. [John & Temperance], b. Oct. 21, 1748; d. Nov. 19, 1749	1	184
Harriet, m. Jacob **WALLS**, b. of Groton, Feb. 15, 1837, by Rev. John G. Wightman	1	56
John, s. Joseph & Dorithy, b. Mar. 10, 1716/7	1	114
John, m. Temperance **AVERY**, Sept. 29, 1743	1	184
John, s. [John & Temperance], b. Jan. 5, 1747	1	184
John, m. Emily **ELDREDGE**, b. of Groton, Aug. 4, 1840, by Rev. John W. Case	1	63
John S., of New London, m. Frances A. **SMITH**, of Groton, Oct. 1, 1850, by Rev. Jared R. Avery	1	90
Jonathan, s. [John & Temperance], b. Nov. 3, 1753	1	184
Joseph, s. Joseph & Dorithy, b. July 28, 1713	1	114
Joseph, m. Marcy **TRACY**, Jan. 3, 1757	1	163
Margaret, of Groton, m. Albert **DENISON**, of Stonington, Mar. 15, 1829, by Nathan Daboll, J.P.	1	30
Mary A., m. Daniel **DAVIS**, b. of Groton, Apr. 9, 1837, by Rev. Mark Meade	1	56
Mercy, 2d w. of Joseph, d. May 31, 1768	1	153
Pedee, of Groton, m. William E. **WHEELER**, of Stonington, Aug. 30, 1831, by Timothy Tuttle	1	38
Phebe, of Groton, m. Thomas **HEWLING**, of New Jersey, July 20, 1843, by Nathan Daboll, J.P.	1	70
Phebe A., of [Groton], m. Stephen **SWEET**, of Franklin, Sept. 29, 1850, by W. Munger	1	92
Reuben, m. Betsey **LAMB**, b. of Groton, June 12, 1825, by Nathan Daball, J.P.	1	16

	Vol.	Page
HEATH, (cont.)		
Samuel, s. [John & Temperance], b. Aug. 31, 1755	1	184
William, m. Exeline **LAMB**, b. of Groton, Nov. 16, 1823, by Philip Gray, J.P.	1	11
HEATON, Marg[a]ret, d. Henry, b. Aug. 28, 1720	1	102
HEDDEN, Benjamin F., of Stonington, m. Clarissa **FITCH**, of Groton, Aug. 21, 1836, by Rev. Roswell Burrows	1	55
HEMINGER, John, s. Chloe **DAVIS**, b. July 13, 1761	1	181
HEMPSTEAD, HEMSTEAD, Abby Amelia, m. Luther **GEER**, Jr., b. of Groton, Oct. 30,1836, by Nathan Daboll, J.P.	1	55
Alymra, of Groton, m. Charles **HANCOCK**, of Stonington, Jan. 3, 1847, by Rev. W[illia]m C. Walker	1	77
Bridget, m. Charles ELDREDGE, b. of Groton, May 28, 1827, by Roswell Fish, J.P.	1	26
Charles G., m. Eliza **CRUMB**, b. of Groton, Apr. 29, 1838, by Rev. John G. Wightman	1	58
Emily, of Groton, m. Champlain **LAMPHEIR**, of Stonington, Dec. 7, 1834, by John G. Wightman, Elder	1	48
Eunice, of Stonington, m. W[illia]m S. **CRANSON**, of Norwich, Mar. 17, 1850, by Rev. W[illia]m C. Walker	1	87
Gurdon, m. Mary L. **NEWTON**, b. of Groton, May 6, 1821, by Ralph Hurlbutt, J.P.	1	3
Lury, m. George **RICHMOND**, Aug. 4, 1828, by Roswell Fish, J.P.	1	28
Mary Ellen, m. W[illia]m Edwin **HANCOCK**, b. of Groton, Mar. 3, 1841, by Rev. Erastus Denison	1	64
Rubua, of Groton, m. Elijah Wait **HINCKLEY**, of Stonington, Dec. 5, 1802, by Amos Geer, J.P.	2	76
HENDERSON, Henry, of Stonington, m. Prudence **CHEATS**, of Groton, Mar. 6, 1825, by Nathan Daball, J.P.	1	16
HERRICK, Ebenezer, of Hudson, N.Y., m. Catharine R. **PARK[E]**, of Groton, Jan. 18, 1843, by Rev. Erastus Denison	1	67
HEWITT, HEWET, HEWETT, HEWIT, Amos, m. Eunice **PACKER**, Sept. 25, 1831, by Erastus Denison	1	38
Bridget W., of N. Stonington, m. Thomas A. **MINER**, of Groton, Dec. 12, 1844, by Rev. Jared R. Avery	1	72
Cyrus, of New London, m. Elizabeth F. **EDGECOMB**, of Groton, June 19, 1847, by Rev. Nicholas T. Allen	1	78
Diadama, of New London, m. Samuel **WOOD**, of Groton, [ ], 1780	2	65
Elisha Jefferson, m. Desire Ann **GALLUP**, b. of Groton, Nov. 27, 1823, by William Williams, J.P.	1	11
Eliza W., m. Alfred **GALLUP**, b. of Groton, Oct. 19, 1823, by William Williams, J.P.	1	11
Eunice, of Groton, m. Charles **STANTON**, of Stonington, July 4, 1843, by Ira R. Steward	1	69
Hannah, of Preston, m. Robert **STANTON**, of Groton, Feb. 27, 1812, by Jonah Witter, J.P.	2	93
Harriet, m. Joshua **STANTON**, b. of Groton, Mar. 25, 1824, by William Williams, J.P.	1	12
Henry P., of Waterford, m. Eunice C. **DENISON**, of Groton, Aug. 26, 1849, by Rev. W. C. Walker	1	86
Isaac, of Preston, m. Mary Ann Caroline **ALLYN**, of Groton, Nov. 28, 1822, by Philip Gray, J.P.	1	8

	Vol.	Page
HEWITT, HEWET, HEWETT, HEWIT, (cont.)		
Nancy, of N. Stonington, m. Erastus **WILLIAMS**, of Groton, Feb. 15, 1818, by Rev. Christopher Avery, of N. Stonington	2	91
Nancy, m. Stephen **CHURCH**, b. of Groton, Oct. 1, 1854, by Rev. Ebenezer Blake	1	96
HEWLETT, HEWLET, HULET, Anne, [d. Josiah], b. Dec. 14, 1765	1	159
Caroline, of Groton, m. Nathaniel **LEWIS**, of Stonington, Aug. 18, 1844, by Nathan Daboll, J.P.	1	71
Jane, [d. Josiah], b. Apr. 8, 1764	1	159
Jenet, of Groton, m. Joseph **SLATE**, of New London, May 23, 1824, by Caleb Avery, J.P.	1	13
Josiah, [s. Josiah], b. Aug. 27, 1769	1	159
Mary A., m. Peter M. **FREEMAN**, Sept. 1, 1833, by Joseph Durfey, J.P.	1	44
Patty, of Groton, m. Alexander **SLATE**, of New London, Nov. 30, 1824, by Caleb Avery, J.P.	1	15
Peter, m. Mary Ann **BENHAM**, b. of Groton, Apr. 18, 1841, by Ira R. Steward	1	64
Phebe, m. Amos BENHAM, b. of Groton, Sept. 7, 1828, by Nathan Daboll, J.P.	1	28
Rachal, of Groton, m. James **JEFFREY**, of New London, Mar. 6, 1838, by Joseph Durfey, J.P.	1	58
Richard, m. Mary **GUYANT**, b. of Groton, Mar. 18, 1835, by John G. Wightman, Eld.	1	49
Sally, m. William **MOTT**, b. of Groton, Mar. 6, 1825, by Caleb Avery, J.P.	1	16
Samuel, s. [Josiah], b. Oct. 1, 1767	1	159
Sarah Alvira, of Groton, m. Peter **McFARLAND**, of New York, Dec. 8, 1839, by Rev. John G. Wightman	1	62
Silvanus, [s. Josiah], b. Aug. 29, 1772	1	159
Sophia, of Groton, m. John **SLATE**, of New London, Apr. 16, 1824, by Caleb Avery, J.P.	1	13
Stephen, [s. Josiah], b. Apr. 23, 1771	1	159
Thomas, of Groton, m. Mary A. **BECKWITH**, of Waterford, Feb. 2, 1841, by Rev. Jared R. Avery	1	64
HEWLING, Thomas, of New Jersey, m. Phebe **HEATH**, of Groton, July 20, 1843, by Nathan Daboll, J.P.	1	70
HEYDEN, Elizabeth E., m. Alfred W. **LYMAN**, Nov. 23, 1845, by Rev. R. Russell	1	74
HICKS, Betsey, b. June 17, 1789; m. Avery MORGAN, Dec. 5, 1809	2	78
Fanny, of Groton, m. Elisha W. **DENISON**, of Stonington, June 5, 1820, by Rev. John G. Wightman	1	1
John, s. Thomas, b. Feb. [ ], 1728/7	1	140
John, s. John & Hannah, b. Aug. 12, 1785	2	17
HIGGINS, Lyman A., of Westbrook, m. Abby Jane **MALLARY**, of Groton, Oct. 8, 1843, by Rev. Erastus Denison	1	70
HILL, Almira, m. Austin **BURROWS**, b. of Groton, May 21, 1826, by Nathan Daboll, J.P.	1	20
Arnold, of Norwich, m. Hannah **STERRY**, of Groton, Aug. 24, 1828, by Elisha Brewster, J.P.	1	28
Esther B., m. Philo **LITTLE**, b. of Groton, Apr. 13, 1845, by Rev. Jared R. Avery	1	73
John, m. Nancy **PERKINS**, b. of Groton, Mar. 14, 1830, by Nathan Daboll, J.P.	1	33

	Vol.	Page
HILL, (cont.)		
Katharine, m. John **BAKER**, Jr., b. of Groton, June 15, 1831, by Nathan Daboll, J.P.	1	37
Mary, of Groton, m. John **MARVIENE**, of New London, Sept. 11, 1825, by Nathan Daboll, J.P.	1	18
Moses, m. Anna **BAKER**, b. of Groton, Aug. 13, 1838, by Rev. John G. Wightman	1	59
Nancy M., m. W[illia]m **BROWN**, b. of Groton, May 14, 1848, by Rev. H. R. Knapp	1	84
HILLHOUSE, Mary, m. Rev. John **OWEN**, Nov. 13, 1744	1	142
HILLIARD, HILLARD, Abigail, [d. Jonathan], b. June 8, 1773	2	11
Abigail, b. June 8, 1773;m. Elijah Perkins **GRAY**, Mar. 24, 1796	2	76
Eliphalet, [s. Jonathan], b. Oct. 30, 1771	2	11
Isaiah, s. Jonathan & Mary **WILLIAMS**, b. May 24, 17[ ]	2	22
Isaiah, [s. Jonathan], b. May 24, 1782	2	11
Jonathan, [s. Jonathan], b. Dec. 3, 1776	2	11
Joseph, [s. Jonathan], b. Oct. 7, 1780	2	11
Mary, [d. Jonathan], b. Apr. 10, 1775	2	11
Sarah, [d. Jonathan], b. Dec. 3, 1778	2	11
William, [s. Jonathan], b. Dec. 30, 1781	2	11
HINCKLEY, Abel, of Stonington, m. Abby E. **BABCOCK**, of Groton, May 5, 1836, by John G. Wightman, Elder	1	53
Elijah, s. [Elijah Wait & Rubua], b. Apr. 9, 1804	2	76
Elijah Wait, of Stonington, m. Rubua **HEMPSTEAD**, of Groton, Dec. 5, 1802, by Amos Geer, J.P.	2	76
Elizabeth, m. William **WALLSWORTH**, Sept. 23, 1742	1	144
Hannah, d. [Elijah Wait & Rubua], b. Feb. 26, 1806	2	76
Sarah, m. George **FISH**, Jan. 20, 1785	2	87
HITCHCOCK, Joseph, m. Prudence **HALLAM**, b. of Stonington, May 13, 1838, by Rev. John G. Wightman	1	58
HOLDREDGE, HOLDRIGE, HOLDRIDGE, Abigail, d. [Samuel & Abigail], b. Sept. 21, 1767	2	38
Allyn, s. Samuel, b. May 24, 1794	2	13
Amanda, m. Benjamin C. **DEWEY**, b. of Groton, Apr. 5, 1847, by Rev. H. R. Knapp	1	83
Ambrose, s. [Samuel & Rhoda], b. Jan. 21, 1800	2	13
Anniss, m. Avery **BROWN**, b. of Groton, July 21, 1833, by John Spicer, J.P.	1	44
Betsey, m. Timothy **ALLYN**, Feb. 7, 1829, by Philip Gray, J.P.	1	29
Charles, s. [Joseph & Content], b. Oct. 13, 1795	2	50
Charles, s. William & Wealthy, b. Aug. 6, 17[ ]	2	19
Coddington, m. Charlotte **LAMB**, b. of Groton, Apr. 19, 1846, by Rev. W. C. Walker	1	76
Content, d. [Samuel & Abigail], b. Sept. 20, 1783	2	38
Cynthia, twin with Sabra, [d. Samuel & Abigail], b. Sept. 21, 1769	2	38
Daniel, s. Nathaniel & Elizabeth, b. Apr. 13, 1741	1	156
Desire, d. [Samuel & Abigail], b. May 17, 1781	2	38
Fanny, d. [Samuel & Rhoda], b. Feb. 27, 1786	2	13
George W., m. Delia **PACKER**, b. of Groton, Apr. 8, 1827, by John G. Wightman, Eld.	1	23
Hannah, d. [Samuel & Abigail], b. Apr. 30, 1778	2	38
Hannah, d. William & Jerusha, b. Jan. 3, 1796	2	54
Henry, s. [Samuel & Rhoda], b. Feb. 25, 1790	2	13
Isaac, s. [Samuel & Abigail], b. Aug. 25, 1773	2	38

	Vol.	Page
HOLDREDGE, HOLDRIGE, HOLDRIDGE, (cont.)		
John, s. Samuel & Rhoda, b. Oct. 9, 1796	2	13
Joseph, s. [Samuel & Abigail], b. Mar. 9, 1775	2	38
Joseph, m. Content **FISH**, Jan. 29, 1795	2	50
Leonard B., m. Nancy **JOHNSTON**, b. of Groton, Dec. 19, 1841, by Rev. Jared R. Avery	1	65
Leonord B., m. Nancy **WATROUS**, b. of Groton, Dec. 5, 1847, by Henry W. Avery, J.P.	1	80
Louisa J., m. Charles E. **BUDDINGTON**, b. of Groton, Jan. 1, 1854, by Geo[rge] H. Woodward	1	95
Manson, s. William, Jr. & Welthy, b. Sept. 15, 1788	2	58
Mariah, d. [Samuel & Rhoda], b. July 15, 1792	2	13
Mary, m. Timothy **LAMB**, Apr. 20, 1766	2	37
Mary, w. Phineas, d. Nov. 9, 1814	2	36
Mary, m. James **STANTON**, b. of Ledyard, Oct. 20, 1841, by Nathan Daboll, J.P.	1	65
Nathan, s. Phinehas & Mary, b. July 10, 1760	2	11
Nathan, d. Oct. 8, 1817	2	3
Nathan, m. Jane **WRIGHT**, b. of Groton, Oct. 18, 1829, by William Williams, J.P.	1	32
Nathan H., s. [Samuel & Rhoda], b. Oct. 25, 1787	2	13
Nathaniel, s. [Samuel & Abigail], b. Sept. 19, 1765	2	38
Phebe, m. William **SISSON**, b. of Groton, Feb. 27, 1806, by Amos Gere, J.P.	2	75
Phinehas, d. Jan. 1, 1815	2	36
Randall, m. Emeline **REED**, b. of Groton, Mar. 25, 1832, by John Spicer, J.P.	1	39
Rhoda, w. Samuel, b. Nov. 1, 1764	2	13
Rhuhamah, m. Nathaniel **BROWN**, 4th, b. of Groton, Jan. 2, 1803, by Amos Gere, J.P.	2	64
Rufus, Jr., m. Waitey **WILLIAMS**, b. of Groton, Dec. 25, 1833, by John G. Wightman, Elder	1	45
Sabra, twin with Cynthia, [d. Samuel & Abigail], b. Sept. 21, 1769	2	38
Sally, m. Nathan **NILES**, b. of Groton, Aug. 31, 1831, by Nathan Daboll, J.P.	1	38
Samuel, b. May 17, 1734; m. Abigail **PERIGO**, Mar. 4, 1762	2	38
Samuel, s. [Samuel & Abigail], b. Oct. 28, 1763	2	38
Samuel, m. Ellen **PARKS**, b. of Groton, Dec. 28, 1834, by Rev. Ira R. Steward	1	49
Samuel, m. Martha Ann **PARK[E]**, b. of Groton, June 15, 1845, by Rev. Simon B. Bailey	1	73
Samuel J., m. Mary **WILLIS**, b. of Groton, June 18, 1843, by Henry W. Avery, J.P.	1	68
Sophia, d. [Samuel & Rhoda], b. Oct. 9, 1796	2	13
William, m. Fanny **STARK**, b. of Groton, Nov. 12, 1826, by Nathan Daboll, J.P.	1	22
Zeboriah, d. Nathaniel & Elizabeth, b. Mar. 25, 1743	1	156
HOLLOWAY, Joseph Edwin, m. Mary **WELSH**, b. of Groton, June 12, 1850, by Rev. Erastus Denison	1	89
Nathan S., of Stonington, m. Harriet N. **BROWN**, of Groton, May 15, 1842, by Rev. B. F. Hedden	1	66
HOLMES, Albert S., of Norwich, Chanango Co., N.Y., m. Eunice **BARNES**, of Groton, Jan. 7, 1833, by William Williams, J.P.	1	42

	Vol.	Page
HOLMES, (cont.)		
Andrew Jackson, [s. Noyes], b. Jan. 31, 1829	2	69
Charles Edwin, s. [Noyes & Lucinda Ann], b. Mar. 30, 1831; d. May 4, 1831	3	14
Esther Ann, d. [Noyes & Lucinda Ann], b. Feb. 22, 1817; d. Nov. 11, 1817	3	14
Hiram C., of Stonington, m. Hannah F. **DENISON**, of Groton, Jan. 30, 1850, by Rev. Jared R. Avery	1	87
Isaac D., of Stonington, m. Ellen **KEMP**, of Groton, Aug. 8, 1837, by Nehemiah B. Cooke	1	57
James Madison, [s. Noyes & Lucinda Ann], b. Feb. 21, 1836	3	14
Katharine, m. Nathan **FISH**, July 24, 1759	2	12
Lucinda Ann, w. Noyes, d. Mar. 6, 1818	3	14
Lucinda Ann Geer, [d. Noyes], b. Aug. 30, 1824	2	69
Manen, of Stonington, m. Nehemiah **SMITH**, of Groton, Dec. 12, 1799, by Joshua Babcock, J.P.	1	168
Mary Wheeler, [d. Noyes], b. Aug. 6, 1826	2	69
Mercy Brown, d. [Noyes & Lucinda Ann], b. Nov. 11, 1834, at Stonington	3	14
Noyes, of N. Stonington, m. Lucinda Ann GERE, of Groton, June 18, 1815	3	14
Noyes, m. Mary Ann **WHEELER**, b. of Stonington, Oct. 13, 1820, by Parle Williams, J.P.	1	2
Sarah, of Stonington, m. Sylvester **WALLWORTH**, of Groton, Apr. 8, 1756, by Rev. Joseph Fish	2	24
Temperance, m. John **SMITH**, May 10, 1727	1	134
William Henry, [s. Noyes], b. June 21, 1822	2	69
HONEYWELL, Mary C., m. Giles H. **PEABODY**, Mar. 10, 1850, by Rev. H. R. Knapp	1	88
HOOKS, Patrick, m. Almira **BROWN**, b. of Groton, Feb. 27, 1831, by William M. Williams, J.P.	1	37
HOPKINS, Luke, m. Mary **HALL**, b. of Charlestown, R.I., Aug. 22, 1847, at Porterville, by Rev. Amos A. Watrous, of Lyme	1	79
HOUGH, Anne, m. Daniel **WHIPPLE**, May 7, 1746	1	175
Mary Ann, m. David **LAMPHEAR**, b. of Stonington, June 9, 1839, by Rev. John G. Wightman	1	60
HOWARD, Benjamin, m. Lucretia **KING**, May 28, 1823, by Noyes Barber, J.P.	1	9
HOWELL, Almira, m. Benjamin F. **PARK[E]**, b. of Groton, Jan. 25, 1835, by John G. Wightman, Elder	1	48
Francis J., of Groton, m. Gurdon **LATHRUPT**, of Towand, Pa., Mar. 13, 1843, by Rev. William S. Simmons, Jr.	1	68
Sally, of Groton, m. Wiliam W. **DENISON**, of Stonington, Sept. 16, 1827, by Rev. John G. Wightman	1	24
HOWLAND, Mary Ann, of Groton, m. James **BENNET[T]**, of Penn., Sept. 28, 1828, by Roswell Fish, J.P.	1	28
HOXEY, Joseph, of Richmond, R.I., m. Ann **BABCOCK**, of Groton, Mar. 6, 1836, by Joseph Durfey, J.P.	1	53
HUB[B]ARD, Lydia, m. John **BURROWS**, Oct. 14, 1700	1	115
HUCHESON, Ann, m. John **STANTON**, of Groton, Mar. 10, 1702	1	104
HUDSON, Mary F., m. Albert G. **LATHAM**, b. of Groton, Aug. 12, 1836, by Rev. Ira R. Steward	1	55
Mary Frances, b. Nov. 23, 1815	3	4
Polly, d. Phinehas & Margaret, b. Sept. 2, 1787	2	37
HULET, see under **HEWLETT**		

	Vol.	Page
HULL, Benjamin G., of Norwich, m. Martha A. **BALDWIN**, of Groton, Oct. 16, 1848, by Rev. Nicholas T. Allen	1	86
Daniel, of S. Kingston, R.I., m. Mary Angeline **CHEATS**, of Groton, Jan. 16, 1848, by Rev. Erastus Denison	1	80
HUNTING, Mary Otis, d. Samuel & Mary, b. July 19, 1806	2	78
HURLBUT, HURLBUTT, Amos, [s. Peter L. & Fanny], b. Nov. 10, 1828	3	29
Asaph, m. Bridget N. **STODDARD**, b. of Groton, Nov. 7, 1830, by Ralph Hurlbutt, J.P.	1	35
Freelove, d. John & Mary, b. Sept. 22, 1739	1	136
Freelove, m. Shapley **MORGAN**, Mar. 24, 1763	2	17
Freelove, d. Stephen & Phebe, b. July 1, 1767	2	5
Hannah, d. John & Mary, b. Feb. 7, 1736/7	1	136
Hannah, d. Stephen & Phebe, b. Mar. 23, 1764	2	5
John, m. Mary **STODDARD**, Oct. 20, 1726	1	136
John, s. John & Mary, b. Mar. 11, 1729	1	136
John, [s. Peter L. & Fanny], b. June 26, 1826	3	29
Mary, d. John & Mary, b. Oct. 29, 1727	1	136
Mary, m. Samuel **WILLIAMS**, July 16, 1746	1	184
Mary, d. Stephen & Phebe, b. July 7, 1760	2	5
Mary, Wid., d. May 22, 1790	2	14
Peter L., m. Fanny **BILL**, b. of Groton, Feb. 3, 1822, by Ralph Hurlbutt, J.P.	1	6
Phebe, d. Stephen & Phebe, b. July 7, 1762	2	5
Ralph, s. John & Mary, b. Aug. 5, 1734	1	136
Ralph, m. Margaret **BOLLES**, Jan. 27, 1833, by Ralph Hurlbutt, J.P.	1	42
Respah, d. John & Ann, b. Jan. 24, 1744	1	137
Rispah, m. Amos **CHAPMAN**, Feb. 26, 1786	2	44
Rufus, s John & Ann, b. May 19, 1742	1	137
Sarah, d. Stephen & Phebe, b. Apr. 25, 1757	2	5
Sarah, [d. Peter L. & Fanny], b. Mar. 13, 1823	3	29
Stephen, s. John & Mary, b. Jan. 11, 1732	1	136
Stephen, m. Phebe **MORGAN**, Oct. 9, 1755	2	5
Stephen Douglass, s. Stephen & Phebe, b. Dec. 19, 1770	2	5
HYDE, Harlam, of Groton, m. Eunice A. **AVERY**, of Greenville, in Norwich, Nov 12, 1833, by Timothy Tuttle	1	45
Joshua L., of Franklin, m. Catharine E. **ASHLEY**, of Groton, Aug. 26, 1832, by Rev. Roswell Burrows	1	41
INGHAM, Abby Ann, d. [Frances & Emily], b. Jan. 1, 1827	3	23
Abby J., m. Moses **WILBUR**, Jr., b. of Groton, June 25, 1848, by David Avery, Elder	1	82
Catharine, m. Erastus **FISH**, b. of Groton, Dec. 4, 1846, by Rev. S. B. Bailey	1	77
Elizabeth, m. Benjamin **ASHBEY**, b. of Groton, Feb. 4, 1847, by Rev. S. B. Bailey	1	77
Francis, m. Emily **CHESTER**, Sept. 11, 1825, by John G. Wightman, Eld.	1	18
Maria, m. Albert **CHESTER**, b. of Groton, Oct. 6, 1833, by Rev. Ira R. Stewart	1	45
Mary, of Groton, m. Peter **WILBUR**, of N. Stonington, Sept. 9, 1827, by Roswell Fish, J.P.	1	26
Narcissa, m. William E. **SPICER**, b. of Groton, Mar. 22, 1846, by Rev. Simon B. Bailey	1	75
Nathan O., m. Elizabeth **DABOLL**, b. of Groton, Aug. 8, 1838, by Ira R. Steward	1	59
William Frances, s. [Frances & Emily], b. Dec. 29,1829	3	23

	Vol.	Page
INGRAHAM, Narcissa, m. Asa **ASHLEY**, b. of Groton, Sept. 5, 1821, by Roswell Burrows	1	4
Prudence M., of Groton, m. Robert **PALMER**, of New London, Jan. 26, 1845, by Rev. Simon B. Bailey	1	72
William, d. May 4, 1721	1	112
IRISH, Betsey E., m. Lyman **BAILEY**, b. of N. Stonington, Dec. 24, 1827, by Rev. Asher Miner	1	33
Peter, of N. Stonington, m. Sally SPICER, of Groton, Nov. 18, 1827, by Roswell Burrows	1	25
William Orson, s. Peter D. & Sarah P., b. Oct. 13, 1828	3	27
IRONS, Dexter, m. Eunice **CRUMB**, b. of Groton, Mar. 1, 1829, by Rev. N. S. Spaulding	1	30
JACKLIN, Isaac, m. Permelia **PIERCE**, Nov. 27, 1845, by Rev. R. Russell	1	74
JACKSON, George, m. Elizabeth **LIMAS**, b. of Groton, June 8, 1834, by John G. Wightman, Elder	1	47
JEFFREY, **JOFFREY**, Anne, d. [John & Elizabeth], b. Oct. 14, 1736	1	178
Anne, m. Joseph **MARCHAND**, Oct. 19, 1755, by Ebenezer Avery, J.P.	1	169
Anne, d. Edward & Hannah, b. Nov. 29, 1761	1	147
Edward, s. [John & Elizabeth], b. Nov. 14, 1738	1	178
Edward, s. Edward & Hannah, b. June 21, 1768	1	147
Edward, Jr., m. Hannah **GODDARD**, Aug. 25, 1799, at Newport, R.I.	2	86
Henry, s. [Edward & Hannah], b. June 23, 1800	2	86
James, of New London, m. Rachal **HULET**, of Groton, Mar. 6, 1838, by Joseph Durfey, J.P.	1	58
Jared, s. [Edward & Hannah], b. May 4, 1803	2	86
John, m. Elizabeth **TURNER**, Dec. 24, 1735	1	178
Nancy, d. [Edward & Hannah], b. Aug. 4, 1810	2	86
Nancy M., m. Waterman Z. **BUD[D]INGTON**, b. of Groton, Sept. 13, 1835, by Timothy Tuttle	1	51
Ozias, s. [Edward & Hannah], b. Nov. 14, 1804	2	86
JOHNSON, Jonathan, s. Lawrence & Sarah, b. Nov. 2, 1751	2	74
Lydia, of Wilkesbarre, Pa., m. Alfred **SMITH**, of Aurelius, N.Y., Sept. 22, 1822, by Timothy Tuttle	1	7
Nancy, m. Leonard B. **HOLDREDGE**, b. of Groton, Dec. 19, 1841, by Rev. Jared R. Avery	1	65
Sarah, d. Lawrence & Sarah, b. Mar. 22, 1753	2	74
JONES, Betsey, m. Young Ledyard **MORGAN**, Feb. 12, 1797	2	84
John Henry, of N.Y., m. Sarah E. **BROWN**, of Groton, Sept. 3, 1848, by David Avery, Elder	1	82
JORDAN, John, of N.Y., m. Mary Ann **DENHAM**, of Groton, Apr. 25, 1847, by Nathan Daboll, J.P.	1	78
KEENEY, Alfred, of Griswold, m. Lucy **BALL**, of Groton, Mar. 12, 1826, by Ralph Hurlbutt, J.P.	1	20
Ezra Moore, of Montville, m. Catharine **CHIPMAN**, of Groton, Jan. 25, 1835, by John G. Wightman, Elder	1	48
KELCIN, Conrad, m. Elizabeth **BRIGHTMAN**, July 27, 1843, by Henry W. Avery, J.P.	1	69
KELLEY, Ellen H., m. Coddington **PACKER**, b. of Groton, Mar. 11, 1829, by John G. Wightman, Eld.	1	30
Emeline, of Groton, m. Jeremiah N. **SAWYER**, of Stonington, July 27, 1826, by Roswell Fish, J.P.	1	22
Reuben, m. Ann Maria **CHESTER**, b. of Groton, May 20, 1844, by Rev. Jared R. Avery	1	71

	Vol.	Page
KELLEY, (cont.)		
Robert, of New London, m. Julia **HARRISON**, of Groton, Aug. 13, 1843, by Rev. Charles C. Lewis	1	69
KEMP, Ellen, of Groton, m. Isaac D. **HOLMES**, of Stonington, Aug. 8, 1837, by Nehemiah B. Cooke	1	57
Mary, m. Denison **NOYES**, b. of Groton, Sept. 1, 1847, by Rev. Erastus Denison	1	79
Phebe J., of Groton, m. Thomas W. **NOYES**, of Stonington, May 11, 1848, by Rev. Nehemiah B. Cooke	1	80
KENNEDY, David, of Norwich, m. Eunice **LESTER**, of Groton, Nov. 21, 1771, by Rev. Jacob Johnson	2	14
KENYON, **KINION**, Amey, m. John G. **THOMPSON**, b. of Groton, Oct. 12, 1828, by Roswell Fish, J.P.	1	29
Bud[d]ington, m. Mary **PRICE**, b. of Groton, Mar. 7, 1827, by Rev. John G. Wightman	1	23
Edward C., m. Sarah A. **BENHAM**, b. of Groton, June 4, 1854, by Rev. Isaac Cheesebrough	1	96
Ellery, of Warwick, R.I., m. Lydia A. **WELCH**, of Groton, Dec. 20, 1829, by Rev. Roswell Burrows	1	32
Mary, m. Samuel **SMITH**, Mar. 31, 1740	1	151
KILLIAM, Lydia, d. Benjamin & Mary, b. June 29, 1733	1	145
Mary, m. Phillip **GRAY**, Nov. 24, 1737	1	149
KIMBALL, Amos Lester, s. [Erastus B. & Lydia], b. Apr. 24, 1826	3	12
Erastus B., of Preston, m. Lydia **LESTER**, of Groton, Dec. 30, 1821, by Jonathan Brewster, J.P., of Preston	1	5
Erastus B., of Preston, m. Lydia **LESTER**, of Groton, Dec. 30, 1821	3	12
Erastus Nathaniel, b. Mar. 30, 1828	3	15
Frank, of Preston, m. Susan **SATTERLEE**, of Groton, Mar. 19, 1826, by John Brewster, J.P.	1	20
Lydia Ann, d. [Erastus B. & Lydia], b. Apr. 23, 1824	3	12
KING, Andrew D., of Norwich, m. Adelia A. **HEATH**, of Groton, Mar. 3, 1844, by Rev. Cha[rle]s C. Lewis	1	70
Caroline Hope, of Groton, m. Enock BURROWS, of Stonington, Dec. 28, 1826, by Rev. Roswell Burrows	1	22
Lucretia, m. Benjamin **HOWARD**, May 28, 1823, by Noyes Barber, J.P.	1	9
Priscilla, of Portersville, in Groton, m. Theodore H. **WHITE**, of Bolton, July 3, 1843, by Rev. S. Simmons	1	69
William, m. Margaret **PARK[E]**, b. of Groton, Sept. 1, 1844, by Rev. Simon B. Bailey	1	71
KINICUM, see **CUNNINGHAM**		
KINNE, **KINNEY**, Aaron, m. Anna **MORGAN**, May 31, 1770	2	19
Aaron, [s. Aaron & Anna], b. Apr. 28, 1773	2	19
Anna, [d. Aaron & Anna], b. Mar. 18, 1771	2	19
Anna, m. Aaron **AVERY**, b. of Groton, Feb. 26, 1798	2	58
Anna, of Groton, m. Aaron **AVERY**, Feb. 26, 1798	2	60
Ashbel, [s. Aaron & Anna], b. Sept. 28, 1798	2	19
Elisha, [s. Aaron & Anna], b. Dec. 11, 1788	2	19
[Luc]y, [d. Aaron & Anna], b. May 20, 1775	2	19
Luther, of Griswold, m. Julia **ALLYN**, of Groton, Nov. 18, 1832, by John G. Wightman, Eld.	1	42
Lydia, [d. Aaron & Anna], b. Mar. 26, 1780	2	19
[M]ary, [d. Aaron & Anna], b. Aug. 16, 1777	2	19
Nathan, [s. Aaron & Anna], b. Mar. 13, 1785	2	19

	Vol.	Page
KINNE, KINNEY, (cont.)		
Solomon, [s. Aaron & Anna], b. Sept. 8, 1786	2	19
Thomas, [s. Aaron & Anna], b. Sept. 6, 1791	2	19
William, [s. Aaron & Anna], b. Aug. 28, 1782	2	19
KINNECUM, KINNICOM, see CUNNINGHAM		
KNAPP, John H., m. Hannah **REED**, b. of Groton, Mar. 31, 1850, by Rev. H. R. Knapp	1	88
KNOWLES, David, m. Emily **AVERY**, b. of Groton, Oct. 3, 1823, by Caleb Avery, J.P.	1	11
Elizabeth, of Groton, m. Francis **PENDLETON**, of Westerly, R.I., May 11, 1826, by John G. Wightman, Eld.	1	20
Sarah H., m. Sidney D. **BUDDINGTON**, b. of Groton, Feb. 7, 1850, by Rev. Nicholas T. Allen	1	87
LAMB, Aaron, [s. Timothy & Mary], b. Jan. 18, 1774	2	37
Abby, Mrs., m. Asa **PARK[E]**, b. of Groton, June 5, 1842, by Nathan Daboll, J.P.	1	66
Abby J., m. Edwin A. **PARK[E]**, b. of Groton, Jan. [ ], 1836, by John G. Wightman, Eld.	1	53
Abby Jane, d. [Asa & Abby], b. Mar. 27, 1819	3	31
Abel, s. [Samuel & Tabitha], b. Dec. 4, 1789	2	26
Abiah, s. [Caleb & Hannah], b. Oct. 31, 1749	1	168
Albert, s. [James & Anna], b. July 7, 1799	2	51
Albert B., of New London, m. Phebe H. **BURROWS**, of Groton, Mar. 7, 1850, by Rev. H. R. Knapp	1	88
Alfred, of Ledyard, m. Lydia Ann **WHIPPLE**, of Groton, Apr. 27, 1845, by Rev. Jared R. Avery	1	73
Allyn, s. [Samuel & Tabitha], b. Apr. 25, 1792	2	26
Ann, d. Daniel & Zeruiah, b. Dec. 18, 1745	1	143
Anna, d. [James & Anna], b. Dec. 17, 1785	2	51
Anne, d. [Nehemiah & Anna], b. June 23, 1764	1	170
Betsey, m. Reuben **HEATH**, b. of Groton, June 12, 1825, by Nathan Daboll, J.P.	1	16
Caleb, m. Hannah **SAMANS**, May 12, 1738	1	168
Catharine, d. [James & Susanna], b. Nov. 12, 1745	1	183
Celinda, see Selinda		
Charlotte, m. Coddington **HOLDREDGE**, b. of Groton, Apr. 19, 1846, by Rev. W. C. Walker	1	76
Content, Mrs., m. Asa **HEATH**, Oct. 27, 1850, by Henry W. Avery, J.P.	1	90
Daniel, m. Zeruiah **BUTTON**, Oct. 5, 1727	1	143
Daniel, s. Daniel & Zeruiah, b. Apr. 5, 1731	1	143
Daniel, s. Daniel & Zeruiah, b. Jan. 22, 1735/6	1	143
Daniel, s. [Samuel & Tabitha], b. Aug. 3, 1783	2	26
Daniel, m. Hannah **CULVER**, Oct. 11, 1802	3	11
Daniel Wightman, s. [Daniel & Hannah], b. Feb. 5, 1809	3	11
Deborah, [d. Timothy & Mary], b. Mar. 7, 1776	2	37
Denison, of Ledyard, m. Sally A. **ASHBEY**, of Groton, May 3, 1840, by Rev. John G. Wightman	1	62
Elisha, m. Sally **CHAPPELL**, b. of Groton, Mar. 25, 1827, by Ralph Hurlbutt, J.P.	1	23
Eliza J., of Groton, m. Simeon **CHURCH**, of Montville, May 25, 1851, by Rev. Nicholas T. Allen	1	91
Emily D., of Groton, m. Isaac N. **FAIRBROTHER**, of Providence, R.I., July 7, 1839, by Rev. John G. Wightman	1	61

	Vol.	Page
LAMB, (cont.)		
Enoch, m. Priscilla **AVERY**, b. of Groton, Mar. 26, 1818, by Rev. John G. Wightman	2	90
Enos, s. [Samuel & Tabitha], b. July 17, 1794	2	26
Erastus Avery, s. Enoch & Prescilla, b. Dec. 31, 1820	2	80
Esther, m. Nehemiah **BARNES**, Mar. 22, 1752	1	171
[E]unis, d. Daniel & Zeruiah, b. Apr. 2, 1729; d. Mar. [ ], 1734/5	1	143
Exeline, m. William **HEATH**, b. of Groton, Nov. 16, 1823, by Philip Gray, J.P.	1	11
Experience, m. William **STARK**, Jr., Apr. 13, 1710	1	112
Ezekiel, s. Daniel & Zeruiah, b. Apr. 5, 1740	1	143
Freeelove, d. Daniel & Zeruiah, b. Jan. 24, 1743	1	143
Freelove, m. Caleb **CHAPMAN**, b. of Groton, May 4, 1760, by Timothy Wightman, Elder	2	26
Hannah, m. Shubael **MAYNARD**, b. of Groton, Nov. 27, 1823, by John G. Wightman	1	11
Hannah C., d. James C. & Jane C., b. Jan. 30, 1840	3	34
Hannah Eliza, d. [Daniel & Hannah], b. Apr. 28, 1824	3	11
Henry, m. Abigail **DEWEY**, b. of Groton, Nov. 21, 1824, by John G. Wightman, Eld.	1	14
Isaac, m. Lydia **RICHARDS**, June 12, 1733	1	148
Isaac, s. Isaac & Lydia, b. Mar. 6, 1736/7	1	148
Isaac, [s. Timothy & Mary], b. Apr. 11, 1775	2	37
Isaac, m. Eliza **ALEXANDER**, b. of Groton, Apr. 3, 1834, by Amos A. Niles, J.P.	1	47
Jacob J., s. [Asa & Abby], b. Sept. 16, 1820	3	31
Jacob J., m. Elizabeth A. **PARK[E]**, b. of Groton, Aug. 16, 1840, by Rev. Ira R. Steward	1	63
James, m. Susanna **WIGHTMAN**, Oct. 31, 1744	1	183
James, m. Anna **RANDALL**, Jan. 22, 1784	2	51
James, s. [James & Anna], b. Apr. 9, 1797	2	51
James Chapman, s. [Daniel & Hannah], b. Aug. 3, 1810	3	11
Jane L., of Groton, m. Henry A. **GATES**, of N. Stonington, June 14, 1835, by W[illia]m M. Williams, J.P.	1	51
Jefferson, m. Mary **CRANDALL**, b. of Groton, Sept. 28, 1823, by William Williams, J.P.	1	10
Jesse, s. Isaac & Lydia, b. Apr. 22, 1738	1	148
Jesse, s. [Samuel & Tabitha], b. Sept. 11, 1787	2	26
John, [s. Timothy & Mary], b. Mar. 6, 1780	2	37
John, s. [Samuel & Tabitha], b. Feb. 13, 1786	2	26
Joseph A., m. Mrs. Mary **FISH**, b. of Groton, Sept. 1, 1839, by Rev. John G. Wightman	1	61
Joseph Austin, s. [Daniel & Hannah], b. Apr. 19, 1814	3	11
Levi, m. Mary Ellen **ASHBEY**, of Groton, Sept. 10, 1843, by Rev. Erastus Denison	1	70
Loanna, m. Levi **CHAPMAN**, 2d, b. of Groton, Dec. 2, 1827, by W[illia]m Williams, J.P.	1	26
Lotte, d. Samuel & Tabitha, b. Apr. 8, 1779	2	26
Lydia, of Groton, m. Hallam **WHITING**, of Stonington, Mar. 11, 1828, by William Williams, J.P.	1	27
Lyman, of Groton, m. Drusilla **MADDEN**, of New London, Nov. 11, 1832, by Nathan Daboll, J.P.	1	41
Mary, m. Timothy **COLVER**, Jan. 11, 1726/7	1	140

	Vol.	Page
LAMB, (cont.)		
Mary, [d. Timothy & Mary], b. Apr. 10, 1771	2	37
Mary, d. [Samuel & Tabitha], b. June 16, 1781	2	26
Mary Ann, d. [Daniel & Hannah], b. Mar. 19, 1822	3	11
Mary Ann, m. Lyman **WILLIAMS**, b. of Groton, July 25, 1836, by Nathan Daboll, J.P.	1	54
Mary Ann J., d. [Asa & Abby], b. July 16, 1817	3	31
Nathan, m. Betsey **CHAPMAN**, b. of Groton, Oct. 14, 1821, by Rev. Levi Nelson, of Lisbon	1	4
Nehemiah, s. Daniel & Zeruiah, b. Mar. 20, 1737/8	1	143
Nehemiah, m. Anna **WOOD**, Dec. 16, 1762	1	170
Nehemiah, s. Sam[ue]ll [& Tabitha], b. Mar. 8, 1777	2	26
Nelson, of Groton, m. Mary **DOUGLASS**, of Stonington, Mar. 19, 1851, by James C. Lamb, J.P.	1	91
Onis, s. Daniel & Zeruiah, b. Nov. 1, 1741	1	143
Permela, d. [Samuel & Tabitha], b. Jan. 12, 1799	2	26
Parmelia, m. Joseph **CULVER**, Jr., Mar. 10, 1822	3	5
Pamela, m. Joseph **CULVER**, Jr., Mar. 10, 1822, by Rev. John G. Wightman	1	6
Permelia, d. [Daniel & Hannah], b. Feb. 16, 1826	3	11
Polly, of Groton, m. Lodowick **WINCHESTER**, of R.I., Nov. 17, 1835, by John G. Wightman, Elder	1	52
Prudence, [d. Timothy & Mary], b. Sept. 11, 1772	2	37
Prudence Ann, of Groton, m. James **BEEBE**, of Norwich, Dec. 20, 1829, by Philip Gray, J.P.	1	32
Roswell Gallup, s. [Daniel & Hannah], b. Apr. 28, 1818	3	11
Rufus, [s. Timothy & Mary], b. Apr. 9, 1778	2	37
Sabrah, [d. Timothy & Mary], b. Mar. 7, 1783	2	37
Samuel, s. Daniel & Zeruiah, b. July 10, 1748	1	143
Samuel, s. [Ebenezer & Mary], b. Dec. 3, 1748	1	164
Samuel, m. Tabitha **WHITMAN**, July 31, 1774, by Timothy Wightman, Elder	2	26
Samuel Stillman, s. [Daniel & Hannah], b. Apr. 21, 1816	3	11
Samuel Whitman, s. Sam[ue]ll [& Tabitha], b. Aug. 23, 1775	2	26
Sanford, of Ledyard, m. Julia **GUYANT**, of Groton, Jan. 26, 1840, by Rev. John G. Wightman	1	62
Sarah, m. Jonathan **CULLVER**, July 19, 1722	1	125
Selinda, d. [Samuel & Tabitha], b. Aug. 21, 1796	2	26
Salinda, m. Joseph **CULVER**, Jr., b. of Groton, June 30, 1816, by John G. Wightman	3	5
Silas, s. Jacob & Jerusha, b. May 17, 1728	2	20
Silas, Jr., s. Silas, b. Apr. 13, 1756	2	58
Silas, Jr., m. Eliza **PERKINS**, b. of Groton, Mar. 21, 1825, by Nathan Daball, J.P.	1	16
Thomas, s. Ebenezer & Mary, b. Dec. 1, 1735	1	164
Timothy, m. Mary **HOLDREDGE**, Apr. 20, 1766	2	37
Timothy, Jr., [s. Timothy & Mary], b. Sept. 28, 1767	2	37
William, [s. Timothy & Mary], b. Apr. 16, 1769	2	37
William R., m. Betsey **ARTHUR**, b. of Groton, Jan. 27, 1833, by Nathan Daboll, J.P.	1	42
Zeruiah, d. Daniel & Zeruiah, b. Mar. 27, 1732/3	1	143

	Vol.	Page
LAMPHERE, LAMPHEAR, LAMPHEIR, Champlain, of Stonington, m. Emily **HEM[P]STEAD**, of Groton, Dec. 7, 1834, by John G. Wightman, Elder	1	48
David, m. Mary Ann **HOUGH**, b. of Stonington, June 9, 1839, by Rev. John G. Wightman	1	60
George, of Groton, m. Mary **FITCH**, of Colchester, Mar. 1, 1758, by Rev. Ichabod Allyn, of Colchester	1	169
Jesse B., of Groton, m. Hannah W. **GRINNELL**, of New Bedford, Mass., July 4, 1850, by Rev. Erastus Denison	1	89
Marian, m. Andrew **DAVIS**, Jr., June 12, 1735	1	183
Rebecca, of Groton, m. Saxton W. **WHEELER**, of Stonington, Nov. 16, 1848, by Rev. Simon B. Bailey	1	82
Thomas W., m. Sarah S. **BROWN**, b. of Groton, Mar. 26, 1843, by Rev. Benjamin C. Phelps, of Mystic	1	68
LANE, William, m. Lucy **ARTHUR**, b. of New London, Jan. 24, 1836, by John G. Wightman, Elder	1	53
LARAY, Charles, m. Mary M. **BALDWIN**, Mar. 9, 1845, at Amos Baldwin's house, by Rev. R. Russell	1	73
LARRABEE, Addam, Capt. m. Hannah Gallup **LESTER**, Sept. 21, 1817	3	6
Adam Allyn, s. [Frederick & Abigail], b. Mar. 14, 1787	2	80
Charles, s. [Capt. Addam & Hannah Gallup], b. June [ ], 1821	3	6
Ellen, d. [Capt. Adam & Hannah Gallup], b. Feb. 19, 1828	3	6
Frederick, m. Abigail **ALLYN**, May [ ], 1786	2	80
Hannah, d. [Capt. Addam & Hannah Gallup], b. Nov. 23, 1825	3	6
Henry, s. [Capt. Addam & Hannah Gallup], b. Apr. 15, 1830	3	6
John, s. [Capt. Addam & Hannah Gallup], b. Nov. 29, 1823	3	6
Julia, d. [Frederick & Abigail], b. Feb. 3, 1789	2	80
Nathan Frederick, s. [Capt. Addam & Hannah Gallup], b. Oct. 11, 1818	3	6
William, s. [Capt. Addam & Hannah Gallup], b. Jan. 20, 1832	3	6
LATHAM, Abby, of Groton, m. Guy C. **STODDARD**, of Ledyard, Feb. 10, 1840, by Rev. Jared R. Avery	1	62
Abby Jane, m. John P. **SPICER**, b. of Groton, Sept. 12, 1830, by Rev. Erastus Denison	1	35
Abigail, m. William **GOOD**, June 24, 1787	2	23
Albert A., m. Lucy A. **GRAY**, of Preston, Dec. 7, 1848, by Rev. H. R. Knapp	1	84
Albert G., m. Mary F. **HUDSON**, b. of Groton, Aug. 12, 1836, by Rev. Ira R. Steward	1	55
Amos, s. [Jasper, Jr. & Deborah], b. July 16, 1759	1	163
Anna, [d. Thomas], b. Apr. 18, 1723	1	107
Asa, s. [Joseph & Deborah], b. Jan. 6, 1782	2	57
Benjamin, s. [Robert & Rebecca], b. Nov. 1, 1787	2	32
Betsey, m. Isaac **FANNING**, Jan. 24, 1836, by W[illia]m M. Williams, J.P.	1	53
Caroline, m. Rufus **AVERY**, Jr., Sept. 3, 1804	2	91
Caroline, m. Joseph B. **MITCHELL**, b. of Groton, Dec. 28, 1834, by Joseph Durfee, J.P.	1	48
Cary, [s. Cary, Jr. & Sarah], b. Jan. 5, 1733/4	1	135
Cary, m. Mary **PACKER**, b. of Groton, Feb. 22, 1761	2	52
Cary, Jr., s. [Cary & Mary], b. Apr. 2, 1773	2	52
Cate, d. [Cary & Mary], b. Mar. 22, 1765	2	52
Catharine, m. George B. **CRARY**, b. of Groton, Aug. 6, 1843, by Rev. Erastus Denison	1	69
Catharine Crary, [d. Henry & Lucy], b. Mar. 22, 1827	3	18

	Vol.	Page
LATHAM, (cont.)		
Catherine D., m. Nathaniel **RANSOM**, Oct. 13, 1845, by Rev. Henry R. Knapp. Recorded Aug. 6, 1895	1	98
Catharine D., m. Nathaniel **RANSOM**, b. of Groton, Dec. 18, 1845, by Rev. H. R. Knapp	1	83
Cyrus, s. [Joseph & Deborah], b. Jan. 16, 1779	2	57
Daniel, [s. Thomas], b. Apr. 26, 1719	1	107
Daniel, m. Delia Ann **DENNISON**, b. of Groton, Sept. 10, 1826, by John G. Wightman, Eld.	1	21
Darius, s. [Joseph & Deborah], b. Aug. 4, 1790	2	57
David, s. Joseph, b. Sept. 18, 1724	1	124
Deborah, d. [Jasper, Jr. & Deborah], b. Feb. 24, 1762	1	163
Deborah, d. [George & Rebecca], b. July 6, 1805	2	71
Deborah, m. Orlando **BAILEY**, b. of Groton, Dec. 23, 1827, by John G. Wightman, Eld.	1	26
Desire, d. [Cary & Mary], b. Mar. 9, 1771	2	52
Ebenezer, s. [Joseph & Deborah], b. Nov. 6, 1776	2	57
Ebenezer, m. Betsey **SMITH**, b. of Groton, Aug. 28, 1803, by Christopher Avery, Pastor	2	66
Eliza, m. Benjamin **RATHBURN**, Oct. 3, 1824, by Rev. Roswell Burrows	1	14
Elizabeth, [d. Joseph], b. Nov. 25, 1726	1	124
Elizabeth, d. [Joseph & Deborah], b. July 23, 1774	2	57
Elizabeth, m. John SPICER, 2d, b. of Groton, Sept. 7, 1794, by Amos Geer, J.P.	2	59
Emblem, [s. Cary, Jr. & Sarah], b. Mar. 14, 1720	1	135
Emeline, m. Simeon A. **BAILEY**, Jr., b. of Ledyard, Apr. 24, 1838, by Rev. John G. Wightman	1	58
Emma C., of Groton, m. Henry B. **LEWIS**, of Westerly, R.I., Apr. 8, 1852, by Rev. James M. Phillips	1	93
Erastus H., m. Charlotte F. **GERE**, b. of Groton, Feb. 7, 1830, by Timothy Tuttle	1	33
Eunice, of Groton, m. Hezekiah **GRAY**, of New York, Oct. 21, 1822, by Rev. Roswell Burrows	1	7
Eunice, m. William **WATROUS**, b. of Groton, May 20, 1840, by Ira R. Steward	1	63
George, s. [Jasper, Jr. & Deborah], b. Nov. 6, 1769	1	163
George, m. Rebecca **BABCOCK**, Nov. 12, 1795	2	71
George, s. [George & Rebecca], b. July 20, 1802	2	71
George, Jr., m. Selinda **NILES**, Nov. 5, 1826, by Rodman Niles, J.P.	1	22
George, Jr., m. Selinda **NILES**, Nov. 5, 1826	3	26
Grace, [d. John], b. Nov. 4,1703	1	112
Griswold, s. [Joseph & Deborah], b. May 12, 1784	2	57
Hannah, [d. William & Hannah], b. Nov. 2, 1700	1	109
Hannah, w. Capt. William, d. Apr. 21, 1727, ae. 53 y.	1	128
Hannah, d. [Cary & Mary], b. Mar. 8, 1767	2	52
Hannah, [d. Jasper, Jr. & Deborah], b. Oct. 6, 1774	1	163
Hannah, d. [Cary & Mary], d. Dec. 7, 1797	2	52
Hannah, of Groton, m. William **ADAMS**, of Ledyard, Feb. 5, 1837, by Rev. Roswell Burrows	1	56
Hannah F., m. Alonzo **WILLIAMS**, b. of Groton, Dec. 18, 1833, by Rev. Ira R. Steward	1	45
Henry, m. Lucy **SPICER**, b. of Groton, Oct. 6, 1822, by Roswell Burrows	1	7

	Vol.	Page
LATHAM, (cont.)		
Holloway, of Groton, m. Hannah **FISH**, of Colchester, Jan. 22, 1815, by Amasa Loomis, Jr.	1	14
James, [s. William & Hannah], b. Jan. 23, 1706	1	109
James, d. Feb. 17, 1728/9, ae. 22 y.	1	129
James A., m. Abby **PALMER**, b. of Groton, June 18, 1832, by Rev. Roswell Burrows	1	40
Jane E., m. Charles H. **GATES**, b. of Groton, Aug. 21, 1851, by Rev. Nicholas T. Allen	1	92
Jasper, Jr. m. Deborah **AVERY**, July 25, 1752	1	163
Jasper, s. [Jasper, Jr. & Deborah], b. Aug. 30, 1754	1	163
Jasper, s. [George & Rebecca], b. July 4, 1809	2	71
Jasper, m. Hannah W. **BAILEY**, b. of Groton, June 14, 1836, by John G. Wightman, Elder	1	54
John, [s. John], b. Nov. 1, 1711	1	112
John, twin with Temperance, s. [Cary & Mary], b. Mar. 18, 1779	2	52
John, of Lebanon, m. Eliza **BROWN**, of Groton, Feb. 17, 1833, by John G. Wightman, Eld.	1	43
John D., m. Emeline **WILBUR**, b. of Groton, May 27, 1838, by Ira R. Steward	1	59
Jonas, s. [Joseph & Deborah], b. May 20, 1772	2	57
Jonathan, [s. William & Hannah], b. May 28, 1716	1	109
Joseph, [s. William & Hannah], b. Sept. 21, 1712	1	109
Joseph, s. Cary, Jr. & Sarah, b. Apr. 8, 1714	1	135
Joseph, m. Patience **SEABURY**, Nov. 28, 1722	1	124
Joseph, [s. Joseph], b. Jan. 27, 1728	1	125
Joseph, s. Joseph & Deborah, b. Feb. 1, 1766	2	57
Joseph, 3d, of Groton, m. Nancy **SCOTT**, of Franklin, Ct., July 3, 1828, by John G. Wightman	1	28
Katharine, of Groton, m. John **RODGERS**, Jan. 20, 1796	2	63
Katy, see Cate		
Lucian Niles, s. [George, Jr. & Selinda], b. Apr. 28, 1829	3	26
Lucretia, [d. Thomas], b. Apr. 4, 1721	1	107
Lucy, [d. William & Hannah], b. May 21, 1709	1	109
Lucy, m. Ebenezer **AVERY**, Jr., June 16, 1726	1	130
Lucy, d. Cary & Mary, b. July 9, 1761	2	52
Lucy Ann, of Groton, m. Nehemiah **MASON**, of Stonington, Sept. 11, 1828, by John G. Wightman	1	28
Lucy E., m. Ambrose H. **BURROWS**, b. of Groton, Sept. 3, 1837, by Nehemiah B. Cooke	1	57
Luke, s. [William & Eunice], b. July 28, 1774	2	59
Lydia, [d. John], b. Oct. 26, 1706	1	112
Lyman, of Preston, m. Mary **GALLUP**, of Groton, Nov. 4, 1829, by Rev. Roswell Burrows	1	32
Malinda B., of Groton, m. John W. **FISK**, of Groton, Oct. 15, 1849, by Rev. Nicholas T. Allen	1	87
Maria, d. [George & Rebecca], b. May 6, 1799	2	71
Mary, [d. William & Hannah], b. Feb. 18, 1698/9	1	109
Mary, [d. John], b. Sept. 20, 1714	1	112
Mary, m. Christopher **AVERY**, Jan. 25, 1719, by Rev. Ephraim Woodbridge	1	119
Mary, m. Christopher **AVERY**, Jr., June 25, 1719	1	133
Mary, m. Johnathan **AVERY**, Jr., Dec. 12, 1734	1	135

	Vol.	Page
LATHAM, (cont.)		
Mary, [d. Joseph], b. July 11, 1735	1	124
Mary, d. [Jasper, Jr. & Deborah], b. July 7, 1752; d. Aug. 10, 1754	1	163
Mary Ann, of Groton, m. Charles S. **RANDALL**, of Havre, France, Oct. 2, 1836, by Ira R. Steward	1	55
Peter, s. James & Elizabeth, b. June 5, 1752	1	120
Polly, d. [Cary & Mary], b. Mar. 14, 1763	2	52
Polly, m. Samuel **GEER**, b. of Groton, July 10, 1804, by Amos Geer, J.P.	2	68
Prudence, d. Joseph & Deborah, b. Feb. 18, 1768	2	57
Rebeckah, d. [Jasper, Jr. & Deborah], b. Sept. 26, 1766	1	163
Rebecca, m. Robert **LATHAM**, Apr. 24, 1783, by Rev. Aaron Kinne	2	32
Rebecca, d. [George & Rebecca], b. Sept. 5, 1796	2	71
Rebecca, of Groton, m. Frank **BAILEY**, of Morgan, Ohio, Sept. 21, 1825, by John G. Wightman, Eld.	1	18
Robert, s. Daniel & Elizabeth, b. Aug. 19, 1756	1	158
Robert, m. Rebecca **LATHAM**, Apr. 24, 1783, by Rev. Aaron Kinne	2	32
Robert, s. [Joseph & Deborah], b. July 30, 1786	2	57
Russell, m. Catharine **FISH**, b. of [ ], Oct. 29, 1848, by Caleb M. Williams, J.P.	1	81
Samuel B., m. Hannah **PACKER**, b. of Groton, Sept. 28, 1834, by Rev. Ira R. Steward	1	48
Sarah, [d. John], b. Apr. 13, 1716	1	112
Sarah, [d. Cary, Jr. & Sarah], b. Sept. 25, 1723	1	135
Sarah M., m. Joseph S. **WIGHTMAN**, b. of Groton, June 12, 1843, by Ira R. Steward	1	69
Sarah Maria, d. [George, Jr. & Selinda], b. Sept. 17, 1827	3	26
Silas, m. Lydia P. **LEWIS**, b. of Groton, Sept. 28, 1834, by Rev. Ira R. Steward	1	48
Susanna, [d. Cary, Jr. & Sarah], b. Sept. 1, 1717	1	135
Temperance, twin with John, d. [Cary & Mary], b. Mar. 18, 1779	2	52
Thomas, [s. Thomas], b. Oct. 15, 1716	1	107
William, m. Hannah **MORGAN**, June 30, 1698	1	109
William, [s. William & Hannah], b. Feb. 24, 1703	1	109
William, d. Nov. 5, 1732, ae. 63 y.	1	129
William, Jr., d. Nov. 9, 1732, ae. 29 y.	1	129
William, s. [Joseph & Deborah], b. Feb. 20, 1770	2	57
William, s. Thomas & Eunice, b. Apr. 2, 1780	2	16
William, m. Mary m. **AVERY**, b. of Groton, Apr. 24, 1836, by Rev. Ira R. Steward	1	54
William F., s. William & Eunice, b. Aug. 18, 1771	2	59
W[illia]m H., m. Hannah **ELDREDGE**, b. of Groton, July 23, 1849, by Rev. H. R. Knapp	1	85
William Henry, [s. Henry & Lucy], b. July 13, 1823	3	18
Willis, s. Jasper & Lydia, b. Jan. 4, 1789	2	58
LATHRUPT, Gurdon, of Towand, Pa., m. Francis J. **HOWELL**, of Groton, Mar. 13, 1843, by Rev. William S. Simmons, Jr.	1	68
LEDYARD, Benjamin, [s. Youngs & Mary], b. Mar. 15, 1753	2	29
Betsey, d. [Youngs & Bridget], b. Apr. 13, 1777	2	6
Caleb, [s. Youngs & Mary], b. Oct. 18, 1762	2	29
Deborah, [d. Youngs & Mary], b. May 19, 1749	2	29
Deborah, m. Christopher **MORGAN**, Feb. 16, 1768	2	1
Fanny, of Groton, m. James **ELLS**, of Harpersfield, N.Y., Apr. 19, 1825, by John G. Wightman, Elder	1	16

	Vol.	Page
LEDYARD, (cont.)		
Isaac, [s. Youngs & Mary], b. Nov. 5, 1754	2	29
Isaac, s. [Youngs & Bridget], b. Nov. 21, 1779	2	6
Lucy, [d. Youngs & Mary], b. July 5, 1761	2	29
Mary, [d. Youngs & Mary], b. Sept. 3, 1758	2	29
Mary, m. Stephen **BILLINGS**, Dec. 12, 1765	1	179
Maryann, m. Gilbert **WILLIAMS**, b. of Groton, Jan. 20, 1823, by John G. Wightman, Eld.	1	9
Nathaniel S., s. Gurdon & Nancy, b. Jan. 25, 1799	2	35
Polly, d. [Youngs & Bridget], b. Sept. 17, 1780	2	6
Youngs, m. Mary **AVERY**, Dec. 8, 1748	2	29
Youngs, [s. Youngs & Mary], b. Jan. 24, 1751	2	29
Youngs, m. Bridget **BILLINGS**, June 24, 1773	2	6
Youngs, s. [Youngs & Bridget], b. Dec. 24, 1775	2	6
Youngs, Lieut., d. Sept. 7, 1781	2	6
LEE, Caleb, m. Ann Amelia Maria **TOPLIFF**, b. of Willington, Mar. 20, 1848, by Rev. L. G. Leonard	1	80
Elizabeth, m. John **BAILEY**, July 2, 1722	1	110
John, m. Mary **PACKER**, b. of Groton, Mar. 28, 1817	3	14
LEEDS, Cary, s. Thomas & Mary, b. May 15, 1720; d. Apr. 10, 1722	1	124
Clarinda, m. Bradley **DANIELS**, b. of Groton, June 29, 1828, by Nathan Daboll, J.P.	1	28
Cynthia, m. Nathan **STARK**, b. of Groton, June 30, 1825, by Timothy Tuttle	1	17
Deborah, [d. Thomas & Mary], b. Oct. 21, 1729	1	124
Ellen, m. Asa **PERKINS**, 2d, b. of Groton, Dec. 16, 1827, by Nathan Daboll, J.P.	1	25
Harriat, s. Cary, b. May 24, 1782	2	32
Harry, s. Cary, b. Feb. 25, 1779	2	32
Jedediah, s. Thomas & Mary, b. Oct. 10, 1717	1	124
Jerusha, d. Cary, b. Apr. 15, 1777	2	32
John, m. Emily **STARK**, b. of Groton, Feb. 16, 1843, by Rev. Erastus Denison	1	67
Julia, m. Caleb **BURROWS**	3	0
Julia Ann, m. Caleb **BURROWS**, b. of Groton, June 10, 1821, by John G. Wightman, Elder	1	3
Mary, [d. Thomas & Mary], b. June 17, 1727	1	124
Mary, of Groton, m. Elihu **HAKES**, Jr., of Preston, Sept. 14, 1829, by John G. Wightman, Eld.	1	31
Nathan, s. Cary, b. Jan. 27, 1775	2	32
Peace C., m. William N. **GRANT**, b. of Groton, May 10, 1837, by Ira R. Steward	1	56
Sarah, d. Thomas & Mary, b. Feb. 28, 1721	1	124
Sarah Ann, d. Cary, b. Oct. 6, 1780	2	32
Thomas, m. Mary **WILLIAMS**, Apr. 17, 1717	1	124
Thomas, [s. Thomas & Mary], b. Sept. 24, 1724	1	124
LEFFINGWELL, Jonathan, s. Jonathan & Lucy, b. Feb. 11, 1742	2	10
Lucy, d. Jonathan & Lucy, b. Nov. 9, 1745	2	10
Lucy, m. John **WOOD**, Feb. 2, 1748/9	1	184
Nathaniel, s. Jona[than] & Lucy, b. Oct. 7, 1739	2	10
Sarah, d. Jonathan & Lucy, b. Aug. 24, 1737	2	10
Sarah, m. Joseph* **CHAPMAN**, b. of Groton, Oct. 18, 1758, by Rev. Jacob Johnson (*Changed to "Joshua" by L.B.B.)	2	17

	Vol.	Page
LESTER, Adeline E., d. [Nicholas S. & Elizabeth S.], b. May 14, 1809	3	2
Adeline Elizabeth, of Groton, m. Earl **WARNER**, of Brooklyn, June 30, 1835, by Timothy Tuttle	1	51
Almy Angell, [d. Jonathan & Almy], b. Feb. 6, 1802	2	27
Amos, Jr., m. Sally **AVERY**, b. of Groton, Jan. 18, 1801, by Amos Geer, J.P.	2	72
Amos, s. Amos & Sally, b. July 20, 1801	2	72
Amos Avery, s. [Amos & Sally], b. Mar. 31, 1805	2	72
Amey, of Groton, m Josiah **ADAMS**, of Stephentown, N.Y., Feb. 14, 1833, by Ralph Hurlbutt, J.P.	1	43
Anna, d. [Peter & Anna], b. Dec. 17, 1736	1	175
Anna, w. Peter, d. May 6, 1790	2	13
Anna, of Groton, m. Oliver S. **TYLER**, of Preston, Jan. 5, 1831, by Levi Meech, Eld.	1	36
Annass, m. Samuel **CHAPMAN**, b. of Groton, Nov. 13, 1814, by W[illia]m Robinson, J.P., in Stonington	2	80
Asa, s. Peter & Delight Hazen, b. Dec. 26, 1761	1	165
Asa, m. Dorothy **LESTER**, Jan. 12, 1785, by Rev. Parke Allyn	2	35
Asa L., m. Eliza M. **LESTER**, b. of Groton, Aug. 16, 1835, by John G. Wightman, Elder	1	51
Austin M., m. Nancy **STODDARD**, b. of Groton, Sept. 16, 1827, by Ralph Hurlbutt, J.P.	1	24
Benjamin, s. [Samuel, Jr. & Abigail], b. Sept. 6, 1743	1	176
Betsey, d. [Christopher & Mary], b. Nov. 22, 1797	2	60
Betsey, m. Latham **AVERY**, July 7, 1816	3	9
Charles, s. [Thomas & Mary], b. Nov. 14, 1768	1	168
Christopher, s. Daniel & Margaret, b. Sept. 10, 1763	1	160
Christopher, m. Mary **FISH**, of Groton, Apr. 10, 1791	2	60
Christopher, s. [Christopher & Mary], b. Mar. 20, 1803	2	60
Christopher, Jr., m. Est[h]er **BAILEY**, b. of Groton, Oct. 23, 1825, by John G. Wightman, Eld.	1	19
Daniel, m. Margaret **AVERY**, Jan. 14, 1760	1	160
Daniel, s. Daniel & Margaret, b. Sept. 15, 1760	1	160
David, m. Elizabeth **STREET**, May 13, 1771	1	176
David, s. [Christopher & Mary], b. Apr. 1, 1796	2	60
Deborah, m. Solomon **PERKINS**, Jan. 2, 1752	1	162
Dorothy, d. John & Dorothy, b. Oct. 21, 1769	2	7
Dorothy, m. Asa **LESTER**, Jan. 12, 1785, by Rev. Parke Allyn	2	35
Ebenezer, s. [Thomas & Mary], b. Aug. 1, 1761	1	168
Elamuel, [s. Sam[ue]ll & Hannah], b. July 18, 1719	1	122
Elijah, s. [Samuel, Jr. & Mary], b. Jan. 5, 1779	2	36
Eliza, of Groton, m. Henry **McCRACKEN**, of Salem, Mar. 23, 1834, by Ralph Hurlbutt, J.P.	1	46
Eliza M., m. Asa L. **LESTER**, b. of Groton, Aug. 16, 1835, by John G. Wightman, Elder	1	51
Eliza M., m. A. C. **ALLEN**, b. of Ledyard, Apr. 2, 1854, by Geo[rge] H. Woodward	1	96
Eliza Maria, d. [Amos & Sally], b. July 26, 1813	2	72
Elizabeth, [d. Sam[ue]ll & Hannah], b. Mar. 13, 1715	1	122
Elizabeth, [d. David & Elizabeth], b. Dec. 29, 1774	1	176
Emeline, of Groton, m. John **SHORT**, of New York, Mar. 23, 1828, by Ralph Hurlbutt, J.P.	1	27

	Vol.	Page
LESTER, (cont.)		
Emily Malvina, m. Elijah Frederick **SMITH**, b. of Groton, Dec. 28, 1825, by Timothy Tuttle	1	19
Eunice, d. Andrew & Abigail, b. Dec. 21, 1754	1	165
[E]unice, m. Elijah **ADAMS**, Mar. 14, 1771	1	151
Eunice, of Groton, m. David **KENNEDY**, of Norwich, Nov. 21, 1771, by Rev. Jacob Johnson	2	14
Frances S., d. [Nicholas S. & Elizabeth S.], b. May 12, 1807	3	2
Hannah, m. James FFARSHEE, Sept. 9, 1708	1	115
Hannah, m. Ralph **STODDARD**, Jan. 3, 1723	1	108
Hannah, [d. Sam[ue]ll & Hannah], b. Jan. 12, 1727/8	1	122
Hannah, d. [Peter & Anna], b. Mar. 17, 1737/8	1	175
Hannah, d. [Christopher & Mary], b. Aug. 13, 1792	2	60
Hannah, m. Isaac **BAILEY**, b. of Groton, June 15, 1828, by Timothy Tuttle	1	27
Hannah Gallup, d. Nathan & Susanna, b. June 8, 1798	2	64
Hannah Gallup, m. Capt. Addam **LARRABEE**, Sept. 21, 1817	3	6
Henry, [s. David & Elizabeth], b. Jan. 30, 1772	1	176
Huldah, d. [Samuel, Jr. & Abigail], b. Apr. 14, 1748	1	176
Isaac Avery, s. [Amos & Sally], b. Mar. 4, 1807	2	72
John, s. [Peter & Anna], b. Oct. 13, 1740	1	175
John, s. [Samuel, Jr. & Abigail], b. Apr. 14, 1748	1	176
John, m. Dorothy **MORGAN**, b. of Groton, Dec, 24. 1767	2	7
John, s. Asa & Dorothy, b. Jan. 1, 1786	2	35
John Henry, s. [Nicholas S. & Elizabeth S.], b. Jan. 29, 1813	3	2
Jonathan, m. Deborah **ALLYN**, Sept. 22, 1724	1	125
Jonathan Greene, [s. Jonathan & Almy], b. Nov. 9, 1804	2	27
Lemuel, s. [Samuel, Jr. & Abigail], b. Apr. 1, 1738	1	176
Lucretia, d. [Samuel, Jr. & Abigail], b. Apr. 14, 1740	1	176
Lucy, d. [Peter & Anna], b. June 4, 1744	1	175
Lydia, d. [Amos & Sally], b. Dec. 19, 1802	2	72
Lydia, of Groton, m. Erastus B. **KIMBALL**, of Preston, Dec. 30, 1821, by Jonathan Brewster, J.P. of Preston	1	5
Lydia, of Groton, m. Erastus B. **KIMBALL**, of Preston, Dec. 30, 1821	3	12
Margaret, [d. Sam[ue]ll & Hannah], b. Feb. 17, 1729	1	122
Marg[a]ret, d. Daniel & Margaret, b. Oct. 23, 1765	1	160
Margaret, w. David, d. Feb. 19, 1771	1	153
Margaret, d. [Christopher & Mary], b. July 18, 1801	2	60
Margaret H., of Groton, m. Alfred A. **WOOD**, of New London, Oct. 2, 1825, by John G. Wightman, Eld.	1	18
Mary, m. Elijah **BAILEY**, Feb. 1, 1750	2	1
Mary, d. [Thomas & Mary], b. Aug. 14, 1756	1	168
Mary, of Groton, m. Samuel **LESTER**, of Groton, Oct. 6, 1763	1	159
Mary, d. Samuel & Mary, b. July 6, 1765	1	159
Mary, d. [Samuel, Jr. & Mary], b. Apr. 14, 1781	2	36
Mary, w. Samuel, d. Dec. 24, 1781	2	36
Mary, d. [Christopher & Mary], b. May 22, 1807	2	60
Mary, m. Amos **ETH[E]RIDGE**, b. of Groton, Feb. 11, 1821, by Ralph Hurlbutt, J.P.	1	3
Mary, m. Amos **ELDREDGE**, b. of Groton, Feb. 11, 1821, by Ralph Hurlbutt, J.P.	2	29
Mary, of Groton, m. Austin **WILLIAMS**, of Stonington, Mar. 1, 1829, by John G. Wightman, Eld.	1	29

	Vol.	Page
LESTER, (cont.)		
Nancy, of Groton, m. Amos **COMSTOCK**, of Montville, Jan. 1, 1832, by Ralph Hurlbutt, J.P.	1	39
Nathan, s. [Peter & Anna], b. July 25, 1742	1	175
Nathan, m. Susanna **GALLUP**, b. of Groton, Apr. 24, 1796	2	64
Nicholas S., s. [Nicholas S. & Elizabeth S.], b. Dec. 19, 1804	3	2
Peter, m. Anna **STREET**, Aug. [ ], 1733	1	175
Peter, s. Peter & Anna, b. Apr. 1, 1734	1	175
Peter, s. Daniel & Margaret, b. Sept. 25, 1767	1	160
Peter, d. Sept. 10, 1789	2	13
Peter, s. [Christopher & Mary], b. May 19, 1801	2	60
Peter, 2d, m. Abby **STODDARD**, b. of Groton, Jan. 2, 1825, by Ralph Hurlbutt, J.P.	1	15
Rebecca Ann, of Groton, m. Avery E. BAILEY, of New London, Mar. 18, 1832, by Ralph Hurlbutt, J.P.	1	39
Sam[ue]ll, m. Hannah **BILL**, Nov. 5, 1707	1	122
Sam[ue]ll, s. Sam[ue]ll & Hannah, b. Sept. 23, 1711	1	122
Samuel, Jr., m. Abigail **MASON**, Dec. 10, 1737	1	176
Samuel, Jr., m. Abigail **MASON**, Dec. 11, 1737	1	147
Samuel, s. [Samuel, Jr. & Abigail], b. Jan. 5, 1745/6	1	176
Samuel, d. Jan. 15, 1750/51, ae. 71 y.	1	152
Samuel, of Groton, m. Mary **LESTER**, of Groton, Oct. 6, 1763	1	159
Samuel, Jr., m. Mary **BAILEY**, Nov. 27, 1777	2	36
Samuel, Jr., m. Hannah **GIFFORD**, of Norwich, Dec. 4, 1782, by Nath[anie]l Waterman, Jr., J.P. of Norwich	2	36
Sarah, [d. Sam[ue]ll & Hannah], b. Jan. 30, 1721/22	1	122
Sarah, m. Asa **WOODWORTH**, Sept. 13, 1739	1	156
Sarah, d. [Christopher & Mary], b. Oct. 4, 1794	2	60
Sarah C., of Groton, m. James **ADAMS**, of Stephenstown, N.Y., Feb. 11, 1821, by Ralph Hurlbutt, J.P.	1	3
Sarah C., of Groton, m. James **ADAMS**, Jr., of Stephentown, N.Y., Feb. 11, 1821, by Ralph Hurlbutt, J.P.	2	29
Simeon, s. Samuel & Mary, b. Feb. 24, 1766	1	159
Susan, m. John **FORSYTH**, b. of Groton, Jan. 1, 1832, by Ralph Hurlbutt, J.P.	1	39
Tabitha, d. [Andrew & Abigail], b. Jan. 8, 1748	1	165
Thomas, m. Mary **ALLYN**, Feb. 28, 1754	1	168
Thomas, s. [Thomas & Mary], b. Mar. 1, 1755	1	168
Waite, s. [Thomas & Mary], b. Dec. 17, 1759	1	168
Zerviah, [d. Sam[ue]ll & Hannah], b. Nov. 11, 1733	1	122
LEWEY, John, m. Frances S. **BURROWS**, b. of Groton, Dec. 8, 1839, by Ira R. Steward	1	62
LEWIS, Abel, of Hopkinton, R.I., m. Prudence **TIFT**, of Groton, Dec. 10, 1829, by William Williams, J.P.	1	32
Abigail, d. Peleg & Abigail, b. May 3, 1783	2	47
Abigail, Jr., m. [A]Eneas **MORGAN**, b. of Groton, Jan. 19, 1800	2	61
Anna, d. [Joseph & Deborah], b. Sept. 8, 1771	1	169
Betsey, m. Andrew **CHESEBRO[UGH]**, b. of Stonington, Mar. 21, 1838, by Rev. John G. Wightman	1	58
Clark, of N. Stonington, m. Lucy **DABOLL**, of Groton, Feb. 26, 1830, by Nathan Daboll, J.P.	1	33
Deborah, d. [Joseph & Deborah], b. June 28, 1773	1	169

	Vol.	Page
LEWIS, (cont.)		
Harriet, of Stonington, m. Theodore **TEAD**, of N.Y., Sept. 18, 1836, by John G. Wightman, Elder	1	55
Henry B., of Westerly, R.I., m. Emma C. **LATHAM**, of Groton, Apr. 8, 1852, by Rev. James M. Phillips	1	93
James, s. [Peleg & Abigail], b. Jan. 5, 1793	2	47
Jepthah, s. [Joseph & Deborah], b. Dec. 8, 1769	1	169
Joseph, s. Joseph & Deborah, b. Feb. 8, 1765	1	169
Lydia, b. June 5, 1790	3	9
Lydia, wid., m. Nathan **MIX**, b. of Groton, Mar. 25, 1825, by Roswell Burrows, Min.	1	16
Lydia P., b. Apr. 27, 1815	3	9
Lydia P., m. Silas **LATHAM**, b. of Groton, Sept. 28, 1834, by Rev. Ira R. Steward	1	48
Mary, d. [Joseph & Deborah], b. Feb. 22, 1768	1	169
Mary A., b. Jan. 18, 1809	3	9
Mary Ann, m. Edwin Barber **WHEELER**, b. of Groton, Sept. 3, 1826, by Roswell Burrows	1	21
Nancy, d. [Peleg & Abigail], b. Apr. 9, 1785	2	47
Nathaniel, of Stonington, m. Caroline **HEWLET**, of Groton, Aug. 18, 1844, by Nathan Daboll, J.P.	1	71
Paul B., b. Apr. 11, 1813	3	9
Peleg, m. Abigail **SMITH**, of Groton, Jan. 27, 1782, by Elder Park Allyn	2	47
Peleg, s. [Peleg & Abigail], b. Mar. 27, 1790	2	47
Peleg, d. Dec. 25, 1792	2	47
Sally, b. June 15, 1787; m. James **GERE**, Jan. 20, 1808	3	0
Sarah, d. [Peleg & Abigail], b. June 15, 1787	2	47
LIMAS, Elizabeth, m. George **JACKSON**, b. of Groton, June 8, 1834, by John G. Wightman, Elder	1	47
Philena, m. Henry **HALLAM**, Apr. 1, 1833, by John G. Wightman, Eld.	1	43
LIRRAS, Elias, of Groton, m. Sarah FREEMAN, of Stonington, May 29, 1828, by Rev. N. S. Spaulding, of Stonington	1	28
LITTLE, Philo, m. Esther B. **HILL**, b. of Groton, Apr. 13, 1845, by Rev. Jared R. Avery	1	73
W[illia]m, m. Catharine **FLINN**, Apr. 23, 1850, at Porterville, by Rev. W. Munger	1	89
LITTLEFIELD, Alva, of Portsmouth, N.H., m. Prudence M. **NILES**, of Groton, Oct. 8, 1843, by Ira R. Steward	1	70
LOMBARD, Elizabeth, m. Josiah **HAYNES**, Mar. 3, 1693	1	102
LOOMIS, Henry, of Hartford, Ct., m. Elizabeth **TIFT**, Nov. 11, 1827, by Rev. Roswell Burrows	1	25
LORD, Hannah, m. Rufus **AVERY**, Mar. 1, 1781	2	34
Louisa, of Groton, m. Lorenzo **BURROWS**, of Albecum, Orleans Co., N.Y., May 11, 1830, by Rev. Roswell Burrows	1	34
Lydia, of Norwich, m. David **AVERY**, of Groton, June 29, 1763, by Benjamin Throop	2	2
LOVEL[L], Charles, of Waterford, m. Mary **BRAMAN**, of Groton, Apr. 23, 1826, by Roswell Fish, J.P.	1	20
James, m. Mary **PIRCY**, b. of Groton, Oct. 2, 1849, by Rev. Simon B. Bailey	1	85
Leonord, of Waterford, m. Cynthia **BRAMAN**, of Groton, May 29, 1825, by Nathan Daboll, J.P.	1	16

	Vol.	Page
LUTHER, John D., m. Lydia **PALMER**, b. of Groton, Sept. 28, 1841, by Ira R. Steward	1	65
LYMAN, Alfred W., m. Elizabeth E. **HEYDEN**, Nov. 23, 1845, by Rev. R. Russell	1	74
MADDEN, Drusilla, of New London, m. Lyman **LAMB**, of Groton, Nov. 11, 1832, by Nathan Daboll, J.P.	1	41
MAGILL, Antonna, of Cape Deyerd Isaldns, m. Lucy **REED**, of Groton, June 13, 1847, by Nathan Daboll, J.P.	1	79
MAIN, MAINE, Aaron, s. [Thomas & Louisa], b. May 14, 1808	2	94
Aaron, m. Nancy **ASHLEY**, b. of Groton, Sept. 24, 1829, by John G. Wightman, Eld.	1	31
Abel, m. Betsey **TIFT**, Nov. 16, 1826, by Perez Hewitt, J.P.	1	23
Abel, of Groton, m. Patty **GAVITT**, of Westerly, R.I., Mar. 9, 1828, by Geo[rge] Ayer, J.P.	1	27
Coridon, m. Loiza **MAIN**, b. of Groton, Sept. 28, 1834, by Oliver Hewitt, J.P.	1	49
Daniel, s. [Thomas & Louisa], b. Oct. 18, 1813	2	94
Daniel, m. Delia A. **ROACH**, b. of Ledyard, Oct. 8, 1838, by Rev. John G. Wightman	1	60
David Morgan, s. John & Matilda, b. Dec. 3, 1813	2	84
Deborah, m. Horace T. **YORK**, b. of Stonington, Dec. 1, 1850, by Rev. James Squier	1	91
John, s. [Thomas & Louisa], b. Aug. 20, 1809	2	94
John, m. Nancy **BARNES**, b. of Groton, Feb. 1, 1835, by W[illia]m M. Williams, J.P.	1	49
Jonas C., M.D., of Stonington, m. Melinda **TURNER**, of Groton, Feb. 1, 1835, by John G. Wightman, Elder	1	49
Loiza, m. Coridon **MAIN**, b. of Groton, Sept. 28, 1834, by Oliver Hewitt, J.P.	1	49
Louisa, d. [Thomas & Louisa], b. Feb. 10, 1815	2	94
Mary Ann, m. Paul **TIFT**, Mar. 4, 1827, by Perez Hewitt, J.P.	1	23
Samuel, Jr., of Groton, m. Martha **TIFT**, Nov. 30, 1823, by Peris Hewitt, J.P.	1	11
Stanten, s. [Thomas & Louisa], b. Feb. 9, 1819	2	94
Thomas, of N. Stonington, m. Louisa BROWN, Apr. 20, 1806	2	94
Thomas B., s. [Thomas & Louisa], b. Feb. 13, 1807	2	94
Thomas B., m. Lydia **HALL**, b. of Groton, Nov. 15, 1835, by John G. Wightman, Elder	1	53
Timothy, s. [Thomas & Louisa], b. Dec. 17, 1810	2	94
William, m. Sally **BROWN**, b. of Groton, Dec. 25, 1834, by Oliver Hewitt, J.P.	1	49
William Leeds, s. [Thomas & Louisa], b. July 4, 1812	2	94
Zerviah, d. [Thomas & Louisa], b. July 8, 1817	2	94
MALLARY, Abby Jane, of Groton, m. Lyman A. **HIGGINS**, of Westbrook, Oct. 8, 1843, by Rev. Erastus Denison	1	70
MALLISON, MALLERSON, MALESON, Abigail, d. Joseph & Phebe, b. July 17, 1751	1	148
Amos, s. Samuel & Lucy, b. Feb. 6, 1773	2	58
Benjain, twin with Phebe, s. Joseph & Phebe, b. Apr. 24, 1744	1	148
Elisha, [s. Joseph & Elizabeth], b. Apr. 15, 1728	1	101
Elisha, [s. Joseph & Elizabeth], b. Apr. 15, 1728	1	133
Elizabeth, d. Joseph & Phebe, b. Oct. 9, 1741	1	148
Ezra, s. Joseph & Phebe, b. Feb. 10, 1739	1	148

	Vol.	Page
MALLISON, MALLERSON, MALESON, (cont.)		
Joseph, m. Elizabeth **STODDARD**, Oct. 4, 1711	1	101
Joseph, m. Elizabeth **STODDARD**, Oct. 4, 1711	1	133
Joseph, s. Joseph & Eliz[abeth], b. Nov. 23, 1712	1	101
Joseph, s. Joseph & Elizabeth, b. Nov. 28, 1712	1	133
Joseph, Jr., m. Phebe **WILLCOCKS**, Nov. 6, 1737	1	148
Joseph, s. Joseph & Phebe, b. Aug. 8, 1738	1	148
Mary, [d. Joseph & Elizabeth], b. Jan. 28, 1719	1	101
Mary, [d. Joseph & Elizabeth], b. Jan. 28, 1721	1	133
Mary, [d. Joseph & Elizabeth], b. Oct. 4, 1725	1	101
Mary, [d. Joseph & Elizabeth], b. Oct. 4, 1725	1	133
Phebe, twin with Benjamin, d. Joseph & Phebe, b. Apr. 24, 1744	1	148
Polly, of Groton, m. John **DARROW**, of Canaan, Dec. 9, 1821, by Timothy Tuttle	1	5
Samuel, s. Joseph & Phebe, b. Aug. 14, 1746	1	148
Tabatha, [d. Joseph & Elizabeth], b. Dec. 11, 1722	1	101
Tabatha, [d. Joseph & Elizabeth], b. Dec. 11, 1722	1	133
Timothy, s. Joseph & Phebe, b. Oct. 8, 1748	1	148
MALONA, Betsey, d. Nathan, b. Dec. 11, 1774	2	24
MANDEVILLE, Henry, of N.Y., m. Mary E. **BRAMAN**, of Groton, Mar. 7, 1848, by Rev. H. R. Knapp	1	84
MANER, Hannah, [d. Zechriah & Mary], b. July 23, 1706	1	106
Mary, [d. Zechriah & Mary], b. Aug. 13, 1711	1	106
Zechriah, m. Mary **GEER**, Sept. 23, 1697	1	106
Zechriah, [s. Zechriah & Mary], b. Apr. 22, 1700	1	106
MANICE, Lucy A., of Groton, m. Alvin **ODELL**, of Kent, Oct. 19, 1851, by Rev. J. R. Avery	1	92
MANIERCE, Benjamin, [s. John & Mary], b. [ ]	3	25
Francis, s. [John & Mary], b. [ ]	3	25
George, s. [John & Mary], b. [ ]	3	25
Hannah, s. [John & Mary], b. [ ]	3	25
John, s. [John & Mary], b. Sept. 11, 1826	3	25
Mary Hellen, s. [John & Mary], b. Sept. 7, 1828	3	25
MANNING, Joseph, of Norwich, m. Cinthia **STORY**, of Groton, Oct. 31, 1824, by Rev. Ashbel Steele, of Pequatanock	1	14
MANWARING, Robert A., of Greenville, m. Ellen BARBER, of Groton, May 15, 1845, by Rev. Jared R. Avery	1	73
William H., of Waterford, m. Emily **PERKINS**, of Groton, June 1, 1828, by Ralph Hurlbutt, J.P.	1	27
MARCHAND, Elizabeth, d. [Joseph & Anne], b. Mar. 5, 1757	1	169
Joseph, m. Anne **JOFFREY**, Oct. 19, 1755, by Ebenezer Avery, J.P.	1	169
MARSTON, Ephraim, m. Mary Angeline **CLARK**, b. of Groton, Aug. 11, 1850, by Rev. James Squier	1	90
MARTIN, Amy, m. Hubbard **BURROWS**, [ ]	3	0
Mary, d. Benjamin & Sarah, b. Apr. 30, 1733	1	112
MARVIENE, John, of New London, m. Mary **HILL**, of Groton, Sept. 11, 1825, by Nathan Daboll, J.P.	1	18
MASON, Abigail, m. Samuel **LESTER**, Jr., Dec. 10, 1737	1	176
Abigail, m. Samuel **LESTER**, Jr., Dec. 11, 1737	1	147
Abigail, d. Peter & Margaret, b. Aug. 5, 1742	1	157
Elnathan, s. [Hobart & Margaret], b. Mar. 17, 1754	1	165
Hannah, of Stonington, m. Henry **GALLUP**, of Groton, Oct. 4, 1750, by Ebenezer Rossiter	2	10

	Vol.	Page
MASON, (cont.)		
Louis, d. Hobart & Margaret, b. Apr. 29, 1752	1	165
Mary, m. Richard **ALLEN**, Sept. 23, 1827, by Geo[rge] Foot, V.D.M.	1	24
Nehemiah, of Stonington, m. Lucy Ann **LATHAM**, of Groton, Sept. 11, 1828, by John G. Wightman	1	28
MA[T]THEWSON, Matilda, of Penn., m. Elisha D. **WIGHTMAN**, of Groton, Nov. 15, 1846, by Rev. W. C. Walker	1	77
MAXSON, Eunice (**CULVER**), w. Ezekiel, d. Feb. 12, 1867	1	189
Ezekiel, of Hopkinton, R.I., m. Eunice **CULVER**, of Groton, Dec. 9, 1813; d. Dec. 11, 1870	1	189
Oliver, s. [Ezekiel & Eunice], b. June 12, 1815; d. June 27, 1873	1	189
Oliver, b. June 12, 1815	2	40
Olive[r], s. Ezekiel & Eunice, b. June 12, 1815	2	74
Sally, d. Ezekiel & Eunice, b. Jan. 13, 1817	2	74
Sally M., d. [Ezekiel & Eunice], b. Jan. 13, 1817; d. May 11, 1831, ae. 14 y.	1	189
MAY, Mary, Mrs., of Windham, m. Asa **STODDARD**, of Groton, May 18, 1836, by Ralph Hurlbutt, J.P.	1	54
MAYNARD, MANARD, Albert, m. Fanny **BRAMAN**, b. of Groton, Oct. 27, 1850, by Rev. Jared R. Avery	1	90
Fanny, m. Marvin **PERKINS**, b. of Groton, Sept. 3, 1824, by John Brewster, J.P.	1	14
Joseph, m. Prudence **MULKEY**, b. of Groton, Aug. 14, 1834, by John Brewster, J.P.	1	48
Lucinda, of Groton, m. James P. **BURDICK**, of Westerly, R.I., Dec. 8, 1833, by John Brewster, J.P.	1	46
Mary, of Groton, m. William C. **PRATT**, of Norwich, Mar. 6, 1832, by Timothy Tuttle	1	39
Roswell E., of Norwich, m. Emeline M. **HEATH**, of Groton, May 10, 1846, by Rev. W. C. Walker	1	76
Sabra, of Groton, m. Barber **SHELDON**, of Richmond, R.I., Mar. 16, 1828, by Elisha Brewster, J.P.	1	27
Shubael, m. Hannah **LAMB**, b. of Groton, Nov. 27, 1823, by John G. Wightman	1	11
MAYNOR, Cynthia, m. George W. **SHOLES**, b. of Groton, May 4, 1835, by Ralph Hurlbutt, J.P.	1	50
Elizabeth, [d. Zachariah & Mary], b. Feb. 14, 1735/6	1	128
Nathan, s. Zachariah & Mary, b. May 31, 1733	1	128
MAYRATH, Jane, of Groton, m. Frances A. **GRISWOLD**, of New London, Aug. 19, 1849, by Rev. Nicholas T. Allen	1	87
McCOLLUM, R. S., of Rochester, N.Y., m. Abby D. **SMITH**, of Groton, Mar. 14, 1828, by Rev. Roswell Burrows	1	27
McCRACKEN, Henry, of Salem, m. Eliza **LESTER**, of Groton, Mar. 23, 1834, by Ralph Hurlbutt, J.P.	1	46
McFARLAND, Peter, of New York, m. Sarah Alvira **HULET**, of Groton, Dec. 8, 1839, by Rev. John G. Wightman	1	62
McFARLING, Margaret, d. Macane & Abigail, b. May 2, 1748	1	147
MEECH, MEACH, Daniel B., of Parma, m. Jerusha **MORGAN**, of Groton, Sept. 26, 1827, by Levi Meech, Elder	1	24
Ezekiel L., of Lisbon, m. Mary B. **CLAPP**, of Groton, Apr. 18, 1832, by Ralph Hurlbutt, J.P.	1	39
Matthew R., of Westerly, R.I., m. Phebe H. **WELLS**, of Groton, July 12, 1846, by Rev. W. C. Walker	1	76

	Vol.	Page
MEIGS, John B., of Washington, D.C., m. Wealthy A. **WILLIS**, of Groton, Oct. 23, 1837, by Rev. John G. Wightman	1	57
MERRILL, Martha, of Groton, m. Stephen **RANDALL**, Jr., of Long Island, Jan. 4, 1821, by Ralph Hurlbutt, J.P.	1	2
MERRITT, MERIT, Delia Ann, m. Joshua E. **BUD[D]INGTON**, b. of Groton, Aug. 4, 1839, by Rev. John G. Wightman	1	61
John A., m. Mary A. **BRAMAN**, b. of Groton, Dec. 8, 1850, by Rev. Nicholas T. Allen	1	90
Meribah, m. Giles **BAILEY**, b. of Groton, June 27, 1824, by Ralph Hurlbutt, J.P.	1	13
MIDDLETON, Mary A., m. Benjamin **BROWN**, b. of Groton, Dec. 30, 1821, by Roswell Burrows, Elder	1	5
Polly, of Groton, m. Andrew **DENISON**, of Stonington, Nov. 14, 1836, by Rev. Roswell Burrows	1	55
MILLER, D. M., Rev., m. Mrs. Lucy E. **BURROWS**, of Groton, Mar. 5, 1848, by Rev. H. R. Knapp	1	84
James W., of New London, m. Almira J. **BURROWS**, of Groton, June 3, 1851, by Rev. Nicholas T. Allen	1	91
Sarah, m. John PACKER, Jr., Mar. 10, 1686	1	106
William, of New London, m. Ann Elizabeth **DEVEROW**, of Groton, Nov. 8, 1825, by Caleb Avery, J.P.	1	19
MILLFIELD, Huldah, of Groton, m. Richard **SAMBER**, of Philadelphia, July 19, 1832, by Rev. Erastus Denison	1	41
MILLS, Hannah, m. Phillip **WARNER**, Oct. 19, 1755	1	170
MINER, MINOR, Abby, m. Anson **DAVIS**, b. of Groton, Sept. 21, 1826, by Nathan Daboll, J.P.	1	22
Adelia H., of Groton, m. Isaac **RANDALL**, of Hartford, Dec. 20, 1831, by Timothy Tuttle	1	38
Anna, m. William **FANNING**, Mar. 17, 1737	1	181
Ardelia Avery, d. May 5, 1887	3	6
Betsey, d. [John Owen & Elizabeth], b. June 18, 1789	2	31
Betsey, m. Asa S. **AVERY**, b. of Groton, Nov. 27, 1806, by John G. Wightman, Elder	2	78
Elias, m. Polly **BURROWS**, b. of Groton, Jan. 28, 1827, by Nathan Daboll, J.P.	1	23
Elisha M., s. [John O., Jr. & Ardelia], b. Apr. 14, 1826	3	6
Elisha M., m. Nancy M. **STRONG**, Oct. 31, 1847, by Rev. Jared R. Avery	1	80
Emeline, m. Elisha **OBRIEN**, b. of Groton, Sept. 13, 1832, by John G. Wightman, Eld.	1	41
Emeline F., m. Nathan G. **FISH**, b. of Groton, Jan. 9, 1833, by Timothy Tuttle	1	42
Hannah, m. Rev. Ebenezer **PUNDERSON**, Aug. [ ], 1732	1	146
Henry Franklin, s. Rufus & Fannie Bailey, d. May 12, 1836, ae. 3 y. 5 m.	1	190
Isaac D., of Stonington, m. Phebe T. **BURROWS**, of Groton, Apr. 28, 1833, by Rev. Erastus Denison	1	43
Joanna, m. John **ALLYN**, July 28, 1726	1	142
John B., s. John W. & Emily A., b. Oct. 17, 1828	3	15
John O., Jr., m. Ardelia **AVERY**, Sept. 9, 1819	3	6
John O., 2d, m. Lucy **AVERY**, b. of Groton, June 13, 1841, by Ira R. Steward	1	64
John O., d. July 22, 1859	3	6
John Owen, m. Elizabeth **AVERY**, Jan. 21, 1785	2	31
John Owen, s. [John Owen & Elizabeth], b. Oct. 26, 1795	2	31

	Vol.	Page
MINER, MINOR, (cont.)		
John W., m. Emily A. **STODDARD**, b. of Groton, Oct. 14, 1827, by Ralph Hurlbutt, J.P.	1	25
Joseph, 2d, of Stonington, m. Sabra E. **AVERY**, of Groton, Nov. 10, 1831, by John G. Wightman, Eld.	1	38
Julia A., m. Dr. B[enjamin] F. **STODDARD**, Nov. 27, 1817	3	9
Lucy Avery, d. [John Owen & Elizabeth], b. Mar. 19, 1798	2	31
Lydia L., m. Eldredge **PACKER**, 3d, b. of Groton, Sept. 8, 1830, by Ralph Hurlbutt, J.P.	1	35
Mariah, m. W[illia]m **WILLIS**, b. of Groton, Feb. 7, 1841, by Ira R. Steward	1	64
Martha Ann, m. William **NEWBURY**, b. of Groton, Aug. 8, 1824, by Ralph Hurlbutt, J.P.	1	13
Mary, of Stonington, m. John **WALLSWORTH**, of Groton, Dec. 4, 1752, by Rev. Nathaniel Eells	2	10
Mary Ann, m. Thomas J. **ALEXENDER**, b. of Groton, July 29, 1830, by Erastus T. Smith, J.P.	1	34
Nancy, d. [John Owen & Elizabeth], b. Oct. 15, 1793	2	31
Nancy A., m. Elisha **AVERY**, Nov. 18, 1810	2	68
Phebe D., of Groton, m. William W. **MINER**, of New London, July 4, 1844, by Rev. Timothy Tuttle, of Ledyard	1	71
Polly, d. [John Owen & Elizabeth], b. July 18, 1791	2	31
Rufus H., of Canterbury, m. Mary **PARK[E]**, of Plainfield, Mar. 6, 1831, by Rev. Levi Kimland, of Canterbury	3	28
Thomas A., s. [John O., Jr. & Ardelia], b. Sept. 5, 1820	3	6
Thomas A., of Groton, m. Bridget W. **HEWITT**, of N. Stonington, Dec. 12, 1844, by Rev. Jared R. Avery	1	72
W[illia]m H., s. [John O., Jr. & Ardelia], b. Aug. 30, 1822	3	6
William W., of New London, m. Phebe D. **MINER**, of Groton, July 4, 1844, by Rev. Timothy Tuttle, of Ledyard	1	71
MITCHELL, Aaron E., m. Lucy Ann **BETHWICK**, b. of Groton, Nov. 24, 1831, by Ralph Hurlbutt, J.P.	1	38
Ebenezer A., of Ashford, m. Nancy Ann **MORGAN**, of Groton, Apr. 2, 1832, by John G. Wightman, Eld.	1	39
Eliza M., m. Dudley **BAILEY**, b. of Groton, Aug. 14, 1842, by Nathan Daboll, J.P.	1	66
[E]unice, of Preston, m. Samuel **WHIPPLE**, Jr., of Groton, Nov. 24, 1740	2	3
Francis F., of Ashford, m. Adeline **STODDARD**, of Groton, Apr. 1, 1830, by Timothy Tuttle	1	34
Hannah A., of Groton, m. Jeremiah **REED**, of Preston, Aug. 12, 1849, by Rev. Levi Walker	1	85
Hannah M., m. Luke W[illia]m **AVERY**, b. of Groton, Sept. 12, 1838, by Rev. Mark Meade	1	60
James R., of New London, m. Elizabeth **BEEBE**, of Groton, Jan. 29, 1837, by John G. Wightman, Elder	1	56
James S., m. Fanny **AVERY**, b. of Groton, Mar. 21, 1824, by Timothy Tuttle	1	12
John D., m. Phebe **WATROUS**, b. of Groton, Sept. 15, 1844, by Rev. Erastus Denison	1	71
Joseph B., m. Caroline **LATHAM**, b. of Groton, Dec. 28, 1834, by Joseph Durfee, J.P.	1	48
Katharine, m. William Henry **PARK[E]**, b. of Groton, Dec. 24, 1828, by John G. Wightman, Eld.	1	29

	Vol.	Page
MITCHELL, (cont.)		
Lucy Ann, of Groton, m. Michael A. **MYERS**, of Apilockicola, Fla., June 19, 1845, by Rev. Jared R. Avery	1	73
Mary, of Groton, m. John **SUTE**, of Lyme, Dec. 5, 1820, by Rev. Lathrop Rockwell, of Lyme	1	2
Phebe, Wid., of Groton, m. Seba **BENJAMIN**, of Preston, Aug. 31, 1845, by W[illia]m C. Walker	1	74
Phebe, of Groton, m. Seba **BENJAMIN**, of Preston, Aug. 31, 1845, by Rev. William C. Walker	1	75
Samuel, of Hartford, Ct., m. Maria **PERKINS**, of Groton, Jan. 26, 1827, by Nathan Daboll, J.P.	1	26
Sanford, of New Shoreham, R.I.*, m. Philena **MURPHEY**, Apr. 1, 1832, by Erastus Denison. (*Block Island written below)	1	39
W[illia]m F., m. Abby Ann **HALEY**, b. of Groton, Apr. 21, 1839, by Rev. John G. Wightman	1	60
W[illia]m F., m. Abby Ann **HALEY**, Apr. 21, 1839	3	0
William F., m. Hannah B. **WOODBRIDGE**, b. of Groton, Mar. 22, 1835, by John G. Wightman, Elder	1	49
MIX, Nathan, m. Wid. Lydia **LEWIS**, b. of Groton, Mar. 25, 1825, by Roswell Burrows, Min.	1	16
MOCKETT, John, of Orange Co., N.Y., m. Louisa **PARK[E]**, of Groton, Feb. 8, 1853, by Rev. Franklin A. Slater	1	94
MOODEY, Albion, of Springville, Pa., m. Temperance **WILLIAMS**, of Groton, Oct. 17, 1830, by William M. Williams, J.P.	1	36
MOON, George, of New York, m. Maria **ROWLAND**, of Groton, Aug. 15, 1833, by Ira R. Steward, Eld.	1	44
MOORE, Bridget, m. Rufus **WILLIAMS**, Jr., b. of Groton, Jan. 13, 1824, by Philip Gray, J.P.	1	12
MORGAN, Abigail, [d. William, Jr. & Hannah], b. Aug. 5, 1727	1	117
Abigail, d. [Samuel & Abigail], b. Sept. 26, 1742	1	165
Abijah, s. Sam[ue]ll & Hannah, b. July 6, 1715	1	113
Adam, s. [Joseph, 2d, & Eunice], b. June 15, 1797	2	34
[A]Eneas, m. Abigail **LEWIS**, Jr., b. of Groton, Jan. 19, 1800	2	61
[A]Eneas, [s. John & Mary], b. Mar. 5, 1827	3	4
Albert, m. Maria **WILBUR**, b. of Groton, Dec. 24, 1840, by Ira R. Steward	1	64
Amanda, d. [Roswell & Jemima], b. Jan. 9, 1822	3	24
Amanda, of Groton, m. Terry **BENNET[T]**, of Stonington, Oct. 18, 1846, by Rev. Simon B. Bailey	1	76
Amos, s. [Samuel & Abigail], b. Nov. 9, 1750	1	165
Ann, [d. William, Jr. & Hannah], b. June 26, 1730	1	117
Ann Jane, d. Elijah B. & Jane M., b. June 8, 1846, at Stonington	3	35
Anna, m. Rev. John **OWEN**, Nov. 25, 1730	1	142
Anna, m. Aaron **KINNE**, May 31, 1770	2	19
Anna, d. Solomon & Mary, b. [ ], 1851	1	157
Avery, b. Oct. 7, 1779; m. Betsey **HICKS**, Dec. 5, 1809	2	78
Bela, s. [Capt. Israel & Elizabeth], b. Dec. 22, 1794	2	52
Caleb, s. [Young Ledyard & Betsey], b. Aug. 22, 1799	2	84
Caroline, of Salem, m. Elisha **MORGAN**, of Groton, Jan. 3, 1819	3	32
Caroline, m. Capt. Benjamin **CHESTER**, b. of Groton, Dec. 25, 1828, by Rev. Roswell Burrows	1	29
Caroline F., m. Frederick A. **WILLIAMS**, Oct. 12, 1837, by Ira R. Steward	1	57
Caroline Fish, d. [Roswell & Jemima], b. Aug. 20, 1818	3	24

	Vol.	Page
MORGAN, (cont.)		
Caroline M., m. James D. **AVERY**, May 26, 1850, at Pequonock Bridge, by Rev. James W. Dennis, of New London	1	89
Caroline Maconda, d. [Elisha & Caroline], b. Sept. 16, 1821	3	32
Charity, m. Amos **CLIFT**, b. of Groton, Jan. 29, 1829, by Timothy Tuttle	1	29
Christopher, s. [William & Temperance], b. Oct. 22, 1747	1	170
Christopher, m. Deborah **LEDYARD**, Feb. 16, 1768	2	1
Christopher, s. [Christopher & Deborah], b. Oct. 15, 1777	2	1
Christopher, Maj., had negro boy Cuff, b. Sept. 28, 1790	2	1
Christopher, Capt., had negro boy Perow, b. Nov. 27, 1786	2	1
Coleby M., s. [Elisha & Caroline], b. Apr. 2, 1832	3	32
Coleby M., [s. Elisha & Caroline], d. Apr. 24, 1862	3	32
Daniel, s. Sanford & Harriet, b. Apr. 13, 1830	3	31
Daniel, of Unidilly, N.Y., m. Frances **BABCOCK**, of Groton, Apr. 29, 1832, by John G. Wightman, Eld.	1	40
Deborah, [d. William & Mary], b. June 26, 1725	1	131
Deborah Calebia, d. [Christopher & Deborah], b. June 17, 1785	2	1
Dorothy, d. [Joseph & Dorothy], b. Jan. 1, 1741/2	1	172
Dorothy, m. Elijah **MORGAN**, Aug. 18, 1763	1	185
Dorothy, m. Elijah **MORGAN**, Aug. 18, 1763	2	95
Dorothy, m. John **LESTER**, b. of Groton, Dec. 24, 1767	2	7
Dorothy, twin with Mary, d. [Capt. Israel & Elizabeth], b. Nov. 23, 1781	2	52
Dudley, s. [William & Lucy], b. Nov. 7, 1795	2	49
Ebenezer, s. [John & Prudence], b. May 30, 1756	1	164
Eben[eze]r, of Groton, m. Olive **PARISH**, of Preston, Apr. 5, 1781, by Jona[tha]n Brewster, J.P.	2	41
Ebenezer, s. [Nathan & Sabra], b. Aug. 9, 1791	2	88
Ebenezer, s. [Joseph, 2d, & Eunice], b. July 8, 1792	2	34
Ebenezer, 2d, m. Levinia **NEWBERRY**, Oct. 28, 1814	2	43
Eleonor, d. [Samuel & Abigail], b. Jan. 6, 1746	1	165
Elias, s. [William & Lucy], b. Sept. 26, 1791	2	49
Elijah, s. Samuell & Hannah, b. Apr. 16, 1712	1	113
Elijah, m. [E]unice **WILLIAMS**, Nov. 13, 1735	1	166
Elijah, m. Dorothy **MORGAN**, Aug. 18, 1763	1	185
Elijah, m. Dorothy **MORGAN**, Aug. 18, 1763	2	95
Elijah, s. [Elijah & [E]unice], b. [ ]	1	166
Elijah Anson, s. [Elijah B. & Mary Ann], b. Aug. 11, 1836, in Stonington	3	35
Elijah B., m. Mary Ann **PERKINS**, Mar. 6, 1832, in Stonington	3	35
Elijah B., m. Jane M. **WIGHTMAN**, b. of Groton, June 8, 1843, by Rev. Erastus Denison	1	69
Elijah Bailey, s. [Nathan & Sabra], b. Mar. 1, 1809	2	88
Elijah S., m. Eliza **TURNER**, b. of Groton, Mar. 20, 1831, by John G. Wightman, Eld.	1	37
Elisha, s. Solomon & Mary, b. Mar. 7, 1762	1	157
Elisha, s. [Elijah & [E]unice], b. Mar. 7, 1762	1	166
Elisha, s. [John & Prudence], b. July 29, 1768	1	164
Elisha, s. [Thomas, Jr. & Joanna], b. Mar. 22, 1800	2	46
Elisha, of Groton, m. Caroline **MORGAN**, of Salem, Jan. 3, 1819	3	32
Elisha, [s. John & Mary], b. July 7, 1834	3	4
Elisha Avery, m. Julia Ann **WILLET**, b. of Groton, July 23, 1820, by Timothy Tuttle	1	1
Eliza, [d. John & Mary], b. Aug. 14, 1842	3	4

	Vol.	Page
MORGAN, (cont.)		
Eliza A., m. Lorenzo D. **BAKER**, b. of Groton, July 18, 1848, by Rev. Jared R. Avery	1	81
Elizabeth, m. Jonathan **STARR**, Jan. 12, 1698/9	1	105
Elizabeth, d. William & Margaret, b. July 10, 1710	1	117
Elizabeth, d. John & Ruth, b. June 12, 1713	1	115
Elizabeth, d. William & Mary, b. Feb. 1, 1718/19	1	131
Elizabeth, d. [Capt.] Israel & Elizabeth, b. Jan. 7, 1779	2	52
Elkana, s. [John, Jr. & Sarah], b. June 8, 1738	1	180
Elkanah, s. [John & Prudence], b. Apr. 30, 1758	1	164
Elkanah, [s. John & Mary], b. Jan. 9, 1839	3	4
Ellen A., d. [Elisha & Caroline], b. May 21, 1830	3	32
Ellen Elizabeth, d. [Elijah B. & Mary Ann], b. Dec. 31, 1832, in Stonington; d. Feb. 24, 1833, At Stonington	3	35
Erastus, s. [William & Lucy], b. Dec. 17, 1793	2	49
[E]unice, d. [Elijah & [E]unice], b. Mar. 25, 1737	1	166
Eunice, d. [John, Jr. & Sarah], b. July 22, 1744	1	180
[E]unice, m. Ezra **BARNES**, Apr. 17, 1754	1	173
Eunice, d. [James, 2d & Eunice], b. Jan. 23, 1792	2	55
Eunice, d. [Joseph, 2d & Eunice], b. Oct. 12, 1795	2	34
Eunice, w. Joseph [2d], d. Mar. 16, 1799	2	34
Eunice, d. [Stephen & Parthenia], b. Sept. 28, 1801	2	41
Eunice, of Groton, m. Amos **GEER**, of Goshen, Apr. 11, 1824, by Timothy Tuttle	1	12
Eunice, m. William **AVERY**, Jr., b. of Groton, Jan. 31, 1830, by John G. Wightman, Eld.	1	33
[E]unice, m. Elijah **BROWN**, [ ]	2	27
Frances, of Groton, m. Thomas B. **COLLINS**, of Stonington, May 27, 1844, by Rev. Simon B. Bailey	1	71
George W., m. Mary A. **BURROWS**, b. of Groton, Feb. 18, 1849, by Rev. S. B. Bailey	1	82
Gilbert William, s. Giles & Julia, b. Sept. 16, 1827	3	13
Giles, s. [Nathan & Sabra], b. Dec. 31, 1794	2	88
Giles, m. Julia **BUD[D]INGTON**, b. of New London, Nov. 9, 1826, by Rev. Ward Stafford, of New York	3	13
Hamilton, of Ledyard, m. Susan **BATTEY**, of Groton, May 26, 1842, by Rev. Erastus Denison	1	66
Hannah, m. William **LATHAM**, June 30, 1698	1	109
Hannah, m. Ephraim **WOODBRIDGE**, May 4, 1704	1	103
Hannah, d. Capt. John & Ruth, b. Dec. 17, 1706	1	115
Hannah, d. Samuell & Hannah, b. Feb. 13, 1713/14	1	113
Hannah, [d. William, Jr. & Hannah], b. July 18, 1725; d. Aug. 21, 1726	1	117
Hannah, m. Thomas **POWERS**, Apr. 3, 1740	1	163
Hannah, d. [Samuel & Abigail], b. May 23, 1748	1	165
Hannah, [d. Nathan & Hannah], b. Nov. 16, 1775	2	25
Hannah, m. Ebenezer **AVERY**, 2d, Sept. 25, 1783	2	44
Hannah, d. [Capt. Israel & Elizabeth], b. May 18, 1787	2	52
Hannah, w. Nathan, d. Oct. 23, 1787, ae. 28 y.	2	88
Hannah, m. Prentice **ASHLEY**, b. of Groton, Nov. 25, 1821, by Rev. John G. Wightman	1	5
Harriet, [d. John & Mary], b. Dec. 5, 1821	3	4
Harriet, d. [Roswell & Jemima], b. Feb. 5, 1825	3	24
Harriet, [d. John & Mary], b. Mar. 14, 1845	3	4

	Vol.	Page
MORGAN, (cont.)		
Harriet L., [d. Sanford & Harriet], b. Feb. 25, 1834; d. Aug. [ ], 1862	3	31
Henrietta, d. [Christopher & Deborah], b. Aug. 2, 1790	2	1
Henry, s. [Elijah & [E]unice], b. Aug. 1, 1741	1	166
Henry E., s. [Elisha & Caroline], b. Oct. 30, 1824	3	32
Hubbard D., m. Lucy A. **AVERY**, b. of Groton, Aug. 7, 1844, by Rev. Erastus Denison	1	71
Isaac, s. [John, Jr. & Sarah], b. Jan. 5, 1750	1	180
Isaac Avery, s. Joseph & Prudence, b. June 23, 1764	2	18
Isham Avery, s. [Young Ledyard & Betsey], b. Mar. 23, 1809	2	84
Israel, s. [William & Temperance], b. July 22, 1757	1	170
Israel F., m. Lucy **STODDARD**, b. of Groton, Dec. 26, 1813	3	4
Israel Fitch, s. [Capt. Israel & Elizabeth], b. Dec. 11, 1792	2	52
James, s. [Elijah & [E]unice], b. May 11, 1750	1	166
James, 2d, m. Eunice **TURNER**, b. of Groton, Apr. 10, 1788	2	55
James, 3d, s. James & Eunice, b. June 21, 1789	2	55
James, 3d, s. [Joseph, 2d & Eunice], b. Mar. 10, 1799	2	34
Jane Ann, m. Jasper S. **FISH**, b. of Groton, Sept. 14, 1843, by Ira R. Steward	1	70
Jemima, d. John & Ruth, b. May 5, 1715	1	115
Jemima, m. Thomas **FISH**, Aug. 25, 1743	1	180
Jemima, d. [Samuel & Abigail], b. Oct. 31, 1754	1	165
Jennette E., d. [Elisha & Caroline], b. June 12, 1828	3	32
Jerusha, d. William & Margaret, b. Jan. 14, 1703	1	117
Jerusha, m. Humphrey **AVERY**, Feb. 1, 1723/4	1	116
Jerusha, m. Humphrey **AVERY**, Feb. 5, 1723/4	1	135
Jerusha, of Groton, m. Daniel B. **MEECH**, of Parma, Sept. 26, 1827, by Levi Meech, Elder	1	24
Jesse Avery, s. [Josphe, 2d, & Eunice], b. Sept. 9, 1788	2	34
Joanna, m. Silas **NILES**, Feb. [ ], 1807	2	77
John, Jr. m. Sarah **COBB**, Apr. 17, 1728	1	180
John, s. [John, Jr. & Sarah], b. July 28, 1729	1	180
John, Jr., m. Prudence **MORGAN**, Feb. 1, 1749/50	1	164
John, s. John & Prudence, b. Dec. 23, 1750	1	164
John, s. [Stephen & Parthenia], b. Jan. 1, 1799	2	41
John, 2d, m. Mary **ALLYN**, b. of Groton, Dec. 31, 1820, by John G. Wightman, Elder	1	2
John, m. Mary **ALLYN**, [ ]	3	4
John A., m. Eunice L. AVERY, Mar. 13, 1846, by Rev. Tho[ma]s J. Greenwood, of New London	1	75
John Albert, s. [Elisha & Caroline], b. Apr. 26, 1823	3	32
John S., [s. John & Mary], b. May 26, 1823	3	4
Jonathan, s. [Elijah & [E]unice], b. June 18, 1755	1	166
Joseph, s. William & Margaret, b. Aug. 10, 1706	1	117
Joseph, m. Dorothy **AVERY**, Dec. 4, 1735	1	172
Joseph, s. [Joseph & Dorothy], b. Jan. 31, 1737/89	1	172
Joseph, s. Joseph, Jr. & Prudence, b. Nov. 28, 1762	2	18
Joseph, 2d, m. Eunice **PERKINS**, b. of Groton, July 3, 1783, by Rev. Parke Allyn, of N. Groton	2	34
Joseph, 3d, s. Joseph, 2d, & Eunice, b. July 3, 1784	2	34
Joseph, Jr., m. Prudence **AVERY**, Dec. 10, 17[ ], by Rev. Jacob Johnson	2	18
Julia, d. [Young Ledyard & Betsey], b. Jan. 10, 1803	2	84
Julia A., m. Osmond P. **CAFLON**, Nov. 6, 1833, by Joseph Durfey, J.P.	1	45

	Vol.	Page
MORGAN, (cont.)		
Julyann, d. [Christopher & Deborah], b. Dec. 31, 1768	2	1
Julian, d. [Ebenezer, 2d & Levinia], b. Apr. 2, 1815	2	43
Lavinia A., m. Benjamin S. **FISH**, b. of Groton, Apr. 1, 1846, by Rev. Erastus Denison	1	75
Lois, m. Thaddeus **BA[I]LEY**, b. of Groton, Dec. 30, 1762, by Rev. Jacob Johnson	2	22
Louis, d. [Elijah & [E]unice], b. Nov. 13, 1745	1	166
Lucinda, d. [Christopher & Deborah], b. Mar. 5, 1780	2	1
Luce, d. Samuel & Hannah, b. May 9, 1717	1	113
Lucy, d. [Elijah & [E]unice], b. May 11, 1750	1	166
Lucy, d. Solomon & Mary, b. Sept. 26, 1756	1	157
Lucy, d. Solomon, b. Sept. 26, 1756; m. Thomas **FISH**, Nov. 12, 1778, by Rev. Aaron Kenne	2	31
Lucy, d. [William & Lucy], b. Aug. 7, 1784	2	49
Lucy, d. [Stephen & Parthenia], b. Aug. 18, 1803	2	41
Lucy, m. Austin **ALLYN**, b. of Groton, Feb. 13, 1824, by Timothy Tuttle	1	12
Lucy Ann, of [Groton], m. Joseph **COLLINS**, of Stonington, Nov. 27, 1850, by W. Munger	1	92
Luther A., [s. John & Mary], b. Oct. 29, 1836	3	4
Lydia, d. [Samuel & Abigail], b. Sept. 27, 1752	1	165
Lydia, m. Caleb **CULVER**, b. of Groton, Aug. 6, 1820, by Timothy Tuttle	1	1
Lydia, m. Caleb **CULVER**, Aug. 6, 1820	1	189
Lydia, m. Horatio N. **FISH**, Aug. 29, 1824, by Rev. Roswell Burrows	1	13
Margaret, d. William & Margaret, b. Sept. 10, 1698	1	117
Margaret, m. Samuel **DAVIS**, Jan. 29, 1718/19	1	127
Margaret, [d. William, Jr. & Hannah], b. Sept. 8, 1723	1	117
Margaret, wid. of Ensign William, d. July 28, 1755, ae. 82 y.	1	153
Margary, d. William & Mary, b. Feb. 26, 1720/1	1	131
Margery, d. [John & Prudence], b. Nov. 21, 1752	1	164
Maria, [d. John & Mary], b. Mar. 25, 1825	3	4
Martha, d. John & Ruth, b. Dec. 12, 1711	1	115
Martha, m. Isaac **GEER**, Jr., May 1, 1741[sic]	1	181
Mary, m. Thomas **STARR**, Jan. 1, 1694/5	1	106
Mary, d. William & Margaret, b. June 5, 1714	1	117
Mary, d. William & Mary, b. May 9, 1717	1	131
Mary, m. Jonas **BELTON**, Aug. 7, 1737	1	151
Mary, d. [Joseph & Dorothy], b. Jan. 6, 1743/4	1	172
Mary, d. Solomon & Mary, b. Aug. 7, 1749	1	157
Mary, m. Peter **WILLIAMS**, b. of Groton, Dec. 7, 1780, by Rev. Paul Allyn, of N. Groton	2	79
Mary, twin with Dorothy, d. [Capt. Israel & Elizabeth], b. Nov. 23, 1781; d. Jan. 11, 1782	2	52
Mary, m. John **ENOS**, b. of Groton, Sept. 24, 1795	2	65
Mary A., m. Asa P. **CHESTER**, b. of Groton, July 29, 1832, by Rev. Roswell Burrows	1	40
Mary A., m. Silas **SPICER**, b. of Groton, Dec. 4, 1839, by Ira R. Steward	1	62
Mary Abby, d. [Elisha & Caroline], b. Mar. 3, 1820	3	32
Mary Abby, m. Nathan D. **SMITH**, b. of Groton, Sept. 12, 1841, by Rev. Erastus Denison	1	65
Mary F., of Groton, m. Moses **MORGAN**, of East Haddam, July 3, 1838, by Rev. Abel McEwen, of New London	1	59
Mary Fermon, d. [Young Ledyard & Betsey], b. Aug. 5, 1806	2	84

	Vol.	Page
MORGAN, (cont.)		
Moses, of East Haddam, m. Mary F. **MORGAN**, of Groton, July 3, 1838, by Rev. Abel McEwen, of New London	1	59
Nancy Ann, of Groton, m. Ebenezer A. **MITCHELL**, of Ashford, Apr. 2, 1832, by John G. Wightman, Eld.	1	39
Nathan, s. [Elijah & [E]unice], b. Oct. 12, 1752	1	166
Nathan, s. Solomon & Mary, b. Jan. 2, 1754	1	157
Nathan, m. Hannah **PERKINS**, b. of Groton, Sept. 8, 1774, by Rev. Aaron Kinne	2	25
Nathan, m. Sabra **CAPRON**, Nov. 27, 1788	2	88
Nathan, s. [Nathan & Sabra], b. Sept. 30, 1789	2	88
Nathan, s. [Joseph, 2d, & Eunice], b. Feb. 9, 1794	2	34
Nelson, s. [Roswell & Jemima], b. July 6, 1827 (1830 in Family Bible)	3	24
Nelson, m. Virginia **HALEY**, [d. Henry & Mary Ann], June 28, 1855	3	0
Nicholas, m. Phebe **AVERY**, b. of Groton, Mar. 1, 1790	2	67
Olive, d. [Stephen & Parthenia], b. Aug. 26, 1792	2	41
Olive, m. Charles **GALLUP**, b. of Groton, Feb. 7, 1821, by Timothy Tuttle	1	3
Osman H., s. [Elisha & Caroline], b. July 10, 1826	3	32
Parthenia, d. [Stephen & Parthenia], b. Sept. 4, 1792	2	41
Parthenia, [d. John & Mary], b. May 26, 1832	3	4
Peddy Elery, d. [Christopher & Deborah], b. Mar. 25, 1783	2	1
Penette E., m. Nathan S. **FISH**, b. of Groton, Mar. 24, 1850, by Rev. J. R. Avery	1	88
Phebe, d. [John, Jr. & Sarah], b. Apr. 9, 1736	1	180
Phebe, m. Stephen **HURLBUTT**, Oct. 9, 1755	2	5
Phebe, d. [Elijah & [E]unice], b. Nov. 15, 1756	1	166
Phebe, d. [William & Lucy], b. Nov. 27, 1787	2	49
Phebe, d. [Thomas, Jr. & Joanna], b. Mar. 31, 1788	2	46
Phebe, m. Avery **BAILEY**, Feb. 22, 1807, by John G. Wightman, Elder	2	80
Polly, twin with May, d. [Capt. Israel & Elizabeth], b. Feb. 27, 1785	2	52
Polly, d. [William & Lucy], b. Oct. 26, 1789	2	49
Polly Avery, d. [Christopher & Deborah], b. Mar. 15, 1774	2	1
Priscilla, of Groton, m. Jabez D. **HALEY**, Jan. 1, 1823, by John G. Wightman	1	9
Prudence, [d. William & Mary], b. Feb. 29, 1727	1	131
Prudence, m. John **MORGAN**, Jr., Feb. 1, 1749/50	1	164
Prudence, d. Joseph & Prudence, b. Apr. 16, 1768	2	18
Prudence, m. Gilbert **SMITH**, Jr., June 12, 1788	2	38
Prudence, d. [Capt. Israel & Elizabeth], b. May 18, 1790	2	52
Prudence, d. [Stephen & Parthenia], b. Aug. 16, 1790	2	41
Prudence, Mrs., m. Silas **BEEBE**, b. of Groton, Jan. 15, 1849, by Rev. H. R. Knapp	1	84
Rachel, d. John & Ruth, b. July 5, 1709	1	115
Rebecca, d. [James, 2d & Eunice], b. Aug. 14, 1793	2	55
Rebecca T., m. Peter A. **GALLUP**, b. of Groton, Apr. 9, 1820, by Roswell Fish, J.P.	3	5
Robert, s. [John, Jr. & Sarah], b. Apr. 9, 1733	1	180
Robert A., m. Sarah S. **AVERY**, b. of Groton, June 7, 1842, by Rev. Jared R. Avery	1	66
Roswell, s. [Elijah & Dorothy], b. June 6, 1764	1	185
Roswell, s. Elijah & Dorothy, b. June 6, 1764	2	95
Roswell A., m. Margaret **WILBUR**, b. of Groton, Oct. 29, 1839, by Ira R. Steward	1	62

	Vol.	Page
MORGAN, (cont.)		
Roswell Augustus, s. [Roswell & Jemima], b. Oct. 14, 1816	3	24
Rufus, [s. John & Mary], b. Jan. 26, 1831	3	4
Sabra, d. [Nathan & Sabra], b. Apr. 18, 1797	2	88
Sabra, of Groton, m. Daniel **STRONG**, of Bolton, Nov. 16, 1825, by Timothy Tuttle	1	19
Samuel, m. Hannah **AVERY**, Dec. 30, 1708	1	113
Samuell, s. Samuell & Hannah, b. Mar. 9, 1710	1	113
Samuel, m. Abigail **HEATH**, Sept. 30, 1741	1	165
Samuel, s. [Samuel & Abigail], b. Mar. 26, 1744	1	165
Sanford, m. Harriet **EDGECOMB**, b. of Groton, Dec. 14, 1828, by John G. Wightman, Eld.	1	29
Sanford, m. Cornelia **AVERY**, b. of Groton, July 9, 1837, by Ira R. Steward, Elder	1	57
Sanford A., m. Lavinia A. **SMITH**, Jan. 1, 1846, by Rev. Jared R. Avery	1	75
Sanford Avery, s. Sanford & Lavina, b. July 9, 1822	3	31
Sarah, d. [Stephen & Parthenia], b. July 21, 1788	2	41
Sarah, m. Phillip **GRAY**, 2d, b. of Groton, Dec. 24, 1801	2	61
Sarah H., d. [Elisha & Caroline], b. Dec. 24, 1835	3	32
Shapley, m. Freelove **HURLBUTT**, Mar. 24, 1763	2	17
Shapley, s. Shapley & Freelove, b. Dec. 28, 1763	2	17
Sibel, see Sybil		
Simeon, s. [Joseph, 2d, & Eunice], b. July 20, 1786	2	34
Solomon, s. William & Margaret, b. Oct. 5, 1708	1	117
Solomon, m. Mary **WALLSWORTH**, July 1, 1742	1	157
Solomon, s. Solomon & Mary, b. Feb. 4, 1744/5	1	157
Solomon, s. [Nathan & Sabra], b. Feb. 7, 1793	2	88
Stephen, s. [John, Jr. & Sarah], b. Feb. 7, 1740	1	180
Stephen, s. [John & Prudence], b. Apr. 19, 1762	1	164
Stephen, m. Parthenia **PARK[E]**, of Groton, Apr. 13, 1788	2	41
Stephen, Jr., of Groton, m. Eliza Maria D. **NOYES**, formerly of Stonington, June 17, 1830, by John G. Wightman, Eld.	1	34
Stephen A., [s. John & Mary], b. Feb. 19, 1834	3	4
Stephen A., s. [Elisha & Caroline], b. Feb. 19, 1834	3	32
Susan, m. Capt. Jeremiah **WILBUR**, b. of Groton, Feb. 25, 1852, by Rev. F. A. Slater	1	93
Susannah, d. Joseph & Prudence, b. July 25, 1766	2	18
Sibel, d. [Capt. Israel & Elizabeth], b. Aug. 27, 1780	2	52
Sibyl, d. [Stephen & Parthenia], b. Nov. 1, 1796	2	41
Sybel, [d. John & Mary], b. Sept. 25, 1840	3	4
Temperance, d. [Capt. Israel & Elizabeth], b. Apr. 27, 1783	2	52
Temperance, d. [Wiliam & Temperance], b. May 4, 1752	1	170
Thomas, s. [John, Jr. & Sarah], b. June 30, 1742	1	180
Thomas, Jr., m. Joanna **ALLYN**, b. of Groton, Jan. 4, 1787, by Rev. Park Allyn, of N. Groton	2	46
Thomas, s. [Thomas, Jr. & Joanna], b. Apr. 15, 1790	2	46
Welthem, d. [Capt. Israel & Elizabeth], b. Jan. 11, 1798	2	52
Welthan, m. Amos **TURNER**, Jr., b. of Groton, Dec. 5, 1824, by John Brewster, J.P.	1	15
William, m. Margaret **AVERY**, July 1, 1696	1	117
William, s. William & Margaret, b. Apr. 7, 1697	1	117
William, m. Mary **AVERY**, July 3, 1716	1	131
William, Jr., m. Hannah **STANTON**, Sept. 21, 1721	1	117

	Vol.	Page
MORGAN, (cont.)		
William, s. William & Mary, b. June 17, 1723	1	131
William, m. Temperance **AVERY**, July 4, 1744	1	170
William, s. Solomon & Mary, b. Nov. 23, 1743/4	1	157
William, s. [William & Temperance], b. Sept. 28, 1745; d. Sept. 29, 1753	1	170
William, s. [Joseph & Dorothy], b. May 25, 1746	1	172
William, Ensign, d. Aug. 26, 1747, ae. 74 y.	1	152
William, of Norwich, m. Sarah **SEABURY**, of Groton, Sept. 24, 1747	1	117
William, s. [John & Prudence], b. Apr. 6, 1754	1	164
William, s. [William & Temperance], b. Nov. 24, 1754	1	170
William, s. Solomon & Mary, b. Sept. 7, 1758	1	157
William, m. Lucy **AVERY**, Jan. 1, 1784	2	49
William, s. [William & Lucy], b. Dec. 6, 1785	2	49
William, s. [Joseph, 2d & Eunice], b. Oct. 7, 1790	2	34
William, s. [Christopher & his 2d w.], b. Mar. 28, 1809	2	1
William, m. Cynthia **BILLINGS**, b. of Groton, Feb. 20, 1836, by Timothy Tuttle	1	53
William P., m. Eunice W. **CHESTER**, b. of Groton, Apr. 14, 1831, by Rev. Roswell Burrows	1	37
Youngs, m. Abby M. **CLARK**, b. of Groton, Apr. 26, 1835, by Ira R. Steward	1	50
Youngs, of Cranston, R.I., m. Phebe **AVERY**, of Groton, May 3, 1835, by Rev. Roswell Burrows	1	50
Youngs, m. Eliza Ann **CLARK**, b. of Groton, Apr. 2, 1837, by Ira R. Steward	1	56
Young Ledyard, s. [Christopher & Deborah], b. Jan. 13, 1772	2	1
Young Ledyard, m. Betsey **JONES**, Feb. 12, 1797	2	84
Youngs Ledyard, s. [Young Ledyard & Betsey], b. Oct. 3, 1797	2	84
Zipporah, d. [Elijah & Dorothy], b. Aug. 13, 1767	1	185
Zipporah, d. Elijah & Dorothy, b. Aug. 13, 1767	2	95
MORRIS, Susanna, d. Josiah & Johanna, b. Dec. 26, 1769	1	171
MORSE, Martha, of Montville, m. William **WATROUS**, of Groton, Jan. 24, 1825, by Nathan Daball, J.P.	1	15
MORTON, William, of Rochester, m. Lucy T. **BROWN**, of Groton, Oct. 22, 1846, by Rev. S. B. Bailey	1	77
MOSELEY, Prudence, of Groton, m. Benjamin **DABOLL**, of Stephentown, N.Y., July 15, 1827, by Nathan Daboll, J.P.	1	24
MOSS, Leonord, m. Bashaba **WATROUS**, b. of Groton, Nov. 25, 1830, by Nathan Daboll, J.P.	1	36
MOTT, William, m. Sally **HULET**, b. of Groton, Mar. 6, 1825, by Caleb Avery, J.P.	1	16
MOXLEY, Albert, of Ledyard, m. Mary A. **EDGECOMB**, of Groton, Feb. 5, 1839, by Ira R. Steward	1	60
Elizabeth, d. John & Mary, b. Mar. 1, 1738	1	178
George William, s. [William & Lucy D.], b. Sept. 14, 1831	3	28
John, d. Feb. 7, 1740	1	178
John Samuel, s. [John & Mary], b. July 5, 1740	1	178
Joseph, s. Joseph & Prudence, b. June 15, 1786	2	10
Joseph, Capt., d. Nov. 10, 1815	2	36
Mary, d. Thomas [& Hannah], b. Oct. 7, 1761	2	10
Mary, m. Washington **AVERY**, b. of Groton, Nov. 26, 1829, by Ralph Hurlbutt, J.P.	1	32
Mary Abby, d. [William & Lucy D.], b. Oct. 14, 1834	3	28

	Vol.	Page
MOXLEY, (cont.)		
Seth, s. Thomas & Hannah, b. Mar. 21, 1759	2	10
William, m. Lydia D. **GEER**, b. of Groton, Feb. 28, 1830, by Nathan Daboll, J.P.	1	33
William, m. Lucy D. **GEER**, Feb. 28, 1830	3	28
MULKEY, Prudence, m. Joseph **MAYNARD**, b. of Groton, Aug. 14, 1834, by John Brewster, J.P.	1	48
Thomas, Jr., m. Mercy **CHAPMAN**, b. of Groton, Feb. 9, 1823, by John Brewster, J.P.	1	9
MUMFORD, Catharine, d. Thomas & Catharine, b. Sept. 16, 1754	1	162
Daniel, [s. Thomas & Abigail], b. Mar. 10, 1731	1	137
Francis, s. Thomas & Catharine, b. June 23, 1770	1	162
Giles, [s. Thomas & Abigail], b. Apr. 21, 1733	1	137
Giles, s. Thomas & Catharine, b. Apr. 16, 1759	1	162
Hannah, d. Thomas & Catharine, b. May 12, 1767	1	162
Thomas, s. Thomas & Abigail, b. Sept. 10, 1728	1	137
Thomas, Jr., m. Catharine **HAVENS**, Dec. 7, 1752	1	162
Thomas Cheesebrough, s. Thomas & Catharine, b. Mar. 22, 1756	1	162
MUNGER, Louisa H., m. W[illia]m O. **CHAFFE**, June 19, 1850, at Porterville, by Rev. W. Munger	1	89
MURDOCK, Enock, of Westbrook, m. Lavina **HAVENS**, of Groton, Dec. 14, 1845, by Rev. Erastus Denison	1	75
Nancy, m. John AVERY, 3d, Jan. 9, 1794	2	47
MURPHY, MURPHEY, MURFIT, [A]Eneas H., m. Rachel **DOUGLASS**, Feb. 17, 1833, by Rev. Erastus Denison	1	43
Betsey, of Groton, m. Adon **BEEBE**, of Waterford, May 10, 1829, by Roswell Fish, J.P.	1	31
Charles, m. Nancy **DABOLL**, b. of Groton, Feb. 11, 1847, by Rev. S. B. Bailey	1	77
Charles H., m. Margary **DOUGLASS**, b. of Douglass(?)*, Apr. 17, 1829, by Asa Fish, J.P. (*Probably Groton)	1	30
Eliza A., m. Frank **BEEBE**, b. of Groton, Aug. 10, 1848, by Rev. H. R. Knapp	1	84
Emily, of Groton, m. Joseph R. **CLARK**, now residing in Stonington, Feb. 7, 1841, by Nathan Daboll, J.P.	1	64
George, of Groton, m. Maria **WATROUS**, of Waterford, Aug. 15, 1827, by Roswell Fish, J.P.	1	26
Hannah P., of Groton, m. Henry G. **BEEBE**, of Waterford, Aug. 30, 1835, by Asa Fish, J.P.	1	51
Leonard D., now residing in Groton, m. Alice **WHIPPLE**, of Groton, Apr. 12, 1834, by Nathan Daboll, J.P.	1	50
Margaret Ellen, m. Alexander **BAIRD**, b. of [Groton], Mar. 30, 1851, by W. Munger	1	92
Mary, of Groton, m. Capt. Jonathan **WHEELER**, of Stonington, Dec. 29, 1828, by Asa Fish, J.P.	1	29
Mary J., m. Silas E. **PARK[E]**, b. of Groton, July 28, 1848, by Rev. Simon B. Bailey	1	81
Mary Jane, m. Nathan W. **MURPHEY**, b. of Groton, July 30, 1834, by Asa Fish, J.P.	1	47
Nathan W., m. Mary Jane **MURPHEY**, b. of Groton, July 30, 1834, by Asa Fish, J.P.	1	47
Philena, m. Sanford **MITCHELL**, of New Shoreham, R.I., *Apr. 1, 1832, by Erastus Denison (*Block Island written below)	1	39

	Vol.	Page
MURPHY, MURPHEY, MURFIT, (cont.)		
Sally Ann, d. [Charles S. & Margaret], b. June 20, 1829	3	17
Stephen, of Westerly, R.I., m. Betsey Ann **ASHBEY**, of Groton, Aug. 5, 1849, by Rev. H. R. Knapp	1	85
MURSER, Antoney, m. Lucy **WHITE**, June 9, 1822, by Caleb Avery, J.P.	1	7
MYERS, MIERS, Michael A., of Apilockicola, Fla., m. Lucy Ann **MITCHELL**, of Groton, June 19, 1845, by Rev. Jared R. Avery	1	73
Nancy, m. John **CHAPMAN**, Jr., b. of Groton, Mar. 1, 1835, by W[illia]m M. Williams, J.P.	1	50
NEWBERRY, NEWBERY, NEWBURY, Davis, [s. Tryal], b. Oct. 4, 1762	1	158
Debora[h], d. Elizabeth, Jr., b. Sept. 24, 1737	1	136
Eliphal, [s. Tryal], b. July 21, 1756	1	158
Elisha, [s. Tryal], b. Apr. 18, 1750	1	158
Elizabeth, [d. John & Elizabeth], b. Feb. 4, 1718	II	382
Elkana, [d. Tryal], b. Apr. 15, 1748	1	158
Hannah, [d. John & Elizabeth], b. Mar. 25, 1726/7	II	382
James, [s. John & Elizabeth], b. Mar. 23, 1720	II	382
John, m. Elizabeth **STARK**, Apr. 5,1707	1	114
John, s. John & Elizabeth, b. Aug. 16, 1710	II	382
John, Jr., m. Zeruiah **BIRCH**, Nov. 26, 1739	1	146
Jonathan, s. John & Zeruiah, b. Sept. 3, 1740	1	146
Joseph, s. John & Elizabeth, b. Mar. 4, 1713	II	382
Levinia, m. Ebenezer **MORGAN**, 2d, Oct. 28, 1814	2	43
Naoma, d. James & Naoma, b. Jan. 27, 1746/7	1	174
Nathan, [s. John & Elizabeth], b. Mar. 3, 1716	II	382
Nathan, of Groton, m. Sarah **STEWART**, of Stonington, Apr. 14, 1743	1	150
Nathan, [s. Tryal], b. Aug. 29, 1759	1	158
Nathaniel, [s. John & Elizabeth], b. Mar. 10, 1724	II	382
Newman, of Groton, m. Lucinda **BOLLES**, of Waterford, Aug. 23, 1835, by Joseph Durfey, J.P.	1	51
Phebe, d. [James & Naoma], b. June 11, 1750	1	174
Rody, d. John & Zeruiah, b. Jan. 8, 1741/2	1	146
Sabra, m. John **SHARP**, b. of Waterfored, Sept. 17, 1826, by Ralph Hurlbutt, J.P.	1	22
Sarah, d. John & Elizabeth, b. June 23, 1712	II	382
Sarah W., of Groton, m. Edwin **PERKINS**, May 14, 1854, at Mr. Newberrry's house, by Rev. Isaac Chees[e]brough	1	96
Susanna, [d. Tryal], b. Aug. 7, 1746	1	158
Trial, [s. John & Elizabeth], b. Feb. 25, 1722	II	382
Tryphenia, [d. Tryal], b. June 20, 1754	1	158
William, m. Martha Ann **MINER**, b. of Groton, Aug. 8, 1824, by Ralph Hurlbutt, J.P.	1	13
NEWTON [see also **NUTON**], Abel Spicer, s. Cyrus, b. Aug. 17, 1815	2	40
Annis, twin with Eunice, d. [Samuel, Jr. & Deborah], b. May 2, 1754	1	164
Bedary, of Groton, m. Moses **PALMER**, of Lyme, Mar. 22, 1829, by Timothy Tuttle	1	30
Bridget, d. [Ebenezer & Anne], b. Mar. 25, 1755	1	182
David, s. [Ebenezer & Anne], b. Dec. 18, 1741	1	182
Deborah, d. [Samuel, Jr. & Deborah], b. Sept. 4, 1749	1	164
Delight, d. [Samuel, Jr. & Deborah], b. Aug. 29,1747	1	164
Ebenezer, m. Anne **PARKE**, Dec. 24, 1736	1	182
Ebenezer, s. [Ebenezer & Anne], b. May 24, 1737	1	182
Elijah, m. Amy **CULVER**, Apr. 4, 1756	1	165

	Vol.	Page
NEWTON, (cont.)		
Elijah, m. Amy **COLVER**, b. of Groton, Apr. 4, 1756, by Rev. Jacob Johnson	1	169
Elizabeth, d. [Samuel, Jr. & Deborah], b. June 2, 1753	1	164
Eunice, twin with Annis, d. [Samuel, Jr. & Deborah], b. May 2, 1754	1	164
Hannah, d. [Samuel, Jr. & Deborah], b. July 21, 1763	1	164
Hannah, b. [ ], 1787	1	188
Hannah, m. Moses **CULVER**, Jan. 22, 1808	1	188
Isaac, s. [Samuel, Jr. & Deborah], b. Feb. 15, 1744/5	1	164
James, s. [Ebenezer & Anne], b. May 11, 1744	1	182
Jesse, s. [Ebenezer & Anne], b. June 1, 1739	1	182
John, s. [Ebenezer & Anne], b. Feb. 8, 1746/7	1	182
Lodowick, s. Abel & Sylvia, b. June 5, 1807	2	16
Mabel, d. [Samuel, Jr. & Deborah], b. Sept. 2, 1751	1	164
Mabel, d. [Elijah & Amy], b. Mar. 24, 1757	1	169
Margery, m. Theophilus **AVERY**, 3d, b. of Groton, Mar. 26, 1797, by Amos Geer, J.P.	2	72
Mary L, m. Gurdon **HEMPSTEAD**, b. of Groton, May 6, 1821, by Ralph Hurlbutt, J.P.	1	3
Prudence, d. [Ebenezer & Anne], b. Dec. 1, 1749	1	182
Roswell, s. [Ebenezer & Anne], b. Oct. 1, 1752	1	182
Ruth, m. Nathaniel **PARK[E]**, Aug. 27, 1747	1	184
Samuel, Jr., m. Deborah **WILLIAMS**, Nov. 11, 1743	1	164
Samuel, s. [Ebenezer & Anne], b. Aug. 28, 1757	1	182
Sarah, d. [Samuel, Jr. & Deborah], b. Dec. 17, 1758	1	164
Sylvia, d. [Samuel, Jr. & Deborah], b. Mar. 9, 1756	1	164
Wateann, of Groton, m. Nathan **SWAN**, Jr., of N. Stonington, Dec. 24, 1820, by Perez Hewitt, J.P.	1	2
NICHOLS, Anna, m. Thomas **DUNBAR**, Apr. 21, 1703	1	103
NILES, A. D., of Groton, m. J. H. **BREACHER**, of Florida, Aug. 24, 1842, by Rev. B. F. Hedden	1	67
Almira, d. [Paul F. & Sabra], b. May 11, 1799	2	85
Amos Avery, b. Mar. 19, 1766; m. Anna **ALLYN**, Mar. 13, 1791	2	92
Anson, m. Emeline **BENTON**, b. of Groton, Apr. 12, 1832, by Nathan Daboll, J.P.	1	39
Bridget, w. Silas, d. Dec. 22, 1805	2	77
Caroline, m. John S. **BURROWS**, b. of Groton, Aug. 10, 1831, by John G. Wightman, Eld.	1	38
Celinda, see Salinda and Selinda		
Cornelia, of Groton, m. John **SEELEY**, of Holesbrough, Me., May 5, 1850, by Rev. W[illia]m C. Walker	1	89
Dorothy, Mrs., of Groton, m. William **AYERS**, of Preston, Nov. 10, 1840, by Ira R. Steward	1	64
Edwin, s. [Amos A. & Anna], b. Nov. 17, 1793	2	92
Elijah, s. [Rodman & Freelove], b. July 22, 1799	2	75
Elisha, m. Elizabeth **WATERMAN**, b. of Groton, Jan. 10, 1836, by Ralph Hurlbutt, J.P.	1	53
Emeline, of Groton, m. Ambrose **REYNOLDS**, of Ledyard, Mar. 22, 1841, by Rev. Erastus Denison	1	64
Frederick Montalbon, s. [Paul F. & Sabra], b. Apr. 13, 1805	2	85
Hannah, d. [Nathan & Mary], b. Nov. 4, 1744	1	174
Hannah, d. [Rodman & Freelove], b. July 19, 1801	2	75
Hiram, [s. Samuel & Bridget], b. Apr. 18, 1805	2	77

	Vol.	Page
NILES, (cont.)		
Horatio Nelson, s. [Amos A. & Anna], b. Sept. 5, 1798	2	92
John A., m. Mary F. **WOODBRIDGE**, b. of Groton, Mar. 3, 1833, by John G. Wightman, Eld.	1	43
John Avery, s. [Amos A. & Anna], b. May 10, 1802	2	92
Julia, of Groton, m. Henry **WILLIAMS**, of Salem, Nov. 26, 1835, by John G. Wightman, Elder	1	52
Julia Ann, d. [Amos A. & Anna], b. Sept. 9, 1810	2	92
Julia Anna, d. [Paul F. & Sabra], b. Feb. 18, 1807	2	85
Katharine, m. Nathan **FISH**, Oct. 13, 1748; d. Jan. [ ], 1759	2	12
Louisa, of Groton, m. Gurdon **GIDDINGS**, of Stonington, Mar. 4, 1838, by Rev. Erastus Denison	1	58
Lucy Ann, of Groton, m. John W. **BREAKER**, of Camden, S.C., May 24, 1837, by John G. Wightman, Elder	1	56
Mary, of Stonington, m. John S. **SIGNIOUS**, of Charleston, S.C., June 17, 1832, by Rev. Erastus Denison	1	40
Mary A., m. John Calvin **BURROWS**, Oct. 7, 1838, by Rev. John G. Wightman	1	60
Mary Elizabeth Charlotte, d. [Paul F. & Sabra], b. July 26, 1811	2	85
Mary J., of Groton, m. William E. **SINGLETON**, of New London, June 19, 1842, by Ira R. Steward	1	66
Nathan, s. [Nathan & Mary], b. Jan. 16, 1737/8	1	174
Nathan, of Stonington, m. Martha **AVERY**, of Groton, July 19, 1820, by Rev. John G. Wightman	1	1
Nathan, m. Sally **HOLDREDGE**, b. of Groton, Aug. 31, 1831, by Nathan Daboll, J.P.	1	38
Nathan Crary, s. Nathan, b. Aug. 16, 1805	2	78
Nathaniel, s. [Nathan & Mary], b. Mar. 23, 1741/2	1	174
Patty Allyn, d. [Amos A. & Anna], b. Nov. 2, 1800	2	92
Patty Allyn, m. Henry **WILLIAMS**, b. of Groton, Dec. 26, 1824, by Anson A. Niles, J.P.	1	15
Paul F., m. Sabra **AVERY**, Oct. 18, 1798, by Amos Geer, J.P.	2	85
Phebe Avery, d. [Paul F. & Sabra], b. Mar. 1, 1803	2	85
Prudence M., of Groton, m. Alva **LITTLEFIELD**, of Portsmouth, N.H., Oct. 8, 1843, by Ira R. Steward	1	70
Robert, s. Nathan & Mary, b. Sept. 2, 1734	1	174
Rodman, b. Aug. 1, 1773; m. Freelove **BAILEY**, Nov. 15, 1797	2	75
Samuel, b. Jan. 10, 1777; m. Bridget **AVERY**, June 24, 1804	2	77
Salinda, d. [Rodman & Freelove], b. Aug. 29, 1803	2	75
Selinda, m. George **LATHAM**, Jr., Nov. 5, 1826, by Rodman Niles, J.P.	1	22
Selinda, m. George **LATHAM**, Jr., Nov. 5, 1826	3	26
Silas, m. Joanna **MORGAN**, Feb. [ ], 1807	2	77
Tabitha, d. [Nathan & Mary], b. Aug. 7, 1736	1	174
Tabitha, m. James **BELTON**, Apr. 3, 1740	1	151
Tabitha, m. Wait **STODDARD**, Jan. 14, 1756	1	160
Thomas North[r]up, s. [Nathan & Mary], b. Dec. 9, 1739	1	174
Thomas North[r]up, s. [Paul F. & Sabra], b. Nov. 11, 1800	2	85
William, of Stonington, m. Esther **GATES**, of Groton, Sept. 25, 1828, by John G. Wightman, Eld.	1	28
William Pitt, s. [Amos A. & Anna], b. Mar. 21, 1792	2	92
NORMAN, George, of Stonington, m. Lucy Ann **BAKER**, of Groton, Dec. 10, 1850, at Noank, by Rev. James M. Phillips	1	90

	Vol.	Page
NORTH[R]UP, Ann C., m. George M. **COLLINS**, b. of Providence, R.I., Aug. 20, 1848, by Rev. Nicholas T. Allen	1	81
NORTON, Anna, d. [Ebenezer & Sarah], b. Mar. 28, 1741	1	183
Ebenezer, s. Hugh & Mary (**BAILEY**), b. Mar. 22, 1715	1	118
Ebenezer, m. Sarah **HARVEY**, July 22, 1736	1	183
Ebenezer, s. [Ebenezer & Sarah], b. May 9, 1745	1	183
Zerviah, d. [Ebenezer & Sarah], b. Apr. 18, 1743	1	183
NOYES, NOYCE, Charles Whiting, s. William & Sibell, b. Mar. 1, 1765. Recorded by Ben A. Gallup, J.P.	1	157
Denison, m. Mary **KEMP**, b. of Groton, Sept. 1, 1847, by Rev. Erastus Denison	1	79
Eliza Maria D., formerly of Stonington, m. Stephen **MORGAN**, Jr., of Groton, June 17, 1830, by John G. Wightman, Eld.	1	34
Eunice, of Groton, m. Paul W. **NOYES**, of Stonington, Feb. 27, 1834, by Rev. Joseph Ayer, Jr.	1	46
James, m. Polly **CHAPPELL**, b. of Groton, Dec. 2, 1827, by Rodman Niles, J.P.	1	26
Nathan, Jr., m. Sarah Ann **BURROWS**, Mar. 18, 1830, by Erastus Denison, Minister	1	33
Oliver J., of Rio Grande, Mexico, m. Hannah C. **TIFT**, of Groton, Aug. 26, 1832, by Timothy Tuttle	1	41
Paul W., of Stonington, m. Eunice **NOYES**, of Groton, Feb. 27, 1834, by Rev. Joseph Ayer, Jr.	1	46
Samuel, s. William & Sibell, b. Nov. 9, 1747	1	157
Sibell, d. William & Sibell, b. Nov. 19, 1745	1	157
Thomas W., of Stonington, m. Phebe J. **KEMP**, of Groton, May 11, 1848, by Rev. Nehemiah B. Cooke	1	80
William, s. William & Sibell, b. Apr. 13, 1743	1	157
William B., of Stonington, m. Abby C. **DENISON**, of Groton, Aug. 23, 1848, by Rev. Erastus Denison, of Waterford	1	81
NUTON, [see also **NEWTON**], Abel, s. Christopher & Deborah, b. Dec. 1, 1746	1	143
Agrippa, s. Christopher & Deborah, b. Apr. 21, 1740	1	143
Christopher, [s. Samuel & Ruth], b. July 13, 1704	1	105
Christopher, m. Deborah **SHOLES**, Feb. 8, 1732	1	143
Christopher, s. Christopher & Deborah, b. Feb. 15, 1742/3	1	143
Ebenezer, [s. Samuel & Ruth], b. Aug. 28, 1714	1	105
Elijah, s. Christopher & Deborah, b. Dec. 19, 1732	1	143
Hannah, [d. Samuel & Ruth], b. Sept. 23, 1720	1	105
Jacob, s. Christopher & Deborah, b. June 29, 1748	1	143
Jane, [d. Samuel & Ruth], b. Apr. 4, 1710	1	105
Mable, d. Christopher & Deborah, b. [ ]	1	143
Marke, s. Christopher & Deborah, b. Aug. 25, 1737	1	143
Nathan, [s. Samuel & Ruth], b. Oct. 4, 1708	1	105
Ruth, [d. Samuel & Ruth], b. Oct. 18, 1712	1	105
Samuel, m. Ruth **SPICER**, Jan. 22, 1702	1	105
Samuel, [s. Samuel & Ruth], b. Oct. 10, 1722	1	105
Sarah, [s. Samuel & Ruth], b. Feb. 3, 1716/17	1	105
OBRIEN, [see also **BRIEN**], Barnard, s. Barnard & Elizabeth, b. Jan. 29, 1785	2	10
Elisha, m. Emeline **MINER**, b. of Groton, Sept. 13, 1832, by John G. Wightman, Eld.	1	41
George, m. Hannah Ann **TURNER**, b. of Groton, June 15, 1823, by Timothy Tuttle	1	9

	Vol.	Page
OBRIEN, (cont.)		
Mary A., of Groton, m. Samuel **GARSIDE**, of Stonington, Oct. 11, 1832, by John G. Wightman, Eld.	1	41
O'CONNELL, see under **CONNELL**		
ODELL, Alvin, of Kent, m. Lucy A. **MANICE**, of Groton, Oct. 19, 1851, by Rev. J. R. Avery	1	92
OWEN, Anna, d. John & Anna, b. Dec. 23, 1731	1	142
Anna, d. John & Anna, b. July 13, 1734	1	142
Anna, d. John & Anna, b. July 10, 1739	1	142
Anna, w. Rev. John, d. May 22, 1743	1	152
John, Rev., m. Anna **MORGAN**, Nov. 25, 1730	1	142
John, s. John & Anna, b. Jan. 20, 1735/6	1	142
John, Rev., m. Mary **HILLHOUSE**, Nov. 13, 1744	1	142
Mary, d. John & Anna, b. Jan. 25, 1733/4	1	142
Mehetable, d. John & Anna, b. Sept. 20, 1741	1	142
PACKER, [see also **PARKER**], Abigail, d. James & Abigail, b. Oct. 23, 1708	1	160
Abigail, d. Ichabod & Abigail, b. Mar. 18, 1734	1	139
Angeline, m. Nathaniel **WILBUR**, Sept. 14, 1831, by Erastus Denison	1	38
Ann, d. James & Abigail, b. Feb. 9, 1719	1	160
Augusta, m. Alfred H. **ASHBEY**, b. of Groton, Aug. 10, 1825, by John G. Wightman	1	18
Avery, s. Avery & Mary, b. May 27, 1803	2	88
Benajah, s. [John], b. June 13, 1790	2	65
Bethiah, m. Joseph **BILL**, Nov. [ ], 1716	1	117
Betsey, m. Benjamin **SAWYER**, b. of Groton, July 9, 1826, by Asa Fitch, J.P.	1	21
Caroline, m. Peter **BAKER**, Jr., b. of Groton, Sept. 25, 1842, by Ira R. Steward	1	67
Charlotte, of Groton, m. Josephus **FITCH**, 2d, May 19, 1822, by Roswell Burrows	1	7
Coddington, m. Ellen H. **KELLEY**, b. of Groton, Mar. 11, 1829, by John G. Wightman, Eld.	1	30
Coshthiah, [d. John, Jr. & Sarah], b. Nov. 20, 1695	1	106
Daniel, s. Ichabod & Abigail, b. Jan. 31, 1732	1	139
David, s. Nathan & Martha, b. Mar. 15, 1774	2	25
Delia, m. George W. **HOLDRIDGE**, b. of Groton, Apr. 8, 1827, by John G. Wightman, Eld.	1	23
Desire, d. James & Abigail, b. Sept. 11, 1712	1	160
Desire, m. John **BURROWS**, Jr., July 1, 1731	1	176
Desire, d. Ichabod & Abigail, b. Jan. 2, 1744/5	1	139
Eldredge, 3d, m. Lydia L. **MINER**, b. of Groton, Sept. 8, 1830, by Ralph Hurlbutt, J.P.	1	35
Eleanor, m. Griswold P. **RATHBURN**, b. of Groton, Oct. 3, 1830, by Rev. Erastus Denison	1	35
Elisha, s. Ichabod & Abigail, b. Sept. 28, 1747	1	139
Ellen W., d. [Dudley & Eleonor], b. Oct. 29, 1822	3	20
[E]onice, d. Ichabod & Abigail, b. Oct. 8, 1740	1	139
Eunice, m. Amos **HEWITT**, Sept. 25, 1831, by Erastus Denison	1	38
Eunice*, m. John **GRAD**, M.D., b. of Groton, Jan. 6, 1848, by Rev. H. R. Knapp [*Written in pencil "Emma, d. of Mason P."]	1	83
Eveline, m. Henry **WILBUR**, b. of Groton, Oct. 1, 1823, by Rev. Roswell Burrows	1	10

	Vol.	Page
PACKER, (cont.)		
Frances L., of Groton, m. William S. **BRAY**, of New Foundland, July 4, 1838, by I. R. Steward. Intention dated July 1, 1838.	1	59
Frederick, m. Loisa **PACKER**, b. of Groton, July 10, 1828, by John G. Wightman, Eld.	1	28
Freelove, d. James & Abigail, b. Jan. 20, 1715	1	160
Gardiner, s. Eunice **BROWN**, b. July 15, 1798	2	61
George, m. Delight **ELDREDGE**, b. of Groton, July 17, 1820, by Rev. John G. Wightman	1	1
George B., m. Lucy **RATHBONE**, b. of Groton, Oct. 15, 1851, by Washington Munger	1	92
George W., s. [George W. & Eliza], b. June 21, 1828	3	23
Hannah, d. Ichabod & Abigail, b. May 8, 1738	1	139
Hannah, d. [John & Hannah], b. July 26, 1748	1	179
Hannah, m. Samuel B. **LATHAM**, b. of Groton, Sept. 28, 1834, by Rev. Ira R. Steward	1	48
Hannah, of Groton, m. Isaac Avery **WIGHTMAN**, of Penn., Apr. 27, 1845, by Rev. Erastus Denison	1	72
Hannah B., m. Robert P. **AVERY**, b. of Groton, Sept. 22, 1841, by Ira R. Steward	1	65
Ichabod, s. James & Abigail, b. Jan. 15, 1707	1	160
Ichabod, m. Abigail **ELDREDGE**, Oct. 30, 1729	1	139
Ichabod, s. Ichabod & Abigail, b. Apr. 26, 1730	1	139
James, s. James & Abigail, b. Nov. 2, 1710	1	160
James, m. Mary Ann **APPLEMAN**, b. of Groton, July 8, 1838, by Ira R. Steward	1	59
Jane A., d. [Dudley & Eleonor], b. Apr. 6, 1826	3	20
Jerusha, m. John A. **WOLF**, b. of Groton, Aug. 24, 1834, by Rev. Ira R. Steward	1	147
John, Jr., m. Sarah **MILLER**, Mar. 10, 1686	1	106
John, [s. John, Jr. & Sarah], b. May 3, 1693	1	106
John, s. James & Abigail, b. Sept. 16, 1720	1	160
John, m. Hannah **AVERY**, Sept. 18, 1746	1	179
John, s. [John], b. Sept. 23, 1784	2	65
Joseph, s. James & Abigail, b. Nov. 2, 1722	1	160
Joshua, s. [Avery & Mary], b. Feb. 5, 1809	2	88
Joshua, m. Lucy **FISH**, b. of Groton, Sept. 27, 1842, by Ira R. Steward	1	67
Loisa, m. Frederick **PACKER**, b. of Groton, July 10, 1828, by John G. Wightman, Eld.	1	28
Lucretia, d. James & Abigail, b. Aug. 2, 1717	1	160
Lucretia, d. [John & Hannah], b. May 23, 1747	1	179
Lucretia, m. Isaac **WHITEMAN**, Oct. 13, 1765	1	158
Lucy, d. [John & Hannah], b. Oct. 23, 1750	1	179
Lucy, d. Ichabod & Abigail, b. Sept. 3, 1751	1	139
Lucy Ann, m. John S. **RATHBUN**, b. of Groton, Sept. 7, 1825, by Asa Fitch, J.P.	1	18
Mary, m. Cary **LATHAM**, b. of Groton, Feb. 22, 1761	2	52
Mary, d. [John], b. June 29, 1799	2	65
Mary, m. John **LEE**, b. of Groton, Mar. 28, 1817	3	14
Mary Ann, m. John M. **PUTNAM**, b. of Groton, July 8, 1841, by Rev. Benjamin C. Phelps	1	65
Mary D., m. Gilbert S. **BAILEY**, b. of Groton, Apr. 16, 1851, by Rev. Simon B. Bailey	1	91

	Vol.	Page
PACKER, (cont.)		
Mason R., m. Polly **FITCH**, b. of Groton, July 6, 1825, by John G. Wightman, Elder	1	17
Phebe A., m. Samuel **RATHBURN**, b. of Groton, Nov. 1, 1835, by Rev. Ira R. Steward	1	52
Prudence A., m. Hezekiah **WILLCOX**, Jr., b. of Groton, July 14, 1839, by I. R. Steward	1	61
Roswell, m. Eliza **FISH**, b. of Groton, Dec. 20, 1820, by John O. Miner, J.P.	1	2
Sabrina, m. Abel **ELDREDGE**, b. of Groton, Sept. 7, 1820, by Roswell Fish, J.P.	1	2
Sarah, [d. John, Jr. & Sarah], b. Oct. 7, 1689	1	106
Sarah, d. Ichabod & Abigail, b. Apr. 16, 1736	1	139
Susan, of Groton, m. Thomas **BROOKS**, of Waterford, July 3, 1836, by Rev. John G. Wightman	1	54
Thankfull, d. James & Rebeckah, b. July 23, 1728	1	184
Thankfull, m. James **CHESTER**, Oct. 17, 1750	1	182
Zerviah, m. Daniel **CHEESEBOROUGH**, Jr., b. of Groton, Sept. 17, 1820, by Rev. John G. Wightman	1	2
PALINS, Susanna, m. Samuell **AVERY**, Oct. 27, 1686	1	121
PALMER, Abby, [d. John & Abby], b. Dec. 25, 1812	3	19
Abby, m. James A. **LATHAM**, b. of Groton, June 18, 1832, by Rev. Roswell Burrows	1	40
Alexander, of Stonington, m. Hannah Adelia **BILLINGS**, of Groton, Jan. 26, 1831, by Timothy Tuttle	1	36
Caroline, [d. John & Abby], b. June 10, 1816	3	19
Caroline, m. Perez **CHAPMAN**, b. of Groton, Oct. 28, 1835, by Rev. Roswell Burrows	1	52
David, of Groton, m. Abigail **GARDINER**, of Westerly, R.I., Nov. 25, 1773, by Joseph Parke, Clerk	2	20
Horace, of Stonington, m. Fanny O. **SPRING**, of Groton, Aug. 27, 1848, by David Avery, Elder	1	82
Jairus B., m. Anna **WHEELER**, b. of N. Stonington, July 3, 1843, by Rev. Erastus Denison	1	69
John, Jr., [s. John & Abby], b. July 16, 1818	3	19
John, Jr., m. Julia **BAKER**, b. of Groton, Jan. 1, 1840, by Ira R. Steward	1	62
Lucy, m. William A. **WILBUR**, b. of Groton, July 25, 1829, by Roswell Burrows, Eld.	1	31
Lucy Clark, d. [John & Abby], b. Oct. 14, 1811	3	19
Lydia, [d. John & Abby], b. Sept. 2, 1821	3	19
Lydia, m. John D. **LUTHER**, b. of Groton, Sept. 28, 1841, by Ira R. Steward	1	65
Mary, [d. John & Abby], b. Oct. 11, 1814	3	19
Mary, of Groton, m. Thomas J. **SAWYER**, of Stonington, June 19, 1832, by Rev. Roswell Burrows	1	40
Moses, of Lyme, m. Bedary **NEWTON**, of Groton, Mar. 22, 1829, by Timothy Tuttle	1	30
Noyes, of Salem, m. Emily **AVERY**, of Groton, June 26, 1836, by Nathan Daboll, J.P.	1	54
Patty, of Groton, m. Samuel **GALLUP**, of New York State, Dec. 2, 1821, by Roswell Burrows	1	5
Robert, [s. John & Abby], b. May 6, 1825	3	19

	Vol.	Page
PALMER, (cont.)		
Robert, of New London, m. Prudence M. **INGRAHAM**, of Groton, Jan. 26, 1845, by Rev. Simon B. Bailey	1	72
Robert, m. Harriet **ROGERS**, b. of Groton, Oct. 25, 1845, by Rev. Simon B. Bailey	1	74
Roswell Burrows, [d. John & Abby], b. Apr. 19, 1828	3	19
William, [s. John & Abby], b. Apr. 5, 1827	3	19
PARISH, Olive, of Preston, m. Eben[eze]r **MORGAN**, of Groton, Apr. 5, 1781, by Jona[tha]n Brewster, J.P.	2	41
PARKE, PARK [see also **PARKS**], Abigail, m. Christopher **AVERY**, Dec. 19, 1704	1	127
Ann C., m. Seth W. **BURROWS**, b. of Groton, Jan. 27, 1849, by Rev. H. R. Knapp	1	84
Anne, m. Ebenezer **NEWTON**, Dec. 24, 1736	1	182
Asa, m. Mrs. Abby **LAMB**, b. of Groton, June 5, 1842, by Nathan Daboll, J. P.	1	66
Benjamin F., m. Almira **HOWELL**, b. of Groton, Jan. 25, 1835, by John G. Wightman, Elder	1	48
Catharine R., of Groton, m. Ebenezer **HERRICK**, of Hudson, N.Y., Jan. 18, 1843, by Rev. Erastus Denison	1	67
Charles C., of N. Stonington, m. Mary J. **SPENCER**, of Stonington, Nov. 27, 1843, by Rev. Erastus Denison	1	70
David, s. Jacob, b. Nov. 8, 1751; m. Anna **STANTON**, of Preston, July 5, 1781, by Levi Hart	2	2
Desire, m. David **EDGECOMB**, b. of Groton, Mar. 29, 1781, by Jonathan Brewster, J.P.	2	79
Dorothy, of Preston, m. Ebenezer **AVERY**, of Groton, June 16, 1708	1	123
Dorothy, m. Mortimer **STODDARD**, b. of Groton, Dec. 6, 1764, by Rev. Jacob Johnson	2	18
Dudley, m. Prudence **HARRISON**, b. of Groton, Dec. 20, 1846, by Rev. H. R. Knapp	1	83
Edwin A., m. Abby J. **LAMB**, b. of Groton, Jan. [ ], 1836, by John G. Wightman, Eld.	1	53
Elizabeth A., m. Jacob J. **LAMB**, b. of Groton, Aug. 16, 1840, by Rev. Ira R. Steward	1	63
Hezekiah, m. Frances **BURROWS**, b. of Groton, July 2, 1837, by John G. Wightman, Elder	1	57
Holthrop, [s. Isaac], b. May 18, 1807	3	26
Holdthrop, m. Elvira **CHIPMAN**, b. of Groton, May 20, 1836, by Roswell Fish, J.P.	1	54
Isaac, Jr., [s. Isaac], b. July 28, 1806, in Stonington	3	26
Jacob, m. Martha **GEER**, July 18, 1723	1	144
Jacob, s. Jacob & Martha, b. Feb. 22, 1724/5	1	144
Jacob, d. Oct. 15, 1752	1	153
James, [s. Isaac], b. Apr. 14, 1813, in Stonington	3	26
James D., m. Ann Maria **CROSSMAN**, b. of Groton, Aug. 2, 1854, by Rev. S. W. Coggeshall, of Mystic Bridge	1	96
John Billings, [s. Isaac], b. Nov. 26, 1808, in Stonington	3	26
John C., of Groton, m. Lara Ann **PARK[E]**, of Stonington, Dec. 31, 1843, by Rev. Cha[rle]s C. Lewis	1	70
Lara Ann, of Stonington, m. John C. **PARK[E]**, of Groton, Dec. 31, 1843, by Rev. Cha[rle]s C. Lewis	1	70

	Vol.	Page
PARKE, PARK, (cont.)		
Ledyard, m. Fanny **BURROWS**, Sept. 23, 1838, by Rev. John G. Wightman	1	59
Louisa, [d. Isaac], b. Aug. 12, 1824	3	26
Louisa, of Groton, m. John **MOCKETT**, of Orange Co., N.Y., Feb. 8, 1853, by Rev. Franklin A. Slater	1	94
Lucy, W[i]d., of Groton, m. William **DOUGLASS**, of Maine, Nov. 16, 1826, by Roswell Fish, J.P.	1	22
Lucy Ann, [d. Isaac], b. Aug. 12, 1826	3	26
Margaret, m. William **KING**, b. of Groton, Sept. 1, 1844, by Rev. Simon B. Bailey	1	71
Martha, d. Jacob & Martha, b. Sept. 27, 1727	1	144
Martha, m. William **DOUGLASS**, Jr., b. of Groton, May 21, 1826, by Roswell Fish, J.P.	1	20
Martha Ann, m. Samuel **HOLDREDGE**, b. of Groton, June 15, 1845, by Rev. Simon B. Bailey	1	73
Mary, b. Dec. 1, 1756, of Groton, m. John **SPICER**, of Groton, Dec. 29, 1774	2	53
Mary, [d. Isaac], b. Dec. 9, 1818	3	26
Mary, of Plainfield, m. Rufus B. **MINER**, of Canterbury, Mar. 6, 1831, by Rev. Levi Kimland, of Canterbury	3	28
Nabby, b. Aug. 10, 1773; m. Sprague **FISH**, June 16, 1789	2	40
Nancy, d. [David & Anna], b. July 9, 1781[sic]	2	2
Nathaniel, m. Ruth **NEWTON**, Aug. 27, 1747	1	184
Nathaniel, s. [Nathaniel & Ruth], b. July 9, 1751	1	184
Parthenia, of Groton, m. Stephen **MORGAN**, Apr. 13, 1788	2	41
Phebe, [d. Isaac], b. Apr. 11, 1815, in Stonington	3	26
Phebe, m. Jabez **WATROUS**, b. of Groton, Mar. 11, 1827, by John G. Wightman	1	23
Phebe E., m. David G. **CLARKE**, Sept. 17, 1850, at Porterville, by Rev. W. Munger	1	89
Polly, m. John **BRAYMAN**, Aug. 1, 1821	3	10
Prentice A., m. Lucy A. **BRAMAN**, b. of Groton, Aug. 13, 1834, by John G. Wightman, Elder	1	47
Prescilla, [d. Isaac], b. Jan. 14, 1811, in Stonington	3	26
Prudence, of Groton, m. John **DUNHAM**, of Stonington, June 6, 1825, by Roswell Fish, J.P.	1	17
Richard, of Island of Wight, G.B., m. Naomi **DEWEY**, of Groton, July 4, 1838, by Rev. John G. Wightman	1	59
Robert, d. Nov. 25, 1779	1	151
Roswell, of Preston, m. Mabel **WILLIAMS**, of Groton, Aug. 3, 1826, by Timothy Tuttle	1	21
Roxana, [d. Isaac], b. Apr. 6, 1820	3	26
Ruth, d. [Nathaniel & Ruth], b. Sept. 3, 1748	1	184
Sibble, m. Daniel **AVERY**, Apr. 27, 1779	2	39
Silas E., m. Mary J. **MURPHY**, b. of Groton, July 28, 1848, by Rev. Simon B. Bailey	1	81
Thomas, m. Mary L. **GRIFFIN**, b. of Groton, Sept. 29, 1845, by Rev. S. B. Bailey	1	74
Timothy, s. Jacob & Martha, b. Nov. 20, 1729	1	144
William Henry, m. Katharine **MITCHELL**, b. of Groton, Dec. 24, 1828, by John G. Wightman, Eld.	1	29

	Vol.	Page
PARKER, [see also **PACKER**], James, of S. America, m. Almira **HALLAM**, of Groton, Apr. 16, 1834, by Rev. Ira R. Steward	1	46
Josephus T., m. Fanny R. **WILBUR**, b. of Groton, Sept. 27, 1846, by Rev. H. R. Knapp	1	83
Thomas E., m. Emma J. **BURROWS**, b. of Groton, July 4, 1849, by Rev. Simon B. Bailey	1	83
PARKS, PARKES, [see also **PARKE**], Abby, m. Russell **BAILEY**, b. of Groton, Aug. 29, 1852, by Nicholas T. Allen, Minister	1	94
Abby C., m. Oliver **BRAMAN**, b. of Groton, July 28, 1833, by John G. Wightman, Eld.	1	44
Abigail, Wid., m. Daniel **BURROWS**, b. of Groton, Jan. 23, 1825, by Roswell Fish, J.P.	1	16
Eliza, of Groton, m. Allyn P. **DENISON**, of Stonington, Dec. 9, 1832, by John G. Wightman, Eld.	1	42
Elizabeth, m. George **SPRING**, b. of Groton, Nov. 15, 1841, by Ira R. Steward	1	65
Ellen, m. Samuel **HOLDREDGE**, b. of Groton, Dec. 28, 1834, by Rev. Ira R. Steward	1	49
Gilbert, Jr., m. Sarah **HARRISON**, b. of Groton, Aug. 4, 1842, by Rev. Ira R. Steward	1	66
James S., of Groton, m. Sarah N. **CLARK**, of Charlestown, R.I., May 17, 1840, by Ira R. Steward	1	63
Roxana, m. Richard **WHEELER**, June 20, 1850, by Rev. W. Munger	1	89
PATTEN, Elizabeth, d. Thomas & Johanna, b. July 31, 1759	1	157
Sarah, d. Thomas & Johanna, b. Aug. 1, 1754	1	157
Thomas, Jr., m. Johanna **ALLEN**, Oct. 9, 1753	1	157
Thomas, s. Thomas & Johanna, b. Aug. 11, 1756	1	157
PEABODY, Benjamin, Jr., of N. Stonington, m. Delia **AVERY**, of Groton, Dec. 26, 1824, by John G. Wightman, Eld.	1	15
Giles H., m. Mary C. **HONEYWELL**, Mar. 10, 1850, by Rev. H. R. Knapp	1	88
Mary, m. Elisha **FITCH**, b. of Groton, Nov. 3, 1822, by Rev. Roswell Burrows	1	8
PECKHAM, Anna, m. Thomas **PROWSER**, b. of Groton, Nov. 26, 1826, by Ralph Hurlbutt, J.P.	1	22
Elizabeth, m. W[illia]m **FITCH**, b. of Groton, July 20, 1851, by Rev. James M. Phillips, of Noank	1	92
Hyram, m. Rhoda **ALLYN**, b. of Groton, Dec. 9, 1824, by Philip Gray, J.P.	1	15
Hyram, m. Julia **ALLYN**, Feb. 7, 1829, by Philip Gray, J.P.	1	29
Hiram, of Ledyard, m. Hannah E. **FISH**, of Groton, Nov. 13, 1853, at Noank, by Rev. James M. Phillips	1	95
Isaac, m. Fanny Maria **PROSSER**, b. of Groton, Nov. 27, 1823, by William Williams, J.P.	1	11
PECOR, Isaac B., of Bridgeport, m. Lucy **GARD**, of Groton, Feb. 1, 1835, by Rev. Ira R. Steward	1	49
PELTON, Elkanah, s. Thomas & Hannah, b. Dec. 14, 1749	1	156
Eunice, d. [Paul & Mary], b. Nov. 24, 1745	1	173
Eunice, d. [Paul & Mary], b. Sept. 15, 1758	1	173
Gideon, s. Thomas & Hannah, b. Feb. 23, 1747/8	1	156
Hannah, d. Thomas & Hannah, b. May 7, 1746	1	156
Hannah, d. [Paul & Mary], b. May 6, 1756	1	173
Henry, m. Mary **ROSE**, Apr. 29, 1712	1	118

	Vol.	Page
PELTON, (cont.)		
Henry, m. Mary **ROSE**, Apr. 29, 1712	1	133
Henry, s. Thomas & Hannah, b. July 2, 1742	1	156
Henry, s. [Rufus & Anne], b. Dec. 16, 1796	2	53
John, s. Thomas & Hannah, b. Aug. 26, 1751	1	156
Lemuel, s. [Henry & Mary], b. Feb. 22, 1723/4	1	133
Mary, d. [Paul & Mary], b.. Oct. 23, 1749	1	173
Paul, s. Henry & Mary, b. May 14, 1720	1	118
Paul, s. [Henry & Mary], b. May 14, 1720	1	133
Paul, m. Mary **AVERY**, Aug. 20, 1743	1	173
Paul, s. [Paul & Mary], b. Feb. 10, 1754	1	173
Preserved, d. Henry & Mary, b. June 24, 1722	1	118
Preserved, d. [Henry & Mary], b. June 24, 1722	1	133
Prudence, d. [Paul & Mary], b. Aug. 12, 1744	1	173
R[e]uben, s. [Henry & Mary], b. Jan. 24, 1725/6	1	133
Robert, s. [Henry & Mary], b. June 9, 1727	1	133
Roswell, s. Thomas & Hannah, b. Apr. 4, 1744	1	156
Samantha, d. Rufus & Anne, b. Feb. 1, 1795	2	53
Samuell, s. Henry & Mary, b. Dec. 16, 1713	1	118
Samuel, s. Henry & Mary, b. Dec. 16, 1713	1	133
Samuel, s. [Paul & Mary], b. Aug. 20, 1751	1	173
Thomas, s. Henry & Mary, b. July 22, 1717	1	118
Thomas, [s. Henry & Mary], b. July 22, 1717	1	133
Thomas, m. Hannah **AVERY**, July 9, 1740	1	156
PENDERSON, Cyrus, of Preston, m. Lucretia **STODDARD**, of Groton, Feb. 11, 1827, by Rev. Thomas R. Peck	1	23
PENDLETON, Almira, residing in Groton, m. John O. **GEER**, of Groton, May 11, 1826, by Rev. Gideon B. Perry, of Stonington	1	20
Amelia, d. Isaac, b. Oct. 25, 18[ ]	2	19
Francis, of Westerly, R.I., m. Elizabeth **KNOWLES**, of Groton, May 11, 1826, by John G. Wightman, Eld.	1	20
Jabez, of Westerly, R.I., m. Eliza W. **DOWNS**, of New York, Nov. 10, 1822, by Elisha Avery, J.P.	1	8
Lucy, of Groton, m. James W. **BRAYTON**, of Providence, R.I., Oct. 2, 1836, by John G. Wightman, Elder	1	55
Peleg, of Norwich, N.Y., m. Lucy Ann **BABCOCK**, of Groton, Sept. 19, 1824, by Rev. John G. Wightman	1	14
William, of Stonington, m. Sally **BREED**, of Groton, June 7, 1821, by Rev. Roswell Burrows	1	3
PENFIELD, Jonathan, s. John & Anna, b. Mar. 25, 1719	1	115
Simeon, s. John & Anna, b. Aug. 2, 1715	1	115
Stephen, s. John & Anna, b. Jan. 28, 1713/14	1	115
PERIGO, PEREGO, Abigail, b. Aug. 8, 1738; m. Samuel **HOLDREDGE**, Mar. 4, 1762	2	38
Abigail, d. John & Hannah, b. Aug. 11, 1738	1	147
Ezekiel, s. John & Hannah, b. June 6, 1743	1	147
Priscilla, d. John & Hannah, b. Feb. 11, 1732/3	1	147
William, s. John & Hannah, b. Jan. 25, 1734/5	1	147
PERKINS, Aaron, s. [Solomon & Deborah], b. May 24, 1756	1	162
Abigail, twin with Bathshua, d. John & Mary, b. Apr. 29, 1738	1	138
Adelia E., m. Oliver E. **BENNET[T]**, b. of Groton, Sept. 29, 1839, by Charles Bennet[t], J.P.	1	61
Alpha Austin, s. [Robert, Jr. & Lucy], b. May 5, 1836	3	31

	Vol.	Page
PERKINS, (cont.)		
Amy, d. [Elnathan & Mary], b. Dec. 23, 1744	1	183
Ann, m. Nathan **ALLYN**, Jr., b. of Groton, June 10, 1821, by Ralph Hurlbutt, J.P.	1	3
Anson G., of Groton, m. Eunice A. **DART**, of Groton, July 1, 1849, by Rev. Nicholas T. Allen	1	86
Asa, s. [Elnathan & Mary], b. Feb. 14, 1748	1	183
Asa, m. Phebe **GARD**, b. of Groton, Jan. 29, 1822, by Ralph Hurlbutt, J.P.	1	6
Asa, 2d, m. Ellen **LEEDS**, b. of Groton, Dec. 16, 1827, by Nathan Daboll, J.P.	1	25
Basheba, m. Gurdon **PERKINS**, b. of Groton, Apr. 11, 1837, by Ralph Hurlbutt, J.P.	1	56
Bathshua, twin with Abigail, d. John & Mary, b. Apr. 29, 1738	1	138
Betsey, m. Charles **HEATH**, b. of Groton, Aug. 28, 1836, by Nathan Daboll, J.P.	1	55
Caleb, s. Obadiah & Emblem, b. Oct. 18, 1784	2	21
Candoia, d. [John & Mary], b. Aug. 20, 1740	1	138
Charles L., m. Nancy **PERKINS**, b. of Groton, June 12, 1831, by Nathan Daboll, J.P.	1	37
Deborah, d. Solomon & Deborah, b. Dec. 18, 1753	1	162
Diana, m. John **BENHAM**, Jr., b. of Groton, Aug. 19, 1827, by Nathan Daboll, J.P.	1	24
Ebenezer, [s. Luke & Lydia], b. Oct. 29, 1720	1	116
Ebenezer, m. Sarah **DAVIS**, July 20, 1749	1	183
Edwin, m. Sarah W. **NEWBURY**, of Groton, May 14, 1854, at Mr. Newberry's house, by Rev. Isaac Chees[e]brough	1	96
Elisha, s. [Elnathan & Mary], b. Jan. 28, 1746	1	183
Elisha, s. Jabez & Rebeckah, b. July 8, 1784	2	49
Eliza, m. Silas **LAMB**, b. of Groton, Mar. 21, 1825, by Nathan Daboll, J.P.	1	16
Elizabeth R., of Groton, m. Thomas **WILSON**, of Sweden, Mar. 25, 1834, by Nathan Daboll, J.P.	1	46
Elnathan, s. Luke & Lydia, b. Sept. 20, 1718	1	116
Elnathan, m. Mary **PHILLIPS**, Dec. 13, 1737	1	183
Emily, of Groton, m. William H. **MANWARING**, of Waterford, June 1, 1828, by Ralph Hurlbutt, J.P.	1	27
Ephraim, s. [Jabez & Rebeckah], b. May 7, 1795	2	49
Eunice, d. Luke & Lydia, b. Jan. 24, 1725/6	1	116
Eunis, [d. Ebenezer & Sarah], b. Oct. 27, 1750	1	183
Eunice, m. Joseph **MORGAN**, 2d, b. of Groton, July 3, 1783, by Rev. Parke Allyn, of N. Groton	2	34
George A., m. Betsey M. **DABOLL**, b. of Groton, June 30, 1839, by Rev. John G. Wightman	1	61
Giles, m. Elizabeth **BENHAM**, Dec. 26, 1821, by Rufus Smith, J.P.	1	5
Gurdon, m. Basheba **PERKINS**, b. of Groton, Apr. 11, 1837, by Ralph Hurlbutt, J.P.	1	56
Hannah, m. Nathan **MORGAN**, b. of Groton, Sept. 8, 1774, by Rev. Aaron Kinne	2	25
Hannah, of Groton, m. Ezekiel **GRAY**, of Montville, Mar. 29, 1829, by Philip Gray, J.P.	1	30
Jabez, s. [Jabez & Rebeckah], b. July 8, 1797	2	49
Jacob, [s. John & Sarah], b. Aug. 1, 1721	1	120
Jacob, s. John & Mary, b. Apr. 7, 1746	1	138

	Vol.	Page
PERKINS, (cont.)		
Jacob, s. Ebenezer & Sarah, b. Oct. 22, 1764	2	16
James, s. Luke & Lydia, b. Feb. 9, 1733/4	1	116
Jefferson, m. Mary C. **PERKINS**, b. of Groton, Jan. 25, 1835, by Nathan Daboll, J.P.	1	48
John, m. Sarah **BAILEY**, Aug. 26, 1711	1	120
John, [s. John & Sarah], b. Aug. 31, 1713	1	120
John, Jr., m. Mary **SHOLES**, July 6, 1737	1	138
John, Jr., [s. John & Mary], b. June 26, 1751	1	138
John, m. Esther **CROWNWELL**, b. of Groton, Dec. 5, 1821, by Rufus Smith, J.P.	1	5
John A., m. Lucinda L. **PERKINS**, b. of Groton, Apr. 21, 1833, by John G. Wightman, Eld.	1	43
John E., of Groton, m. Sarah A. **DART**, of Groton, May 29, 1850, by Rev. Nicholas T. Allen	1	88
Keziah, d. [Solomon & Deborah], b. Feb. 19, 1764	1	162
Lemuel A., m. Eliza H. **STARR**, b. of Groton, Mar. 1, 1850, by Rev. Jared R. Avery	1	87
Levinia, d. [Jabez & Rebeckah], b. Dec. 16, 1799	2	49
Lois, of Groton, m. Enos **DAVIS**, of Preston, June 22, 1826, by Ralph Hurlbutt, J.P.	1	20
Lois, of Groton, m. Thomas A. **ADGATE**, of Montville, Mar. 11, 1835, by Ralph Hurlbutt, J.P.	1	49
Loiza, m. Cyrus **WILLIAMS**, b. of Groton, Dec. 2, 1830, by John G. Wightman, Eld.	1	36
Lorenzo D., m. Prudence M. **CHAPMAN**, b. of Groton, May 11, 1852, by Rev. Nicholas T. Allen	1	93
Lucinda L., m. John A. **PERKINS**, b. of Groton, Apr. 21, 1833, by John G. Wightman, Eld.	1	43
Lucy Ann, d. [Robert, Jr. & Lucy], b. Feb. 28, 1825	3	31
Lucy C., Mrs., m. Benjamin **BURROWS**, b. of Groton, Nov. 10, 1844, by Rev. Simon E. Bailey	1	72
Luke, Jr. m, Lydia **DAVIS**, Dec. 12, 1715	1	116
Luke, s. Obadiah & Emblem, b. July 31, 1786	2	21
Lydia, d. Luke & Lydia, b. Dec. 18, 1722	1	116
Lydia, Mrs., m. Russell **PERKINS**, b. of Groton, May 6, 1832, by Ralph Hurlbutt, J.P.	1	40
Marina, d. [Jabez & Rebeckah], b. Dec. 30, 1802	2	49
Martha, of Groton, m. Daniel **THOMPSON**, of Norwich, July 5, 1829, by Joseph Durfey, J.P.	1	31
Marvin, d. [Jabez & Rebeckah], b. Apr. 21, 1804	2	49
Marvin, m. Fanny **MA[Y]NARD**, b. of Groton, Sept. 3, 1824, by John Brewster, J.P.	1	14
Mary, [d. John & Mary], b. Oct. 3, 1753	1	138
Mary, m. Joseph **WOODMANSEE**, b. of Groton, Oct. 3, 1830, by Ralph Hurlbutt, J.P.	1	35
Mary Ann, m. Elijah B. **MORGAN**, Mar. 6, 1832, in Stonington	3	35
Mary C., m. Jefferson **PERKINS**, b. of Groton, Jan. 25, 1835, by Nathan Daboll, J.P.	1	48
Meria, of Groton, m. Samuel **MITCHELL**, of Hartford, Ct., Jan. 26, 1827, by Nathan Daboll, J.P.	1	26
Moses, s. [Solomon & Deborah], b. Mar. 27, 1758	1	162
Moses, s. Jabez & Rebeckah, b. Aug. 21, 1786	2	10

	Vol.	Page
PERKINS, (cont.)		
Moses, s. [Jabez & Rebeckah], b. Aug. 23, 1786	2	49
Nabby, m. John **WOOD**, b. of Groton, June 21, 1784	2	55
Nancy, m. John **HILL**, b. of Groton, Mar. 14, 1830, by Nathan Daboll, J.P.	1	33
Nancy, m. Charles L. **PERKINS**, b. of Groton, June 12, 1831, by Nathan Daboll, J.P.	1	37
Nancy C., Mrs., of Groton, m. Lyman **ROGERS**, of Montville, Feb. 22, 1846, by Belton A. Copp, J.P.	1	75
Nathan W., s. [Robert, Jr. & Lucy], b. May 29, 1823	3	31
Noyes, of Stephenstown, N.Y., m. Caroline **GARD**, of Groton, Jan. 20, 1822, by Rufus Smith, J.P.	1	6
Obadiah, s. [Elnathan & Mary], b. Apr. 2, 1741	1	183
Oliver, m. Mary **CHESTER**, b. of Groton, Dec. 3, 1832, by Nathan Daboll, J.P.	1	41
Peabury, s. [Jabez & Rebeckah], b. May 24, 1788	2	49
Peter, twin with Prudence, s. [Solomon & Deborah], b. Feb. 9, 1762	1	162
Phebe J., m. Alfred H. **WILCOX**, Apr. 6, 1845, at Ezra Bailey's house, by Rev. R. Russell	1	73
Phinehas, Jr., m. Frances **CROMWELL**, b. of Groton, July 3, 1825, by John G. Wightman	1	17
Prudee, d. John & Mary, b. Oct. 19, 1748	1	138
Prudence, twin with Peter, d. [Solomon & Deborah], b. Feb. 9, 1762	1	162
Robert, Jr. m. Lucy Beers **ROB[B]INS**, b. of Groton, Nov. 11, 1821, by Rufus Smith, J.P.	1	5
Rufus, s. John & Mary, b. Sept. 28, 1743	1	138
Russell, Jr., m. Francina **BAILEY**, b. of Groton, Mar. 13, 1828, by Ralph Hurlbutt, J.P.	1	27
Russell, m. Mrs. Lydia **PERKINS**, b. of Groton, May 6, 1832, by Ralph Hurlbutt, J.P.	1	40
Russell, Jr., m. Charlotte **GRAY**, b. of Groton, Apr. 2, 1848, by Rev. Jared R. Avery	1	80
Sarah, [d. John & Mary], b. Mar. 9, 1756	1	138
Simeon, s. [Solomon & Deborah], b. Mar. 27, 1760	1	162
Sivilian, m. Lucy **POTTER**, b. of Groton, Aug. 9, 1832, by Rev. Roswell Burrows	1	40
Solomon, s. Luke & Lydia, b. Oct. 26, 1716; d. Dec. 9, 1725	1	116
Solomon, s. Luke & Lydia, b. July 16, 1729	1	116
Solomon, m. Deborah **LESTER**, Jan. 2, 1752	1	162
Solomon, s. Solomon & Deborah, b. Oct. 2, 1752	1	162
Solomon, Capt., d. Nov. 4, 1809	2	21
Theodie, d. Elnathan & Mary, b. Nov. 4, 1738	1	183
William, [s. John & Sarah], b. Aug. 13, 1718	1	120
William, m. Eunice **BILL**, b. of Groton, July 25, 1830, by Ralph Hurlbutt, J.P.	1	34
PERRY, Nehemiah D., of Colchester, m. Betsey A. **AVERY**, of Groton, Mar. 16, 1834, by John G. Wightman, Eld.	1	46
PHELPS, Harriet, of Stonington, m. Joseph **CRUMB**, of Groton, Apr. 29, 1838, by Rev. John G. Wightman	1	58
Isabel, m. Roswell **FISH**, Feb. 2, 1797	2	53
Peggy, of West Springfield, Mass., m. Lodowick **GALLUP**, of Groton, Feb. 28, 1799	2	69
PHILLIPS, Mary, m. Elnathan **PERKINS**, Dec. 13, 1737	1	183

	Vol.	Page
PIERCE, PEIRCE, Adame, [s. Ebenezer & Marg[a]ret], b. Sept. 12, 1717	1	114
Ebenezer, [s. Ebenezer & Marg[a]ret], b. May 28, 1719	1	114
Francis W., m. Frances M. **GUYANT**, b. of Groton, Jan. 26, 1851, by Rev. F. A. Slater	1	91
Jerusha, [s. Ebenezer & Marg[a]ret], b. Jan. 30, 1720	1	114
Margaret, [d. Ebenezer & Marg[a]ret], b. Apr. 8, 1723	1	114
Martha, d. Ebenezer & Marg[a]ret, b. Nov. 7, 1715	1	114
Permelia, m. Isaac **JACKLIN**, Nov. 27, 1845, by Rev. R. Russell	1	74
Stephen W., of Mass., m. Permelia **ROYCE**, of Groton, June 10, 1838, by Joseph Durfey, J.P.	1	58
PINCHION, Daniel, of Albany, Ga., m. Frances A. **TIFT**, of Groton, Sept. 26, 1844, by Nehemiah B. Cook	1	72
PIRCY, Mary, m. James **LOVEL[L]**, b. of Groton, Oct. 2, 1849, by Rev. Simon B. Bailey	1	85
PITCHER, Betsey, Mrs., of Groton, m. Griswold **HARRIS**, of New London, May 31, 1820, by Thomas Avery, J.P.	1	1
POOLER, Elizabeth, d. John & Eleoner, b. Feb. 1, 1708	1	116
Humphrey, [s. John & Eleoner], b. Apr. 7, 1714	1	116
John, m. Eleoner **DORE**, Feb. 20, 1707	1	116
John, [s. John & Eleoner], b. Aug. 7, 1710	1	116
Mary, [d. John & Eleoner], b. Aug. 5, 1715	1	116
POTTER, Abby, m. Abner B. **SPENCER**, Nov. 11, 1810	3	19
Abby, d. [Joseph & Mercy], b. Sept. 28, 1818	3	20
Abby M., m. Latham **ASHBEY**, b. of Groton, Jan. 5, 1836, by Ira R. Steward, Eld.	1	53
Abigail, d. [Thomas & Lavina], b. Nov. 27, 1787	3	20
Eliza, [d. Joseph & Mercy], b. Oct. 3, 1826	3	20
Ellen, [d. Joseph & Mercy], b. Sept. 5, 1828	3	20
Emeline, of Groton (Noank), m. John A. **FORSYTH**, of New London, Oct. 2, 1850, at Noank, by Rev. W[illia]m A. Smith	1	90
Hannah, d. [Thomas & Lavina], b. Sept. 6, 1785	3	20
Henrietta, [d. Thomas & Lavina], b. July 9, 1804	3	20
Heneretta, m. Luther **RATHBURN**, b. of Groton, Oct. 22, 1826, by Rev. Roswell Burrows	1	22
James, [s. Thomas & Lavina], b. July 3, 1806	3	20
James, s. James & Lucretia, b. Aug. 30, 1829	3	24
James, of Groton, m. Grace **COBB**, of New London, July 12, 1835, by John G. Wightman, Elder	1	51
James, m. Mrs. Grace **COBB**, of Groton, Feb. 24, 1842, by Caleb M. Williams, J.P.	1	65
Joseph, [s. Thomas & Lavina], b. Mar. 22, 1779	3	20
Joseph, s. [Joseph & Mercy], b. May 24, 1816	3	20
Lucy, d. [Joseph & Mercy], b. May 23, 1814	3	20
Lucy, m. Sivilian **PERKINS**, b. of Groton, Aug. 9, 1832, by Rev. Roswell Burrows	1	40
Nancy, m. Ebenezer **CLEVERLY**, b. of Groton, Nov. 15, 1846, by Nathan Daboll, J.P.	1	77
Prudence, [d. Joseph & Mercy], b. Dec. 23, 1823	3	20
Prudence, of Groton, m. Charles H. **CHESEBRO]UGH]**, of Stonington, Oct. 19, 1844, by Rev. Simon B. Bailey	1	72
Richard, [s. Thomas & Lavina], b. Oct. 7, 1800	3	20
Richard, m. Nancy **BURROWS**, b. of Groton, Sept. 19, 1830, by Rev. Erastus Denison	1	35

	Vol.	Page
POTTER, (cont.)		
Sally, [d. Thomas & Lavina], b. Feb. 10, 1797	3	20
Thomas, s. [Thomas & Lavina], b. Oct. 8, 1785	3	20
William, [s. Thomas & Lavina], b. May 24, 1775	3	20
William H., m. Bridget **RATHBURN**, b. of Groton, Apr. 4, 1842, by Ira R. Steward	1	66
POTTS, Abigail, [d. Jonathan & Mary], b. Sept. 11, 1715	1	109
Elizabeth, [d. Jonathan & Mary], b. Jan. 10, 1723	1	109
Jeremiah, of New London, m. Lydia **DANIELS**, of Groton, Apr. 7, 1834, by John G. Wightman, Eld.	1	46
Joanna, [d. Jonathan & Mary], b. Nov. 20, 1722	1	109
Jonathan, m. Mary **GEER**, Nov. 10, 1713	1	109
Mary, [d. Jonathan & Mary], b. Feb. 14, 1714	1	109
Mary S., of Groton, m. Orlando **SAY**, of New London, Apr. 17, 1837, by Joseph Durfey, J.P.	1	56
Rebeckah, [d. Jonathan & Mary], b. Dec. 6, 1717	1	109
William, [s. Jonathan & Mary], b. Oct. 13, 1719	1	109
POWERS, Avery, s. [Thomas & Hannah], b. Oct. 21, 1748	1	163
Elizabeth, d. Lawrence & Elizabeth, b. Jan. 18, 1733/4	1	143
Hannah, d. [Thomas & Hannah], b. Apr. 12, 1744	1	163
Hannah, m. Samuel **WILLIAMS**, 3d, b. of Groton, July 11, 1765	2	20
John, s. Lawrence & Elizabeth, b. Nov. 10, 1730	1	143
John, s. [Thomas & Hannah], b. Apr. 20, 1745	1	163
Lawrence, m. Elizabeth **STOGERS**, Feb. 11, 1729/30	1	143
Thomas, m. Hannah **MORGAN**, Apr. 3, 1740	1	163
Thomas, s. [Thomas & Hannah], b. Jan. 14, 1742	1	163
PRATT, William C., of Norwich, m. Mary **MAYNARD**, of Groton, Mar. 6, 1832, by Timothy Tuttle	1	39
PRAY, John, m. Hannah **FITCH**, b. of Groton, Aug. 20, 1848, by Rev. Simon B. Bailey	1	81
PRENTICE, Amos, s. Amos & Anna, b. Sept. 28, 1770	2	8
David N., m. Margaret **RATHBUN**, b. of Groton, Apr. 22, 1846, by Nehemiah B. Cooke	1	75
[E]unice, m. Christopher **AVERY**, Jr., Sept. 10, 1735	1	146
Jonas, s. Jonas & Amy, b. Oct. 27, 1768	1	159
Jonas, of Stonington, m. Amy **SMITH**, of Groton, Nov. 5, 1768, by Sam[ue]ll Prentice, J.P.	1	159
Mary Ann, of Stonington, m. Lynds **TINKER**, of Lyme, Dec. 8, 1833, by John G. Wightman, Eld.	1	45
Patty, of Stonington, m. Christopher **GALLUP**, of Groton, Apr. 13, 1792, by Jona[tha]n Palmer, Jr., J.P.	2	66
William, s. Amos & Anna, b. Aug. 23, 1772	2	8
PRICE, Mary, m. Bud[d]ington **KENYON**, b. of Groton, Mar. 7, 1827, by Rev. John G. Wightman	1	23
PRIDE, Lydia, of Preston, m. James **SPICER**, of Groton, Dec. 28, 1801	2	74
PROSSER, PROWSER, Fanny Maria, m. Isaac **PECKHAM**, b. of Groton, Nov. 27, 1823, by William Williams, J.P.	1	11
Lusana, m. Asa **GRAY**, b. of Groton, Feb. 15, 1821, by Stephen Billings, J.P.	1	3
Thomas, m. Anna **PECKHAM**, b. of Groton, Nov. 26, 1826, by Ralph Hurlbutt, J.P.	1	22
PUNDERSON, Cyrus, s. Ebenezer & Hannah, b. Apr. 17, 1737	1	146
Ebenezer, Rev., m. Hannah **MINER**, Aug. [ ], 1732	1	146

	Vol.	Page
PUNDERSON, (cont.)		
Ebenezer, s. Ebenezer & Hannah, b. Sept. 28, 1735	1	146
Ebenezer, m. Prudence **GEER**, Sept. 21, 1757	1	171
Hannah, d. Ebenezer & Hannah, b. June 16, 1733	1	146
Prudence, d. [Ebenezer & Prudence], b. July 28, 1758	1	171
PUTNAM, John M., m. Mary Ann **PACKER**, b. of Groton, July 8, 1841, by Rev. Benjamin C. Phelps	1	65
Mary Ann, m. W[illia]m Parkinson **HADLEY**, b. of Groton, Apr. 20, 1845, by Rev. Erastus Denison	1	72
QUIMBY, Phillip, d. Oct. 28, 1723	1	128
RAMSDELL, Albert N., of New London, m. Caroline A. **WHITE**, of Groton, Sept. 2, 1839, by Rev. Jared R. Avery	1	61
RANDALL, Adelia Mercy, d. Isaac & Adelia H., b. Sept. 1, 1832	3	35
Anna, m. James **LAMB**, Jan. 22, 1784	2	51
Betsey Ann, m. Albert D. **CULVER**, b. of Groton, Apr. 14, 1844, by Rev. Erastus Denison	1	71
Caroline M., m. Stephen **BUDDINGTON**, b. of Groton, Aug. 13, 1843, by Timothy Tuttle	1	69
Charles S., of Havre, France, m. Mary Ann **LATHAM**, of Groton, Oct. 2, 1836, by Ira R. Steward	1	55
Eliza, m. Simeon **FISH**, Oct. 15, 1823, by Roswell Burrows, Min.	1	10
Elizabeth Frances, d. [Isaac & Adelia H.], b. Mar. 3, 1834	3	35
Frances, of Groton, m. W[illia]m **SMITH**, of Rochester, Aug. 5, 1839, by Ira R. Steward	1	61
Frank, m. Betsey **FREEMAN**, Sept. 28, 1851, by Rev. Reuben Palmer	1	92
Hannah T., of Stonington, m. Jesse **BREED**, of Litchfield, July 3, 1825, by Timothy Tuttle	1	17
Isaac, of Hartford, m. Adelia H. **MINER**, of Groton, Dec. 20, 1831, by Timothy Tuttle	1	38
Jedediah, s. [Isaac & Adelia H.], b. Sept. 3, 1835	3	35
John Frederic, s. [Isaac & Adelia H.], b. Sept. 13, 1839	3	35
Julia Ann, d. [Isaac & Adelia H.], b. Apr. 18, 1837	3	35
Mary, m. James **ADAMS**, b. of Groton, Aug. 3, 1756, in Westerly, by Silas Greenman, J.P. Intention of marriage signed by Ebenezer Avery, J.P.	1	167
Mary Ann, m. Roswell S. **BURROWS**, b. of Groton, Jan. 16, 1822, by Roswell Burrows, Elder	1	6
Nathan, s. [Isaac & Adelia H.], b. Mar. 11, 1841	3	35
Patent, of Stonington, m. Adeline **WELLS**, of Groton, Nov. 26, 1835, by Nathan Daboll, J.P.	1	52
Polly, m. Josiah **GALLUP**, Nov. 11, 1792	2	45
Preserved*, m. Lemuel **DARROW**, Sept. 19, 1751 (*Preserved, wid. of Capt. Jonathan)	2	9
Stephen, Jr., of Long Island, m. Martha **MERRILL**, of Groton, Jan. 4, 1821, by Ralph Hurlbutt, J.P.	1	2
RANSOM, Nathaniel, m. Catherine D. **LATHAM**, Oct. 13, 1845, by Rev. Henry R. Knapp. Recorded Aug. 6, 1895.	1	98
Nathaniel, m. Catharine D. **LATHAM**, b. of Groton, Dec. 18, 1845, by Rev. H. R. Knapp	1	83
RATHBURN, RATHBONE, RATHBUN, Alden, m. Hannah L. **AVERY**, b. of Groton, June 13, 1838, by Ira R. Steward	1	59
Benjamin, s. [Samuel & Abigail], b. May 8, 1801	3	22
Benjamin, m. Eliza **LATHAM**, Oct. 3, 1824, by Rev. Roswell Burrows	1	14

	Vol.	Page
RATHBURN, RATHBONE, RATHBUN, (cont.)		
Benjamin Franklin, s. [Benjamin & Eliza], b. May 6, 1829	3	18
Betsey, d. [Samuel & Abigail], b. Apr. 8, 1796	3	22
Betsey, m. Joseph **FISH**, b. of Groton, Sept. 29, 1824, by Gideon B. Perry, Minister	1	15
Bridget, m. William H. **POTTER**, b. of Groton, Apr. 4, 1842, by Ira R. Steward	1	66
Calvin, s. [Samuel & Abigail], b. Dec. 6, 1816	3	22
Desire, d. [Samuel & Abigail], b. Sept. 15, 1800	3	22
Desire, m. William E. **CHESTER**, b. of Groton, Mar. 23, 1842, by Caleb M. Williams, J.P.	1	66
Elisha, Jr., m. Wealthy Ann **WOLF**, Aug. 18, 1830, by Rev. Erastus Denison	1	34
Eliza J., m. James W. **DOUGLASS**, b. of Groton, June 4, 1848, by Nathan Daball, J.P.	1	80
Eliza Jane, d. [Benjamin & Eliza], b. July 13, 1826	3	18
Frances, m. Harlem **BAKER**, b. of Noank, Dec. 23, 1849, in Noank, by Rev. William A. Smith, of Noank	1	87
Frances Sabrina, d. [Benjamin & Eliza], b. Sept. 10, 1827	3	18
Griswold P., m. Eleanor **PACKER**, b. of Groton, Oct. 3, 1830, by Rev. Erastus Denison	1	35
Hannah, m. Simeon W. **ASHLEY***, b. of Groton, Sept. 9, 1830, by Rev. Erastus Denison (***ASHBEY**)	1	35
Hannah, Mrs., m. Gurdon **ALLEN**, b. of Groton, Sept. 19, 1842, by Ira R. Steward	1	67
Henrietta, d. [Samuel & Abigail], b. Dec. 13, 1807	3	22
Henrietta, m. William E. **CHESTER**, b. of Groton, July 10, 1831, by Rev. Roswell Burrows	1	37
John, s. [Samuel & Abigail], b. Nov. 21, 1803	3	22
John, of New London, m. Almira **BAILEY**, of Groton, Apr. 19, 1846, by Rev. Simon B. Bailey	1	75
John S., m. Lucy Ann **PACKER**, b. of Groton, Sept. 7, 1825, by Asa Fitch, J.P.	1	18
Joshua, m. Mary **WHITEMAN**, Feb. 5, 1723/4, by Eph[rai]m Woodbridge	1	116
Lathan, s. [Samuel & Abigail], b. Dec. 8, 1809	3	22
Latham, m. Eleoner Jane **WILBUR**, b. of Groton, Oct. 27, 1835, by Rev. Roswell Burrows	1	52
Lucretia, d. Capt. Elisha, m. Ransford **ASHBEY**, b. of Groton, Aug. 23, 1824, by Rev. Roswell Burrows	1	13
Lucy, m. George B. **PACKER**, b. of Groton, Oct. 15, 1851, by Washington Munger	1	92
Lucy A., m. Gilbert B. **WILCOX**, b. of Groton, Dec. 27, 1846, by Rev. Simon B. Bailey	1	77
Lucy Ann, d. [Luther & Henrietta], b. Oct. 6, 1829	3	21
Luther, s. [Samuel & Abigail], b. Sept. 8, 1805	3	22
Luther, m. Heneretta **POTTER**, b. of Groton, Oct. 22, 1826, by Rev. Roswell Burrows	1	22
Luther, m. Mary **CHIPMAN**, b. of Groton, July 3, 1836, by Rev. Ira R. Steward	1	54
Margaret, m. David N. **PRENTICE**, b. of Groton, Apr. 22, 1846, by Nehemiah B. Cooke	1	75
Mary E., m. Henry S. **STARK**, b. of Groton, Aug. 10, 1843, by Nehemiah B. Cooke	1	69

	Vol.	Page
RATHBURN, RATHBONE, RATHBUN, (cont.)		
Nancy, d. [Samuel & Abigail], b. Oct. 25, 1798	3	22
Nathan Warren, s. [Luther & Henrietta], b. Sept. 10, 1827	3	21
Samuel, s. [Samuel & Abigail], b. May 8, 1813	3	22
Samuel, m. Phebe A. **PACKER**, b. of Groton, Nov. 1, 1835, by Rev. Ira R. Steward	1	52
Wealthy Ann, Mrs., m. Dan G. **BAILEY**, b. of Groton, Nov. 28, 1833, by Rev. Erastus Denison	1	45
William, s. [Samuel & Abigail], b. Dec. 4, 1811	3	22
William, m. Harriet **RICE**, b. of Groton, Feb. 17, 1833, by Rev. Roswell Burrows	1	43
REED, READ, REID, Dolly, m. Giles **BAILEY**, b. of Groton, Oct. 21, 1821, by Rev. John G. Wightman	1	4
Emeline, m. Randall **HOLDREDGE**, b. of Groton, Mar. 25, 1832, by John Spicer, J.P.	1	39
Hannah, of Groton, m. William R. **BAGSLEY**, of St. Helena, Aug. 23, 1840, by Rev. John G. Wightman	1	63
Hannah, m. John H. **KNAPP**, b. of Groton, Mar. 31, 1850, by Rev. H. R. Knapp	1	88
James, of New York, m. Rebecca **TUFT**, of Groton, June 26, 1825, by Roswell Fish, J.P.	1	17
Jeremiah, of Preston, m. Hannah A. **MITCHELL**, of Groton, Aug. 12, 1849, by Rev. Levi Walker	1	85
Judith, of Norwich, m. William **GALLUP**, of Groton, June 9, 1752, in Norwich, by Rev. Jabez White	1	167
Lucy, of Groton, m. Antonna **MAGILL**, of Cape Deverd Islands, June 13, 1847, by Nathan Daboll, J.P.	1	79
Mary, m. Erastus **BALDWIN**, b. of Groton, Jan. 28, 1821, by Ralph Hurlbutt, J.P.	1	3
Mary Ann, m. Robert **WILCOX**, b. of Groton, Apr. 4, 1824, by William Williams, J.P.	1	12
Olive, of Norwich, m. Robert **ROSE**, of Groton, Aug. 10, 1772, by Elisha Lathrop, J.P.	2	21
Phebe, of Groton, m. Richard **BLACKSTONE**, of S. Atlantic Ocean, June 28, 1838, by Rev. John G. Wightman	1	59
Rebecca, Mrs., of Groton, m. Edward **SANDS**, a European, June 1, 1836, by Roswell Fish, J.P.	1	54
Sally, m. John **BINKS**, b. now residing in Groton, June 13, 1847, by Nathan Daboll, J.P.	1	79
Sarah, m. John **CHESTER**, b. of Groton, Aug. 17, 1829, by Joseph Durfey, J.P.	1	31
REEVE, Nancy, m. George **BABCOCK**, Mar. 15, 1818	2	83
REMICK, Isaac, d. May 8, 1724, ae. 19 y.	1	125
RENHAM, Anna, m. Seabury **BRAMAN**, b. of Groton, Jan. 11, 1852, by Rev. Nicholas T. Allen	1	93
REYNOLDS, RENOLDS, Alfred, of Groton, m. Almira **GAVITT**, July 5, 1829, by John G. Wightman, Eld.	1	31
Ambrose, of Ledyard, m. Emeline **NILES**, of Groton, Mar. 22, 1841, by Rev. Erastus Denison	1	64
Anna, of Preston, m. Thomas **BEN[N]ET**, of New London, Oct. 29, 1713, by Salmon Treat	1	109
Elmira, m. Allen T. **BRAMAN**, b. of Groton, Aug. [ ], 1837, by John G. Wightman, Elder	1	56

	Vol.	Page
REYNOLDS, RENOLDS, (cont.)		
Evan, of R.I., m. Frances **WELLS**, of Groton, Nov. 17, 1822, by John G. Wightman	1	8
Henry, m. Esther **EDGECOMB**, b. of Groton, Sept. 4, 1827, by John G. Wightman, Eld.	1	24
Jonathan, Jr., m. Eliza **FITCH**, b. of Groton, Nov. 3, 1833, by Ira R. Steward, Minister	1	45
Nathan C., of Griswold, m. Almira **STERRY**, of Groton, Sept. 16, 1827, by Ralph Hurlbutt, J.P.	1	24
Samuel, a European, now residing in New London, m. Wid. Nancy **SWEET**, of Groton, Apr. 23, 1827, by Roswell Fish, J.P.	1	26
Susannah, m. Thomas **HARTLEY**, Oct. 24, 1830, by Rev. Erastus Denison	1	35
RHODES, Caroline, m. John **WESLEY**, Apr. 18, 1841, at Portersville in Groton, by James Gallup, J.P.	1	64
RICE, Abishai, s. Gershom & Elizabeth, b. Oct. 16, 1701	1	112
Elizabeth, d. Gershom & Elizabeth, b. Oct. 20, 1798[sic]1698	1	112
Harriet, m. William **RATHBURN**, b. of Groton, Feb. 17, 1833, by Rev. Roswell Burrows	1	43
Joseph W., of Stonington, m. Mary **ELDREDGE**, of Groton, Aug. 5, 1804, by Rev. Christ[opher] Avery	2	68
Joseph William, s. [Joseph W. & Harry], b. July 20, 1805	2	68
Matthais, s. Gershom & Elizabeth, b. Jan. 26, 1707/8	1	112
Ruth, d. Gershom & Elizabeth, b. Apr. 11, 1710	1	112
Sarah, d. Gershom & Elizabeth, b. Feb. 9, 1703	1	112
RICHARDS, Lydia, m. Isaac **LAMB**, June 12, 1733	1	148
RICHMOND, George, m. Lury **HEM[P]STEAD**, Aug. 4, 1828, by Roswell Fish, J.P.	1	28
RIDENT, William M., of Quincy, Mass., m. Mary H. **BAKER**, of Pembroke, Mass., July 22, 1838, by Rev. Nathan Paine	1	60
ROACH, Delia A., m. Daniel **MAIN**, b. of Ledyard, Oct. 8, 1838, by Rev. John G. Wightman	1	60
Nathaniel, m. Lydia **BAKER**, June 4, 1761	2	17
Thomas, s. Nathaniel & Lydia, b. Apr. 15, 1762	2	17
ROATH, Eliza, of Stonington, m. George **FREEMAN**, of Groton, Jan. 27, 1850, by Nathan Daboll, J.P.	1	87
Elizabeth, d. Thomas & Sarah, b. Oct. 12, 1726; d. Sept. 20, 1727	1	129
Hannah, d. Thomas & Sarah, b. Apr. 26, 1720	1	129
Huldah, of Norwich, m. Elihu **SPICER**, of Groton, Apr. 30, 1850, by Rev. Nicholas T. Allen	1	88
Lois, d. Thomas & Sarah, b. Oct. 11, 1728	1	129
Nathaniel, s. Thomas & Sarah, b. June 2, 1722	1	129
Sarah, d. Thomas & Sarah, b. Jan. 19, 1730	1	129
Thomas, m. Sarah **CHAPPELL**, Feb. 26, 1719	1	129
Thomas, d. Jan. 3, 1730/31	1	129
ROBBINS, ROBINS, Daniel, of Exeter, m. Mary **TYLER**, of Groton, June 20, 1760	2	28
Daniel, [s. Daniel & Mary], b. Dec. 8, 1763	2	28
Davenport, [s. Daniel & Mary], b. June 14, 1773	2	28
Dolly, [d. Daniel & Mary], b. Dec. 8, 1761	2	28
Job, [s. Daniel & Mary], b. Feb. 21, 1770	2	28
Lucy Beers, m. Robert **PERKINS**, Jr., b. of Groton, Nov. 11, 1821, by Rufus Smith, J.P.	1	5

	Vol.	Page
ROBBINS, ROBINS, (cont.)		
Polly Washington, [d. Daniel & Mary], b. May 15, 1778	2	28
Whitefield, [s. Daniel & Mary], b. Mar. 30, 1776	2	28
William, [s. Daniel & Mary], b. Dec. 20, 1768	2	28
William, Jr., m. Mary Ann **SHAW**, b. of Groton, July 12, 1840, by Rev. Erastus Denison	1	63
ROBERTSON, Mary C., of New London, m. Willis **CLARKE**, of Providence, R.I., Mar. 28, 1832, by Rev. Abel McEwen, of New London	1	39
ROBINSON, Abial, m. Samuel **CUNNINGHAM**, May 8, 1755 (Changed to 1725 by L.B.B.)	1	172
Mary, [d. William], b. Mar. 9, 1720	1	101
William, [s. William], b. Apr. 24, 1722	1	101
ROCKWELL, Amasa, of Mass., m. Jenette **GARD**, of Groton, July 20, 1826, by Nathan Daboll, J.P.	1	21
Amasa, Jr., s. Amasa & Jennette, b. Sept. 2, 1827	3	35
Eureta P., d. [Amasa & Jennette], b. Jan. 8, 1839	3	35
Henry H., s. [Amasa & Jennette], b. Feb. 7, 1831	3	35
Henry H., m. Sabrina L. **SPICER**, Sept. 12, 1852, by Rev. Nicholas T. Allen	1	94
Sarah Jane, d. [Amasa & Jennette], b. Jan. 28, 1843	3	35
RODMAN, Christopher G., m. Letilia F. **CHAPMAN**, b. of Preston, Sept. 24, 1833, by John Brewster, J.P.	1	45
ROGERS, RODGERS, Alexander, s. [John & Katharine], b. Jan. 14, 1800	2	63
Azubah, m. Obadiah **BAILEY**, Jr., Dec. 9, 1747	1	174
Bathsheba, m. Robert **STODDARD**, Jr., Dec. 21, 1727	1	134
Ebenezer, m. Grace **GALLUP**, b. of Groton, Jan. 8, 1824, by Rev. Roswell Burrows	1	12
Eliza, d. [Zabdial & Fanny], b. Apr. 27, 1792	2	35
Frances A., m. Henry N. **SPENCER**, b. of Groton, Oct. 1, 1843, by Ira R. Steward	1	70
Harriet, of Bridgeport, m. David H. **STARR**, of Groton, Dec. 10, 1837, by Joseph Durfey, J.P.	1	57
Harriet, m. Robert **PALMER**, b. of Groton, Oct. 25, 1845, by Rev. Simon B. Bailey	1	74
Henry, formerly of Waterford, m. Amey **WATROUS**, of Groton, Feb. 8, 1835, by Zephaniah Watrous	1	49
Isaac C., m. Anna **BAILEY**, b. of Groton, Oct. 12, 1829, by Ralph Hurlbutt, J.P.	1	32
James, s. [John & Katharine], b. Jan. 1, 1802	2	63
James Stevens, s. [Stephen & Mary], b. May 13, 1825	3	7
John, m. Katharine **LATHAM**, of Groton, Jan. 20, 1796	2	63
John, s. [John & Katharine], b. Dec. 12, 1796	2	63
Jonathan, m. Mary Ann **CULVER**, b. of Groton, Jan. 16, 1825, by John Brewster, J.P.	1	16
Lyman, m. Almira **TURNER**, b. of Groton, Sept. 9, 1821, by Amos A. Niles, J.P.	1	4
Lyman, m. Nancy Maria **TURNER**, b. of Groton, Apr. 27, 1835, by John G. Wightman, Eld.	1	50
Lyman, of Montville, m. Mrs. Nancy C. **PERKINS**, of Groton, Feb. 22, 1846, by Belton A. Copp, J.P.	1	75
Mary, m. Stephen **ROGERS**, Mar. 2, 1820, by Thomas Avery, Esq.	3	7
Mary, m. Joseph S. **ALLYN**, b. of Groton, Jan. 11, 1824, by Ralph Hurlbutt, J.P.	1	12

	Vol.	Page
ROGERS, RODGERS, (cont.)		
Orlando, of New London, m. Polly M. **WATROUS**, of Groton, Aug. 16, 1847, by Nathan Daball, J.P.	1	79
Paul Allen Comstock, of Waterford, m. Lucy Ann **STARR**, of Groton, Jan. 26, 1840, by Rev. Jared R. Avery	1	62
Stephen, m. Mary **ROGERS**, Mar. 2, 1820, by Thomas Avery, Esq.	3	7
Stephen Abigail, d. Stephen & Mary, b. Apr. 27, 1822	3	7
Theophilus, s. [Zabdial & Fanny], b. Nov. 6, 1794	2	35
Ursula M., m. Simeon **CHAPMAN**, b. of Groton, Mar. 14, 1824, by Timothy Tuttle	1	12
Zabdial, m. Fanny **ELDREDGE**, Feb. 27, 1791	2	35
Zabdial, s. [Zabdial & Fanny], b. Oct. 2, 1793	2	35
ROSE, Dorcas, m. Nathaniel **BELLOWS**, Nov. 15, 1704	1	110
Johan[n]ah, m. Edward **AVERY**, June 3, 1699	1	111
Loice, d. Lydia, b. Mar. 20, 1734	1	131
Mary, m. Henry **PELTON**, Apr. 29, 1712	1	118
Mary, m. Henry **PELTON**, Apr. 29, 1712	1	133
Robert, of Groton, m. Olive **READ**, of Norwich, Aug. 10, 1772, by Elisha Lathrop, J.P.	2	21
ROSS, James, of Ledyard, m. Margaret **HALEY**, of Groton, June 2, 1840, by Rev. John G. Wightman	1	63
Jesse, s. Jesse & May Daboll, b. Nov. 22, 1787	2	17
ROUSE, Benjamin, of Stonington, m. Eunice **GALLUP**, of Groton, Mar. 16, 1823, by William Williams, J.P.	1	9
Harriet Cornelia, d. Benjamin & Eunice, b. July 7, 1826	3	11
ROWLAND, Eldredge Pierre, m. Emma Ann **WOLF**, b. of Groton, July 25, 1841, by Rev. Erastus Denison	1	65
Maria, of Groton, m. George **MOON**, of New York, Aug. 15, 1833, by Ira R. Stewart, Eld.	1	44
ROYCE, Parmelia, of Groton, m. Stephen W. **PEIRCE**, of Mass., June 10, 1838, by Joseph Durfey, J.P.	1	58
RUSSELL, Mary M., m. Frederick C. **BEMAN**, Aug. 9, 1846, by Rev. R. Russell	1	76
RYAN, Thomas, m. Mary A. **BROWN**, b. residing in Groton, Apr. 30, 1838, by Nathan Daboll, J.P.	1	58
SALTER, W[illia]m, of Stonington, m. Lucy R. **STRONG**, of Groton, Mar. 25, 1851, by Rev. Nicholas T. Allen	1	91
SAMBER, Richard, of Philadelphia, m. Huldah **MILLFIELD**, of Groton, July 19, 1832, by Rev. Erastus Denison	1	41
SAMON, SAMANS, Bial, m. Hannah **ALGER**, Mar. 28, 1715/6	1	114
Hannah, d. Bial & Hannah, b. Jan. 24, 1717	1	114
Hannah, m. Caleb **LAMB**, May 12, 1738	1	168
Mary, m. James **BA[I]LEY**, Jr., Oct. 20, 1730	1	144
SANDS, Edward, a European, m. Mrs. Rebecca **REED**, of Groton, June 1, 1836, by Roswell Fish, J.P.	1	54
SARLES, Catharine, of Groton, m. Donald **FISHER**, of Norwich, Nov. 24, 1827, by Elisha Brewster, J.P.	1	26
SATTERLEE, SATTERLY, SATERLEY, Abigail, d. William & Ann, b. Apr. 12, 1720	1	136
Ann, d. William & Ann, b. May 16, 1718	1	136
Benedick, s. William & Anna, b. Aug. 11, 1714	1	136
Dwight Alden, s. [Elisha & Sally], b. Apr. 17, 1814	2	82
Elisha, m. Sally **AVERY**, b. of Groton, Apr. 3, 1796	2	82

	Vol.	Page
SATTERLEE, SATTERLY, SATERLEY, (cont.)		
Elisha, m. Hester **STODDARD**, b. of Groton, Aug. 28, 1825, by Ralph Hurlbutt, J.P.	1	18
Elisha Avery, s. [Elisha & Sally], b. Nov. 10, 1800	2	82
Jemima, d. William & Mary, b. May 14, 1737	1	174
John, s. William & Mary, b. May 14, 1737	1	136
Jonas, s. [Elisha & Sally], b. Mar. 28, 1803	2	82
Julian, d. [Elisha & Sally], b. Mar. 15, 1808	2	82
Lucy, d. William & Ann, b. Jan. 6, 1725/6	1	136
Lydia, d. [Elisha & Sally], b. Nov. 8, 1798	2	82
Lydia, m. Samuel G. **ALLYN**, June 17, 1821, by Stephen Meech, J.P.	1	3
Mary, d. William & Ann, b. June 6, 1722	1	136
Rebeckah, d. William & Ann, b. Mar. 1, 1723/4	1	136
Susan, d. [Elisha & Sally], b. June 25, 1805	2	82
Susan, of Groton, m. Frank **KIMBALL**, of Preston, Mar. 19, 1826, by John Brewster, J.P.	1	20
William, m. Ann **AVERY**, Sept. 6, 1711	1	136
William, s. William & Ann, b. Nov. 7, 1712	1	136
SAUNDERS, Albert, of Groton, m. Nancy D. **WILLIAMS**, of Stonington, Nov. 10, 1841, in Stonington, by Ira R. Steward	1	65
SAVANEY, Charles P., m. Hannah E. **CROMWELL**, of Groton, Jan. 18, 1849, by Rev. H. R. Knapp	1	84
SAWYER, Alva, m. Harriet **BROWN**, Aug. 29, 1850, by Rev. W. Munger	1	89
Ann E., m. Charles C. **SISSON**, b. of Groton, Aug. 24, 1851, by W. Munger	1	92
Asa, of Stonington, m. Lucy P. **ASHLEY**, of Groton, Aug. 29, 1832, by Rev. Roswell Burrows	1	41
Asa, m. Phebe **WILBUR**, b. of Groton, June 11, 1840, by Ira R. Steward	1	63
Benjamin, m. Betsey **PACKER**, b. of Groton, July 9, 1826, by Asa Fitch, J.P.	1	21
Elcey, m. John H. **SAWYER**, b. of Groton, Aug. 24, 1825, by Asa Fish, J.P.	1	17
Frances J., m. Thomas E. **WOLF**, b. of Groton, Aug. 1, 1852, at Mystic River, by Rev. Franklin A. Slater	1	94
James, s. James & Mary, b. May 5, 1797	2	12
Jeremiah N., of Stonington, m. Emeline **KELLEY**, of Groton, July 27, 1826, by Roswell Fish, J.P.	1	22
John H., m. Elcey **SAWYER**, b. of Groton, Aug. 24, 1825, by Asa Fish, J.P.	1	17
Mary Ann, m. Asa **ASHBEY**, b. of Noank, Mar. 25, 1850, in Noank, by Rev. William A. Smith	1	88
Nancy B., of Portersville, Groton, m. Charles **BRIGGS**, of Pembroke, N.Y., Aug. 13, 1845, by Rev. H. R. Knapp	1	74
Phebe, m. George **ELDREDGE**, Jr., b. of Groton, Sept. 6, 1825, by Asa Fitch, J.P.	1	18
Thomas J., of Stonington, m. Mary **PALMER**, of Groton, June 19, 1832, by Rev. Roswell Burrows	1	40
Winthrop, m. Allice **BRIA**, b. of Groton, Aug. 5, 1821, by Rev. Roswell Burrows	1	3
SAY, Orlando, of New London, m. Mary S. **POTTS**, of Groton, Apr. 17, 1837, by Joseph Durfey, J.P.	1	56
SCHRIDER, John, of New York, m. Eunice **DODGE**, of Stonington, Dec. 8, 1839, by Rev. John G. Wightman	1	62

	Vol.	Page
SCOTT, Amelia, d. [Zebadiah & Phebe], b. June 26, 1748	1	185
Amelia, d. Zebadiah & Phebe, b. June 26, 1748	2	95
David, m. Lydia **WATROUS**, b. of Groton, Nov. 26, 1820, by Amos Watrous	1	2
David, m. Mary **BURROWS**, Apr. 23, 1848, by Rev. H. R. Knapp	1	84
John, s. Zedediah & Phebe, b. Dec. 8, 1746	1	84
John, s. Zebediah & Phebe, b. Dec. 8, 1746	2	95
Nancy, of Franklin, Ct., m. Joseph **LATHAM**, 3d, of Groton, July 3, 1828, by John G. Wightman	1	28
SEABURY, Caleb, s. Samuel & Abigail, b. Feb. 27, 1728/9	1	137
David, [s. John & Elizabeth], b. Jan. 16, 1699	1	103
David, s. Nathaniel & Michal, b. Mar. 21, 1738	1	148
Easter, d. John & Est[h]er, b. May 4, 1734	1	147
Elizabeth, [d. John & Est[h]er], b. July 4, 1738	1	147
John, m. Elizabeth **ALDEN**, of Duxbury, Mass., Dec. 9, 1697	1	103
John, s. [John & Elizabeth], b. Nov. 25, 1700; d. Nov. 25, 1700	1	103
John, [s. John & Elizabeth], b. May 22, 1704	1	103
John, s. John & Est[h]er, b. Jan. 12, 1735/6	1	147
Mary, [s. (*dau*) John & Elizabeth], b. Nov. 11, 1708	1	103
Mary, m. Jonathan **STARR**, Jr., Oct. 10, 1728	1	137
Nathaniel, [s. John & Elizabeth], b. July 31, 1720	1	103
Nathaniel, s. Nathaniel & Michal, b. Nov. 20, 1736	1	148
Patience, [d. John & Elizabeth], b. May 5, 1702	1	103
Patience, m. Joseph **LATHAM**, Nov. 28, 1722	1	124
Samuel, [s. John & Elizabeth], b. July 8, 1706	1	103
Samuel, s. Samuel & Abigail, b. Nov. 30, 1729	1	137
Sarah, [d. John & Elizabeth], b. Mar. 16, 1710	1	103
Sarah, of Groton, m. William **MORGAN**, of Norwich, Sept. 24, 1747	1	117
SEARLES, see under **SARLES**		
SEELEY, John, of Holesbrough, Me., m. Cornelia **NILES**, of Groton, May 5, 1850, by Rev. W[illia]m C. Walker	1	89
SEWALL, Henry, Jr., m. Grace **HALLAHAN**, now residing in Stonington, Sept. 16, 1834, by Rev. John G. Wightman	1	48
SHALER, Julia Ann, of Colchester, m. William **GLASSENDER**, of Groton, Aug. 24, 1850, by Rev. Jared R. Avery	1	89
SHANE, Lucy, of Groton, m. Horatio N. **AMSBURY**, of Stonington, Mar. 9, 1836, by Elias Brown, J.P.	1	53
SHARP, John, m. Sabra **NEWBURY**, b. of Waterford, Sept. 17, 1826, by Ralph Hurlbutt, J.P.	1	22
SHAW, Lydia, of Stonington, m. Perez **CHIPMAN**, of Groton, Feb. 16, 1840, in Stonington, by Ira R. Steward	1	62
Mary Ann, m. John **FELLOWS**, b. of Groton, Feb. 10, 1830, by Nathan Daboll, J.P.	1	33
Mary Ann, m. William **ROBBINS**, Jr., b. of Groton, July 12, 1840, by Rev. Erastus Denison	1	63
SHEALES, [see also **SHOLES**], Deborah, [d. John], b. Aug. 6, 1709	1	120
Elizabeth, [d. John], b. Oct. 15, 1706	1	120
Hannah, [d. John], b. Jan. 4, 1704	1	120
Hutcheson, [s. John], b. Nov. 13, 1720	1	120
John, [s. John], b. Oct. 1, 1714	1	120
Lucretia, [d. John], b. June 7, 1724	1	120
Mary, [d. John], b. Mar. 23, 1718	1	120
Sarah, [d. John], b. Apr. 15, 1712	1	120

	Vol.	Page
SHELDON, Barber, of Richmond, R.I., m. Sabra **MAYNARD**, of Groton, Mar. 16, 1828, by Elisha Brewster, J.P.	1	27
SHERD, Peter, m. Sally Louisa **CHIPMAN**, June 24, 1831, by Joseph Durfey, J.P.	1	37
SHERLEY, Albert, of Stonington, m. Dianah **FRANKLIN**, of Groton, Feb. 18, 1838, by Caleb M. Williams, J.P.	1	57
SHOLES, [see also **SHEALES**], Aaron, s. [Hutchinson & Temperance], b. Oct. 5, 1754	1	174
Abel, s. John, Jr. & Lydia, b. Apr. 15, 1735	1	150
Abel, s. [Jonathan & Lydia], b. Nov. 20, 1792	2	62
Betsey, d. [Jonathan & Lydia], b. Dec. 26, 1794	2	62
Betsey Clark, [d. Jabez & Sarah], b. Dec. 31, 1799	2	62
Cary Wheeler, s. [Hutchinson & Temperance], b. Jan. 28, 1742/3	1	174
Christopher, s. Levy & Elizabeth, b. Mar. 14, 1765	2	14
Cyrus, s. [Hurchinson & Temperance], b. Feb. 2, 1748	1	174
Deborah, m. Christopher **NUTON**, Feb. 8, 1732	1	143
Deborah, d. [John & Lois], b. Apr. 17, 1770	2	62
Elizabeth, d. John & Lydia, b. July 6, 1739	1	150
Eunice, d. [Jonathan & Lydia], b. Apr. 2, 1800; d. May 9, 1801	2	62
Fanny, d. [John & Lois], b. Sept. 20, 1776	2	62
George W., s. [Jonathan & Lyida], b. Oct. 13, 1797	2	62
George W., m. Cynthia **MAYNOR**, b. of Groton, May 4, 1835, by Ralph Hurlbutt, J.P.	1	50
Giles, s. [John & Lois], b. Sept. 2, 1778; d. Jan. 10, 1780	2	62
Giles, s. [Jonathan & Lydia], b. Apr. 9, 1791	2	62
Hutchinson, m. Temperance **BAILEY**, May 28, 1741	1	174
Jabez, s. John & Lydia, b. Dec. 24, 1753	1	150
Jabez, m. Sarah **BAKER**, b. of Groton, June 5, 1791	2	62
James, s. [Stanton & Abigail], b. Feb. 19, 1796	2	65
John, s. John & Lydia, b. Aug. 30, 1742	1	150
John, m. Lois **DILL**, b. of Groton, May 12, 1764	2	62
John, f. of John & Jabez, d. July 13, 1799	2	62
Jonathan, s. John & Lydia, b. Mar. 13, 1744	1	150
Jonathan, s. Levy & Elizabeth, b. Sept. 28, 1766	2	14
Jonathan, 2d, s. [John & Lois], b. July 3, 1768	2	62
Jonathan, m. Lydia **SHOLES**, b. of Groton, Dec. 15, 1790	2	62
Joseph, s. John & Lyida, b. Feb. 6, 1747	1	150
Joseph, s. Levy & Elizabeth, b. June 17, 1771	2	14
Levi, s. [Hutchinson & Temperance], b. Apr. 4, 1746	1	174
Levy, m. Elizabeth **STODDARD**, b. of Groton, May 10, 1764	2	14
Lucy, d. [Stanton & Abigail], b. Dec. 29, 1797	2	65
Lydia, m. Jonathan **SHOLES**, b. of Groton, Dec. 15, 1790	2	62
Mahala, d. Stanton & Abigail, b. May 24, 1794	2	65
Mary, m. John **PERKINS**, Jr., July 6, 1737	1	138
Richard, s. [Jabez & Sarah], b. June 25, 1792; d. June 22, 1794	2	62
Sarah, d. John & Lydia, b. Feb. 2, 1736	1	150
Sarah, 2d, d. [John & Lois], b. Feb. 12, 1767	2	62
Stanton, s. Abel & Lucy, b. Mar. 14, 1772; m. Abigail **AVERY**, b. of Groton, Mar. 14, 1793	2	65
Stanton, s. [Stanton & Abigail], b. Dec. 13, 1799	2	65
Temperance, d. Levy & Elizabeth, b. Mar. 7, 1769	2	14
William, s. [John & Lois], b. Apr. 2, 1773	2	62

	Vol.	Page
SHORT, John, of New York, m. Emeline **LESTER**, of Groton, Mar. 23, 1828, by Ralph Hurlbutt, J.P.	1	27
Margaret, m. Isaac **SPICER**, b. of Groton, Sept. 28, 1823, by Timothy Tuttle	1	10
SHORTMAN, Phebe, [s. Abigail], b. Dec. 28, 1781	1	169
William, [s. Abigail], b. Apr. 14, 1776	1	169
SIGNIOUS, John S., of Charleston, S.C., m. Mary **NILES**, of Stonington, June 17, 1832, by Rev. Erastus Denison	1	40
SINGLETON, William E., of New London, m. Mary J. **NILES**, of Groton, June 19, 1842, by Ira R. Steward	1	66
SISSON, Charles C., m. Ann E. **SAWYER**, b. of Groton, Aug. 24, 1851, by W. Munger	1	92
Frances L., m. Rufus C. **BURROWS**, July 1, 1850, at Porterville, by Rev. W. Munger	1	89
William, m. Phebe **HOLDREDGE**, b. of Groton, Feb. 27, 1806, by Amos Gere, J.P.	2	75
SKINNER, Prentice P., of Marlborough, m. Hannah E. **SMITH**, of Groton, Feb. 10, 1833, by Timothy Tuttle	1	42
SLATE, Alexander, of New London, m. Patty **HEWLETT**, of Groton, Nov. 30, 1824, by Caleb Avery, J.P.	1	15
John, of New London, m. Sophia **HULET**, of Groton, Apr. 16, 1824, by Caleb Avery, J.P.	1	13
Joseph, of New London, m. Jenet **HEWLETT**, of Groton, May 23, 1824, by Caleb Avery, J.P.	1	13
Sophia, Mrs., m. Edward **CHAPEL**, Feb. 25, 1839, by Rev. John G. Wightman	1	60
SMITH, Abby D., of Groton, m. R. S. **McCOLLUM**, of Rochester, N.Y., Mar. 14, 1828, by Rev. Roswell Burrows	1	27
Abigail, [d. Isaac & Esther], b. Feb. 15, 1740; d. Nov. 4, 1760	1	138
Abigail, d. [Simeon & Eunice], b. Jan. 27, 1779	1	168
Abigail, of Groton, m. Peleg **LEWIS**, Jan. 27, 1782, by Elder Park Allyn	2	47
Abigail, m. Rufus **SMITH**, May 17, 1786	2	90
Abigail, d. Nehemiah, Jr. & Abigail, b. May 10, 1793	2	49
Abigail, w. Nehemiah, d. July 8, 1797	1	168
Abigail, d. [Rufus & Abigail], b. Aug. 15, 1808	2	90
Albert F., m. Julia A. **BUCKLEY**, b. of Groton, Dec. 24, 1837, by Rev. John G. Wightman	1	57
Albert G., of Rochester, N.Y., m. Julia Ann **BURROWS**, of Groton, May 12, 1830, by Rev. Roswell Burrows	1	34
Albert Gallitan, s. [Rufus & Abigail], b. [ ]	2	90
Alfred, s. [Nehemiah, Jr. & Abigail], b. Aug. 31, 1796	2	49
Alfred, of Aurelius, N.Y., m. Lydia **JOHNSON**, of Wilkesbarre, Pa., Sept. 22, 1822, by Timothy Tuttle	1	7
Allethiah, d. Jonathan & Deborah, b. Jan. 29, 1714/15	1	112
Almira W., m. William T. **BURROWS**, b. of Groton, July 4, 1833, by Ira R. Stewart, Eld.	1	44
Amos, s. Isaac & Esther, b. Dec. 13, 1732	1	138
Amos Denison, s. [Gilbert & Eunice], b. Nov. 14, 1778	2	37
Amy, d. [Jabez & Amy], b. Jan. 18, 1746/7	1	178
Amy, of Groton, m. Jonas **PRENTICE**, of Stonington, Nov. 5, 1768, by Sam[ue]ll Prentice, J.P.	1	159
Ann, Mrs., of Groton, m. Caleb **BECKWITH**, of Waterford, Nov. 30, 1848, by Rev. Jared R. Avery	1	83

	Vol.	Page
SMITH, (cont.)		
Ann E., m. Gurdon **DUNBAR**, b. of Groton, Apr. 23, 1854, by Rev. Isaac Cheesebrough	1	96
Anna, b. Nov. 1, 1717	1	114
Anna, d. [Nehemiah & Abigail], b. Dec. 8, 1765	1	168
Anna, d. [Joshua & Sabra], b. Apr. 26, 1793	2	67
Anne, d. [Jabez & Amy], b. Dec. 4, 1754	1	178
Anne, m. Capt. Isaac **GALLUP**, b. of Groton, Oct. 5, 1786, by Benedam Gallup, J.P.	2	36
Austin, s. [Rufus & Abigail], b. Mar. 2, 1795; d. Mar. 1, 1798	2	90
Betsey, m. Ebenezer **LATHAM**, b. of Groton, Aug. 28, 1803, by Christopher Avery, Pastor	2	66
Betsey F., m. Austin **GRAY**, Jan. 5, 1834, by W[illia]m M. Williams, J.P.	1	46
Betsey F., m. George L. **DABOLL**, b. of Groton, May 26, 1839, by Rev. John G. Wightman	1	60
Carlton, s. [Rufus & Abigail], b. Mar. 20, 1789; d. Apr. [ ], 1789	2	90
Caroline C., Mrs., m. William V. **DABOLL**, b. of Groton, Feb. 2, 1835, by Rev. Ira R. Steward	1	49
Charles, m. Hannah **STEWARD**, Oct. 13, 1771, by Timothy Whitman	2	21
Charles, s. [Simeon & Eunice], b. Feb. 24, 1775	2	40
Charles A., of Ledyard, m. Amanda **COLVER**, of Groton, Mar. 31, 1842, by Rev. Erastus Denison	1	66
Charles A., m. Betsey A. **HEATH**, b. of Groton, Sept. 7, 1851, by Rev. Nicholas T. Allen	1	92
Charles G., of Westerly, R.I., m. Eliza B. **STANDISH**, of Preston, July 17, 1825, by Elisha Ayer, J.P.	1	18
Charles G., m. Frances A. **STODDARD**, b. of Norwich, May 19, 1833, by Rev. Erastus Denison	1	44
Charles S., m. Hannah **WILLIAMS**, Jan. 26, 1792, by Christopher Avery, J.P.	2	45
Charles Steward, [s. Charles & Hannah], b. Oct. 30, 1772	2	21
Charles Williams, s. [Charles S. & Hannah], b. Jan. 18, 1793	2	45
Cynthia, d. [Joshua & Sabra], b. May 30, 1800	2	67
Daniel, s. Isaac & Esther, b. Dec. 1, 1730; d. Oct. 2, 1753	1	138
David, s. John & Temperance, b. Dec. 10, 1735	1	134
David Joshua, s. Joshua & Lucy, b. Sept. 26, 1780	2	24
Deborah, d. Jonathan & Deborah, b. Nov. 3, 1712	1	112
Denison B., m. Eliza **WOODBRIDGE**, Sept. 2, 1845, by Rev. R. Russell	1	74
Desire, d. [Jabez & Desire], b. July 31, 1737	1	178
Dorothy, d. Aug. 26, 1697; d. Jan. 4, 1697[/8]	1	114
Doretha, d. [Nathan & Mary], b. Apr. 18, 1729	1	107
Dudley, s. [Joshua & Sabra], b. Feb. 9, 1798	2	67
Elias, d. [Rufus & Abigail], b. Aug. 2, 1787	2	90
Elijah, s. [Simeon & Eunice], b. Nov. 16, 1776	2	40
Elijah, s. [Rufus & Abigail], b. Dec. 13, 1792	2	90
Elijah Frederick, m. Emily Malvina **LESTER**, b. of Groton, Dec. 28, 1825, by Timothy Tuttle	1	19
Elisha, s. Jonathan & Deborah, b. Mar. 16, 1710	1	112
Elisha, m. Elizabeth **STREET**, Nov. 30, 1732	1	164
Elisha, s. Jonathan & Jemima, b. Nov. 8, 1748	1	141
Eliza, d. [Nathan & Mary], b. May 2, 1736	1	107
Eliza, m. Charles **DAVIS**, b. of Groton, Feb. 9, 1834, by Joseph Durfey, J.P.	1	46

	Vol.	Page
SMITH, (cont.)		
Eliza Denison, d. Joseph D. & Eliza F., b. Apr. 16, 1819	2	76
Eliza F., of Groton, m. Joseph D. **SMITH**, of Lyme, Jan. 28, 1817, by Rev. Silas Burrows	2	76
Eliza J., of Groton, m. Caleb O. **BURROWS**, of Ledyard, July 23, 1845, by Rev. Erastus Denison	1	74
Elizabeth, b. Nov. 17, 1700	1	114
Elizabeth, m. James **AVERY**, Jr., Dec. 13, 1719	1	124
Elizabeth, [d. Jon[a]than, Jr. & Elizabeth], b. Oct. 27, 1738	1	141
Elizabeth, w. Jonathan, Jr., d. Mar. 14, 1747	1	141
Ephraim, m. Hannah **CHAPMAN**, Apr. 12, 1722	1	102
Erastus Tennant, s. [Gilbert, Jr. & Prudence], b. June 24, 1789	2	38
Esther, twin with Hannah, [d. Isaac & Esther], b. Aug. 9, 1734; d. Aug. 18, 1734	1	138
Easter, [d. Simeon & [E]unice], b. Nov. 21, 1769	2	15
Esther, d. [Simeon & Eunice], b. Nov. 21, 1769	2	40
Eunice, d. [Jabez & Amy], b. Feb. 25, 1748/9	1	178
[E]unice, [d. Simeon & [E]unice], b. June 24, 1772	2	15
Eunice, d. [Simeon & Eunice], b. June 24, 1772	2	40
Eunice, d. [Gilbert & Eunice], b. Oct. 31, 1772	2	37
Eunice, d. [Joshua & Sabra], b. Oct. 23, 1795	2	67
Fanny, Mrs., m. Comfort **DAVIS**, b. of Groton, Feb. 13, 1825, by Amos A. Niles, J.P.	1	16
Frances, of Stonington, m. Ansel **WEST**, of Providence, R.I., Oct. 26, 1851, at Mystic River, by Rev. Franklin A. Slater	1	93
Frances A., of Groton, m. John S. **HEATH**, of New London, Oct. 1, 1850, by Rev. Jared R. Avery	1	90
Frances Ann, of Groton, m. Luther **TUCKER**, of Ontario, N.Y., Oct. 18, 1825, by John G. Wightman, Eld.	1	19
George, m. Emeline **WOOD**, July 26, [1832], by Rev. James Porter	1	41
Gilbert, s. [Nathan & Mary], b. Apr. 2, 1742	1	107
Gilbert, m. Eunice **DENISON**, Aug. 2, 1764	2	37
Gilbert, s. [Gilbert & Eunice], b. Sept. 25, 1766	2	37
Gilbert had negro boy Ceazer, b. Dec. 4, 1784; Melia, negro girl, b. Feb. 5, 1787; Rose and June, negro girls, b. Apr. 10, 1789	2	37
Gilbert, Jr., m. Prudence **MORGAN**, June 12, 1788	2	38
Gilbert A., of Springfield, Mass., m. Eliza D. **BARBER**, of Groton, June 8, 1823, by Timothy Tuttle	1	9
Gilbert Avery, s. [Gilbert, Jr. & Prudence], b. Sept. 15, 1796	2	38
Gilbert T., m. Emma M. **STARR**, b. of Groton, May 22, 1854, by Rev. Isaac Chees[e]brough	1	96
Hannah, b. Feb. 20, 1699	1	114
Hannah, [d. Jon[a]than, Jr. & Elizabeth], b. May 20, 1733	1	141
Hannah, twin with Esther, [d. Isaac & Esther], b. Aug. 9, 1734; d. June 15, 1736	1	138
Hannah, d. Nathan & Mary, b. July 19, 1745	1	175
Hannah, m. Thomas **AVERY**, July 7, 1768	2	28
Hannah, [d. Charles & Hannah], b. July 6, 1780	2	21
Hannah, m. David **AVERY**, b. of Groton, Jan. 24, 1804, by John G. Wightman, Elder	2	67
Hannah E., of Groton, m. Prentice P. **SKINNER**, of Marlborough, Feb. 10, 1833, by Timothy Tuttle	1	42

	Vol.	Page
SMITH, (cont.)		
Harriet L., m. Noyes P. **DENISON**, b. of Groton, Dec. 9, 1830, by Timothy Tuttle	1	36
Henry, m. Eliza **CHESTER**, b. of Groton, June 29, 1828, by Nathan Daboll, J.P.	1	28
Henry W., of Williamstown, Mass., m. Amanda M. **WOODBRIDGE**, of Groton, Apr. 8, 1832, by Timothy Tuttle	1	39
Isaac, b. Dec. 29, 1707	1	114
Isaac, m. Esther **DENISON**, Nov. 4, 1729	1	138
Jabez, b. Feb. 17, 1714	1	114
Jabez, m. Desire **DENISON**, Nov. 11, 1736	1	178
Jabez, m. Amy **AVERY**, May 26, 1742	1	178
Jabez, s. [Nathan & Mary], b. May 9, 1748	1	175
Jabez, s. [Jabez & Ammy], b. Aug. 31, 1751	1	178
Jabez, s. [Simeon & Eunice], b. Aug. 25, 1783	2	40
James, s. Samuel & Mary, b. Dec. 12, 1740	1	151
Jane, d. [Nathan & Mary], b. Jan. 13, 1731	1	107
Jeremiah, s. Jonathan & Deborah, b. July 8, 1705	1	112
Jesse, [s. Jonathan & Jemima], b. Jan. 19, 1750/51	1	141
Jesse D., of Groton, m. Mary J. **STODDARD**, of Ledyard, Apr. 20, 1851, by Rev. J. R. Avery	1	91
Jesse Denison, s. [Nathaniel D. & Eliza], b. Apr. 18, 1830	3	31
John, b. June 14, 1704	1	114
John, m. Temperance **HOLMES**, May 10, 1727	1	134
John, s. John & Temperance, b. Mar. 26, 1728	1	134
John, [s. Jonathan & Jemima], b. May 21, 1753	1	141
John, s. [Jabez & Amy], b. Apr. 11, 1757; d. Feb. [ ], 1759	1	178
John, s. [Jabez & Amy], b. Apr. 10, 1762	1	178
John, s. [Nehemiah & Abigail], b. Apr. 9, 1771	1	168
John, b. Apr. 9, 1771	2	26
John, of Groton, m. Patty **BROWN**, of Stonington, June 13, 1792, by Eleazer Brown, Elder	2	43
John, Jr., s. John & Patty, b. Feb. 1, 1794	2	43
John, m. Hopea **WHIPPLE**, June 23, 1822, by Silas Whipple	1	7
John D., m. Ann **ALDERMAN**, b. of Stonington, Nov. 21, 1830, by Nathan Daboll, J.P.	1	36
John Owen, s. [Prentice P. & Maria], b. Oct. 6, 1819	2	94
Jonathan, s. Jonathan & Deborah, b. Dec. 31, 1706	1	112
Jon[a]than, Jr., m. Elizabeth **WILLIAMS**, June 8, 1732	1	141
Jonathan, Jr., m. Jemima **HARDEN**, Aug. 7, 1747	1	141
Joseph, [s. Jon[a]than, Jr. & Elizabeth], b. Dec. 25, 1735	1	141
Joseph, [s. Simeon & [E]unice], b. Mar. 25, 1767	2	15
Joseph, s. [Simeon & Eunice], b. Mar. 25, 1767	2	40
Joseph Aborn, of New London, m. Sarah Augusta **AVERY**, of Groton, June 24, 1832, by John G. Wightman, Elder	1	40
Joseph D., of Lyme, m. Eliza F. **SMITH**, of Groton, Jan. 28, 1817, by Rev. Silas Burrows	2	76
Joseph Washington, s. Joseph D. & Eliza F., b. Apr. 30, 1821	2	76
Joseph Washington, of New London, m. Sarah Elizabeth **SMITH**, of Groton, Sept. 7, 1847, by Rev. Erastus Denison	1	79
Joshua, s. John & Temperance, b. June 31,[sic] 1729	1	134
Joshua, m. Sabra **BILL**, b. of Groton, Oct. 9, 1786, by Elder Park Allyn	2	67
Joshua, s. [Joshua & Sabra], b. Aug. 22, 1790	2	67

	Vol.	Page
SMITH, (cont.)		
Latham Avery, s. James & Annise, b. May 2, 1781	2	16
Lavinia A., m. Sanford A. **MORGAN**, Jan. 1, 1846, by Rev. Jared R. Avery	1	75
Lucy, [d. Isaac & Esther], b. Nov. 11, 1746	1	138
Lucy, d. [Joshua & Sabra], b. May 20, 1802	2	67
Lucy, of Groton, m. Russell **HARRIS**, of R.I., Oct. 11, 1835, by Rev. Ira R. Steward	1	52
Lydia, b. Jan. 24, 1712/13	1	114
Lydia, d. Nehemiah, d. Oct. 24, 1723, ae. 78 y.	1	128
Lyman, of Montville, m. Emeline **FANNING**, of Groton, Jan. 25, 1829, by William Williams, J.P.	1	30
Mariah, d. [Rufus & Abigail], b. May 11, 1798	2	90
Martha, d. [Gilbert & Eunice], b. May 24, 1776	2	37
Mary, b. Nov. 16, 1709	1	114
Mary, d. [Nathan & Mary], b. Oct. 1, 1726	1	107
Mary, [d. Isaac & Esther], b. Nov. 15, 1743	1	138
Mary, d. [Jabez & Amy], b. Oct. 31, 1759	1	178
Mary, d. [Simeon & Eunice], b. June 1, 1781	2	40
Mary, d. [Nehemiah, Jr. & Abigail], b. Apr. 21, 1795; d. Aug. 8, 1795	2	49
Mary, d. [Nehemiah, Jr. & Abigail], b. May 4, 1800	2	49
Mary (Chester), m. Noyes **BARBER**, Aug. 11, 1814	2	83
Nancy, d. [John & Patty], b. Aug. 11, 1796	2	43
Nancy, d. [Nathaniel D. & Eliza], b. Oct. 28, 1835	3	31
Nathan, b. Sept. 16, 1702	1	114
Nathan, m. Mary **DENISON**, Dec. 5, 1723	1	107
Nathan, [s. Nathan & Mary], b. Sept. 18, 1724	1	107
Nathan D., m. Mary Abby **MORGAN**, b. of Groton, Sept. 12, 1841, by Rev. Erastus Denison	1	65
Nathaniel D., m. Eliza **WILLIAMS**, b. of Groton, June 17, 1827, by John G. Wightman, Eld.	1	23
Nehemiah, m. Dorothy **WHEELER**, Apr. 22, 1696	1	104
Nehemiah, m. Elizabeth **HARRIS**, Sept. 9, 1724	1	128
Nehemiah, Jr., d. Nov. 15, 1724, ae. 51 y.	1	128
Nehemiah, s. John & Temperance, b. Oct. 30, 1733	1	134
Nehemiah, m. Abigail **AVERY**, May 3, 1758	1	168
Nehemiah, s. [Nehemiah & Abigail], b. Apr. 21, 1767	1	168
Nehemiah, Jr., m. Abigail **GERE**, b. of Groton, Dec. 9, 1792, by A. Gere, J.P.	2	49
Nehemiah, of Groton, m. Manen **HOLMES**, of Stonington, Dec. 12, 1799, by Joshua Babock, J.P.	1	168
Nehemiah, d. Aug. 13, 1803	2	49
Noah, s. Joshua & Lucy, b. Apr. 26, 1779	2	24
Oliver, s. [Nathan & Mary], b. Apr. 27, 1739	1	107
Perez Swan, s. [Jabez & Amy], b. July 15, 1766	1	178
Phebe, d. Samuel & Mary, b. Nov. 10, 1742	1	151
Phebe, [d. Isaac & Esther], b. Apr. 18, 1752; d. Oct. 28, 1760	1	138
Prentice Orrin, s. [Prentice P. & Maria], b. Aug. 3, 1817	2	94
Prentice P., m. Maria **AVERY**, b. of Groton, Dec. 1, 1814, by Daniel Eldredge, J.P.	2	94
Priscilla, m. Richard **STARR**, Jan. 15, 1740/41	1	156
Prudence, w. Gilbert, b. Apr. 16, 1768; m. Vine **STODDARD**, Jr., Nov. 23, 1803	3	10

	Vol.	Page
SMITH, (cont.)		
Prudence, of Lyme, m. Samuel **FISH**, Jr., of Groton, Nov. 5, 1820, by Roswell Burrows, Elder	1	2
R.W., m. Eliza **HALEY**, Nov. 23, 1838	3	0
Reuben P., of Waterford, m. Caroline B. **CHAPMAN**, of Groton, Aug. 12, 1827, at the dwelling of Noah Chapman, by Rev. Reuben Palmer	1	24
Richard William, m. Eliza **HALEY**, b. of Groton, Nov. 23, 1838, by Rev. John G. Wightman	1	60
Roswell, of Waterford, m. Mary S. **CHAPMAN**, of Groton, Oct. 13, 1826, by John G. Wightman, Eld.	1	19
Rufus, s. [Simeon & Eunice], b. Oct. 14, 1762	2	40
Rufus, [s. Simeon & [E]unice], b. Jan. 9, 1765	2	15
Rufus, m. Abigail **SMITH**, May 17, 1786	2	90
Rufus, s. [Rufus & Abigail], b. Jan. 29, 1802	2	90
Russell, [s. Charles & Hannah], b. May 3, 1777	2	21
Sabra, d. [Joshua & Sabra], b. May 30, 1788	2	67
Sally Maria, d. [Prentice P. & Maria], b. Sept. 30, 1815	2	94
Samuel, m. Mary **KINION**, Mar. 31, 1740	1	151
Samuel, s. Samuel & Mary, b. Dec. 26, 1744	1	151
Sarah, b. July 14, 1719	1	114
Sarah, d. [Nehemiah & Abigail], b. Aug. 9, 1761	1	168
Sarah, Wid., & d. Lawrence **JOHNSON**, m. Robert **STODDARD**, Nov. 30, 1791	2	74
Sarah Elizabeth, d. [Nathaniel D. & Eliza], b. May 26, 1828	3	31
Sarah Elizabeth, of Groton, m. Joseph Washington **SMITH**, of New London, Sept. 7, 1847, by Rev. Erastus Denison	1	79
Shubael, s. John & Temperance, b. Sept. 27, 1731	1	134
Shueball, [s. Charles & Hannah], b. Feb. [ ], 1775	2	21
Silas, [s. Isaac & Esther], b. Apr. 18, 1752; d. Apr. 28, 1762	1	138
Simeon, m. [E]unice **WALLWORTH**, Jan. 7, 1762	2	15
Simeon, m. Eunice **WALWORTH**, Jan. 7, 1762	2	40
Simeon, [s. Simeon & [E]unice, b. Oct. 14, 1762	2	15
Simeon, s. [Simeon & Eunice], b. Oct. 14, 1762	2	40
Simeon, s. [Rufus & Abigail], b. Sept. 6, 1790	2	90
Simon, [s. Isaac & Esther], b. June 9, 1738	1	138
Temperance, twin with Thankfull, d. [Nehemiah & Abigail], b. Jan. 1, 1769	1	168
Thankfull, twin with Temperance, d. [Nehemiah & Abigail], b. Jan. 1, 1769; d. Sept. 6, 1770	1	168
Thankfull, d. [Nehemiah & Abigail], b. Jan. 21, 1775	1	168
Thankfull, b. Jan. 21, 1775	2	26
William, b. May 10, 1706	1	114
William, [s. Isaac & Esther], b. Oct. 26, 1749	1	138
W[illia]m, of Rochester, m. Frances **RANDALL**, of Groton, Aug. 5, 1839, by Ira R. Steward	1	61
William B., m. Mary Abby **EDGECOMB**, b. of Groton, June 1, 1851, in Porterville, by Rev. A. F. Slater	1	91
William Burrows, s. [Nathaniel D. & Eliza], b. Sept. 4, 1833	3	31
William E., of Stonington, m. Sophia **GALLUP**, of Groton, Aug. 10, 1834, by John G. Wightman, Elder	1	47
W[illia]m W., m. Sally **DAVID**, b. of Groton, May 16, 1841, by Rev. Jared R. Avery	1	64
________, d. [Rufus & Abigail], b. Apr. 15, 1797; d. May 3, 1797	2	90

	Vol.	Page
SMITH, (cont.)		
________, m. Sally **HALEY**, d. Caleb, Jr. & Sally, [ ]	3	0
SOUTHERLAND, Margaret, d. James & Sarah, b. May 15, 1766	1	150
SPAULDING, Fanny C., of Groton, m. James D. **GILLSON**, of Worcester, Mass., May 4, 1835, by Ira D. Steward	1	50
SPENCER, Abner, of Groton, m. Eliza A. **WEEKS**, of Thompson, Dec. 31, 1851, at Thompson, by Rev. Allen Darrow	1	97
Abner B., m. Abby **POTTER**, Nov. 11, 1810	3	19
Charles, of Griswold, m. Betsey **HALLETT**, of Groton, Mar. 14, 1830, by William Williams, J.P.	1	34
Ezra S., s. [Abner B. & Abby], b. June 6, 1813	3	19
Ezra S., m. Fanny **FITCH**, b. of Groton, Dec. 26, 1836, by Rev. Roswell Burrows	1	55
Fanny, m. John **SPENCER**, b. of Groton, Sept. 5, 1847, by Rev. Simon B. Bailey	1	79
Fanny F., [d. Abner B. & Abby], b. May 23, 1825	3	19
Fanny F., m. Harris **FOWLER**, b. of Groton, May 30, 1847, by Rev. Simon B. Bailey	1	78
Grace, m. Aaron **BRIGGS**, b. of Stonington, Aug. 30, 1835, by Joseph Durfey, J.P.	1	51
Hannah, [d. Abner B. & Abby], b. Mar. 16, 1819	3	19
Hannah C., m. John **BAKER**, s. Peter, b. of Groton, July 3, 1836, by Rev. Roswell Burrows	1	54
Henry N., [s. Abner B. & Abby], b. Oct. 22, 1820	3	19
Henry N., m. Frances A. **ROGERS**, b. of Groton, Oct. 1, 1843, by Ira R. Steward	1	70
John, m. Fanny **SPENCER**, b. of Groton, Sept. 5, 1847, by Rev. Simon B. Bailey	1	79
John R., [s. Abner B. & Abby], b. Apr. 28, 1823	3	19
Louisa, m. John L. T. **WHEELER**, b. of Groton, Aug. 27, 1837, by Rev. Ira R. Steward	1	57
Louisa N., [d. Abner B. & Abby], b. Apr. 15, 1817	3	19
Lurena P., [d. Abner B. & Abby], b. Sept. 3, 1815	3	19
Mary Ann, d. [Abner B. & Abby], b. Sept. 11, 1811	3	19
Mary Ann, of Groton, m. Harris **FOWLER**, of New London, Apr. 17, 1838, by Ira R. Steward	1	58
Mary J., of Stonington, m. Charles C. **PARK[E]**, of N. Stonington, Nov. 27, 1843, by Rev. Erastus Denison	1	70
Richard P., [s. Abner B. & Abby], b. June 18, 1827	3	19
Serena, of Groton, m. Gilbert **FOWLER**, of New London, Sept.6, 1835, by Ira R. Steward	1	52
Thomas S., [s. Abner B. & Abby], b. May 20, 1829	3	19
SPICER, Abel, [s. John & Mary], b. Mar. 9, 1736	1	102
Abel, of Groton, m. Sarah **ALLEN**, of Groton, Jan. 14, 1762, by Jacob Johnson	2	7
Abel, s. [John & Mary], b. June 10, 1762	2	181
Abel, s. [Abel & Sarah], b. June 12, 1775	2	7
Abigail, d. Edward, b. Apr. 8, 1708	1	114
Abigail, d. John & Mary, b. Dec. 16, 1729	1	102
Abigail, d. [John, 2d, & Elizabeth], b. Aug. 21, 1797	2	59
Abigail, m. James **GALLUP**, 2d, b. of Groton, June 5, 1820, by John G. Wightman	1	1
Alethea, d. [Oliver & Alethea], b. Feb. 26, 1749/50	1	165

	Vol.	Page
SPICER, (cont.)		
Althea, d. Oliver & Althea, b. Feb. 26, 1750/1	1	174
Allyn, m. Anna **WILLIAMS**, b. of Groton, Dec. 4, 1825, by Timothy Tuttle	1	19
Amos, s. [Oliver & Alethea], b. Feb. 20, 1762	1	165
Ann, m. Peter **TIFFT**, Dec. 13, 1722	1	135
Anna, d. Edward, b. May 28, 1703	1	114
Anne, d. [Abel & Sarah], b. Sept. 22, 1771	2	7
Benjamin, 2d, m. Clarissa **ALLYN**, b. of Groton, Mar. 24, 1822, by Philip Gray, J.P.	1	6
Betsey, m. Christopher **BROWN**, b. of Groton, Dec. 10, 1824, by Robert Avery, J.P.	1	14
Catren, d. Edward, b. Oct. 6, 1696	1	114
Clarissa, d. [John & Mary], b. Dec. 30, 1785	2	53
Cynthia, see Synthia		
Cyrus, s. [John & Mary], b. Mar. 13, 1750/51	1	181
Damaris, [d. John G. & Clarissa[, b. Apr. 9, 1842	3	30
Deborah, d. [Oliver & Alethea], b. Apr. 26, 1757	1	165
Edmund, s. [John, 2d & Elizabeth], b. Jan. 11, 1812	2	59
Edward, m. Hannah **BILL**, Oct. 17, 1743	1	184
Edwin, s. John & Mary, b. Apr. 4, 1721	1	102
Eldredge, s. [L:evi & Prudence], b. Jan. 23, 1799	3	18
Elihu, s. [Elisha & Jemima], b. Apr. 13, 1825	3	18
Elihu, of Groton, m. Huldah **ROATH**, of Norwich, Apr. 30, 1850, by Rev. Nicholas T. Allen	1	88
Elihu, Jr., Capt., m. Mary M. **DUDLEY**, b. of Groton, Jan. 21, 1852, by Rev. Franklin A. Slater	1	93
Elihu P., s. [Levi & Prudence], b. Oct. 1, 1796	3	18
Elizabeth, [d. William & Hannah], b. Sept. 21, 1704	1	106
Elizabeth, d. [Oliver & Alethea[, b. July 25, 1764	1	165
Elizabeth, d. [John, 2d & Elizabeth], b. Feb. 21, 1815	2	59
Emeline, d. [Elisha & Jemima], b. June 16, 1823	3	18
Eunice, d. Abel & Sarah, b. Mar. 18, 1767	2	7
Eunice, d. [John & Mary], b. Feb. 26, 1782	2	53
Fanny, d. [John, 2d & Elizabeth], b. Aug. 20, 1804	2	59
Gurdon Bill, s. [John, 2d & Elizabeth], b. Nov. 14, 1806	2	59
Hannah, [d. William & Hannah], b. Nov. 6, 1709	1	106
Hannah, of Groton, m. Gardner N. **WILCOX**, of Preston, Oct. 15, 1848, by David Avery, Elder	1	82
Hannah, d. [Edward & Hannah], b. Jan. 5, 1748/9	1	184
Hannah, d. [John & Mary], b. Dec. 25, 1777	2	53
Hannah, d. [Eldredge & Lydia G.], b. [ ], 1829	3	18
Harriet Ann, [d. John G. & Clarissa], b. Dec. 16, 1837	3	30
Herbert P., s. [James & Lydia], b. Nov. 17, 1806	2	74
Isaac, [s. John, 2d & Elizabeth], b. Sept. 19, 1799	2	59
Isaac, m. Margaret **SHORT**, b. of Groton, Sept. 28, 1823, by Timothy Tuttle	1	10
Isaac, of Preston, m. Francina **CHAPMAN**, Feb. 25, 1827, by Zelotes Fuller, Minister	1	23
James, s. [John & Mary], b. Nov. 30, 1779	2	53
James, of Groton, m. Lydia **PRIDE**, of Preston, Dec. 28, 1801	2	74
Jemimmia, d. Edward, b. Apr. 14, 1710	1	114
Jerushe, d. Edward, b. Aug. 2, 1706	1	114

	Vol.	Page
SPICER, (cont.)		
Jerusha, d. [Oliver & Alethea], b. July 9, 1774	1	165
John, s. Edward, b. Jan. 1, 1698	1	114
John, m. Mary **GEER**, Oct. 22, 1720	1	102
John, [s. John & Mary], b. Feb. 17, 1724	1	102
John, m. Mary **CHAPMAN**, Oct. 25, 1744	1	181
John, s. [John & Mary], b. Apr. 8, 1749	1	181
John, b. Apr. 20, 1749; of Groton, m. Mary **PARK[E]**, of Groton, Dec. 29, 1774	2	53
John, d. Aug. 28, 1753	1	153
John, 2d, s. Edward & Abigail, b. Aug. 14, 1770; m. Elizabeth **LATHAM**, b. of Groton, Sept. 7, 1794, by Amos Geer, J.P.	2	59
John G., s. [James & Lydia], b. Nov. 26, 1804	2	74
John Orrin, s. John G. & Clarissa, b. Sept. 19, 1835	3	30
John P., s. [Levi & Prudence], b. Sept. 14, 1808	3	18
John P., m. Abby Jane **LATHAM**, b. of Groton, Sept. 12, 1830, by Rev. Erastus Denison	1	35
John Seabury, s. [John, 2d & Elizabeth], b. Apr. 30, 1802	2	59
John Stanton, s. [Eldredge & Lydia G.], b. [ ], 1827	3	18
Katherine, d. [Edward & Hannah], b. Nov. 22, 1746	1	184
Kazia, d. [John & Mary], b. Mar. 13, 1755	1	181
Levi C., s. [Levi & Prudence], b. Dec. 7, 1793	3	18
Lucy, d. [Oliver & Alethea], b. May 3, 1770	1	165
Lucy, m. Henry **LATHAM**, b. of Groton, Oct. 6, 1822, by Roswell Burrows	1	7
Lucy C., d. [Levi & Prudence], b. Jan. 8, 1803	3	18
Lucy L., of Groton, m. Winthrop **WARD**, of Stonington, May 24, 1853, by Rev. James M. Phillips	1	95
Lydia Ann, d. [Eldredge & Lydia G.], b. [ ], 1824	3	18
Marcy, d. [John & Mary], b. Aug. 5, 1764	1	181
Martha, d. [Oliver & Alethea], b. Mar. 30, 1755	1	165
Mary, d. Edward, b. May 28, 1701	1	114
Mary, d. [John & Mary], b. Jan. 28, 1746/7	1	181
Mary, d. [Oliver & Alethea], b. Feb. 27, 1751/2	1	165
Mary, d. [John & Mary], b. Nov. 24, 1775	2	53
Mary Avery, d. [John, 2d & Elizabeth], b. Mar. 28, 1809	2	59
Molly, d. [John & Mary], b. Jan. 27, 1753	1	181
Moses, s. Hannah, b. Nov. 25, 1721	1	126
Oliver, [s. John & Mary], b. May 28, 1726	1	102
Oliver, m. Alethea **ALLYN**, Aug. 15, 1749	1	165
Oliver, s. [Oliver & Alethea], b. Nov. 20, 1766	1	165
Peter, [s. William & Hannah], b. June 21, 1712	1	106
Phebe, d. Abel & Sarah, b. Oct. 24, 176[ ]	2	7
Prudence, d. John, 2d & Elizabeth, b. May 1, 1795	2	59
Prudence, m. Erastus **DENISON**, b. of Groton, June 25, 1815, by John G. Wightman, Elder	2	87
Prudence, d. [Elisha & Jemima], b. May 19, 1821	3	18
Prudence, m. Pardon T. **BROWN**, b. of Groton, July 31, 1842, by Ira R. Steward	1	66
Prudence A., m. George P. **WILBUR**, b. of Groton, [Oct.] 26, [1853], by Rev. James M. Phillips	1	95
Ruth, m. Samuel **NUTON**, Jan. 22, 1702	1	105

	Vol.	Page
SPICER, (cont.)		
Sabrain L., m. Henry H. **ROCKWELL**, Sept. 12, 1852, by Rev. Nicholas T. Allen	1	94
Sally, d. [Levi & Prudence], b. Nov. 10, 1806	3	18
Sally, of Groton, m. Peter **IRISH**, of N. Stonington, Nov. 18, 1827, by Roswell Burrows	1	25
Sarah, d. Abel & Sarah, b. Nov. 1, 176[ ]	2	7
Seth, s. Abel & Sarah, b. June 12, 1769	2	7
Silas, s. [Edward & Hannah], b. Jan. 22, 1744/5	1	184
Silas, s. [Levi & Prudence], b. Apr. 29, 1811	3	18
Silas, m. Mary A. **MORGAN**, b. of Groton, Dec. 4, 1839, by Ira R. Steward	1	62
Susan, [d. John G. & Clarissa], b. Dec. 24, 1839	3	30
Synthia, d. [John, 2d & Elizabeth], b. Sept. 5, 1817	2	59
Thankfull, [d. William & Hannah], b. June 28, 1707	1	106
William, m. Hannah **WROTH**, Nov. 25, 1703	1	106
William, [s. William & Hannah], b. Feb. 9, 1714	1	106
William, s. [James & Lydia], b. Feb. 9, 1803	2	74
William A., m. Elizabeth H. **CHAPMAN**, of Groton, Oct. 31, 1852, by Rev. Nicholas T. Allen	1	94
William E., m. Narcissa **INGHAM**, b. of Groton, Mar. 22, 1846, by Rev. Simon B. Bailey	1	75
William Eldredge, s. [Eldredge & Lydia G.], b. [ ], 1822	3	18
SPRING, Fanny O., of Groton, m. Horace **PALMER**, of Stonington, Aug. 27, 1848, by David Avery, Elder	1	82
George, m. Elizabeth **PARKS**, b. of Groton, Nov. 15, 1841, by Ira R. Steward	1	65
Mary A., m. William E. **WILLCOX**, b. of Groton, Oct. 26, 1845, by Rev. Simon B. Bailey	1	74
SPRINGER, Sarah, m. John **COOK**, Dec. 22, 1703	1	120
SQUIER, William, of New York, m. Eliza **WELCH**, of Groton, Apr. 23, 1843, by Rev. Erastus Denison	1	68
SQUILE, Betsey, of Groton, m. Ce[a]sar **WAITE**, of Exeter, R.I., July 4, 1824, by William Williams, J.P.	1	13
STAFFORD, Jonas, of New York, m. Lucy **FISH**, of Conn., Aug. 12, 1841, by Rev. Erastus Denison	1	65
STALLIN, Elizabeth, m. John **BAILEY**, Dec. 25, 1713	1	108
STANDISH, Eliza B., of Preston, m. Charles G. **SMITH**, of Westerly, R.I., July 17, 1825, by Elisha Ayer, J.P.	1	18
Levi, of Preston, m. Eunice **CHAPMAN**, of Groton, Aug. 4, 1834, by John Brewster, J.P.	1	48
STANTON, Amos, s. [John & Prudence], b. Nov. 27, 1750	1	181
Amos, s. [Joseph & Hannah], b. June 10, 1773	2	92
Angelence, [d. John & Bathsheba], b. Apr. 13, 1807	3	32
Angelina, m. Ebenezer **GALLUP**, b. of Groton, Dec. 10, 1826, by William Williams, J.P.	1	22
Ann, [d. John & Bathsheba], b. July 21, 1803	3	32
Anna, [d. John & Ann], b. Nov. 3, 1703	1	104
Anna, d. [John & Mary], b. Mar. 14, 1726/7	1	183
Anna, d. Thomas & Lucy, b. July 10, 1740; d. Nov. 20, 1751	1	145
Anna, m. James **ALLYN**, Dec. 15, 1768	2	69
Anna, d. [Joseph & Hannah], b. Aug. 13, 1771; d. Apr. 3, 1779	2	92
Anna, d. [Joseph & Hannah], b. May 2, 1779	2	92

	Vol.	Page
STANTON, (cont.)		
Anna, of Preston, m. David **PARK[E]**, s. Jacob, of Groton, July 5, 1781, by Levi Hart	2	2
Anny, m. William **WILLIAMS**, Jr., b. of Groton, Oct. 13, 1799, by Rev. Christopher Avery, of Stonington	3	8
Benjamin, [s. John & Ann], b. Aug. 30, 1721	1	104
Bridgett, m. James **BA[I]LEY**, Feb. 8, 1721	1	126
Cassandra, b. Jan. 29, 1763; m. Robert **GEER**, 3d, [Dec. 5, 1782]	2	42
Cassandara, m. Robert **GEER**, 3d, b. of Groton, Dec. 5, 1782, by Amos Geer, J.P.	2	42
Charles, of Stonington, m. Eunice **HEWIT[T]**, of Groton, July 4, 1843, by Ira R. Steward	1	69
Charles H., m. Lavinia S. **GALLUP**, b. of Ledyard, Nov. 28, 1847, by Rev. Erastus Denison	1	80
Desirah, d. [Joseph & Hannah], b. June 10, 1775	2	92
Desire, m. Henry **GALLUP**, Jr., b. of Groton, Nov. 17, 1793, by Christ[ophe]r Avery, Elder	2	47
Dorothia, [d. John & Ann], b. June 28, 1715	1	104
Elisha, s. Samuel & Sarah, b. Jan. 13, 1785	2	17
Hannah, m. William **MORGAN**, Jr., Sept. 21, 1721	1	117
Hannah, d. [Joseph & Hannah], b. May 22, 1783	2	92
Huldah, m. Thomas **BAILEY**, Jr., Apr. 13, 1739	1	174
Isaac Wheeler, s. [Robert & Hannah], b. Mar. 25, 1819	2	93
James, s. [John & Prudence], b. Dec. 28, 1745	1	181
James, s. [John & Bathsheba], b. Mar. 16, 1796	3	32
James, m. Mary **HOLDREDGE**, b. of Ledyard, Oct. 20, 1841, by Nathan Daboll, J.P.	1	65
John, of Groton, m. Ann **HUCHESON**, Mar. 10, 1702	1	104
John, [s. John & Ann], b. Jan. 24, 1705	1	104
John, m. Mary **COLLVER**, Feb. 12, 1725	1	183
John, m. Prudence **CHEESEBROUGH**, Feb. 27, 1736/7	1	181
John, s. [John & Prudence], b. May 17, 1745	1	181
John, s. [Joseph & Hannah], b. July 25, 1767	2	92
John, [s. John & Bathsheba], b. Apr. 2,1817	3	32
John, m. Bathsheba **GILES**, [ ]	3	32
Joseph, [s. John & Ann], b. Jan. 26, 1717	1	104
Joseph, m. Hannah [ ], Apr. 22, 1767	2	92
Joseph, s. [Joseph & Hannah], b. May 17, 1769	2	92
Joshua, s. [Joseph & Hannah], b. Apr. 1, 1777; d. Mar. 28, 1779	2	92
Joshua, m. Harriet **HEWITT**, b. of Groton, Mar. 25, 1824, by William Williams, J.P.	1	12
Joshua C., s. [Joseph & Hannah], b. June 1, 1781	2	92
Lavinia, [d. John & Bathsheba], b. Mar. 8, 1801	3	32
Lavinia, m. Ebenezer **GALLUP**, b. of Groton, Apr. 27, 1823, by William Williams, J.P.	1	9
Lucy, d. Thomas & Lucy, b. Apr. 10, 1734	1	145
Lucy, [d. John & Bathsheba], b. June 14, 1812	3	32
Lucy, m. Sanford A. **WILLIAMS**, b. of Groton, Oct. 28, 1832, by William Williams, J.P.	1	41
Lydia, of Groton, m. Oliver **CHAMPLAIN**, of Preston, Oct. 12, 1823, by Jona[than] Brewster, J.P.	1	10
Mary, d. [John & Mary], b. Sept. 21, 1725	1	183

	Vol.	Page
STANTON, (cont.)		
Mary, of Stonington, m. David **GERE**, of Groton, May 17, 1781, by Rev. Nath]anie]l Eells	2	64
Mary, d. [Joseph & Hannah], b. July 4, 1785	2	92
Mary Ann, d. [Robert & Hannah], b. Dec. 29, 1813	2	93
Pacience, [d. John & Ann], b. Nov. 10, 1710	1	104
Prudence, d. [John & Prudence], b. Nov. 7, 1754	1	181
Prudence M., [d. John & Bathsheba], b. Feb. 1, 1815	3	32
Robert, s. [Joseph & Hannah], b. May 6, 1787	2	92
Robert, [s. John & Bathsheba], b. June 7, 1810	3	32
Robert, of Groton, m. Hannah **HEWET[T]**, of Preston, Feb. 27, 1812, by Jonah Witter, J.P.	2	93
Robert Austin, s. [Robert & Hannah], b. May 12, 1816	2	93
Sabra, of Groton, but residing in Preston, m. Phillip **GRAY**, 2d, of Groton, Feb. 9, 1797	2	61
Samuel, s. [John & Mary], b. Nov. 13, 1729	1	183
Samuel, s. [John & Prudence], b. Nov. 10, 1747	1	181
Sarah Cheesebrough, d. [John & Prudence], b. July 31, 1739	1	181
Thomas, [s. John & Ann], b. Apr. 17, 1708	1	104
Thomas, m. Lucy **BA[I]LEY**, Mar. 12, 1731/32	1	145
Thomas, s. Thomas & Lucy, b. Jan. 14, 1745; d. Oct. 20, 1751	1	145
William, [s. John & Bathsheba], b. June 8, 1819	3	32
Zerviah, d. [John & Prudence], b. Sept. 11, 1742	1	181
Zerviah, d. Mar. 13, 1766	1	185
Zerviah (**ELDREDGE**), [d. Charles & Mary **ELDREDGE**], d. Mar. 13, 1766	2	96
STAPLES, Experience, [d. Joseph], b. May 7, 1714	1	134
Hannah, [d. Joseph], b. June 21, 1711	1	134
Isaac, [s. Joseph], b. Dec. 21, 1721	1	134
Jacob, [s. Joseph], b. Mar. 11, 1716	1	134
James, [s. Joseph], b. Mar. 7, 1709	1	134
John, [s. Joseph], b. Dec. 12, 1719	1	134
Sarah, [d. Joseph], b. Apr. 1, 1707	1	134
STAPLINGS, Giles, of Salem, m. Sibel **CHAPMAN**, of Groton, Jan. 27, 1833, by W[illia]m M. Williams, J.P.	1	42
STARK, **STARKE**, Aaron, s. Christopher & Joanna, b. Mar. 3, 1732/3	1	101
Aaron, s. Christopher & Phebe, b. Mar. 3, 1732/3	1	149
Albert G., m. Hannah **WOLFE**, b. of Groton, Mar. 1, 1846, by Rev. Erastus Denison	1	75
Celinda, see Selenda		
Charles, m. Sally **BURROWS**, [ ]	3	0
Christopher, m. Joanna **WALSWORTH**, Apr. 1, 1722	1	101
Christopher, m. Johanna **WALLSWORTH**, Apr. 1, 1722	1	149
Christopher, s. Christopher & Joanna, b. Sept. 27, 1728	1	101
Christopher, s. Christopher & Phebe, b. Sept. 27, 1728	1	149
Eliza A., m. Caleb E. **TAFTS**, b. of Groton, Aug. 5, 1838, by Ira R. Steward	1	59
Eliza Ann, d. John & Charlotte, b. Jan. 21, 1812	2	71
Elizabeth, m. John **NEWBERRY**, Apr. 5, 1707	1	114
Elizabeth, d. William & Experience, b. Aug. 26, 1718	1	112
Elizabeth, d. Christopher & Joanna, b. Dec. 23, 1730	1	101
Elizabeth, d. Christopher & Phebe, b. Dec. 23, 1730	1	149

	Vol.	Page
STARK, STARKE, (cont.)		
Emily, m. John **LEEDS**, b. of Groton, Feb. 16, 1843, by Rev. Erastus Denison	1	67
Est[h]er, [d. Stephen & Hannah], b. Dec. 26, 1718	1	125
Fanny, m. William **HOLDREDGE**, b. of Groton, Nov. 12, 1826, by Nathan Daboll, J.P.	1	22
Hannah, m. Isaac **FOX**, Apr. 21, 1707	1	110
Hannah, d. Stephen & Hannah, b. Dec. 7, 1709	1	125
Henry S., m. Mary E. **RATHBUN**, b. of Groton, Aug. 10, 1843, by Nehemiah B. Cooke	1	69
Ichabod, s. Stephen & Hannah, b. May 22, 1713	1	125
Jacob, m. Martha **GREER**, July 18, 1728	1	114
James, s. Christopher & Phebe, b. May 22, 1734	1	149
John, m. Martha **WALWORTH**, Nov. 10, 1715	1	116
John, s. John & Martha, b. Nov. 11, 1716	1	116
John, m. Charlotte **BABCOCK**, b. of Groton, June 19, 1803, by John G. Wightman, Eld.	2	71
John, s. John & Charlotte, b. Dec. 1, 1804	2	71
Jonathan, s. William & Experience, b. Dec. 10, 1712	1	112
Mary, m. Joseph **COLVER**, Jan. 29, 1707	1	125
Mary, d. Christopher & Phebe, b. Feb. 26, 1738	1	149
Moses, s. William & Experience, b. June 17, 1716	1	112
Nathan, m. Cynthia **LEEDS**, b. of Groton, June 30, 1825, by Timothy Tuttle	1	17
Phebe, d. Christopher & Joanna, b. Aug. 1, 1726	1	101
Phebe, d. Christopher & Johanna, b. Aug. 1, 1726	1	149
Samuel, [s. Stephen & Hannah], b. Oct. 19, 1722	1	125
Sands, s. Solomon & Waitstill, b. Mar. 5, 1783	2	16
Selenda, d. John & Charlotte, b. July 23, 1809	2	71
Stephen, m. Hannah **CULVER**, Feb. 15, 1708	1	125
Stephen, [s. Stephen & Hannah], b. Nov. 15, 1717	1	125
Timothy, [s. Stephen & Hannah], b. Dec. 6, 1720	1	125
William, Jr., m. Experience **LAMBE**, Apr. 13, 1710	1	112
William, s. Christopher & Phebe, b. Feb. [ ], 1745	1	149
Zeruiah, d. Christopher & Joanna, b. Feb. 23, 1723	1	101
Zerviah, d. Christopher & Johanna, b. Feb. 23, 1723	1	149
STARKWEATHER, James, s. James & Sarah **BAKER**, b. May 6, 1781	2	10
James, s. Sarah BAKER, b. May 6, 1801	2	62
STARR, Abigail, d. Jonathan & Mary, b. Apr. 25, 1733	1	137
Austin D.*, m. Rhoda **COLVER**, b. of Groton, Dec. 30, 1844, by Rev. Erastus Denison (*Perhaps "S")	1	72
Benjamin, s. [Nicholas & Hannah], b. July 10, 1781	2	15
David H., of Groton, m. Harriet **ROGERS**, of Bridgeport, Dec. 10, 1837, by Joseph Durfey, J.P.	1	57
Deborah, d. Richard & Priscilla, b. May 15, 1749	1	156
Elijah, s. Richard & Priscilla, b. Feb. 3, 1756	1	156
Elisha, s. Richard & Priscilla, b. Mar. 6, 1741/2	1	156
Eliza H., m. Samuel A. **PERKINS**, b. of Groton, Mar. 1, 1850, by Rev. Jared R. Avery	1	87
Elizabeth, [s. Jonathan & Elizabeth], b. Aug. 19, 1701	1	105
Elizabeth, d. Jonathan & Mary, b. July 13, 1729	1	137
Emma M., m. Gilbert T. **SMITH**, b. of Groton, May 22, 1854, by Rev. Isaac Chees[e]brough	1	96

	Vol.	Page
STARR, (cont.)		
Hannah, [d. Thomas & Mary], b. Aug. 29, 1698	1	106
Hannah, d. Jonathan & Elizabeth, b. Dec. 10, 1710	1	105
Hannah, m. Joseph **BUTTOLPH**, Mar. 17, 1719	II	369
Hannah, m. Nicholas **STARR**, Oct. 31, 1771	2	15
Hannah, of Groton, m. Elnathan **APPLEY**, of Canterbury, Feb. 6, 1843, by Rev. Jared R. Avery	1	67
James, [s. Thomas & Mary], b. Oct. 18, 1708	1	106
James, s. [Nicholas & Hannah], b. Mar. 30, 1777	2	15
Jared, [s. Jonathan & Mary], b. Jan. 14, 1748	1	137
Jerusha, [d. Thomas & Mary], b. Feb. 8, 1702/3	1	106
Jesse, s. Vine & Mary, b. Nov. 30, 1753	1	155
Jonathan, m. Elizabeth **MORGAN**, Jan. 12, 1698/9	1	105
Jonathan, s. Jonathan & Elizabeth, b. Aug. 19, 1705	1	105
Jonathan, Jr., m. Mary **SEABURY**, Oct. 10, 1728	1	137
Jonathan, [s. Jonathan & Mary], b. Sept. 19, 1742	1	137
Jonathan, Capt., d. Aug. 26, 1747, ae. 74 y.	1	152
Joseph, s. Jonathan & Elizabeth, b. July 17, 1713	1	105
Joseph, s. [Nicholas & Hannah], b. Sept. 6, 1775	2	15
Joseph, Capt. had negroes Brunitta, b. Aug. 1, 17[ ], Brister, b. Mar. 1, 17[ ]	2	25
Katharine, [d. Jonathan & Elizabeth], b. Feb. 18, 1724	1	105
Lousey, d. Jonathan & Elizabeth, b. July 18, 1708	1	105
Lucy Ann, of Groton, m. Paul Allen Comstock **ROGERS**, of Waterford, Jan. 26, 1840, by Rev. Jared R. Avery	1	62
Mary, [d. Thomas & Mary], b. June 29, 1696	1	106
Mary, m. Joseph **CULVER**, Jan. 29, 1707 (Should be Mary Stark)	1	186
Mary, m. John **CHESTER**, Nov. 1, 1716	1	108
Mary, [d. Jonathan & Elizabeth], b. Aug. 30, 1722	1	105
Mary, [d. Jonathan & Mary], b. Sept. 3, 1737	1	137
Mary, m. Charles **ELDREDGE**, Apr. 23, 1741	1	185
Mary, m. Charles **ELDREDGE**, Apr. 23, 1741	2	96
Mary, d. Richard & Priscilla, b. Oct. 29, 1759	1	156
Mary S., m. Alfred P. **HALLOWAY**, b. of Groton, Feb. 22, 1852, by Rev. N. T. Allen	1	93
Nicholas, m. Hannah **STARR**, Oct. 31, 1771	2	15
Nicholas, s. [Nicholas & Hannah], b. Oct. 3, 1772	2	15
Nicholas, m. Abbeline **TIFT**, b. of Groton, Nov. 29, 1829, by Rev. Roswell Burrows	1	32
Rachel, [d. Thomas & Mary], b. Sept. 15, 1705	1	106
Rachel, d. Richard & Priscilla, b. No[ ]	1	156
Rebeckah, [d. Jonathan & Mary], b. July 24, 1750	1	137
Richard, [s. Jonathan & Elizabeth], b. May 14, 1718	1	105
Richard, m. Priscilla **SMITH**, Jan. 15, 1740/41	1	156
Richard, s. Richard & Priscilla, b. June 26, 1745	1	156
Samuel, [s. Jonathan & Elizabeth], b. Nov. 5, 1699	1	105
Sarah, [d. Jonathan & Mary], b. Apr. 4, 1740	1	137
Susan, of Groton, m. Youngs A. **TURNER**, of Ledyard, Apr. 16, 1843, by Rev. Jared R. Avery	1	68
Thomas, m. Mary **MORGAN**, Jan. 1, 1694/5	1	106
Thomas, [s. Thomas & Mary], b. Sept. 26, 1700; d. [ ], 1701	1	106
Thomas, [s. Thomas & Mary], b. Apr. 10, 1711	1	106
Vine, [s. Jonathan & Elizabeth], b. Jan. 19, 1716	1	105

	Vol.	Page
STARR, (cont.)		
Vine, m. Mary **STREET**, Apr. 14, 1737	1	155
Vine, s. Vine & Mary, b. Feb. 17, 1739/40	1	155
Vine, s. Vine & Mary, b. Feb. 3, 1757	1	155
STEAD, Jemima, of Swanzey, m. Joshua **CHAPMAN**, of Groton, Jan. 27, 1783, in Swanzey, by Russell Mason, J.P.	2	2
STEBBINS, John, m. Sarah **CLARK**, b. of Waterford, Oct. 8, 1853, by Rev. William A. Smith	1	95
John, m. Sarah **CLARK**, b. of Waterford, Oct. 8, 1853, by Rev. William A. Smith	3	35
STEDMAN, Braddock, s. Joanna, b. Mar. 12, 1763	1	176
Clementine, of Groton, m. Christopher **CHAPMAN**, of Bozrah, Feb. 20, 1833, by Nathan Daboll, J.P.	1	42
STEELE, Ashbel, Rev., of Waterbury, Ct., m. Clarissa **BREWSTER**, of Waterville, N.Y., June 28, 1825, in St. James Church, by Rev. S. B. Paddock, of Norwich	1	17
W[illia]m, m. Ruth **BAILEY**, [ ]	1	114
STERRY, Almira, of Groton, m. Nathan C. **REYNOLDS**, of Griswold, Sept. 16, 1827, by Ralph Hurlbutt, J.P.	1	24
Hannah, of Groton, m. Arnold **HILL**, of Norwich, Aug. 24, 1828, by Elisha Brewster, J.P.	1	28
Sally, m. Joseph **BOLLES**, b. of Montville, Feb. 3, 1830, by Philip Gray, J.P.	1	33
STEWARD, Emily, d. Ira R. & Mary, b. May 5, 1833; d. Dec. 25, 1833	3	29
Eunice, H., m. James A. **AVERY**, b. of Groton, June 11, 1843 by Ira R. Steward	1	69
Hannah, m. Charles **SMITH**, Oct. 13, 1771, by Timothy Whitman	2	21
Ira R., m. Matilda **AVERY**, b. of Groton, Feb. 4, 1834, by Rev. Roswell Burrows	1	46
Ira W., s. Ira R. & Matilda, b. Apr. 25, 1835	3	27
Mary, w. Elder Ira R., d. Oct. 1, 1833	3	27
STEWART, [see also **STUART**], Sarah, of Stonington, m. Nathan **NEWBURY**, of Groton, Apr. 15, 1743	1	150
STILLMAN, Matthew, of Westerly, R.I., m. Francina **HAVENS**, of Groton, Aug. 1, 1832, by John G. Wightman, Elder	1	40
Nathaniel, of New London, m. Wealthy **CLARK**, of Groton, Feb. 10, 1822, by Ralph Hurlbutt, J.P.	1	6
STODDARD, Abby, m. Peter **LESTER**, 2d, of Groton, Jan. 2, 1825, by Ralph Hurlbutt, J.P.	1	15
Abigail, d. Robert & Bathsheba, b. Aug. 6, 1745	1	134
Abigail, d. [Robert, Jr. & Bathsheba], b. Aug. 6, 1745	1	173
Abigail, d. Thomas & Abigail, b. Nov. 29, 1772	2	16
Adeline, of Groton, m. Francis F. **MITCHELL**, of Ashford, Apr. 1, 1830, by Timothy Tuttle	1	34
[A]Eneas Morgan, s. [Ebenezer & Lydia], b. June 26, 1824	3	13
Albert Monroe, [s. Sanford & Polly], b. July 8, 1818	2	85
Almira, of Groton, m. Franklin **BREWSTER**, of Norwich, Nov. 29, 1832, by Timothy Tuttle	1	42
Anna, d. [Robert, Jr. & Lucy], b. Dec. 14, 1759	2	27
Anna, d. [Jonathan], b. Mar. 2, 1798	2	93
Anselia, d. [Sanford & Polly], b. July 5, 1811	2	85
Asa, s. Ichabod & Tabitha, b. Apr. 29, 1771	2	6

	Vol.	Page
STODDARD, (cont.)		
Asa, of Groton, m. Mrs. Mary **MAY**, of Windham, May 18, 1836, by Ralph Hurlbutt, J.P.	1	54
Baththia, d. Robert & Bathsheba, b. Aug. 25, 1732	1	134
Bathsheba, d. [Robert, Jr. & Lucy], b. Jan. 11, 1755	2	27
Bathsheba, [d. Mortimer & Dorothy], b. Apr. 3, 1774	2	18
Benecey, s. Robert & Sarah, b. Sept. 15, 1728	1	140
B[enjamin] F., Dr., b. Jan. 26, 1792; m. Julia A. **MINER**, Nov. 27, 1817	3	9
Bridget N., m. Asaph **HURLBUTT**, b. of Groton, Nov. 7, 1830, by Ralph Hurlbutt, J.P.	1	35
Bridget Niles, [d. Sanford & Polly], b. Feb. 12, 1807	2	85
Caroline, m. Alfred **ALLYN**, b. of Groton, Sept. 4, 1831, by John G. Wightman, Eld.	1	38
Caroline L., of Ledyard, m. Frederick A. **WILLIAMS**, of Groton, June 20, 1843, in Ledyard, by Ira R. Steward	1	69
Catharine, d. Robert & Sarah, b. Dec. 25, 1732/3	1	140
Cephas, [s. Ichabod & Tabitha], b. Nov. 8, 1775; d. Apr. 6, 1778	2	6
Cephas, s. [Ichabod & Tabitha], b. Sept. 28, 1784	2	6
Charity, d. [Ebenezer & Lydia], b. Apr. 29, 1820	3	13
Clarissa, d. [Daniel & Lucretia], b. Feb. 10, 1795	2	90
Clarissa, d. [Ebenezer & Lydia], b. Sept. 9, 1818	3	13
Daniel, s. [Robert, Jr. & Lucy], b. Nov. 6, 1761	2	27
Daniel, b. Nov. 6, 1761; m. Lucretia **BELLOWS**, Jan. 1, 1784	2	90
Daniel, s. [Daniel & Lucretia], b. June 5, 1787	2	90
Daniel, 3d, s. Daniel & Fanny, b. Apr. 25, 1824	3	7
David, s. Moses & Mary, b. June 6, 1749	1	150
Deborah, d. Moses & Mary, b. June 3, 1755	1	150
Easther, d. Ralph, Jr. & Hannah, b. May [ ], 1740	1	139
Easther, m. Simeon **ALLYN**, Sept. 1, 1771	2	15
Ebenezer, s. Moses & Mary, b. Feb. 13, 1737/8	1	150
Ebenezer, s. Moses & Mary, b. Sept. 19, 1759	1	150
Ebenezer, s. [James, Jr. & Charity], b. Jan. 23, 1786	2	59
Ebenezer, m. Lydia **WILLIAMS**, Nov. 11, 1811	3	13
Ebenezer Morgan, s. [Stephen & Sally], b. Oct. 22, 1835[sic]	3	30
Edmund, s. [Daniel & Lucretia], b. Jan. 28, 1802	2	90
Edmond, m. Lucy **ALLYN**, b. of Groton, May 9, 1830, by Ralph Hurlbutt, J.P.	1	34
Elisha, s. Moses & Mary, b. Sept. 17, 1757	1	150
Elisha Denison, s. [Stephen & Sally], b. Nov. 27, 1815	3	30
Eliza, of Groton, m. Daniel **CONGDON**, of Norwich, Mar. 29, 1829, by John Brewster, J.P.	1	30
Elizabeth, m. Joseph **MALESON**, Oct. 4, 1711	1	101
Elizabeth, m. Joseph **MALLISON**, Oct. 4, 1711	1	133
Elizabeth, d. Moses & Mary, b. Oct. 5, 1740	1	150
Elizabeth, d. Robert & Bathsheba, b. Mar. 11, 1749/50	1	180
Elizabeth, d. Mortimer & Dorothy, b. July 6, 1766	2	18
Elizabeth, m. Levy **SHOLES**, b. of Groton, May 10, 1764	2	14
Elizabeth, d. Daniel, Jr. & Fanny, b. Mar. 12, 1822	3	7
Elkanah, s. Ralph, Jr. & Hannah, b. Aug. [ ], 1743	1	139
Elkana, s. Wait & Tabitha, b. Jan. 29, 1771	1	160
Emelia Avery, [d. Sanford & Polly], b. Dec. 26, 1804	2	85
Emily A., m. John W. **MINER**, b. of Groton, Oct. 14, 1827, by Ralph Hurlbutt, J.P.	1	25

	Vol.	Page
STODDARD, (cont.)		
Enoch V., s. [Vine, Jr. & Prudence], b. Sept. 14, 1804	3	10
Ephraim, s. [Ebenezer & Lydia], b. June 16, 1815	3	13
[E]unis, d. Ralph, Jr. & Hannah, b. Mar. 9, 1735/6	1	139
Fanny, d. [Ebenezer & Lydia], b. Nov. 11, 1813	3	13
Frances A., m. Charles G. **SMITH**, b. of Norwich, May 19, 1833, by Rev. Erastus Denison	1	44
Guy C., of Ledyard, m. Abby **LATHAM**, of Groton, Feb. 10, 1840, by Rev. Jared R. Avery	1	62
Hannah, d. Ralph & Hannah, b. May 4, 1727	1	108
Hannah, m. Nathan **AVERY**, Mar. 27, 1746	1	178
Hannah, d. Ichabod & Tabitha, b. July 20, 1773	2	6
Hannah, d. [James, Jr. & Charity], b. Feb. 1, 1787	2	59
Hannah, d. [Ebenezer & Lydia], b. July 19, 1812; d. Sept. 15, 1813	3	13
Hannah, d. [Seth], b. June 5, 1825	2	93
Harriet, d. [Vine, Jr. & Sabra], b. Feb. 27, 1802	3	10
Henry, s. [Jonathan], b. Nov. 16, 1812	2	93
Hester, m. Elisha **SATTERLEE**, b. of Groton, Aug. 28, 1825, by Ralph Hurlbutt, J.P.	1	18
Hibbard, s. James, Jr. & Charity, b. Mar. 26, 1783	2	59
Ichabod, s. Robert & Bathsheba, b. Jan. 10, 1741/2	1	134
Ichabod, m. Tabitha **BILLINGS**, b. of Groton, May 10, 1767, by Jacob Johnson, Elder	2	6
Ichabod, s. Ichabod & Tabitha, b. Sept. 13, 1767	2	6
Ichabod, s. [Seth], b. Mar. 15, 1817	2	93
Increase, s. [Robert, Jr. & Lucy], b. Oct. 22, 1767	2	27
James, s. Robert & Sarah, b. Feb. 17, 1735/6	1	140
James, s. [James, Jr. & Charity], b. May 14, 1784	2	59
James A., of Ledyard, m. Lucy C. **EDGECOMB**, of Groton, Sept. 6, 1846, by Rev. H. R. Knapp	1	83
Jane, m. William G. **DEWEY**, b. of Groton, June 28, 1829, by John G. Wightman, Eld.	1	31
Jonathan, s. Ralph & Hannah, b. Oct. 19, 1731	1	108
Jonathan, s. Robert & Bathsheba, b. Nov. 28, 1737	1	134
Jonathan, s. [Robert, Jr. & Lucy], b. Nov.14, 1765	2	27
Jonathan, s. Mark & Lucy, b. Mar. 16, 1783	2	3
Jonathan, s. [Jonathan], b. Jan. 12, 1789	2	93
Joseph, s. Moses & Mary, b. May 8, 1747	1	150
Josephus, s. [Seth], b. Mar. 17, 1821	2	93
Julia, d. [Ebenezer & Lydia], b. Apr. 7, 1817	3	13
Lucretia, d. [Daniel & Lucretia], b. Sept. 29,1784	2	90
Lucretia, of Groton, m. Cyrus **PENDERSON**, of Preston, Feb. 11, 1827, by Rev. Thomas R. Peck	1	23
Lucy, d. Robert & Bathsheba, b. Apr. 10, 1747	1	134
Lucy, d. [Robert, Jr. & Bathsheba], b. Apr. 10, 1747	1	173
Lucy, d. [Daniel & Lucretia], b. Oct. 17, 1798	2	90
Lucy, m. Israel F. **MORGAN**, b. of Groton, Dec. 26, 1813	3	4
Lydia, d. [Jonathan], b. Jan. 4, 1796	2	93
Lyman, s. Daniel & Fanny, b. Feb. 17, 1826	3	7
Mariah, d. [Daniel & Lucretia], b. Apr. 10, 1797	2	90
Maria, m. Christopher **ALLYN**, Nov. 19, 1820, by Timothy Tuttle	1	2
Mark, s. Ralph, b. Feb. 14, 1702	1	117
Mark, m. Joannah **AVERY**, Feb. 13, 1724/3	1	109

	Vol.	Page
STODDARD, (cont.)		
Mark, d. Jan. 27, 1724/5	1	109
Mark, s. Ralph & Hannah, b. May 1, 1725; d. Sept. 29, 1726	1	108
Mark, s. Robert & Bathsheba, b. Oct. 10, 1743	1	134
Mark, s. Robert, Jr. & Bathsheba, b. Oct. 10, 1743	1	173
Marvin Wait, s. [Wait & Sarah], b. Aug. 4, 1796	2	81
Mary, d. Ralph, b. July 20, 1705	1	117
Mary, m. William **CHAPMAN**, Jan. 8, 1718/19	1	155
Mary, d. Mark & Joannah, b. Aug. 4, 1725	1	109
Mary, d. Mark & Joannah, b. Aug. 4, 1725	1	109
Mary, m. John **HURLBUTT**, Oct. 20, 1726	1	136
Mary, d. Ralph, Jr. & Hannah, b. Dec. 12, 1733	1	139
Mary, d. Robert & Bathsheba, b. July 21, 1734	1	134
Mary, d. Robert & Bathsheba, b. Mar. 10, 1739/40	1	134
Mary, m. Timothy **WIGHTMAN**, May 13, 1747	1	175
Mary, m. John **WIGHTMAN**, Nov. 9, 1752; d. Mar. 13, 1768	1	158
Mary, d. Moses & Mary, b. Aug. 19, 1753	1	150
Mary, d. Moses & Mary, b. Oct. 5, 1761	1	150
Mary, d. Wait & Tabitha, b. Jan. 19, 1762	1	160
Mary Ann, m. Urban **AVERY**, b. of Groton, Jan. 5, 1836, by Ira R. Steward, Eld.	1	53
Mary D., of Grootn, m. Silas **FISH**, of Stonington, Apr. 10, 1851, by Rev. Nehemiah B. Cooke, of Stonington	1	91
Mary J., of Ledyard, m. Jesse D. **SMITH**, of Groton, Apr. 20, 1851, by Rev. J. R. Avery	1	91
Mercy, m. William **CHAPMAN**, Jan. 8, 1718	1	108
Mortemore, s. Robert & Bathsheba, b. Mar. 16, 1735/6	1	134
Mortimer, m. Dorothy **PARKE**, b. of Groton, Dec. 6, 1764, by Rev. Jacob Johnson	2	18
Mortimer, s. Mortimer & Dorothy, b. Sept. 12, 1771	2	18
Moses, s. Moses & Mary, b. June 6, 1742	1	150
Nancy, m. Austin M. **LESTER**, b. of Groton, Sept. 16, 1827, by Ralph Hurlbutt, J.P.	1	24
Nathan, s. Wait & Tabitha, b. May 28, 1758	1	160
Orlando, s. Daniel & Fanny, b. Dec. 1, 1827	3	7
Phebe, d. [Daniel & Lucretia], b. Oct. 4, 1792	2	90
Polly, [d. Ichabod & Tabitha], b. July 10, 1782	2	6
Pollie, d. [Jonathan], b. Oct. 16, 1791	2	93
Polly, of Groton, m. Henry **BILLINGS**, of Waterford, Nov. 9, 1806, by Amos Geer, J.P.	2	81
Polly Cordelia, [d. Sanford & Polly], b. Feb. 20, 1821	2	85
Prentice S., s. [Vine, Jr. & Sabra], b. June 20, 1803	3	10
Priscilla, d. Ralph, Jr. & Hannah, b. Mar. 12, 1737/8	1	139
Priscilla L., of Groton, m. Nathan **GEER**, Jr., of Griswold, Feb. 5, 1824, by Timothy Tuttle	1	12
Prudence, d. [Vine, Jr. & Prudence], b. Feb. 25, 1807; d. Oct. 30, 1808	3	10
Ralph, s. Ralph, b. May 21, 1697	1	117
Ralph, m. Hannah **LESTER**, Jan. 3, 1723	1	108
Ralph, s. Ralph & Hannah, b. July 30, 1723	1	108
Ralph, Jr., m. Susannah **AVERY**, Apr. 3, 1746	1	184
Ralph, s. [Ralph, Jr. & Susannah], b. Feb. 4, 1751	1	184
Robert, Jr., m. Bathsheba **RODGERS**, Dec. 21, 1727	1	134
Robert, s. Robert & Bathsheba, b. Aug. 26, 1729	1	134

	Vol.	Page
STODDARD, (cont.)		
Robert, Jr., m. Lucy **BILLINGS**, of Groton, June 18, 1752	2	27
Robert, 3d, s. [Robert, Jr. & Lucy], b. June 2, 1757	2	27
Robert, m. Wid. Sarah **SMITH**, d. Lawrence **JOHNSON**, Nov. 30, 1791	2	74
Robert A., s. Mortimer & Dorothy, b. Jan. 26, 1769	2	18
Sabra, s. Vine, d. Aug. 7, 1803	3	10
Sally L., of Groton, m. William **GREENE**, of Pitcher, N.Y., Oct. 13, 1833, by Timothy Tuttle	1	45
Sally Maria, d. [Wait & Sarah], b. Apr. 16, 1793	2	81
Samuel, s. Robert & Sarah, b. Sept. 13, 1730	1	140
Sanford, m. Polly **AVERY**, b. of Groton, Feb. 22, 1804, by Amos Geer, J.P.	2	85
Sanford Billings, [s. Sanford & Polly], b. Dec. 4, 1812	2	85
Sarah, d. Robert & Sarah, b. Aug. 1, 1718	1	140
Sarah, m. Increase **BILLINGS**, July 26, 1751, by Ebenezer Punderson, Missionary	1	175
Sarah Elmira, d. [Stephen & Sally], b. June 20, 1813	3	30
Seth, s. [Ichabod & Tabitha], b. Jan. 19, 1787	2	6
Shapley, s. Seth, b. Oct. 16, 1811	2	93
Sidney, s. [Daniel & Lucretia], b. Aug. 24, 1799	2	90
Sidney, m. Wealthy **ALLYN**, b. of Groton, July 12, 1823, by Timothy Tuttle	1	10
Silas, s. Wait & Tabitha, b. Dec. 7, 1759	1	160
Simeon, s. Wait & Tabitha, b. May 29, 1768	1	160
Sophia. [d. Ichabod & Tabitha], b. July 1, 1780; d. July 8, 1780	2	6
Sophia. [d. Sanford & Polly], b. Mar. 4, 1809	2	85
Stanford, [s. Ichabod & Tabitha], b. July 25, 1778	2	6
Stephen, s. Robert & Sarah, b. Mar. 2, 1739/40	1	140
Stephen, [s. Stephen], b. Mar. 18, 1768	1	180
Stephen, s. [James, Jr. & Charity], b. May 10, 1788; d. Jan. 2, 1799	2	59
Stephen Morgan, s. [Stephen & Sally], b. Apr. 21, 1811	3	30
Susanna, d. Robert & Sarah, b. Aug. 23, 1737	1	140
Tabitha, d. Ichabod & Tabitha, b. Mar. 14, 1769	2	6
Thomas, s. Moses & Mary, b. Dec. 12, 1744	1	150
Thomas, m. Abigail **CULVER**, b. of Groton, May 3, 1772	2	16
Vine, s. [Ralph, Jr. & Susannah], b. Feb. 27, 1748/9	1	184
Vine, Jr., b. Oct. 28, 1775; m. Sabra **AVERY**, June 11, 1801	3	10
Vine, Jr., m. Prudence **SMITH**, Nov. 23, 1803	3	10
Wait, s. Ralph & Hannah, b. July 14, 1729	1	108
Wait, m. Tabitha **NILES**, Jan. 14, 1756	1	160
Wait, s. Wait & Tabitha, b. May 30, 1766	1	160
Wait, m. Sarah **ALLYN**, b. of Groton, Dec. 4, 1791	2	81
Welthy, d. Stephen, b. Feb. 12, 1764	1	180
William, [s. Stephen], b. Nov. 8, 1766	1	180
William Henry, [s. Sanford & Polly], b. Apr. 18, 1816	2	85
STOGERS, Elizabeth, m. Lawrence **POWERS**, Feb. 11, 1729/30	1	143
La[w]rence, m. Elizabeth **DOWNING**, June 19, 1718	1	110
STORER, Frederick, of Mansfield, m. Eliza **CHEESEBOROUGH**, of Groton, Apr. 29, 1822, by Rev. John G. Wightman	1	6
STORY, Abby, of Groton, m. James **WINCHESTER**, Jr., of Norwich, Dec. 30, 1827, by Rev. David N. Bentley	1	26
Cinthia, of Groton, m. Joseph **MANNING**, of Norwich, Oct. 31, 1824, by Rev. Ashbel Steele, of Pequatanock	1	14

	Vol.	Page
STORY, (cont.)		
Mary Ann, of Groton, m. Isaac **WILLIAMS**, of Stonington, Sept. 26, 1830, by Ebenezer Avery, J.P.	1	35
Sarah, m. Solomon **BENHAM**, b. of Groton, Sept. 4, 1831, by Nathan Daboll, J.P.	1	38
STREET, Anna, d. Nicholas & Jerusha, b. Nov. 24, 1710	1	111
Anna, m. Peter **LESTER**, Aug. [ ], 1733	1	175
Elizabeth, m. Elisha **SMITH**, Nov. 30, 1732	1	164
Elizabeth, m. David **LESTER**, May 13, 1771	1	176
Jerusha, d. Nicholas & Jerusha, b. [ ], 1715	1	111
Mary, d. Nicholas & Jerusha, b. Nov. 25, 1716	1	111
Mary, m. Vine **STARR**, Apr. 14, 1737	1	155
Nicholas, s. Nicholas & Jerusha, b. July 29, 1713	1	111
Nicholas, d. July 10, 1733	1	171
Rebeccah, [d. Nicholas & Jerusha], b. Feb. 10, 1727/8	1	111
Samuel, s. [Nicholas & Jerusha], b. Sept. 6, 1718	1	111
Sarah, [d. Nicholas & Jerusha], b. Aug. 31, 1720; d. Sept. 7, 1720	1	111
Susanna, [d. Nicholas & Jerusha], b. Dec. 19, 1722	1	111
STRICKLAND, James, of Waterford, m. Sally **CONGDON**, of Groton, Nov. 29, 1840, by Nathan Daboll, J.P.	1	64
STRONG, Amanda M., m. George C. **BRICK**, b. of Groton, Jan. 8, 1853, by Rev. Nicholas T. Allen	1	94
Daniel, of Bolton, m. Sabra **MORGAN**, of Groton, Nov. 16, 1825, by Timothy Tuttle	1	19
Lucy R., of Groton, m. W[illia]m **SALTER**, of Stonington, Mar. 25, 1851, by Rev. Nicholas T. Allen	1	91
Nancy M., m. Elisha M. **MINOR**, Oct. 31, 1847, by Rev. Jared R. Avery	1	80
Sabra Emeline, of Groton, m. George F. **BURDICK**, of Norwich, Mar. 30, 1847, by Rev. Jared R. Avery	1	78
STUART, [see also **STEWART**], Alexander, Jr., of Griswold, m. Lucy L. **BARROWS**, of Groton, Feb. 22, 1821, by Roswell Burrows, Minister	1	3
SUTE, John, of Lyme, m. Mary **MITCHELL**, of Groton, Dec. 5, 1820, by Rev. Lathrop Rockwell, of Lyme	1	2
SUTTON, Robert, of the town of Maraland, m. Hannah **COTTRELL**, of Groton, June 6, 1830, by John G. Wightman, Eld.	1	34
SWADDLE, SWADLE, Anna, m. Comfort **DAVIS**, July 18, 1708	1	113
Elizabeth, [d. W[illia]m & Elizabeth], b. Mar. 31, 1724	1	113
James, s. W[illia]m & Elizabeth, b. Dec. 23, 1719	1	113
Samuel, [s. W[illia]m & Elizabeth], b. June 26, 1726	1	113
William, m. Elizabeth **CROCKER**, Jan. 22, 1718	1	113
SWAN, Abigail, of Hancock, Mass., m. Thomas **WELLS**, of Groton, Mar. 8, 1808, by William Douglass, Jr., J.P. in Rennsalear County, N.Y.	2	80
Cyrus Wolcott, s. Cyrus, b. May 24, 1818	2	58
Lucy, of Stonington, m. Isaac **AVERY**, of Groton, June 11, 1771, in Stonington	2	58
Nathan, Jr., of N. Stonington, m. Wateann **NEWTON**, of Groton, Dec. 24, 1820, by Perez Hewitt, J.P.	1	2
Timothy, m. Hannah **WELLS**, Apr. 11, 1824, by Philip Gray, J.P.	1	13
SWEET, Nancy, Wid., of Groton, m. Samuel **REYNOLDS**, a European now residing in New London, Apr. 23, 1827, by Roswell Fish, J.P.	1	26
Stephen, of Franklin, m. Phebe A. **HEATH**, of [Groton], Sept. 29, 1850, by W. Munger	1	92
TAYLOR, Avery, s. [John & Elizabeth], b. Aug. 1, 1795	2	73

	Vol.	Page
TAYLOR, (cont.)		
Edna, d. [John & Elizabeth], b. Sept. 4, 1798	2	73
George W., of Groton, m. Mary **BRIGHTMAN**, of Stonington, Dec. 23, 1832, by John G. Wightman, Eld.	1	42
Gurdon, s. [John & Elizabeth], b. Mar. 22, 1791	2	73
John C., s. [John & Elizabeth], b. Sept. 20, 1787	2	73
Marybe, of Groton, m. Thomas W. **BROOKS**, of Waterford, Apr. 28, 1828, by N. S. Spaulding	1	27
Samuel, of Greenville, Norwich, m. Abby L. **TURNER**, of Groton, May 20, 1845, by Rev. D. H. Cheney, of Greenville	1	73
Sile, d. [John & Elizabeth], b. Nov. 6, 1784	2	73
William, s. William & Sally, b. Mar. 28, 1796	2	13
TEAD, Theodore, of N.Y., m. Harriet **LEWIS**, of Stonington, Sept. 18, 1836, by John G. Wightman, Elder	1	55
TEFFT, TEFTS, see under **TIFT**		
THOMAS, Alfred, s. [Daniel & Eunice], b. May 26, 1795	2	54
Betsey, d. [Daniel & Eunice], b. Mar. 31, 1783	2	54
Daniel, m. Eunice **BAKER**, b. of Groton, Jan. 11, 1781	2	54
Daniel, s. [Daniel & Eunice], b. Mar. 12, 1798	2	54
Eunice, d. [Daniel & Eunice], b. Mar. 31, 1789	2	54
Jerusha, d. [Daniel & Eunice], b. Feb. 2, 1792	2	54
Seabury, s. [Daniel & Eunice], b. Aug. 22, 1802; m. Hannah Avery **HALEY**, Sept. 18, 1825	2	54
Seabury, m. Hannah **HALEY**, b. of Groton, Sept. 18, 1825, by John G. Wightman, Eld.	1	18
Sebra(?), m. Hannah **HALEY**, d. Caleb, Jr. & Sally [ ]	3	0
Steward, s. [Daniel & Eunice], b. Mar. 21, 1787	2	54
Welthen, d. [Daniel & Eunice], b. Nov. 21, 1784	2	54
Welthian, m. Avery **CHAPMAN**, b. of Groton, Nov. 20, 1804, by Amos Geer, J.P.	2	73
THOMPSON, THOMSON, Daniel, of Norwich, m. Martha **PERKINS**, of Groton, July 5, 1829, by Joseph Durfey, J.P.	1	31
John G., m. Amey **KENYON**, b. of Groton, Oct. 12, 1828, by Roswell Fish, J.P.	1	29
Julia Ann, of N. Stonington, m. Charles H. **DAVIS**, of Westerly, July 23, 1842, by Ira R. Steward	1	67
Lucy Ann, m. Austin **WHITE**, b. of Stonington, Sept. 19, 1830, by Ralph Hurlbutt, J.P.	1	35
Martin, of Groton, m. Abby **GILES**, of New York, Aug. 30, 1834, by Nathan Daboll, J.P.	1	47
THURBER, Mary, m. Ebenezer ALLYN, Apr. 27, 1726	1	132
THURSTON, John, of Boxford, Mass., m. Nancy **CULVER**, of Groton, May 10, 1835, by John G. Wightman, Eld.	1	50
TIFT, TEFTS, TIFFT, TEFT, TUFT, Abby Ann, d. Ezekiel & Ann, b. June 18, 1814	3	16
Abbeline, m. Nicholas **STARR**, b. of Groton, Nov. 29, 1829, by Rev. Roswell Burrows	1	32
Betsey, m. Abel **MAINE**, Nov. 16, 1826, by Perez Hewitt, J.P.	1	23
Caleb E., of Groton, m. Eliza A. **STARK**, of Groton, Aug. 5, 1838, by Ira R. Steward	1	59
Caleb Ezekiel, s. [Ezekiel & Ann], b. Mar. 20, 1816	3	16
Daniel, s. Peter & Ann, b. July 23, 1725	1	135

	Vol.	Page
TIFT, TEFTS, TIFFT, TEFT, TUFT, (cont.)		
Elizabeth, m. Henry **LOOMIS**, of Hartford, Ct., Nov. 11, 1827, by Rev. Roswell Burrows	1	25
Elizabeth J., m. Isaac D. **CLIFT**, b. of Groton, Oct. 5, 1853, by Rev. Walter R. Seny, of Mystic Bridge	1	96
Elizabeth R., b. July 21, 1808	3	9
Frances A., of Groton, m. Daniel **PINCHION**, of Albany, Ga., Sept. 26, 1832, by Timothy Tuttle	1	72
Hannah C., of Groton, m. Oliver J. **NOYES**, of Rio Grande, Mexico, Aug. 26, 1832, by Timothy Tuttle	1	41
Joseph, s. Solomon & Eunice, b. Oct. 18, 1782	2	17
Joseph, Jr., of N. Stonington, m. Maria **WHITTLES**, of Groton, May 2, 1833, by Philip Gray, J.P.	1	44
Joseph B., b. Oct. 18, 1782	3	9
Martha, m. Samuel **MAINE**, Jr., of Groton, Nov. 30, 1823, by Peris Hewitt, J.P.	1	11
Paul, m. Mary Ann **MAINE**, Mar. 4, 1827, by Perez Hewitt, J.P.	1	23
Peleg Spicer, of R.I., m. Mary **AVERY**, of Groton, Dec. 7, 1831, by John Brewster, J.P.	1	38
Peter, m. Ann **SPICER**, Dec. 13, 1722	1	135
Peter, s. Peter & Ann, b. Feb. 5, 1724	1	135
Phebe, m. Samuel **CHIPMAN**, b. of Groton, Aug. 30(?), 1821, by Rev. Roswell Burrows	1	4
Prudence, of Groton, m. Abel **LEWIS**, of Hopkinton, R.I., Dec. 10, 1829, by William Williams, J.P.	1	32
Rebecca, of Groton, m. James **REED**, of New York, June 26, 1825, by Roswell Fish, J.P.	1	17
Rebecca A., b. Jan. 21, 1790	3	9
Solomon, s. Solomon & Eunice, b. May 4, 1786	2	10
TILER, [see also **TYLER**], Amy, d. Job & Bial, b. Mar. 5, 1742	1	159
Anne, d. Job & Bial, b. Oct. 28, 1739	1	159
Bial, d. Job & Bial, b. July 28, 1748	1	159
Daniel, m. Anne **GARE**, May 28, 1700	1	105
Daniel, Jr., [s. Daniel & Anne], b. Feb. 22, 1700/1	1	105
Job, [s. Daniel & Anne], b. Feb. 14, 1710/11	1	105
Job, m. Bial **WILLIAMS**, Aug. 24, 1732	1	159
Job, s. Job & Bial, b. Apr. 18, 1746	1	159
John, [s. Daniel & Anne], b. Mar. 24, 1705	1	105
Martha, m. Robert **GEERE**, Apr. 3, 1700	1	103
Molly, d. Job & Bial, b. Mar. 29, 1744	1	159
Sarah, [, d. Daniel & Anne], b. Aug. 16, 1702	1	105
Solomon, s. Job & Bial, b. Jan. 25, 1734	1	159
Solomon, s. Job, b. Jan. 25, 1734/5	1	172
TILVEST, Martin, m. Mary **ADELY**, b. of Groton, Jan. 9, 1849, by Rev. Simon B. Bailey	1	82
TINKER, Jonathan, of Lyme, m. Bridget Caroline **WIGHTMAN**, of Groton, July 24, 1842, by Rev. Erastus Denison	1	66
Lynds, of Lyme, m. Mary Ann **PRENTICE**, of Stonington, Dec. 8, 1833, by John G. Wightman, Eld.	1	45
TOPLIFF, Ann Amelia Maria, m. Caleb **LEE**, b. of Willington, Mar. 20, 1848, by Rev. L. G. Leonard	1	80
TOURTELETT, Abraham, of Dudley, Mass., m. Martha Louisa **BUD[D]ING-TON**, of Groton, Oct. 20, 1825, by Caleb Avery, J.P.	1	19

	Vol.	Page
TRACY, Marcy, m. Joseph **HEATH**, Jan. 3, 1757	1	163
Margaret, of Norwich, m. Samuel **WILLIAMS**, of Groton, May 28, 1758, by Rev. Stephen White	1	171
Margaret, of Norwich, m. Samuel **WILLIAMS**, of Groton, May 28, 1758	2	24
TRAIL, James, of Svotland, m. Harriet **WILLIAMS**, of Groton, Nov. 10, 1850, by Rev. Nicholas T. Allen	1	90
TRENCHARD, Anna Culver, d. Mar. 6, 1840	1	189
Henry, m. Anna **CULVER**, Nov. 9, 1807	1	189
TRUMAN, Horace, of Norwich, m. Bridget **EDGECOMB**, of Groton, Aug. 1, 1847, by Rev. Nicholas T. Allen	1	79
TUCKER, Luther, of Ontario, N.Y., m. Frances Ann **SMITH**, of Groton, Oct. 18, 1825, by John G. Wightman, Eld.	1	19
Wealthy A., of Groton, m. John D. **WHEELER**, of N. Stonington, July 2, 1849, by Rev. H. R. Knapp	1	85
TURNER, Abby L., of Groton, m. Samuel **TAYLOR**, of Greenville, Norwich, May 20, 1845, by Rev. D. H. Cheney, of Greenville	1	73
Alfred, of Groton, m. Mary A. **TURNER**, of Ledyard, June 5, 1851, by Rev. Nicholas T. Allen	1	91
Almira, m. Lyman **ROGERS**, b. of Groton, Sept. 9, 1821, by Amos A. Niles, J.P.	1	4
Allyn, of Groton, m. Nancy C. **BECKWITH**, of Salem, Oct. 27, 1833, by Ralph Hurlbutt, J.P.	1	45
Amos, [s. Ezekiel & Baradel], b. Sept. 1, 1744	1	144
Amos, 2d, s. [Ezekiel & Rebecca], b. [ ], 1764	1	187
Amos, Jr., m. Welthan **MORGAN**, b. of Groton, Dec. 5, 1824, by John Brewster, J.P.	1	15
Amos, d. Feb. 15, 1826, ae. 82 y.	1	190
Amos, 2d, d. Apr. 1, 1847, ae. 83 y.	1	190
Charles, s. Amos & Thankfull, d. Feb. 8, 1795, ae. 4 y.	1	190
Eliza, m. Elijah S. **MORGAN**, b. of Groton, Mar. 20, 1831, by John G. Wightman, Eld.	1	37
Elizabeth, m. John **JEFFREY**, Dec. 24, 1735	1	178
Erastus, m. Betsey **FISH**, b. of Ledyard, June 25, 1849, by Rev. W. C. Walker	1	86
Eunice, [d. Ezekiel & Baradel], b. July 24, 1740	1	144
Eunice, m. James **MORGAN**, 2d, b. of Groton, Apr. 10, 1788	2	55
Eunice, d. [Ezekiel & Rebecca], b. [ ], 17[ ]	1	187
Ezekiel, m. Theoder **WILLIAMS**, Apr. 29, 1723	1	107
Ezekiel, m. Baradel **DENISON**, May 11, 1729	1	144
Ezekiel, [s. Ezekiel & Baradel], b. Jan. 27, 1733/4	1	144
Ezekiel, s. Ezekiel & Boredell Denison, b. Jan. 27, 1734	1	187
Ezekiel, m. Rebecca **ALLYN**, May [ ], 1756	1	187
Ezekiel, s. [Ezekiel & Rebecca], b. July 8, 1770	1	187
Ezekiel, s. Ezekiel & Rebeckah, b. July 8, 1770	2	2
Ezekiel, d. Apr. 7, 1826, ae. 93 y.	1	190
Fannie, w. Rufus, d. Jan. 12, 1862, ae. 76 y.	1	190
Hannah Ann, m. George **O'BRIEN**, b. of Groton, June 15, 1823, by Timothy Tuttle	1	9
Jane E., m. Ezra G. **BAILEY**, b. of Groton, Apr. 30, 1837, by John G. Wightman, Elder	1	56
Lucy, d. [Ezekiel & Rebecca], b. Dec. 20, 1757	1	187
Lucy, m. Moses **CULVER**, [ ], 1775/6	1	187
Lucy, d. [Ezekiel & Rebecca], b. Feb. 2, 1831, ae. 73 y.	1	187

	Vol.	Page
TURNER, (cont.)		
Mary, b. Nov. 3, 1750; m. Samuel **ELDREDGE**, Dec. 17, 1771	2	32
Mary A., of Ledyard, m. Alfred **TURNER**, of Groton, June 5, 1851, by Rev. Nicholas T. Allen	1	91
Melinda, of Groton, m. Jonas C. **MAINE**, M.D., of Stonington, Feb. 1, 1835, by John G. Wightman, Elder	1	49
Nancy Maria, m. Lyman **ROGERS**, b. of Groton, Apr. 27, 1835, by John G. Wightman, Eld.	1	50
Prudence, [d. Ezekiel & Baradel], b. Mar. 8, 1731/2	1	144
Prudence, w. Amos, d. Sept. 27, 1834, ae. 83 y.	1	190
Rebecca, w. Ezekiel, d. Aug. 17, 1822, ae. 84 y.	1	190
Rebecca, d. [Ezekiel & Rebecca], b. [ ], 17[ ]	1	187
Rufus, d. Dec. 15, 1867, ae. 82 y.	1	190
Thankfull, w. Amos, d. May 19, 1839, ae. 77 y.	1	190
Theody, [d. Ezekiel & Baradel], b. Aug. 14, 1730	1	144
Youngs A., of Ledyard, m. Susan **STARR**, of Groton, Apr. 16, 1843, by Rev. Jared R. Avery	1	68
TUTTLE, Daniel, b. Oct. 31, 1826	3	12
Joseph T., of Groton, m. Clarissa G. **CAPRON**, of Preston, Sept. 5, 1830, by W[illia]m M. Williams, J.P.	1	35
Ursula, b. June 12, 1821	3	12
TYLER, [see also **TILER**], Mary, of Groton, m. Daniel **ROBBINS**, of Exeter, June 20, 1760	2	28
Oliver S., of Preston, m. Anna **LESTER**, of Groton, Jan. 5, 1831, by Levi Meech, Eld.	1	36
VAN BRUNT, Charles, of Shrewsbury, N.J., m. Eliza **ASHBEY**, of Groton, Feb. 5, 1853, at Noank, by Rev. James M. Phillips	1	95
VINCENT, John R., m. Sarah T. **YORK**, b. of Stonington, Sept. 29, 1846, by Belton A. Copp, J.P.	1	76
VORHIS, VORES, Rebec[c]a, m. Dudley **HALEY**, s. Stephen & Lucy, [ ]	2	79
Rebecca, m. Dudley **HALLEY**, [s. Stephen & Lucy], [ ]	3	0
WAIT, Betsey, m. Reuben **AARON**, Apr. 28, 1833, by Geo[rge] Ayer, J.P.	1	43
Ce[a]sar, of Exeter, R.I., m. Betsey **SQUILE**, of Groton, July 4, 1824, by William Williams, J.P.	1	13
WALDEN, Hannah, d. Isaac & Judith, b. Sept. 12, 1771	2	16
John, [s. Isaac & Judith], b. Mar. 18, 1773	2	16
WALEY, Ephraim, m. Eunice **CHAPMAN**, June 16, 1793	2	43
WALLS, Jacob, m. Harriet **HEATH**, b. of Groton, Feb. 15, 1837, by Rev. John G. Wightman	1	56
WALSWORTH, WALWORTH, WALLWORTH, Abigail, [d. William & Mary], b. Nov. 29, 1736	1	141
Abigail, [d. Sylvester & Sarah], b. Apr. 8, 1769	2	24
Amos, s. W[illia]m & Mary, b. Jan. 30, 1728/9	1	119
Edward, [s. Sylvester & Sarah], b. June 1, 1766	2	24
Edward, Jr., m. Mary **COMSTOCK**, b. of Groton, Apr. 24, 1825, by Rev. Roswell Burrows	1	16
Elizabeth, w. Joshua, d. Jan. 10, 1821, ae. 63 y.	2	30
[E]unic[e], d. William & Elizabeth, b. June 4, 1743	1	144
[E]unice, m. Simeon **SMITH**, Jan. 7, 1762	2	15
Eunice, m. Simeon **SMITH**, Jan. 7, 1762	2	40
George, [s. Sylvester & Sarah], b. Sept. 1, 1759	2	24
Hannah, [d. Samuel & Hannah], b. July 27, 1769	2	18
Hannah, m. William **AVERY**, Mar. 16, 1775	2	23

	Vol.	Page
WALSWORTH, WALWORTH, WALLWORTH, (cont.)		
Henry, s. [Joshua], b. Oct. 7, 1784; d. Mar. 28, 1830	2	30
Holmes, [s. Sylvester & Sarah], b. Mar. 31, 1768	2	24
James, s. William & Mary, b. Sept. 2, 1734	1	141
Joanna, m. Christopher **STARK**, Apr. 1, 1722	1	101
Johanna, m. Christopher **STARKE**, Apr. 1, 1722	1	149
John, of Groton, m. Mary **MINER**, of Stonington, Dec. 4, 1752, by Rev. Nathaniel Eells	2	10
John, s. John & Mary, b. Mar. 19, 1755	2	10
John, [s. Samuel & Hannah], b. June 10, 1765	2	18
Joshua, d. Dec. 14, 1831. Burned to death by falling into the fire in a fit.	2	30
Lucy, [d. W[illia]m & Mary], b. Dec. 3, 1732	1	119
Lucy, d. Sylvester & Sarah, b. Apr. 9, 1758	2	24
Martha, m. John **STARK**, Nov. 10, 1715	1	116
Mary, d. William & Mary, b. Sept. 29, 1721	1	119
Mary, m. Solomon **MORGAN**, July 1, 1742	1	157
Nathan, [s. William & Mary], b. Oct. 17, 1724	1	119
Philenah, [d. Sylvester & Sarah], b. Nov. 24, 1760	2	24
Samuel, s. John & Sarah, b. Jan. 15, 1725/6; d. May 5, 1733, ae. 48 y.	1	130
Samuel, m. Hannah **WOODBRIDGE**, Jan. 10, 176[ ]	2	18
Samuel, s. Samuel & Hannah, b. Mar. [ ], 176[ ]	2	18
Samuel, s. [Joshua], b. July 11, 1782; d. Sept. 30, 1787	2	30
Sarah, wid of Capt. John, d. Nov. 5, 1778	1	154
Susan Angeline, m. John **FISH**, 2d, b. of Groton, Sept. 8, 1833, by John G. Wightman, Eld.	1	45
Susannah, d. W[illia]m & Mary, b. Oct. 22, 1726	1	119
Sylvester, of Groton, m. Sarah **HOLM[E]S**, of Stonington, Apr. 8, 1756, by Rev. Joseph Fish	2	24
Selvester, [s. Sylvester & Sarah], b. Nov. 4, 1762	2	24
William, m. Mary **AVERY**, Jan. 16, 1720, by Rev. Ephraim Woodbridge	1	119
William, m. Elizabeth **HINCKLEY**, Sept. 23, 1742	1	144
William, s. [Joshua], b. Apr. 4, 1796; d. Mar. 7, 1863	2	30
WARD, Huntington, m. Frances Louisa **HEATH**, b. of Norwich, Sept. 28, 1853, by Rev. S. W. Coggeshall	1	95
Winthrop, of Stonington, m. Lucy L. **SPICER**, of Groton, May 24, 1853, by Rev. James M. Phillips	1	95
WARDEN, Collins, of Richmond, Mass., m. Mary H. **BALDWIN**, of Groton, Oct. 9, 1846, by Rev. Jared R. Avery	1	76
WARNER, Anne, d. [Phillip & Hannah], b. Oct. 11, 1758	1	170
Earl, of Brooklyn, m. Adeline Elizabeth **LESTER**, of Groton, June 30, 1835, by Timothy Tuttle	1	51
Jabez, s. [Phillip & Hannah], b. July 21, 1756	1	170
Phillip, m. Hannah **MILLS**, Oct. 19, 1755	1	170
WASHINGTON, Amey, relict of John, d. Apr. 24, 1889, ae. 61 y.	2	84
John, 1st, s. John, b. Jan. 27, 1818	2	84
John, of Island of Gernsey, d. Nov. 19, 1829, ae. 42 y.	2	84
Mary E., of Portersville, Groton, m. William H. **BREED**, Aug. 17, 1845, by Rev. H. R. Knapp	1	74
WATERMAN, Elizabeth, m. Elisha **NILES**, b. of Groton, Jan. 10, 1836, by Ralph Hurlbutt, J.P.	1	53
WATROUS, Alexander, m. Esther **WATROUS**, b. of Groton, Oct. 9, 1831, by Zephaniah Watrous	1	38

	Vol.	Page
WATROUS, (cont.)		
Amey, of Groton, m. Henry **ROGERS**, formerly of Waterford, Feb. 8, 1835, by Zephaniah Watrous	1	49
Amos, Jr., m. Hopewell **WATROUS**, of Groton, Aug. 20, 1820, by Amos Watrous	1	1
Bashaba, m. Leonord **MOSS**, b. of Groton, Nov. 25, 1830, by Nathan Daboll, J.P.	1	36
Content, m. Henry **WATROUS**, Jr., Apr. 5, 1835, by Zephaniah Watrous	1	50
Cynthia, of Groton, m. Joseph **WATROUS**, of Ledyard, Apr. 11, 1847, by Rev. Simon B. Bailey	1	78
Delight, m. Zachariah **CH[R]OUCH**, b. of Groton, Apr. 20, 1834, by Zephaniah Watrous	1	47
Elisha, m. Cordelia **HEATH**, b. of Groton, June 7, 1840, by Rev. John W. Case	1	63
Esther, m. Alexander **WATROUS**, b. of Groton, Oct. 9, 1831, by Zephaniah Watrous	1	38
Henry, Jr., m. Content **WATROUS**, Apr. 5, 1835, by Zephaniah Watrous	1	50
Henry, Jr., m. Mary **CROUCH**, b. of Ledyard, Nov. 29, 1848, by Nathan Daball, J.P.	1	82
Hopewell, of Groton, m. Amos **WATROUS**, Jr., Aug. 20, 1820, by Amos Watrous	1	1
Jabez, m. Phebe **PARK[E]**, b. of Groton, Mar. 11, 1827, by John G. Wightman	1	23
John, m. Esther **CULVER**, 28 of the 12th mo., 1719/20, by Peter Crandall, Justice	1	121
John, m. Rebecca **WATROUS**, Aug. 22, 1841, by Zephaniah Watrous	1	65
Joseph, m. Rebecca **WATROUS**, b. of Groton, Oct. 17, 1821, by Zephaniah Watrous	1	4
Joseph, of Ledyard, m. Cynthia **WATROUS**, of Groton, Apr. 11, 1847, by Rev. Simon B. Bailey	1	78
Julia, m. Alexander **WILKINSON**, b. of Groton, Sept. 18, 1850, by Nathan Daboll, J.P.	1	90
Lydia, m. David **SCOTT**, b. of Groton, Nov. 26, 1820, by Amos Watrous	1	2
Maria, of Waterford, m. George **MURPHY**, of Groton, Aug. 15, 1827, by Roswell Fish, J.P.	1	26
Martha, m. Gilbert **HEATH**, b. of Groton, Aug. 8, 1846, by Rev. W. C. Walker	1	76
Mary, m. Nathan **CHAPMAN**, b. of Groton, Mar. 1, 1829, by Zephaniah Watrous	1	30
Nancy, m. Daniel **CROUGH**, b. living in Groton, Sept. 2, 1827, by Zephaniah Watrous	1	24
Nancy, of Groton, m. Elisha **BENNET[T]**, of Stonington, [ ], by Rev. Roswell Burrows. Recorded July 25, 1831	1	37
Nancy, m. Leonord B. **HOLDREDGE**, b. of Groton, Dec. 5, 1847, by Henry W. Avery, J.P.	1	80
Olivia, m. P. David **WATROUS**, b. of Groton, Dec. 8, 1833, by Zephaniah Watrous	1	46
P. David, m. Olivia **WATROUS**, b. of Groton, Dec. 8, 1833, by Zephaniah Watrous	1	46
Phebe, m. John D. **MITCHELL**, b. of Groton, Sept. 15, 1844, by Rev. Erastus Denison	1	71
Polly M., of Groton, m. Orlando **ROGERS**, of New London, Aug. 16, 1847, by Nathan Daball, J.P.	1	79

	Vol.	Page
WATROUS, (cont.)		
Rachal, m. John **CROUCH**, b. of Groton, July 29, 1821, by Zephaniah Watrous	1	4
Rebecca, m. Joseph **WATROUS**, b. of Groton, Oct. 17, 1821, by Zephaniah Watrous	1	4
Rebecca, m. John **WATROUS**, Aug. 22, 1841, by Zephaniah Watrous	1	65
Sarah, m. Jabez **WHIPPLE**, b. of Groton, Aug. 27, 1820, by Amos Watrous	1	1
Silas, m. Mary **CROUCH**, Sept. 14, 1823, by Zephaniah Watrous	1	10
William, of Groton, m. Martha **MORSE**, of Montville, Jan. 24, 1825, by Nathan Daball, J.P.	1	15
William, m. Eunice **LATHAM**, b. of Groton, May 20, 1840, by Ira R. Steward	1	63
Zephaniah, m. Abiah **CHAPMAN**, b. living in Groton, [ ], by Zephaniah Watrous. Recorded Oct. 15, 1827.	1	25
WEAVER, Nathan S., of Stonington, m. Lydia Ann **BRIGGS**, of Groton, May 17, 1835, by John G. Wightman, Elder	1	50
WEEKS, Eliza A., of Thompson, m. Abner **SPENCER**, of Groton, Dec. 31, 1851, at Thompson, by Rev. Allen Darrow	1	97
WELCH, [see also **WELSH**], Eliza, of Groton, m. William **SQUIER**, of New York, Apr. 23, 1843, by Rev. Erastus Denison	1	68
Lydia A., of Groton, m. Ellery **KENYON**, of Warwick, R.I., Dec. 20, 1829, by Rev. Roswell Burrows	1	32
WELLS, **WELLES**, Adeline, of Groton, m. Patent **RANDALL**, of Stonington, Nov. 26, 1835, by Nathan Daboll, J.P.	1	52
Cylora A., m. John S. **BURROWS**	3	0
Frances, of Groton, m. Evan **REYNOLDS**, of R.I., Nov. 17, 1822, by John G. Wightman	1	8
Hannah, m. Timothy **SWAN**, Apr. 11, 1824, by Philip Gray, J.P.	1	13
Joseph, of Long Island, m. Hannah Jane **WILBUR**, of Groton, Mar. 16, 1843, by Rev. Erastus Denison	1	68
Phebe H., of Groton, m. Matthew R. **MEACH**, of Westerly, R.I., July 12, 1846, by Rev. W. C. Walker	1	76
Thomas, of Groton, m. Phebe **EAGLETON**, of Stonington, Mar. 21, 1782, in Stonington, by Eleazer Brown, Elder	2	22
Thomas, of Groton, m. Abigail **SWAN**, of Hancock, Mass., Mar. 8, 1808, by William Douglass, Jr., J.P., in Rennsalear County, N.Y.	2	80
WELSH, [see also **WELCH**], Abby Jane, of Groton, m. Capt. Joseph **BRERETON**, of Manchester, England, July 18, 1847, by Rev. Erastus Denison	1	79
Mary, m. Joseph Edwin **HOLLOWAY**, b. of Groton, June 12, 1850, by Rev. Erastus Denison	1	89
WENTWORTH, Hannah, m. Walter **CAPRON**, Oct. 28, 1738	1	179
WESLEY, John, m. Caroline **RHODES**, Apr. 18, 1841, at Portersville, in Groton, by James Gallup, J.P.	1	64
WEST, Ansel, of Providence, R.I., m. Frances **SMITH**, of Stonington, Oct. 26, 1851, at Mystic River, by Franklin A. Slater	1	93
Lois, of Lee, Mass., m. Isaac W. **HAKES**, of N. Stonington, Oct. 1, 1827, by Ralph Hurlbutt, J.P.	1	25
WESTERN, Katharine, m. Daniel **WHITMAN**, Nov. 11, 1725	1	126
WHEELER, Anna, m. Jairus B. **PALMER**, b. of N. Stonington, July 3, 1843, by Rev. Erastus Denison	1	69
Dorothy, m. Nehemiah **SMITH**, Apr. 22, 1696	1	104

	Vol.	Page
WHEELER, (cont.)		
Dudley, of Stonington, m. Nancy **WHEELER**, of Groton, Sept. 4, 1820, by Rev. Roswell Burrows	1	2
Edwin Barber, m. Mary Ann **LEWIS**, b. of Groton, Sept. 3, 1826, by Roswell Burrows	1	21
Emily, m. Charles **BURROWS**	3	0
Giles, of Stonington, m. Hannah Ann **AVERY**, of Groton, Dec. 4, 1825, by John G. Wightman, Eld.	1	19
Hannah, d. David & Abigail, b. May 12, 1707	1	126
Hannah, m. Nathaniel **ADAMS**, Jan. 23, 1731/32	1	152
Hannah, of Groton, m. Thomas **WILLIAMS**, of Ledyard, Nov. 15, 1854, by Rev. S. B. Bailey	1	97
Ira, of Stonington, m. Amelia M. **WILLIAMS**, of Groton, Jan. 9, 1825, by John G. Wightman, Eld.	1	15
James, m. Hannah **CHIPMAN**, b. of Groton, Oct. 18, 1829, by Roswell Fish, J.P.	1	33
John D., of N. Stonington, m. Wealthy A. **TUCKER**, of Groton, July 2, 1849, by Rev. H. R. Knapp	1	85
John H., of Stonington, m. Est[h]er H. **BUD[D]INGTON**, of Groton, Nov. 22, 1821, by Caleb Avery, J.P.	1	5
John L. T., m. Louisa **SPENCER**, b. of Groton, Aug. 27, 1837, by Rev. Ira R. Steward	1	57
Jonathan, Capt., of Stonington, m. Mary **MURPHEY**, of Groton, Dec. 29, 1828, by Asa Fish, J.P.	1	29
Mary A., of Waterford, m. Nathan P. **WHITING**, of Stonington, May 19, 1847, by Rev. W[illia]m O. Walker	1	78
Mary Ann, m. Noyes **HOLMES**, b. of Stonington, Oct. 13, 1820, by Parkle Williams, J.P.	1	2
Mary Esther, m. Hubbard **BURROWS**, [ ]	3	0
Nabby, of Stonington, m. Isaac **AVERY**, Jr., of Groton, Apr. 27, 1800	2	74
Nancy, of Groton, m. Dudley **WHEELER**, of Stonington, Sept. 4, 1820, by Rev. Roswell Burrows	1	2
Prudence, m. Christopher **AVERY**, Apr. 1, 1714	1	127
Prudence, m. Ebenezer **GEER**, Jan. 2, 1734/5	1	154
Prudence, m. Giles **HALEY**, [ ], in Stonington	3	0
Richard, of Stonington, m. Cinthia **GALLUP**, of Groton, Nov. 23, 1824, by John G. Wightman, Eld.	1	14
Richard, m. Roxana **PARKS**, June 20, 1850, by Rev. W. Munger	1	89
Samuel, of Stonington, m. Hannah **HAVENS**, of Groton, May 1, 1845, by Elias Brown, J.P.	1	73
Samuel B., of N. Stonington, m. Delia Ann **AVERY**, of Groton, Nov. 27, 1827, by Timothy Tuttle	1	25
Samuel P., of Stonington, m. Amanda M. **AVERY**, of Groton, Nov. 22, 1838, by Mark Meade, V.D.M.	1	60
Saxton W., of Stonington, m. Rebecca **LAMPHERE**, of Groton, Nov. 16, 1848, by Rev. Simon B. Bailey	1	82
William E., of Stonington, m. Pedee **HEATH**, of Groton, Aug. 30, 1831, by Timothy Tuttle	1	38
(Sarah, m. Richard **WILLIAMS**, Jan. 19, 1688	LR2	0)
WHELDON, Nancy, of Stonington, m. Andrew **GALLUP**, of Groton, Dec. 16, 1792, by Rev. Valentine W. Rathburn	2	46
WHIPPLE, Abby, m. John **WHIPPLE**, b. of Ledyard, Aug. 16, 1852, at William M. Haley's in Groton, by Zephaniah Watrous	1	94

	Vol.	Page
WHIPPLE, (cont.)		
Ales, d. Samuel, Jr., b. June 5, 1754	2	3
Alice, of Groton, m. Leonard D. **MURFIT**, now residing in Groton, Apr. 12, 1834, by Nathan Daboll, J.P.	1	50
Anna, twin with Elizabeth, d. [Daniel & Anne], b. Feb. 15, 1746/7	1	175
Benjamin, of Brattleborough, m. Elizabeth **WHIPPLE**, of Groton, Feb. 14, 1774	2	6
Christian, m. Noah **WHIPPLE**, b. of Groton, Aug. 16, 1835, by Zephaniah Watrous	1	51
Content, m. Ori **CHAPMAN**, Aug. 24, 1834, by Zephaniah Watrous	1	47
Dames, d. [Timothy & Elizabeth], b. July 5, 1768	1	171
Daniel, m. Anne **HOUGH**, May 7, 1746	1	175
Ebenezer, s. [Daniel & Anne], b. June 4, 1755	1	175
Elenor, d. [Timothy & Elizabeth], b. Apr. 10, 1756	1	171
Elizabeth, twin with Anna, d. [Daniel & Anne], b. Feb. 15, 1746/7	1	175
Elizabeth, d. Timothy & Elizabeth, b. Jan. 2, 1754	1	171
Elizabeth, d. Samuel, Jr. & [E]unice, b. June 8, 1756	2	3
Elizabeth, of Groton, m. Benjamin **WHIPPLE**, of Brattleborough, Feb. 14, 1774	2	6
Elizabeth, m. Ichabod **DAVIS**, b. of Groton, Aug. 27, 1820, by Amos Watrous	1	1
Elizabeth, m. David **CHROUCH**, Jan. 26, 1834, by Zephaniah Watrous	1	46
Eunice, d. Noah & Hopea, b. June 16, 1764	2	3
Eunice, m. John **CROUCH**, Jr., b. of Groton, Dec. 30, 1826, by Zephaniah Watrous	1	23
Ezra, s. Samuel, Jr., & [E]unice, b. Jan. 13, 1761	2	3
Hannah, m. Thomas **GEER**, b. of Groton, Oct. 7, 1821, by Zephaniah Watrous	1	4
Hopea, m. Noah **WHIPPLE**, b. of Groton, Nov. 7, 1762	2	3
Hopea, m. John **SMITH**, June 23, 1822, by Silas Whipple	1	7
Isaac, s. Samuel, Jr. & [E]unice, b. Apr. 14, 1764	2	3
Jabez, m. Sarah **WATROUS**, b. of Groton, Aug. 27, 1820, by Amos Watrous	1	1
Jeremiah, s. [Daniel & Anne], b. Mar. 1, 1751	1	175
Jerome*, s. Samuel, Jr. , b. Apt. 5, 1752 (*Perone, Mrs. J. C. Frost)	2	3
John, s. [Timothy & Elizabeth], b. Feb. 7, 1765	1	171
John, m. Abby **WHIPPLE**, b. of Ledyard, Aug. 16, 1852, at William M. Haley's in Groton, by Zephaniah Watrous	1	94
Jonathan, s. Samuel, Jr., b. Dec. 12, 1748	2	3
Joseph, s. Samuel, Jr., b. Dec. 12, 1748	2	3
Joseph, of Groton, m. Jennet **CAMBBEL**, of Voluntown, Dec. 10, 1772	2	1
Julian, of Waterford, m. James B. **ADAMS**, of Newport, R.I., Oct. 21, 1821, by Philip Gray, J.P.	1	4
Lucretia, d. Samuel, Jr., b. Nov. 18, 1744	2	3
Lucretia, d. [Daniel & Anne], b. June 15, 1748	1	175
Lydia Ann, of Groton, m. Alfred **LAMB**, of Ledyard, Apr. 27, 1845, by Rev. Jared R. Avery	1	73
Mary, [d. Joseph & Jennet], b. Apr. 4, 1774	2	1
Mary G., of Groton, m. Orlando H. **BEARS**, of Sag Harbour, L.I., Nov. 4, 1838, by Mark Meade, V.D.M.	1	60
Nathan, s. Samuel, Jr. & [E]unice, b. Apr. 2, 1759	2	3
Noah, s. Samuel, Jr., b. Jan. 10, 1742	2	3
Noah, m. Hopea **WHIPPLE**, b. of Groton, Nov. 7, 1762	2	3

	Vol.	Page
WHIPPLE, (cont.)		
Noah, s. Noah, b. Aug. 9, 1771	2	3
Noah, m. Christian **WHIPPLE**, b. of Groton, Aug. 16, 1835, by Zephaniah Watrous	1	51
Phebe, d. [Daniel & Anne], b. Mar. 11, 1753	1	175
Priscilla, d. [Daniel & Anne], b. Feb. 4, 1757	1	175
Samuel, m. Ruth CARD, Nov. 15, 1720	1	124
Samuel, s. Samuel & Ruth, b. [ ], 1722	1	124
Samuel, Jr., of Groton, m [E]unice **MITCHELL**, of Preston, Nov. 24, 1740	2	3
Samuel, 3d, s. Noah & Hopea, b. Nov. 28, 1766	2	3
Silas, s. N[oah], b. July 25, 1773	2	3
Thankful, m. Thomas **GERE**, b. of Groton, Dec. 11, 1825, by Nathan Daboll, J.P.	1	19
Timothy, [s. Samuel & Ruth], b. A[ ], 1723	1	124
William, s. [Timothy & Elizabeth], b. Feb. 17, 1763	1	171
Zipporah, d. [Timothy & Elizabeth], b. Mar. 17, 1757	1	171
WHITE, Austin, m. Lucy Ann **THOM[P]SON**, b. of Stonington, Sept. 19, 1830, by Ralph Hurlbutt, J.P.	1	35
Caroline A., of Groton, m. Albert N. **RAMSDELL**, of New London, Sept. 2, 1839, by Rev. Jared R. Avery	1	61
Edwin, m. Adeline **BUD[D]INGTON**, b. of Groton, Aug. 29, 1836, by Joseph Durfey, J.P.	1	55
Hannah, m. Frederick **DANIELS**, b. of Groton, May 10, 1829, by John G. Wightman, Eld.	1	30
Joseph, s. Christopher & Mary, b. Mau. 15, 1785	2	69
Lucy, m. Antoney **MURSER**, June 9, 1822, by Caleb Avery, J.P.	1	7
Seabury, m. Carolina **ALLYN**, of Groton, Nov. 3, 1822, by Timothy Tuttle	1	8
Theodore H., of Bolton, m. Priscilla **KING**, of Portersville, in Groton, July 3, 1843, by Rev. S. Simmons	1	69
Thomas, m. Nancy **CROMWELL**, b. of Groton, July 1, 1826, by Nathan Daboll, J.P.	1	21
WHITEMAN, [see also **WIGHTMAN** & **WHITMAN**], Avery, [s. Isaac & Lucretia], b. Jan. 24, 1777	1	158
Daniel, [s. Isaac & Lucretia], b. Nov. 14, 1766	1	158
Deborah, [d. Isaac & Lucretia], b. Aug. 27, 1778	1	158
Hannah, [d. Isaac & Lucretia], b. Jan. 11, 1769	1	158
John, [s. Isaac & Lucretia], b. Apr. 11, 1787(?)	1	158
Lucretia, [d. Isaac & Lucretia], b. Aug. 27, 1772	1	158
Mary, m. Joshua **RATHBONE**, Feb. 5, 1723/4, by Eph[rai]m Woodbridge	1	116
Nathan, [s. Isaac & Lucretia], b. Sept. 27, 1780	1	158
WHITING, Hallam, of Stonington, m. Lydia **LAMB**, of Groton, Mar. 11, 1828, by William Williams, J.P.	1	27
Nathan P., of Stonington, m. Mary A. **WHEELER**, of Waterford, May 19, 1847, by Rev. W[illia]m C. Walker	1	78
WHITMAN, [see also **WHITEMAN** and **WIGHTMAN**], A. L., Rev., of Greenville, m. Mary E. **BARBER**, of Groton, Apr. 26, 1843, by Rev. J. R. Avery	1	68
Daniel, m. Katharine **WESTERN**, Nov. 11, 1725	1	126
Tabitha, m. Samuel **LAMB**, July 31, 1774, by Timothy Wightman, Elder	2	26
WHITMARSH, Susanna, of Dighton, Mass., m. Benjamin **GEER**, 2d, of Groton, Sept. 12, 1779, by Rufus Allyn, Elder	2	30

	Vol.	Page
WHITNEY, Angelina, [d. Shubael], b. Dec. 11, 1818	3	2
Ann, [d. Shubael], b. May 29, 1802	3	2
Asa, [s. Shubael], b. Mar. 19, 1797	3	2
Betsey, [d. Shubael], b. Feb. 6, 1807	3	2
Clarissa, [d. Shubael], b. Jan. 1, 1809	3	2
George W., [s. Shubael], b. Mar. 23, 1816	3	2
Joshua, [s. Shubael], b. Jan. 1, 1799	3	2
Lucy A., [d. Shubael], b. Nov. 16, 1812	3	2
Sally, [d. Shubael], b. Aug. 1, 1804	3	2
Sally M., of Groton, m. Reuben B. **DEWEY**, of N. Stonington, Mar. 22, 1825, by William Williams, J.P.	1	16
WHITTEMORE, Charles S., m. Caroline A. **BAILEY**, Apr. 30, 1844, by Rev. Simon B. Bailey	1	71
WHITTLES, Maria, of Groton, m. Joseph **TIFT**, Jr., of N. Stonington, May 2, 1833, by Philip Gray, J.P.	1	44
WIDGER, Amy, d. Benjamin & Tabitha, b. Jan. 30, 1749	1	171
Edward Bunnet, s. Tabitha, b. Nov. 3, 1741	1	171
Eli, s. [Benjamin & Tabitha], b. May 5, 1756	1	171
Susannah, d. [Benjamin & Tabitha], b. July 25, 1751	1	171
WIGHTMAN, [see also **WHITMAN** and **WHITEMAN**], Abraham, [s. Valentine], b. 15th of 5th mo., 1711	1	122
Allyn, s. [Timothy & Mary], b. June 27, 1748	1	175
Amy, d. [Timothy & Mary], b. Dec. 2, 1751	1	175
Amy, d. [Timothy, Jr. & Mary], b. Feb. 26, 1795	2	39
Asa, s. [Timothy, Jr. & Mary], b. Jan. 19, 1784	2	39
Bridget, d. [John Gano & Mercy], b. Jan. 11, 1798	2	38
Bridget Caroline, of Groton, m. Jonathan **TINKER**, of Lyme, July 24, 1842, by Rev. Erastus Denison	1	66
Daniell, s. Val[entine], b. 23d of 9th mo. 1703	1	122
Elisha D., of Groton, m. Matilda **MA[T]THEWSON**, of Penn., Nov. 15, 1846, by Rev. W. C. Walker	1	77
Elisha Daboll, s. [John G. & Bridget], b. Feb. 4, 1822	2	38
Elizabeth, [d. John Gano & Mercy], b. Aug. 3, 1792	2	38
Easther, d. John & Mary, b. May 26, 1760	1	158
Esther B., m. David A. **DABOLL**, June 27, 1839, by Rev. John G. Wightman	1	61
Esther Burrows, d. [John G. & Bridget], b. May 13, 1820	2	38
Eunice, d. John & Mary, b. Oct. 5, 1755	1	158
Hannah, d. John & Mary, b. Sept. 25, 1753	1	158
Hannah, d. [Timothy & Mary], b. May 22, 1761	1	175
Isaac, [s. Valentine], b. 12th of 8th mo., 1715	1	122
Isaac, s. [Timothy & Jane], b. Mar. 13, 1744	1	175
Isaac Avery, of Penn., m. Hannah **PACKER**, of Groton, Apr. 27, 1845, by Rev. Erastus Denison	1	72
Jacob, [s. Valentine], b. 1st of 7th mo., 1717	1	122
Jane, w. Timothy, d. Mar. 14, 1744/5	1	175
Jane M., m. Elijah B. **MORGAN**, b. of Groton, June 8, 1843, by Rev. Erastus Denison	1	69
Jane Maria, d. [John G. & Bridget], b. Nov. 3, 1823	2	38
Jesse, s. [Timothy & Mary], b. Jan. 22, 1764	1	175
Jesse, [s. John Gano & Mercy], b. Oct. 4, 1789	2	38
Joanna Elizabeth, [d. Jesse & Mercy], b. Aug. 27, 1816	3	28
John, [s. Valentine], b. 8th of 6th mo., 1723 (Written "Whitman")	1	122

	Vol.	Page
WIGHTMAN, (cont.)		
John, m. Mary **STODDARD**, Nov. 9, 1752	1	158
John, s. John & Mary, b. Mar. 15, 1758	1	158
John Clark, [s. Jesse & Mercy], b. Mar. 4, 1818	3	28
John G., m. Bridget **ALLYN**, July 7, 1817	2	38
John Gano, m. Mercy **CLARK**, Jan. 22, 1789	2	38
John Gene, s. [Timothy & Mary[, b. Aug. 16, 1766	1	175
John L, [s. John Gano & Mercy], b. June 6, 1794	2	38
Joseph Culver, [s. Jesse & Mercy], b. Jan. 3, 1828	3	28
Joseph Latham, s. [John G. & Bridget], b. May 19, 1818	2	38
Joseph S., m. Sarah M. **LATHAM**, b. of Groton, June 12, 1843, by Ira R. Steward	1	69
Julia, [d. Jesse & Mercy], b. June 1, 1830	3	28
Mary, [c. Valentine], b. 18th of 12th mo., 1704	1	122
Mary, d. [Timothy & Mary], b. Jan. 20, 1749/50; d. Oct. 5, 1751	1	175
Mary, d. [Timothy & Mary], b. Jan. 21, 1754	1	175
Mary, w. John, d. Mar. 13, 1768	1	158
Mary, [d. John Gano & Mercy], b. Mar. 14, 1796	2	38
Mary, d. [John Gano & Mercy], b. Dec. 8, 1803	2	38
Mary Avery, [d. Jesse & Mercy], b. Jan. 4, 1823	3	28
Mercy, w. John G., d. May 29, 1816	2	38
Mercy C., of Groton, m. Erastus **WILLIAMS**, of Stonington, Nov. 11, 1827, by Rev. John G. Wightman	1	25
Palmer Gallup, [s. Jesse & Mercy], b. Feb. 16, 1820	3	28
Polly, d. [Timothy, Jr. & Mary], b. Sept. 16, 1788	2	39
Sally, d. [John Gano & Mercy], b. Nov. 3, 1801	2	38
Samuel, s. [Timothy, Jr. & Mary], b. Nov. 17, 1785	2	39
Sarah, [d. Valentine], b. 5th of 6th mo., 1721 (Written "Whitman")	1	122
Sarah, of Groton, m. Eliakim **WILLIAMS**, of Stonington, Dec. 3, 1823, by John G. Wightman	1	11
Susanna, [d. Valentine], b. 24th of 11th mo., 1712/13	1	122
Susanna, m. James LAMB, Oct. 31, 1744	1	183
Tabitha, d. [Timothy & Mary], b. Sept. 18, 1758	1	175
Timothy, [s. Valentine], b. 20th of 9th mo., 1719	1	122
Timothy, m. Jane **FISH**, June 1, 1743	1	175
Timothy, m. Mary **STODDARD**, May 13, 1747	1	175
Timothy, Jr., m. Mary **AVERY**, Apr. 17, 1783	2	39
Timothy, s. [Timothy, Jr. & Mary], b. June 20, 1799	2	39
Timothy Tuttle, [s. Jesse & Mercy], b. Sept. 19, 1825	3	28
Vallentine, [s. Valentine], b. 26th of 10th mo., 1706	1	122
Valentine, s. John & Mary, b. Oct. 13, 1762	1	158
Zerviah, d. [John Gano & Mercy], b. Jan. 30, 1800	2	38
WILBUR, Ann Maria, d. [Moses & Maria], b. June 10, 1828	3	23
Anna Maria, m. Elisha **FITCH**, Dec. 2, 1849, in Noank, by Rev. H. R. Knapp	1	88
Betsey, m. Charles **CHESTER**, b. of Groton, Sept. 9, 1821, by John G. Wightman, Elder	1	4
Calvin, s. [James & Betsey], b. Oct. 19, 1812	3	21
Calvin, m. Lucy **FITCH**, b. of Groton, Sept. 30, 1835, by Ira R. Steward	1	52
Charles Henry, s. [James & Betsey], b. June 28, 1814	3	21
Eleanor Jane, d. [William & Sally], b. June 2, 1818	3	21
Eleonor Jane, m. Latham **RATHBURN**, b. of Groton, Oct. 27, 1835, by Rev. Roswell Burrows	1	52

	Vol.	Page
WILBUR, (cont.)		
Eliza, m. Latham **FITCH**, b. of Groton, July 17, 1836, by Rev. Ira R. Steward	1	55
Elizabeth, d. [James & Betsey], b. Apr. 25, 1816	3	21
Emeline, d. [William & Sally], b. Aug. 13, 1820	3	21
Emeline, m. John D. **LATHAM**, b. of Groton, May 27, 1838, by Ira R. Steward	1	59
Fanny R., m. Josephus T. **PARKER**, b. of Groton, Sept. 27, 1846, by Rev. H. R. Knapp	1	83
Frances, m. Henry **DAVIS**, b. of Groton, May 4, 1848, by David Avery, Elder	1	81
George P., m. Prudence A. **SPICER**, b. of Groton, [Oct.] 26, [1853], by Rev. James M. Phillips	1	95
Hannah Jane, d. [James & Betsey], b. Aug. 4, 1818	3	21
Hannah Jane, of Groton, m. Joseph **WELLES**, of Long Island, Mar. 16, 1843, by Rev. Erastus Denison	1	68
Henry, s. [Moses & Maria], b. Aug. 26, 1818	3	23
Henry, m. Eveline **PACKER**, b. of Groton, Oct. 1, 1823, by Rev. Roswell Burrows	1	10
James, 2d, m. Mary **FITCH**, b. of Groton, Sept. 8, 1822, by Roswell Burrows	1	7
James Edwin, s. [James & Betsey], b. Oct. 12, 1820	3	21
Jeremiah, Capt., m. Susan **MORGAN**, b. of Groton, Feb. 25, 1852, by Rev. F. A. Slater	1	93
John, m. Betsey **BURROWS**, b. of Groton, Aug. 1, 1829, by Roswell Fish, J.P.	1	31
Julia Ann, d. [James & Betsey], b. May 21, 1804	3	21
Juliann, m. Charles **WOLF**, b. of Groton, Sept. 19, 1826, by John G. Wightman, Eld.	1	22
Lucretia, m. Ray S. **WILBUR**, Sept. 26, 1831, by Erastus Denison	1	38
Lucretia A., d. [James & Betsey], b. June 12, 1811	3	21
Margaret, d. [William & Sally], b. May 24, 1822	3	21
Margaret, m. Roswell A. **MORGAN**, b. of Groton, Oct. 29, 1839, by Ira R. Steward	1	62
Mariah, d. [Elam & Caroline], b. Oct. 9, 1823	3	22
Maria, m. Albert **MORGAN**, b. of Groton, Dec. 24, 1840, by Ira R. Steward	1	64
Mary, m. Shubael **GEER**, b. of Groton, Aug. 5, 1827, by Rev. Roswell Burrows	1	24
Mary Ann, d. [William & Sally], b. July 16, 1825	3	21
Mary Ann, m. Elihu **CHESEBRO[UGH]**, b. of Groton, Nov. 13, 1842, by Ira R. Steward	1	67
Melissa B., [d. James & Betsey], b. Dec. 26, 1827	3	21
Melissa B., m. James P. **FERRIS**, b. of Groton, Apr. 22, 1849, by Rev. Simon B. Bailey	1	83
Moses, s. [Moses & Maria], b. Oct. 19, 1822	3	23
Moses, Jr., m. Abby J. **INGHAM**, b. of Groton, June 25, 1848, by David Avery, Elder	1	82
Nathaniel, m. Angeline **PACKER**, Sept. 14, 1831, by Erastus Denison	1	38
Peter, of N. Stonington, m. Mary **INGHAM**, of Groton, Sept. 9, 1827, by Roswell Fish, J.P.	1	26
Phebe, m. Asa **SAWYER**, b. of Groton, June 11, 1840, by Ira R. Steward	1	63
Ray S., m. Lucretia **WILBUR**, Sept. 26, 1831 by Erastus Denison	1	38

	Vol.	Page
WILBUR, (cont.)		
Ray S., m. Harriet P. **FITCH**, b. of Groton, Apr. 28, 1850, by Rev. N. E. Shailer	1	88
Robert Niles, s. [James & Betsey], b. May 20, 1806	3	21
Sally Sawyer, d. [James & Betsey], b. July 16, 1806	3	21
Sally T., of Groton, m. Isaac C. **AMIDON**, of Rome, N.Y., Oct. 25, 1829, by Rev. Roswell Burrows	1	32
Sary, w. William, d. Jan. 13, 1822	2	94
Sarah, d. [William & Sally], b. June 4, 1829	3	21
Sarah, of Groton, m. Daniel **CLARKE**, of Con[e]y Island, N.Y., May 28, 1848, by David Avery, Elder	1	81
Whitman, m. Charlotte N. **DABOLL**, b. of Groton, July 10, 1844, by Rev. Simon B. Bailey	1	71
William, d. Jan. 24, 1822	2	94
William A., m. Lucy **PALMER**, b. of Groton, July 25, 1829, by Roswell Burrows, Eld.	1	31
WILCOX, **WILLCOCKS**, Alfred H., m. Phebe J. **PERKINS**, Apr. 6, 1845, at Ezra Bailey's house, by Rev. R. Russell	1	73
Calvin S., m. Freelove **GRUMBY**, b. of Groton, Jan. 27, 1851, by Rev. James M. Phillips	1	91
Daniel, Jr., m. Betsey (born Elizabeth), d. Moses & Lucy Turner **CULVER**, Sept. 13, 1812, at Preston	1	188
Deborah, m. Joseph **CRANDALL**, Jr., b. of Groton, Sept. 3, 1826, by William Williams, J.P.	1	21
Gardner N., of Preston, m. Hannah **SPICER**, of Groton, Oct. 15, 1848, by David Avery, Elder	1	82
Gilbert B., m. Lucy A. **RATHBUN**, b. of Groton, Dec. 27, 1846, by Rev. Simon B. Bailey	1	77
Hezekiah, Jr., m. Prudence A. **PACKER**, b. of Groton, July 14, 1839, by I. R. Steward	1	61
Idutha, of Stonington, m. Dudley E. **CHESEBRO[UGH]**, Dec. 7, 1848, by Rev. H. R. Knapp	1	84
Jared, of New York, m. Mary Elizabeth **ASHBEY**, of Groton, Apr. 16, 1843, by Rev. Erastus Denison	1	68
Jeremiah, of Stonington, m. Sabra **BROWN**, of Groton, Dec. 11, 1831, by Robert S. Avery, J.P.	1	39
Mary A., of Groton, m. Gurdon **HALL**, of Westerly, R.I., Aug. 2, [1853], by Rev. James M. Phillips	1	95
Nancy, of Stonington, m. Andrew **CHESEBRO[UGH]**, of Groton, July 14, 1847, by Rev. H. R. Knapp	1	83
Phebe, m. Joseph **MALLISON**, Jr., Nov. 6, 1737	1	148
Robert, m. Mary Ann **REED**, b. of Groton, Apr. 4, 1824, by William Williams, J.P.	1	12
W[illia]m E., m. Caroline E. **CHIPMAN**, b. of Groton, Sept. 1, 1840 by Rev. John G. Wightman	1	63
William E., m. Mary A. **SPRING**, b. of Groton, Oct. 26, 1845, by Rev. Simon B. Bailey	1	74
WILKINSON, Alexander, m. Julia **WATROUS**, b. of Groton, Sept. 18, 1850, by Nathan Daboll, J.P.	1	90
WILLEA, Jane, m. Thomas **BAILEY**, June 13, 1711	1	119
WILLET, Julia Ann, m. Elisha Avery **MORGAN**, b. of Groton, July 23, 1820, by Timothy Tuttle	1	1

	Vol.	Page
WILLEY, Sophroney R., of New Shoram, R.I., m. William F. **CLARK**, of Stonington, May 27, 1832, by John G. Wightman, Eld.	1	40
[On January 26, 1926, the following entries were copied from a leaf preceding page 1 of Volume 2 of Groton Land Records by Mr. Frank Farnsworth Starr, of Middletown. These entries do not appear in the Arnold Copy of Groton Vital Records, now in the Connecticut State Library:]		
WILLIAMS, David, [s. Richard & Sarah], b. Aug. 14, 1692	LR2	0
Deborah, [d. Richard & Sarah], b. May 29, 1708	LR2	0
Elizabeth, [d. Richard & Sarah], b. July 19, 1700	LR2	0
John, [s. Richard & Sarah], b. Sept. 29, 1703	LR2	0
Mary, [d. Richard & Sarah], b. Sept. 1, 1697	LR2	0
Nathan, [s. Richard & Sarah], b. Apr. 1, 1705	LR2	0
Richard, [s. Richard & Sarah], m. Sarah **WHEELER**, Jan. 19, 1688	LR2	0
Richard, [s. Richard & Sarah], b. Nov. 25, 1694	LR2	0
Sarah, [d. Richard & Sarah], b. Oct. 7, 1689	LR2	0
WILLIAMS, Abigail, d. Henry & Mary, b. Mar. 17, 1756	2	9
Abigail, of Groton, m. John **AVERY**, of Griswold, Dec. 9, 1824, by Timothy Tuttle	1	14
Adrian M., of N.Y., m. Margarette **ASHBEY**, of Noank, Ct., Sept. 16, 1849, in Noank, by Rev. William A. Smith, of Noank	1	85
Alfred, [s. Caleb], b. Dec. 21, 1776	2	23
Alonzo, [s. Jesse & Elizabeth], b. June 26, 1808	3	1
Alonzo, m. Hannah F. **LATHAM**, b. of Groton, Dec. 18, 1833, by Rev. Ira R. Steward	1	45
Amanda, m. Thomas B. **GRAY**, b. of Groton, Nov. 2, 1823, by William Williams, J.P.	1	11
Amelia M., of Groton, m. Ira **WHEELER**, of Stonington, Jan. 9, 1825, by John G. Wightman, Eld.	1	15
Ann, d. Benjamin & Sarah, b. Sept. 27, 1728	1	140
Anna, d. [Richard & Anna], b. Oct. 19, 1746	1	177
Anna, [d. Caleb], b. Nov. 4, 1784	2	23
Anna, m. Allyn **SPICER**, b. of Groton, Dec. 4, 1825, by Timothy Tuttle	1	19
Asa, s. Daniel & Elizabeth, b. Mar. 17, 1757[sic]	1	169
Asenith, m. Capt. Isaac W. **GEER**, b. of Groton, Jan. 9, 1825, by Park Williams, J.P.	1	15
Asseneth, m. Capt. Isaac W. **GERE**, b. of Groton, Jan. 9, 1825, by Park Williams, J.P.	3	14
Austin, of Stonington, m. Mary **LESTER**, of Groton, Mar. 1, 1829, by John G. Wightman, Eld.	1	29
Avery, [s. Samuel & Hannah], b. July 2, 1774	2	20
Avery, s. [Samuel & Hannah], b. Oct. 13, 1783	2	20
Betsey, of Groton, m. William **BARROWS**, of Mansfield, May 11, 1823, by Philip Gray, J.P.	1	9
Bial, m. Job **TILER**, Aug. 24, 1732	1	159
Caleb, Jr., [s. Caleb], b. Jan. 13, 1781	2	23
Caleb M., [s. Jesse & Elizabeth], b. Mar. 30, 1806	3	1
Caleb M., m. Sabrina **GALLUP**, b. of Groton, Nov. 22, 1829, by John G. Wightman, Eld.	1	32
Catharine, d. Benjamin & Sarah, b. Apr. 7, 1731	1	140
Christopher, of Taunton, Mass., m. Margaret H. **AVERY**, of Groton, July 9, 1835, by Timothy Tuttle	1	51
Clarissa, of Groton, m. John C. **BAKER**, of Griswold, Mar. 9, 1821, by William Williams, J.P.	1	3

	Vol.	Page
WILLIAMS, (cont.)		
Cornelius, [s. Samuel & Margaret], b. Mar. 20, 1763	2	24
Cyrus, s. [Daniel & Elizabeth], b. Mar. 22, 1767	1	169
Cyrus, [s. Samuel & Hannah], b. Nov. 11, 1772(?) (See date of Prudence)	2	20
Cyrus, m. Loiza **PERKINS**, b. of Groton, Dec. 2, 1830, by John G. Wightman, Eld.	1	36
Daniel, m. Est[h]er **AVERY**, b. of Groton, Mar. 17, 1758, by William Williams, J.P.	1	169
Daniel, s. [Daniel & Elizabeth], b. Apr. 6, 1762	1	169
Daniel, m. Dianna **BOLLES**, b. of Groton, May 29, 1825, by Ralph Hurlbutt, J.P.	1	17
Daniel R., of Stonington, m. Matilda **APPLEMAN**, of Groton, June 21, 1832, by John G. Wightman, Eld.	1	40
David, m. Experience **BA[I]LEY**, June 18, 1721	1	124
Deborah, [d. Jonathan & Elizabeth], b. Mar. 16, 1720	II	369
Deborah, [d. Nathaniel & Deborah], b. Sept. 24, 1720	1	118
Deborah, m. Waitstill **AVERY**, Sept. 18, 1729	1	138
Deborah, d. Nathan & Deborah, b. Feb. 14, 1731/2	1	154
Deborah, w. Nathan, d. May 8, 1732	1	154
Deborah, m. Samuel **NEWTON**, Jr., Nov. 11, 1743	1	164
Delacy, of Groton, m. Silas **HAZARD**, of Stonington, Dec. 10, 1823, by Rufus Smith, J.P.	1	10
Denison B., of Ledyard, m. Eliza **AVERY**, of Groton, Nov. 21, 1850, by Rev. Nicholas T. Allen	1	90
Desire, m. William **CROUCH**, Sept. 8, 1731	1	149
Ebenezer, [s. Jonathan & Elizabeth], b. Sept. 5, 1727	II	369
Ebenezer, [s. Samuel & Margaret], b. June 6, 1768	2	24
Ebenezer A., [s. Jesse & Elizabeth], b. June 7, 1811; d. Sept. 23, 1811	3	1
Edmond, [s. Caleb], b. Mar. 18, 1788	2	23
Eliakim, of Knox, N.Y., m. Hannah **WOLF**, of Groton, June 16, 1822, by John G. Wightman	1	7
Elikim, of Stonington, m. Sarah **WIGHTMAN**, of Groton, Dec. 3, 1823, by John G. Wightman	1	11
Elias Hewitt, s. [Erastus & Nancy], b. July 23, 1819	2	91
Elisha, s. William & Margaret, b. Aug. 14, 1746	1	155
Elisha, [s. Samuel & Margaret], b. Oct. 13, 1773	2	24
Eliza, d. [Jesse & Elizabeth], b. Dec. 22, 1803	3	1
Eliza, m. Nathaniel D. **SMITH**, b. of Groton, June 17, 1827, by John G. Wightman, Eld.	1	23
Elizabeth, [d. Jonathan & Elizabeth], b. Jan. 14, 1717	II	369
Elizabeth, m. Obadiah **BA[I]LEY**, July 10, 1718	1	122
Elizabeth, [d. Nathaniel & Deborah], b. Dec. 26, 1722	1	118
Elizabeth, d. Benjamin & Sarah, b. June 28, 1726	1	140
Elizabeth, m. Jon[a]than **SMITH**, Jr., June 8, 1732	1	141
Elizabeth, d. [Richard & Anna], b. May 12, 1748	1	177
Erastus, of Groton, m. Nancy **HEWITT**, of N. Stonington, Feb. 15, 1818, by Rev. Christopher Avery, of N. Stonington	2	91
Erastus, of Stonington, m. Mercy C. **WIGHTMAN**, of Groton, Nov. 11, 1827, by Rev. John G. Wightman	1	25
Est[h]er, d. [Daniel & Elizabeth], b. Oct. 3, 1764	1	169
[E]unice, m. Elijah **MORGAN**, Nov. 13, 1735	1	166
Eunice, m. Erastus **GALLUP**, b. of Groton, Oct. 2, 1823, by Timothy Tuttle	1	10

	Vol.	Page
WILLIAMS, (cont.)		
Experience, d. David [& Experience], b. Nov. 20, 1721	1	124
Frederic A., [s. Jesse & Elizabeth], b. May 11, 1816	3	1
Frederick A., m. Caroline F. **MORGAN**, Oct. 12, 1837, by Ira R. Steward	1	57
Frederic A., of Groton, m. Caroline L. **STODDARD**, of Ledyard, June 20, 1843, in Ledyard, by Ira R. Steward	1	69
Gilbert, m. Maryann **LEDYARD**, b. of Groton, Jan. 20, 1823, by John G. Wightman, Eld.	1	9
Giles, m. Mary Ann **BROWN**, b. of Stonington, Aug. 5, 1833, by John G. Wightman, Eld.	1	44
Giles, of Pomfret, m. Fanny Maria **GALLUP**, of Groton, Sept. 16, 1833, by Rev. Jared R. Avery	1	45
Gurdon, [s. Henry], b. Aug. 22, 1766	1	177
Hannah, d. William & Margaret, b. Sept. 23, 1753	1	155
Hannah, d. Sam[[ue]l & Hannah, b. Sept. 11, 1767	2	20
Hannah, d. [Samuel & Hannah], b. Apr. 28, 1778	2	20
Hannah, [d. Caleb], b. Dec. 6, 1790	2	23
Hannah, m. Charles S. **SMITH**, Jan. 26, 1792, by Christopher Avery, Elder	2	45
Hannah E., of Groton, m. George T. **FISH**, of New London, May 11, 1846, by Rev. Jared R. Avery	1	76
Harriet, of Groton, m. James **TRAIL**, of Scotland, Nov. 10, 1850, by Rev. Nicholas T. Allen	1	90
Henry, Jr., m. Mary **BOARDMAN**, Oct. 12, 174[ ]	2	9
Henry, s. Henry & Mary, . Dec. 27, 1749	2	9
Henry, s. [Samuel & Hannah], b. Aug. 19, 1781	2	20
Henry, m. Patty Allyn **NILES**, b. of Groton, Dec. 26, 1824, by Anson A. Niles, J.P.	1	15
Henry, of Salem, m. Julia **NILES**, of Groton, Nov. 26, 1835, by John G. Wightman, Elder	1	52
Isaac, of Stonington, m. Mary Ann **STORY**, of Groton, Sept. 26, 1830, by Ebenezer Avery, J.P.	1	35
James B., m. Sabra **GRAY**, b. of Groton, May 25, 1823, by William Williams, J.P.	1	9
James Barton, [s. William, Jr. & Anny], b. Sept. 19, 1802	3	8
Jefferson, [s. William, Jr. & Anny], b. Aug. 11, 1806; d. Aug. 13, 1822	3	8
Jennett, [d. William, Jr. & Anny], b. Sept. 8, 1815	3	8
Jeremiah, [s. Samuel & Margaret], b. May 2, 1759	2	24
Jesse, [s. Caleb], b. June 28, 1774	2	23
Jesse, m. Elizabeth **AVERY**, of Groton, Oct. 13, 1802, by Ebenezer Avery, Esq.	3	1
John, [s. Jonathan & Elizabeth], b. July 14, 1715	II	369
John, s. Henry & Mary, b. Sept. 9, 174[ ]	2	9
John, s. Sam[ue]l & Hannah, b. Apr. 22, 1766	2	20
Jonathan, m. Elizabeth **ALLEN**, Jan. 24, 1711	II	369
Jonathan, [s. Jonathan & Elizabeth], b. Sept. 30, 1711	II	369
Joseph S., of Stonington, m. Julia Ann **GALLUP**, of Groton, Dec. 9, 1824, by Timothy Tuttle	1	14
Julia E., of Groton, m. Nathan S. **EDGECOMB**, of N. Stonington, Dec. 9, 1824, by William Williams, J.P.	1	14
Laura, [d. William, Jr. & Anny], b. Oct. 23, 1817	3	8
Lucretia, [d. David & Experience], b. Nov. 29, 1723	1	124
Lucretia, m. Asa **AVERY**, Dec. 22, 1742	1	178

	Vol.	Page
WILLIAMS, (cont.)		
Lucretia, d. Daniel & Elizabeth, b. Oct. 30, 1759	1	169
Lucy, [d. Jonathan & Elizabeth], b. Dec. 5, 1724	II	369
Lucy A., m. Joseph C. **BENTLEY**, b. of Groton, Nov. 19, 1835, by W[illia]m M. Williams, J.P.	1	52
Lydia, m. Ebenezer **STODDARD**, Nov. 11, 1811	3	13
Lydia, m. William A. **WILLIAMS**, b. of Groton, Dec. 24, 1820, by Philip Gray, J.P.	1	2
Lydia Ann, [d. Jesse & Elizabeth], b. May 1, 1813	3	1
Lydia P., of Groton, m. Ebenezer **BALDWIN**, of Yonkers, N.Y., Dec. 29, 1847, by Rev. Nicho[la]s T. Allen	1	80
Lyman, m. Mary Ann **LAMB**, b. of Groton, July 25, 1836, by Nathan Daboll, J.P.	1	54
Mabel, of Groton, m. Roswell **PARK[E]**, of Preston, Aug. 3, 1826, by Timothy Tuttle	1	21
Margaret, d. Henry & Margaret, b. Aug. 31, 1708	1	136
Margaret, d. William & Margaret, b. Feb. 19, 1748	1	155
Margaret Griswold, [d. Samuel & Margaret], b. June 5, 1766	2	24
Martha, m. Moses **FISH**, Nov. 5, 1713	1	121
Martha, m. William **BAILEY**, Dec. 24, 1796	2	82
Mary, m. Thomas **LEEDS**, Apr. 17, 1717	1	124
Mary, d. William & Margaret, b. Oct. 24, 1743	1	155
Mary, d. Henry & Mary, b. Aug. 16, 1747	2	9
Mary, d. [Samuel & Mary], b. Feb. 26, 1749/50	1	184
Mary, [d. Samuel & Margaret], b. June 12, 1770	2	24
Mary, m. Joseph **COLVER**, Nov. 17, 1782	2	29
Mary Ann, m. Charles W. **CHESTER**, b. of Groton, July 15, 1849, by Rev. Jared R. Avery	1	85
Mary L., m. Rufus L. **FANNING**, b. of Groton, Dec. 12, 1830, by W[illia]m M. Williams, J.P.	1	36
Mary Loiza, [d. William, Jr. & Anny], b. Feb. 25, 1811	3	8
Matilda, of Groton, m. Joshua **HAILEY**, Jr., of Stonington, Jan. 1, 1851, by Rev. Jared R. Avery	1	90
Miner, [s. Caleb], b. Mar. 28, 1779	2	23
Nathan, m. Deborah **AVERY**, Feb. 17, 1726/7	1	154
Nathaniel, m. Deborah **DAVIS**, Dec. 9, 1717, by Justice Chesebrough. Witnesses: Samuel Buston, Robert Davis.	1	118
Nathaniel, s. Nathaniel & Deborah, b. Sept. 18, 1718	1	118
Nancy D., of Stonington, m. Albert **SAUNDERS**, of Groton, Nov. 10, 1841, in Stonington, by Ira R. Steward	1	65
Oliver, s. [Samuel & Hannah], b. Nov. 3, 1779	2	20
Peleg, s. Henry & Mary, b. Mar. 26, 1753	2	9
Peter, m. Mary **MORGAN**, b. of Groton, Dec. 7, 1780, by Rev. Paul Allyn, of N. Groton	2	79
Peter, Jr., m. Amy **DANIELS**, b. of Groton, Nov. 21, 1821, by Caleb Avery, J.P.	1	5
Peter, of Groton, m. Lydia A. **BARNES**, of Ledyard, July 15, 1849, by Rev. Jared R. Avery	1	85
Phillip, [s. Jonathan & Elizabeth], b. Dec. 17, 1734	II	369
Phillip, s. Jonathan & Elizabeth, b. Dec. 17, 1736	II	369
Prentice, s. [Daniel & Elizabeth], b. June 7, 1773	1	169
Prudence, d. Sam[ue]ll & Hannah, b. Apr. 18, 1772(?) (see date of Cyrus)	2	20
Prudence Anna, d. [Erastus & Nancy], b. Sept. 11, 1821	2	91

	Vol.	Page
WILLIAMS, (cont.)		
Quash, m. Hannah, Apr. 10, 1824, by Rufus Smith, J.P.	2	24
Ralph, of Groton, d. Aug. 6, 1822, ae. 63 y.	2	48
Rebecca, d. William & Margaret, b. Sept. 20, 1760	1	155
Richard, [s. Nathaniel & Deborah], b. Jan. 22, 1725	1	118
Richard, m. Anna **BROWN**, Nov. 6, 1745	1	177
Robert, s. Jonathan & Elizabeth, b. May 17, 1732	1	109
Robert, [s. Jonathan & Elizabeth], b. May 17, 1732	II	369
Roger*, [s. Henry], b. Dec. 24, 1763 (*and Mary, see will)	1	177
Roswell*, [s. Henry], b. Nov. 26, 1769 (*or Russell) (*and Mary, see will)	1	177
Rufus, Jr., m. Bridget **MOORE**, b. of Groton, Jan. 13, 1824, by Philip Gray, J.P.	1	12
Samuel, s. Henry & Margaret, b. Jan. 10, 1710/11	1	136
Samuel, s. Henry & Margaret, b. Jan. 10, 1710/11	1	168
Sam[ue]., [s. Jonathan & Elizabeth], b. July 17, 1722	II	369
Samuel, m. Mary **HURLBUTT**, July 16, 1746	1	184
Samuel, s. [Samuel & Mary], b. Dec. 11, 1747	1	184
Samuel, m. Deborah **MORGAN**, Apr. 20, 1748	1	179
Samuel, of Groton, m. Margaret **TRACY**, of Norwich, May 28, 1758, by Rev. Stephen White	1	171
Samuel, of Groton, m. Margaret **TRACY**, of Norwich, May 28, 1758	2	24
Samuel, 3d, m. Hannah **POWERS**, b. of Groton, July 11, 1765	2	20
Sanford A., m. Lucy **STANTON**, b. of Groton, Oct. 28, 1832, by William Williams, J.P.	1	41
Sarah, d. Nathan & Deborah, b. Dec. 29, 1729	1	154
Sarah, d. William & Margaret, b. May 13, 1756	1	155
Sarah, of Groton, m. Elisha **AYER**, of Northampton, Mass., Feb. 10, 1822, by William Williams, J.P.	1	6
Sarah, m. Jacob **GALLUP**, b. of Groton, Oct. 15, 1829, by Timothy Tuttle	1	31
Senaca, of Groton, m. Joan[n]a **ANDREWS**, of N. Stonington, Jan. 2, 1825, by William Williams, J.P.	1	15
Seth*, [s. Henry], b. Jan. 21, 1761 (*and Mary, see will)	1	177
Seth, m. Anna **GALLUP**, b. of Groton, Jan. 30, 1825, by Timothy Tuttle	1	16
Sibel, d. Sam[ue]l & Hannah, b. Mar. 10, 1769	2	20
Sophia Christina, d. William & Margaret, b. July 25, 1738	1	155
Temperance, [d. Samuel & Margaret], b. Sept. 7, 1761	2	24
Temperance, of Groton, m. Albion **MOODEY**, of Springville, Pa., Oct. 17, 1830, by William M. Williams, J.P.	1	36
Theoder, m. Ezekiel **TURNER**, Apr. 29, 1723	1	107
Thomas, [s. Jonathan & Elizabeth], b. Feb. 8, 1729/30	II	369
Thomas, [s. Samuel & Hannah], b. Sept. 23, 1776	2	20
Thomas, Capt., of Stonington, m. Lucretia **DUDLEY**, of Groton, Dec. 24, 1826, by John G. Wightman, Eld.	1	23
Thomas, of Ledyard, m. Hannah **WHEELER**, of Groton, Nov. 15, 1854, by Rev. S. B. Bailey	1	97
Waitey, m. Rufus **HOLDREDGE**, Jr., b. of Groton, Dec. 25, 1833 by John G. Wightman, Elder	1	45
William, s. William & Mary, b. Jan. 15, 1708/9	1	112
William, Jr., m. Marg[a]ret **COOKE**, Nov. 10, 1736	1	155
William, s. William & Margaret, b. Feb. 6, 1740	1	155
William, 3d, b. Oct. 13, 1780	3	8
William, Jr., m. Anny **STANTON**, b. of Groton, Oct. 13, 1799, by Rev. Christopher Avery, of Stonington	3	8

	Vol.	Page
WILLIAMS, (cont.)		
William, 3d, [s. William, Jr. & Anny], b. Nov. 8, 1800	3	8
William, [s. William, Jr. & Anny], b. Aug. 26, 1821	3	8
William, s. [Erastus & Nancy], b. May 29, 1823	2	91
William A., m. Lydia **WILLIAMS**, b. of Groton, Dec. 24, 1820, by Philip Gray, J.P.	1	2
Zipporah, m. James **GEER**, Mar. 24, 1736/7	1	179
WILLIS, Anne, d. William & Mary, b. Oct. 29, 1726	1	140
Caleb, m. Mary **CROUCH**, b. of Groton, Oct. 29, 1821, by Zephaniah Watrous	1	4
James, [s. William & Mary], b. Apr. 21, 1731	1	140
Mary, m. Samuel J. **HOLDREDGE**, b. of Groton, June 18, 1843, by Henry W. Avery, J.P.	1	68
Wealthy A., of Groton, m. John B. **MEIGS**, of Washington, D.C., Oct. 23, 1837, by Rev. John G. Wightman	1	57
William, [s. William & Mary], b. Oct. 21, 1728	1	140
W[illia]m, m. Mariah **MINER**, b. of Groton, Feb. 7, 1841, by Ira R. Steward	1	64
WILLIT, John, m. Mary CLARK, Nov. 19, 1719	1	125
John, s. [John & Mary], b. Jan. 25, 1723; d. [ ]	1	125
John, s. [John & Mary], b. May 1, 1727	1	125
John, s. John & Mary, b. May 1, 1727	1	121
Mary, d. John & Mary, b. Aug. 8, 1721	1	125
WILSON, WILLSON, John, m. Mary **CONINGHAM**, Sept. 3, 1730	1	146
John Capen, s. John & Mary, b. Dec. 16, 1733	1	146
Susanna, d. John & Mary, b. May 21, 1732	1	146
Thomas, of Sweden, m. Elizabeth R. **PERKINS**, of Groton, Mar. 25, 1834, by Nathan Daboll, J.P.	1	46
WINCHESTER, James, Jr., of Norwich, m. Abby **STORY**, of Groton, Dec. 30, 1827, by Rev. David N. Bentley	1	26
Lodowick, of R.I., m. Polly **LAMB**, of Groton, Nov. 17, 1835, by John G. Wightman, Elder	1	52
WITTER, Abigail, d. Robert & Abigail **GERE** & w. Ebenezer, d. Jan. [ ], 1791	2	35
Lura, of Preston, m. Joseph **GERE**, of Groton, Feb. 21, 1816, by Rev. John Hyde	2	89
WOLF, WOOLF, WOLFE, Abby Jane, m. Henry **ASHBEY**, b. of Groton, July 8, 1823, by John G. Wightman	1	10
Albert G., of Groton, m. Mary **COMIT**, of N.Y., Sept. 6, 1835, by Ira R. Steward	1	51
Charles, m. Juliann **WILBUR**, b. of Groton, Sept. 19, 1826, by John G. Wightman, Eld.	1	22
Charles, m. Katharine **BURROWS**, b. of Groton, June 12, 1833, by John G. Wightman, Eld.	1	44
Eldredge D., m. Prudence **FITCH**, b. of Groton, Aug. 2, 1824, by Rev. Roswell Burrows	1	13
Emma Ann, m. Eldredge Pierre **ROWLAND**, b. of Groton, July 25, 1841, by Rev. Erastus Denison	1	65
Hannah, of Groton, m. Eliakim **WILLIAMS**, of Knox, N.Y., June 16, 1822, by John G. Wightman	1	7
Hannah, m. Albert G. **STARK**, b. of Groton, Mar. 1, 1846, by Rev. Erastus Denison	1	75

	Vol.	Page
WOLF, WOOLF, WOLFE, (cont.)		
John A., m. Jerusha **PACKER**, b. of Groton, Aug. 24, 1834, by Rev. Ira R. Steward	1	47
Thomas E., m. Frances J. **SAWYER**, b. of Groton, Aug. 1, 1852, at Mystic River, by Rev. Franklin A. Slater	1	94
Wealthy Ann, m. Elisha **RATHBURN**, Jr., Aug. 18, 1830, by Rev. Erastus Denison	1	34
William H., s. [Charles & Julia Ann], b. Mar. 30, 1829	3	16
WOOD, Alfred A., of New London, m. Margaret H. **LESTER**, of Groton, Oct. 2, 1825, by John G. Wightman, Eld.	1	18
Anna, m. Nehemiah **LAMB**, Dec. 16, 1762	1	170
Emeline, m. George **SMITH**, July 26, [1832], by Rev. James Porter	1	41
John, m. Lucy **LEFFINGWELL**, Feb. 2, 1748/9	1	184
John, m. Nabby **PERKINS**, b. of Groton, June 21, 1784	2	55
Lucy, had d. Anne **BULKLEY**, b. Mar. 9, 1734	2	10
Mary, d. [John & Lucy], b. Aug. 29, 1751	1	184
Ruth, d. [John & Lucy], b. Dec. 3, 1749	1	184
Samuel, of Groton, m. Diadama **HEWIT[T]**, of New London, [ ], 1780	2	65
Samuel, s. Sam[ue]l & Diadama, b. Feb. 13, 1802	2	65
WOODBRIDGE, Amanda M., of Groton, m. Henry W. **SMITH**, of Williamstown, Mass., Apr. 8, 1832, by Timothy Tuttle	1	39
Augustus, [s. Ephraim & Hannah], b. Oct. 29, 1710	1	103
Benjamin, s. Dudley, b. Dec. 15, 1757; d. Apr. [ ], 1770	2	13
Christopher, s. Oliver & Susanna, b. July 4, 1756	1	161
Dudley, [s. Ephraim & Hannah], b. Apr. 21, 1705	1	103
Dudley, s. Dudley, b. Oct. 9,1747	2	13
Eliza, m. Denison B. **SMITH**, Sept. 2, 1845, by Rev. R. Russell	1	74
Elizabeth, d. Dudley, b. May 13, 1752	2	13
Elizabeth, d. Dudley, b. Dec. 26, 1761	2	13
Ephraim, m. Hannah **MORGAN**, May 4, 1704	1	103
Ephraim, Rev., d. Dec. 1, 1725, ae. 45 y.	1	128
Hannah, [d. Ephraim & Hannah], b. Feb. 9, 1713	1	103
Hannah, m. Samuel **WALWORTH**, Jan. 10, 176[ ]	2	18
Hannah B., m. William F. **MITCHELL**, b. of Groton, Mar. 22, 1835, by John G. Wightman, Elder	1	49
Henry, s. Oliver & Susanna, b. Oct. 28, 1750	1	161
John, s. Samuel, Jr., b. Feb. 28, 1775	2	40
Joseph, s. Dudley, b. Jan. 1, 1750	2	13
Lucy, d. Oliver & Susanna, b. Apr. 14, 1753; d. Aug. 21, 1754	1	161
Lucy, d. Dudley, b. May 4, 1760	2	13
Mary, [d. Ephraim & Hannah], b. Oct. 22, 1717	1	103
Mary, d. Oliver & Susanna, b. Sept. 20, 1760	1	161
Mary F., m. John A. **NILES**, b. of Groton, Mar. 3, 1833, by John G. Wightman, Eld.	1	43
Oliver, [s. Ephraim & Hannah], b. Dec. 3, 1723	1	103
Oliver, m. Susanna **AVERY**, Dec. 28, 1749	1	161
Oliver, s. Oliver & Susanna, b. Apr. 3, 1763	1	161
Paul, [s. Ephraim & Hannah], b. Mar. 12, 1707	1	103
Sally, d. [Samuel, Jr.], b. Feb. 20, 1779	2	40
Samuel, s. Dudley, b. Oct. 31, 1755	2	13
Sarah, d. Dudley, b. June 28, 1767	2	13
Sarah, m. Thomas **FERGO**, Jan. 4, 1790	2	48

	Vol.	Page
WOODBRIDGE, (cont.)		
Susanna, w. Oliver, d. Jan. 4, 1767	1	153
Susanna, w. Oliver, d. Jan. 4, 1768 (Entry made in pencil)	2	161
William, s. Dudley, b. July 18, 1745	2	13
WOODBURN, Anna, d. George & Mary, b. Sept. 25, 1761	1	189
George, of Stonington, m. Mary **CULVER**, of Groton, July 22, 1759, by Timothy Wightman, Elder	1	189
George, s. George & Mary, b. Aug. 26, 1760	1	189
John, s. George & Mary, b. Apr. 25, 1765	1	189
WOODMANSEY, WOODMANSEE, Joseph, d. Dec. 10, 1813	2	9
Joseph, m. Mary **PERKINS**, b. of Groton, Oct. 3, 1830, by Ralph Hurlbutt, J.P.	1	35
Sarah, m. Zebadiah **GATES**, Nov. 9, 1742	2	8
WOODWARD, Experience, m. Capt. Lemuel **BURROWS**, Aug. 12, 1832, by Rev. Erastus Denison	1	40
George, m. Nancy **BURROWS**, b. of Groton, Aug. 25, 1830, by Rev. John G. Wightman	1	34
Nancy, m. Gurdon **DANIELS**, b. of Groton, Sept. 1, 1850, by Rev. William C. Walker	1	90
WOODWORTH, Asa, m. Sarah **LESTER**, Sept. 13, 1739	1	156
Asa, s. Asa & Sarah, b. Apr. 25, 1744	1	156
Caleb, s. Asa & Sarah, b. Oct. 22, 1753	1	156
Eunice, d. Asa & Sarah, b. Jan. 24, 1748	1	156
Jasper, s. Asa & Sarah, b. Oct. 7, 1740	1	156
Joseph Ellery, s. Azel & Hannah, b. Dec. 9, 1799	2	17
Joseph Ellery, m. Phebe Williston **FISH**, b. of Groton, July 14, 1822, by Timothy Tuttle	1	7
Ruth, s. Asa & Sarah, b. June 26, 1751	1	156
Sarah, d. Asa & Sarah, b. Aug. 20, 1746	1	156
WRIGHT, George N., of Montville, m. Eliza D. **DABOLL**, of Groton, Aug. 18, 1840, by Rev. Erastus Denison	1	63
Jane, m. Nathan **HOLDREDGE**, b. of Groton, Oct. 18, 1829, by William Williams, J.P.	1	32
WROTH, Hannah, m. William **SPICER**, Nov. 25, 1703	1	106
YEOMAN, YEOMANS, YEAMAN, Dorothy, m. Samuel **CHAPEL**, Dec. 3, 1737	1	147
Rebeckah, m. David **DODGE**, May 15, 1717	1	119
Sally, Mrs., of Groton, m. Johnathan **CHESEBRO[UGH]**, of Stonington, Nov. 9, 1849, by Henry W. Avery, J.P.	1	86
YORK, Horace T., m. Deborah **MAINE**, b. of Stonington, Dec. 1, 1850, by Rev. James Squier	1	91
Mary Ann, m. Emerson **BIBBER**, b. of Groton, July 18, 1852, at Noank, by Rev. James M. Phillips	1	94
Sarah T., m. John R. **VINCENT**, b. of Stonington, Sept. 29, 1846, by Belton A. Copp, J.P.	1	76
Saunders, of Hopkinton, R.I., m. Rhoda E. **BROWN**, of N. Stonington, Oct. 25, 1847, by Rev. Erastus Denison	1	79
NO SURNAME		
Hannah, m. Joseph **STANTON**, Apr. 22, 1767	2	92
Hannah, m. Quash **WILLIAMS**, Apr. 10, 1824, by Rufus Smith, J.P.	2	24
Susanna, m. Moses **CULVER**, of Groton, [ ], 1735	1	186